WITHDRAWN

A
William Butler Yeats
Encyclopedia

A
WILLIAM BUTLER YEATS
Encyclopedia

Sam McCready

GREENWOOD PRESS
Westport, Connecticut

Library of Congress Cataloging-in-Publication Data

McCready, Sam.
    A William Butler Yeats encyclopedia / Sam McCready.
        p.   cm.
    Includes bibliographical references and index.
    ISBN 0–313–28371–0 (alk. paper)
        1. Yeats, W. B. (William Butler), 1865–1939—Encyclopedias.
    2. Poets, Irish—19th century—Biography—Encyclopedias.   3. Poets,
    Irish—20th century—Biography—Encyclopedias.   4. Ireland—
    Intellectual life—Encyclopedias.   5. Ireland—In literature—
    Encyclopedias.   I. Title.
    PR5906.M44   1997
    821'.8—dc21   96–50288

British Library Cataloguing in Publication Data is available.

Library of Congress Catalog Card Number: 96–50288
ISBN: 0–313–28371–0

First published in 1997

Greenwood Press, 88 Post Road West, Westport, CT 06881
An imprint of Greenwood Publishing Group, Inc.

Printed in the United States of America

The paper used in this book complies with the
Permanent Paper Standard issued by the National
Information Standards Organization (Z39.48–1984).

10 9 8 7 6 5 4 3 2 1

For
Mary O'Malley
and the
Lyric Players Theatre, Belfast

Contents

Acknowledgments

My interest in W. B. Yeats began when I was a member of the Lyric Players Theatre in Belfast, Northern Ireland, then the only theater in the world devoted to the study and presentation of the plays of Yeats. During those first years, I traveled to Sligo with the company and saw at firsthand the landscape that inspired the poet throughout his life. I met, too, many Yeatsian scholars whose love of Yeats transcended mere scholarship and reputation. My interest in Yeats was fixed for life, and since then, I have written about Yeats, taught the poetry of Yeats, and directed and acted in his plays, in both the United States and Europe. A lifetime study. Thus, I dedicate this book to Mary O'Malley, the founder of the Lyric Players Theatre, to whom I am eternally grateful.

My wife Joan was a member of that theater troupe, and she has worked alongside me in this latest Yeatsian enterprise, devoting many hours to reading and correcting the manuscript. She is a constant source of love and care.

I am indebted to the many Yeats scholars whose work I have delved into and borrowed from. I thank my colleagues at the University of Maryland, Baltimore County, and my theater students, who have helped me in more ways than I can name. Diana Attuso was a willing secretary when things got really tough and made a major contribution to the final presentation of the book.

Dr. George F. Butler has guided me through the process of writing this book and has inspired me with his enthusiasm and belief in the project.

I thank my many friends and especially my family, Julian, Richard, and Florence, for their continuing support.

Introduction

W. B. Yeats was not only a major poet but also a playwright, politician, theater founder, and literary critic. In his early life, he immersed himself in Irish folk stories and mythology, skillfully and unself-consciously weaving these threads into the fabric of his major poems and plays. He devoted himself to occult studies and philosophy. He developed, too, a rare sense of place, finding dignity and significance in an Irish mountain, village, holy well, places steeped in local history and mythology, and created a new Ireland, one imagined by the poets, "terrible and gay." Yet he had time for his friends—the many women who fascinated him throughout his life as well as his fellow-writers whom he attacked and defended, often in print and sometimes from the stage of the national theater he founded in Dublin. He never moved far from his family, with whom he lived until he was thirty years of age. His father was a major influence on him, shaping the young poet through nightly reading and study of the classics and contemporary masters and providing for him an example of a life devoted more to living than to art. His sisters were his constant care. W. B. Yeats's family, friends, studies, and professional life all provided themes that his imagination translated into poetry. All became the stuff of his consummate art.

Books on Yeats proliferate, many of them by eminent scholars who bring a dazzling intelligence to the explication of his poetry, his plays, his stories, and his innumerable essays and reviews. In recent years, Macmillan, who has published Yeats from the 1930s, has undertaken the publication of Yeats's *Collected Works*, in fourteen volumes, scrupulously edited by major authorities under the general editorship of Richard J. Finneran and George Mills Harper. Clarendon Press is publishing the *Collected Letters of W. B. Yeats*, in a number of volumes, edited by John Kelly and others. An authorized biography, *The Apprentice Mage*, has been written by Irish historian R. F. Foster. There is a need for a reference work that brings together the vast amount of biographical material on Yeats and his circle that is currently available only in disparate sources.

The aim of this book is to make available basic information about W. B. Yeats's life and work and to guide the reader to sources for further study. There is nothing new in the book. All the material has been drawn from reliable biographical and interpretative sources. Any virtue it may have is that it makes a maximum amount of information accessible between two covers.

Yeats is at the center of this book, and each entry has been written from his perspective. In the interest of space and volume, it has not been possible to include every person, place, or topic referred to by Yeats, but through a detailed reading of his *Collected Works*, a selection has been made of those that are important to an understanding of the author and the world he lived in. The book contains almost a thousand entries, with a Chronology, a Selected Bibliography, and an Index. All entries are cross-referenced.

CATEGORIES OF ENTRY

Entries may be categorized as follows:

1. Brief account of the content of each of Yeats's major collections. These entries include his collections of verse, essays, stories, and autobiography. Each entry contains a publication history.
2. Summary of the plots of Yeats's published plays, with production histories and brief character sketches of the leading figures in each play.
3. Guide to the mythological figures in the poems and plays. Most of these are from the Irish mythological cycles, but reference is also made to Greek, Roman, and Hindu myth.
4. Guide to the places associated with Yeats, including his homes, schools, and those places mentioned in the *Collected Works*.
5. Organizations to which Yeats belonged.
6. Biographies. They include members of Yeats's family, including his ancestors and extended family, in addition to biographies of literary and political figures associated with Yeats and his writings. There are also biographies of those contemporaries and historical figures referred to in the major poems, plays, novels, and essays.

In these entries, information is given that may be helpful in the reading and understanding of Yeats's work, and any attempt to offer an interpretation or to guide a reading has been avoided. In entries on Irish places, the original Gaelic and its transliteration have been provided, where this has been thought helpful. Yeats's sometimes eccentric spelling and capitalization have been retained in references to characters from his plays and the titles of his poems. Quotations from Yeats and others have been kept to a minimum.

READING LISTS

Where appropriate, short reading lists have been provided at the end of each entry. In the interest of space, these lists have been limited, where possible, to works that have some bearing on Yeats, although there is an attempt to include a biography for each of the major historical and literary figures. References to periodical literature have been kept to a minimum.

FORMS OF REFERENCE

The major works of W. B. Yeats are referred to in detail in all entries. Each has been given a cue-title, which may be found in Abbreviations. The information in the entries has been drawn from hundreds of sources, and a reference is not usually given. Besides general works of reference such as *Dictionary of National Biography, Who's Who, Encyclopedia Britannica,* and *The Columbia Encyclopedia,* information has been obtained from the standard biographies of Yeats, most notably from Joseph Hone's *W. B. Yeats: 1865–1939,* A. Norman Jeffares's *Yeats: Man and Poet,* and Frank Tuohy's *Yeats.* With the Wade *Letters,* and the two available volumes of *Collected Letters,* edited by John Kelly and others, detailed page references are provided. Where a particular book has been consulted for many entries—for example, Robert Hogan's *Dictionary of Irish Biography* and James P. McGarry's *Place Names in the Writings of William Butler Yeats*—it is listed, for convenience, under each entry. Every attempt has been made to keep the presentation simple so that entries may be found easily. Cross-references are systematically given to other entries in the encyclopedia by the use of bold type on the first mention. Throughout, Yeats himself is referred to as WBY. No cross-reference is given, and the abbreviation is in ordinary type.

CHRONOLOGY

Here are listed the main events of Yeats's life, with major publications and so on. Some notable historical events, such as the Easter Rising of 1916, are given because they are significant to Yeats and his work. Detailed information about Yeats's life will be found in the main body of the encyclopedia.

SELECTED BIBLIOGRAPHY

The main bibliography, which appears at the end of the book, is divided into sections covering bibliographical and reference works, the standard editions of the *Collected Works,* other editions, letters, biography, and general criticism. The list contains only a selection of the available material and represents those books that have been found useful in the preparation of this encyclopedia. Articles have been omitted. Many distinguished studies have been excluded, although reference to these has been made in the reading list for each entry.

INDEX

The Index is designed to make the work as efficient as possible. Page references are given for all topics, titles, persons, places, and characters in the main text. Where there is a separate entry, the page reference appears in bold type.

While writing this encyclopedia, my interest in the work of W. B. Yeats turned to fanaticism as I became more and more consumed with the man himself, the range and quality of his output, the depth of his reading, his unerring aesthetic and political convictions, and his intense, unswerving loyalty to his friends. His is a life that must fill many such volumes.

Chronology

1865	June	WBY born in **George's Ville**, Sandymount Ave., Dublin.
1866	Aug.	**Susan Mary (Lily)** born in **Sligo**.
1867	Mar.	**John B. Yeats** enrolls at Heatherley's Art School, London.
	July	Family joins him at 23 **Fitzroy Road**.
1868	Mar.	**Elizabeth Corbet (Lolly)** born in London.
1871	Aug.	**John Butler (Jack)** born in London.
1872	July	**Susan Yeats** returns with WBY and her other children to Sligo for an extended stay with grandparents, **William** and **Elizabeth Pollexfen**, at **Merville**.
1874	Oct.	Family returns to London. Settles at **Edith Villas**.
1876	Fall	While rest of family holiday in Sligo, WBY joins father at **Farnham Royal**.
1877	Jan.	Susan Yeats and family return to Edith Villas.
		WBY enrolls at **Godolphin School**, Hammersmith.
1879	Spring	Yeats family moves to **Woodstock Road** in **Bedford Park**, London.
1881	Summer	Yeats family returns to Ireland. Settles at **Balscadden Cottage, Howth**.
	Fall	WBY attends **Erasmus Smith High School**, Dublin, where he meets **Charles Johnston**.
1882	Spring	Yeats family moves to **Island View**, Howth.
	Fall	WBY meets **Laura Armstrong**.

1883	Dec.	WBY leaves Erasmus Smith High School.
1884	Jan.	Writes the play *Vivien and Time* for Laura Armstrong.
	Spring	Yeats family moves to **Ashfield Terrace**, South Dublin.
	May	WBY enrolls at **Metropolitan School of Art**, Dublin. Meets **AE**.
1885	Jan.	**John O'Leary** returns to Dublin from exile. WBY meets him later in the year.
	Mar.	First poems published in the *Dublin University Review*.
	June	Founds **Dublin Hermetic Society** with AE and Charles Johnston. Meets **Katharine Tynan**.
	Nov.	Attends early meeting of **Contemporary Club**, founded by **C. H. Oldham**.
1886	Apr.	Leaves Metropolitan School of Art. Meets **William Morris** in Dublin.
	Oct.	*Mosada* published.
1887	Apr.	Returns with family to London. They settle at **Eardley Crescent**.
	May	Meets **Ernest Rhys**. Visits **Madame Blavatsky**. Joins the **Theosophical Society**.
1888	Mar.	Yeats family moves to **Blenheim Road**, Bedford Park.
	Sept.	Publication of *Fairy and Folk Tales of the Irish Peasantry*.
	Nov.	Joins the Esoteric Section of the Theosophical Society.
1889	Jan.	*The Wanderings of Oisin and Other Poems* published. Meets **Maud Gonne**. Begins study of **William Blake's** Prophetic Books.
	Feb.	Begins writing *The Countess Cathleen*.
1890	Jan.	Founds **Rhymers' Club** with Ernest Rhys.
	Mar.	Initiated into **The Order of the Golden Dawn**.
	May	Attends performance of **John Todhunter's** *A Sicilian Idyll*.
1891	Aug.	WBY proposes to Maud Gonne but is refused.
	Oct.	Death of **Charles Stewart Parnell**.
	Nov.	*John Sherman and Dhoya* published.
1892	May	**Irish Literary Society** founded in London.

	Aug.	**National Literary Society** founded in Dublin.
		The Countess Kathleen and Various Legends and Lyrics published.
	Sept.	Controversy over **New Irish Library** begins.
	Oct.	Death of grandmother, Elizabeth Pollexfen.
	Nov.	Death of grandfather, William Pollexfen.
1893	Jan.	*The Works of William Blake*, eds. WBY and Ernest Rhys.
	July	Gaelic League founded by **Douglas Hyde**.
	Dec.	*The Celtic Twilight*.
1894	Feb.	Visits Paris. Attends performance of **Villiers de L'Isle-Adam's** *Axël*.
		Meets **Paul Verlaine**.
	Mar.	*The Land of Heart's Desire* produced in London.
	Apr.	Meets **Olivia Shakespear**.
	Aug.	**Iseult Gonne** born.
	Nov.	Visits Sligo. Stays with **Gore-Booth** family at **Lissadell**.
1895	May	Arrest and trial of **Oscar Wilde**. WBY offers support.
	Aug.	*Poems* published.
	Oct.	Takes rooms with **Arthur Symons** in **Fountain Court**.
1896	Feb.	Takes rooms at **Woburn Buildings**.
		Begins affair with Olivia Shakespear.
	Aug.	Visits **Edward Martyn** at **Tulira Castle**.
		Meets **Lady Gregory**.
	Dec.	Meets **J. M. Synge** in Paris.
1897	Apr.	*The Secret Rose* published.
	July	Stays at **Coole Park**. Spends summer collecting folklore.
		Discusses the founding of the **Irish Literary Theatre** with Lady Gregory, Edward Martyn, and **George Moore**.
1898	Apr.	Meets **Wilfred Scawen Blunt**.
		Visits **MacGregor Mathers** in Paris.
	June	Stays at Coole Park through mid-August.
	Dec.	WBY and Maud Gonne embark on a mystical marriage.
1899	Feb.	Visits Maud Gonne in Paris and again proposes marriage.
	Apr.	*The Wind among the Reeds* published.

	May	*The Countess Cathleen* performed by the Irish Literary Theatre in Dublin.
		WBY goes to Coole Park for the summer and early fall.
	Nov.	Begins collaboration with George Moore on **Diarmuid and Grania**.
1900	Jan.	Death of mother, Susan Yeats.
	Feb.	Second season of the Irish Literary Theatre in Dublin.
	Mar.	Queen Victoria visits Dublin.
		Jubilee riots.
	Apr.	Quarrel with MacGregor Mathers over The Order of the Golden Dawn. WBY evicts Aleister Crowley from the Golden Dawn headquarters in London.
	June	Goes to Coole Park for the summer and early fall.
1901	Mar.	Admires **Gordon Craig's** scenery for *Dido and Aeneas* and *The Masque of Love*.
	Oct.	*Diarmuid and Grania* produced in Dublin.
1902	Apr.	**Cathleen Ni Houlihan**, with Maud Gonne in the title role, produced by **W. G. Fay**.
		Gives lectures with **Florence Farr** on verse speaking to the psaltery.
	Aug.	Meets **John Quinn**.
	Summer	Meets **James Joyce**.
	Oct.	Death of **Lionel Johnson**.
		The Pot of Broth produced by **Irish National Dramatic Society**.
	Nov.	Setting up of **Dun Emer Press** by Lolly Yeats.
1903	Feb.	Maud Gonne marries **John MacBride**.
	May	**Irish National Theatre Society's** first visit to London.
		Ideas of Good and Evil published.
	Aug.	**In the Seven Woods**.
	Nov.	Leaves for first U.S. **Lecture Tour**.
1904	Mar.	Returns to London from United States.
	June	**Where There Is Nothing** produced by the London Stage Society.
	Dec.	**Abbey Theatre** opens with *On Baile's Strand*.
1905	Sept.	Irish National Theatre Society reorganized. WBY becomes codirector.
1906	Sept.	*The Poems of Spenser* published.
1907	Jan.	Synge's *Playboy of the Western World* opens at Abbey.

	Mar.	Death of John O'Leary.
	May	Visits Italy with Lady Gregory and her son **Robert**.
	Dec.	*Discoveries* published.
		John B. Yeats leaves permanently for New York.
1908	Jan.	W. G. Fay and brother **Frank** resign from Abbey Theatre.
	Sept.	First volumes of *Collected Works* published.
	Nov.	**Mrs. Patrick Campbell** in *Deirdre* in Dublin and London.
	Dec.	Visits Maud Gonne (now estranged from MacBride) in Paris.
1909	Mar.	Death of Synge.
	Aug.	Quarrel with John Quinn.
1910	May	Stays with Maud Gonne in Normandy.
		Death of Edward VII. Quarrel with **Annie F. Horniman**.
	Aug.	Granted a Civil List pension of £150 per annum in England—with the proviso that he may take part in political activities in Ireland.
	Sept.	Death of **George Pollexfen**.
	Dec.	*The Green Helmet and Other Poems*.
1911	Sept.	Accompanies Abbey Theatre company to United States.
	Oct.	Returns to London.
		Meets **Georgie Hyde-Lees**.
1912	June	Meets **Rabindranath Tagore**.
	Nov.	*The Cutting of an Agate*.
1913	Spring	Supports **Hugh Lane's** plans for Gallery of Modern Art in Dublin.
	Oct.	*Poems Written in Discouragement*.
	Nov.	Rents **Stone Cottage** with **Ezra Pound**.
1914	Jan.	Leaves for U.S. Lecture Tour.
	Mar.	Resumes friendship with John Quinn.
	Apr.	Returns to London.
	May	*Responsibilities: Poems and a Play*.
	Aug.	World War I begins.
	Fall	WBY starts writing his autobiography.
1915	May	Hugh Lane drowned on the *Lusitania*.
	Dec.	Refuses a knighthood from King George V.

1916	Mar.	*Reveries over Childhood and Youth.*
	Apr.	*At the Hawk's Well* produced in London.
		Easter Rising in Dublin.
	May	Execution of leaders of Rising, including John Mac-Bride.
	July	Visits Maud Gonne in Normandy. Renews offer of marriage.
	Oct.	Campaign to have Hugh Lane pictures brought to Dublin.
1917	Mar.	Buys **Thoor Ballylee**.
	Aug.	Proposes marriage to Iseult Gonne in Normandy and is refused.
	Oct.	Marries Georgie Hyde-Lees.
	Nov.	*The Wild Swans at Coole.*
1918	Jan.	Settles in **Oxford**.
		Per Amica Silentia Lunae.
		Death of Robert Gregory.
	Sept.	Moves into renovated Thoor Ballylee.
		Rents Dublin home at 73 St. Stephen's Green from Maud Gonne.
	Nov.	Georgie Yeats ill with pneumonia.
		Quarrel with Maud Gonne.
		End of World War I.
1919	Jan.	*Two Plays for Dancers.*
	Feb.	Birth of daughter **Anne**.
	May	London Stage Society produces *The Player Queen*.
	June	Gives up London apartment at Woburn Buildings.
	Oct.	Civil unrest in Ireland.
1920	Jan.	Leaves with Georgie Yeats for U.S. Lecture Tour.
		First Black and Tans arrive in Ireland.
	May	Returns from United States.
1921	Feb.	*Michael Robartes and the Dancer.*
	July	Truce in Ireland.
	Aug.	Birth of **Michael Yeats**.
	Oct.	*Four Plays for Dancers.*
	Dec.	Anglo-Irish Treaty signed in London.
1922	Jan.	Civil War in Ireland. WBY sympathizes with the pro-Treaty side.
	Feb.	John B. Yeats dies in New York.

	Mar.	Settles in **Merrion Square**, Dublin.
	Apr.	*The Only Jealousy of Emer* produced in Amsterdam.
	July	Honorary degree from **Trinity College**, Dublin.
	Aug.	Bridge at Thoor Ballylee blown up by Republicans.
	Oct.	*The Trembling of the Veil*.
	Dec.	Elected to the **Irish Senate**.
1923	Nov.	*Plays and Controversies*.
	Dec.	In Stockholm to receive **Nobel Prize for Literature**.
1924	July	Death of John Quinn.
	Nov.	Suffering from high blood pressure, WBY holidays in **Sicily** and Rome.
1925	June	Senate speech on divorce.
1926	Jan.	*A Vision*.
	Feb.	**O'Casey's** *The Plough and the Stars* opens at Abbey Theatre.
	June	Chairman of Senate Committee on new Irish coinage.
	Nov.	*Autobiographies* published.
1927	July	Assassination of **Kevin O'Higgins**.
	Nov.	Winters in **Algeciras**. Ill with congestion of the lungs.
1928	Feb.	Visits **Rapallo** to rent an apartment.
		The Tower.
	June	O'Casey's *The Silver Tassie* rejected by Abbey board.
	July	Sells house in Merrion Square and moves to rented apartment at 42 Fitzwilliam Square, Dublin.
	Sept.	Resigns from Irish Senate.
1929	Mar.	Meets **George Antheil** in Rapallo.
	Summer	Last stay in Thoor Ballylee.
	Dec.	Dangerously ill in Rapallo with Malta fever.
1930	Jan.	Recuperates in Italy. Reads **Jonathan Swift**.
	July	Lady Gregory seriously ill. Stays with her at Coole Park.
	Nov.	*The Words upon the Window-Pane* opens at Abbey Theatre.
1931	Sept.	Broadcasts from **BBC** in Belfast. Spends most of fall and winter with Lady Gregory at Coole Park.
1932	Feb.	**Eamon de Valera's** party wins Irish General Election. WBY at Coole Park.
	May	Death of Lady Gregory.
	July	Buys lease on **Riversdale**, Rathfarnham, Dublin (county).

	Sept.	Founder member of **Irish Academy of Letters**.
	Oct.	Starts last American Lecture Tour.
	Nov.	***Words for Music Perhaps***.
1933	Jan.	Returns from New York.
	July	Involved with **Blueshirts** in Dublin.
	Sept.	***The Winding Stair and Other Poems*** published by Macmillan.
	Nov.	***Collected Poems***.
1934	April	Undergoes Steinach operation in London.
	July	Premiere of ***The Resurrection*** and ***The King of the Great Clock Tower***.
	Oct.	Meets **Margot Ruddock**.
	Nov.	***Wheels and Butterflies***.
		Collected Plays.
1935	July	Death of AE.
	Aug.	Stays with **Dorothy Wellesley** at Penns in the Rocks.
	Nov.	***A Full Moon in March***.
	Dec.	In **Majorca** with **Shri Purohit Swami**.
		Dramatis Personae.
1936	Jan.	Health deteriorates.
	Oct.	Broadcasts from BBC in London.
	Nov.	Controversial ***Oxford Book of Modern Verse*** published.
1937	Apr.	Begins friendship with **Edith Shackleton Heald**.
		Gives series of poetry broadcasts for the BBC.
	May	Retires from public life.
	Aug.	Irish Academy of Letters dinner in Dublin.
	Oct.	Revised edition of *A Vision*.
1938	Jan.	Spends winter in the South of France.
	May	*New Poems*.
	Aug.	First production of ***Purgatory***.
		Final public appearance.
	Oct.	Death of Olivia Shakespear.
	Nov.	Leaves London for the South of France.
1939	Jan.	Dies at Cap Martin. Buried at **Roquebrune**.
	July	**Last Poems and Two Plays**.
	Sept.	World War II. ***On the Boiler***.
1941		Coole Park pulled down.
1948		WBY reinterred in **Drumcliff**, Sligo (county).

Abbreviations

WBY   William Butler Yeats.

A.   Yeats, W. B. *Autobiographies*. 1955. Reprint, London: Macmillan, 1956.

AV.   Yeats, W. B. *A Vision*. London: Macmillan, 1937.

CP.   Yeats, W. B. *The Collected Poems of W. B. Yeats*. 1950. Reprint, London: Macmillan, 1982.

CPl.   Yeats, W. B. *The Collected Plays of W. B. Yeats*. 1952. Reprint, London: Macmillan, 1977.

EI.   Yeats, W. B. *Essays and Introductions*. New York: Macmillan, 1961.

EX.   Yeats, W. B. *Explorations*. Selected by Mrs. W. B. Yeats. New York: Macmillan, 1962.

JS.   Finneran, Richard J., ed. *John Sherman and Dhoya: The Collected Works of W. B. Yeats*. Vol. XII. New York: Macmillan, 1991.

KLI.   Kelly, John, and Domville, Eric, eds. *The Collected Letters of W. B. Yeats*. Vol. I, 1865–1895. Oxford: Clarendon Press, 1986.

KLIII.   Kelly, John, and Schuchard, Ronald, eds. *The Collected Letters of W. B. Yeats*. Vol. III, 1901–1904. Oxford: Clarendon Press, 1994.

LE.   O'Donnell, William H., ed. *Later Essays: The Collected Works of W. B. Yeats*. Vol. V. New York: Charles Scribner's Sons, 1994.

LNI.   Bornstein, George, and Witemeyer, Hugh, eds. *Letters to the New Island: The Collected Works of W. B. Yeats*. Vol. VII. New York: Macmillan, 1989.

M.   Donoghue, Denis, ed. *W. B. Yeats: Memoirs: Autobiography-First Draft, Journal*. London: Macmillan, 1972.

MY.   Yeats, W. B. *Mythologies*. New York: Macmillan, 1959.

OS.   O'Shea, Edward. *A Descriptive Catalog of W. B. Yeats's Library.* New York and London: Garland, 1985.

PI.   O'Donnell, William H., ed. *Prefaces and Introductions: The Collected Works of W. B. Yeats.* Vol. VI. New York: Macmillan, 1989.

UM.   Bornstein, George, ed. *Under the Moon: The Unpublished Early Poetry by William Butler Yeats.* New York: Scribner, 1995.

UP1.   Frayne, John P., ed. *Uncollected Prose by W. B. Yeats 1: First Reviews and Articles, 1886–1896.* New York: Columbia University Press, 1970.

UP2.   Frayne, John P., ed. *Uncollected Prose by W. B. Yeats 2: Reviews, Articles and Other Miscellaneous Prose, 1897–1939.* New York: Columbia University Press, 1975.

VP.   Allt, Peter, and Alspach, Russell K., eds. *The Variorum Edition of the Poems of W. B. Yeats.* New York: Macmillan, 1968.

VPl.   Alspach, Russell K., ed. *The Variorum Edition of the Plays of W. B. Yeats.* London: Macmillan, 1966.

WL.   Wade, Allan, ed. *The Letters of W. B. Yeats.* New York: Octagon Books, 1980.

THE W. B. YEATS ENCYCLOPEDIA

A

ABBEY, setting for WBY's play *The Dreaming of the Bones*. The First Musician in the play describes a village called Abbey near the ruined Cistercian abbey of **Corcomroe**. There is no village of Abbey in that part of Ireland. WBY may have had in mind the nearby townland of Abbey, consisting of Abbey East and Abbey West.

REFERENCE: McGarry, James P. *Place Names in the Writings of William Butler Yeats.* Gerrards Cross: Colin Smythe, 1976.

ABBEY OF WHITE FRIARS, ruined friary in the center of **Sligo** (town). Known as Sligo Abbey, it was built in 1253 by Maurice Fitzgerald for the Dominicans. It was pillaged and burned in 1641 by **Cromwell's** troops, commanded by Sir Frederick Hamilton. In "The Curse of the Fires and the Shadows" (*MY.* 177), WBY graphically describes the destruction of the abbey. See also "The Crucifixion of the Outcast" (*MY.* 147, 148).

REFERENCE: McGarry, James P. *Place Names in the Writings of William Butler Yeats.* Gerrards Cross: Colin Smythe, 1976.

ABBEY THEATRE, home of the Irish National Theatre Society. It grew out of the ideals of the **Irish Literary Theatre** and the **Irish National Dramatic Society**, formed in 1902 by **W. G. Fay** and his brother **Frank**. In 1903, the latter company became the Irish National Theatre Society. Among its stated aims was the creation of a national theater to produce plays by Irish writers and significant works by foreign authors. At the inaugural meeting of the society, WBY was elected president. During their first season in the **Molesworth Hall**, Dublin, March 1903, the society produced *The Hour-Glass* by WBY and *Twenty-Five* by **Lady Gregory**. Between the plays, WBY gave a lecture on

"The Reform of the Theatre." In May 1903, when the society made a visit to London, the enthusiasm of the London critics encouraged the founders to think seriously about finding a permanent home. In April 1904, with financial help from **Annie F. Horniman**, the society acquired premises in Lower Abbey Street, Dublin. These consisted of a small music hall theater within the **Mechanics Institute** and an adjacent property that had been, in former times, a bank, the home of a nationalist debating society, a recruiting office for the Fenian movement, and the city morgue. Miss Horniman held the lease at a cost of £170 a year. After overcoming objections by other Dublin theaters to the granting of a patent, the Abbey Theatre, renovated by Miss Horniman at a cost of nearly £3,000, opened 27 December 1904 with a program that included WBY's *On Baile's Strand*. The distinguished opening night audience included **J. M. Synge, John B. Yeats, Hugh Lane**, and **John Masefield**. Lady Gregory was prevented from attending because of influenza. Initially, seasons were given biannually, in the spring and late fall; only from 1910 were plays performed throughout the year. In its early history, the society encountered opposition. That the Abbey had been leased and renovated by an Englishwoman fomented resentment among the nationalists in Dublin, while the Catholic clergy took exception to the morality of some plays. Audiences were generally small. When the plays of J. M. Synge were performed, the opposition became acrimonious and vindictive, culminating in the *Playboy* riots of 1907. There were also quarrels in 1926 over *The Plough and the Stars* by **Sean O'Casey**. Internal tensions led to the withdrawal from the company of **AE, Edward Martyn**, and **Padraic Colum**, but the most serious blow to the early development of the Abbey was the departure of the Fays. Important foundation members, they had modeled the company on the work of the French director Antoine, evolving a naturalistic acting style suited to the folk and peasant dramas for which the Abbey became famous. The Fays wished to have artistic control, but WBY thought such control would be detrimental to a national theater. In the ensuing struggle, the Fays resigned. Later, talented actors like **Sara Allgood** and her sister **Máire O'Neill** also left, to be replaced by a second generation of outstanding performers, among them **Barry Fitzgerald** and **F. J. McCormick**. In 1925, the Abbey extended its premises to house the **Peacock**, a small experimental theater. The Abbey School of Acting was established, and choreographer **Ninette de Valois** directed the Abbey School of Ballet. Until 1934, the Abbey Theatre board consisted of WBY and two others. In 1935, the board was increased to seven members, and WBY withdrew from active decision making—although his opinion still carried weight. There was wrangling among the seven board members, so that after WBY's death the Abbey Theatre went into decline. The original theater was destroyed by fire in 1951, to be replaced by a modern theater on the same site in July 1966. WBY was associated with the Abbey from its formation until his death in 1939. Regardless of health and other commitments, he maintained almost daily contact with the management of the theater. He read and recommended plays, wrote encouraging letters to new playwrights, and supervised productions of his own plays. He fought publicly with those who opposed the Abbey's choice of plays, and he was the theater's finest publicist. In his statements of artistic policy, he not only outlined the objectives of the Abbey but communicated these ideas to an international public through a series of publications, **Samhain** and *The Arrow* (*EX*. 73–243), and **Beltaine**. After the early productions of his own poetic plays, the Abbey Theatre became increasingly identified with peasant drama. It was with frustration that he turned in 1916 to presenting his dance plays, modeled on the Japanese **Noh**, in the drawing rooms of fashionable London houses. Yet he never turned his back on the Abbey nor lost his enthusiasm for the ideals he articulated at the setting up of the Irish Literary Theatre. He was a visionary, ruthless in his dealings with actors and directors if he thought they were not serving the needs of the theater he envisaged (*M*. 143).

REFERENCES: Flannery, James W. *W. B. Yeats and the Idea of a Theatre: The Early Abbey Theatre in Theory and Practice*. New Haven: Yale University Press, 1976; Frazier, Adrian. *Behind the Scenes: Yeats, Horniman, and the Struggle for the Abbey Theatre*. Berkeley: University of California Press, 1990; Miller, Liam. *The Noble Drama of W. B. Yeats*. Dublin: Dolmen, 1977; Robinson, Lennox. *Ireland's Abbey Theatre*. London: Sidgwick & Jackson, 1951; Saddlemyer, Ann, ed. *Theatre Business: The Correspondence of the First Abbey Theatre Directors: W. B. Yeats, Lady Gregory, and J. M. Synge*. University Park: Penn State University Press, 1982.

ABIEGNOS [also Abiegnus], mountain of spiritual struggle and the sacred Rosicrucian Mountain of Initiation. According to the beliefs of **The Order of the Golden Dawn**, Abiegnos is the central mountain in the world, to be climbed only by those who achieve the highest level of spiritual purification. **Father Christian Rosenkreuz** was said to have been buried there, in the Mountain of the Caverns in the center of the earth. In *The Unicorn from the Stars* (*CPl*. 382), the dying hero Martin speaks of climbing the Mountain of Abiegnos to the vineyards of **Eden**.

REFERENCE: Regardie, Israel. *The Golden Dawn: An Account of the Teachings, Rites and Ceremonies of the Order of the Golden Dawn*. St. Paul, Minn.: Llewellyn Publications, 1995.

ACHILLES, a leading warrior in the Trojan War. He was the son of **Peleus** and **Thetis**. At his birth, his mother, aware of a prophecy that he would be killed at **Troy**, attempted to make him invulnerable by bathing him in the River Styx, but the water did not touch his heel. He died at Troy, after being wounded in the heel by **Paris** in revenge for the death of **Hector**. WBY refers to Achilles in the poem "Upon a Dying Lady" (*CP*. 177).

ADAM, first man, according to the Judaic-Christian Bible. The account of his creation and expulsion from **Eden** is told in Genesis, chapters 2 and 3. In the poem "Adam's Curse" (*CP*. 88), WBY identifies with Adam's disillusionment, while in "Under Ben Bulben" (*CP*. 397), he refers to **Michelangelo's** painting of Adam on the ceiling of the **Sistine Chapel**.

ADAMS, HENRY [BROOKS] (1838–1918), American historian, philosopher, and literary scholar. He was born in Boston, the grandson of John Quincy Adams, and graduated from Harvard in 1858. After a period as private secretary to his father, Charles Francis Adams, minister to Great Britain during the Lincoln administration, he returned to the United States in 1868 as a newspaper correspondent for *The Nation*. In 1870, he was appointed to teach medieval history at Harvard. He resigned in 1877 and moved to Washington, D.C., where he devoted himself to writing the political satire *Democracy* (1880), followed by *History of the United States of America* (1889–91), a nine-volume study of the administrations of Thomas Jefferson and James Madison. After the suicide of his wife in 1885, he devoted himself increasingly to philosophy and to travel, especially in France, where he investigated thirteenth-century life as a fixed point from which modern history might be traced. He published his findings in the important book *Mont-Saint-Michel and Chartres* (1904). His depressing view of America was expressed in his autobiography, *The Education of Henry Adams* (1906). A later work, *The Degradation of the Democratic Dogma* (1919), contained three outstanding essays on his philosophy of history. In a letter to **AE**, written in 1921 (*WL*. 666), WBY claims to have read "all Adams," and he quotes him in *On the Boiler* (*LE*. 237) when discussing the theories of the French mathematician Jules Henri Poincaré. WBY had copies of *The Degradation of the Democratic Dogma, The Education of Henry Adams* (two copies), and *Mont-Saint-Michel and Chartres* in his personal library (*OS*. nos. 16–19).

REFERENCES: Chalfant, Edward. *Better in Darkness: A Biography of Henry Adams: His Second Life, 1862–91*. Cambridge, Mass.: Harvard University Press, 1989; Contosta, David R., and Muccigrosso, Robert. *Henry Adams and His World*. Philadelphia: American Philosophical Society, 1993; O'Toole, Patricia. *The Five of Hearts: An Intimate Portrait of Henry Adams and His Friends, 1880–1918*. New York: Clarkson Potter, 1990; Samuels, Ernest. *Henry Adams*. Cambridge, Mass.: Harvard University Press, 1989.

ADONIS, a beautiful young man in Greek mythology. He was loved by the goddesses Aphrodite and Persephone. After he was killed by a boar, Zeus brought him back to life and ordered him to spend half the year above the ground with Aphrodite and the other half in the underworld with Persephone. His death and resurrection are symbolic of the seasonal cycle of the year. In his essay on **Edmund Spenser** (*EI*. 356–83), WBY celebrates the pagan imagery of Spenser's *The Faerie Queen*, with its references to Venus (the Roman Aphrodite) and to the gardens of Adonis.

AE. *See* **RUSSELL, GEORGE [WILLIAM]**.

AEACUS, son of Zeus in Greek mythology. He was known for his justice and was reputed to have ruled the Myrmidons so justly that, after his death, he was appointed a judge of the Greek underworld. In his essay ''Bishop Berkeley'' (*LE*. 111), WBY praises **Berkeley** by placing him in the pantheon with the major Greek scholars and philosophers, including Aeacus.

AEDH, name of many figures in Irish mythology. In his reference to Aedh in *The Wanderings of Oisin* (*CP*. 425), WBY has in mind the Irish god of death (*VP*. 794). All who heard him play his golden harp died. WBY's source is **Standish [James] O'Grady**, who claims in his *History of Ireland* (1878–80) that Aedh appeared to the dying **Cuchulain**. In some early poems from *Crossways* (1889) and *The Secret Rose* (1897), WBY uses Aedh as the mask of the lover. In a note, he explains that Aedh is the Irish word for fire and that in these poems Aedh is myrrh and frankincense, offered by the imagination to the beloved (*VP*. 803). In WBY's play *The Herne's Egg*, Aedh is the feuding king who is killed in battle by his rival **Congal**. This may be a reference to Aedh, High King of Ireland in the fourth century B.C.
  REFERENCE: Ellis, Peter Berresford. *Dictionary of Celtic Mythology*. New York: Oxford University Press, 1992.

AENGUS [also Aonghus] (Irish: *Aonghus Óg*), god of love, youth, and poetry. He was reputedly very handsome, with four doves, representing kisses, always around his head. He played a golden harp, which made such sweet music that no one could hear and not be enchanted. Aengus was the foster father of **Diarmuid**. When Diarmuid was killed by a wild boar, Aengus took him to his palace, which overlooked the river **Boyne** at Brugh na Boinne. There, he brought the body back to life. **Midhir**, son of the Dagda, enlists Aengus's help in making the beautiful **Étain** fall in love with him. In ''The Song of Wandering Aengus'' (*CP*. 66) and ''The Harp of Aengus'' (*CP*. 471), the god becomes a mask for the poet as he addresses his love to **Maud Gonne**. Aengus is also referred to in the poems ''Under the Moon'' (*CP*. 91), *The Wanderings of Oisin* (*CP*. 409), and ''The Old Age of Queen Maeve'' (*CP*. 451) and in the plays *The Land of Heart's Desire* (*CPl*. 69), *The Shadowy Waters* (*CPl*. 163), and *The King of the Great Clock Tower* (*CPl*. 637).
  REFERENCES: Ellis, Peter Berresford. *Dictionary of Celtic Mythology*. New York: Oxford University Press, 1992; Green, Miranda J. *Dictionary of Celtic Myth and Legend*. London: Thames & Hudson, 1992; Mac Cana, Proinsias. *Celtic Mythology*. Feltham, Middlesex: Newnes, 1983.

AHERNE, fictional character. He appears in WBY's Rosicrucian stories ''Rosa Alchemica'' and ''The Tables of the Law,'' first published in 1897. He allegedly delivered the manuscript of *A Vision* (1925) to WBY at **Thoor Ballylee**, but in his introduction to *A Vision* (1937), WBY admits authorship. Aherne holds a dialogue with **Michael Robartes** in ''Phases of the Moon'' (*CP*. 183), summarizing the central ideas of *A Vision*. WBY, very likely with his tongue in his cheek, thought he may have read the name Aherne among those prosecuted for creating a disturbance at the first production of *The Playboy of the Western World* (*VP*. 852). See also "Owen Aherne and his Dancers" (*CP*. 247).

AIBRIC, pirate sailor in WBY's play *The Shadowy Waters*. He admonishes his master **Forgael** for following the mysterious birds, the "souls of the dead," but he is loyal to Forgael and prevents his murder by the other sailors. He leads the capture of the ship carrying **Dectora** and brings her to Forgael. Finally, having failed to dissuade Forgael from altering a course that he believes will lead to certain death, he returns to port with the other sailors on the ship they have captured. The role of Aibric in the first production of *The Shadowy Waters* in Dublin, 1904, was played by **Seamus O'Sullivan**.

AILILL [also Ailell], mythological king of **Connacht**. His seat was at **Cruachan**, in modern County Roscommon. Ailill is the ineffectual husband of **Maeve**, who is envious of the White Bull in his possession. When she undertakes war on **Ulster** because the Ulstermen refuse to let her have the Brown Bull of Cooley, Ailill is killed by **Conall Caernach** in retaliation for the death of **Fergus**. In WBY's poem "The Old Age of Queen Maeve" (*CP*. 451), the dead Ailill is the person through whom the love god **Aengus** speaks to Maeve and asks for her help. Ailill is also the name of the brother of **Eochaid**, the High King of Ireland, who falls in love with **Étain**, his brother's wife. The story is told in "The Two Kings" (*CP*. 503), although WBY changes the name Ailill to **Ardan**.
    REFERENCES: Ellis, Peter Berresford. *Dictionary of Celtic Mythology*. New York: Oxford University Press, 1992; Green, Miranda J. *Dictionary of Celtic Myth and Legend*. London: Thames & Hudson, 1992; Mac Cana, Proinsias. *Celtic Mythology*. Feltham, Middlesex: Newnes, 1983.

AILLINN, daughter of **Lugaidh**, King of **Munster**. Having discouraged the attentions of the young men of her own province, she falls in love with Baile, the son of **Buan** and heir to the throne of **Ulster**. Their families are opposed to the union, but the lovers arrange to leave home and meet at **Muirthemne**, near **Dun Dealgan**. While he is on his way, Baile, who is so sweetly spoken he is known as Baile of the Honey-Mouth, is approached by a stranger. When he is told Aillinn has died because she has been prevented from coming to meet him, Baile dies of a broken heart. The stranger then seeks out Aillinn and tells her of Baile's death. She, too, dies of a broken heart. Baile is buried at **Baile's Strand**, and a yew tree is planted on his grave. On Aillinn's grave, an apple tree is planted. Later, poets cut branches from the two trees and bring them to **Tara**. There, they spring together and cannot be separated. The lovers' story, which **Lady Gregory** includes in her *Cuchulain of Muirthemne* (1902), is the subject of WBY's dramatic poem "Baile and Aillinn" (*CP*. 459). In WBY's version, the stranger who approaches Baile and Aillinn is **Aengus**, who wishes the lovers to die and be united in **Tir-nan-Oge**. WBY celebrates the miracle of their union after death in ''Ribh at the Tomb of Baile and Aillinn'' (*CP*. 327).

REFERENCE: Ellis, Peter Berresford. *Dictionary of Celtic Mythology*. New York: Oxford University Press, 1992.

ALEEL, a leading character in *The Countess Cathleen*. Called Kevin in the original 1892 version of the play, he is a poet in love with the **Countess** and accompanies her throughout the action. The Countess decides to sell all she has to feed the starving peasants. Aleel, claiming to have been warned by **Aengus** that some terrible death awaits her, implores her instead to accompany him to safety among the hills. She refuses and dies, having sold her soul to the devil. Aleel does not feature in the version of the story that appears in WBY's *Fairy and Folk Tales of the Irish Peasantry* (1888). He is an invention of WBY, and subsequent revisions of the play develop the role until Aleel appears in every scene. It may be that WBY increasingly identified the self-sacrifice of the Countess Cathleen with the political fanaticism of **Maud Gonne** and saw himself in the role of the rejected poet, unsuccessfully offering an alternative existence in dreams and poetry. At the first performance in the **Antient Concert Rooms**, Dublin, 8 May 1899, the part of Aleel was played by **Florence Farr**.

ALEXANDER THE GREAT (356–323 B.C.), king of Macedon (now Macedonia). The son of Philip II of Macedon, he was given a model education by his tutor, **Aristotle**. He succeeded to the throne of Macedon when he was twenty and set about subduing the restive cities of Greece and thwarting uprisings in Thrace and Illyria. After crossing the Hellespont, he defeated the Persians, took command of Syria, and entered Egypt. There he founded **Alexandria**, before returning to Asia and conquering Afghanistan. He overran the Punjab in India, but his army, growing increasingly disillusioned with his leadership, refused to go any further. Returning to Greece through Afghanistan and Iran, he discovered that the leaders he had chosen to govern were largely corrupt. The people deplored the harshness of his punishments, and his generals mutinied, feeling alienated by his visions of equality and by his behavior and mode of dress, which he modeled on the East. The mutiny was unsuccessful, but Alexander, planning a voyage around Arabia by sea, caught a fever and died. He is remembered for his manly beauty, his impulsiveness, his visionary schemes, and his sense of his own divinity but above all for his military strategies and leadership. One of the outstanding leaders of all time, he is referred to by WBY in ''The Saint and the Hunchback'' (*CP*. 189) and ''On a Picture of a Black Centaur by Edmund Dulac'' (*CP*. 242).

REFERENCE: Green, Peter. *Alexander of Macedon, 356–323 B.C.: A Historical Biography*. Berkeley: University of California Press, 1991.

ALEXANDRIA, largest seaport in Egypt. Founded in 332 B.C. by **Alexander**, Alexandria is situated on the Mediterranean Sea, west of the Nile delta. It was an important center of Greek and Jewish culture, with a university and two royal libraries, whose collections have not survived. In 30 B.C., Alexandria was conquered by the Romans. It later became part of the Byzantine Empire, but after the Muslim Arabs took the city in A.D. 642, its importance as a center of learning declined. In WBY's play *The Resurrection* (*CPl.* 580), **The Greek** claims to have come from Alexandria where he saw the worshippers of **Dionysus** carousing in the streets. He declares that the resurrected **Christ** has come to destroy the beliefs of Alexandria, Rome, and Athens. In ''Blood and the Moon'' (*CP* 267), WBY makes reference to the tower of Pharos, a lighthouse built off the coast of Alexandria, c. 280 B.C. Considered one of the wonders of the ancient world, Pharos was destroyed by an earthquake during the fourteenth century.

REFERENCE: Forster, E. M. *Alexandria: A History and a Guide.* Gloucester, Mass.: P. Smith, 1968.

ALGECIRAS, Mediterranean seaport in the Bay of Algeciras in southern Spain, opposite Gibraltar. In November 1927, WBY stayed at the Hotel Reina Cristina in Algeciras, recovering from congestion of the lungs. He moved to Seville, then to Cannes, and finally to **Rapallo** in February 1928. He visited Algeciras again in the fall of 1928 (*AV.* 20). There, he conceived the idea for ''At Algeciras—A Meditation upon Death'' (*CP.* 278).

ALLEN. *See* **ALMHUIN.**

ALLGOOD, MOLLY (1887–1952), actress and sister of **Sara Allgood**. She was born into a working-class family in Dublin. After her father's early death, she grew up in a Protestant orphanage. She was eighteen and an apprentice dressmaker when she joined the **Abbey Theatre** company in 1906, using the stage name Máire O'Neill. She played one of the Musicians in the first production of *Deirdre* by WBY, November 1906, and **Biddy Lally** in *The Unicorn from the Stars*, 1907. She created the role of Conall's Wife in the first production of WBY's play *The Golden Helmet*, March 1908. An intense relationship developed between her and **J. M. Synge**, and they became engaged. Her performance of Pegeen in the first production of *The Playboy of the Western World* was a personal triumph, and Synge was writing *Deirdre of the Sorrows* for her when he died in 1909. After his death, she directed and starred in the play at the Abbey Theatre, 13 January 1910. In 1911, she married the drama critic of the *Manchester Guardian*, George Herbert Mair, and continued her acting career in England with much success. She acted with the Liverpool Repertory Theatre, with **Beerbohm Tree** and J. B. Fagan, and played the role of **Decima** in *The Player Queen*, premiered by the London Stage Society at King's Hall, Covent Garden, May 1919. With the death of her husband in 1926, she returned to Ireland. There, she married actor Arthur Sinclair, and together they acted in the plays of **Sean O'Casey**, both at the Abbey Theatre and on tour. After a divorce and the death of her son in an accident, her final years were clouded with money problems and alcohol. WBY was most impressed with her acting talent (*A.* 563–64) and classified her as a tragic actress (*LE.* 226).

REFERENCES: Coxhead, Elizabeth. *Daughters of Erin: Five Women of the Irish Renascence.* London: Secker & Warburg, 1965; Robinson, Lennox. *Ireland's Abbey Theatre.* London: Sidgwick & Jackson, 1951; Saddlemyer, Ann, ed. *Letters to Molly: John Millington Synge to Máire O'Neill.* Boston: Harvard University Press, 1971.

ALLGOOD, SARA (1883–1950), Irish stage and film actress. A member of the original **Abbey Theatre** company and sister of the actress **Máire O'Neill**, Sara Allgood was born into a working-class family in Dublin. On leaving school, she was apprenticed to an upholsterer, and it was only when she joined Inghínidhe na hÉireann (Daughters of Ireland), the militant nationalist organization founded by **Maud Gonne**, that she gained her first acting experience. Among the cultural activities of the Inghínidhe na hÉireann was a drama class taught by the brothers **Frank** and **W. G. Fay**. When WBY and the Fays formed the **Irish National Theatre Society** in 1903, Sara Allgood was elected to the company, although she continued to work full-time as an apprentice upholsterer. Her first acting role with the Irish National Theatre Society was a "walk-on" in *Twenty-Five* by **Lady Gregory**, March 1903. She then played the part of the daughter Cathleen in the premiere of *Riders to the Sea* by **J. M. Synge**, January 1904. She had her first major success, however, on the opening night of the Abbey Theatre, 27 December 1904, when she played the role of Mrs. Fallon in Lady Gregory's farcical comedy *Spreading the News.* In 1905, she became a full-time actress, and during the next eight years at the Abbey, she developed depth of feeling and vocal power in a range of dramatic roles, including Molly Byrne in Synge's *The Well of the Saints*, February 1905; Widow Quinn in Synge's *The Playboy of the Western World*, January 1907; Feemy Evans in *The Shewing-Up of Blanco Posnet* by **George Bernard Shaw**, August 1909; Lavarcham in Synge's *Deirdre of the Sorrows*, January 1910; and Mary **Bruin** in the first production at the Abbey of WBY's play ***The Land of Heart's Desire***, February 1911. She served as manager for a short time after W. G. Fay's resignation in February 1908 and appeared as Isabella in William Poel's production of *Measure for Measure* at the Gaiety Theatre, Manchester, in April 1908. She left the Abbey in 1913 to perform with the Liverpool Repertory Theatre and other leading English repertory companies. In 1915, at the height of her reputation, she accepted a role in the commercial comedy *Peg O' My Heart.* The production was hugely successful and, in 1916, toured Australia and New Zealand. In Melbourne, September 1916, she married her leading man, Gerald Hensen. In 1918, a daughter died soon after birth, followed some months later by Gerald's death during an influenza epidemic. After a period in London, during which she played Mrs. O'Flaherty in Shaw's *O'Flaherty VC* at the Lyric, Hammersmith, she returned to the Abbey in 1923 and played Juno, one of her most memorable roles, in **Sean O'Casey's** *Juno and the Paycock*, March 1924. She reprised all her O'Casey roles in New York during the 1920s. She went into films in 1929, in

Alfred Hitchcock's *Blackmail*, and after appearing in London in a series of undistinguished plays, she moved to Hollywood in 1940. She appeared in such films as *Lady Hamilton, How Green Was My Valley*, and *Jane Eyre*, but the stereotypical parts she was offered failed to capitalize on her talent. She became an American citizen in 1945 and died in Hollywood on 13 September 1950. She appeared in the premieres of five plays by WBY, playing The Princess in **The King's Threshold** (1903), the Chorus in **On Baile's Strand** (1904), First Musician in **Deirdre** (1906), and **Emer** in both **The Golden Helmet** (1908) and **The Green Helmet** (1910). For WBY, she was one of the greatest of the Abbey actors (*A.* 563–64).

REFERENCES: Coxhead, Elizabeth. *Daughters of Erin: Five Women of the Irish Renascence.* London: Secker & Warburg, 1965; Hunt, Hugh. *The Abbey: Ireland's National Theatre, 1904–1978.* Dublin: Gill and Macmillan, 1979; McCann, Sean, ed. *The Story of the Abbey Theatre.* London: New English Library, 1967; Robinson, Lennox. *Ireland's Abbey Theatre.* London: Sidgwick & Jackson, 1951.

ALLINGHAM, WILLIAM (1824–89), poet and editor. Born in Ballyshannon in the north of Ireland, he was educated at Wray's School, Church Lane, Ballyshannon, and at a boarding school in Killieshandra, County Cavan. At fourteen, he began working in the Provincial Bank of Ireland (now the Allied Irish Bank) where his father was manager. In 1846, he entered the civil service as a customs official and had various placements in Ireland and England. His first collection, *Poems* (1850), was dedicated to the poet Leigh Hunt. A subsequent volume, *Day and Night Songs* (1854), was illustrated by **Dante Gabriel Rossetti**, with whom he had a warm friendship, and by John Everett Millais. In 1864, with the publication of *The Ballad Book*, he was granted a Civil List pension, and in 1874, having retired from the civil service, he moved to London to devote himself to writing. As the editor of *Frazer's Magazine* from 1874 to 1879, he was at the center of London's literary set, numbering among his friends **Alfred, Lord Tennyson** and **Robert Browning**. His later publications included *Irish Songs and Poems* (1887) and *Flower Pieces and Other Poems* (1888). In his writing, he had much understanding and sympathy for his own country and for the native Irish. This is apparent in his narrative poem *Laurence Bloomfield in Ireland* (1864), which focused on the conflict between the Anglo-Irish landlord and the Irish peasant. Yet Allingham was not a nationalist—a severe limitation on his craft, according to WBY in a review of the collected poems (*UP1.* 209–12). He died in Hampstead, London, 18 November 1889, and his ashes were brought back to Ballyshannon for burial. The bridge in the center of Ballyshannon is named after him, while a commemorative bust stands outside the local Allied Irish Bank. WBY admired the Ballyshannon poet, although he had reservations about his ultimate stature as a writer. His article on Allingham, ''The Poet of Ballyshannon,'' appeared in the *Providence Journal*, 2 September 1888, and was reprinted in **Letters to the New Island** (1934). In 1892, he contributed a sketch of Allingham to Alfred Miles's anthology *The Poets and Poetry of the*

Century (*UP1*. 259–61), and he prepared an edition of *Sixteen Poems by William Allingham* (1905) for the **Dun Emer Press**. He named Allingham's *Irish Songs and Poems* (1887) in his list of "Best Irish Books" (*UP1*. 387), and he included Allingham's poems in his collections *Fairy and Folk Tales of the Irish Peasantry* (1888) and *A Book of Irish Verse* (1895). Allingham's lyrical celebrations of Ireland, in particular of the area around Ballyshannon, had a profound influence on WBY, encouraging the younger poet to write about his native **Sligo**. He was influenced by Allingham's treatment of fairy lore; indeed, the early fairy poems and ballads of WBY in *Crossways* (1889) and *The Rose* (1893) are full of echoes of Allingham. In a letter written to Allingham's widow in 1904, WBY graciously acknowledged his debt (*WL*. 446). He had three volumes of poetry and a play by Allingham in his library (*OS*. nos. 33–36).

REFERENCES: Hill, George Birkbeck, ed. *Letters of Dante Gabriel Rossetti to William Allingham, 1854–1870*. London: Fisher Unwin, 1897; Marcus, Phillip L. *Yeats and the Beginning of the Irish Renaissance*. Syracuse: Syracuse University Press, 1987; Warner, Alan. *William Allingham*. Lewisburg, Pa.: Bucknell University Press, 1975; Warner, Alan. "William Allingham: Bibliographical Survey." *Irish Booklore* 2 (1976); Welch, Robert. "William Allingham: The Power and Zest of All Appearance." In *Irish Poetry from Moore to Yeats*. Totowa, N.J.: Barnes & Noble, 1980.

ALMHUIN, Hill of Allen, County Kildare. It was the site of a fortress built by Nuada, the chief druid of Cahir Mór, and was later associated with his descendant **Fionn Mac Cumhal. Grania** was brought here by Fionn after the death of her lover **Diarmuid**. Almhuin is referred to by **Oisin** in *The Wanderings of Oisin* (*CP*. 430), while in *The King's Threshold* (*CPl*. 110), the poet **Seanchan**, weak from his hunger strike, imagines he is in Almhuin with Fionn and **Oscar**. It was the scene of the battle in which the poet Donn Bó, after being decapitated, sang a song in praise of his slain master Fergal Mac Máile Dúin. A different version of the story is told in WBY's story "The Binding of the Hair" (*UP1*. 390–93). In "Gods and Fighting Men" (*EX*. 14), WBY describes a visit he made to the hill of Almhuin on a hot, sunny day.

REFERENCES: Ellis, Peter Berresford. *Dictionary of Celtic Mythology*. New York: Oxford University Press, 1992; McGarry, James P. *Place Names in the Writings of William Butler Yeats*. Gerrards Cross: Colin Smythe, 1976.

ALT (Irish: *Alt dubh*) [black glen], known locally as the Glen, the Glen at Alt, or the Black Glen. Alt is a rocky glen on the north side of **Knocknarea**, in **Sligo** (county). It is the setting for one of WBY's last poems, "The Man and the Echo" (*CP*. 393), written July–October 1938.

REFERENCE: McGarry, James P. *Place Names in the Writings of William Butler Yeats*. Gerrards Cross: Colin Smythe, 1976.

AMERGIN. *See* **INVER AMERGIN**.

AMRITA, drink of the gods and the elixir of immortality in Hindu mythology. In WBY's poem "Anashuya and Vijaya" (*CP*. 10), the suitor **Vijaya**, when challenged by the priestess **Anashuya**, claims Amrita is his mother's name and then that it is the name of his former lover.

REFERENCE: Zimmer, Heinrich. *Myths and Symbols in Indian Art and Civilization.* Ed. Joseph Campbell. Washington, D.C.: Bollingen Foundation, 1946.

ANASHUYA, daughter of Daksha and wife of Atri in Hindu mythology. Her name means "uncomplaining." In WBY's poem "Anashuya and Vijaya" (*CP*. 10), she is a priestess of the temple who challenges the young suitor **Vijaya** to forget his former lover and love only her. Anashuya is also the name of a character in the Sanskrit drama *Shakuntala* by the poet and dramatist Kalidasa. WBY is believed to have read this play in a translation by Monier Williams.

REFERENCE: O'Flaherty, Wendy Doniger, trans. *Hindu Myths: A Sourcebook Translated from the Sanskrit.* Harmondsworth, Middlesex: Penguin, 1975.

ANGEL, character in *The Countess Cathleen* and *The Hour-Glass*. In *The Countess Cathleen*, a group of Angels appears as the Countess dies. When the poet **Aleel** demands to know her fate, one of the Angels assures him she has gone to Heaven. In *The Hour-Glass*, an Angel, upturning an hourglass, tells the **Wise Man** that he will die in an hour and go to Hell. When challenged by the Wise Man, the Angel tells him he may go to Heaven if he finds, before the sand runs out, one person who believes in God. The Angel (then named a spirit) in the first production of *The Countess Cathleen*, May 1899, was played by Dorothy Paget, niece of **Florence Farr**. When *The Hour-Glass* was produced by the **Irish National Theatre Society**, March 1903, the role of the Angel was performed by Máire Nic Shiubhlaigh.

ANTHEIL, GEORGE (1900–1959), pianist, composer, and writer. Of German descent, Antheil was born in Trenton, New Jersey. His first music teacher of importance was Constantine von Sternberg, a former pupil of Liszt. He studied in New York with the composer Ernest Bloch (1880–1959) and, in 1922, moved to Berlin to pursue a career as a concert pianist. A year later, 4 October 1923, he performed three of his piano compositions, including *Mechanisms* and *Airplane Sonata*, at the glamorous Théâtre des Champs-Élysées in Paris. The distinguished audience included Pablo Picasso, Igor Stravinsky, Serge Diaghilev, **T. S. Eliot**, and **James Joyce**. A near-riot ensued, and overnight Antheil became celebrated among the French avant-garde. He composed the score for an experimental film by Fernand Léger, *Ballet Mécanique* (1923), although it was not used. The score was written for an unusual arrangement of instruments, including eight pianos, gongs and rattles, door bells, xylophones, and an airplane propeller driven by two electric motors. At the first American performance in Carnegie Hall, New York, the audience considered the composition more of a joke than serious music and responded audibly, especially when the airplane propeller blew a stream of cold air into the auditorium. In Paris, Antheil met **Ezra Pound**, who believed him a genius. Not only did Pound write the influential *Antheil and the Theory of Harmony*, but he also tried to procure him financial support so that he could give up the concert platform to concentrate on composition. It was Pound who introduced Antheil to WBY at the cafe of the Hotel Rapallo, **Rapallo**, Italy, where WBY dined regularly with Pound, T. S. Eliot, and Gerhart Hauptmann, among others. According to Antheil in his autobiography *Bad Boy of Music*, all these writers were voracious readers of detective stories, so he decided to write a thriller for them under the pseudonym Stacey Bishop. The novel, *Death in the Dark*, was published by Faber and Faber in 1930. WBY was impressed with Antheil and, in March 1929, wrote excitedly to **Lady Gregory**, telling her that Antheil had already started work on musical settings for a production in Vienna of *At the Hawk's Well, On Baile's Strand*, and *Fighting the Waves* (*WL.* 757–60). The production never took place, and only *Fighting the Waves* was set to music by Antheil. Its premiere was given at the **Abbey Theatre**, August 1929, with choreography by **Ninette de Valois**. The music, with its unusual combination of instruments, aroused some controversy, but WBY comments favorably on it in *Wheels and Butterflies* (1934) and in his introduction to *Fighting the Waves* (*VPl.* 571). Antheil also composed settings for several of WBY's poems. In 1933, he moved to Hollywood, where he wrote film scores and worked on two major works, *Symphony No. 3* and *Symphony No. 4*. Among his other compositions are *Sonata Sauvage* (1922), *Jazz Symphonietta* (1926), and a trio of operas: *Transatlantic*, which premiered at the Frankfurt Opera House, May 1930; *Helen Retires*, which was performed in New York, 1934; and *Volpone*, first performed in New York in 1953. He composed the incidental music for **Sophocles's** *Oedipus Rex* at the Berlin State Theater in 1929.

REFERENCES: Antheil, George. *Bad Boy of Music*. Garden City, N.J.: Doubleday, 1945; Gilder, Eric. *The Dictionary of Composers and Their Music*. New York: Wings Books, 1985; Rossi, Nick, and Choate, Robert A. *Music of Our Time: An Anthology of Works of Selected Contemporary Composers of the 20th Century*. Boston: Crescendo, 1969.

ANTIENT CONCERT ROOMS, Brunswick Street (now Pearse Street), Dublin. This large hall, which seated about 800 people, had a fairly large stage, suitable for play production. Under a new Irish Local Government Act permitting the Municipality of Dublin to license public halls for theatrical performances, the first production of WBY's play *The Countess Cathleen* was given in the Antient Concert Rooms by the **Irish Literary Theatre**, May 1899. The first performance of WBY's one-act play *The Pot of Broth*, produced by **W. G. Fay's** Irish National Dramatic Company, was presented there, 30 October 1902, while WBY and **Padraic Pearse** shared the platform at the Antient Concert Rooms during the **Thomas Davis** Centenary Celebrations, November 1914.

AOIFE, legendary Scottish queen. She is the daughter of Ard-Greimne and sister of **Scathach**. When her sister, accompanied by the youthful **Cuchulain**, opposes her in battle, Aoife challenges Cuchulain to a duel. He wins but spares her life on condition she make peace with her sister. She becomes his lover and bears him a son, **Connla**, whom she raises to hate his father. She sends the boy to Ireland to challenge him in single combat. Cuchulain accepts, and the boy is killed. At the conclusion of WBY's play *At the Hawk's Well*, the young Cuchulain leaves to fight with Aoife, while in *The Death of Cuchulain*, Aoife appears when the fatally wounded warrior is about to die and ties his body to a stake so that he may die upright. See also "The Grey Rock" (*CP*. 115) and *On Baile's Strand* (*CPl*. 252, 274–76).

REFERENCE: Ellis, Peter Berresford. *Dictionary of Celtic Mythology*. New York: Oxford University Press, 1992.

ARAN ISLANDS, islands off the coast of **Galway** (county) in the west of Ireland. They consist of three islands: Inishmore (Irish: *Árainn Mhor*), the largest; Inishmaan (*Inis Meáin*); and Inisheer (*Inis Óirr*), the smallest. Inishmore is also known as Aranmor. The islands are rich in megalithic monuments, most notably the stone fort of Dun Aengus, built on the edge of a 300-foot cliff on Inishmore. Also of note are the monastic settlements. In the 1890s, the Aran Islands were renowned for a way of life that had changed little for centuries. WBY visited the islands with **Arthur Symons** during a tour of the west of Ireland, summer 1896, ostensibly to research fairy lore for his novel *The Speckled Bird*—a novel that he never completed (Symons's account of the visit was published in the *Savoy*, October–December 1896). WBY claims to have had mystical dreams on the islands, including one of a woman shooting an arrow among the stars, and in "What is 'Popular Poetry'?" (*EI*. 9), he quotes a version of a poem spoken by an Aran Islander. In WBY's play *The Dreaming of the Bones*, the **Young Man** is dressed like an Aran fisherman, with his *bainín* (white woollen coat) and *pampooties* (hide shoes without heels). In the course of the play, the Young Man looks from the Irish mainland and is moved by the sight of the islands in the early light of dawn. The Aran Islands made a profound impression on WBY, and when he first met **J. M. Synge** in Paris, he urged him to go there and to write of the people and their way of life. WBY tells the story in his preface to Synge's *The Well of the Saints* (*EI*. 299). Synge spent his summers on the islands, from 1898 to 1902, and his one-act tragedy *Riders to the Sea* takes place there. **Lady Gregory** visited the islands in search of folklore.

REFERENCES: Robinson, Tim. *Stones of Aran: Pilgrimage*. Mullingar: Lilliput/Wolfhound, 1988; Synge, J. M. *The Aran Islands*. Dublin: Maunsel, 1907; Waddell, John; O'Connell, J. W.; and Korff, Anne. *The Book of Aran: The Aran Islands, Co. Galway*. Newtownlynch, Kinvara, Co. Galway: Tír Eolas, 1994.

ARCADY [Arcadia], mountainous region of southern Greece. It was reputed to be the rural paradise of the ancient Greek world. The Arcadians were shepherds and hunters who lived a simple, natural life, isolated from the rest of the world. In his poem "The Song of the Happy Shepherd" (*CP*. 7), WBY regrets the passing of Arcady. See also *The Island of Statues* (*VPl*. 1224).

ARDAN, brother of **Eochaid**, the High King of Ireland. In WBY's dramatic poem "The Two Kings" (*CP*. 503), Ardan falls in love with his brother's wife, **Étain**, who is shocked when she discovers his secret. She contrives for him to fall into a magic sleep. When he awakens, he is miraculously cured of his infatuation. Ardan is also the name of one of the two brothers of **Naoise**. He is killed by **Conchubar** when he returns with his brothers to Ireland from Scotland. He does not appear in WBY's play *Deirdre*. See also **Ailill**.

REFERENCES: Ellis, Peter Berresford. *Dictionary of Celtic Mythology*. New York: Oxford University Press, 1992; Green, Miranda J. *Dictionary of Celtic Myth and Legend*. London: Thames & Hudson, 1992; Mac Cana, Proinsias. *Celtic Mythology*. Feltham, Middlesex: Newnes, 1983.

ARDRAHAN (Irish: *Ard-rathain*) [height of the ferns], a village on the main **Galway** to **Limerick** road. It is about eight miles north of **Gort**, County Galway. In the area is **Tulira Castle**, home of **Edward Martyn**, with whom WBY stayed while on a tour of Ireland during the summer of 1896. In "Dust Hath Closed Helen's Eye" (*MY*. 26), WBY recalls an old woman from **Ballylee** who had seen **Mary Hynes** and claimed she was more beautiful than Mary Guthrie from Ardrahan.

REFERENCE: McGarry, James P. *Place Names in the Writings of William Butler Yeats*. Gerrards Cross: Colin Smythe, 1976.

ARISTOTLE (384–322 B.C.), Greek teacher and thinker. He was born in Stagira, the son of a doctor. After studying for twenty years with **Plato**, he tutored **Alexander the Great** from 343 to 336 B.C.—a role that WBY alludes to in the poem "Among School Children" (*CP*. 242). In 335 B.C., Aristotle opened a school in Athens, but after the death of Alexander in 323 B.C., he fled to Chalcis and died a year later. Aristotle left little writing, but his principles and ideas, including the treatises *De Anima, De Poetica*, and *Rhetoric*, were passed down through lecture notes taken by his pupils. WBY characterized **Lady Gregory** by quoting Aristotle: "[T]o write well one should express oneself like the common people, but think like a wise man" (*UP2*. 494). He entitled one of the stories, collected when in the company of Lady Gregory, "Aristotle of the Books" (*MY*. 66).

REFERENCES: Barnes, Jonathan, ed. *The Cambridge Companion to Aristotle*. Cambridge and New York: Cambridge University Press, 1995; Evangeliou, Christos. *Aristotle's Categories and Porphyry*. New York: Leiden, 1988; Jaspers, Karl. *The Great Philosophers*. Trans. Edith Ehrlich and Leonard Ehrlich. New York: Harcourt Brace, 1994.

ARMSTRONG, [EDITH] LAURA (1862–?), youngest daughter of Sergeant Richard Armstrong, a Dublin barrister and distant relative of WBY through his Corbet relations. Reputedly the first of many women to attract WBY, she met the poet for the first time in 1882, when she asked him to ride with her in her pony carriage at **Howth**, County Dublin. She was three years older than WBY and lived with her family at 60 St. Stephen's Green, Dublin. Although she was engaged to be married, WBY became her confidant, and they carried on a literary flirtation in which she was "Vivien" to his "Clarin." In January 1884, he wrote his first play, *Vivien and Time*, later published as **Time and the Witch Vivien**. She played the part of Vivien in an amateur performance of the play given at the home of Judge Wright in Howth, and WBY began writing for her **The Island of Statues**. In September 1884, she married her fiance, Henry Morgan Byrne, a solicitor, in St. Peter's Church, Dublin. The marriage ended in divorce. She is subsequently reported to have married a Welsh gardener from whom she also separated, but later events in her life are sketchy and without confirmation. She is thought to have had two children. She is very likely the model for the flighty Margaret Leland in WBY's novel **John Sherman and Dhoya**, written a few years later. In an unpublished lyric, "A Double Moon or More Ago" (*UM*. 34), WBY appears to have had Laura Armstrong in mind.

REFERENCE: Murphy, William M. "William Butler Yeats's *John Sherman*: An Irish Poet's Declaration of Independence." *Irish University Review* 9, no. 1 (spring 1979).

ARNOLD, MATTHEW (1822–88), influential English poet and critic, and professor of poetry at Oxford University, 1857–67. He was the son of Thomas Arnold, headmaster of Rugby. For a considerable period of his life, he was an inspector of schools. Considered one of the most important Victorian writers, he exercised a major influence over the younger poets, especially through his essays on literary criticism. Arnold emphasized the need for objectivity in poetry and promoted a literature based on Christian morality. Among his important books of literary criticism are *On Translating Homer* (1861), *Essays in Criticism* (1865, 1888), and *Culture and Anarchy* (1869). WBY rejected Arnold's central belief that poetry was "a criticism of life," and in his own early work retreated into the imaginative world of faery. Yet he formulated his aesthetic theory by reading Arnold, whom he consistently quoted, although sometimes in a negative context. He found support for his interest in Celtic myth in Arnold's seminal work *The Study of Celtic Literature* (1896), responding to it in his essay "The Celtic Element in Literature" (*EI*. 173–88). Arnold was a classical scholar and read the works of **Plato** and **Dante**. This may have alienated WBY, who had no knowledge of Greek or Latin and was forced to read the classical writers in translation—a further reason for his intense investigations into Celtic mythology. Arnold's greatest poems, "The Scholar Gypsy" and "Dover Beach," dealing with themes of loneliness and pessimism, disturbed WBY by their psychological perplexity. While in **Oxford** in the late 1880s, he visited the places mentioned in Arnold's poetry (*WL*. 135). There is a suggestion that Arnold's dramatic poem

''Sohrab and Rustum'' may have influenced some of the action in WBY's play *On Baile's Strand*. WBY had *Letters of Matthew Arnold* (1895), *On Translating Homer* (1862), *Poetical Works* (1892), and *The Study of Celtic Literature* (1891) in his library (*OS*. nos. 52–55).

REFERENCES: Honan, Park. *Matthew Arnold: A Life*. New York: McGraw-Hill, 1981; Kelleher, John V. ''Matthew Arnold and the Celtic Revival.'' In *Perspectives of Criticism*. Ed. Harry Levin. Cambridge, Mass.: Harvard University Press, 1950; Rowse, A. L. *Matthew Arnold: Poet and Prophet*. London: Thames & Hudson, 1976; Trilling, Leonard. *Matthew Arnold: Poet*. New York: Harcourt Brace Jovanovich, 1979.

ARTHUR, KING OF BRITAIN, arguably the best known of the Celtic heroes. He may have been based on a historical figure who lived in Britain during the sixth century A.D. There are references to Arthur in *De Excidio et Conquesta Britanniae* by the monk Gildas (500–570) and in *Historia Brittonum*, in which the historian Nennius (c. 800) claims Arthur led the Celts to victory in a number of battles against the Anglo-Saxons. According to the *Annales Cambriae* (c. 955), Arthur was killed at the battle of Camluan in 537. These historical references were elaborated by Geoffrey of Monmouth, who in his *Historia Regum Britanniae* (c. 1135) portrayed Arthur as the conqueror of Europe. Subsequent writers added to the legend. The Norman poet Wace, in his *Roman de Brut* (c. 1155), introduced the knights of the Round Table, while the twelfth-century French poet Chrétien de Troyes added courtly love and the legend of the Holy Grail. Sir Thomas Malory completed the transformation of the Celtic chieftain to medieval English monarch in *Le Morte d'Arthur* (1485). This has remained the model for future writers, among them **Tennyson** and **William Morris**. WBY believed that much of Arthurian legend developed from the exploits of **Fionn Mac Cumhal** and the **Fianna**, and from **Cuchulain** and the knights of the **Red Branch**. Thus, in his essay ''The Celtic Element in Literature'' (*EI*. 185) he insists that the Celt has been close to the mainstream of European literature for many centuries. In his notes to *Visions and Beliefs in the West of Ireland* (*LE*. 260), WBY also claims that Mongan, who is reputed to have killed Arthur, was the reincarnation of Fionn.

REFERENCES: Barber, Richard W. *Arthur of Albion: An Introduction to the Arthurian Literature and Legends of England*. London: Barrie & Rockliff, 1961; Gurteen, Stephen H. V. *The Arthurian Epic*. New York: Haskell, 1965; Loomis, Roger Sherman. *Celtic Myth and Arthurian Romance*. New York: Haskell, 1967.

ARTISSON, ROBERT, a spirit or demon. According to St. John D. Seymour in his *Irish Witchcraft and Demonology* (1913), Robert Artisson was the incubus of **Lady Alice Kyteler**, a witch in Kilkenny during the fourteenth century, and had sexual intercourse with her. He appeared in different animal forms, such as a cat or a hairy black dog. WBY gives symbolic significance to the relationship between this demon and Lady Kyteler in "Nineteen Hundred and Nineteen" (*CP*. 232). See also *VP*. 433.

REFERENCES: Jeffares, A. Norman. *A New Commentary on the Poems of W. B. Yeats*. Stanford, Calif.: Stanford University Press, 1984; Seymour, St. John D. *Irish Witchcraft and Demonology*. 1913. Reprint, New York: Barnes & Noble, 1972.

ASHFIELD TERRACE, Yeats family residence. In 1884, because of financial problems, **John B. Yeats** moved with his family from **Howth**, Dublin (county), to 10 Ashfield Terrace (now 418 Harold's Cross Road), Dublin. It was a red brick villa in Terenure, a suburb two and a half miles south of the center of the city. While there, WBY enrolled at the **Metropolitan School of Art**. He was not happy in Ashfield Terrace, feeling alienated by both the people and the environment (*A*. 83–85). Nevertheless, he remained there with his family until they returned to London in 1887.

ATHENE [also Pallas Athene], virgin goddess of war and peace in Greek mythology. She was also associated with wisdom and with arts and crafts. In his poems, WBY frequently compares **Maud Gonne** with Athene, as in "A Thought from Propertius" (*CP*. 172) and "Beautiful Lofty Things" (*CP*. 348). In "The Phases of the Moon" (*CP*. 183), Athene instructs **Achilles** on the actions he must follow in battle—an incident derived from the *Iliad*, Book xxii, 330. In "Michael Robartes and the Dancer" (*CP*. 197), WBY presents Athene as representative of that Unity of Being that is achieved by those women who think not only with the mind but also with the whole body.

ATHENRY (Irish: *Ath-na-Riogh*) [ford of the kings], town in **Galway** (county). It is referred to by WBY in "Happy and Unhappy Theologians" (*MY*. 46) when the Unhappy Theologian recalls a vision in which he thought he saw a soldier who was descended from King O'Connor of Athenry. In 1316, Felim O'Conor, King of **Connacht**, was killed outside the town in a battle against the Anglo-Normans.

REFERENCE: McGarry, James P. *Place Names in the Writings of William Butler Yeats*. Gerrards Cross: Colin Smythe, 1976.

AT THE HAWK'S WELL, one-act verse play by WBY. Subtitled *The Well of Immortality, At the Hawk's Well* was modeled in style and presentation on the Japanese **Noh**. It was performed privately for the first time in Lady Cunard's drawing room at Cavendish Square, London, 2 April 1916. In the audience were **T. S. Eliot** and Sir Thomas Beecham. It was revived 4 April 1916 in Lady Islington's drawing room at Chesterfield Gardens as a war benefit, before an audience of 300, including Queen Alexandra, Princess Victoria, the Grand Duchess George of Russia, the Duchess of Marlborough, and Lady Randolph Churchill. Before the performance, WBY gave a lecture that Queen Alexandra asked to be cut short. She left soon afterward. The innovative production of this verse

play made use of masks, stylized movement, a climactic dance, and a choreographed ritual for the opening and closing of the curtain. It was played on a
small platform without special lighting, the audience seated on three sides, and
the actors entered and left by the same door as the audience. Features of the
production were the dancing of **The Guardian of the Well** by the Japanese
Michio Ito and the music and costumes by **Edmund Dulac**. According to the
stage directions, the action of the play takes place during the Heroic Age. A
chorus of three musicians, accompanying the action on flute, gong, and zither,
describes the barren mountain setting and the dry well at the foot of three bare
hazel trees. The well is represented by a square blue cloth. The Guardian of the
Well crouches on the ground, covered by a black cloth, while an **Old Man**
climbs up the mountain to keep vigil by the well. The action begins when a
young man, who identifies himself as **Cuchulain**, arrives to drink from the
miraculous water of the well of immortality. The Old Man advises him that the
water only bubbles for a few moments, and since he has been waiting there for
the past fifty years, he has the right to drink first. The Young Man promises to
share the water, but he is interrupted by the Guardian of the Well, who slowly
transforms into a hawk-woman, having been possessed by the **Sídhe**. The Old
Man warns Cuchulain that if he looks in her eyes, he will be cursed, but the
Young Man ignores the warning, and while the water bubbles up, he is led
offstage by the hawk-woman, as in a dream. The Old Man falls asleep, and
when he wakes, he finds the stones of the well are wet. When the Young Man
returns, having failed to capture the hawk-woman, he hears the clashes of swords
and shields on a nearby mountain. Excited by the noise of battle, he goes off
to fight **Aoife**, no longer in a dream. The Old Man, thwarted once again, leaves
the stage to the Musicians who close the ritual curtain with a song that extols
a quiet, pastoral life. There is no basis for this story in the legends of Cuchulain,
but there are precedents in Irish mythology for a well that possesses magical
powers. WBY was familiar with **William Morris's** *The Well at the World's
End* and the Noh drama *Yoro* (The sustenance of age) by Zeami (1363–1443),
in which a peasant and his son are questioned by a court official about a miraculous fountain of youth. *At the Hawk's Well* was first published in *Harper's
Bazaar* in March 1917 and in *Today* in June 1917. It was included in the collection ***The Wild Swans at Coole*** (1917), in ***Four Plays for Dancers*** (1921),
the latter printing containing drawings by Dulac of the masks and costumes, and
in ***Plays and Controversies*** (1923). From 1934, it was included in all subsequent
printings of WBY's ***Collected Plays***. The cast of the first production was as
follows: Old Man, Allan Wade; **Young Man**, Henry Ainley; Guardian of the
Well, Michio Ito; Three Musicians, Edmund Dulac, Mrs. Mann, Mr. Foulds.
The production was photographed by American photographer Alvin Langdon
Coburn.

REFERENCES: Bjersby, Birgit. *The Interpretation of the Cuchulain Legend in the
Works of W. B. Yeats.* Folcroft, Pa.: Folcroft, 1969; Ellis, Sylvia C. *The Plays of W. B.
Yeats: Yeats and the Dancer.* London: Macmillan, 1995; Miller, Liam. *The Noble Drama*

of W. B. Yeats. Dublin: Dolmen, 1977; Taylor, Richard. *A Reader's Guide to the Plays of W. B. Yeats*. New York: St. Martin's, 1984.

ATTRACTA, priestess in WBY's late play ***The Herne's Egg***. Attracta claims to be betrothed to the Great Herne. She is raped by **Congal** and the other warriors but insists that it was the Great Herne that came to her in the night and made love to her. She prophesies that the warriors will be reincarnated as animals. When Congal is fatally wounded by the **Fool**, a donkey is heard coupling with another donkey. Attracta's prophecy has been fulfilled. WBY based the character on St. Attracta, a fifth-century priestess who kept a hospice for travelers in **Cool-a-vin**. In the first production of the play by the Lyric Theatre, Dublin, October 1950, Attracta was played by Eithne Dunne.

AUBEG (Irish: *Abhann Beag*) [little river], river in **Cork** (county). It runs through a large area of land owned by the Elizabethan poet and statesman **Edmund Spenser**. In his essay "Edmund Spenser" (*EI*. 360), WBY identifies the Aubeg as the Mulla in Spenser's *The Faerie Queen*.
    REFERENCE: McGarry, James P. *Place Names in the Writings of William Butler Yeats*. Gerrards Cross: Colin Smythe, 1976.

AUDEN, W[YSTAN] H[UGH] (1907–73), poet and playwright. He was born in York, England, and educated at Gresham's School, Holt, and **Christ Church** College, **Oxford**. From 1930 to 1935, he taught at Malvern College. With his fellow poets **Stephen Spender, Louis MacNeice**, and **C. Day Lewis**, Auden was a member of a postdepression generation that saw poetry as a means to effect social and political change. In 1939, on the outbreak of World War II, he moved to the United States, becoming an American citizen in 1946. He returned to England and was elected Professor of Poetry at Oxford, 1956–61. In his numerous collections of verse, among them *The Double Man* (1941), *Collected Poetry* (1945), *The Age of Anxiety* (1947), *Nones* (1951), and *About the House* (1965), he reveals himself to be an original and satirical writer with a natural command of language. WBY was out of sympathy with much of Auden's poetry, criticizing him for obscurity and lack of form (*LE*. 193). Nevertheless, he included four of his poems in ***The Oxford Book of Modern Verse*** (1936) and admitted to **Dorothy Wellesley** that he admired Auden more than he had acknowledged in the anthology (*WL*. 886). With Christopher Isherwood, Auden wrote verse plays, including *The Ascent of F6* (1936), referred to by WBY in ***On the Boiler*** (*LE*. 248). On the death of WBY in 1939, Auden composed the moving and uplifting elegy "In Memory of W. B. Yeats." WBY had four of Auden's books in his library, *Look Stranger* (1936), *The Orators* (1932), *Poems* (1933), and *The Dog beneath the Skin* (1935), coauthored with Christopher Isherwood (*OS*. nos. 64–67).
    REFERENCES: Callan, Edward. *Auden: A Carnival of Intellect*. New York: Oxford University Press, 1983; Carpenter, Humphrey. *W. H. Auden: A Biography*. London; Bos-

ton: Allen & Unwin, 1981; Hynes, Samuel. "Yeats and the Poets of the Thirties." In *Modern Irish Literature*. Ed. Raymond J. Porter and James D. Brophy. New York: Twayne, 1972; Levy, Alan. *In the Autumn of the Age of Anxiety*. Sag Harbor, N.Y.: Permanent, 1983; Maxwell, D. E. S. *Poets of the Thirties*. New York: Barnes & Noble, 1969; Osborne, Charles. *W. H. Auden: The Life of a Poet*. London: Methuen, 1979; Rowse, A. L. *Poet Auden: A Personal Memoir*. London: Methuen, 1987.

AUGHANISH (Irish: *Each-Inis*) [island of the horse], rocky promontory in Galway Bay, six miles northwest of **Kinvara, Galway** (county). In a note to the poem "The Host of the Air" (*VP*. 804), WBY tells of a young bride from Aughanish who was taken by the **Sídhe** and drowned. Aughanish is the location of a barracks in *The Unicorn from the Stars* (*CPl*. 370), while in *The Dreaming of the Bones* (*CPl*. 437), the **Stranger** speaks of the cocks of Aughanish.
   REFERENCE: McGarry, James P. *Place Names in the Writings of William Butler Yeats*. Gerrards Cross: Colin Smythe, 1976.

AUGHRIM (Irish: *Each-dhruim*) [ridge of the horse], village, two miles southeast of Kilconnell in **Galway** (county). The Battle of Aughrim was fought on a nearby ridge in July 1691, when the Catholic army under James II was defeated by the Protestant forces of **William III**. The outcome of this battle determined the future course of Irish history. In *Purgatory* (*CPl*. 683), the **Old Man** claims to be descended from those who fought at Aughrim (most likely on the Protestant side). The Battle of Aughrim, together with the Siege of Londonderry (1689) and the Battle of the **Boyne** (1690), has taken on mythic status with many of the Protestants of **Ulster**.
   REFERENCE: McGarry, James P. *Place Names in the Writings of William Butler Yeats*. Gerrards Cross: Colin Smythe, 1976.

AUTOBIOGRAPHIES. WBY finished the draft of his autobiography in late 1914. It covered his childhood, adolescence, and young adulthood up to 1900. He chose not to publish this draft, but over the next years, he revised and released the material in sections, beginning with *Reveries over Childhood and Youth*, published by the **Cuala Press** in 1915. This covered his life in **Sligo**, Dublin, and London, up to 1886. The second part of his autobiography, *The Trembling of the Veil*, which was published by T. Werner Laurie in 1922, was completed at **Thoor Ballylee** in 1922. It included reminiscences of his schooldays in **Bedford Park**, his infatuation with **Maud Gonne**, his contacts with **W. E. Henley, Oscar Wilde**, and **William Morris**, and character analyses of those members of the **Rhymers' Club** whom he classified collectively as the "Tragic Generation." *Reveries over Childhood and Youth* and *The Trembling of the Veil* were published together in 1926 under the title *Autobiographies*. The third part of the autobiography, *Estrangement*, was published by Cuala Press in 1926. It was followed by *The Death of Synge* (1928). Both of these publications consisted of journal entries for the year 1909. The final section of the autobiography,

Dramatis Personae, was published by Cuala Press in 1935. It was principally an account of **Coole Park** and the beginnings of the **Abbey Theatre**. All these publications, in addition to *The Bounty of Sweden* (1925), which told of WBY's visit to Sweden to receive the **Nobel Prize for Literature**, were brought together in *The Autobiography of William Butler Yeats* (1938), reprinted in 1955 as *Autobiographies*. The published volumes of WBY's autobiography, six in all, differ in content and detail from the first draft of the autobiography and the entries in his journal (transcribed and edited by Denis Donoghue in *W. B. Yeats: Memoirs* (1972). While new material is added, the poet omits, among other things, some conversations with Maud Gonne and intimate details of his relationship with **Olivia Shakespear**.

REFERENCES: Fletcher, Ian. "Rhythm and Pattern in Yeats's *Autobiographies*." In *W. B. Yeats and His Contemporaries*. Brighton, Sussex: Harvester, 1987; Ronsley, Joseph. *Yeats' Autobiography: Life as Symbolic Pattern*. London: Oxford, 1968.

AUTOBIOGRAPHY OF WILLIAM BUTLER YEATS, THE. *See AUTOBIOGRA-PHIES*.

B

BABAR [also Baber, Babur](1483–1530), founder of the Mogul empire of India. A descendant of **Tamerlane**, Babar succeeded to a small principality in central Asia when he was fifteen. From there, he established a kingdom in Afghanistan in 1504. He captured Delhi in 1526 and took control of northern India. Babar was an accomplished musician and writer. His autobiography is his outstanding work. He is referred to by WBY in "Upon a Dying Lady" (*CP*. 177).
   REFERENCE: Lane–Poole, Stanley. *Babar*. Dehli: S. Chand, 1964.

BAILE. *See* **AILLINN**.

BAILE'S STRAND (Irish: *Traigh mBaile*), now called Seatown, County Louth. Baile's Strand was near **Dun Dealgan**. It was associated with **Cuchulain**, who had a fortress nearby. The legendary hero killed his only son at Baile's Strand (*CPl*. 247, 699, 701).
   REFERENCE: McGarry, James P. *Place Names in the Writings of William Butler Yeats*. Gerrards Cross: Colin Smythe, 1976.

BAILEVELEHAN (Irish: *Baile-Ui-Mhaolachain*) [place of the pathway], in northern **Clare** (county), between New Quay and **Corcomroe Abbey**. The **Stranger** refers to it in *The Dreaming of the Bones* (*CPl*. 437).
   REFERENCE: McGarry, James P. *Place Names in the Writings of William Butler Yeats*. Gerrards Cross: Colin Smythe, 1976.

BALLAGHADEREEN [also Ballaghaderreen] (Irish: *Bealach an Doirin*) [road of the little oakwood], cathedral town of the Diocese of Achonry, County Roscommon. When discussing the beginnings of the Irish Dramatic Movement in *Sam-*

hain (1903) (*EX.* 98), WBY recalls an amateur company from Ballaghadereen performing **Douglas Hyde's** *An Posadh* in the Rotunda, Dublin. Ballaghadereen was previously in **Mayo** (county).
REFERENCE: McGarry, James P. *Place Names in the Writings of William Butler Yeats.* Gerrards Cross: Colin Smythe, 1976.

BALLINA (Irish: *Bel-an-atha*) [mouth of the ford], market town and seaport in northeast **Mayo** (county). Seven miles from **Killala**, it is the setting for WBY's play *Cathleen Ni Houlihan*. In the play, Bridget reminds her husband Peter of driving lambs to the market at Ballina.
REFERENCE: McGarry, James P. *Place Names in the Writings of William Butler Yeats.* Gerrards Cross: Colin Smythe, 1976.

BALLINAFAD (Irish: *Bel-an-atha-fada*) [mouth of the long ford], village in the parish of Aughanagh, between **Sligo** (town) and Boyle, County Roscommon. Ballinafad is mentioned by WBY in "The Ballad of Father O'Hart" (*CP.* 23). The area is rich in megalithic sites.
REFERENCE: McGarry, James P. *Place Names in the Writings of William Butler Yeats.* Gerrards Cross: Colin Smythe, 1976.

BALLISODARE [also Ballysadare, Ballisadare] (Irish: *Baile eas-dara*) [town of the waterfall of the oak], small town, south of **Sligo** (town), at the mouth of the Owenmore River. WBY's great-uncle **William Middleton** lived during the winter at Avena House, near the **Pollexfen** flour mills at Ballisodare. As a child, WBY visited the Middletons, and it was at Ballisodare that he was introduced to the local belief in fairies. He recalls his terror as a child when passing a haunted spot by the river in Ballisodare (*LE.* 289). He based "Down by the Salley Gardens" (*CP.* 22) and "The Host of the Air" (*CP.* 63) on a folk song and ballad sung by an old woman in Ballisodare (*VP.* 797, 803).
REFERENCE: McGarry, James P. *Place Names in the Writings of William Butler Yeats.* Gerrards Cross: Colin Smythe, 1976.

BALLYGAWLEY HILL[S] (Irish: *Baile Dhalaigh*), range of hills, south of **Sligo** (town). It is mentioned by WBY in his play *The Land of Heart's Desire* (*CPl.* 68), in which the **Faery Child** claims to be older than the eagle-cock on Ballygawley Hill. In "Red Hanrahan's Curse" (*MY.* 238–45), the poet **Hanrahan** puts a curse on the old eagle-cock of Ballygawley Hill and on the gray pike of **Castle Dargan** Lake, which is near the town of Ballygawley. A high point in the Ballygawley Hills is **Birds' Mountain**.
REFERENCE: McGarry, James P. *Place Names in the Writings of William Butler Yeats.* Gerrards Cross: Colin Smythe, 1976.

BALLYLEE (Irish: *Baile O'Liagh*), townland in **Galway** (county). It gave its name to the Norman tower, Ballylee Castle (which WBY renamed **Thoor Bal-**

lylee), three miles from **Gort**. WBY visited Ballylee in 1900. He spoke with the miller who lived in the tower about **Mary Hynes**, the famous beauty associated with the area. He describes his visit in "Dust Hath Closed Helen's Eye" (*MY*. 22–30). Ballylee, which is on the link road to **Coole Park**, is the setting for WBY's tribute to **Lady Gregory**, "Coole Park and Ballylee, 1931" (*CP*. 275).

REFERENCE: McGarry, James P. *Place Names in the Writings of William Butler Yeats*. Gerrards Cross: Colin Smythe, 1976.

BALLYMONEY (Irish: *Baile-Mhuine*). There are a number of towns or townlands in Ireland with the name Ballymoney, although possibly the best known is the market town in County Antrim, in the northeast of Ireland. **John Corbet**, the Cambridge student and skeptic in *The Words upon the Window-Pane*, is said to be related to the Corbets of Ballymoney. WBY's paternal grandmother was **Jane Grace Corbet Yeats**, and WBY was born near **Sandymount Castle**, which belonged to his uncle **Robert Corbet**. No family connection can be traced to Ballymoney in County Antrim.

REFERENCE: McGarry, James P. *Place Names in the Writings of William Butler Yeats*. Gerrards Cross: Colin Smythe, 1976.

BALOR [Balor of the Evil Eye], Irish god of death. Balor was king of the **Fomorians**, a mythical race of demons who came from the sea and were associated with darkness and death. When the **Tuatha dé Danaan** inhabited Ireland, the Fomorians, who were grossly misshapen, harried them with harsh taxes and demands. Anyone who failed to meet their expectations was punished by having his nose cut from his face. Balor had one eye that could kill anyone it looked on. As he grew older, the eyelid became so heavy that it had to be raised by servants with pulleys and ropes. He lived in fear of a prophecy that he would be killed by his own grandson. When his daughter Eithne gave birth to triplets, Balor hurled the babies into the sea. One was saved and given the name **Lugh**. He fulfilled the prophecy when he joined the Tuatha dé Danaan in the second Battle of **Moytura**. He cast a spear at Balor with such force that the eye was driven through the back of Balor's head, killing the king and most of the Fomorian army behind him. In *The Countess Cathleen* (*CPl*. 45, 49), **Aleel** describes Balor in hell, in the company of **Barach, Cailitin**, and **Conchubar**. In *On Baile's Strand* (*CPl*. 251), the **Fool** sings about the Fomor (or Fomorians) who steal children. See also *The Wanderings of Oisin* (*CP*. 438).

REFERENCES: Dames, Michael. *Mythic Ireland*. 1992. Reprint, New York: Thames & Hudson, 1996; Ellis, Peter Berresford. *Dictionary of Celtic Mythology*. New York: Oxford University Press, 1992; Green, Miranda J. *Dictionary of Celtic Myth and Legend*. London: Thames & Hudson, 1992; Mac Cana, Proinsias. *Celtic Mythology*. Feltham, Middlesex: Newnes, 1983.

BALSCADDEN COTTAGE, Kilrock Road, **Howth**, Dublin (county). After leaving London in 1881, **John B. Yeats** and his family (with the exception of **Jack**, who was with his grandparents in **Sligo**) lived in Balscadden Cottage, from late fall 1881 to spring 1882. WBY describes the cottage as "a long thatched house" (*A.* 55). In early 1882, they moved to a house overlooking the harbor at Howth, Island View—a name recalled in the title of the early play *The Island of Statues*, begun while he was living there. In the spring of 1884, they were forced for financial reasons to leave the pleasant atmosphere of Howth for the less desirable **Ashfield Terrace** in the suburbs of Dublin. During this time, 1881–83, WBY attended the **Erasmus Smith High School**.

REFERENCE: Eglinton, John. "Yeats and his Story." In *Irish Literary Portraits*. London, Macmillan, 1935.

BALZAC, HONORÉ DE (1799–1850), French novelist and short story writer. Early in his career, Balzac wrote sensational novels in order to survive financially, then embarked upon his memorable work *La Comédie humaine*. Written over a twenty-year period, it comprises forty volumes of novels and short stories that re-create French society in the early nineteenth century. Among the novels are *La Peau de Chagrin* (1831), *Louis Lambert* (1832–35), *Père Goriot* (1834–35), *Séraphita* (1834–35), *About Catherine de Medici* (1842–43), and *Cousin Bette* (1847). His short stories include "The Unknown Masterpiece" (1832). WBY was still a child when he was introduced to the works of Balzac by his father **John B. Yeats** (*A.* 48). The influence remained with him throughout his life. He owned the entire forty volumes of *La Comédie humaine* (*WL.* 449) and was reading them in Paris, December 1908, and visiting places mentioned in the novels (*WL.* 513). By October 1909, he had read all but four or five (*WL.* 536). In his essay "If I were Four-and-Twenty" (*LE.* 38–40), he compares Balzac favorably with **Dante** and tells how, as a child, he heard that reading Balzac had changed people's lives. He wrote an essay on *Louis Lambert* for the *London Mercury*, July 1934, naming it among his "sacred" books and including Balzac among those authors who had most moved him (*LE.* 123–29), the others being **Shakespeare** and **William Morris**. In his introduction to *The Holy Mountain* (*LE.* 139–55), he adds that when tempted to go to the East for his philosophy, Balzac brings him back, convincing him he cannot escape from the *comédie humaine*.

REFERENCES: Pritchett, V. S. *Balzac*. New York: Knopf, 1973; Rogers, Samuel. *Balzac and the Novel*. New York: Octagon, 1969; Stanfield, Paul S. "Yeats and Balzac." In *Yeats and Politics in the 1930s*. New York: St. Martin's, 1988; Stowe, William W. *Balzac, James, and the Realistic Novel*. Princeton, N.J.: Princeton University Press, 1983.

BANACHAS (BONACHAS), Irish wood sprites and goblins. In the play *On Baile's Strand* (*CPl.* 251), the **Fool** claims that **Cuchulain** has killed the Banachas and Bonachas. He is very likely referring to *bannanach* (white-faced goblins) and *boccanach* (puck-faced goblins).

BANIM, JOHN (1798–1842), novelist and short story writer. He was born in Kilkenny, the son of a prosperous Catholic shopkeeper, and attended the prestigious St. John's College, Kilkenny, a Protestant school where Congreve and **Swift** had also been pupils. In 1813, he moved to Dublin to study drawing at the Academy of the Royal Dublin Society. He returned to Kilkenny to teach, but in the early 1820s, after **Sir Walter Scott** had praised his poem ''The Celt's Paradise,'' and the actor-manager William Charles Macready had produced his verse tragedy *Damon and Pythias* (1821), he traveled to London to establish himself as a writer. In 1826, he and his brother Michael Banim (1796–1874), under the pseudonym O'Hara Brothers, embarked on a series of historical novels, in which they attempted to create a distinctive Anglo-Irish literature and to bridge the cultural gap between Ireland and England. Each contributed chapters to the books, but John Banim was the more prolific and better novelist. The writing ranged from vignettes of pre-Famine life to the historical novels set during the Williamite Wars, the Penal Age, and the Rebellion of 1798. Arguably the best from their twenty-four novels are *The Nowlans* (1826) and *The Boyne Water* (1826), the latter being compared with the best of Sir Walter Scott. John Banim married in 1822, but chronic ill-health forced him to retire to Kilkenny on a small Civil List pension. After his death, his brother Michael, a prosperous merchant, produced little of value. When he lost his fortune in 1840, his health deteriorated, and he died three years later. WBY began reading the Banims in 1889 and was enthusiastic. In a letter to Father Matthew Russell (*WL*. 143–44), he compared John Banim with **William Carleton**, and he included *The Nowlans* and *John Doe* (1825) in his collection *Representative Irish Tales* (London: Putnam, 1891). These novels and *Father Connell* (1842) are included in WBY's list of ''Best Irish Books'' (*UP1*. 385).

REFERENCES: Flanagan, Thomas. *The Irish Novelists: 1800–1850*. New York: Columbia University Press, 1959; Hawthorne, Mark D. *John and Michael Banim (the 'O'Hara Brothers')*. Salzburg, Austria: Institut für Englishche Sprache und Literatur, 1975; Hogan, Robert, ed. *Dictionary of Irish Literature*. Rev. ed., Westport, Conn.: Greenwood, 1996.

BANIM, MICHAEL. *See* **BANIM, JOHN**.

BARACH, treacherous knight in the **Red Branch**. Barach plots with **Conchubar** to invite **Fergus** to a feast on the night when **Deirdre** and **Naoise** return from Scotland. Fergus, having given an oath not to refuse a feast from Barach, is forced to remain with him while Deirdre and Naoise go to meet Conchubar. In Fergus's absence, Conchubar revenges himself on Deirdre by killing Naoise. In *The Countess Cathleen* (*CPl*. 45), Barach is pictured in hell with Conchubar, **Balor**, and **Cailitin**. See also *The Wanderings of Oisin* (*CP*. 437).

REFERENCE: Gregory, Lady Augusta. *Cuchulain of Muirthemne*. Gerrards Cross: Colin Smythe, 1976.

BARHAIM, possibly Bahrám Gur, who was king of Persia from 420 to 430. Bahrám, a famed hunter, was distinguished for his courage. After his cousin was chosen king, Bahrám placed the crown between two raging lions. When his cousin refused to pick it up, Bahrám claimed the crown. He appears in Quatrain 19 of the *Rubáiyát of Omar Khayyám* (1859), translated by Edward Fitzgerald (1809–83). In WBY's poem "Upon a Dying Lady" (*CP*. 177), he compares the courage of the dying **Mabel Beardsley** with that of Barhaim and others.

BARLOW, JANE (1857–1917), popular writer of poems and sketches of Irish life. Daughter of the Reverend James W. Barlow (vice provost of **Trinity College**), she was born in Clontarf, Dublin (county). Her first volume of verse, *Bog-Land Studies*, was published in 1892. It contained narrative poems in dialect, many of them melodramatic and sentimental. She followed this with *Irish Idylls* (1892), a collection of stories set in the small, fictional village of Lisconnel. The stories were so popular that the book went to some eight editions. She produced at least twenty further volumes of stories and verse on Irish peasant life, including the novel *Flaws* (1911). WBY, who claimed to know her only slightly, thought she observed peasant life in admirable detail (*UP1*. 370). He was favorably disposed to her work and included her *Irish Idylls* in his list of "Best Irish Books" (*UP1*. 386). He reluctantly omitted her from his list of "Thirty Best Irish Books" (*WL*. 248).

REFERENCE: Hogan, Robert, ed. *Dictionary of Irish Literature*. Rev. ed. Westport, Conn.: Greenwood, 1996.

BATTLE, MARY (d. 1908), elderly housekeeper of WBY's uncle **George Pollexfen**. Mary Battle was a clairvoyant, gifted with second sight, who reported omens and visions. Originally from **Mayo**, she had a vast store of tales about fairies, leprechauns, and ghosts (*WL*. 305). WBY listened avidly to her stories. He claimed that much of his writing in *The Celtic Twilight* was but her daily speech (*A*. 71). She advised him about **Maud Gonne**, and when WBY and his uncle later explored the supernatural and magic together, Mary Battle acted as a medium. In dreams, she would call up wild men riding the mountains of **Ben Bulben** and **Knocknarea**. One is reminded of the image of ghostly horsemen that WBY uses in his final poems, among them "Three Songs to the One Burden" (*CP*. 371) and "Under Ben Bulben" (*CP*. 397).

BAX, SIR ARNOLD [EDWARD TREVOR] (1883–1953), composer. He was born in Streatham, near London, and studied at the Royal Academy of Music. In 1902, he made his first visit to Ireland. He was captivated by the landscape and the people, so that for the remainder of his life, he strongly identified with Celtic folklore and culture. He discovered WBY, **AE**, and **J. M. Synge** and was so impressed with WBY's poem *The Wanderings of Oisin* (*CP*. 409) that it inspired his first orchestral pieces, *Into the Twilight* (1908) and *In the Faery Hills* (1909). He spent many summers in Ireland, and after his marriage in 1911, he lived for two years in Dublin. There he made the acquaintance of the emerging Irish writers, among them **Padraic Colum, James Stephens**, and **Seamus O'Sullivan**. The influence of Irish mythology and folklore is especially evident in his tone poems *The Garden of Fand* (1916), *Moy Mell* (1917), *November Woods* (1917), and *Tintagel* (1919). His opera *Deirdre* was not completed. In a broadcast for the **BBC** in 1949, he claimed to have been the first composer to express the hidden Ireland in musical terms. He also wrote Celtic stories and poetry under the pseudonym Dermot O'Byrne. The first of these, *The Sisters* and *Green Magic*, were published in 1912. They were followed by *Children of the Hills* (1913) and *Wrack, and Other Stories* (1918). In 1916, to celebrate friends like **Padraic Pearse** and **Countess Markiewicz** who had fought in the Easter Rising, he wrote *A Dublin Ballad & Other Poems*. It was banned by the British censor as seditious and dangerous, but copies were given to friends and sympathizers. Despite his nationalist sympathies, he was knighted in 1937 and appointed Master of the King's Music in 1942. Throughout his life, Bax acknowledged his debt to WBY, whose poetry, he said on a number of occasions, meant more to him than all the music of the centuries. He was reluctant to set any of WBY's poems to music, however, apart from ''The Fiddler of Dooney'' (*CP*. 82), because he thought they were already so musical. In 1936, he met WBY in Grosvenor Square, the first time he had seen him in thirty years, and they recalled earlier times (*WL*. 858).

REFERENCES: Bax, Arnold. *Farewell My Youth, and Other Writings*. Aldershot: Scolar, 1992; Foreman, Lewis. *Bax: A Composer and His Times*. London and Berkeley: Scolar, 1983; Scott-Sutherland, Colin. *Arnold Bax*. London: Dent, 1973.

BBC. *See* **BROADCASTS**.

BEARDSLEY, AUBREY [VINCENT] (1872–98), one of the outstanding illustrators of the fin de siècle period in England and a prominent member of the **Rhymers' Club**. He was born in Brighton, the son of impoverished parents. A frail child, he contracted tuberculosis when he was seven and was sent to a school in Sussex. He then attended Brighton Grammar School but left at the age of fifteen to work in London, first in a surveyor's office and later with the Guardian Life and Fire Insurance Company. Encouraged by a visit that he and his sister **Mabel** made in 1891 to the Pre-Raphaelite painter **Edward Burne-Jones**, he decided to devote himself to painting and illustration. Despite having minimal art training, his first commissioned illustrations for Sir Thomas Malory's *Le Morte d'Arthur* (1893–94) demonstrated not only his mastery of line but also imagination. He found inspiration for his early black-and-white illustrations in the formalized art of Japan and in eighteenth-century rococo architecture. He created a unique artificial style, without precedent in English nineteenth-century graphic art. With the publication of his drawings for **Oscar Wilde's** *Salomé* (1894), he aroused much criticism and hostility because of the erotic nature of the work. He established a relationship with Oscar Wilde and the personalities of the literary underworld, including **Leonard Smithers**. His distinctive, ironic style of illustration led to his appointment, in 1894, as art editor of the avant-garde publication the *Yellow Book*. He later contributed to

Smithers's prestigious *Savoy* magazine, 1895–96, and continued to explore his original talent with the detailed rococo illustrations for *The Rape of the Lock* (1896) and the sexually explicit *Lysistrata* (1896). He was art editor of the *Yellow Book* until 1895, when he was dismissed in response to the wave of moral indignation that followed the trial of Oscar Wilde. He died of tuberculosis two years later, at the age of twenty-five. Shortly before his death, he became a Roman Catholic and denounced his illustrations for *Lysistrata* as obscene. He asked Smithers to have them destroyed, but his request was not carried out. He died in Menton, France, and was buried in the local Protestant cemetery. WBY and Beardsley had frequent contact through the Rhymers' Club and shared the same circle of friends. WBY admired the patterns and rhythmical lines of Beardsley's illustrations, observing that though the images of human life were faded, the drawings continued to hold the interest (*UP2.* 134). He owned reproductions of eleven of the fifteen drawings for *Salomé*. Beardsley designed the blue and green poster for the premiere of WBY's play **The Land of Heart's Desire**, Avenue Theatre, London, 1894, and it later hung in WBY's rooms in **Woburn Buildings**, London. In 1896, Beardsley was commissioned by Leonard Smithers to work on six illustrations for WBY's play **The Shadowy Waters**. He completed one but died before he could finish the rest. In ''The Tragic Generation'' (*A.* 322–25, 331–33), WBY writes movingly of the public rejection of Beardsley. He had much admiration for his courage, not only in dealing with an incurable illness but also with the stand that he took against a hostile society that he was powerless to change (*M.* 90–92). Beardsley's influence on WBY may be seen in the formal, hieratic style that the poet adopted for his dance plays.

REFERENCES: Berkovitz, Miriam J. *Aubrey Beardsley: An Account of His Life.* New York: Putnam, 1981; Brophy, Brigid. *Black and White: A Portrait of Aubrey Beardsley.* New York: Stein & Day, 1969; Easton, Malcolm. *Aubrey and the Dying Lady: A Beardsley Riddle.* London: Secker & Warburg, 1972; Fletcher, Ian. *Aubrey Beardsley.* Boston: Twayne, 1987; Zatlin, Linda Gertner. *Aubrey Beardsley and Victorian Sexual Politics.* New York: Oxford University Press, 1990.

BEARDSLEY, MABEL (1871–1916), friend and confidante of her younger brother, **Aubrey**. She was born in Brighton, England. As a child, she played piano duets with her brother and recited excerpts from Dickens. When the family moved to London in 1888, she won a scholarship to Newnham College, Cambridge, but was forced to turn it down because of her family's meager finances. She became a teacher at the Polytechnic School for Girls in Langham Place. After a short time, she left to follow a career as an actress and, in 1894, appeared in the Haymarket Theatre, London, in **Oscar Wilde's** *A Woman of No Importance.* She was a striking woman, above-average height, with red hair. She was devoted to her brother and was his constant companion at meetings and social gatherings. Indeed, it was suggested by some of their associates that their relationship was incestuous. She was with her brother when he died in Menton,

France, in 1898. She married George Bealby Wright, a talented but unappreciated actor, in 1903. She was diagnosed with cancer in 1912 and died in 1916. WBY met Mabel Beardsley in the company of her brother, and she was an occasional guest at his Monday evening "At Homes." He visited her frequently during her last illness (*WL*. 574–75). He saw in her the same courage he had admired in her brother, and in his sequence of seven poems "Upon a Dying Lady" (*CP*. 177), she became for him an image of doomed heroic youth triumphing in the face of disaster. **Victor Plarr**, a member of the **Rhymers' Club**, also wrote a poem about Mabel Beardsley. According to Austin Clarke (*Shenandoah*, summer 1965), Plarr's "Stand not uttering sedately" may have inspired WBY.

REFERENCE: Easton, Malcolm. *Aubrey and the Dying Lady: A Beardsley Riddle*. London: Secker & Warburg, 1972.

BEATRICE, woman who inspired the *Divine Comedy* and *Vita Nuova* of **Dante**. She is thought to have been Beatrice Portinari (1266–90), a noble woman of Florence. The poet first saw Beatrice when she was eight years old, and she remained his ideal and inspiration until his death in 1321. WBY makes connections between Beatrice and his own muse **Maud Gonne**. See also "Ego Dominus Tuus" (*CP*. 180).

BEDFORD PARK, suburb near Chiswick, southwest London. Built on the estate of Bedford House, this garden suburb of winding streets and large trees was a new departure in nineteenth-century urban planning. Jonathan T. Carr (1845–1915), a property speculator, began building the estate in 1875. He conceived it largely as an artists' colony, with all the advantages and atmosphere of an English country village. It boasted more artists per acre than any other area in London, although other professionals also made their home there. The houses, which were predominantly in the Queen Anne style, were designed by significant contemporary architects, principally Ernest L. Godwin (1833–86), Norman Shaw, E. J. May, and Maurice B. Adams. The interiors of the houses were mainly in the style of **William Morris**. Many of them boasted an adjoining studio and a small cottage garden. The houses were grouped around a clubhouse, intended as the focus of the artistic endeavors of the community. The exterior of the clubhouse was plain and undistinguished, but the interior was hung with Japanese paper and old tapestries. **John B. Yeats** was one of the first artists to take up residence in Bedford Park. He moved with his family to **Woodstock Road** in 1879. For the fourteen-year-old WBY, the architecture and the interior decoration transported him to an exotic world that he associated with literature. It was in Bedford Park that WBY met **John Todhunter** and **Maud Gonne** and where he saw **Florence Farr** act in the Bedford Park Amateur Dramatic Club's production of Todhunter's *A Sicilian Idyll*, presented in the clubhouse in 1890. There was a debating society, the Calumet, which John B. Yeats attended, and frequent social gatherings. WBY valued Bedford Park for the social contacts, but he felt out of sympathy with the artistic views of many of the artists and writers who lived there (*A*. 115).

REFERENCE: Fletcher, Ian. "Bedford Park: Aesthete's Elysium?" In *W. B. Yeats and His Contemporaries*. Brighton, Sussex: Harvester, 1987.

BEERBOHM, [SIR] MAX (1872–1956), English novelist, essayist, critic, caricaturist, and wit. He was born in Kensington, London, and educated at Charterhouse and Merton College, **Oxford**. His family lived at 48 Upper Berkeley Street, Marylebone, and it was there that he wrote his essays *The Works of Max Beerbohm* (1896) and *Zuleika Dobson* (1911), the latter a fantasy about Oxford, begun in 1898. While at Charterhouse, he met **Oscar Wilde** and became an admirer. Wilde's influence is evident in *The Happy Hypocrite* (1896), in which Beerbohm tells the story of Lord George Hell who, under the mask of a saint called Lord George Heaven, falls in love and woos an innocent girl. In other writings, Beerbohm parodied the literary styles of Henry James, H. G. Wells, and **Rudyard Kipling**. With **Aubrey Beardsley**, he was on the staff of the *Yellow Book*, and later he became the drama critic of the *Saturday Review*, 1898–1912, succeeding **George Bernard Shaw**. In 1910, he married and settled in Italy, except for the periods of the two world wars. In the early 1940s, he began a series of broadcasts for the **BBC**, later collected as *Mainly on the Air* (1946, 1957). These were a popular feature of British radio during World War II. He was buried in St. Paul's Cathedral. WBY knew and admired Beerbohm, who was enthusiastic about the work of the **Irish National Theatre Society** when it was presented in London in 1904. Today, Beerbohm is best known for witty and biting caricatures of his contemporaries, among them "Celtades Ambo: **Edward Martyn** and W. B. Yeats" (1899) and "Mr. W. B. Yeats presenting Mr. **George Moore** to the Queen of the Fairies." WBY is included in the Beerbohm drawing "Some Persons of 'the Nineties,' " along with Beardsley, Wilde, George Moore, and Sir William Rothenstein.

REFERENCES: Behrman, S. N. *Portrait of Max: An Intimate Memoir of Sir Max Beerbohm*. New York: Random, 1960; Cecil, Lord David. *Max: A Biography*. London: Constable, 1966; Hart-Davies, Sir Rupert. *A Catalogue of the Caricatures of Max Beerbohm*. Cambridge, Mass.: Harvard University Press, 1972; McElderry, Bruce R. *Max Beerbohm*. New York: Twayne, 1972; Viscusi, Robert. *Max Beerbohm: Or the Dandy Dante*. Baltimore: Johns Hopkins University Press, 1986.

BELSHRAGH, small lake on the top of **Slieve Echtge**, near the town of **Loughrea, Galway** (county). In "The Death of Hanrahan" (*MY*. 253), the poet **Hanrahan** spends many hours by the remote lake. Belshragh is known locally as Rashragh.

REFERENCE: McGarry, James P. *Place Names in the Writings of William Butler Yeats*. Gerrards Cross: Colin Smythe, 1976.

BELTAINE [also Beltene], ancient Celtic festival. One of four major festivals, it was held annually on May Eve and the first day of May. It officially marked the beginning of summer. The festival was in honor of Bel, the Celtic god of life and death. Household fires were extinguished and bonfires lit by torches from the rays of the sun, symbolizing a fresh start for the whole community. *Beltaine* was the name given by WBY to the publication in which he announced his plans and ideas for the **Irish Literary Theatre**. There were three issues of the magazine, May 1899, February 1900, and April 1900.

REFERENCES: Dames, Michael. *Mythic Ireland*. 1992. Reprint, New York: Thames & Hudson, 1996; Ellis, Peter Berresford. *Dictionary of Celtic Mythology*. New York: Oxford University Press, 1992; Green, Miranda J. *Dictionary of Celtic Myth and Legend*. London: Thames & Hudson, 1992; Mac Cana, Proinsias. *Celtic Mythology*. Feltham, Middlesex: Newnes, 1983.

BEN BULBEN (Irish: *Beann Ghulban*) [Gulban's Peak], flat-topped limestone mountain in **Sligo** (county). The long, bare mountain, with its waterfalls, dominates the surrounding landscape. Ben Bulben is mentioned in a number of WBY's poems, including "Towards Break of Day" (*CP*. 208), "The Tower" (*CP*. 218), "The Alternative Song for the Severed Head" (*CP*. 324), and "Under Ben Bulben" (*CP*. 397). It is on Ben Bulben that **Diarmuid**, the lover of **Grania**, is mortally wounded, and it is the setting for the final two acts of *Diarmuid and Grania* (1901) by WBY and **George Moore**. The poet **Hanrahan** has a vision on Ben Bulben in which he meets the ghosts of **Diarmuid MacMurrough** and **Dervorgilla** (*MY*. 246–52). The mountain had special associations for WBY (*EX*. 29). He climbed it as a boy and fished its streams, regarding it as a place inhabited by the **Sídhe**. At sunset, he believed, fairy riders swept down from the mountain over the plains of **Drumcliff** below (*MY*. 90). It was in the shadow of Ben Bulben, at Drumcliff, that WBY chose to be buried.

REFERENCES: Mac Cana, Proinsias. *Celtic Mythology*. Feltham, Middlesex: Newnes, 1983; McGarry, James P. *Place Names in the Writings of William Butler Yeats*. Gerrards Cross: Colin Smythe, 1976.

BERA [Beare Island], Bantry Bay, **Cork** (county). The island was named after Beara, a legendary Spanish princess, wife of Eoghan Mor, king of **Munster**. In *The Wanderings of Oisin* (*CP*. 442), **Oisin** speaks of Bera in the southwest and **Rachlin** in the northeast, to indicate the length of Ireland.

REFERENCE: McGarry, James P. *Place Names in the Writings of William Butler Yeats*. Gerrards Cross: Colin Smythe, 1976.

BERENICE II (c. 273–221 B.C.), queen of ancient Egypt. She was the daughter of King Magus of Cyrene. After the death of her father, there was an attempt by her mother, Apama, to have her married to Demetrius of Macedon. She successfully led a rebellion, putting her mother and suitor to death. Subsequently, she married the King of Egypt, Ptolemy III (c. 284–221 B.C.). According to legend, she offered her hair for the safe return of her husband from war.

Her petition granted, a constellation of stars was named Berenice's Hair (*Coma Berenices*). After her husband's death, she ruled jointly with her son, Ptolemy IV, until he had her murdered. WBY uses her hair as a symbol of romantic love in "Veronica's Napkin" (*CP*. 270) and in "Her Dream" (*CP*. 299).

BERKELEY, GEORGE (1685–1753), Bishop of Cloyne and Ireland's outstanding philosopher. He was born in Kilkenny and spent his early years at the family home, Dysert Castle, near Thomastown. He attended Kilkenny College and graduated from **Trinity College**, Dublin, in 1704. He founded the Trinity College Philosophical Society in 1705 and was ordained into the Church of Ireland in 1710. By then, he had developed his theory that matter does not exist, a doctrine known as *immaterialism*, which he published in his major works *Essay Towards a New Theory of Vision* (1709), *The Principles of Human Knowledge* (1710), and *Three Dialogues between Hylas and Philonous* (1713). He spent some years in England, where he wrote for the *Guardian* (1713), and made the acquaintance of **Jonathan Swift**. In 1724, he returned to Ireland, to the prestigious appointment of dean of Derry. In 1729, newly married, he moved to the United States, hoping to found a school to train Christian missionaries to the American Indians. He bought a house and farm in Newport, Rhode Island, and formed friendships with leading American clerics. He gained considerable financial support for his school, but frustrated by the unwillingness of the British government to let him have a promised grant, he returned to London in 1731. Nevertheless, he left his mark on American philosophy and gave an impetus to American education. As a mark of gratitude, the town of Berkeley, California, was named after him. In 1734, he was appointed bishop of Cloyne, a diocese some twenty miles from **Cork** (city) and the site of an abbey founded in the sixth century by the poet Colman MacLenini. Berkeley remained at Cloyne for seventeen years, exerting a profound influence in the diocese. He instituted technical training programs, organized cultural events, and raised money for the poor. He promoted tar water as the universal cure for sickness, having learned about it from the American Indians. His concern for the economic and social welfare of the Irish was evident in his writings in *Querist* (1735–37), work that continued to be admired into the twentieth century by generations of Irish nationalists. In late 1752, Berkeley retired to **Oxford** and died a short time afterward. Among his most influential writings are: *Word to the Wise, or an Exhortation to the Roman Catholic Clergy of Ireland* (1749) and *A Defence of Free-Thinking in Mathematics* (1735). WBY initially rejected Berkeley as an Irish author because he did not deal with Irish subjects (*UP1*. 352). He later revised his opinion and, in 1931, wrote a long, laudatory introduction to *Bishop Berkeley: His Life, Writings, and Philosophy* by Joseph Hone and Mario Rossi (*EI*. 396–411). He credited Berkeley with the creation of modern philosophy (*LE*. 237) and thought his work should be taught in colleges in Ireland since it was impossible not to be influenced by Berkeley when discussing any modern philosophical question (*UP2*. 458). Two copies of *Berkeley's Commonplace Book* (1930) and *The Works of George Berkeley* (2 vols., 1784) were in WBY's library (*OS*. nos. 159, 159a, 160). He includes Berkeley among "The Seven Sages" (*CP*. 271).

REFERENCES: Berman, David. "George Berkeley (1685–1753): Pictures by Goldsmith, Yeats and Luce." *Hermathena*, 1985; Houghton, Raymond W.; Berman, David; and Lapan, Maureen T., eds. *Images of Berkeley*. Dublin: National Gallery of Ireland/ Wolfhound, 1986; Luce, A. A. *Life of George Berkeley, Bishop of Cloyne*. London: Thomas Nelson, 1949.

BESANT, ANNIE. *See* **WOOD, ANNIE BESANT**.

BEST, RICHARD I[RVINE] (1872–1959), one of the outstanding Celtic scholars of his generation. Best was born in Derry, in the north of Ireland. He studied Old Irish with **Kuno Meyer**, and together they founded the School of Irish Learning in 1903. In 1906, he married Edith Oldham (1868–1950), an accomplished musician, and sister of **C. H. Oldham** of **Trinity College**, Dublin. Best was assistant director of the **National Library of Ireland** from 1904 to 1923 and director from 1924 to 1940. His appointment, in 1940, as senior professor of Celtic Studies, Dublin Institute of Advanced Studies, confirmed his preeminence as a Celtic scholar. He was chairman of the Irish Manuscripts Commission, 1948–56, and president of the **Royal Irish Academy**, 1943–46. He retired in 1947, although he continued to publish until his death. Best was on intimate terms with all the Irish writers of the period, including **Synge** (with whom he roomed as a student in Paris), and appears in the Scylla and Charybdis, and Circe episodes of **James Joyce's** *Ulysses*. He wrote a critical review of **Lady Gregory's** *Cuchulain of Muirthemne* (1902), regretting the pagan tendencies in the writing. This response did not endear him to WBY. He had a special friendship with **George Moore** when the novelist was living near the National Library in Dublin. Best's translation of **Henri d'Arbois de Jubainville's** influential *Irish Mythological Cycle and Celtic Mythology* (1903) was widely read and studied, but his major contribution to Celtic studies was his two-volume *Bibliography of Printed Irish Literature* (1913) and *Bibliography of Irish Philology and Manuscript Literature* (1941). His other publications include *Bibliography of the Publications of Kuno Meyer* (1923), *The Martyrology of Tallaght* (1931), and *The Book of Leinster* (1954). Portraits of Best are now in the Irish National Portrait Gallery and in the Royal Irish Academy.

REFERENCES: Boylan, Henry. *A Dictionary of Irish Literature*. Dublin: Gill & Macmillan, 1978; Welch, Robert, ed. *The Oxford Companion to Irish Literature*. Oxford: Clarendon, 1996.

BIGGER, FRANCIS JOSEPH (1863–1926), lawyer, antiquarian, and local historian. He was born into a well-to-do Presbyterian family in the north of Ireland. In the early 1900s, his Belfast home, "Ardrigh," was the center of the Gaelic revival in **Ulster** and visited by the outstanding Ulster writers, among them Shane Leslie, George A. Birmingham, Forrest Reid, **Alice Milligan**, and Rutherford Mayne. Another visitor was Eoin MacNeill, who assisted **Douglas Hyde** with the formation of the Gaelic League in 1893. In 1903, Bigger toured **Donegal** (county) with **Joseph Campbell** and the musicologist Herbert Hughes to collect folk melodies, which they published as *Songs of Uladh* (1904). Bigger also published a number of books on Irish cultural history and edited the *Ulster Journal of Archaeology*, 1894–1914. When WBY visited Belfast in 1893 to lecture to the Belfast Naturalists' Field Club on "Irish Fairy Lore," Bigger took him on a brief tour of Northern Ireland. On his death, he bequeathed his considerable collection of books of Irish interest to the Belfast Public Library.

REFERENCE: Bardon, Jonathan. *A History of Ulster*. Belfast: Blackstaff, 1992.

BINYON, [ROBERT] LAURENCE (1869–1943), poet, art historian, and critic. He was born in Lancaster, the son of a clergyman, and educated at Trinity College, **Oxford**. His long poem *Persephone* won the Newdigate Prize in 1890, but it was only with the publication of *London Visions* (1908) that he revealed his talent for characterization and lyrical speech. Later collections, most notably his *Odes* (1901) and *The Secret* (1920), show greater depth of thought and delicate, restrained musical flow. He wrote critical works and was especially interested in comparing literature to the other arts, as in *Painting in the Far East* (1908) and *English Poetry in Its Relation to Painting and the Other Arts* (1919). His *Collected Poems* appeared in 1931. From 1893 until his death, he worked in the **British Museum**, first as an assistant in the Department of Prints and Drawings and, from 1913, as Keeper of Oriental Prints and Drawings. WBY, who shared his enthusiasm for **Edward Calvert** and **Samuel Palmer**, had a close friendship with Binyon. From the late 1890s they met often, sometimes in the company of **T. Sturge Moore**. WBY was impressed with Binyon as a poet, critic, and art historian, and in *The Academy*, 7 December 1901, he named his *Odes*, which included the three-part poem "The Death of Tristram," as one of his "books of the year." In 1915, he suggested, unsuccessfully, that Binyon succeed **Hugh Lane** at the **National Gallery of Ireland**. WBY included Binyon's long poem "Tristram's End" in *The Oxford Book of Modern Verse* (1936).

REFERENCE: Hatcher, John. *Laurence Binyon: Poet, Scholar of East and West*. Oxford: Clarendon, 1995.

BIRDS' MOUNTAIN [also Bird Mountain] (Irish: *Sliabh-da-En*). Known now as Slieve Daeane, the mountain of the two birds, it stretches from Ballygawley to **Lough Gill**, both in **Sligo** (county). On the south side of the mountain is a stone monument associated locally with the Cailleach Beare, the legendary Old Woman of Beare. In "The Untiring Ones" (*MY*. 79), WBY refers to Lough Ia (Loch Dagea), a small lake on the top of Birds' Mountain.

REFERENCE: McGarry, James P. *Place Names in the Writings of William Butler Yeats*. Gerrards Cross: Colin Smythe, 1976.

BISCAY [Bay of Biscay], large bay on the west coast of Europe, between France and Spain. In "Pardon, old Fathers" (*CP*. 113), WBY remembers his maternal great-grandfather, **William Middleton**, who brought goods from South America to his depot in the Channel Islands by way of the Bay of Biscay. As a child, WBY envied his great-grandfather, who had the courage to jump overboard in the Bay of Biscay to retrieve an old hat (*A*. 36).

BLAKE, WILLIAM (1757–1827), poet, artist, and visionary. He was born into a well-to-do family in London, where he spent most of his life. His parents belonged to the Swedenborgian Church, and from an early age, he was encouraged to take seriously **Emanuel Swedenborg's** accounts of his visions and experiences of the spiritual world. In 1782, after completing an apprenticeship as an engraver, he married Catherine Boucher, the daughter of a greengrocer. With her assistance, he illustrated and published all his major poetry, including *Songs of Innocence* (1789) and *Songs of Experience* (1794), using printing techniques that he claimed had been revealed to him in a vision. He published his "Prophetic Books," among them *The Book of Thel* (1789), *The Marriage of Heaven and Hell* (1790), *The First Book of Urizen* (1794), *Milton* (1804), and *Jerusalem* (1804). In these, he created a personal mythology in which he transformed friends, enemies, and historical figures like **John Milton, Isaac Newton**, Francis Bacon, and **John Locke** into allegorical figures—apocalyptic forces warring among themselves for control of the universe. His visionary writings and his engraving techniques found little appreciation from contemporary critics, while his books were expensive to produce and did not sell. Eccentric in his ideas and behavior, and frustrated by his lack of success, he became increasingly hostile to critics and fellow-artists, among them Sir Joshua Reynolds, and was frequently characterized as a madman. Even after his death, he found little acceptance until he was adopted as a forerunner by the Pre-Raphaelites. WBY was sixteen years old when his father introduced him to Blake's work (*A*. 114). From 1889, he collaborated with **Edwin J. Ellis** on the three-volume edition of *The Works of William Blake, Poetic, Symbolic and Critical* (1893), gaining a thorough knowledge of Blake's poetry and evolving a highly personal interpretation of Blake's symbolism (*A*. 161–62, 164, 403). He recognized that Blake had much in common doctrinally with Emanuel Swedenborg and learned from Blake to "hate all abstraction" (*A*. 181). Blake's insistence that the arts were the source of divine revelation confirmed the young WBY's instinctive belief in the primacy of art. This he argues in his essay "William Blake and the Imagination" (*EI*. 111–15). The impact of Blake on WBY was so powerful that he referred with marked frequency in his letters and essays to Blake's visionary poetry and paintings, quoting him in support of his arguments. When he published a collection of essays in 1903, he chose for his title a phrase from Blake, *Ideas of Good and Evil*, and considered using Blake's "Paola and Francesca" as the frontispiece (*WL*. 377). His walls at **Woburn Buildings** were hung with seven illustrations from Blake's *Divine Comedy*, while in his 1937 introduction to a complete edition of his work, he recalls that, as a young man, the engravings of Blake had been his "particular study" (*EI.* vii). In the visionary Blake, WBY found confirmation for his cyclic view of history and the unity of all opposites: self and soul, good and evil, life and death. In *The Bounty of Sweden* (*A.* 550), he names Blake among the significant myth makers and mask makers, while in the poem "An Acre of Grass" (*CP.* 346), he includes him with the frenzied heroes **Timon** and King Lear.

REFERENCES: Adams, Hazard. *Blake and Yeats: The Contrary Vision.* Ithaca, N.Y.: Cornell University Press, 1955; Binyon, Laurence. *The Followers of William Blake: Edward Calvert, Samuel Palmer, George Richmond and Their Circle.* New York: B. Blom, 1968; Loizeaux, Elizabeth Bergmann. *Yeats and the Visual Arts.* New Brunswick and London: Rutgers University Press, 1986; Pinto, Vivian de Sola. *The Divine Vision: Study in the Poetry and Art of William Blake.* New York: Haskel, 1968; Raine, Kathleen. *William Blake.* New York: Oxford University Press, 1970.

BLANID (Irish: *Blathnát*), daughter of Mend, king of Inis Fer Falga. Blanid was in love with **Cuchulain**. Cú Roí, son of the king of **Munster**, helped Cuchulain against Mend and carried off Blanid as his prize. She was taken to his fortress, constructed so that no one could gain access. Blanid enabled Cuchulain to find an entrance by pouring milk into a stream that ran through the fort. He killed Cú Roí, but as the victorious procession left the castle, a servant of Cú Roí took Blanid by the waist and, jumping from a high rock, carried her to her death. The tragic Blanid is recalled in *The Wanderings of Oisin* (*CP.* 437).

REFERENCES: Ellis, Peter Berresford. *Dictionary of Celtic Mythology.* New York: Oxford University Press, 1992; Mac Cana, Proinsias. *Celtic Mythology.* Feltham, Middlesex: Newnes, 1983.

BLAVATSKY, MADAME [HELENA PETROVNA] (1831–91), founder of the Theosophical Society. She was born in Ekaterinoslav in southern Russia, the daughter of Colonel Peter von Hahn. At eighteen, she married the middle-aged Nikifor V. Blavatsky, vice governor of the Province of Yerivan, but left him shortly after the marriage and traveled widely in Europe. In 1851, she claimed to have met in London her Master, a mystic of Rajput birth, who told her of the important religious work she must undertake. In 1873, after undergoing occult training in Tibet, she went to New York. Two years later, with Colonel Henry Steel Olcott and William Quan Judge, she founded the Theosophical Society. In 1877, she published her *Isis Unveiled* to provide a master-key to theosophical thought, and in 1878, she traveled with Olcott to India. There, they both took Buddhist vows and bought an estate at Adyar that became the headquarters of the Theosophical Society. In 1884, her credibility was undermined by allegations that she had forged records of psychic phenomena. In 1885, despondent and in poor health, she resigned as corresponding secretary of the Theosophical Society and returned to Europe with the Indian **Mohini Chatterjee**. It was while she was lodging with **Mabel Collins** in Upper Norwood, London, in early 1887, that WBY first visited her, with an introduction from **Charles Johnston**. She intrigued him, and he called on her regularly every six weeks. In the fall of 1887, she formally established the Blavatsky Lodge of the Theosophical Society in Holland Park. WBY joined the Esoteric Section of the Society in December 1888 and became a member of the Recording Committee for Occult Research in December 1889. He contributed an article on Irish fairies and other phenomena to the theosophical magazine *Lucifer*, 15 January 1889 (*UP1*. 130–37). In 1890, much to his regret, he was asked to resign because of his participation in an unauthorized experiment (*M*. 23–24). He had also written an article critical of *Lucifer* for *Weekly Review*, edited by Charles Johnston. WBY was ambivalent in his attitude to Madame Blavatsky and in 1893 discussed her at length in an interview for the *Irish Theosophist* (*UP1*. 298–302). In her appearance, she reminded him of an old Irish peasant woman, and he noted in his correspondence her vast and shapeless body, her perpetual rolling of cigarettes, and her constant writing, which he claimed she did for twelve hours a day. He admired her sense of humor, her dislike of formalism, her abstract idealism, and her intense passionate nature (*M*. 24–26). He took pleasure in watching her deal with other members of her lodge, as on the occasion when she expelled for flirting not only the president of the lodge but also an American woman who gossiped about it (*WL*. 123–24, 125). WBY saw in Madame Blavatsky an example of someone who evolved a philosophy from many sources—a model he was to follow when he worked on *A Vision*. She gave him practical advice, persuading him not to deliver a lecture inexpressively from a manuscript but to extemporize. (He followed her advice, even when receiving the **Nobel Prize** in 1923.) She also advised him that removing his beard would cause him a serious illness within six months through the loss of the mesmeric forces that lodge in the beard (*WL*. 145). He disregarded her advice and shaved off his beard! Madame Blavatsky died in May 1891 and was cremated at Woking, Surrey. Her book *The Secret Doctrine* was published in 1888.

REFERENCES: Cranston, Sylvia. *The Extraordinary Life & Influence of Helena Blavatsky: Founder of the Modern Theosophical Movement*. New York: Putnam, 1993; Johnston, Charles. ''A Memory of Madame Blavatsky.'' In *Lucifer*. London: Theosophical Publishing Society, June 1891.

BLENHEIM ROAD, a Yeats family residence in London. **John B. Yeats** moved into 3 Blenheim Road, **Bedford Park**, on Saturday, 24 March 1888. With him were WBY, **Jack**, and **Lily**. His wife **Susan** and elder daughter, **Lolly**, who were in Yorkshire, arrived on 13 April 1888. The house was large and airy, with a balcony and a little garden shaded by a large chestnut tree (*A*. 113–14). The rent was reasonable, at £45 per annum, but with little income coming into the home, there was a dire shortage of money. Often there was no food. The family had to walk rather than take a cab or public transport, and the Yeats sisters wore hand-me-downs from generous neighbors. Yet it was a period of consolidation for the family, who dined together each evening, apart from Susan

Yeats, who, because of her illness, ate alone in her room. WBY and his sisters joined in the active social life at the Bedford Park Clubhouse. It was at 3 Blenheim Road that WBY first met **Maud Gonne. Lady Gregory** visited the Yeats family there, and writer **Susan Mitchell** stayed as a paying guest, from late 1897 to late 1899. The Yeats family lived at Blenheim Road until 1902, although WBY moved, October 1895, to his own rooms in **Fountain Court**. Susan Yeats died at Blenheim Road in 1900. On the initiative of the Bedford Park Society, 7 September 1991, a house plaque, to mark the residence of WBY, his father John B. Yeats, and his brother Jack, was unveiled by **Anne Yeats**.

REFERENCE: Fletcher, Ian. ''Bedford Park: Aesthete's Elysium?'' In *W. B. Yeats and His Contemporaries*. Brighton, Sussex: Harvester, 1987.

BLIND BEGGAR, character in *The Cat and the Moon*. At the opening of the play, he and his companion, the **Lame Beggar**, are traveling to **St. Colman's Well**. The Blind Beggar carries the other on his back. When offered the choice of his sight or to be blessed, the Blind Beggar chooses his sight. When the miracle happens, he sees everything except the saint who has effected the cure. After beating the Lame Beggar, because he has supposedly stolen a sheepskin from him, the Blind Beggar goes on his way alone. The role of the Blind Beggar in the first production of *The Cat and the Moon* at the **Abbey Theatre**, September 1931, was taken by Michael J. Dolan.

BLIND MAN, a character in *On Baile's Strand* and *The Death of Cuchulain*. In *On Baile's Strand*, the Blind Man, called Fintain in the first production, anticipates the action, telling the audience that **Conchubar**, the High King, has demanded that **Cuchulain** take an oath of allegiance and that the son of **Aoife** is coming to challenge Cuchulain in battle. The Blind Man knows that the young man is Cuchulain's son but will not reveal the secret. He cheats the **Fool** out of the hen they have stolen, leaving him only the feathers. This action provides an ironic parallel to the central action of the play in which Cuchulain is exploited by Conchubar. The Blind Man, who wears a grotesque mask, was played by **Seamus O'Sullivan** in the first production, December 1904. In *The Death of Cuchulain*, the Blind Man, with a knife and a bag, appears as Cuchulain is dying. He claims that **Queen Maeve** has promised twelve pennies for Cuchulain's head. In Ireland, the Blind Man has traditionally been gifted with second sight.

BLIND RAFTERY. *See* **RAFTERY, [ANTHONY]**.

BLUESHIRTS. *See* **FASCISM**.

BLUNT, WILFRED SCAWEN (1840–1922), explorer, horseman, painter, poet, and essayist. He was educated at the Jesuit School for Boys in Lancashire,

England. After leaving school in 1858, he entered the British Diplomatic Service, a profession for which he was not particularly suited. In 1872, soon after his retirement from the Diplomatic Service, he inherited Crabbet Park, in Worth, East Sussex, and married Anne Noel, an Arabic scholar. He visited India in 1878 and 1883–84. Strongly anti-imperialist, especially on Egypt and Ireland, he was imprisoned in **Galway** in 1887 for organizing a mass protest meeting of the oppressed tenants of the Clanricarde estates near Portumna. He described the experience in his sonnet sequence *In Vinculis* (1889), while his journal of the period became the basis of *Land War in Ireland* (1912). In 1895, he took possession of Newbuildings Place, Southwater, West Sussex, an estate that had belonged to his family from 1757, and commissioned a tapestry from **William Morris**, an illustration of **Botticelli's** *Primavera*. At Newbuildings Place, he entertained many friends, including WBY, who read his poems aloud to him. He lived there until his death in 1922 and is buried on the grounds. Among his published works are *Sonnets and Songs of Proteus* (1875), *Esther* (1892), *Collected Poems* (1914), and *My Diaries* (1920). A limited edition of *The Love-Lyrics & Songs of Proteus* was published by William Morris at the Kelmscott Press in 1892, bound in white vellum. WBY was introduced to Blunt by **Lady Gregory** on 1 April 1898. They became friends, and Blunt attended meetings of the **Irish Literary Society** in London. Because of his action in Galway, Blunt became for WBY something of a heroic model, although he does not figure in any of the major poems. Encouraged by their friendship, Blunt completed a verse play, *Fand of the Fair Cheek*, produced by the **Abbey Theatre** in 1907. WBY thought Blunt an amateur poet but with a touch of greatness. He wrote a review of Blunt's *Love Song of Proteus*, published in *United Ireland*, 28 January 1888 (*UP1*. 124–30). In 1914, to celebrate Blunt's seventy-fourth birthday, WBY attended a celebratory dinner at Newbuildings Place in the company of **T. Sturge Moore, Victor Plarr, Ezra Pound**, and others, at which (at WBY's suggestion) a peacock was served in full plumage, and a tribute in verse was read by Ezra Pound. An account of the dinner, attributed to WBY, appeared in *The Times*, 20 January 1914 (*UP2*. 410–11). Six poems by Scawen Blunt were included in WBY's selection for ***The Oxford Book of Modern Verse*** (1936).

REFERENCES: Blunt, Wilfred S. *My Diaries*. London: Martin & Secker, 1919; Going, William T. "A Peacock Dinner: The Homage of Pound and Yeats to Wilfred Scawen Blunt." *Journal of Modern Literature*, March 1971.

BOANN, Irish goddess of water. The wife of Nechtan, she disobeys her husband by visiting the sacred well of inspiration. The waters, which rise up and drown her, flow through the countryside to form the River **Boyne**. In another version of her story, the Dagda, father of all the gods, having lusted after her, sends her husband Nechtan on a journey. He puts a spell on the sun, causing it to stand still for nine months, during which time he lies with Boann and she bears him a son. The child is the love god **Aengus**. In WBY's play *On Baile's Strand* (*CPl.* 248), the **Fool** claims to enjoy the company of Boann.

REFERENCES: Ellis, Peter Berresford. *Dictionary of Celtic Mythology.* New York: Oxford University Press, 1992; Green, Miranda J. *Dictionary of Celtic Myth and Legend.* London: Thames & Hudson, 1992; Mac Cana, Proinsias. *Celtic Mythology.* Feltham, Middlesex: Newnes, 1983.

BOCACH, JOHNNY, beggar. He is a character in *The Unicorn from the Stars*, and in early versions of the play, is called Johnny Bacach. The name is derived from the Irish *bacac* (lame man) and was commonly used in the early nineteenth century for a disreputable beggar. The role of Johnny Bocach in the first production of *The Unicorn from the Stars,* **Abbey Theatre**, November 1907, was played by **W. G. Fay**.

BOEHME, JACOB [also Böhme, Behmen] (1575–1624), German philosopher and mystic who claimed divine inspiration. Boehme wrote more than thirty religious books, including *Aurora* (1612) and *The First Book of Urizen* (1794). When his works were published in England, societies of Behmenites were established. WBY thought that **William Blake** might have been familiar with his teachings and consulted his books in his efforts to find a system whereby Blake's poetry could be explained. Thus, Boehme became a major influence on WBY, who regarded him as the greatest of the Christian mystics (*WL.* 262) and one of his chief mystical authorities (*WL.* 592). A copy of Franz Hartmann's *The Life and Doctrines of Jacob Boehme, the God-Taught Philosopher* (1891), heavily annotated by WBY and **Edwin J. Ellis**, was among the books in WBY's private library (*OS.* no. 853), in addition to six other works by Boehme (*OS.* nos. 234–39). In a letter to **Olivia Shakespear** (*WL.* 234), WBY recommended Boehme's major work, *The Morning Redness* (1612), as suitable reading for one of her characters in her novel *Beauty's Hour* (1896).

REFERENCE: Jaspers, Karl. *The Great Philosophers.* Trans. Edith Ehrlich and Leonard Ehrlich. New York: Harcourt Brace, 1994.

BOG OF ALLEN (Irish: *Moin Almhaine*), the central plain in Ireland. The Bog of Allen consists principally of marshy bog land. In *The Countess Cathleen* (*CPl.* 30), one of the **Merchants** claims to have seen a servant of the **Countess** drowned in the Bog of Allen.

REFERENCE: McGarry, James P. *Place Names in the Writings of William Butler Yeats.* Gerrards Cross: Colin Smythe, 1976.

BOG OF CLOONE. *See* **CLOONE BOG**.

BORU, BRIAN [Irish: *Borúmba*] (c. 940–1014), High King of Ireland. Brian Boru has been a national heroic figure since he defeated the Norsemen at **Clontarf** in 1014, successfully ending Norse rule in Ireland. Soon after his victory, he was murdered, and the nation fell into anarchy. WBY recalls a conversation centered around **Lady Gregory's** *Kincora* (1907), a play on Brian Boru, in which he claims that when he was young, every Irish nationalist knew as much about Boru as he did about **St. Patrick** (*M.* 197). In his appreciation, "Major Robert Gregory" (*UP2.* 430), he notes that **Robert Gregory** designed the staging for *Kincora* at the **Abbey Theatre**, while in "Ireland and the Arts" (*EI.* 206), WBY asserts that even with subjects like Brian Boru and St. Patrick, a writer should not consciously try to make his work popular.

REFERENCES: Dames, Michael. *Mythic Ireland.* 1992. Reprint, New York: Thames & Hudson, 1996; Ellis, Peter Berresford. *Dictionary of Celtic Mythology.* New York: Oxford University Press, 1992.

BOTTICELLI, SANDRO (c. 1445–1510), major Renaissance painter. He was born Alessandro di Mariano Filepepi, in Florence. A student of Fra Lippo Lippi, he became a favorite of Lorenzo the Magnificent and his Medici circle—patricians, literati, and scholars who were confirmed Neoplatonists. It was for a member of this elite group that Botticelli painted *The Birth of Venus* (c. 1485). Botticelli's finest work is distinguished by subtle colors and by the shallow modeling of the figures, producing a friezelike effect on the canvas. His lack of concern for three-dimensional effects and deep space is apparent in his mythological works *Primavera* (c. 1477) and *Mars and Venus.* In his final years, he turned to apocalyptic religious scenes, among them *Mystic Nativity* (1501). After his death, his reputation declined. It was only in the late nineteenth century that his work was acclaimed and given recognition by **Dante Gabriel Rossetti** and the Pre–Raphaelites. WBY had a reproduction of *Primavera* in his bedroom at **Riversdale** (*WL.* 865), while his room at **Coole Park** was hung with a number of prints, among them several by Botticelli (*M.* 189). He compares him favorably with **William Blake** in "Blake's Illustrations to Dante" (*EI.* 143–45). While admitting that Botticelli has superior skills to Blake in the handling of the figure and drapery, he finds his work lacks mystery and spiritual significance.

REFERENCE: Ripley, Elizabeth. *Botticelli: A Biography.* London: Oxford University Press, 1960.

BOUNTY OF SWEDEN, THE, essay. An account of the visit that WBY made to Sweden in December 1923 to receive the **Nobel Prize for Literature**. The essay includes reflections on the Swedish court and on Swedish art and architecture, together with observations on WBY's journey through Denmark and some people he encountered on the way. He wrote *The Bounty of Sweden* in January 1924, soon after his return from Sweden. He refers to it in letters to **Lady Gregory** and **Edmund Dulac** (*WL.* 701, 703). It was still on his mind in 1934, when he sent a copy to **Olivia Shakespear**, with a letter recounting a conversation in which **Mrs. Yeats** was told that the Swedish royal family had liked her husband better than all the other Nobel Prize winners, thinking him to have the manners of a courtier (*WL.* 827). *The Bounty of Sweden* first appeared in the *London Mercury* and in *The Dial*, September 1924. It was published by the **Cuala Press** in May 1925, provoking a nitpicking review from **Sir Edmund Gosse** in *The Sunday Times* (*UP2*. 453–54). *The Bounty of Sweden* was subsequently included in ***Dramatis Personae*** (1936), ***The Autobiography of William Butler Yeats*** (1938), and ***Autobiographies*** (1958). Included with the essay was the text of the lecture that WBY delivered to the Royal Swedish Academy, dictated months afterward, since he spoke to the Academy without notes.

BOYLE, WILLIAM (1853–1923), playwright. He was born in Dromiskin, County Louth, and educated at St. Mary's College, **Dundalk**. An excise officer by profession, he was an authority on **James Clarence Mangan**, and he enjoyed the friendship of eminent politicians like **Charles Stewart Parnell** and **John Redmond**. His first three successful plays were *The Building Fund* (1905), *The Eloquent Dempsey* (1906), and *The Mineral Workers* (1906). These rural dramas were among the most popular of the plays produced by the **Irish National Theatre Society** in the early years. They were presented at the **Abbey Theatre** during the 1905 and 1906 seasons and featured the leading players, among them **W. G. Fay, Frank Fay**, and **Sara Allgood**. While his plays were popular and exposed the hypocrisies of contemporary Irish life, Boyle left the Abbey in 1907 in protest against the production of *The Playboy of the Western World*. He returned again in 1912, when the Abbey produced his play *Family Failing*. Although WBY did not approve of Boyle's work, he nevertheless publicly supported it in *The Arrow* (*UP2*. 345–46, 349), arguing that in defending **J. M. Synge** he was also ensuring artistic freedom for Boyle. In a letter to **Florence Farr**, written in 1905, WBY expressed the view that in the future Boyle and **Lady Gregory** would be the most popular Abbey playwrights (*WL*. 464). While writing to **John Quinn** in 1907, he compared Boyle with Synge, remarking that Boyle's plays were more readily accepted in Ireland because the moral was so obvious (*WL*. 495). According to **Lennox Robinson** (*Ireland's Abbey Theatre*), Boyle's plays occupy an important place in the Abbey canon, since he was the first Abbey playwright to focus on the intrigues and corruptions of an Irish town. Among his other writings is a collection of short stories of Irish life, *A Kish of Brogues* (1899).
REFERENCES: Hogan, Robert, ed. *Dictionary of Irish Literature*. Rev. ed. Westport, Conn.: Greenwood, 1996; Robinson, Lennox. *Ireland's Abbey Theatre*. London: Sidgwick and Jackson, 1951.

BOYNE, river that flows through County Louth to the Irish Sea a few miles from the town of Drogheda. It derived its name from **Boann**, the Irish water goddess, whose home was reputedly at Brugh-na-Bóinne (Palace of the Boyne), a prehistoric burial site on the banks of the river at New Grange. The Boyne was the scene of a historic battle in 1690, when **William III**, Prince of Orange, defeated the Catholic James II. In "Pardon, old Fathers" (*CP*. 113), WBY recalls that one of his ancestors, a **Butler** or an Armstrong, fought on William's side in the battle. There are references to the Boyne in other writings by WBY, including *The Green Helmet* (*CPl.* 232), *The King of the Great Clock Tower* (*CPl.* 637), and *Purgatory* (*CPl.* 683).

REFERENCES: Ellis, Peter Berresford. *Dictionary of Celtic Mythology.* New York: Oxford University Press, 1992; Green, Miranda J. *Dictionary of Celtic Myth and Legend.* London: Thames & Hudson, 1992; Mac Cana, Proinsias. *Celtic Mythology.* Feltham, Middlesex: Newnes, 1983; McGarry, James P. *Place Names in the Writings of William Butler Yeats.* Gerrards Cross: Colin Smythe, 1976.

BRADLEY, KATHARINE [HARRIS] (1846–1914), playwright and poet. She was educated at Newnham College, Cambridge. She formed a special friendship with her niece Edith [Emma] Cooper (1862–1913), who was born in Kenilworth. From 1878, the two women lived together in Stoke Bishop, a suburb of Bristol. There they wrote *Bellerophon* (1881). In 1885, they adopted the pseudonym Michael Field for their play *Callirrhoë.* In 1888, while living in Reigate, Surrey, they became members of the Fellowship of the New Life, founded by Thomas Davidson. In 1899, they moved to Richmond, London, becoming part of a social group that included **Charles Ricketts**. WBY, who was introduced to Edith Cooper by Charles Ricketts, was favorably disposed toward the early plays of Michael Field, which included *The Father's Tragedy, William Rufus, Loyalty in Love*, and *Brutus Ultor.* In 1892, he wrote a negative review of the poetry collection *Sight and Song* (*UP1.* 225–27), asserting that the poems, inspired by paintings, were overly intellectual and lacking in originality. In 1903, having invited Michael Field to submit a five-act version of *Deirdre* for consideration by the **Abbey Theatre** (*KLIII.* 384), he turned down the play (*WL.* 407). In ''Modern Poetry: A Broadcast'' (*LE.* 93), he claimed that under the influence of Ricketts, Edith Cooper had written a series of short, simple poems reminiscent of the lyrics of **Walter Savage Landor**, and he included nine poems by Michael Field in *The Oxford Book of Modern Verse* (1936). The poems are from the anthology *A Selection from the Poems of Michael Field* (London: Poetry Bookshop, 1923), which was in WBY's library (*OS.* no. 670). In *Works and Days: From the Journal of Michael Field* (London, 1933), the two women provide a long, unsympathetic portrait of WBY.

REFERENCE: Field, Michael. *A Selection from the Poems of Michael Field.* Ed. Mary C. Sturgeon and T. Sturge Moore. London: Poetry Bookshop, 1923.

BRAHMA, Hindu deity. He is associated with the creation of the universe. **Anashuya**, the priestess, sings praises to Brahma in WBY's love poem ''Anashuya and Vijaya'' (*CP.* 10).

REFERENCES: O'Flaherty, Wendy Doniger, trans. *Hindu Myths: A Sourcebook Translated from the Sanskrit.* Harmondsworth, Middlesex: Penguin, 1975; Zimmer, Heinrich. *Myths and Symbols in Indian Art and Civilization.* Ed. Joseph Campbell. Washington, D.C.: Bollingen Foundation, 1946.

BRAN, one of the three hounds of **Fionn Mac Cumhal.** In *The Wanderings of Oisin* (*CP*. 409), **Oisin** nostalgically remembers Bran, Lomair, and Sceolan, the three hounds that accompanied the **Fianna** on their adventures. Bran and Sceolan were nephews to Fionn, having been born to his sister Tuireann while she was transformed into a hound by her husband's mistress. Other sources claim the hounds were born to Uirne, Fionn's aunt. Bran was also the name of the brother of **Branwen.**

REFERENCE: Ellis, Peter Berresford. *Dictionary of Celtic Mythology*. New York: Oxford University Press, 1992.

BRANWEN, tragic figure from the Welsh *Mabinogion*. She was the daughter of Llyr. She married Matholwch, King of Ireland, and had a son, Gwern. In response to an assertion that her half brother Efnisien had insulted Matholwch, she was forced to do menial work in the castle. A starling brought the news of this indignity to her brother **Bran,** ruler of the Island of the Mighty. He protested to Matholwch. When Branwen was about to be restored to her former dignity, Efnisien again intervened, throwing her child Gwern into the fire. In the battle that followed, everyone, except five pregnant women and some soldiers, was killed. When Branwen saw the devastation, she died of a broken heart. In his poem "Under the Moon" (*CP*. 91), WBY recalls her dignity and restraint.

REFERENCES: Ellis, Peter Berresford. *Dictionary of Celtic Mythology*. New York: Oxford University Press, 1992; Green, Miranda J. *Dictionary of Celtic Myth and Legend*. London: Thames & Hudson, 1992; Mac Cana, Proinsias. *Celtic Mythology*. Feltham, Middlesex: Newnes, 1983.

BREIFFNY [also Breffny, Breffni] (Irish: *Breifne*), ancient Irish kingdom that included parts of counties **Sligo,** Leitrim, and Cavan. It was ruled over by Tiernan O'Rourke, husband of **Dervorgilla.** Her elopement with **Diarmuid MacMurrough** contributed to the invasion of Ireland by the Normans in the twelfth century. In WBY's story "Proud Costello," the old piper plays a tune called "The Princes of Breffny" (*MY*. 199).

REFERENCE: McGarry, James P. *Place Names in the Writings of William Butler Yeats*. Gerrards Cross: Colin Smythe, 1976.

BRIAN, feisty old servant in WBY's play *The King's Threshold*. He brings food to his master **Seanchan** and tries to persuade him to eat. When Seanchan refuses, Brian defends his honor against the **Mayor of Kinvara,** who speaks on behalf of King **Guaire.** The role of Brian, in the first production of *The King's Threshold*, October 1903, was played by P. Josephs.

BRICRIU [also *Bricriu Nemthenga*, or Bricriu of the Poisoned Tongue]. He is one of the champions of the mythological **Red Branch** in **Ulster.** Malicious and mean, he antagonizes all with whom he comes in contact. In **Lady Gregory's** version of "Bricriu's Feast" in *Cuchulain of Muirthemne* (1902), Bricriu causes trouble, not only among **Cuchulain** and the other champions but also among their wives. When judging the contest between the Brown Bull of Cooley and the White Bull from **Connacht**, Bricriu is trampled to death by the fighting bulls. In *The Only Jealousy of Emer* (*CPl.* 287), he admits to causing trouble between the gods and men.

REFERENCES: Ellis, Peter Berresford. *Dictionary of Celtic Mythology*. New York: Oxford University Press, 1992; Green, Miranda J. *Dictionary of Celtic Myth and Legend*. London: Thames & Hudson, 1992; Mac Cana, Proinsias. *Celtic Mythology*. Feltham, Middlesex: Newnes, 1983.

BRIDGES, ROBERT [SEYMOUR] (1844–1930), lyric poet, playwright, and critic. He was educated at Eton and Corpus Christi College, Oxford. He qualified as a physician and practiced at St. Bartholomew's and the Hospital for Sick Children, Great Ormonde Street, two of London's major hospitals. In 1881, after an illness, he gave up medicine to devote himself to writing and moved from London, first to Yattendon, near Newbury, Berkshire, and later to Boar's Hill, near **Oxford**. Between 1873 and 1884, he published four collections of verse, all titled *Poems*, but it was only with his *Shorter Poems* (1890) that he achieved a critical following. Bridges was made Poet Laureate in 1913. He formed a friendship with Gerard Manley Hopkins and was later responsible for the publication of Hopkins's poems. WBY admired Bridges and believed his verse had an emotional purity and a delicacy of rhythm unmatched by his contemporaries. He spoke of him with much enthusiasm in his introduction to *The Oxford Book of Modern Verse* (*LE.* 181, 188). Their friendship began when Bridges wrote to WBY in 1896 after reading his *Poems* (1895). WBY visited the older poet at Yattendon in March 1897, and although they met infrequently thereafter, they regularly corresponded. Three of Bridges's poems were included in the recitals given in 1901 by **Florence Farr**, accompanied by the psaltery, and WBY helped Bridges with his anthology *The Spirit of Man* (1916). He subscribed to the purchase of a clavichord for Bridges's eightieth birthday (*WL.* 707). In 1913, Bridges expressed his admiration for WBY's introduction to *Gitanjali* by **Rabindranath Tagore** (*WL.* 580). His other publications include *Poetical Works* (1953), *Collected Essays* (1927–36), and his poetic dramas, among them *Achilles in Scyros* (1890), *Palicio* (1890), and *The Return of Ulysses* (1896), which WBY thought one of the most beautiful and dramatic of modern plays (*EI.* 167, 198–202). Six poems by Bridges were included in WBY's selection for *The Oxford Book of Modern Verse* (1936).

REFERENCES: Finneran, Richard J., ed. *The Correspondence of Robert Bridges and W. B. Yeats*. Toronto: Macmillan, 1977; Phillips, Catherine. *Robert Bridges: A Biography*. Oxford: Oxford University Press, 1992; Sparrow, John H. A. *Robert Bridges*. London: Longmans, Green, 1962; Stanford, Donald E. *In the Classic Mode: The Achievement of Robert Bridges*. Newark: University of Delaware Press, 1978.

BRIDGET, wife of the **Wise Man** in *The Hour-Glass*. The role of Bridget in the first production of *The Hour-Glass* by the **Irish National Theatre Society**,

March 1903, was played by Maire T. Quinn. Bridget is also the name of the mother in both *The Land of Heart's Desire* and *Cathleen Ni Houlihan*. See **Bruin** and **Gillane**.

BRITISH MUSEUM, established in 1753 to house the national collection of treasures in science and art. The British Museum is in Bloomsbury, London— conveniently placed to WBY's home at **Woburn Buildings**. The museum has a library and extensive departments of archaeology, antiquities, prints and draw- ings, coins and medals, and ethnography. The library is a nonlending, reference library only and is a copyright depository. It houses one of the world's outstand- ing collections of rare books and manuscripts. WBY was a frequent visitor to the British Museum, both to the reference library, with its domed reading room completed in 1857, and to the many special collections of paintings, drawings, and sculpture. In 1888, he did some copying work on folklore in the library for the publisher David Nutt, and in his essay ''Certain Noble Plays of Japan'' (*EI*. 231, 234), he recalls looking at Japanese prints and screens in the museum. In other writings, he refers to two unidentified statues in the Egyptian Room (*LE*. 72). A *Guide to the First and Second Egyptian Rooms* (1904) at the British Museum and the Department of Manuscripts' *Reproductions from Illuminated Manuscripts* were in WBY's personal library (*OS*. nos. 284, 285). A number of WBY's friends and acquaintances worked in the British Museum. **Laurence Binyon** was Keeper of Oriental Prints and Drawings, while **Standish Hayes O'Grady** compiled the *Catalogue of Irish Manuscripts in the British Museum*. It was in the library of the British Museum that WBY met **MacGregor Mathers** in 1890.

REFERENCE: Harris, P. R., ed. *The Library of the British Museum*. London: British Library, 1991.

BROADCASTS. WBY made his first radio broadcast for the British Broadcasting Corporation (BBC) from the Belfast studios, 8 September 1931. The program included the poems ''The Lake Isle of Innisfree'' (*CP*. 44), ''The Fiddler of Dooney'' (*CP*. 82), ''The Song of Wandering Aengus'' (*CP*. 66), ''Running to Paradise'' (*CP*. 129), and ''In Memory of Eva Gore-Booth and Con Markiew- icz'' (*CP*. 263). In March 1932, he made two broadcasts for the BBC from London. On 17 March 1934, he made a further broadcast from Belfast. This consisted of a talk entitled ''The Growth of a Poet'' illustrated by a selection from his poetry, including ''The Song of the Old Mother'' (*CP*. 67), ''A Faery Song'' (*CP*. 43), ''The Fiddler of Dooney,'' ''Running to Paradise,'' ''The Fisherman'' (*CP*. 166), and ''Down by the Salley Gardens'' (*CP*. 22). The talk appeared in *The Listener*, 4 April 1934 (*UP2*. 495–99). After the publication of *The Oxford Book of Modern Verse* (1936), he gave a forty-five-minute lecture for the BBC in London, 11 October 1936, on ''Modern Poetry'' (*LE*. 89–102). The lecture, which was later published in *The Listener*, 14 October 1936, was the eighteenth in a BBC series of ''Broadcast National Lectures.'' He discussed with the producer George Barnes the possibility of developing a series of broadcasts of poetry, with light musical accompaniment—whistle, concertina, drum, solo violin or viola. While these discussions were continuing, he tried out the idea in a program from the **Abbey Theatre**, broadcast on 1 February 1937 by Radio Éireann. According to WBY, the broadcast, which included "Roger Casement" (*CP*. 351) and "Come Gather Round Me, Parnellites" (*CP*. 355), was not a success (*WL*. 879). Nevertheless, WBY continued his discussions with the BBC, and two programs—with musical interludes—were broadcast from London: "In the Poet's Pub" (2 April 1937) and "In the Poet's Parlour" (22 April 1937). These were successful and encouraged the production of "My Own Poetry" (3 July 1937) and his final broadcast, "My Own Poetry Again" (29 October 1937). These last four programs were produced by George Barnes, and the readers were **Margot Ruddock** and **V. C. Clinton-Baddeley**. Three additional programs were planned for 1938 but did not materialize, although the text of one of them—"I Became an Author"—appeared in *The Listener*, 4 August 1938 (*UP2*. 506–9). It was WBY's last publication, apart from *The Autobiography of William Butler Yeats* (1938).

REFERENCES: Clinton-Baddeley, V. C. *Words for Music*. Cambridge: Cambridge University Press, 1941; Gould, Warwick, ed. "George Barnes's 'W. B. Yeats and Broadcasting' 1940." *Yeats Annual, No. 5*. London: Macmillan, 1987.

BROWNE, SIR THOMAS (1605–82), author and physician. His intense faith and highly elaborate prose style made him an important figure in English literary history. In his major work *Religio Medici* (c. 1635), Browne attempted to reconcile science and religion. A new edition of *Religio Medici, Urn-Burial, Christian Morals, and Other Essays*, with an introduction by John Addington Symonds, was published by Walter Scott, 1886, a copy of which was in WBY's library (*OS*. no. 290). He was clearly familiar with Browne's work and cites him authoritatively in a number of essays and articles. See *LE*. 66, 72, 213, 227; *UP1*. 408.

REFERENCE: Patrides, C. A., ed. *Approaches to Sir Thomas Browne*. Columbia: University of Missouri Press, 1982.

BROWNING, ROBERT (1812–89), poet. He was born in London, the son of a bank clerk of independent wealth. His plays *Strafford* (1837) and *A Blot in the 'Scutcheon* (1843) were performed with William Charles Macready in the leading roles, but he only established his reputation with his dramatic monologues—keen psychological portraits in verse of a range of characters, many of them from medieval Italy. These monologues included "My Last Duchess," "Fra Lippo Lippi," and "Andrea del Sarto." In 1846, he eloped to Italy with the poet Elizabeth Barrett (1806–61). After her death, he returned to England. Browning experimented with rhythm and structure and had a well-informed mind and creative imagination, but he did not achieve the national popularity of his contemporary, **Lord Tennyson**. Only with the publication of *The Ring* *and the Book* (1868–69), a murder story told in ten dramatic monologues, did he find national recognition. In his introduction to *The Oxford Book of Modern Verse* (*LE*. 194), WBY cites this long poem as one of two poems that caught the attention of the Victorian public. He quotes lines from Browning's "Pauline" (1833) in a number of his writings, including "Are You Content?" (*CP*. 370), "William Blake and the Imagination" (*EI*. 112), and "Thoughts on Lady Gregory's Translations" (*PI*. 127). In a letter to **Katharine Tynan**, written in 1887, he admits he has not been reading Browning (*WL*. 46), while in a letter to **Olivia Shakespear**, 2 March 1929 (*WL*. 759), he claims Browning to be a dangerous influence. He read Browning's "How They Brought the Good News from Ghent to Aix" and "The Pied Piper of Hamelin" to his children when they visited him in **Rapallo** in 1930 (*WL*. 776).

REFERENCES: Irvine, William, and Honan, Park. *The Book, the Ring, and the Poet: Biography of Robert Browning*. New York: McGraw-Hill, 1974; Markus, Julia. *Dared and Done: The Marriage of Elizabeth and Robert Browning*. New York: Knopf, 1995; Ryals, Clyde de L. *Life of Robert Browning: A Critical Biography*. Oxford: Blackwell, 1993; Thomas, Donald S. *Robert Browning: A Life within Life*. New York, Viking, 1983.

BRUIN, family name. The action of WBY's play *The Land of Heart's Desire* is set in the Bruin household in **Sligo**. The mother, Bridget Bruin, complains about the laziness of her new daughter-in-law, Mary Bruin. Mary's husband Shawn and father-in-law Maurteen take sides in the argument, but when Maurteen unwittingly brings the **Faery Child** into the house, Mary is torn between her wish to go with the fairy and her love for her husband. She chooses the fairy life and dies at the conclusion of the play.

BUAL'S HILL [also Anbuail's Hill], associated with the **Sídhe**. The name is derived from Ethal Anbuail, who was the father of the beautiful fairy woman Cáer Ibormeith. Bual's Hill is referred to in WBY's poem "The Old Age of Queen Maeve" (*CP*. 451).

REFERENCES: Ellis, Peter Berresford. *Dictionary of Celtic Mythology*. New York: Oxford University Press, 1992; McGarry, James P. *Place Names in the Writings of William Butler Yeats*. Gerrards Cross: Colin Smythe, 1976.

BUAN, Ulster goddess. Buan married Mesgedra, and at his death, her wailing could be heard from **Tara** to the **Bog of Allen**. Her son was **Baile**, heir to the kingdom of Ulster. His tragic story is told by WBY in "Baile and Aillinn" (*CP*. 459).

BUCHANAN, ROBERT [WILLIAM] (1841–1901), English poet, critic, and novelist. He earned a reputation by publishing provocative statements about religion and literature. These initiated much correspondence from fellow writers and journalists, among them **Richard Le Gallienne** who challenged his remark that religion was "played out." His collection *Poems* was published in 1866, while the *Complete Poetical Works of Robert Buchanan* was published in 1901. His best-known poem was *The Wandering Jew* (1893), which WBY reviewed unfavorably for *The Bookman*, April 1893 (*UP1*. 264–66). His novels include *Annan Water* (1883), *Foxglove Manor* (1884), and *Idyls and Legends of Inverburn* (1865).

REFERENCES: Cassidy, John A. *Robert W. Buchanan*. New York: Twayne, 1974; Jay, Harriett. *Robert Buchanan: Some Account of His Life, His Life's Work, and His Literary Friendships*. New York: AMS, 1970.

BUCKLEY'S FORD, over the river Garavogue in **Sligo** (town). In "The Crucifixion of the Outcast" (*MY*. 152), the gleeman Cumhal is thrown into the river by the Brothers of the **Abbey of White Friars** at a place afterward called Buckley's Ford.

REFERENCE: McGarry, James P. *Place Names in the Writings of William Butler Yeats*. Gerrards Cross: Colin Smythe, 1976.

BUDDHA, [SIDDHARTHA GAUTAMA] (c. 568–c. 483 B.C.), philosopher and founder of Buddhism. He was reputedly the son of a wealthy ruler in the north of India, near Nepal. After leading a sheltered life in which he married and had a son, he discovered human misery. At the age of twenty-nine, he rejected his luxurious lifestyle to become a hermit and a wanderer. At Buddh Gaya, under a bo tree, he was rewarded for his holy asceticism by "the great enlightenment," and he learned the principles on which Buddhism is based. He became a teacher and disseminated his beliefs through his disciples. In Sanskrit, the name Buddha means "the enlightened one." In his "Introduction to 'An Indian Monk' " (*LE*. 134), WBY asserts that no single image of **Christ**, Krishna, or Buddha represents God to the exclusion of other images. Buddha is referred to in WBY's poem "The Double Vision of Michael Robartes" (*CP*. 192).

BULLEN, A[RTHUR] H[ENRY] (1857–1920), publisher and scholar. Born in London, the son of George Bullen from **Cork**, he set up a publishing house with Harold Lawrence in 1891. Together they published *The Poems of William Blake* (1893), edited by WBY, followed by **The Celtic Twilight** (1893, 1902) and **The Secret Rose** (1897). The partnership with Lawrence was dissolved in 1900, but Bullen continued to publish the work of WBY, including **Cathleen Ni Houlihan** (1902, 1909), **Ideas of Good and Evil** (1903), **The King's Threshold** (1904), and **Plays for an Irish Theatre** (1911). In 1904, he joined with Frank Sidgwick to form the Shakespeare Head Press at Stratford-upon-Avon. They published, with the financial assistance of **Annie F. Horniman,** *The Collected Works in Verse and Prose of William Butler Yeats* (1908), followed by **Deirdre** (1911) and **The Green Helmet** (1911). Bullen was a strong supporter of WBY, and in his efforts to promote the sale of his books, he encountered hostility from booksellers in Ireland (*A*. 447; *WL*. 350, 352). At WBY's suggestion, he considered opening a business in Dublin to publish Irish books, but the plan did not materialize (*WL*. 361). WBY thought Bullen a fine scholar of poetry (*EI*. 20) and supported his application for a Civil List pension in 1912. Yet he was frustrated by him, believing him unresponsive to ideas, and he thought his poor business methods were responsible for delays in publication and payment (*WL*. 397, 426).

BURKE, EDMUND (1729–97), political writer and statesman. He was born in Dublin, the son of a Protestant lawyer. He graduated from **Trinity College**, Dublin, and studied at the Middle Temple, London. When he was not called to the Bar, he embarked on the publication of two philosophical essays—*A Vindication of Natural Society* (1756) and *A Philosophical Inquiry into the Origin of Our Ideas of the Sublime and the Beautiful* (1756). In 1759, he became editor of the *Annual Register* and formed a friendship with Samuel Johnson and members of his elite literary circle. In 1765, he became private secretary to the prime minister, Lord Rockingham, and entered Parliament. Despite his harsh voice and awkward gestures, he became an influential political orator, urging conciliation rather than coercion in the dispute with the American colonies. He published influential pamphlets, most notably *Thoughts on the Cause of the Present Discontents* (1770), *American Taxation* (1774), *Conciliation with the Colonies* (1775), and *A Letter to the Sheriffs of Bristol* (1777). He promoted a policy of conciliation and legislative independence for Ireland, a position that cost him his seat in Parliament. He returned to the government as paymaster-general in 1782 but later resigned. In 1787, he instigated the impeachment of Warren Hastings, governor-general of India, on corruption charges. The trial lasted for eight years and ended with Hastings's acquittal. In 1790, his most famous work, *Reflections on the Revolution in France*, in which he expressed his opposition to the French Revolution, was published throughout Europe. It generated many critical responses, including Thomas Paine's *The Rights of Man* (1791, 1792). A man of integrity and deep insight, Burke's stand for tradition and inherited values appealed to the mature WBY, who identified with him in the poems ''The Tower'' (*CP*. 218) and ''Blood and the Moon'' (*CP*. 267). He notes Burke's conciliation policy to the American colonies in ''The Seven Sages'' (*CP*. 271).

REFERENCES: Ayling, Stanley E. *Edmund Burke: His Life and Opinions*. New York: St. Martin's, 1988; O'Brien, Conor Cruise. *The Great Melody: A Thematic Biography and Commented Anthology of Edmund Burke*. Chicago: University of Chicago Press, 1992.

BURNE-JONES, SIR EDWARD [COLEY] (1833–98), painter and designer. He was born in Birmingham, England, and educated at Exeter College, **Oxford**, where he was a fellow student of **William Morris**. After meeting the painter **Dante Gabriel Rossetti** in 1856, he left Oxford without completing his degree and settled in London. He began studying under Rossetti, and as a member of the Pre-Raphaelites, he explored in his paintings an imaginative, medieval world of chivalry, much influenced by the Italian masters Fra Lippo Lippi and **Botticelli**. His first success came in 1877, when he exhibited his *Days of Creation* and *The Beguiling of Merlin*. He consolidated his reputation as one of the leading British painters with his major work *King Cophetua and the Beggar Maid* (1884) and *Merlin and Nimue* (1858–59). He contributed eighty-seven designs for the Kelmscott *Chaucer*, published by Morris's Kelmscott Press, and designed tapestries, tiles, and ecclesiastical stained glass, and it is as a designer that his reputation has been sustained through the twentieth century. Burne-Jones devoted some of his spare time to the study of Celtic romances, and in her tribute to her husband, *Memorials of Edward Burne-Jones* (1904), Lady Burne-Jones cites examples of his sympathy for Irish nationalism. Burne-Jones's dreamlike, romantic females appealed to the young WBY, who, though fascinated with women, could still not deal with the reality of sex (*A.* 143; *M.* 33). He admired a cartoon for a stained glass window exhibited at an 1890 Arts and Crafts Exhibition, although he preferred the earlier Burne-Jones who was much more under the influence of Rossetti (*UP1.* 184). Nevertheless, writing in 1913, he observes that he could still be moved by Burne-Jones's *King Cophetua and the Beggar-Maid*, a later picture (*EI.* 347). In ***Reveries over Childhood and Youth*** (*A.* 140), he recalls the impression made upon him at the home of William Morris by a cupboard painted by Burne-Jones. He treasured a copy of the Kelmscott *Chaucer*, a fortieth birthday present, and when he moved into his home at **Riversdale**, he proudly displayed a stained-glass window by Burne-Jones, given to him by **Charles Ricketts**.

REFERENCE: Loizeaux, Elizabeth Bergmann. *Yeats and the Visual Arts*. New Brunswick and London: Rutgers University Press, 1986.

BURNS, ROBERT (1759–96), poet. He was born at Alloway, Ayrshire, the oldest of seven children, and worked on his father's farm. He was encouraged to educate himself by reading the Scottish writers and the works of Pope, **Locke**, and **Shakespeare**. He tried a variety of farming jobs but was unsuccessful. His poems were circulated in manuscript, but he did not achieve recognition until the publication of *Poems, Chiefly in the Scottish Dialect* (1786). With the earnings from this collection, Burns intended emigrating to Jamaica with Mary Campbell, one of his lovers, but with her death, he decided not to leave. He toured the Highlands, then settled in Edinburgh where he became a figure of social importance. In 1788, he married his mistress Jean Armour, who already had four children with him. He retired to a farm at Ellisland, and when it failed, he moved in 1791 to Dumfries as exciseman. He died of rheumatic fever, five years later, at the age of thirty-seven. Robert Burns is remembered best for his simple but moving songs, among them "The Banks o' Doon," "Flow Gently, Sweet Afton," "A Red, Red Rose," "Auld Lang Syne," and "Comin' thro' the Rye." He was the author of longer poems, among them *Tam o' Shanter, The Cotter's Saturday Night*, and the satirical *Death of Dr. Hornbook*. Written in broad Scottish dialect, these works are distinguished by their humor and deep humanitarianism, qualities that elevate the work from the merely provincial to the universal. WBY makes numerous references to Burns in his writings, but the majority of these are negative and critical. Despite Burns's lowly birth and popular appeal, WBY believed him to be a poet not of the people but of the middle class. In his essay "What is 'Popular Poetry'?" (*EI.* 6), he finds Burns's verse, despite the expressive speech, to be sterile in ideas and trivial in emotion. Yet in "The Symbolism of Poetry" (*EI.* 155, 156), he uses two lines of Burns's to illustrate symbolic writing. *The Poetry of Robert Burns*, in four volumes, edited by **W. E. Henley** and Thomas F. Henderson (1896–97), was in WBY's library (*OS.* no. 310), with many pages uncut.

REFERENCES: Bold, Alan N. *A Burns Companion*. New York: St. Martin's, 1991; Daiches, David. *Robert Burns and His World*. London: Thames & Hudson, 1978; Low, Donald A. *Robert Burns*. Edinburgh: Scottish Academic, 1986.

BURREN (Irish: *Boireann*), rocky limestone outcrop on the edge of the Atlantic, in the north of **County Clare**. The Burren is an area of about 100 square miles of outstanding geological interest, with distinctive flora and fauna. Before the tenth century, it was known as *Corcumruadh Ninnis*, giving its name to **Corcomroe Abbey**, which is in the vicinity. The apparent barrenness of the area led to the comment, attributed to one of **Cromwell's** generals, that the place hadn't enough trees to hang a man, wood to burn him, or water to drown him. In "Ireland and the Arts" (*EI.* 209), WBY recalls that **Robert Gregory** found a distinctive artistic style when he painted in the Burren. He also remembers standing on **Slieve Echtge**, with the Burren on his left, looking out over the plains of **Galway** (*EI.* 211). In "And Fair, Fierce Women" (*MY.* 58), WBY recalls meeting a young man in the Burren Hills who spoke of an old poet who claimed he had made love to **Queen Maeve**.

REFERENCE: McGarry, James P. *Place Names in the Writings of William Butler Yeats*. Gerrards Cross: Colin Smythe, 1976.

BURROUGH, the name by which the slum area in **Sligo** (town) was commonly known. The Burrough lay between the site of Sligo Castle (now the Town Hall) and the river Garavogue. For a time, **George Pollexfen** lived near the Burrough, then a disreputable part of the town, according to WBY (*A.* 257). In "Hanrahan and Cathleen" (*MY.* 234), the poet **Hanrahan** meets the prostitute Margaret Rooney and stays with her and her friend Mary Gillis in the Burrough. See also "Red Hanrahan's Curse" (*MY.* 238). The area is no longer known as the Burrough.

REFERENCE: McGarry, James P. *Place Names in the Writings of William Butler Yeats*. Gerrards Cross: Colin Smythe, 1976.

BUTLER, Yeats family name. WBY believed he could trace his family back to James Butler, Duke of Ormonde (1610–88). His son, James Butler, the second Duke of Ormonde (1665–1746), who fought in the Battle of the **Boyne**, was

Lord Lieutenant of Ireland and a friend of **Jonathan Swift**. He was impeached for high treason in 1705. Edmond Butler, thought to be a descendant of the third Earl of Ormonde, was the father of **Mary Butler Yeats**, WBY's paternal great-great-grandmother. It was through her marriage in 1773 to **Benjamin Yeats** that the family inherited 560 acres of land in Thomastown, County Kildare, together with a house in Dorset Street, Dublin, and a silver cup inscribed with the Ormonde coat of arms. WBY was proud of the aristocratic connection and attempted to research it in detail, although evidence was inconclusive. He recalls James Butler, the second Duke of Ormonde, in the poem ''Pardon, old Fathers'' (*CP*. 113). In *The Words upon the Window-Pane* (*CPl*. 601), **Dr. Trench** comments that three of Swift's friends, including the second Duke of Ormonde, have been dismissed from power. Portraits of the Ormonde family, which hang in the **National Gallery of Ireland**, are referred to in ''Demon and Beast'' (*CP*. 209). They are part of the **Hugh Lane** bequest. See also ''Are You Content'' (*CP*. 370).

REFERENCE: Fitzgerald, Brian. *The Anglo–Irish, Three Representative Types: Cork, Ormonde, Swift, 1602–1745*. London and New York: Staples Press, 1952.

BUTT, ISAAC (1813–79), writer, orator, and politician. He was born in Glenfin, **Donegal** (county), the son of a Protestant clergyman. A lawyer by profession, he was educated at **Trinity College**, Dublin, where he met WBY's grandfather **William Butler Yeats** and cofounded the *Dublin University Magazine* (1833). Although he was reared in a staunchly Unionist family, he revealed a depth of nationalist feeling in his early political writings, but he was only fully converted to the cause of Irish nationalism during his valiant but unsuccessful defense of the Fenians, 1865–68. He was elected Conservative M.P. for Youghal, **Cork** (county), 1852–65. In 1870, he founded the Home Government Association and returned to the British Parliament the following year as leader of the Irish Party, promoting Home Rule. A brilliant orator, he was endowed with enormous physical and mental energy and was credited with making the term *Home Rule* a household word. Nevertheless, although he wanted an Irish Parliament elected by the people, he saw it emphatically within the British Empire. He did not think it important that Ireland should be independent from England. In his political dealings with the English, he remained the Anglo-Irish gentleman and was no match for the shrewder, more hardheaded **Charles Stewart Parnell**, who successfully challenged him for the leadership of the Irish Party in 1877. Butt's death in 1879 marked the end of the law-respecting tradition of Irish constitutional nationalism. The Yeats family was devoted to Isaac Butt. WBY's father, **John B. Yeats**, painted two portraits of him, one of which now hangs in the **National Gallery of Ireland**. Butt had a major influence on the political thinking of John B. Yeats, and WBY inherited this influence. His father deplored violence and assumed that England would eventually be persuaded by constitutional means to treat Ireland fairly. WBY never moved far from this thinking until the 1920s. Apart from his books on politics and history, Butt wrote fiction, including *The Gap of Barnesmore, Chapters of College Romance*, and *Irish Life in Court and Castle*.

REFERENCES: McCaffrey, Lawrence J. *Irish Federalism in the 1870s: A Study in Conservative Nationalism*. Philadelphia: American Philosophical Society, 1962; Thornley, David. *Isaac Butt and Home Rule*. Westport, Conn.: Greenwood, 1976.

BUTT, ROSA (1839–1926), writer and reviewer. She was the daughter of the political leader **Isaac Butt** and became a close acquaintance of the Yeats family when they lived in **Bedford Park**. WBY's father, **John B. Yeats**, was a frequent visitor to her home in Oakley Street, London. They became platonic friends, and John B. Yeats painted her portrait in 1900. Indeed, a rumor circulated in Dublin that the widowed painter had proposed marriage. She contributed articles and reviews to various journals, including a favorable review of WBY's *The Wanderings of Oisin* in the *Irish Monthly*, May 1889.

REFERENCE: Murphy, William M. "John Butler Yeats and Rosa Butt." In *Family Secrets*. New York: Syracuse University Press, 1995.

BYRNE, BILLY, fictional beggar who appears in "Under the Round Tower" (*CP*. 154). In the poem, WBY associates Billy Byrne with William (Billy) Byrne of Ballymanus, County Wicklow, a member of the United Irishmen who was hanged for his part in the 1798 Rebellion.

BYRON, LORD [GEORGE GORDON NOEL] (1788–1824), poet. He was born lame, and after the early death of his father, he suffered from the excessive attentions and violent mood swings of an adoring mother. His contempt for her was later directed toward all women. He succeeded to his title at the age of ten, and after attending Dulwich College and Harrow, he graduated from Trinity College, Cambridge. A gifted storyteller, his first volume of verse was *Poems on Various Occasions* (1807), followed by *Hours of Idleness* (1807). After the latter was severely criticized by the *Edinburgh Review*, he responded with *English Bards and Scotch Reviewers* (1809), a satire in heroic couplets. This immediately brought him fame. He left England and toured through Spain, Portugal, Italy, and the Balkans. On his return to London, he confirmed his literary promise with the publication of Cantos I and II of *Childe Harold* (1812). His social reputation, however, was adversely affected by his many love affairs, most notably with Lady Caroline Lamb and with Claire Clairmont, sister-in-law to **Percy Bysshe Shelley**. It was also rumored that he was having an affair with his half sister, Mrs. Augusta Leigh. His marriage to Anne Isabella Milbanke in 1815 lasted only one year. In 1816, he left England and spent some time with Shelley in Switzerland. There he wrote Canto III of *Childe Harold*, before settling in Venice in 1817. He completed Canto IV of *Childe Harold* in 1818 and began working on his epic satire *Don Juan* (1819–24), his acknowledged masterpiece in ottava rima. He became involved in the movement for Greek independence and worked tirelessly to unify the divergent Greek forces. The effort proved physically overwhelming, and he died of exposure. Other writings by Byron include the Faustian tragedy *Manfred* (1817), in which a romantic hero lives haunted by some past crime (*LE*. 109, 121; *UP1*. 271; *WL*. 548). WBY admired Byron, the adventurous man of action, but felt he had sacrificed his stature as a writer to his style of living (*WL*. 467). He read with enthusiasm a privately published account of Byron's affair with Mrs. Augusta Leigh (*WL*. 468). WBY had four books of Lord Byron's in his library: *The Letters and Journals of Lord Byron* (1886), *Lord Byron's Correspondence* (1922), *Poetical Works of George Lord Byron* (1853), and *The Poetical Works of Lord Byron* (1889) (*OS*. nos. 323–26).

REFERENCES: Coote, Stephen. *Byron: The Making of a Myth*. London: Bodley Head, 1988; Gunn, Peter. *My Dearest Augusta: A Biography of Augusta Leigh—Byron's Half-Sister*. New York: Atheneum, 1968; Longford, Elizabeth. *Life of Byron*. Boston: Little, Brown, 1976; Noel, Roden Berkeley. *Life of Lord Byron*. Port Washington, N.Y.: Kennikat, 1972.

BYZANTIUM, ancient city on the Bosporus. It was founded by the Greeks in 658 B.C. and rebuilt as Constantinople (now Istanbul) in A.D. 300 by the Roman emperor Constantine I (c. 287–337). It became the capital of the Byzantine Empire and a center for a distinctive art style that had a profound influence on many countries in Europe as late as the twentieth century. Influenced by the East, Byzantine art emphasized decoration and ornamentation, as well as flat-line harmony. After Christianity became the official religion, these principles were applied to religious subjects, especially in colorful mosaics composed of glass tesserae in a range of colors but predominantly gold, silver, and purple. The best examples may be seen at **Ravenna** (which WBY visited with **Lady Gregory** in 1907). Sculpture was characterized by even, flat surfaces, with no attempt to produce realistic gradations of light and shade. Stone carving of decorative subjects such as fruit and flowers was prevalent, while ivory carving was a popular art form. The elaborate illustration of manuscripts was practiced, and among the minor arts, enameled icons and gold ornaments confirm the delicate and decorative workmanship characteristic of Byzantine art. WBY's encounter with Byzantine art in Ravenna in 1907 does not appear to have made an impression on him at that time. Later, he admired the Byzantine mosaics when he visited Palermo, **Sicily**, November 1924, and Byzantium became a symbol of the search for the spiritual in art. It has an important role to play in *A Vision* (1937) and is the subject of his poems ''Sailing to Byzantium'' (*CP*. 217) and ''Byzantium'' (*CP*. 280).

REFERENCES: Gordon, D. J., ed. ''Byzantium.'' In *W. B. Yeats: Images of a Poet*. Manchester: University of Manchester, 1961; Lister, Raymond. *Beulah to Byzantium: A Study of Parallels in the Works of W. B. Yeats, William Blake, Samuel Palmer & Edward Calvert*. Dolmen Press Centenary Papers, vol. II. Dublin: Dolmen, 1965; Melchiori, Giorgio. *The Whole Mystery of Art: Pattern and Poetry in the Work of W. B. Yeats*. London: Routledge & Kegan Paul, 1960.

C

CAESAR, [CAIUS] JULIUS (c. 102 B.C.–44 B.C.), statesman and military commander. He was born into an old, established Roman family and was appointed a priest of Jove in 87 B.C. When he refused to obey an order to divorce his wife, he was proscribed and fled the city. Through his powerful connections, he was pardoned, and he returned to Rome in 78 B.C. to embark on a political career. As a member of the popular party, led by Pompey, he agitated for the reform of the government, quickly gaining a reputation as a dynamic young statesman and fine orator. He was appointed military tribune and, in 69 B.C., helped Pompey obtain the supreme command of the army in the East. In 63 B.C., he became a member of the First Triumvirate, a coalition made up of Pompey, the wealthy Marcus Licinius Crassus, and himself, in which he held the balance of power. In 58 B.C., he was appointed ruler in Gaul and firmly established his military leadership when he reduced all of Gaul to Roman control. Because of his military success, Pompey and the Roman senate, feeling threatened, ordered him to disband his army. He refused and, in 49 B.C., made a triumphal march on Rome, where he was elected consul. In 44 B.C., he was appointed dictator for life. His increasing popularity and absolute dictatorial powers aroused resentment, and on 15 March 44 B.C., he was assassinated. His heir was the eighteen-year-old Octavian, later Augustus Caesar. Caesar's achievements were considerable. Not only did he unite all of Italy and expand the borders of Roman rule, but he also established a system of government that was more conscious of its responsibilities to the people. In addition to his military achievements, he was a gifted writer. His commentaries on the Gallic Wars and on the civil war are among the world's literary masterpieces. In "Long-Legged Fly" (*CP*. 381), WBY pictures Caesar, contemplating in silence the superhuman role he must play in world affairs. In *Per Amica Silentia Lunae*

(*LE*. 27), he recalls Caesar's son by Cleopatra, Caesarion, who ruled Egypt from 44 to 30 B.C. and was killed by Augustus Caesar, while in *The Cat and the Moon* (*CPl*. 469), the **Lame Beggar** includes Caesar with the notorious emperors, Nero and Herod.

REFERENCES: Balsdon, J. P. *Julius Caesar: A Political Biography*. New York: Atheneum, 1967; Bradford, Ernle. *Julius Caesar: The Pursuit of Power*. London: Hamish Hamilton, 1984.

CAHEL, DELIA, fictional character. In WBY's play *Cathleen Ni Houlihan*, the young woman, Delia Cahel, is to be married the next day to Michael **Gillane**. When her future husband chooses instead to follow the poor old woman, **Cathleen Ni Houlihan**, she tries to dissuade him. In the first production of the play, April 1902, the role of Delia Cahel was played by Máire Nic Shiublaigh.

CAILITIN [also Calatin], magician of the Druids. He is commanded by **Queen Maeve** to cast a spell on **Cuchulain** during the battle for the Brown Bull of Cooley in the epic *Táin Bó Cuailnge*. Cailitin has twenty-seven sons, each of whom has a hand or foot missing. They are sent to lure Cuchulain to his death, but he kills all of them. In *The Countess Cathleen* (*CPl*. 45), **Aleel** refers to Cailitin casting a spell over Cuchulain.

REFERENCE: Ellis, Peter Berresford. *Dictionary of Celtic Mythology*. New York: Oxford University Press, 1992.

CALLANAN, J[EREMIAH] J[OSEPH] [also James Joseph, Jeremiah John] (1795–1829), poet. Born in **Cork**, he was educated at Maynooth College and **Trinity College**, Dublin. Unable to complete his studies for lack of money, he enlisted in the British army but was quickly bought out by friends. He returned to Cork, where a friendship with the Irish poet and journalist William Maginn (1793–1842) enabled him to have his poetry published in *Blackwood's Magazine*. He spent some years traveling throughout Ireland, collecting ballads and legends and rivaling **Blind Raftery** in popularity (*MY*. 125). Sadly, many of the manuscripts containing his poems and transcriptions were lost. He contracted tuberculosis and in 1829 went to Portugal to recover. His condition worsened, and he died in Lisbon. Callanan is credited with being one of the first writers to introduce a Gaelic influence into Anglo-Irish poetry (*UP1*. 362). His collections include *Gougane Barra* (1826), *The Recluse of Inchidony and Other Poems* (1830), *The Poems of J. J. Callanan* (1847), and *Gems of the Cork Poets: Comprising the Complete Works of Callanan, Condon, Casey, Fitzgerald, and Cody* (1883). WBY was initially enthusiastic about Callanan, admiring his simplicity, his rude, instinctive passion and sincerity. He gave a short biographical account of him in ''Popular Ballad Poetry of Ireland'' (*UP1*. 151–52) and included his poem ''Cusheen Loo'' in his *Fairy and Folk Tales of the Irish*

Peasantry (1888). Later, he listed Callanan among those who, while inspired by Gaelic poetry, lacked inspiration themselves (*KLI.* 451).

REFERENCES: Hogan, Robert, ed. *Dictionary of Irish Literature.* Rev. ed. Westport, Conn.: Greenwood, 1996; MacCarthy, Bridget G. "Jeremiah J. Callanan. Part I: His Life. Part II: His Poetry." *Studies* 35 (1946); Monahan, Michael. *Nova Hibernia: Irish Poets and Dramatists of Today and Yesterday.* Freeport, N.Y.: Books for Libraries, 1967.

CALLIMACHUS, fifth-century B.C. Greek sculptor. He is reputed to have designed the capital on the Corinthian pillar and to have invented a drill to simulate the folds of drapery in marble. He made the gold lamp on the Erechtheum in Athens. Comparing him with the more naturalistic **Phidias**, WBY believed that Callimachus had been influenced by Asiatic stylization (*EI.* 225) and revived, in his sculpture, a pure Ionic style. In the poem "Lapis Lazuli" (*CP.* 338), WBY describes the genius of Callimachus in more detail, noting his stylized drapery and a lamp chimney, shaped like a palm.

REFERENCES: Bowra, C. M. "The Lock of Berenice: Callimachus and Catullus." In *Greek Poetry and Life*, ed. F.A. Barber. Freeport, N.Y.: Books for Libraries, 1967; Ferguson, John. *Callimachus.* Boston: Twayne, 1980.

CALVARY, one-act play by WBY. First published by Macmillan and Company in *Four Plays for Dancers* (1921), this short play dramatizes **Christ's** reliving of his journey to Calvary to be crucified. On the way, he encounters **Lazarus, Martha**, three **Marys**, and **Judas**. At the conclusion of the action, three Roman Soldiers dice for Christ's clothes and dance victoriously around the cross. The play, which is written in the style of the Japanese **Noh**, opens and closes with a lyric sung by the three Musicians. WBY acknowledged **Oscar Wilde's** story "The Doer of Good" (1894) as a major source for the play, but the theme emerges in an early short story by WBY, "The Tables of the Law" (1897) (*MY.* 293–307), in which the hero claims he is not one of those for whom Christ died. The play was not performed in WBY's lifetime, although WBY read it aloud at the home of **Oliver St. John Gogarty**, when the poetry appeared to disturb the spirits of the house (*WL.* 729).

REFERENCES: Bradley, Anthony. *William Butler Yeats.* New York: Frederick Ungar, 1979; Ellis, Sylvia C. *The Plays of W. B. Yeats: Yeats and the Dancer.* London: Macmillan, 1995; Miller, Liam. *The Noble Drama of W. B. Yeats.* Dublin: Dolmen, 1977; Taylor, Richard. *A Reader's Guide to the Plays of W. B. Yeats.* New York: St. Martin's, 1984.

CALVERT, EDWARD (1799–1883), visionary painter and illustrator. He was born in Appledore, near Bideford, Devon, the son of Rowland Calvert, a captain in the Devonshire Yeomanry. Educated at Bodmin Grammar School, he joined the Royal Navy as a midshipman but, in 1820, left the navy to devote himself to art. He married and went to live in London where he met **Samuel Palmer** and became a member of "The Ancients," a group of artists who frequented the idyllic countryside near Shoreham, Kent. By day, these disciples of **William**

Blake sketched and swam in the River Darent; by night, often by moonlight, they sang and read poetry. Calvert was influenced by the art of ancient Greece that he had seen while serving in the British navy, so that many of his figures and compositions may be traced back to Greek models, as in the engravings *The Ploughman* (1827), *The Bride* (1828), *The Sheep of His Pasture* (1828), *Ideal Pastoral Life* (1829), and *The Brook* (1829). An early interest in Christianity turned in later years to paganism. It is likely that WBY became familiar with Calvert's illustrations when he was working with **Edwin J. Ellis** on Blake. He was attracted by their pastoral, Arcadian mood and planned to write a short monograph on Calvert for the Unicorn Press. It was announced in the *Dome* (vol. 1, no. 3) as being in preparation, but it never materialized. In 1918, while working at the Bodleian Library, **Oxford**, his table was covered with etchings by Calvert and Palmer (*WL*. 646), and he included thirteen slides of scenes by Calvert and Palmer in a lecture, "William Blake and His School," given in the **Abbey Theatre**, 14 April 1918, and on his American **Lecture Tour** in 1920. In *A Vision* (1937), he may have been influenced by Calvert's cyclic theory of history in which each phase was given the name of a Greek god. In the poem "Under Ben Bulben" (*CP*. 397), he names him with Palmer, **Claude Lorrain**, and **Richard Wilson**. In *The Bounty of Sweden* (*A*. 550), he includes Calvert with Blake, **Puvis de Chavannes**, and **Rossetti** among the "great myth-makers" (*A*. 550), while in the introduction to **W. T. Horton's** *A Book of Images* (1898), he associates Calvert with Blake and **Wagner** (*EI*. 149). His final home, **Riversdale**, reminded WBY of a farmhouse in a woodcut by Calvert (*WL*. 799). In his monograph *Beulah to Byzantium*, Raymond Lister examines connections between the imagery of Calvert's *A Primitive City* and WBY's city of **Byzantium**.

REFERENCES: Binyon, Laurence. *The Followers of William Blake: Edward Calvert, Samuel Palmer, George Richmond and Their Circle.* New York: B. Blom, 1968; Gordon, D. J., ed. *W. B. Yeats: Images of a Poet.* Manchester: University of Manchester, 1961; Lister, Raymond. *Beulah to Byzantium: A Study of Parallels in the Works of W. B. Yeats, William Blake, Samuel Palmer & Edward Calvert.* Dolmen Press Centenary Papers, Vol. II. Dublin: Dolmen, 1965; Lister, Raymond. *Edward Calvert.* London: G. Bell, 1962; Loizeaux, Elizabeth Bergmann. *Yeats and the Visual Arts.* New Brunswick and London: Rutgers University Press, 1986.

CAMDEN STREET HALL, premises at 34 Lower Camden Street, Dublin. From August 1902 until 1904, the Camden Street Hall provided a base for the newly formed **Irish National Theatre Society**. WBY's one-act farce *The Pot of Broth* was performed there, December 1902. The unheated hall, which was behind a shop and was approached down a long, dark passageway, held an audience of about fifty persons, sitting on rough benches. The stage was small, with a depth of only six feet, and there were no dressing rooms or backstage accommodation, the actors dressing at the side of the stage. Nevertheless, in the early days of the Irish National Theatre Society, this hall acted as an important meeting place for writers and actors, a place where they could discuss and argue the merits of plays and production methods. Even when the company moved to the larger **Molesworth Hall** in March 1903, the Camden Street Hall continued to be used as a rehearsal space and workshop for the building of costumes and scenery, until the company moved to the **Abbey Theatre** in December 1904. Years later, the Camden Street Hall was used by **Countess Markiewicz** as a drill hall for her boy scouts, which she called Na **Fianna**. It was unused for a time and eventually fell into disrepair. In *Samhain* (*EX*. 100), WBY notes the hall was useful only for rehearsals.

REFERENCE: McGarry, James P. *Place Names in the Writings of William Butler Yeats.* Gerrards Cross: Colin Smythe, 1976.

CAMPBELL, JOSEPH (1879–1944), poet, patriot, and scholar. He was born in Belfast, the son of a building contractor. In 1902, he was introduced to WBY and other leading figures of the Irish Literary Revival and published articles and poems in *The United Irishman* and *All Ireland Review*. He collaborated with Herbert Hughes in the publication of *Songs of Uladh* (1904), providing the lyrics for the traditional airs that Hughes had collected in **Donegal** (county). These included two of Campbell's best-known songs, "My Lagan Love" and "The Ninepenny Fiddle." He contributed to the contemporary journal *Uladh*. Through the nationalist **Francis Joseph Bigger**, he became associated with the Ulster Literary Theatre, both as an actor and as a playwright. In 1905, he moved to London to teach English at a local high school. He became secretary of the **Irish Literary Society** and assistant to Eleanor Hull of the Irish Texts Society. He married and returned to Ireland in 1911 to pursue a literary career, settling at Glencree in the Wicklow mountains. His play *Judgement* was produced at the **Abbey Theatre**, April 1912. He became active in nationalist politics and was interned during the Civil War. On his release in 1923, he immigrated to the United States and set about promoting his cultural heritage with fervor and enthusiasm. He founded a school of Irish Studies in New York in 1925, but the venture failed. He taught Irish literature at Fordham University, 1927–38, and founded the *Irish Review* in 1934. In 1939, he returned to Ireland. His collections of verse, some of which are illustrated with his own drawings, include *The Garden of the Bees* (1905), *The Rushlight* (1906), *The Gilly of Christ* (1907), *The Mountainy Singer* (1909), *Irishry* (1913), and *Earth of Cualann* (1917). All his poems are marked by freshness and a pleasing lyricism, owing much to early Gaelic poetry in their austerity and simplicity. As a native of Belfast, Campbell was never fully accepted in the south of Ireland, although he lived near Dublin for some years and was active politically. This may help to explain why his contribution to the emerging Irish Literary Movement has been unjustly ignored. WBY makes few references to him in his writings but acknowledges that Campbell's poems, like those of **Padraic Colum**, have become part of the folk tradition (*LE*. 186, 247). His poem ''The Dancer'' was included in WBY's selection for *The Oxford Book of Modern Verse* (1936).

REFERENCES: Austin Clarke, ed. *The Poems of Joseph Campbell*. Dublin: Allen Figgis, 1963; Hogan, Robert, ed. *Dictionary of Irish Literature*. Rev. ed. Westport, Conn.: Greenwood, 1996; O'Hegarty, P. S. *A Bibliography of Joseph Campbell—Seosamh Mac Cathmaoil*. Dublin: A. Thom, 1940.

CAMPBELL, MRS. PATRICK (1865–1940), actress. She was born Beatrice Stella Tanner, her father the heir to a wealthy Anglo-Indian family and her mother the daughter of an Italian political exile. After attending school in London and Brighton, she won a scholarship to study piano at the Guildhall School of Music in London. She was expected to continue her studies in Germany, but she eloped with Patrick Campbell and within two years had two children. Her husband went to Australia to make his fortune (he was later killed in the Boer War), leaving her to cope with her young family. She was beautiful, with a pleasing voice, so she decided to earn her living on the stage. She made her London debut in 1888 with some success, but she did not establish her reputation as a major actress until 1893, when she played the title role in Sir Arthur W. Pinero's *The Second Mrs. Tanqueray*. After appearing with **Beerbohm Tree** in his 1894–95 season at the Haymarket Theatre, she joined the Forbes-Robertson company to play a range of classic roles, including Juliet, Ophelia, Lady Teazle, and Mélisande in **Maeterlinck's** *Pelléas and Mélisande*. From 1902, she made successful tours of the United States with her own company, but she became increasingly demanding with her actors, gaining a reputation for rudeness and sharpness of tongue, a reputation alluded to by WBY in *Per Amica Silentia Lunae* (*LE*. 5). In 1904, she acted opposite Sarah Bernhardt in a memorable production of *Pelléas and Mélisande*, a production that was seen in Dublin, but perhaps her crowning success as an actress was her portrayal of Eliza Doolittle in **George Bernard Shaw's** *Pygmalion* (1914), a role that she had been reluctant to perform. After a triumphant opening in London, she took the play to New York and toured throughout the United States. It was her last success before she settled into retirement in France. WBY was impressed when he saw her acting in 1901 (*WL*. 360) and must have been familiar with her style, since she frequently played in Dublin. By 1906, he had altered his stance, thinking her too emotional compared with the more restrained acting style then current (*WL*. 475), but at the height of her popularity, when she performed in a revival of *Deirdre* at the **Abbey Theatre** in 1908, he thought her performance ''magnificent'' (*WL*. 512). She toured London and the provinces with the production before a further run at the Court Theatre, June 1909. At her request, he completed *The Player Queen*, but after hearing it read, she lost interest. In *On the Boiler* (*LE*. 226), written in 1938, he recalls her passionate performance of **Deirdre**.

REFERENCES: Campbell, Mrs. Patrick. *My Life and Some Letters*. New York: Dodd, Mead, 1922; Dent, Alan, ed. *Bernard Shaw, Mrs. Patrick Campbell: Their Correspon-*

dence. London: Gollancz, 1952; Dent, Alan. *Mrs. Patrick Campbell*. 1961. Reprint, Westport, Conn.: Greenwood, 1973; Peters, Margot. *Mrs. Pat: The Life of Mrs. Patrick Campbell*. New York: Knopf, 1984.

CAOILTE [also Cáilte, Caolte] [the thin man], poet and warrior of the **Fianna**. He was reputed to be the fastest runner among the Fianna, so that the name is synonymous with the wind. In *The Wanderings of Oisin* (*CP*. 409, 412), Caoilte is the companion of **Fionn** and **Oisin**. He appears as a character in *Diarmuid and Grania* by WBY and **George Moore**. See also "The Hosting of the Sidhe" (*CP*. 61).
    REFERENCE: Mac Cana, Proinsias. *Celtic Mythology*. Feltham, Middlesex: Newnes, 1983.

CARLETON, WILLIAM (1794–1869), short story writer and novelist. He was born at Prolusk near Clogher, County Tyrone, the son of a poor Catholic tenant farmer. He had no formal schooling, but with the help of a local hedge-schoolmaster, he rose to popularity as a prolific novelist and short story writer. A robust man, with a reputation for drinking and womanizing, he was torn between a passion for education and a desire to join the priesthood. Unable to commit himself to either, he set out for Dublin, gathering stories of evictions, famine, superstition, and trickery. These, together with the many characters he encountered on his journey, became the material for his short stories and novels, among them *Traits and Stories of the Irish Peasantry* (1830–33), generally considered his best writing. He married Jane Anderson and alienated himself from many of his readers and critics by becoming a Protestant and contributing sketches of Irish country life to the *Christian Examiner*, a propagandist paper intended to expose the influence of the Roman Catholic priesthood in rural Ireland. His later writing could be interpreted as didactic and rhetorical. He spent his final years on an unfinished biography. Overall, Carleton's writing is distinguished by its authenticity and truthfulness, especially in its observations of nineteenth-century Irish peasant life. His finest novel is *The Black Prophet* (1847), a story of the painful sufferings of the peasants during the Famine. Carleton was a major inspiration to the writers of the Irish Literary Revival, especially in his reproduction of native Irish speech with its mixture of English vocabulary and Irish syntax. WBY was an early advocate of Carleton (*UP1*. 138–39). He included six of his tales in *Fairy and Folk Tales of the Irish Peasantry* (1888), edited the *Stories of William Carleton*, published in the Camelot Series (1889), included excerpts from Carleton in *Representative Irish Tales* (1891), and contributed an anonymous review of *The Red-Haired Man's Wife* for the *Scots Observer* (*UP1*. 141–46). He defended Carleton against charges of sectarianism and anti-Catholic bias (*UP1*. 167–69, 306–7, 394–97; *WL*. 147) and named *Fardorougha the Miser* (1839), *The Black Prophet* (1847), and *Traits and Stories of the Irish Peasantry* among his "Best Irish Books" (*UP1*. 383–

87) and "Thirty Best Books" (*WL*. 246–48). In time, his enthusiasm for Carleton waned, and he recognized that some of his early novels like *Valentine McClutchy, the Irish Agent* (1845) and *Willy Reilly and His Dear Colleen Bawn* (1855) were formless, and the later work was didactic (*UP1*. 335, 383, 394–97).

REFERENCES: Flanagan, Thomas. *The Irish Novelists 1800–1850*. New York: Columbia University Press, 1959; Hogan, Robert, ed. *Dictionary of Irish Literature*. Rev. ed. Westport, Conn.: Greenwood, 1996; Hyland, Paul, and Sammells, Neil, eds. *Irish Writing: Exile and Subversion*. New York: St. Martin's, 1991; Kiely, Benedict. *Poor Scholar*. New York: Sheed & Ward, 1948; Sullivan, Eileen A. *William Carleton*. Boston: Twayne, 1983.

CARLYLE, THOMAS (1795–1881), essayist and historian. He was born in Scotland and attended Edinburgh University, intending to enter the church. Instead, he became a teacher of mathematics, before studying law. From law, he turned to the study of German Romanticism and quickly gained a literary reputation with his major publication *Life of Schiller* (1825) and a translation of **Goethe's** *Wilhelm Meister* (1824). In 1826, he married Jane Baillie Welsh, a woman of strong temperament, who did much to further his literary career. In 1828, they moved to her farm at Craigenputtock to enable him to devote himself to writing. Rejecting eighteenth-century materialism and influenced by the philosophical ideas of Immanuel Kant, Carlyle embarked on a spiritual autobiography, *Sartor Resartus* (1838), written under the pseudonym Herr Diogenes Teufelsdröckh. In 1834, he and his wife moved to London, where he intensified his relationship with the philosopher and economist John Stuart Mill and began writing his memorable work *French Revolution* (1837). In this dramatic account, he gave an engaging interpretation of the events of the revolution and warned that reforms in England were overdue. The book gained him enormous popularity and influence. He believed that the social and political injustices in English society must be set right and that, while change was possible and desirable, it could only be achieved through the leadership of outstanding men or "heroes." He expressed these ideas in *On Heroes, Hero-Worship, and the Heroic in History* (1841) and in *Past and Present* (1843) and followed their publication with an edition of *Oliver Cromwell's Letters and Speeches* (1845) and a mammoth biography of *Frederick the Great* (1858–65). After the death of his wife in 1866, he retired from public life and wrote little. Carlyle was a major influence on the writers and thinkers of the late nineteenth century. WBY was aware of this influence through his contact with **William Morris** (*A*. 146; *EI*. 248) and **John F. Taylor** (*A*. 214) and saw its doubtful effect on writers like **Standish [James] O'Grady** and **John Mitchel** (*LE*. 207; *UP1*. 361). He regretted that the writers of the Young Ireland movement had looked to Carlyle for a model and not to the heroic past; **Sir Charles Gavan Duffy**, for example, arranged for someone to read him Carlyle after dinner (*A*. 224). WBY recognized that Carlyle dealt

only in vulgar abstractions and rhetoric, not with people. By 1916, his influence
had waned, and he was already old-fashioned and out of date (*WL*. 608).
  REFERENCES: Campbell, Ian. *Thomas Carlyle*. London: Hamilton, 1974; Kaplan,
Fred. *Thomas Carlyle: A Biography*. Ithaca, N.Y.: Cornell University Press, 1983.

CARRICKFERGUS (Irish: *Carraig Fhearghasa*) [Rock of Fergus], port on the
shores of Belfast Lough, eleven miles from Belfast. Carrickfergus is notable for
its fine, well-preserved Norman castle and church of St. Nicholas, which date
from the twelfth century. **Louis MacNeice** lived in the town from early childhood until he went to school in England and to Cambridge University. In ''A
Remonstrance with Scotsmen'' (*MY*. 107), WBY discusses the opposing attitudes of the Scots and Irish to fairies and witches and recalls a story in which
a witch in Carrickfergus has her eye put out with a cabbage stalk by Scotsmen
in 1711.
  REFERENCE: McGarry, James P. *Place Names in the Writings of William Butler Yeats*.
Gerrards Cross: Colin Smythe, 1976.

CASEMENT, SIR ROGER [DAVID] (1864–1916), diplomat and patriot. He was
born in Ireland and educated at Ballymena Academy, County Antrim. He went
to Africa in 1884 and joined the British consular service there in 1892. From
1895 to 1912, he exposed the inhuman treatment of native workers in the Belgian Congo and in the Putumayo region of Peru and was knighted for his public
services. In a growing wave of nationalist feeling among intellectuals in the
north of Ireland, he joined the Gaelic League and contributed articles to the
nationalist press under the pseudonym ''Sean Bhean Bhocht.'' In 1913, after
retiring from the British diplomatic service, he joined the Irish Volunteers. A
year later, he went to Germany to solicit aid for a rebellion and to recruit an
Irish Brigade from prisoners of war in Berlin. In April 1916, just as a shipment
of arms from Germany for use in the planned rebellion was intercepted off the
coast of Ireland and blown up by the British, Casement returned to Ireland in a
German submarine, intending to persuade the leaders to call off the Easter Rising. He was arrested and taken to England, where he was convicted of high
treason and sentenced to death. To counteract the strong public reaction to the
sentence, particularly in the United States, the British government released diaries, supposedly belonging to Casement, that documented homosexual practices. Public opinion turned against Casement, and he was hanged in Pentonville
Prison. In 1965, his remains were returned to Ireland and reinterred in **Glasnevin**, Dublin, after a state funeral. WBY appears to have had little reaction in
1916 to the execution of Casement. Only in the 1930s does he turn to the Irish
patriot as a subject for verse. He recalls Casement's portrait ''The Court of
Criminal Appeal,'' by **Sir John Lavery**, in ''The Municipal Gallery Revisited''
(*CP*. 368) and celebrates him as a wronged political hero in the ballads ''Roger
Casement'' (*CP*. 351) and ''The Ghost of Roger Casement'' (*CP*. 352). Both
ballads were written in November 1936 after he read Dr. Maloney's *The Forged*

Casement Diaries, in which the author argued Casement's innocence. WBY's response to the book and his writing of the ballads are documented in letters he wrote to **Ethel Mannin** (*WL.* 867–68) and to **Dorothy Wellesley** (*WL.* 868–69, 870–71, 876).

REFERENCES: Hyland, Paul. *Black Heart: A Voyage into Central Africa.* New York: Holt, 1989; Inglis, Brian. *Roger Casement.* New York: Jovanovich, 1974; MacColl, Rene. *Roger Casement: A New Judgement.* New York: Norton, 1957; Reid, Benjamin Lawrence. *Lives of Roger Casement.* New Haven: Yale University Press, 1976; Sawyer, Roger. *Casement: The Flawed Hero.* London: Routledge & Kegan Paul, 1984.

CASHEL. *See* **ROCK OF CASHEL**.

CASHEL-NA-GAEL (Irish: *Caisle-Geala*) [white castle], rocky townland on the side of **Cope's Mountain** in **Sligo** (county). In "The Curse of the Fires and the Shadow" (*MY.* 177–83), five English troopers are led to their deaths in the abyss of **Lugnagall**, by way of the pass between **Ben Bulben** and Cashel-na-Gael.

REFERENCE: McGarry, James P. *Place Names in the Writings of William Butler Yeats.* Gerrards Cross: Colin Smythe, 1976.

CASHELNORE (Irish: *Caiseal-an-Oir*) [fort of the spring], raised mound or rath in Glencolumcille, **Donegal** (county). Cashelnore is overlooked by Slieve League. In "The Three O'Byrnes and the Evil Faeries" (*MY.* 86–87), WBY writes of the treasure that is supposedly buried under Cashelnore.

REFERENCE: McGarry, James P. *Place Names in the Writings of William Butler Yeats.* Gerrards Cross: Colin Smythe, 1976.

CASTIGLIONE, COUNT BALDASSARE (1478–1529), Italian statesman and man of letters. He was born near Mantua and educated in Milan. From 1496, he was attached to the court of the Duke of Milan, but he returned to Mantua in 1500 after the duke was imprisoned and taken to France. In 1504, he entered the service of **Guidobaldo**, Duke of **Urbino**, a noted patron of the arts and letters. There, he began writing his masterpiece, *Il Libro del Cortegiano* (The book of the courtier). With the death of Guidobaldo, he served his successor, Francesco Maria della Rovere, until 1516, when he was appointed papal nuncio to Spain. He was later made Bishop of Avila, but in the subsequent sacking of Rome by the French in 1527, he was accused of treachery and spent his final days in disgrace in Toledo. *The Book of the Courtier*, which celebrates aristocratic courtesy and values at the court of Urbino, was published in 1528. It almost immediately achieved an international reputation. Sir Thomas Hoby's English translation appeared in 1561 and was a major influence on the thought, literature, and religion of Elizabethan England. Written in four sections, *The Book of the Courtier* provided a vivid account of Italian court life during the Renaissance, presented as a series of discussions that took place in the ducal palace on four evenings in March 1507, under the supervision of the gracious Duchess Eliza-betta Gonzaga, wife of Guidobaldo. The topics discussed ranged from politics and ethics to dress, manners, and relationships between the sexes. In *The Bounty of Sweden* (*A.* 545), WBY recalls **Lady Gregory** reading to him from *The Book of the Courtier* (possibly during the summer of 1903 at **Coole Park**, when WBY's eyesight was especially poor). As Corinna Salvadori argues in her study *Yeats and Castiglione* (1965), WBY was fascinated by the work, not only be-cause it celebrated aristocratic values but also because it provided him with a symbol for unity of culture and tradition. In his Journal, written 6 February 1909 (*M.* 163), WBY recalls how moved he was to discover, in the final section of the book, that all those who took part in the discussions, including Elizabetta, were dead. WBY refers to the duchess and her courtiers in "The People" (*CP.* 169), while in "To a Wealthy Man Who Promised a Second Subscription to the Dublin Municipal Gallery if it were proved the People wanted Pictures" (*CP.* 119), he contrasts the values of the Italian Renaissance court with the attitudes of contemporary Irish patrons like Lord Ardilaun. In *On the Boiler* (*LE.* 234), written in 1938, he returns to the court of Urbino, extolling the virtues of the Renaissance courtier, a perfect symbol for unity of being. A copy of Hoby's translation of *The Book of the Courtier*, published by David Nutt (Lon-don: 1900), was in WBY's library (*OS.* no. 351).

REFERENCE: Salvadori, Corinna. *Yeats and Castiglione: Poet and Courtier.* Dublin: Allen Figgis, 1965.

CASTLE DARGAN (Irish: *Caiseal-Deargain*), ruined castle on the edge of Castle Dargan Lake near Ballygawley, **Sligo** (county). A Middleton cousin of WBY was married to the owner of the castle. They lived in a house nearby. When WBY was a child, he visited Castle Dargan and observed in rich detail the antics of its eccentric owner (*A.* 53–55). Castle Dargan is the setting for the final lyric in the play *The King of the Great Clock Tower* (*CPl.* 640). WBY may have been thinking of the castle when he described the ruined house in *Purgatory* (*CPl.* 681), and it is very likely the uninhabited house mentioned in the poem "Crazy Jane on God" (*CP.* 293). In "Red Hanrahan's Curse" (*MY.* 238–45), **Hanrahan** puts a curse on the gray pike in Castle Dargan Lake, as well as on local places and people. On Castle Dargan Lake was Castle Fury, a large, uninhabited house that WBY saw when he visited his cousin at Castle Dargan. It had been lived in by a family called Furey but was now derelict and in ruins. According to WBY, the last of the family were two elderly ladies who kept a boarding house in Sligo (*A.* 54).

REFERENCE: McGarry, James P. *Place Names in the Writings of William Butler Yeats.* Gerrards Cross: Colin Smythe, 1976.

CASTLE FURY. *See* **CASTLE DARGAN.**

CASTLE HACKETT, mansion set on some 900 acres in **Galway** (county). Castle Hackett is located about three miles from **Tuam**. Ruins of the original castle may still be found on the estate. In "Kidnappers" (*MY*. 74), WBY tells the story of the owner of Castle Hackett, John Kirwan, who had some good fortune. He was in England to race his horse, when he met a changeling boy who claimed that he had been stolen as a baby from a cottage on the Castle Hackett estate and that his mother still lived there. The boy warned Kirwan there would be a fire where he had thought of stabling the horse. The fire occurred, just as he had predicted. Next day, as a reward, he begged to be allowed to ride Kirwan's horse in the race. He advised Kirwan to make a large bet. He won the race for Kirwan and was never seen again.

REFERENCE: McGarry, James P. *Place Names in the Writings of William Butler Yeats*. Gerrards Cross: Colin Smythe, 1976.

CASTLE HYDE. *See* **HYDE, DOUGLAS**.

CASTLE ROCK [also Castle Island, MacDermot's Castle], island in Lough Key (*Loch Cé*), County Roscommon. WBY discovered the island while he was staying with **Douglas Hyde** at Frenchpark in the spring of 1895 (*M*. 123). The small island was dominated by a sound but uninhabited castle, the stronghold of the MacDermot family. Although their lands had been forfeited in Elizabethan times, the MacDermots had lived on the island until the early 1800s. At the invitation of the ruling head of the MacDermot clan, Castle Rock had been a gathering place for the poets of Ireland in 1540 and 1549—a tradition established by the Gaelic chieftains from the fourteenth century. WBY enthusiastically evolved a plan to establish the island as the center of an Order of Celtic Mysteries, in which the castle would be known as the Castle of the Heroes. Elaborate plans were drawn up and discussed with **Maud Gonne, George Pollexfen, Lady Gregory**, and others, but the mystical Order was never founded.

REFERENCE: McGarry, James P. *Place Names in the Writings of William Butler Yeats*. Gerrards Cross: Colin Smythe, 1976.

CASTLE TAYLOR, home of the Taylor family, near Craughwell, **Galway** (county). The house was built in 1802 when part of the old castle, *Caislean MacCraith*, which had stood on the site, was incorporated into the building. The Taylors were neighbors of **Lady Gregory**, and Castle Taylor is mentioned by WBY in the poem "In Memory of Major Robert Gregory" (*CP*. 148).

REFERENCE: McGarry, James P. *Place Names in the Writings of William Butler Yeats*. Gerrards Cross: Colin Smythe, 1976.

CAT AND THE MOON, THE, one-act farce by WBY. It was written in 1917 but not published until 1924, when it was included in *The Cat and the Moon and Certain Poems*. It was subsequently printed in *Wheels and Butterflies* (1934), where it was dedicated to **John Masefield**, and in *The Collected Plays of W. B. Yeats* (1934, 1952). WBY planned to include the farce, which is in the style of a Japanese *kyogen*, in his *Four Plays for Dancers* (1921). He decided against this, however. In the play, two beggars, one lame and the other blind, journey to the holy well of St. Colman, hoping to be cured. One of the Musicians, speaking the lines of the saint, offers them the choice of blessedness or physical well-being. The garrulous **Blind Beggar** chooses his sight, but the **Lame Beggar** is content to remain lame so that he will be blessed. The Blind Beggar is given his sight and, after beating the Lame Beggar, goes off on his own. The saint climbs on the back of the Lame Beggar and tells him to dance. Miraculously, the Lame Beggar begins to move. He throws his stick away and dances joyously around the stage. The play opens and concludes with a chorus. **Minnaloushe**, the cat described in the opening and closing lyrics, belonged to **Maud Gonne**. The play very likely owed its genesis to the sole *kyogen* among the papers of **Ernest Fenollosa,** *Kikazu Zato*, in which a blind man and a deaf man play malevolent tricks on each other. **J. M. Synge's** *The Well of the Saints* (1905) is another likely source, while WBY, in a note to the play (*VP*. 805), half remembers a story in which a lame Man and a blind Man come to **St. Colman's Well** to be cured. In *Dramatis Personae* (*A*. 402), WBY claims to have dramatized in the play, somewhat wickedly, the friendship between **George Moore** and **Edward Martyn**. In the first production of *The Cat and the Moon*, presented by the Dublin Drama League at the **Abbey Theatre**, May 1926, the cast was as follows: Blind Beggar, Michael J. Dolan; Lame Beggar, W. O'Gorman; Musicians, John Stephenson, T. Moran, **Lennox Robinson**. The play was directed by Lennox Robinson, under the supervision of WBY.

REFERENCES: Bradley, Anthony. *William Butler Yeats*. New York: Frederick Ungar, 1979; Ellis, Sylvia C. *The Plays of W. B. Yeats: Yeats and the Dancer*. London: Macmillan, 1995; Miller, Liam. *The Noble Drama of W. B. Yeats*. Dublin: Dolmen, 1977; Taylor, Richard. *A Reader's Guide to the Plays of W. B. Yeats*. New York: St. Martin's, 1984.

CAT AND THE MOON AND CERTAIN POEMS, THE, collection of verse by WBY. It was printed in a limited edition of 500 copies by the **Cuala Press** in 1924. In addition to the one-act farce *The Cat and the Moon*, the collection included the poems "Meditations in Time of Civil War" (*CP*. 225), "Youth and Age" (*CP*. 237), "Leda and the Swan" (*CP*. 241), and "Owen Aherne and his Dancers" (*CP*. 247).

CATHLEEN NI HOULIHAN, synonym for Ireland or Mother Ireland. The concept of Ireland as a woman is rooted in mythology. When the Gaels arrived in Ireland, according to legend, they were greeted by the goddess Ériu. Later, the poets of the seventeenth and eighteenth century continued to portray Ireland as a beautiful woman yearning for the return of her land and her lover or as a shameless whore who shared her favors with the usurping English. WBY drew on the tradition when he celebrated the land of Ireland through the symbol of Cathleen, daughter of Houlihan, in his poem "Red Hanrahan's Song about Ireland" (*CP*. 90) and in the play *Cathleen Ni Houlihan*. An early version of the figure appears in the story ''Hanrahan and Cathleen, the Daughter of Houlihan,'' published in *Stories of Red Hanrahan* (1897) (*MY.* 234).

CATHLEEN NI HOULIHAN, one-act play by WBY. It was first performed by **W. G. Fay's** Irish National Dramatic Company in Dublin, April 1902, with **Maud Gonne** in the title role. The complete text was printed in **Samhain**, October 1902. The play was published by **A. H. Bullen** in 1902, and subsequently in many collections of WBY's plays, including *The Hour-Glass and Other Plays* (1904), *The Unicorn from the Stars and Other Plays* (1908), *Collected Works of W. B. Yeats*, Vol. IV (1908), ***Plays for an Irish Theatre*** (1911), *Plays in Prose and Verse* (1922), *Nine One-Act Plays* (1937), and ***The Collected Plays of W. B. Yeats*** (1934, 1952). There is no known source for the story of the play, which WBY claimed came to him in a dream. According to **Michael B. Yeats**, in his article ''W. B. Yeats and Irish Folk Song'' (*Southern Folk Lore Quarterly*, June 1966), the title of the play was inspired by a song composed by William Heffernan, a blind Gaelic poet. With *Cathleen Ni Houlihan*, which he dedicated to the memory of the young Irish writer **William Rooney**, WBY had his first popular success. It became a rallying cry to the militant Irish nationalists, a fact alluded to by WBY in his poem ''The Man and the Echo'' (*CP.* 393), written in July 1938. In the play, set in 1798, Michael **Gillane**, a young Irishman soon to be married, is persuaded by an Old Woman to fight the English by joining the French troops arriving at **Killala** Bay. The Old Woman is **Cathleen Ni Houlihan**, a symbol for Ireland. While he was in Sweden to receive the **Nobel Prize for Literature**, WBY saw a well-researched production of the play, presented in his honor, but some of the production details troubled him (*A.* 556–57). The cast of the first production was: Cathleen, Maud Gonne; Delia Cahel, Máire Nic Shiubhlaigh; Bridget Gillane, Maire T. Quinn; Patrick Gillane, C. Caulfield; Michael Gillane, Dudley Digges; and Peter Gillane, W. G. Fay. The play was directed by W. G. Fay.

REFERENCES: Bradley, Anthony. *William Butler Yeats.* New York: Frederick Ungar, 1979; Jeffares, A. Norman, and Knowland, A. S. *A Commentary on the Collected Plays of W. B. Yeats.* London: Macmillan, 1975; Miller, Liam. *The Noble Drama of W. B. Yeats.* Dublin: Dolmen, 1977; Taylor, Richard. *A Reader's Guide to the Plays of W. B. Yeats.* New York: St. Martin's, 1984.

CATULLUS, [CAIUS VALERIUS] (c. 84–c. 54 B.C.), poet. He is considered one of the outstanding lyric poets of all time for his purity and simplicity of style. Born in Verona, Italy, of a wealthy family, he moved to Rome. After he fell in love, he wrote many poems, ranging from poems of adoration to poems of disillusionment after the discovery of his mistress's infidelity. He wrote epics and an epithalamium on **Thetis** and **Peleus**. In ''Modern Poetry: A Broadcast'' (*LE.* 92, 183), WBY recalls that members of the **Rhymers' Club** admired Catullus and tried to emulate his purity of style. WBY refers to Catullus in ''The Scholars'' (*CP.* 158).

CAVALCANTI, GUIDO (c. 1250–1300), poet and friend of **Dante**. He is referred to as Guido in WBY's poem "Ego Dominus Tuus" (*CP.* 180). Cavalcanti aligned himself with the White faction in a struggle with the Guelphs in Florence and was banished to Sarzana. There he became ill and died soon after his reinstatement in Florence. A love poet, his major work is to be found in *Canzone d'Amore* and in *Sonnets and Ballate of Guido Cavalcanti*, translated by **Ezra Pound** (1912). Two copies of the latter were in WBY's library (*OS.* nos. 356, 356a), in addition to Cavalcanti's *Rime* (*OS.* no. 355). In *Per Amica Silentia Lunae* (*LE.* 7), WBY quotes Cavalcanti on Dante.

CELBRIDGE (Irish: *Cill-Droichid*) [church of the bridge], County Kildare. Celbridge is the location of Castletown House, reputedly the largest and finest house in Ireland. In his introduction to *The Words upon the Window-Pane* (*EX.* 349), WBY challenges **Jonathan Swift's** claim, made in 1730, that there were no new buildings in Ireland, citing Castletown House, built for the speaker of the Irish Parliament, 1719–32. **Hester van Homrigh** lived at nearby Celbridge Abbey.
    REFERENCE: McGarry, James P. *Place Names in the Writings of William Butler Yeats.* Gerrards Cross: Colin Smythe, 1976.

CELTIC TWILIGHT, THE, a collection by WBY of short essays, folktales, and anecdotes. *The Celtic Twilight* was first published by **Lawrence and Bullen** in 1893 and reprinted, with additions, in 1902. The first edition contained twenty-two essays, while the 1902 edition contained thirty-nine essays (one of the essays from the first edition had been removed and twenty new essays added). In 1925, the essays from *The Celtic Twilight* were included in *Mythologies* with stories from *The Secret Rose* (1897) and *Per Amica Silentia Lunae* (1917). *The Celtic Twilight* is based on a diary that WBY carried with him as he collected folklore around **Sligo** and the Irish countryside in the late 1880s. In the diary, he noted down sketches and folktales heard by the roadside or told him by local people like Paddy Flynn of **Ballisodare**, the subject of the first story, "A Teller of Tales" (*MY.* 5–6). *The Celtic Twilight* is valuable for the insight it provides into WBY's early interest in fairy lore and the world of spirits, and his rooted sense of place, especially Sligo and the west of Ireland. It contains fresh and lively descriptions of local characters like **Blind Raftery** and **Mary Hynes** and of places that WBY visited on his youthful travels, among them **Kiltartan**, near the home of **Lady Gregory**, and the old Norman castle at **Ballylee**, which WBY bought some twenty-five years later. *The Celtic Twilight* is important because it provides an early glimpse of source material that the poet later turned into verse, as in "Drumcliff and Rosses" (*MY.* 88–94), in which he refers to the faery riders rushing in the evenings from a square door in the side of **Ben Bulben** over the plain of **Drumcliff** below, a reference he was to return to in his late poems.
    REFERENCES: Greene, David. H. "Yeats's Prose Style: Some Observations." In *Modern Irish Literature*, ed. Raymond J. Porter and James D. Brophy. New York: Twayne,

1972. Thuente, Mary Helen. *W. B. Yeats and Irish Folklore*. Totowa, N.J.: Barnes & Noble, 1981.

CHAMBERLAIN [Lord High Chamberlain], fictional character. In WBY's play *The King's Threshold*, he is the representative of King **Guaire**. He claims to be a court poet and aggressively tries to persuade the rebel poet **Seanchan** to break his hunger strike. In the first production, October 1903, the part of the Chamberlain was played by **Seamus O'Sullivan**.

CHARLEMAGNE (742–814), king of the Franks. The elder son of Pepin the Short, he became king of the Franks in 771. He invaded Lombardy in support of Pope Adrian I in 773 and in 774 was crowned king of the Lombards. After successfully conquering northeast Spain from the Moors in 778, he annexed Bavaria and continued an ongoing battle to subjugate the Saxons. When the new pope, Leo III, was threatened with deposition by the Romans, he appealed to Charlemagne. In 800, he confirmed Leo III as pope and, on Christmas Day, was crowned emperor of the Holy Roman Empire. His final years were troubled with raids by Norse and Danish pirates. Charlemagne's rule was distinguished by the efficiency of his administration. He was reputed for enlightened care of the poor and his imposition of strict measures to eradicate abusive practices in the church and state. His court at Aachen was the center of a lively intellectual and artistic revival. After his death, his reputation grew until it reached mythic proportions, and he became the central figure of a medieval romance cycle. WBY refers to his "world transforming" achievements in the poem "Whence Had They Come?" (*CP*. 332).
    REFERENCES: Chamberlin, E. R. *Charlemagne: Emperor of the Western World*. London: Grafton, 1986; King, P. D. *Charlemagne*. London: Methuen, 1986.

CHATTERJEE, [BABU] MOHINI [also Chatterji] (1858–1936), Indian philosopher and lawyer. Mohini Chatterjee was born in Calcutta, a descendant of the Hindu reformer Raja Rammonhun Roy. A leading Bengali Brahmin, Mohini Chatterjee was one of the first and most brilliant members of the **Theosophical Society** in India. He was a close associate of **Madame Blavatsky** and traveled with her when she visited Europe in 1884. Later in life, as Blavatsky's reputation declined and he became more celebrated as a guru, they became estranged. The poems "Anashuya and Vijaya" (*CP*. 10), "The Indian upon God" (*CP*. 14), and "The Indian to His Love" (*CP*. 15) were all written by WBY after Mohini Chatterjee's visit to Dublin in 1885. In "The Way of Wisdom," first published in *The Speaker* (14 April 1900) and reprinted as "The Pathway" in *Collected Works* (Vol. 8, 1908), WBY describes the Brahmin's visit to Dublin and acknowledges the influence that he exerted over him. Indeed, Chatterjee was the source of many Indian anecdotes that WBY told throughout his life. He is the subject of the poem "Mohini Chatterjee" (*CP*. 279), written in early 1929 and first published in *A Packet for Ezra Pound* (1929).

REFERENCE: Cranston, Sylvia. *The Extraordinary Life & Influence of Helena Blavatsky: Founder of the Modern Philosophical Movement*. New York: Putnam, 1993.

CHESHIRE CHEESE, YE OLDE, long-established coffeehouse at 145 Fleet Street, London. WBY and fellow members of the **Rhymers' Club** met regularly at the Cheshire Cheese during the early 1890s. They ate and drank downstairs in the old coffeehouse boxes and then retired to a smoking room upstairs to read their poems aloud. WBY acknowledges his debt to the Rhymers' Club and the Cheshire Cheese in his poem "The Grey Rock" (*CP*. 115). He refers to it in his essays "Art and Ideas" (*EI*. 349) and "Modern Poetry: A Broadcast" (*EI*. 491) and in his introduction to *The Oxford Book of Modern Verse* (*LE*. 185).

REFERENCES: Beckson, Karl. "Yeats and the Rhymers' Club." *Yeats Studies* 1 (1971); Gardner, Joann. *Yeats and the Rhymers' Club: A Nineties' Perspective*. New York: Peter Lang, 1989.

CHESSON, NORA. *See* **HOPPER, NORA**.

CHESTERTON, G[ILBERT] K[EITH] (1874–1936), journalist, novelist, poet, and essayist. He was born in Kensington, London, and educated at St. Paul's School and University College, London. A prolific writer, he produced critical studies of **Robert Browning** (1903) and **George Bernard Shaw** (1909), among others, but he is best remembered as an essayist and the author of detective fiction featuring Father Brown. He converted to Catholicism in 1900, largely through the influence of his friend Hilaire Belloc. When Chesterton courted his future wife, Frances Blogg, a resident of **Bedford Park**, he met the Yeats family. They became lifelong friends. WBY spent time in Chesterton's company and introduced him to many Irish writers, including **J. M. Synge**. Curiously, there are no references to Chesterton in WBY's published writings, with the exception of a few allusions in letters and some sentences in "An Undelivered Speech" (*UP2*. 451), in which he challenges Chesterton's views on divorce. Chesterton gives a witty description of WBY and his family in his *Autobiography* (1936). Two of his poems, including the long narrative *Lepanto*, were included in WBY's selection for *The Oxford Book of Modern Verse* (1936).

REFERENCES: Belloc, Hilaire. *On the Place of Gilbert Chesterton in English Letters*. Shepherdstown, W. Va.: Patmos, 1977; Chesterton, G. K. *Autobiography*. London: Hutchinson, 1936; Ward, Maisie. *Gilbert Keith Chesterton*. New York: Sheed & Ward, 1943.

CHOU, powerful ruling dynasty of China, c. 1122–256 B.C. Most of the influential works of Chinese philosophy were written during the turbulent Chou dynasty, including the Five Classics of Confucianism and the chief literature of

Taoism. In "Vacillation" (*CP*. 284), WBY refers to the lord of Chou, possibly Chou-Kung who ruled China during the twelfth century B.C.

CHRIST [Jesus Christ], the Son of God in the Christian tradition. According to the gospels of Matthew and Luke, he was born in Bethlehem, Judea, the son of **Mary** and her husband Joseph, a carpenter from Nazareth. When he was about thirty years of age, he gathered together a group of disciples and began preaching. He proclaimed himself the Messiah, or the anointed one of God, and called upon his listeners to be baptized and repent their sins in preparation for the coming of the kingdom of God. He taught through the medium of parables and was reputed to have performed miracles. He attacked the hypocrisy of the High Priests, the Scribes, and the Pharisees and advocated sympathy for the poor and socially oppressed. While in Jerusalem to celebrate the Feast of the Passover, he was betrayed to the Jewish authorities by **Judas**, one of his disciples. After taking part in a Seder (known now as the Last Supper), he was arrested and handed over to the Romans, who sentenced him to death. He was taken to Calvary, where he was crucified. After three days, his tomb was found empty. He appeared to several of the disciples and, after forty days, ascended to heaven. In his one-act play *Calvary*, WBY shows Christ reliving his journey to Calvary and his crucifixion. In *The Resurrection*, he appears to the terrified disciples in an upper room after he has risen from the dead. He is referred to in WBY's poem "Ego Dominus Tuus" (*CP*. 180). WBY, who came from a religious background, attended an Anglican church when he lived in London as a young man. He insisted that his children should be raised in the Protestant tradition, and he chose the churchyard at **Drumcliff** as his final resting place. For WBY, Christ was an image of perfection, a symbol of the artistic imagination, and the dominant figure in the 2,000-year cycle of history that began with his birth. Although WBY might not be described as adopting orthodox Christianity, nothing in his beliefs in astrology, spiritism, and reincarnation is inconsistent with enlightened Christian teaching. See also "Conjunctions" (*CP*. 333).

REFERENCES: Moore, Virginia. "Was Yeats a Christian?" In *The Unicorn: William Butler Yeats' Search for Reality*. New York: Octagon Books, 1973; Williams, Melvin G. "Yeats and Christ: A Study in Symbolism." *Renascence* 20 (1968).

CHRIST CHURCH, college founded in **Oxford** during the sixteenth century by Cardinal Wolsey. In the poem "All Souls' Night" (*CP*. 256), WBY refers to the tolling of the great bell of Christ Church. WBY was living on Broad Street, Oxford, when he wrote the poem in November 1920.

CHRONOS [also Cronos], Greek word for time. It was personified by Pindar as "the father of all." WBY refers to Chronos in "The Song of the Happy Shepherd" (*CP*. 7). In Greek mythology, Chronos, one of the Titans, was ruler of the universe and father of Zeus, Hera, and Poseidon.

CHURCH ISLAND, largest island on **Lough Gill** in **Sligo** (county). Church Island contains the ruins of a sixth century monastery, destroyed by fire in 1416. The O'Cuirnins, hereditary poets to the O'Rourke family of **Breiffny**, had a school of poetry on the island from the thirteenth century, but their books and manuscripts were destroyed in the fire. Church Island is the setting for WBY's story "The Heart of Spring" (*MY.* 171–76).

REFERENCE: McGarry, James P. *Place Names in the Writings of William Butler Yeats.* Gerrards Cross: Colin Smythe, 1976.

CICERO, [MARCUS TULLIUS] [also known as Tully] (106–43 B.C.), Roman author, philosopher, and politician. He is generally regarded as the greatest Roman orator. As a senator, he vehemently opposed **Julius Caesar** and was the leader of a party that threatened Caesar's leadership and caused him to form the triumvirate at Lucca (56 B.C.). He fought with Pompey against Caesar at Pharsalia, but on his return to Rome after the Civil War, Caesar received him with honor. He opposed Mark Antony in the senate with his First and Second Philippics, and after Augustus Caesar became ruler, Antony was responsible for Cicero's execution. He is best known for his philosophical writings in which his outstanding mastery of Latin prose is much in evidence. WBY refers to him in the poem "Mad as the Mist and Snow" (*CP.* 301).

REFERENCES: Fuhrman, Manfred. *Cicero and the Roman Republic.* Trans. W. E. Yuill. Oxford: Blackwell, 1992; Mitchell, Thomas N. *Cicero, the Senior Statesman.* New Haven: Yale University Press, 1991; Rawson, Elizabeth. *Cicero: A Portrait.* Ithaca, N.Y.: Cornell University Press, 1983.

CITY HALL, Dublin. Built in 1769–79 as the Royal Exchange, it was taken over in 1850 by the City of Dublin Corporation. In "Three Songs to the One Burden" (*CP.* 371), WBY refers to the occupation of the City Hall by the insurgents during the Easter Rising of 1916 and to the **Abbey Theatre** actor, Sean Connolly, the first person to be killed in the Rising.

CLAN-NA-GAEL [Family of the Gaels], oath-bound Irish-American organization. It was formed in New York in 1867 to promote the cause of Irish independence. The organization was affiliated with the Irish Republican Brotherhood (IRB) from 1877, recognizing the Supreme Council of the IRB as the legitimate government of Ireland. It provided money and ideological support to the parent organization. In the 1880s, the Clan was divided over whether to promote Irish independence by supporting terrorism or by a program of political and economic pressures. Among opposing members of the Clan were Alexander Sullivan (1847–1913), an Irish-American lawyer in Chicago and first president of Clan-na-Gael, and the more cautious John Devoy (1842–1928). A leading Fenian, Devoy was born in Ireland and immigrated to the United States in 1871, having been imprisoned by the British for five years and released on condition of exile. He advocated political pressure on England as the solution to the Irish question, while Sullivan supported violent action. After Sullivan was discredited when implicated in the murder of a fellow Fenian in 1889, Devoy became the most powerful Irish American. WBY wrote to him before his first American tour (*KL III.* 465) and, at his invitation, gave an important address at the anniversary celebrations for **Robert Emmet**, promoted by the Clan in the Academy of Music, New York, 28 February 1904. Clan-na-Gael continued to be associated with radical Irish nationalism until the 1930s.

CLARE (Irish: *Clar*) [level place], county on the western seaboard of Ireland. It takes its name from a village in the area, now called Clarecastle. Clare is a remote, barren county, long associated with the **Firbolg**. It was the home of **Brian Boru**, who ruled from his castle at Kincora, on the River Shannon. Clare was part of **Thomond** until 1580, when it officially became a county in the province of **Munster**. A noted geological feature of County Clare is the **Burren**. WBY makes references to Clare in his writings, most notably in *The Dreaming of the Bones* (*CPl.* 435, 439) and *The Herne's Egg* (*CPl.* 647, 667). He refers to the rocky landscape of Clare in his poem ''In Memory of Major Robert Gregory'' (*CP.* 148), while **Biddy Early's** association with Clare is mentioned in ''Dust Hath Closed Helen's Eye'' (*MY.* 22) and *Dramatis Personae* (A. 401).
    REFERENCE: McGarry, James P. *Place Names in the Writings of William Butler Yeats.* Gerrards Cross: Colin Smythe, 1976.

CLARE-GALWAY (Irish: *Baile an Chlair*) [town of the plain], town and windswept townland in **Galway** (county). The Atlantic winds that blow across this plain are mentioned by the Musicians in WBY's play *The Dreaming of the Bones* (*CPl.* 445).
    REFERENCE: McGarry, James P. *Place Names in the Writings of William Butler Yeats.* Gerrards Cross: Colin Smythe, 1976.

CLAREMORRIS (Irish: *Clar Chlainne Muiris*) [plain of the Murris family]. Claremorris is a thriving market town, formerly in **Galway** (county) but now in **County Mayo**. In his story ''Kidnappers'' (*MY.* 75), WBY tells of a poor woman from Claremorris whose cow was taken away by the fairies.
    REFERENCE: McGarry, James P. *Place Names in the Writings of William Butler Yeats.* Gerrards Cross: Colin Smythe, 1976.

CLAUDE [Claude Lorrain] (1600–1682), landscape painter. He was born Claude Gellée, the son of poor parents in Lorraine, France. After the early death of his parents, he traveled to Rome, where he studied landscape painting and made detailed topographical drawings of the nearby countryside, the Roman Campagna. These early sketches and compositions, which were published in *Liber Veritatis* (1777), provided the source material for his paintings. In them he explored idyllic landscapes, suffused with nostalgia, in which he presented a classical view of nature more beautiful and harmonious than nature itself. These landscapes, many of which contain classical ruins and pastoral figures, exercised a major influence on English painters of the eighteenth and early nineteenth centuries, among them **Richard Wilson**. The antique world of Claude, pictured in the hazy light of morning or in the warm glow of late afternoon, appealed to WBY. In 1902, he used Claude's idealized style in support of an argument that the harmony and integration found in classical painting no longer existed in modern art (*EI*. 377–78). See also "Swedenborg, Mediums, and the Desolate Places" (*LE*. 52) and "Under Ben Bulben" (*CP*. 397).

REFERENCES: Cotte, Sabine. *Claude Lorrain*. New York: G. Braziller, 1971; Kitson, Michael. *The Art of Claude Lorrain*. London: Arts Council of Great Britain, 1969; Langdon, Helen. *Claude Lorrain*. Oxford: Phaidon, 1989; Manwaring, Elizabeth Wheeler. *Italian Landscape in 18th Century England: A Study Chiefly of the Influence of Claude Lorrain and Salvator Rosa on English Taste, 1700–1800*. New York: Russell and Russell, 1965.

CLIFTON, HENRY [Harry] (1907–78), poet. He was educated at **Christ Church**, Oxford, and published two volumes of verse, *Dielma and Other Poems* (1932) and *Flight* (1934), both of which were in WBY's library (*OS*. nos. 395, 396). In July 1935, as a seventieth birthday present, he gave WBY a gift of an eighteenth-century Chinese lapis lazuli medallion. On the medallion were carved the figures of an old man and a servant, referred to in the short fourth stanza of WBY's poem "Lapis Lazuli" (*CP*. 338). WBY dedicated the poem to Harry Clifton, who owned Kildalton Castle, Islay, in the north of Scotland.

CLINTON-BADDELEY, V[ICTOR] C. (1900–1970), British radio actor and mystery writer. Clinton-Baddeley was one of the readers in the poetry programs that WBY made for the **BBC**: "In the Poet's Pub," 2 April 1937; "In the Poet's Parlour," 22 April 1937; "My Own Poetry," 3 July 1937; and "My Own Poetry Again," 29 October 1937. Although he had his own ideas on how poetry should be spoken, Clinton-Baddeley submitted himself to WBY's direction and proved so indispensable that the poet postponed a further broadcast because he was not available. In his book *Words for Music* (1941), Clinton-Baddeley confirms that experiments to find the most satisfactory way of performing poetry became an absorbing passion of WBY's final years. He insists that to please WBY a reading had to be ceremonious and hieratical and that the poet detested triviality. In 1958, Clinton-Baddeley recorded a selection of the poems that WBY and he had worked on together. These may be heard on *Poems by W. B. Yeats: Spoken According to His Own Directions* (Jupiter). Clinton-Baddeley published a number of mystery novels, including *Death's Bright Dart* (1967), *My Foe Outstretch'd Beneath the Tree* (1968), *Only a Matter of Time* (1969), and *To Study a Long Silence* (1972).

REFERENCE: Clinton-Baddeley, V. C. *Words for Music*. Cambridge: Cambridge University Press, 1941.

CLONTARF (Irish: *Cluain-tarbh*) [meadow of the bulls], site of the decisive battle in 1014 in which **Brian Boru** defeated the Vikings. Clontarf is now a suburb of Dublin. In a journal entry for 7 January 1910 (*M*. 241), WBY recounted a dream in which he felt he should express all his bitter feelings about Ireland by writing a poem about Dubhlaing Ua hArtacáin, an Irish soldier who, despite the entreaties of his sweetheart, left his home to fight and die at the Battle of Clontarf. In his essay "J. M. Synge and the Ireland of His Time" (*EI*. 337), WBY makes reference to the traditional Norse account of the Battle of Clontarf, which is sober compared with the more exuberant Irish account. In *Cathleen Ni Houlihan* (*CPl*. 83), the Old Woman, attempting to recruit the young men to her cause, recalls a man named Brian who died at Clontarf.
    REFERENCE: McGarry, James P. *Place Names in the Writings of William Butler Yeats.* Gerrards Cross: Colin Smythe, 1976.

CLOONE BOG (Irish: *Cluain*) [meadow], **Galway** (county). Formerly on the Gregory estate, the Cloone Bog is two miles from the home of **Lady Gregory** at **Coole Park**. It is referred to in "The Tower" (*CP*. 218). The incident of the man who drowned in Cloone Bog on his way to visit the beautiful **Mary Hynes** is recorded by WBY in "Dust Hath Closed Helen's Eye" (*MY*. 6).
    REFERENCE: McGarry, James P. *Place Names in the Writings of William Butler Yeats.* Gerrards Cross: Colin Smythe, 1976.

CLOOTH-NA-BARE (Irish: *Cailleach Beare*) [Old Woman of Beare]. The Old Woman of Beare, a goddess who symbolized longevity, having passed repeatedly through the cycles of youth and age, tried to drown her fairy life in Lough Ia on the top of **Birds' Mountain** in **Sligo** (county). The stone monument on Slieve Daeane, not far from Lough Dagea, is known as the House of the Cailleach Beare. In "The Untiring Ones" (*MY*. 79), WBY gives an account of the Old Woman of Beare's search for a lake in which she can drown her fairy life. WBY makes references to Clooth-na-Bare in his poems "The Hosting of the Sidhe" (*CP*. 61) and "Red Hanrahan's Song about Ireland" (*CP*. 90).
    REFERENCE: McGarry, James P. *Place Names in the Writings of William Butler Yeats.* Gerrards Cross: Colin Smythe, 1976.

CLOVER HILL (Irish: *Cnoc-na-Seamar*) [hill of the shamrocks], **Sligo** (county). Clover Hill is adjacent to the megalithic cemetery at Carrowmore. The **Faery Child** in *The Land of Heart's Desire* (*CPl*. 59) is initially thought by Maurteen to be a visiting stranger from Clover Hill.
    REFERENCE: McGarry, James P. *Place Names in the Writings of William Butler Yeats.* Gerrards Cross: Colin Smythe, 1976.

CLOYNE. *See* **BERKELEY, GEORGE**.

CNOC-NA-SIDHA. *See* **KNOCKNASHEE**.

COCHRANE, WILLIAM (1823–1907), borough engineer. He was responsible for the building of the Sligo Waterworks. Known as Cochrane of the Glen, he lived at Glen Lodge, Cullinamore, **Sligo** (county), not far from **Alt**. He was a man of enlightened ideas. WBY recalls dining with him and **George Pollexfen** in 1895 and speaking of the trial of **Oscar Wilde** (*A.* 284–85; *M.* 79).

COLERIDGE, SAMUEL TAYLOR (1772–1834), poet, critic, and philosopher. He was born in Ottery St. Mary, Devonshire, the son of a vicar who was master of the local grammar school. After his father's death, the nine-year-old boy attended school at Christ's Hospital, London. There he met the essayist Charles Lamb. A brilliant student, he graduated from Jesus College, Cambridge, in 1794, but he already showed the signs of mental instability, which later turned into drug dependence. He was a close friend of Robert Southey, and in 1795, after marrying the sister of Southey's fiancée, he moved to Bristol, and then to Nether Stowey, in Somerset. In 1797, **William Wordsworth** settled nearby, and together they wrote *Lyrical Ballads* (1798), the seminal work of English Romanticism, in which Coleridge published "The Rime of the Ancient Mariner" and "The Foster Mother's Tale." In 1800, he and his family moved to Keswick in the Lake District to be closer to Southey. There he wrote "Kubla Khan," "Christabel," "Dejection: An Ode," and "The Pains of Sleep," but as his drug dependence increased, he became estranged from his family and moved to London. He published a number of short-lived periodicals, and his play *Remorse* (1813) had a successful London production. In 1818, in a desperate attempt to cure his opium addiction, he went to live with Dr. James Gillman and remained with him for the rest of his life. He continued to publish critical and philosophical essays, including *Biographia Literaria* (1817), *Aids to Reflection* (1825), and *Essay on Church and State* (1830). WBY read Coleridge avidly and responded to his fiery belief in the divine power of the imagination in poetry, a concept inherited from the German mystic **Jacob Boehme**. In his "Introduction to 'An Indian Monk' " (*LE.* 134), WBY notes the Asiatic influences on Coleridge's "Kubla Khan" and "Christabel" and later quotes from Coleridge's poem "What Is Life" (1805) (*LE.* 149). In the essay "Bishop Berkeley" (*EI.* 410), he refers to Coleridge's observations in his *Lectures and Notes on Shakespere and Other English Poets* (1883) that the Nurse in *Romeo and Juliet* was drawn from observation, while Hamlet came from the playwright's inner self. WBY had eight books of Coleridge in his library, including *Biographia Literaria* and *The Poetical Works of Samuel Taylor Coleridge* (1925) (*OS.* nos. 400–406).

REFERENCES: Ashton, Rosemary. *The Life of Samuel Taylor Coleridge: A Critical Biography*. Oxford: Blackwell, 1996; Doughty, Oswald. *Perturbed Spirit: The Life and Personality of Samuel Taylor Coleridge*. Rutherford, N.J.: Fairleigh Dickinson University Press, 1981; Weissman, Stephen M. *His Brother's Keeper: A Psychobiography of Samuel Taylor Coleridge*. Madison, Conn.: International Universities Press, 1989.

COLLECTED PLAYS OF W. B. YEATS, THE, collection of plays. The volume was published by Macmillan and Company in 1934. It contained twenty-one plays, in the following order: *The Countess Cathleen* (1892), *The Land of Heart's Desire* (1894), *Cathleen Ni Houlihan* (1902), *The Pot of Broth* (1904), *The King's Threshold* (1904), *The Shadowy Waters* (1911), *Deirdre* (1907), *At the Hawk's Well* (1917), *The Green Helmet* (1910), *On Baile's Strand* (1903), *The Only Jealousy of Emer* (1919), *The Hour-Glass* (1914), *The Unicorn from the Stars* (1908), *The Player Queen* (1922), *The Dreaming of the Bones* (1919), *Calvary* (1920), *The Cat and the Moon* (1926), *Sophocles' King Oedipus* (1928), *Sophocles' Oedipus at Colonus* (1934), *The Resurrection* (1931), and *The Words upon the Window-Pane* (1934). When the collection was republished in 1952 by Macmillan and Company, the following plays were added: *A Full Moon in March* (1935), *The King of the Great Clock Tower* (1935), *The Herne's Egg* (1938), *Purgatory* (1939), and *The Death of Cuchulain* (1939).

COLLECTED POEMS OF W. B. YEATS, THE, standard one-volume collection of WBY's verse. In 1932, while plans were delayed for Macmillan and Company to publish a seven-volume deluxe edition of WBY's work, WBY suggested that a one-volume *Collected Poems* should be released as soon as possible. The first volume of the Edition de Luxe was already in proof, but Macmillan suggested a different order for the poems, arguing successfully that the collection would be more appealing to the casual buyer if the longer narrative and dramatic poems like *The Wanderings of Oisin* were moved to the back of the volume. The collection would then begin with the shorter poems and lyrics from *Crossways* and *The Rose*. WBY approved this ordering of his poems, which was followed in *The Collected Poems of W. B. Yeats* (1933). After WBY's death, a second edition of the *Collected Poems* was published by Macmillan in 1950. This contained poems from *A Full Moon in March* (1935), *New Poems* (1938), and *Last Poems and Two Plays* (1939), in addition to those included in the earlier *Collected Poems*. A new edition of *The Poems of W. B. Yeats*, edited by Richard J. Finneran, was published by Macmillan in 1983. It contains three previously unknown poems and the unpublished ''Reprisals,'' a poem dedicated to **Major Robert Gregory**.

COLLINS, MABEL (1851–1927), minor novelist and leading member of the **Theosophical Society** in London. She was the daughter of the writer Mortimer Collins (1827–76). After her marriage to Keningale Robert Cook in 1871, she continued to write, under her maiden name, a number of novels and books of occult instruction, including *The Light on the Path* (1885) and *Through the Gates of Gold* (1887). In 1887, **Madame Blavatsky** lodged with Mabel Collins at Maycott, Upper Norwood, London, and together they edited a monthly magazine, *Lucifer*. Later, she was expelled from the Blavatsky Lodge of the Theosophical Society for flirting with the president, T. B. Harbottle (*A.* 177).

REFERENCES: Wood, Annie Besant. *H. P. Blavatsky and the Masters of the Wisdom.* Krotona, Calif.: Theosophical Publishing House, 1918; Cranston, Sylvia. *The Extraordinary Life & Influence of Helena Blavatsky, Founder of the Modern Theosophical Movement.* New York: G. P. Putnam, 1993.

COLLIS, MARGOT. *See* **RUDDOCK, MARGOT.**

COLLOONEY (Irish: *Cuil Mhuine*) [corner thicket], village near **Ballisodare** in **Sligo** (county). Collooney was the site of a fortified castle, built in the twelfth century by Turlough O'Conor, High King of Ireland. **Father Terence O'Rorke**, author of *The History of Sligo; Town and County*, was the parish priest at Collooney. It was there, in the nineteenth century, that the kindly priest of ''The Ballad of Father O'Hart'' (*CP.* 23) lived in a house called Cloonamahon.

REFERENCE: McGarry, James P. *Place Names in the Writings of William Butler Yeats.* Gerrards Cross: Colin Smythe, 1976.

COLONUS [also known as Colonus of the Horses], district a mile north of Athens. Colonus was associated with the worship of Poseidon, the god who gave horses to mankind. It is the setting for the play by WBY, *Sophocles' Oedipus at Colonus*.

COLUM, PADRAIC [MacCORMACK] (1881–1972), poet, playwright, novelist, and author of stories for children. He was born in County Longford and attended the local Glasthule National School. At the age of seventeen, he became a railway clerk in Dublin and furthered his education with frequent visits to the **National Library**. A member of the Gaelic League and the Irish Republican Brotherhood, and a friend of **Arthur Griffith**, his early poetry and plays were published in the *United Irishman* and the *Irish Independent*. The plays brought him into contact with **W. G. Fay** and the Inghínidhe na Éireann (Daughters of Erin), and he became a founding member of the **Irish National Theatre Society**. His realistic plays *Broken Soil* (later retitled *The Fiddler's House*) (1903), *The Land* (1905), and *Thomas Muskerry* (1910) were all produced by the Society, and he became an intimate friend of WBY, **Lady Gregory**, and **AE**. He acted with the company in AE's *Deirdre* and in WBY's *The Hour-Glass* and *The King's Threshold*. WBY regarded Colum as the most talented of the younger poets and believed he might become the most influential playwright in the Irish theater. Unfortunately, Colum thought the attitudes of WBY and members of the Irish National Theatre Society too dictatorial, and he withdrew from the company, associating himself with **Edward Martyn** and a breakaway group, the Theatre of Ireland. In retrospect, this was a serious error of judgment from which Colum never recovered. In 1908, after the publication of his first collection of poems, *Wild Earth*, he was given a five-year scholarship by a wealthy

American patron, Thomas Hughes Kelly, and returned to full-time study at University College, Dublin. There he met Mary Catherine Gunning Maguire (1887–1957), and they married in 1912. He formed a close relationship with AE and became one of his inner circle. WBY deeply lamented this association, believing that with AE, Colum would not discover the discipline and respect for poetic technique necessary to develop as a poet (*M.* 147–48). In 1914, Colum visited the United States with his wife on a protracted honeymoon and remained throughout most of his life, writing children's stories for the *New York Sunday Tribune* and lecturing on Irish literature at Columbia and other American universities and colleges. He spent a period in Hawaii where he completed three volumes of Hawaiian folklore (1937) for use in local schools. He wrote sixty-one books, including many volumes of verse, and hundreds of essays and articles. Among his best-known publications are *The King of Ireland's Son* (1916), *The Adventures of Odysseus* (1918), *The Boy Apprenticed to an Enchanter* (1920), *Anthology of Irish Verse* (1922), *At the Gateways of the Day* (1924), *The Fountain of Youth* (1927), *The Flying Swans* (1957), *The Poet's Circuits: Collected Poems of Ireland* (1960), and *Irish Elegies: Memorabilia of Roger Casement* (1976). The *Collected Poems of Padraic Colum* was published in 1953 while he and his wife collaborated on an intimate account of their friendship with **James Joyce** in *Our Friend James Joyce* (1958). He contributed "Early Days in the Irish Theatre" to the *Dublin Magazine*, October 1949 and January 1950. A sound recording *Padraic Colum Reading from His Tales and Poems* (1966) is available from Folkways. One of the last links with WBY and the early years of the Irish Literary Revival, Colum died in Enfield, Connecticut, and his remains were returned to Ireland for burial. WBY gave him scant attention in his writings, but he included four poems by Colum in his selection for *The Oxford Book of Modern Verse* (1936).

REFERENCES: Bowen, Zack. *Padraic Colum: A Biographical-Critical Introduction.* Carbondale: Southern Illinois University Press, 1970; Bowen, Zack, and Henderson, Gordon, eds. *The Journal of Irish Literature*: Padraic Colum Number, January 1973; Colum, Mary. *Life and the Dream.* London: Macmillan, 1928; Denson, Alan. "Padraic Colum: An Appreciation, with a Checklist of His Publications." *Dublin Magazine* 6 (spring 1967); Sternlicht, Sanford. *Padraic Colum.* Boston: Twayne, 1985.

CONALL CAERNACH [also Conall of the Victories], mythological **Ulster** warrior. Regarded as the bravest of the older generation of Ulster warriors, Conall Caernach appears as a major character in WBY's play *The Green Helmet*. At the opening of the play, he is in hiding from the **Red Man**, whose head he has cut off two years previously in a game. He is afraid that the Red Man will come to claim his share of the bargain. When the Red Man appears and offers a green helmet to be worn by the greatest of Ulster's champions, Conall claims the prize, vigorously supported by his wife proclaiming her husband's supremacy. Conall is eventually thwarted by **Cuchulain**, who is recognized by the Red Man as the true hero of Ulster. Conall avenges Cuchulain's death in the saga of the cattle raid of Ulster (*Táin Bó Cuailnge*). The **Morrigu** confirms this in WBY's play *The Death of Cuchulain* (*CPl.* 703). In the first production of *The Green Helmet*, February 1910, the role of Conall Caernach was played by Arthur Sinclair.

REFERENCES: Ellis, Peter Berresford. *Dictionary of Celtic Mythology*. New York: Oxford University Press, 1992; Green, Miranda J. *Dictionary of Celtic Myth and Legend*. London: Thames & Hudson, 1992; Mac Cana, Proinsias. *Celtic Mythology*. Feltham, Middlesex: Newnes, 1983.

CONAN, warrior of the **Fianna**. He was known as *Conan Maol*, or Bald Conan. Characterized as a parasite-buffoon and a loud-mouthed braggart, he appears with **Fionn** and **Caoilte** in WBY's narrative poem *The Wanderings of Oisin* (*CP.* 409).

REFERENCE: Ellis, Peter Berresford. *Dictionary of Celtic Mythology*. New York: Oxford University Press, 1992.

CONCHUBAR [Mac NESSA], mythological king of **Ulster**. The son of **Nessa** and Cathbad and uncle of the hero **Cuchulain**, he rules Ulster from his seat at **Emain Macha**. He gains the kingship when his mother promises herself to **Fergus Mac Roich** if he gives up the throne in favor of her son for one year. Fergus agrees. When Conchubar, who is popular with the people, refuses to give back the throne, Fergus goes into exile to the court of **Maeve**. In all the stories of the **Red Branch**, Conchubar appears as wily and manipulative. He is portrayed as a cunning statesman in WBY's *On Baile's Strand* (1903) and *Deirdre* (1907). He is referred to by WBY in the early poems "Fergus and the Druid" (*CP.* 36) and "Cuchulain's Fight with the Sea" (*CP.* 39).

REFERENCES: Dames, Michael. *Mythic Ireland*. 1992. Reprint, New York: Thames & Hudson, 1996; Ellis, Peter Berresford. *Dictionary of Celtic Mythology*. New York: Oxford University Press, 1992; Green, Miranda J. *Dictionary of Celtic Myth and Legend*. London: Thames & Hudson, 1992; Mac Cana, Proinsias. *Celtic Mythology*. Feltham, Middlesex: Newnes, 1983.

CONEELY, JOHN, elderly husband in WBY's play *The Pot of Broth*. In the play, he and his wife, **Sibby Coneely**, are tricked by a **Tramp** into parting with a chicken in return for a worthless stone.

CONEELY, SIBBY, wife in WBY's play *The Pot of Broth*. She is married to a much older husband, **John Coneely**, whom she dominates. Through her arrogance and pride, she is deceived by the wily **Tramp** into believing a stone can work all kinds of culinary miracles.

CONGAL, king of **Connacht**. He is a character in WBY's play *The Herne's Egg*, in which he feuds with **Aedh**, king of **Tara**. When the two kings arrange a truce to enable them to prepare for their next battle, Congal steals the sacred eggs from the Great Herne to serve at a celebratory banquet. As a punishment, he meets his death at the hands of a **Fool** and is reincarnated as a donkey.

CONNACHT [also Connaught], one of the four provinces of modern Ireland. The name is most likely derived from Conn of the Hundred Battles, who once was High King of Connacht. The province occupies the western part of Ireland and comprises the modern counties of **Sligo**, Leitrim, **Mayo, Galway**, and Roscommon. In ancient Ireland, it was one of five provinces and was ruled over by **Queen Maeve** from her capital at **Cruachan**. WBY had many associations with Connacht. His mother's family, the **Pollexfens** and the **Middletons**, and the aristocratic **Gore-Booth** family lived in Sligo. His great-grandfather, **Reverend John Yeats**, was rector of a church in **Drumcliff. Lady Gregory, George Moore**, and **Edward Martyn** had homes in Galway, close to WBY's home in the west of Ireland, **Thoor Ballylee. Douglas Hyde** lived in Roscommon. Connacht was rich in fairy and folklore, since it was reputed to be the place to which the **Tuatha dé Danaan** had fled after their defeat by the Milesians. It was in the peasant homes of Sligo and Galway that WBY heard the stories of **Blind Raftery** and **Mary Hynes** and collected legends and folktales. These he included in *The Celtic Twilight* (1893), *The Secret Rose* (1897), and *Stories of Red Hanrahan* (1897). WBY's home in the west of Ireland, Thoor Ballylee, was in Galway. Among the most notable of the references to the name Connacht are *The Green Helmet* (*CPl.* 224, 228, 235); *The Herne's Egg* (*CPl.* 645, 658, 659, 663, 676); and *The Death of Cuchulain* (*CPl.* 695).

REFERENCES: Dames, Michael. *Mythic Ireland.* 1992. Reprint, New York: Thames & Hudson, 1996; Ellis, Peter Berresford. *Dictionary of Celtic Mythology.* New York: Oxford University Press, 1992; Mac Cana, Proinsias. *Celtic Mythology.* Feltham, Middlesex: Newnes, 1983; McGarry, James P. *Place Names in the Writings of William Butler Yeats.* Gerrards Cross: Colin Smythe, 1976.

CONNELL, F. NORREYS. *See* **O'RIORDAN, CONAL [HOLMES O'CON-NELL].**

CONNEMARA, wild, mountainous area of **Galway** (county). Connemara is bordered to the north by Clew Bay, to the south by Galway Bay, and to the west by the Atlantic Ocean. There are few towns in the region but many lakes, streams, and mountains. The name is believed to have come from the Conmaicne-Mara, descendants of **Queen Maeve** and **Fergus Mac Roich**. In ''The Fisherman'' (*CP.* 166), WBY describes a man in gray Connemara clothes to whom he hopes to write a poem. Connemara is referred to in ''The Dedication to a Book of Stories Selected from the Irish Novelists'' (*CP.* 51) and ''The Phases of the Moon'' (*CP.* 183).

REFERENCE: McGarry, James P. *Place Names in the Writings of William Butler Yeats.* Gerrards Cross: Colin Smythe, 1976.

CONNLA (Irish: *Conlaí*), son of **Cuchulain** and the warrior queen **Aoife**. Aoife rears Connla to revenge Cuchulain's desertion of her. When he is old enough, the boy travels from Scotland to Ireland. He defeats **Conall Caernach**, then challenges Cuchulain. Despite an ominous warning from his wife **Emer**, the **Ulster** hero fights with Connla, mortally wounding him. As he dies, the young man reveals his identity. Connla appears as the Young Man in *On Baile's Strand* (*CPl.* 264). In a dialogue with Aoife in *The Death of Cuchulain* (*CPl.* 699–700), the dying Cuchulain poignantly recalls the birth and death of his son. The story of Connla is told in "Cuchulain's Fight with the Sea" (*CP*. 37–40), although in the poem, WBY does not follow the mythological version. Instead, it is Emer who sends her son to kill his father when she learns that Cuchulain has taken a younger concubine.

REFERENCES: Dames, Michael. *Mythic Ireland*. 1992. Reprint, New York: Thames & Hudson, 1996; Ellis, Peter Berresford. *Dictionary of Celtic Mythology*. New York: Oxford University Press, 1992; Mac Cana, Proinsias. *Celtic Mythology*. Feltham, Middlesex: Newnes, 1983.

CONNOLLY, JAMES (1868–1916), labor leader and political activist. Connolly was born in Edinburgh, Scotland, the son of an **Ulster** farm laborer. At fourteen, he joined the British army and was posted to Ireland. He deserted to marry an Irish girl in Scotland. In 1896, he returned to Ireland as the organizer of the Dublin Socialist Club and published the first Irish socialist paper, *The Workers' Republic*. He founded the Irish Socialist Republican Party and, from 1903, spent seven years in the United States, where he formed the Irish Socialist Federation in New York, published a monthly magazine, *The Harp*, and helped found the International Workers of the World. On his return to Ireland in 1910, he became Ulster organizer for the recently formed Irish Transport and General Workers' Union. In 1911, he visited Belfast. Work conditions there were intolerable, and he successfully organized strikes to improve them. In 1913, after James Larkin (1876–1947), the organizer of the Irish Transport and General Workers' Union strike in Dublin, was imprisoned, Connolly took control. Later in the year, he formed the Irish Citizen Army, modeled on private armies already recruited in Ulster. Initially dedicated to economic freedom, the 200-strong Irish Citizen Army gradually expanded to include revolutionaries from other fringe movements, and the objectives became more political. In the Easter Rising (1916), Connolly was one of the seven signatories of the Proclamation of the Irish Republic. He was appointed military commander of the Republican forces in Dublin, and while holding the **General Post Office** against the British, he was wounded and taken prisoner. His execution, seated in a chair because of his wounds, acted as a major catalyst to the growth of anti-British feeling that swept many parts of Ireland and led to the partition of Ireland in 1921. Among his writings on labor and revolutionary socialism, his book *Labour in Irish History* (1910) is his best-known work. WBY first met him during the anti-Jubilee demonstrations of 1897. Connolly, then little known, had invited **Maud Gonne** to speak to his Socialist Club. Maud Gonne was not a Socialist, and when she discovered she was to speak at an open-air meeting, she declined. Responding to Connolly's disappointment, WBY persuaded her to address the large crowd. Her anti-British remarks led to rioting in which some 200 people were injured and 1 woman killed (*M.* 111–12). The anti-Jubilee demonstrations were a personal triumph for Maud Gonne and for Connolly. WBY and Connolly were both members of the committee for the **Wolfe Tone** Centenary Celebrations in 1898, at which WBY gave an oration. WBY pays tribute to the heroic Connolly in a number of poems, including the elegy "Easter 1916" (*CP.* 202). He is referred to in "Sixteen Dead Men" (*CP.* 205), "The Rose Tree" (*CP.* 206), and "The O'Rahilly" (*CP.* 354), and in the concluding lyric of *The Death of Cuchulain* (*CPl.* 704). (The Connolly referred to in "Three Songs to the One Burden" [*CP.* 371] is not James but Sean Connolly, a young actor from the **Abbey Theatre**, the first man to be killed in the Easter Rising.)

REFERENCES: Anderson, W. K. *James Connolly and the Irish Left.* Dublin: Irish Academic Press, 1994; Hogan, Robert, ed. *Dictionary of Irish Literature.* Rev. ed. Westport, Conn.: Greenwood, 1996; Metscher, Priscilla. *Republicanism and Socialism in Ireland.* Frankfurt am Main and New York: P. Lang, 1986; Morgan, Austen. *James Connolly: A Political Biography.* Manchester: Manchester University Press, 1988.

CONSTANT, ABBÉ [ALPHONSE LOUIS] [pseud. Éliphas Lévi] (1810–75), French occultist. According to WBY, he claimed to be the voice of an ancient magical society (*LE.* 271–72). WBY refers to him in a note to "An Image of a Past Life" (*VP.* 822). Two books by Lévi were in WBY's library, *The Magical Ritual of the Sanctum Regnum Interpreted by the Tarot Trumps* (trans. W. Wynn Westcott. London: George Redway, 1896) and *Transcendental Magic* (trans. Arthur Edward Waite. London: George Redway, 1896) (*OS.* nos. 1108, 1109).

REFERENCE: Lévi, Éliphas. *The History of Magic, Including a Clear and Precise Exposition of Its Procedure, Its Rites and Its Mysteries.* Trans. Arthur Edward Waite. London: Rider, 1913.

CONTEMPORARY CLUB. Formed in 1885 by **C. H. Oldham**, the Protestant Home Ruler and editor of the *Dublin University Review*, the club aimed to provide the Dublin intelligentsia with an opportunity to debate current issues. The name of the club was chosen by C. H. Oldham because the members needed nothing more in common than to be contemporaries. It met initially every Saturday evening in Oldham's rooms at **Trinity College**, Dublin. Because of Oldham's nationalist views, the group was forced by the conservative college authorities to change the venue and met above Ponsonby's Book Shop at 116 Grafton Street, Dublin. To encourage frank and open debating, the club was forbidden by its rules from taking public action. Membership was at first limited to fifty but was later raised to seventy-five. Women were not admitted in the early years, although "Ladies Night" eventually became a popular feature. Among the members were **John O'Leary, Michael Davitt, John F. Taylor,**

George Sigerson, Douglas Hyde, John B. Yeats, and **T. W. Rolleston**. WBY, who attended the club between 1885 and 1887, joined to develop self-confidence in debate and conversation. Although he was not especially popular, the youthful writer made a deep impression on the other members, among them **Stephen Gwynn**, who was convinced WBY was going to be "a better poet than we have yet seen in Ireland." Domiciled in London from 1888, WBY continued to attend meetings of the Contemporary Club on his occasional visits to Ireland. Indeed, in *Reveries over Childhood and Youth* (*A*. 93), he writes in some detail about the club, which provided him with an early model for the **Rhymers' Club**.

REFERENCE: Nicholl, Harry. "Memories of the Contemporary Club." *Irish Times* (20 December 1965).

COOLANEY, village in **Sligo** (county), some five miles west of **Collooney**. In *The Land of Heart's Desire* (*CPl*. 65), the **Faery Child** recalls the reeds that dance beside Coolaney Lake. According to James P. McGarry, *Place Names in the Writings of W. B. Yeats* (1976), there is no lake at Coolaney.

COOL-A-VIN [also Coolavin] (Irish: *Cuil O'bhFinn*) [corner of Finn's country], townland on the borders of **Sligo** (county) and County Roscommon. Finn was the son of **Fergus [Mac Roich]**. The land was later owned by the MacDermot family, who were known as Princes of Coolavin. In WBY's story "Proud Costello" (*MY*. 196–210), Cool-a-vin is the home of Una MacDermot, who loves Costello. The area is associated with St. Attracta, who kept a hospice there during the fifth century. **Attracta**, the Priestess in WBY's play *The Herne's Egg*, is modeled on her.

REFERENCE: McGarry, James P. *Place Names in the Writings of William Butler Yeats*. Gerrards Cross: Colin Smythe, 1976.

COOLE PARK, home of **Lady Gregory**. The Gregory family lived on the estate from 1768, when Richard Gregory, a chairman of the East India Company, bought 600 acres of land in **Galway** (county). He built an undistinguished house of local stone, started a fine collection of books and pictures, and extended the estate by purchasing an additional 1,000 acres. On her marriage to Sir William Gregory in 1880, Lady Gregory became the mistress of Coole, although a large part of the estate had been sold by Sir William to pay off debts. When he died in 1892, the estate was passed to their son, **Robert Gregory**, with the proviso that Lady Gregory should continue to live there. After the death of Robert Gregory, the house was sold to the Irish Land Commission, to whom Lady Gregory paid rent until her death in 1932. The house stood empty until 1941, when it was demolished by a local building contractor for the value of the stone. Nothing remains today but the walled garden, the ruins of the stables, and the Autograph Tree, the copper beech on which distinguished visitors like **George Bernard Shaw** and **Sean O'Casey** carved their initials. WBY stayed at Coole Park for the first time in 1897, when, suffering from nervous exhaustion, he was nursed back to health by Lady Gregory. For the next twenty years, the house and the estate became his summer refuge in the west of Ireland. There, he found an ordered, aristocratic life, steeped in tradition, a place where he could write undisturbed. He was stimulated by congenial companions with whom he explored his ideas on literature and the founding of an Irish National Theatre. He found an inner peace as he walked in the **Seven Woods** or fished for trout in the lake, especially through those periods of his life when he suffered from deep personal stress. After his marriage in 1917, he went to live in the renovated **Thoor Ballylee**, once part of the Gregory demesne, although after Lady Gregory's death, he never returned there. The quality of life at Coole is described by WBY in *Dramatis Personae* (*A.* 388–95), in that section of his autobiography that deals with the late 1890s and the setting up of the **Irish Literary Theatre**. He refers to Coole in the poems, principally, ''The Wild Swans at Coole'' (*CP.* 147), ''In the Seven Woods'' (*CP.* 85), ''Coole Park, 1929'' (*CP.* 273), ''Coole Park and Ballylee, 1931'' (*CP.* 275), and ''I Walked Among the Seven Woods of Coole'' (*CP.* 469).

REFERENCES: Gordon, D. J., ed. *W. B. Yeats: Images of a Poet.* Manchester: University of Manchester, 1961; Masefield, John. *Some Memories of W. B. Yeats.* New York: Macmillan, 1940; Smythe, Colin. *A Guide to Coole Park, Co. Galway: Home of Lady Gregory.* Gerrards Cross: Colin Smythe, 1973.

COOPER, EDITH [EMMA]. *See* **BRADLEY, KATHARINE [HARRIS]**.

COPE'S MOUNTAIN, Sligo (county). Cope's Mountain lies to the south of **Glencar**, with the townland of **Lugnagall** at its foot, opposite **Ben Bulben**. See also ''A Knight of the Sheep'' (*MY.* 31).

REFERENCE: McGarry, James P. *Place Names in the Writings of William Butler Yeats.* Gerrards Cross: Colin Smythe, 1976.

CORBET, JOHN, fictional character. In WBY's play *The Words upon the Window-Pane*, Corbet is a young skeptic from Cambridge University who attends a séance organized by the Dublin Spiritualists' Association. He is studying **Jonathan Swift** for his doctorate and identifies the spirits of Swift, **Stella**, and **Vanessa** when they are called up by the medium **Mrs. Henderson**. In the first production of the play at the **Abbey Theatre**, November 1930, the role was played by Arthur Shields. WBY's paternal grandmother was **Jane Grace Corbet Yeats**.

CORBET, ROBERT (d. 1872), great-uncle of WBY. He lived with his mother, Grace Armstrong Corbet (1774–1861), and aunt, Jane Armstrong Clendenin, in a large house, **Sandymount Castle**, on the outskirts of Dublin. His brother Arthur Corbet, who worked in a Dublin bank, lived with them. A stockbroker with the Court of Chancery and later the Landed Estates Court, Robert Corbet made his fortune through a fortuitous political appointment and lived the comfortable life of an Anglo-Irish gentleman. He was generous but snobbish and condescending to those not of his class. Despite his wealth, Robert Corbet did not have a good business head and, after falling on difficult times, left Sandymount Castle to take lodgings on Upper Mount Street, Dublin. Terminally ill, depressed, and penniless, he committed suicide by jumping from a steamer crossing the Irish Sea. His death made a profound impression on WBY, who recalled him years later in a diary entry for 1930 (*EX.* 319) and in the poem "Are You Content" (*CP.* 370).

REFERENCES: Murphy, William M. *Prodigal Father: The Life of John Butler Yeats (1839–1922)*. London and Ithaca: Cornell University Press, 1978; Yeats, John Butler. *Early Memories*. Dublin: Cuala, 1923.

CORCOMROE ABBEY (Irish: *Corca Modhruadh*) [children of Modhruadh—son of **Queen Maeve**], ruined Cistercian abbey four miles east of Ballyvaughan in **County Clare**. Corcomroe Abbey, known also as St. Mary-of-the-Fertile Rock because of its location between two limestone hills, is situated at the foot of Abbey Hill. It was founded in 1182 by Donal O'Brien, king of **Munster**, and is the setting for WBY's play *The Dreaming of the Bones*. The tomb of the fourteenth-century **Donough O'Brien** may still be seen close to the altar of the ruined church. WBY may have become familiar with Corcomroe while visiting **Lady Gregory** at her summer home, Vernon Lodge, four miles from the Abbey ruins.

REFERENCE: McGarry, James P. *Place Names in the Writings of William Butler Yeats*. Gerrards Cross: Colin Smythe, 1976.

CORK (Irish: *Corcaigh*) [marsh], city and county in the province of **Munster**. The city of Cork dates from the seventh century, when St. Finnbarr founded a monastery on the site of the present cathedral. It was occupied by the Vikings in the ninth century and passed to English control in 1172. Cork suffered much deprivation during the Great Famine of the 1840s. As a result, the area was defiantly nationalist during the nineteenth and twentieth centuries. It was the scene of bloody skirmishes during the Irish Civil War. Among the distinguished writers and critics from Cork who took part in the Irish Renaissance were **Frank O'Connor** and **Lennox Robinson**. While WBY makes references to Cork in his writings, none deal directly with the city. His major literary interest in Cork was its associations with **Edmund Spenser**, who lived in Cork (county) after his appointment to the secretaryship of Ireland in 1580. His home was Kilcolman Castle, which had belonged to the rebel Earl of Desmond, and as WBY observed in the essay "Edmund Spenser" (*EI.* 360), Spenser used the landscape around this area of Cork, including **Aubeg** and Ballyvaughan Hills, in his lyric poetry.

REFERENCE: McGarry, James P. *Place Names in the Writings of William Butler Yeats*. Gerrards Cross: Colin Smythe, 1976.

CORMAC [Mac CUILLEANÁIN] (d. 1138), king and cleric. He was a twelfth-century Irish king of **Munster** who, after marriage, chose to follow an ancient tradition of consecration as a king-bishop and lead a life of celibacy. He built an exquisite Romanesque chapel on the **Rock of Cashel**. The chapel, which is now in ruins, was consecrated in 1134. It is these ruins that are referred to by WBY in "The Double Vision of Michael Robartes" (*CP*. 192).

REFERENCE: Mac Cana, Proinsias. *Celtic Mythology*. Feltham, Middlesex: Newnes, 1983.

CORNEY, rustic servant. In WBY's play *The Herne's Egg*, he is servant to the priestess **Attracta**. After the death of **Congal**, Attracta asks him to copulate with her so that Congal will be reincarnated as a human. In *The Words upon the Window-Pane*, the gambler, Cornelius Patterson, refers to himself as Corney Patterson.

COSGRAVE, WILLIAM T[HOMAS] (1880–1965), Irish politician. He was born in Dublin and educated by the Christian Brothers. He was keenly interested in local and national politics and was elected to Dublin Corporation in 1909. A member of the Irish Volunteers from their formation in 1913, he fought in the Easter Rising (1916) and was sentenced to death. The sentence was commuted to life imprisonment, and he was released under a general amnesty. After his election as Sinn Fein M.P. for Kilkenny in a by-election, 1917, and again at the general election of 1918, he was appointed minister for local government in **Dáil Éireann**. He supported the 1921 Treaty with Britain and became acting chairman of the provisional government of Ireland in 1922. With the death of **Arthur Griffith**, he was appointed the first president of the Executive Council of the Irish Free State, a position he held until 1932, when his party, Cumann na nGaedheal, was defeated in the general election by the party led by **Eamon de Valera**. WBY had known Cosgrave as a sympathetic member of the Dublin Corporation at the time of the controversy over the **Hugh Lane** pictures, and was distressed when he heard Cosgrave had been sentenced to death for his part in the Easter Rising (*WL*. 612). It was Cosgrave who nominated WBY for the Irish Free State Senate in 1922. WBY was opposed to the Cosgrave government's attitude toward divorce and wrote one of his strongest Senate speeches condemning it (*UP2*. 450, 451). He refers to Cosgrave in "Parnell's Funeral" (*CP*. 320).

REFERENCES: Freyer, Grattan. *W. B. Yeats and the Anti-Democratic Tradition*. Dublin: Gill & Macmillan, 1981; Krimm, Bernard G. *W. B. Yeats and the Emergence of the Irish Free State, 1918–1939: Living in the Explosion*. Troy, N.Y.: Whitston, 1981; Stanfield, Paul S. *Yeats and Politics in the 1930s*. New York: St. Martin's, 1988.

COSIMO. *See* **MEDICI, COSIMO DE'**.

COUNTESS CATHLEEN [also Countess Kathleen], tragic heroine. She is the leading character in WBY's drama *The Countess Cathleen*. Distressed because her people are starving, she decides to sell her soul to demons who are masquerading as **Merchants**. Her loyal servant **Oona** and the poet **Aleel** try to dissuade her, but she persists with her plan. As she dies, angels appear to re-assure Aleel and Oona that the Countess is in heaven. The part was inspired by **Maud Gonne**, but in the first performance of the play, May 1899, the Countess was played by Dame May Whitty.

COUNTESS CATHLEEN, THE, WBY's first full-length play. It was written in verse and first published by **T. Fisher Unwin** in the collection *The Countess Kathleen and Various Legends and Lyrics* (1892). It was subsequently printed in all of the major anthologies of WBY's works. He returned to the play again and again, so that there are five published versions, the last being included in *Poems* (1919). It is this version that appears in *The Collected Plays of W. B. Yeats* (1934, 1952). In a long introduction to the play, published in the 1927 revision of *Poems* (1895), WBY gives a detailed account of the genesis of the play and its subsequent revisions. He read the story in a newspaper while col-lecting material for *Fairy and Folk Tales of the Irish Peasantry* (1888) and later found it was a translation of *Les Matinées de Timothé Trimm* by Léo Lespès. The closest Irish source is a story in William Larminie's *West Irish Folk Tales and Romances* (1893) of a woman who goes to hell for ten years to save her husband. *The Countess Cathleen* takes place in early Ireland during a famine, when a noblewoman, the **Countess Cathleen**, sells her soul in return for food to feed her starving people. Although it was written for **Maud Gonne** to act in Dublin, and dedicated to her, she never performed in it. Before the opening performance, the Catholic hierarchy in Dublin decided the play was blasphe-mous and irreligious and demanded a boycott. WBY gives an account of the tension generated at the opening in *Dramatis Personae* (*A*. 413–18). The first performance of the play, at which there was a riot, was given by the **Irish Literary Theatre**, 8 May 1899, with the following cast: Countess, Dame May Whitty; **First Merchant**, Marcus St. John; **Second Merchant**, Trevor Lowe; **Shemus Rua**, Valentine Grace; **Teigue**, Charles Sefton; **Mary Rua**, Madame San Carolo; **Aleel, Florence Farr; Oona**, Anna Mather; Herdsman, Claude Holmes; Gardener, Jack Wilcox; Sheogue, Dorothy Paget; Peasant Woman, M. Kelly; Servant, F. E. Wilkinson. **George Moore** assisted with the casting and directing of the first production, which was rehearsed in London.

REFERENCES: Clark, David R. ''Vision and Revision: Yeats's *The Countess Cath-leen*.'' In *The World of W. B. Yeats*, ed. Robin Skelton and Ann Saddlemyer. Seattle: University of Washington Press, 1967; Ellis, Sylvia C. *The Plays of W. B. Yeats: Yeats and the Dancer*. London: Macmillan, 1995; Miller, Liam. *The Noble Drama of W. B. Yeats*. Dublin: Dolmen, 1977; Sidnell, M. J. ''Yeats's First Work for the Stage.'' In *W. B. Yeats 1865–1939: Centenary Essays*, ed. D. E. S. Maxwell and S. B. Bushrui. Ibadan: Ibadan University Press, 1965.

COUNTESS KATHLEEN AND VARIOUS LEGENDS AND LYRICS, THE, collec-tion of verse. It was published in September 1892 by **T. Fisher Unwin** in the

"Cameo Series." In addition to WBY's full-length verse play *The Countess Cathleen*, the collection contained the majority of those poems later included in *The Rose* section of the *Collected Poems* (1952), together with "The Ballad of Father O'Hart" (*CP*. 23) and "The Ballad of the Foxhunter" (*CP*. 27). Five hundred and thirty copies of the book, which was WBY's second collection of verse, were printed. The frontispiece was by **J. T. Nettleship**.

COUNTRY-UNDER-WAVE (Irish: *Tir-Fa-Tonn*). After their defeat by the Milesians, the **Tuatha dé Danaan** went underground to fairy mounds in the west of Ireland. Some inhabited places under water, which came to be known as the Country-under-Wave. WBY makes references to the Country-under-Wave in his plays *The Countess Cathleen* (*CPl*. 28), *On Baile's Strand* (*CPl*. 258, 268, 269), and *The Only Jealousy of Emer* (*CPl*. 290).
   REFERENCE: McGarry, James P. *Place Names in the Writings of William Butler Yeats.* Gerrards Cross: Colin Smythe, 1976.

COUNTY CLARE. *See* **CLARE**.

COUNTY DOWN. *See* **DOWN**.

COUNTY MAYO. *See* **MAYO**.

COUSINS, JAMES H[ENRY SPROULL] (1873–1956), writer and teacher. He was born in Belfast but moved to Dublin as a ledger clerk in 1897. After meeting WBY and other prominent writers of the Irish Literary Revival, he determined to become a writer. His plays *The Sleep of the King* and *The Racing Lug* were produced by **W. G. Fay** during the 1902 season at the **Antient Concert Rooms**. Although his plays were poetic versions of Irish stories, WBY was not enthusiastic, and after squashing a production of Cousins's comedy *Sold*, he ruthlessly ousted him from the theater movement in Dublin (*WL*. 379–80, 417). In 1903, Cousins married Margaret E. Gillespie (1878–1954) and became an English teacher. He published a series of collections of verse, including *The Bell-Branch* (1908), and became the butt of unflattering jibes from literary notables like **James Joyce**. In 1908, he joined the **Theosophical Society**, and in 1915, at the invitation of **Annie Besant Wood**, he and his wife moved to India, where he became subeditor of the theosophical publication *New India*. Before he left Dublin, he was given a special benefit evening by his theater friends. WBY gave £5 to the benefit and wrote him an enthusiastic letter of recommendation. Cousins appears to have had no further contact with WBY, since he remained in India for the rest of his life, with occasional lecturing tours of Japan, Europe, and the United States. He was art adviser to the Maharajah of Mysore and formed the first public collection of art and sculpture for the Maharajah of Travancore. He was a prolific writer, producing over 100 books, the majority of which were published in India, including *Collected Poems, 1894–1940, Re-*

flections before Sunset (1946), and *Twenty-four Sonnets* (1949). Donagh Mc-Donagh included two of Cousins's poems in his anthology *The Oxford Book of Irish Verse* (1950). Much of Cousins's prose writing is concerned with aesthetics and belief, as in his *The Faith of the Artist* (1941) and his essays on Jean Delville (b. 1867) and Nicholas Roerich (1874–1947), published in *The Great Theosophist Painters* (1925). Among his best literary criticism is his book on **Percy Bysshe Shelley,** *The Work Promethean* (1933). His wife, a free-spirited, enthusiastic feminist, was an accomplished writer and musician. Their autobiography, *We Two Together*, was published in Madras in 1950. Cousins is interesting to Yeats scholars because his removal from the Dublin literary scene was a demonstration of the ruthlessness with which WBY pursued those whose work, he believed, was detrimental to the reputation of the **Irish National Theatre Society.**

REFERENCES: Denson, Alan. *James H. Cousins and Margaret E. Cousins, a Bio-Bibliographical Survey*. Kendal: Alan Denson, 1967; Hogan, Robert, ed. *Dictionary of Irish Literature*. Rev. ed. Westport, Conn.: Greenwood, 1996.

CRACKED MARY. *See* **CRAZY JANE.**

CRAGLEE. *See* **GREY ROCK.**

CRAIG, [EDWARD] GORDON (1872–1966), designer and theater innovator. The son of the actress Ellen Terry and E. W. Godwin, architect and theatrical designer, Gordon Craig started his career as an actor with the Lyceum company in London in 1885. Increasingly disillusioned with attempts at realistic staging and mannered acting in the theater, he devoted himself to reeducating his contemporaries to a fresh appreciation of the drama in all its presentational aspects, in acting, production, and staging. His first stage designs were for the Purcell Operatic Society's productions of *Dido and Aeneas*, May 1900; *The Masque of Love*, January 1901; and *Acis and Galatea*, 1902. The special design features of these three productions were the stretched backcloths, one painted bright purplish blue, placed behind a stretched gauze, and the stage lighting, which dispensed with footlights and made use of side and overhead sources of illumination. The visual presentation was revolutionary in its simplicity and style. WBY saw a repeat performance of *Dido and Aeneas*, presented with *The Masque of Love* in 1901. He was impressed (*EI*. 100–101; *WL*. 366) and asked the designer's sister, Edith Craig, to take him backstage to see how the lighting was done (*WL*. 380). Under Craig's influence, WBY became increasingly interested in the effects of light on the painted scene and in the use of shadows thrown on the backcloth by the two arc lights on the balcony of the **Abbey Theatre**. WBY's fascination with lighting and set design was further encouraged by the set of screens that Craig gave to the Abbey in 1911, after first presenting the playwright with a model stage for his own use. The Craig screens were of varying heights, ran on swivel wheels, and were plain ivory in surface and tone.

They were capable of being moved easily and were open to many arrangements so that a stage scene could be quickly and effortlessly changed—even in view of the audience. The screens were used at the Abbey Theatre in 1911 for *The Deliverer* by **Lady Gregory**, and a revival of WBY's play ***The Hour-Glass*** (*M.* 276; *WL.* 555). While there were reservations from the press and the actors about the effectiveness of the screens, they were used in 1913 for *The Post Office* by **Rabindranath Tagore**, in 1924 for *The Story Brought by Brigit*, by Lady Gregory, and in the twenty-fifth anniversary production of *The Hour-Glass*, 1926. Despite the opposition, WBY anticipated productions of all his plays using the Craig screens and continued to write plays for them, namely, ***The Player Queen*** and ***The King of the Great Clock Tower***. Craig designed screens for a production of *Hamlet* at the Moscow Art Theatre in 1912, but they were too heavy and problematic in performance. He moved to Florence, Italy, in 1907. There he experimented with his model stage and ran a school for the Art of the Theatre. He published his theories in *The Mask*, 1908–29. Craig has been a major, if controversial, influence on the development of European theater in this century, principally through his writings in *The Art of the Theatre* (1905), *Towards a New Theatre* (1913), and *Scene* (1923). He had a profound effect on WBY as a playwright, not only pointing the way toward simplicity and harmony in scenic staging but also confirming WBY's ideas on stylization and the use of the mask.

REFERENCES: Bablet, Denis. *Edward Gordon Craig*. Trans. Daphne Woodward. London: Heinemann, 1966; Craig, Edward. *Gordon Craig: The Story of His Life*. London: Gollancz, 1968; Dorn, Karen. "Dialogue into Movement: W. B. Yeats's Theatre Collaboration with Gordon Craig." In *Yeats and the Theatre*, ed. Robert O'Driscoll and Lorna Reynolds. Niagara Falls, N.Y.: Maclean-Hunter, 1975; Flannery, James W. *W. B. Yeats and the Idea of a Theatre: The Early Abbey Theatre in Theory and Practice*. New Haven: Yale University Press, 1976; Loizeaux, Elizabeth Bergmann. *Yeats and the Visual Arts*. New Brunswick and London: Rutgers University Press, 1986.

CRAOIBHIN AOIBHINN, AN. *See* **HYDE, DOUGLAS**.

CRAZY JANE, character in a series of erotic poems written by WBY between 1929 and 1938. WBY originally called the character Cracked Mary, the nickname of a local eccentric who lived in a cottage near **Gort, Galway** (county), but after the first printing, he changed the name to Crazy Jane. In a note to his play ***The Pot of Broth*** (1904), WBY claims that the song "There's Broth in the Pot" came from Cracked Mary (*VPl.* 254), while in a letter to **Olivia Shakespear**, November 1931, he writes that the local stories of Cracked Mary were "of an epic magnificence" (*WL.* 785–86). Cracked Mary is the name of the leading female character, a strange and eccentric younger woman, in *The Full Moon* (1910) by **Lady Gregory**.

REFERENCE: Hardy, Barbara. "The Wildness of Crazy Jane." In *Yeats, Sligo and Ireland*, ed. A. Norman Jeffares. Gerrards Cross: Colin Smythe, 1980.

CREON, brother of Jocasta. At the opening of ***Sophocles' King Oedipus***, Creon returns to **Thebes** after visiting the oracle at **Delphi**. He brings news that the death of King Laius, murdered on his way to Delphi, must be avenged. Later in the play, his brother-in-law **Oedipus** accuses him of treachery. After Oedipus goes into exile, Creon becomes regent. He supports Eteocles in his struggle with his brother Polyneices for control of the kingdom. When the brothers kill each other, Creon buries Eteocles with honor, but he has Antigone put to death for performing the funeral rites for Polyneices. The part of Creon in the first production of *Sophocles' King Oedipus*, December 1926, was taken by **Barry Fitzgerald**.

CREVROE (Irish: *Craobh ruadh*) [**Red Branch**], the building where the Red Branch knights lived at **Emain Macha**. The name is retained today in Creeveroe, County Armagh. Crevroe is recalled as a feasting place of the old gods in WBY's dramatic poem *The Wanderings of Oisin* (*CP.* 444).
    REFERENCES: Ellis, Peter Berresford. *Dictionary of Celtic Mythology.* New York: Oxford University Press, 1992; McGarry, James P. *Place Names in the Writings of William Butler Yeats.* Gerrards Cross: Colin Smythe, 1976.

CROMWELL, OLIVER (1599–1658), Lord Protector of the Commonwealth. He was a brilliant military strategist, and after the Commonwealth was proclaimed in England in 1649, he was sent to Ireland as commander in chief and Lord Lieutenant. There, he waged a cruel and punitive campaign to dispossess the native Irish. He stormed Drogheda and Wexford, burning homes and churches, massacring the people, and causing a succession of towns and cities to surrender. He left Ireland, May 1650, having been there for nine months. He masterminded the Act of Settlement of 1652 and the Act of Sequestration of 1653, as a result of which much of the land in Ireland was confiscated, and Irish landowners were driven to **Connacht**. He became Lord Protector of the Commonwealth in 1654. Opinions of Cromwell differ. Many appreciate his military genius and force of character, but he is chiefly remembered in Ireland for his barbaric cruelty. In his essay "Edmund Spenser" (*EI.* 375–76), WBY condemns Cromwell's actions, calling him the "Great Demagogue," and he writes of Cromwell's ruthless destruction of Ireland in "The Curse of Cromwell" (*CP.* 350).
    REFERENCES: Esson, Denis M. R. *The Curse of Cromwell: A History of the Ironside Conquest of Ireland, 1649–53.* London: Leo Coope, 1971; Foster, R. F. *Modern Ireland 1600–1972.* 1988. Reprint, London: Penguin, 1989.

CROOK, WILLIAM [MONTGOMERY] (1860–1945), teacher and scholar. Born in **Sligo**, he read classics at **Trinity College**, Dublin, before taking up a post as classics master at Wesley College, Dublin. When he accepted a post at Manor House School, Clapham, London, in 1887, he met frequently with WBY, whom he had encountered at the **Contemporary Club**. For a time, they were close friends. He became interested in theosophy and corresponded with **Charles**

Johnston in Dublin. Crook, a Protestant Home Ruler, joined the Liberal Party and stood unsuccessfully as Liberal candidate for Wandsworth in 1892. In the same year, he helped WBY found the **Irish Literary Society** in London. He later became a journalist with the *Methodist Times*.

CRO-PATRICK [also Croaghpatrick] (Irish: *Cruach Phádraig*) [Patrick's Hill], mountain near Westport, **County Mayo**. It is known as Ireland's holiest mountain because of its association with **St. Patrick**. A midsummer pilgrimage is held there each year on the last Sunday in July, Garland Sunday, when pilgrims climb to the summit where St. Patrick is reputed to have fasted. In *The Countess Cathleen* (*CPl.* 20), the poet **Aleel** tells the Countess's loving nurse **Oona** that she will never be pardoned, even if she does penance by climbing Cro-Patrick. The mountain is a setting for the poem "The Dancer at Cruachan and Cro-Patrick" (*CP.* 304).
  REFERENCES: Dames, Michael. *Mythic Ireland.* 1992. Reprint, New York: Thames & Hudson, 1996; McGarry, James P. *Place Names in the Writings of William Butler Yeats.* Gerrards Cross: Colin Smythe, 1976.

CROSSWAYS, a selection of early verse by WBY. The verse was taken from *The Wanderings of Oisin and Other Poems* (1889) and *The Countess Kathleen and Various Legends and Lyrics* (1892) and was included in *Poems* (1895) under the title *Crossways.* WBY used the title to reflect the changes of direction in his early work. All sixteen poems in the collection, which is dedicated to **AE**, were written by WBY before he was twenty. They range from the self-conscious verse inspired by classical antiquity to ballads and songs based on Irish folklore. All the poems in *Crossways* are romantic in mood and heavily influenced by the Pre-Raphaelites in subject matter, language, and imagery. The epigraph to the collection is from the poem "Night the Ninth" by **William Blake**.

CRUACHAN (Irish: *Cruach*) [a round hill], ancient capital of **Connacht** and seat of **Queen Maeve**. Cruachan, now called Rathcroghan, is near the village of Tulsk, in County Roscommon. One of the oldest royal sites, it originally consisted of five concentric circular forts, many of which still survive today. It is reputedly the burial ground of the legendary Irish heroes, including **Dathi**, the last High King of pagan Ireland. In close proximity to Cruachan is the Cave of Cruachan, fabled to be the entrance to the underworld. It was to Cruachan that **Fergus** went when he lost the throne of **Ulster** to **Conchubar**, and it was from Cruachan that Maeve set out with her army to challenge the men of Ulster in the epic tale "The Brown Bull of Cooley" (*Táin Bó Cuailnge*). Cruachan is referred to by WBY in the poem "The Hour before Dawn" (*CP.* 130). It is the setting for "The Dancer at Cruachan and Cro-Patrick" (*CP.* 304), "Tom at Cruachan" (*CP.* 306), and "The Old Age of Queen Maeve" (*CP.* 451). In *On*

Baile's Strand (*CPl*. 255), **Cuchulain** recalls routing Maeve of Cruachan in battle.

REFERENCES: Ellis, Peter Berresford. *Dictionary of Celtic Mythology*. New York: Oxford University Press, 1992; Green, Miranda J. *Dictionary of Celtic Myth and Legend*. London: Thames & Hudson, 1992; Mac Cana, Proinsias. *Celtic Mythology*. Feltham, Middlesex: Newnes, 1983; McGarry, James P. *Place Names in the Writings of William Butler Yeats*. Gerrards Cross: Colin Smythe, 1976.

CRUACHMAA [also Knockmaa] (Irish: *Cruach Magh*) [hill of the plain], low-lying hill near **Tuam, Galway** (county). Cruachmaa was associated with the **Sídhe**. WBY named it as one of the holy places in Ireland (*EI*. 295), and in his essay "The Galway Plains" (*EI*. 211), he recalls looking over Cruachmaa from **Slieve Echtge**. It was in this area that the blind poet **Raftery** lived and traveled, and **Lady Gregory** researched material for her collection of poems and stories *Poets and Dreamers* (1903).

REFERENCE: McGarry, James P. *Place Names in the Writings of William Butler Yeats*. Gerrards Cross: Colin Smythe, 1976.

CUALA PRESS, publishing house. It was started in 1908 by **Elizabeth (Lolly) Yeats**, who had previously been involved in the **Dun Emer Press**. Housed in a small cottage at Churchtown, near Dundrum, County Dublin, it took its name from the barony in which the cottage stood. Cuala Press concentrated on the publication of hand-printed books of artistic merit, but it also printed a series of hand-colored prints by **Jack B. Yeats** and others, in addition to book plates and greeting cards. In August 1923, the press was moved from Churchtown to the basement of WBY's house, 82 **Merrion Square**, Dublin. Later, in February 1925, a shop and workrooms were acquired at 133 Lower Baggot Street, Dublin. WBY, who was the literary editor and closely supervised the choice of literary material, brought distinction to the press when he allowed it to publish the first editions of many of his major books, including *The Green Helmet and Other Poems* (1910), *The Hour-Glass* (1914), *The Wild Swans at Coole* (1917), *Michael Robartes and the Dancer* (1921), *A Packet for Ezra Pound* (1929), *Words for Music Perhaps* (1932), *The Words upon the Window-Pane* (1934), and *Dramatis Personae* (1935). The Cuala Press published the work of other writers, among them **Lady Gregory, J. M. Synge**, and **Oliver St. John Gogarty**, so that most of the important Irish writers of the first fifty years of the century appeared over its imprint. Sixty titles (in addition to private publications) were produced before Cuala ceased book publication in 1946, although it continued to issue hand-colored prints and greeting cards. After the death of Lolly Yeats in 1941, **Georgie Yeats** managed the press from her home at Palmerston Road, Dublin. In 1969, the press was reorganized. It moved to 116 Lower Baggot Street, with **Michael B. Yeats, Anne Yeats**, Liam Miller, and Thomas Kinsella as directors, and the publication of books was resumed.

REFERENCES: Miller, Liam. "The Dun Emer and the Cuala Press." In *The World of W. B. Yeats*, ed. Robin Skelton and Ann Saddlemyer. Seattle: University of Washington

Press, 1965; Miller, Liam. *The Dun Emer, Later the Cuala Press*. Dublin: Dolmen, 1973; Murphy, William M. *Family Secrets: William Butler Yeats and His Relatives*. Syracuse, N.Y.: Syracuse University Press, 1995.

CUCHULAIN (Irish: *Cú Chulainn*), mythological champion of the ancient province of **Ulster**. He was the son of the sun god **Lugh** and Dechtiré, daughter of the Druid Cathbad. He was named Sétanta but was given the name Cuchulain, the Hound of Culann, after killing Culann's savage watchdog. Cuchulain is the hero of the tales of the **Red Branch**. He is called upon to endure personal trials, among them the slaying of his son **Connla** and the killing of his best friend Ferdia at the Battle of the Ford, when he single-handedly protects Ulster from **Queen Maeve** and the warriors of **Connacht**. Cuchulain became for WBY a personal symbol for the heroic as well as the national ideal. He was not only his mask or alter ego but also the chief representative of that heroic age to which WBY wished Ireland to aspire. He is the protagonist in a cycle of plays written by WBY over a span of thirty-five years. The plays, which trace Cuchulain's life from early manhood to death, are *On Baile's Strand* (1903), *The Green Helmet* (1910), *At the Hawk's Well* (1916), *The Only Jealousy of Emer* (1919), and *The Death of Cuchulain* (1939). In *The Only Jealousy of Emer*, Cuchulain's inert body (called the Figure of Cuchulain) is taken over by **Bricriu**, while the Ghost of Cuchulain is revealed with **Fand**. Cuchulain is the central figure in the dramatic "Cuchulain's Fight with the Sea" (*CP*. 37), first published in *United Ireland*, 11 June 1892, and he is referred to in the poems "To the Rose upon the Rood of Time" (*CP*. 35) and "The Secret Rose" (*CP*. 77).

REFERENCES: Bjersby, Birgit. *The Interpretation of the Cuchulain Legend in the Works of W. B. Yeats*. Folcroft, Pa.: Folcroft, 1969; Ellis, Peter Berresford. *Dictionary of Celtic Mythology*. New York: Oxford University Press, 1992; Green, Miranda J. *Dictionary of Celtic Myth and Legend*. London: Thames & Hudson, 1992; Mac Cana, Proinsias. *Celtic Mythology*. Feltham, Middlesex: Newnes, 1983.

CUMHAL, leader of the **Fianna** and father of **Fionn**. He eloped with Murna of the White Neck, with whom he had a son. In revenge, Murna's father arranged to have him killed by **Goll** Mac Morna at the Battle of Knock. In "The Crucifixion of the Outcast" (*MY*. 147–56), the gleeman who is nailed to the cross is Cumhal, son of Cormac. In the poem "The Blessed" (*CP*. 75), WBY writes of Cumhal visiting **Dathi**, the last pagan High King of Ireland, but it is unclear to which Cumhal this refers.

CUMMEN STRAND (Irish: *Cuimín*) [little common], **Sligo** (county). Referred to in "Red Hanrahan's Song about Ireland" (*CP*. 90), the Cummen townland and strand run along the southern shore of Sligo Bay, from Sligo (town) to Strandhill.

REFERENCE: McGarry, James P. *Place Names in the Writings of William Butler Yeats*. Gerrards Cross: Colin Smythe, 1976.

CURRAGH (Irish: *Currach*) [racetrack], plain in County Kildare. There has been a race course at the Curragh of Kildare from earliest times. It has long been used for the training of world-class race horses and show jumpers and is the major center of the bloodstock industry in Ireland. It is home to Ireland's finest horse-racing track, where the Turf Club, established in the eighteenth century to control equestrian sport, disburses some of the highest prizes in the horse-racing world. In *Purgatory* (*CPl.* 683), the **Old Man** boasts that his well-to-do mother had a horse stabled at the Curragh, and it was there she had met her future husband, a groom in one of the stables. There has been an established military camp on the Curragh since 1646.

REFERENCE: McGarry, James P. *Place Names in the Writings of William Butler Yeats.* Gerrards Cross: Colin Smythe, 1976.

CURTIN, JEREMIAH (1835–1906), collector of Irish folktales. He was born of Irish parents in Detroit, Michigan. After a period as a translator with the U.S. government in Russia, 1864–70, he joined the staff of the Smithsonian Institution, Washington, D.C., 1883–91. In this capacity, he made many trips to the west of Ireland, collecting stories and folklore with the aid of a translator, since his Irish was poor. His major collections of Irish stories include *Myths and Folklore of Ireland* (1890, 1911), *Hero Tales of Ireland* (1894), and *Tales of the Fairies and the Ghost World* (1893). In a note to **The Countess Kathleen and Various Legends and Lyrics** (*VP.* 799), WBY states that one of his poems, "Cuchulain's Fight with the Sea" (*CP.* 37), is based on a legend taken from Curtin's *Myths and Folklore of Ireland.* He praises this collection in an article in the *National Observer*, 28 February 1891 (*UP1.* 188), and includes *Hero Tales of Ireland, Myths and Folklore of Ireland*, and *Tales of the Irish Fairies* in his list of "Best Irish Books" (*UP1.* 386).

REFERENCE: Boylan, Henry. *A Dictionary of Irish Biography.* Dublin: Gill & Macmillan, 1978.

CUTTING OF AN AGATE, THE, collection of essays written between 1902 and 1916. The volume, which was published in 1919 by Macmillan and Company, contains ten essays. The first American edition, which appeared in 1912, did not include the important essay "Certain Noble Plays of Japan" (1916).

D

DÁIL ÉIREANN, Irish Parliament. The first Dáil Éireann met in the **Mansion House**, Dublin, 21 January 1919, and declared independence from England, despite the opposition of the British Parliament. **Eamon de Valera** was appointed president. When the assembly was declared illegal, Dáil Éireann voted funds for the intensification of the war against Britain. After a truce was signed in July 1921, Dáil Éireann appointed delegates to the Anglo-Irish Conference, which negotiated the Anglo-Irish Treaty, signed 6 December 1921. Thereafter, Dáil Éireann became the established Parliament of the Irish Republic, though not before a civil war was fought and the terms of the Anglo-Irish Treaty rejected by de Valera and his supporters. WBY was appointed to the Irish Senate, the upper house of Dáil Éireann, in 1922, one of three members appointed to advise the new Irish government on matters relating to education, literature, and the arts. He applied himself to his senatorial duties with relish, making a number of persuasive and powerful speeches, frequently against majority opinion. In 1925, he vehemently but unsuccessfully opposed legislation outlawing divorce, insisting that such a law discriminated against Protestants who had made such a contribution to the identity of modern Ireland. He retired from the Senate in November 1928.

REFERENCES: Farrell, Brian. *The Founding of Dáil Éireann: Parliament and Nation Building*. Dublin: Gill & Macmillan, 1971; Fitzpatrick, David. ''W. B. Yeats in Seanad Éireann.'' In *Yeats and the Theatre*, ed. Robert O'Driscoll and Lorna Reynolds. Niagara Falls, N.Y.: Maclean–Hunter, 1975; Freyer, Grattan. *W. B. Yeats and the Anti-Democratic Tradition*. Dublin: Gill & Macmillan, 1981; Krimm, Bernard G. *W. B. Yeats and the Emergence of the Irish Free State, 1918–1939: Living in the Explosion*. Troy, N.Y.: Whitston, 1981; Pearce, Donald R. *The Senate Speeches of W. B. Yeats*. Bloomington: Indiana University Press, 1960.

DANTE [ALIGHIERI] (1265–1321), poet. He was born in Florence, Italy. As a young man, he made a study of philosophy and Provençal poetry, and in 1290, after the death of his beloved **Beatrice**, he wrote *La Vita Nuova* (c. 1292), a narrative in poetry and prose that celebrated ideal love. In 1302, he was banished from Florence because of his political activities, and in exile, he completed his outstanding work *The Divine Comedy*, begun prior to 1308 and finished before his death in 1321, a poem of 100 cantos, written as a memorial to Beatrice. In it, he tells of a journey through Hell and Purgatory, guided by **Virgil**, and through Heaven, accompanied by Beatrice. Dante spent the rest of his life wandering throughout Italy and died in **Ravenna**. In his frustrated and passionate love for **Maud Gonne**, WBY identified with Dante's love for Beatrice, yet he claimed not to have been a Dante scholar and to have read him only in translation (*LE.* 7). Nevertheless, he was profoundly influenced by the Italian poet, not only in his use of the vernacular in his later poetry but also in his poetic theories. In his search for Unity of Being (a phrase taken from Dante), he acknowledged his influence (*A.* 190), while in "Ego Dominus Tuus" (*CP.* 180), a title taken from *La Vita Nuova* (*LE.* 4), he cited Dante to support his theory of the Mask. Copies of Dante were in WBY's library (*OS.* nos. 466–77).

REFERENCES: Bornstein, George. "Yeats's Romantic Dante." In *Poetic Remaking: The Art of Browning, Yeats, and Pound*. University Park: Pennsylvania State University Press, 1988.

D'ARBOIS DE JUBAINVILLE, [MARIE] HENRI (1827–1910), archaeologist and professor of Celtic Languages and Literature at the Collège de France in Paris. He was the founder of the *Revue Celtique*, a periodical devoted to the study and publication of scholarly material on Celtic mythology and literature. He exerted a powerful influence on the Celtic revival in Europe through his lectures at the Sorbonne, which **J. M. Synge** attended, and his twelve-volume series *Cours de littérature celtique*. The second volume in the series was *Le Cycle mythologique irlandais et la mythologie celtique* (Paris, 1884). It was translated into English in 1903 by **Richard Best**, later director of the **National Library of Ireland**, thus making the old Celtic myths and legends available to WBY and his contemporaries. Having read Best's translation, WBY declared that no right knowledge of the pagan myths of Ireland was possible without it, and he recommended it among the "Best Irish Books" (*WL.* 246–51). WBY pays tribute to de Jubainville in his article "Celtic Beliefs about the Soul," which he contributed to *The Bookman*, September 1898 (*UP2.* 119). In the article, he confirms his belief that *Le Cycle mythologique irlandais*, a copy of which was in his library (*OS.* no. 1047), was one of three books essential to an understanding of Celtic legends.

REFERENCES: D'Arbois de Jubainville, Henri. *Irish Mythological Cycle and Celtic Mythology*. Trans. Richard I. Best. New York: Lemma, 1970; Marcus, Phillip L. *Yeats and the Beginning of the Irish Renaissance*. Syracuse: Syracuse University Press, 1987.

DARLEY, ARTHUR, composer and conductor. He was a descendant of the nine-teenth-century Irish poet George Darley. He formed the first **Abbey Theatre** orchestra in 1905 and toured with the company. A fine violin player who spe-cialized in traditional Irish airs, he had met **J. M. Synge** in Paris and played in an orchestra with him. He left the Abbey after a short stay, apparently because as a solo violinist he found the shifting of scenery during the intermissions too noisy. He provided the musical settings for the first production of WBY's *Deirdre* in November 1906.

DATHI, High King. He was the last king of pagan Ireland, succeeding Niall of the Nine Hostages in A.D. 405. In the poem ''The Blessed'' (*CP*. 75), Dathi is shown embracing the two worlds of the pagan Celt and the new Christianity. He is reputed to have been killed by lightning while crossing the Alps (*UP1*. 163).

DATTATREYA, Brahmin saint. He is the son of Atri and **Anashuya** and is believed to be an incarnation of the Hindu god Vishnu or a composite of the three gods Vishnu, **Brahma**, and Siva. In *An Indian Monk: His Life and Adventures* (1934), **Shri Purohit Swami** tells of his decision to worship the divine Dattatreya, the first Yogi (*LE*. 158–60).
  REFERENCE: O'Flaherty, Wendy Doniger, trans. *Hindu Myths: A Sourcebook Translated from the Sanskrit*. Harmondsworth, Middlesex: Penguin, 1975.

DAVIDSON, JOHN (1857–1909), poet and literary editor. He was born at Barr-head, Renfrewshire, Scotland, and taught in various public schools before mov-ing to London with his wife and two children in 1889. He attempted to make a living as a writer and became a prominent member of the **Rhymers' Club**, where he met WBY. In 1890, he was editor of the short-lived *Weekly Review of Magazines, Books and Newspapers, and Index of Periodical Literature*, to which WBY contributed book reviews, and edited a literary column in *The Speaker* and the *Daily Chronicle*. He achieved a sudden but short-lived popu-larity with his *Ballads and Songs* (1895) and *New Ballads* (1897). In addition to his poems and ballads, including *In the Music Hall and Other Poems* (1891) and *Fleet Street Eclogues* (1893), he wrote plays, among them *Bruce* (1886) and *Scaramouche in Naxos* (1889). After 1900, Davidson became increasingly neurotic, a condition that rendered his verse rhetorical, melodramatic, and shrill. He jumped to his death from the cliffs at Penzance in the southwest of England. WBY admired the passion in Davidson's verse, but he did not have a close friendship with Davidson (*A*. 168). It was very likely Davidson who wrote a negative review of WBY's *The Countess Cathleen* in the *Daily Chronicle*, 1 September 1892 (*KL1*. 320), possibly in retaliation for the poor review that WBY gave to his ballads. Nevertheless, WBY writes movingly about Davidson in ''The Tragic Generation'' (*A*. 315–18), concluding that while he had the passion to be a memorable poet, he lacked discipline and commitment to his poetic craft.

REFERENCES: Halladay, Jean R. *Eight Late Victorian Poets Shaping the Artistic Sensibility of an Age*. Lewiston, N.Y.: E. Mellen, 1993; Sloan, John, ed. *Selected Poems and Prose of John Davidson*. Oxford: Clarendon, 1995; Stanford, Derek, ed. *Three Poets of the Rhymers' Club: Ernest Dowson, Lionel Johnson, John Davidson*. Cheadle: Carcenet, 1974.

DA VINCI, LEONARDO (1452–1519), painter, sculptor, architect, and engineer. He was born in Vinci, Tuscany, the son of a Florentine notary and a peasant woman. As a child, he showed a precocious skill in drawing and painting and, at the age of fourteen, was apprenticed to the Italian master Verrocchio, at whose studios in Florence he met **Botticelli**. In 1482, Da Vinci was appointed to the court of Ludovico Sforza, in Milan. There, he painted the famous *Madonna of the Rocks* (1483) and his fresco *The Last Supper* (c. 1495–98), in addition to working on architectural plans and elevations for the restoration of the cathedrals at Pavia and Piacenza. In 1500, he returned to Florence, and having pursued studies in mathematics and anatomical research, he was appointed military engineer to Cesare Borgia. It was in Florence, during this period, that he painted some of his masterpieces, among them *Mona Lisa*, *St. Anne, Mary, and the Child* (1510), and *St. John the Baptist* (c. 1513). In 1513, he went to Rome to complete several commissions for the newly elected Pope Leo X. Shortly after 1515, he accepted an invitation from Francis I of France to retire to the castle of Cloux, near Amboise, where he pursued his original ideas in engineering and design until his death. In his appreciation of Leonardo, WBY was influenced by **Walter Pater** (*UP2*. 260). When he closed his eyes and repeated the word *Christianity*, he saw a painting by Leonardo—possibly *The Madonna of the Rocks* (*LE*. 40). In "Four Years: 1887–1891" (*A*. 155), he recalled that the females in Leonardo's paintings reminded him of women he had seen in Dublin.

REFERENCES: Bramly, Serge. *Leonardo: Discovering the Life of Leonardo Da Vinci*. Trans. Sian Reynolds. New York: Harper Collins, 1991; Loizeaux, Elizabeth Bergmann. *Yeats and the Visual Arts*. New Brunswick and London: Rutgers University Press, 1986; Raboff, Ernest L. *Leonardo Da Vinci*. New York: Lippincott, 1987.

DAVIS, THOMAS [OSBORNE] (1814–45), poet, leader of the Young Ireland movement, and cofounder of *The Nation* (1842–92). Born into a Protestant family at Mallow, **Cork** (county), the posthumous son of a British army surgeon, Davis graduated from **Trinity College**, Dublin, and was called to the Bar in 1838. He had immense personal charm and a persuasive personality, and he wrote with style and feeling about Irish cultural life and the Irish language. His spirited writing in verse and prose presented a vision of a free Ireland and so captured the national imagination that his rousing ballads "A Nation Once Again" and "The West's Asleep" continued to be popular through the twentieth century. He was the main inspiration behind the nationalist movement in Ireland from the mid-1800s to modern times, in literary as well as political affairs, influencing the major writers **Sir Samuel Ferguson, John Mitchel** and **Sir Charles Gavan Duffy**. He was the unofficial leader of the Young Irelanders and stood up to **Daniel O'Connell** over the issue of nondenominational education. He worked ceaselessly for a number of societies, including the **Royal Irish Academy**, his main objective being to define the parameters of Irish nationality. He died in Dublin of scarlet fever at the age of thirty-one. **John O'Leary** was a disciple and introduced WBY to Davis's essays and poems (*A.* 95). In 1892, WBY recommended to **Katharine Tynan** five poems by Davis for her anthology *Irish Love-Songs* (*WL.* 204), and in the poem "To Ireland in the Coming Times" (*CP.* 56), he names himself in the tradition of Davis, Ferguson, and **James Clarence Mangan**, a claim that drew much criticism from his contemporaries for its lack of modesty (*WL.* 213). Initially, WBY valued Davis for his nationalism but later agreed with John O'Leary that he was too propagandist and a dangerous model as a poet. He criticized Davis for encouraging his literary friends to write uninspired, propagandist plays on Irish subjects (*UP2.* 33–35), and he castigated **Sir Charles Gavan Duffy**, who cofounded *The Nation*, for insisting on naming Davis a great poet (*UP1.* 408). For WBY, Davis's major influence came from his intellectual ideas and the high moral principles displayed in his political actions (*M.* 211–12, 213). In 1893, he unsuccessfully challenged the publication of Davis's *The Patriot Parliament of 1689* by the **New Irish Library** because he thought its dry content of little appeal to the general reader. According to WBY, the New Irish Library series was doomed by that first publication (*A.* 228; *UP1.* 333). WBY, however, delivered a eulogy on Davis at the centenary celebrations organized by the Gaelic Society of Trinity College, Dublin, 20 November 1914, sharing the platform at the **Antient Concert Rooms** with **Padraic Pearse**. He praised Davis for his magnanimity and scrupulousness in argument, illustrating his speech with a reading of Davis's poem "Lament for the Death of Eoghan Ruadh O'Neill" (*LE.* 41), included in WBY's selection for *A Book of Irish Verse* (1895).

REFERENCES: Marcus, Phillip L. *Yeats and the Beginning of the Irish Renaissance.* Syracuse: Syracuse University Press, 1987; Monahan, Michael. *Nova Hibernia: Irish Poets and Dramatists of Today and Yesterday.* Freeport, N.Y.: Books for Libraries, 1967; Sullivan, Eileen A. *Thomas Davis.* Cranberry, N.J.: Associated University Press, 1977; Yeats, William Butler. *Tribute to Thomas Davis.* Cork: Cork University Press, 1947; Yeats, William Butler, and Kinsella, Thomas. *Davis, Mangan, Ferguson?: Tradition and the Irish Writer.* Dublin: Dolmen, 1971.

DAVITT, MICHAEL (1846–1906), political leader. He was born in **County Mayo** and emigrated with his family to the north of England in 1851. As a youth, Davitt became involved in the struggle for Irish independence, joining the Fenian movement in 1865. As organizing secretary of the Irish Republican Brotherhood, he was imprisoned for his part in the abortive uprising of 1867. After his release from prison in 1877, he formed the Land League, which combined agitation for land reform with demands for Home Rule. In 1882, he was elected M.P. for North **Meath**, as a member of the Home Rule Party led by **Charles Stewart Parnell**, whom he gradually came to regard as dictatorial and antidemocratic in his leadership. When the scandal over Parnell's liaison with Kitty O'Shea broke, Davitt denounced him. In 1898, he cofounded the United Irish League, in which he attempted to reconcile the opposing demands for revolutionary and constitutional nationalism, but he alienated some Irishmen by visiting Russia in 1903 and meeting with the revolutionaries. His book *The Fall of Feudalism in Ireland* was published in 1904. WBY was unsympathetic to Davitt and his anti-Parnellite policies (*A.* 140). After meeting him, however, he connected with the more inward side of Davitt's nature, recognizing in him a man more suited to being an artist than a political activist (*A.* 356–57).

REFERENCES: Foster, R. F. *Modern Ireland 1600–1972.* 1988. Reprint, London: Penguin, 1989; Moody, T. W. *Davitt and the Irish Revolution.* New York: Oxford University Press, 1981.

DAY LEWIS, C[ECIL] (1904–72), poet and novelist. He was born in Ballintubber, **County Mayo**, but spent most of his life in England. In 1927, while completing his degree at Oxford University, he edited, with **W. H. Auden,** *Oxford Poetry.* His first book of poems, *Country Comets*, was published the following year. He became identified with the socially conscious poetry of the 1930s, as in his collections *The Magnetic Mountain* (1933) and *A Time to Dance and Other Poems* (1935), written while he was a teacher at Cheltenham College, 1930–35. He joined the Communist Party but resigned during World War II when he began working for the Ministry of Information. He was Professor of Poetry at Oxford, 1951–55. In 1958, he moved to Crooms Hill, London, where he published his autobiography, *The Buried Day* (1960), together with his collections *The Gate and Other Poems* (1962), *The Room and Other Poems* (1965), and *Whispering Roots* (1970). He was appointed Poet Laureate in 1968. Day Lewis was conscious of his Irish roots, but WBY discounted them, choosing to classify him with the socially committed English poets of the 1930s (*LE.* 95). He included eight poems by Day Lewis in his selection for *The Oxford Book of Modern Verse* (1936) and had copies of *Collected Poems, 1929–1933* (1935), *From Feathers to Iron* (1931), *A Hope for Poetry* (1935), and *A Time to Dance and Other Poems* in his library (*OS.* nos. 1111–14).

REFERENCES: Day Lewis, C. *Notable Images of Virtue.* 1954. Reprint, Philadelphia: R. West, 1977; Hogan, Robert, ed. *Dictionary of Irish Literature.* Rev. ed. Westport, Conn.: Greenwood, 1996; Maxwell, D. E. S. *Poets of the Thirties.* New York: Barnes & Noble, 1969; Stanford, Derek. *Stephen Spender, Louis MacNeice, Cecil Day Lewis: A Critical Essay.* Grand Rapids: Eerdmans, 1969.

DEATH OF CUCHULAIN, THE, last play written by WBY. It was completed in 1939, during the last months of his life, and he was still correcting it a few days before he died. The plot is based on a story from the **Ulster** Cycle of mythology,

"The Death of Cúchulainn," telling of Ulster's defeat and how **Cuchulain** was lured to his death by the sons of **Cailitin**. The play tells of the final hours of Cuchulain, the Ulster hero. Despite a warning from his wife that he should wait until morning before engaging in battle, he chooses to fight. He is fatally wounded and dies, tied to a standing stone. The play opens with a prologue spoken by an **Old Man** and concludes with an ironic chorus performed by a modern Irish trio. It was published in *Last Poems and Two Plays* (1939). The first production was given by the Lyric Theatre Company, Dublin, 2 December 1945, with the following cast: Old Man, Art O'Murnaghan; Cuchulain, Enda McGarry; **Eithne Inguba**, Ronnie Masterson; **Aoife**, Marjorie Williams; **Emer**, Christine Kane; **Morrigu**, Máiréad Connaughton; **Blind Man**, Oliver Bradley; Servant, John O'Riordan; Street Singer, Edward Farrell. The music was played by Hilda Layng (flute), and the setting and costumes were designed by **Anne Yeats**.

REFERENCES: Bjersby, Birgit. *The Interpretation of the Cuchulain Legend in the Works of W. B. Yeats.* Folcroft, Pa.: Folcroft, 1969; Bradley, Anthony. *William Butler Yeats.* New York: Frederick Ungar, 1979; Marcus, Phillip L., ed. *The Death of Cuchulain: Manuscript Materials.* Ithaca and London: Cornell University Press, 1982; Miller, Liam. *The Noble Drama of W. B. Yeats.* Dublin: Dolmen, 1977; Taylor, Richard. *A Reader's Guide to the Plays of W. B. Yeats.* New York: St. Martin's, 1984.

DECIMA, character in *The Player Queen*. She is the leading member of the traveling theater troupe that is to present a play at the court of the **Queen**. She feels betrayed by the drunken poet **Septimus** and prepares to kill herself but is interrupted by the Queen, who wishes to leave the castle and lead a simple life elsewhere. Decima convincingly assumes the role of the Queen and forbids the traveling players ever to return to her kingdom. The role of Decima in the first production, presented by the Stage Society in London, May 1919, was played by **Abbey Theatre** actress Christine Hayden.

DECTORA, character in *The Shadowy Waters*. After the slaying of her husband, Queen Dectora is taken prisoner by **Forgael**. She contemplates suicide and threatens to kill her captor. She falls under the spell of his magic harp, and they sail away together. The role of Dectora in the first production in Dublin, January 1904, was played by **Florence Farr**.

DEIRDRE, fated heroine. According to a prophecy, the beautiful Deirdre is doomed at birth to bring ruin on the warriors of **Ulster**. The Ulstermen decide to kill her, but **Conchubar**, who plans to marry her when she grows up, hides her in the woods, with Lavarcham as her only companion. By chance, years later, Deirdre sees the warrior **Naoise** and falls in love. She persuades him to elope with her to Scotland, accompanied by his brothers **Ardan** and Ainnle. They remain there for seven years, but with the promise of a pardon, Conchubar encourages them to return home. When they arrive at his castle at **Emain Macha**, he has Naoise and his brothers treacherously murdered. Grief-stricken Deirdre takes her own life.

REFERENCES: Ellis, Peter Berresford. *Dictionary of Celtic Mythology*. New York: Oxford University Press, 1992; Fackler, Herbert V. *That Tragic Queen: The Deirdre Legend in Anglo-Irish Literature*. Salzburg, Austria: University of Salzburg, 1978; Green, Miranda J. *Dictionary of Celtic Myth and Legend*. London: Thames & Hudson, 1992; Mac Cana, Proinsias. *Celtic Mythology*. Feltham, Middlesex: Newnes, 1983.

DEIRDRE, one-act play by WBY. It was first published in 1907 and included in many subsequent anthologies, including the *Poetical Works of W. B. Yeats* (1907), *Collected Works of W. B. Yeats* (1908), and **Collected Plays of W. B. Yeats** (1934, 1952). The story of **Deirdre** and **Naoise** appears in the **Ulster** Cycle of mythology as "The Tragical Death of the Sons of Uisnech." WBY's version is freely based on a retelling of the story by **Lady Gregory** in her *Cuchulain of Muirthemne* (1902). The action of the play takes place after Deirdre and her lover Naoise have been persuaded to return from Scotland to **Conchubar's** home at **Emain Macha**. There, Conchubar has Naoise treacherously put to death, and Deirdre kills herself, leaving an exultant Conchubar to speak the final lines. The Deirdre legend has been dramatized by a number of the Irish playwrights, including **Sir Samuel Ferguson, J. M. Synge, AE**, and **James Stephens**. In *Deirdre*, which is written in verse, WBY introduces for the first time in his drama Musicians who tell the story and play a minor part in the action. The play was first performed at the **Abbey Theatre**, November 1906, with the following cast: Deirdre, Miss Darragh (Letitia Marion Dallas); Naoise, **Frank Fay; Fergus**, Arthur Sinclair; Dark-faced Messenger, Udolphus Wright; Conchubar, J. M. Kerrigan; Dark-faced Executioner, Arthur Power; Musicians, **Sara Allgood, Máire O'Neill**, Brigid O'Dempsey. The scenery and costumes were designed by **Robert Gregory**, with music for the Musicians' songs by **Arthur Darley**. The role of Deirdre was subsequently played at the Abbey Theatre by **Mrs. Patrick Campbell**, to whom WBY dedicated the play.

REFERENCES: Ellis, Sylvia C. *The Plays of W. B. Yeats: Yeats and the Dancer*. London: Macmillan, 1995; Miller, Liam. *The Noble Drama of W. B. Yeats*. Dublin: Dolmen, 1977; Oppel, Frances Nesbitt. *Mask and Tragedy: Yeats and Nietzsche, 1902–10*. Charlottesville: University Press of Virginia, 1987; Taylor, Richard. *A Reader's Guide to the Plays of W. B. Yeats*. New York: St. Martin's, 1984.

DE JUBAINVILLE, HENRI. *See* **D'ARBOIS DE JUBAINVILLE, [MARIE] HENRI**.

DELACROIX, [FERDINAND VICTOR] EUGÈNE (1798–1863), painter. He was the outstanding painter of the nineteenth-century Romantic movement in France. His exuberant use of color and his dramatic renderings of large-scale scenes from literature and mythology contrasted dramatically with the neo-classical style of his contemporaries, like David. He was noted for his portraits and studies of animals. WBY compares the painting of **Charles Ricketts** with the rich coloring of Delacroix (*LE*. 92, 227). In the poem "A Nativity" (*CP*. 387), WBY makes a somewhat obscure reference to Delacroix's ability to paint drapery.

REFERENCE: Deslandres, Yvonne. *Delacroix: A Pictorial Biography*. Trans. Jonathan Griffin. New York: Viking, 1963.

DELPHI, seat of the Delphic oracle. Located on the slopes of Mount Parnassus in Ancient Greece, it was the principal shrine of Apollo. Housed in the Temple of Apollo, which was built in the sixth century B.C., the oracle answered questions on all matters, public and private, through a virgin priestess called Pythia—hence, the temple was also known as the Pythian House. The priestess sat on a golden dais and in a trancelike state uttered words and sounds that were interpreted for the enquirer by a priest. At the opening of **Sophocles' King Oedipus, Oedipus** waits for the arrival of **Creon**, whom he has sent to Delphi to consult the oracle. When Creon returns, he brings news that the death of King Laius, murdered on his way to Delphi, must be revenged. Delphi was later pillaged by the Romans, and the oracle was abolished by the emperor Theodosius in A.D. 390. WBY refers to Delphi in the poems "The Delphic Oracle upon Plotinus" (*CP*. 306) and "News for the Delphic Oracle" (*CP*. 376). See also *The Player Queen* (*CPl*. 420, 422, 423).

DERMOT. *See* **MacMURROUGH, DIARMUID**.

DERVORGILLA (1108–93), daughter of the king of **Meath** and wife of Tiernan O'Rourke, prince of **Breiffny**. Dervorgilla was abducted by **Diarmuid MacMurrough**, king of **Leinster**. For his action, Diarmuid was banished from Leinster and appealed to Henry II for help. In response, Henry II sent an army under Strongbow and successfully reinstated Diarmuid. While some accounts suggest that Dervorgilla went willingly with Diarmuid, the version in the *Annals of the Four Masters* claims that Diarmuid carried Dervorgilla off against her will and that she was restored to her husband the following year. Apparently, she survived her husband by twenty-one years and died in the Abbey of Mellifont at the age of eighty-five. In his play *The Dreaming of the Bones*, WBY dramatizes Dervorgilla's remorse for her part in bringing the Normans to Ireland. Her story is also movingly told by WBY in "Hanrahan's Vision" (*MY*. 250–51). There is a version of the story by **Lady Gregory,** *Dervorgilla*, first performed at the **Abbey Theatre** in May 1908, with **Sara Allgood** in the title role.

DE VALERA, EAMON (1882–1975), politician, prominent in the setting up of the Irish Republic, and the dominant force behind the political shaping of modern Ireland. De Valera was born in New York of a Spanish father and Irish mother. He grew up in Ireland and was educated at Christian Brothers School, Charleville, **Limerick** (county), at Blackrock College, and University College, Dublin. As a young man he joined the Gaelic League. In 1913, he became a member of the Irish Volunteers and fought in the 1916 Easter Rising against

British rule. He was the last commander to surrender to the British. He avoided the death sentence, possibly because of his American citizenship, and was sentenced to life imprisonment. He was later released under a general amnesty. In 1917, he was elected Sinn Féin M.P. for East **Clare**. Working rigorously to avoid a split between the political wing of Sinn Féin and the militant Volunteers, he was declared president of the new Sinn Féin in the same year. In 1918, he was again imprisoned, made an audacious escape, and was elected president of the revolutionary assembly, **Dáil Éireann**. He resigned in opposition to the 1921 Treaty with Britain that established the Irish Free State, arguing that it did not give Ireland absolute freedom. He fought on the anti-Treaty side in the Irish Civil War. He was arrested and imprisoned, 1923–24. In 1926, he resigned from Sinn Féin, founded the separatist Fianna Fáil Party, and led them to victory in the 1932 parliamentary elections, a popular victory that WBY opposed, agreeing with **Olivia Shakespear** when she compared de Valera with Hitler or Mussolini (*WL*. 805–6). One of the first actions of the new de Valera government was the reduction by one fourth of the state subsidy to the **Abbey Theatre**. When the Abbey planned its 1933 American tour, de Valera publicly advised caution in the selection of plays, so as not to offend Irish Americans. Only after discussions between de Valera and the directors of the Abbey Theatre was a compromise reached (*UP2*. 500). As president of the Executive Council, 1932–37, de Valera intensified his efforts to separate Ireland from Britain, removing all references to the monarch and the governor-general from the Irish Constitution. He became Taoiseach (prime minister) and minister of external affairs in 1937 and was instrumental in making Ireland a sovereign state and in maintaining its neutrality during World War II. He was Taoiseach, 1937–48, 1951–54, 1957–59, and president of Ireland, 1959–73. In 1937, aware of de Valera's record as a tough negotiator with the British, WBY acquainted him with the controversy over the **Hugh Lane** pictures (*WL*. 877) but to no avail. In "Parnell's Funeral" (*CP*. 319), written in 1934, WBY referred to de Valera, who, he believed, had risen to power on the shoulders of the mob, as a "loose-lipped demagogue." There is a further reference to him in "The Statesman's Holiday" (*CP*. 389).

REFERENCES: Coogan, Tim Pat. *Eamon de Valera: The Man Who Was Ireland*. New York: HarperCollins, 1995; Dwyer, T. Ryle. *De Valera: The Man and the Myths*. Swords, Ireland: Poolbeg, 1992; Edwards, Owen Dudley. *Eamon de Valera*. Washington, D.C.: Catholic University of America Press, 1987; Freyer, Grattan. *W. B. Yeats and the Anti-Democratic Tradition*. Dublin: Gill & Macmillan, 1981; Krimm, Bernard G. *W. B. Yeats and the Emergence of the Irish Free State, 1918–1939: Living in the Explosion*. Troy, N.Y.: Whitston, 1981; Stanfield, Paul S. *Yeats and Politics in the 1930s*. New York: St. Martin's, 1988.

DE VALOIS, [DAME] NINETTE (b. 1898), stage name of dancer and choreographer Edris Stannus. She was born in Baltinglass, County Kildare. As a child, she was a member of a dancing troupe, "The Wonder Children," which toured seaside resorts in England. From 1914 to 1919, she danced in the annual pantomime at the Lyceum Theatre, London, and from 1917 to 1923, she appeared in music hall. From 1923 to 1925, she was a member of Diaghilev's *Ballets Russes*. In 1926, she opened the Academy of Choreographic Arts in London and coached movement and dance at the Old Vic/Sadler's Wells Theatre. She choreographed WBY's *On Baile's Strand* for the Cambridge Festival Theatre in January 1927. She was introduced to WBY in May 1927, at a performance of *The Player Queen* produced by the Cambridge Festival Theatre and directed by her cousin Terence Gray. At WBY's invitation, she returned to Dublin to establish a school of ballet at the **Peacock Theatre**, the experimental wing of the **Abbey Theatre**. In August 1929, she choreographed *Fighting the Waves*, with music by **George Antheil** and masks by **Hildo Krop**. Dancers from her school performed the chorus, and she danced the nonspeaking role of **Fand**. She choreographed the first production of WBY's dance play *The Dreaming of the Bones*, and in July 1933, she choreographed a revival of *At the Hawk's Well* in which she danced the role of the **Guardian of the Well**. Throughout this period, she maintained her connections with the Old Vic, and in 1934, after the opening of *The King of the Great Clock Tower*, in which she danced the part of the **Queen**, she reluctantly told WBY she now had to devote herself fully to the Sadler's Wells School of Ballet—later the Royal Ballet—which had been formed in London in 1931. She was director of the Royal Ballet until 1963 and distinguished herself as one of the foremost choreographers and teachers of dance in England. Much of the success of the Royal Ballet was due to her enthusiasm and untiring efforts to train dancers—qualities that WBY so admired when she was working with him in Ireland. As a tribute, he dedicated to her his play *The King of the Great Clock Tower*. In his "Introduction to Essays" (*LE*. 218), WBY fantasizes about a new marriage service to be devised by **T. S. Eliot** and Ninette de Valois, while in *On the Boiler* (*LE*. 226), he names among those moments at the Abbey Theatre that dominate his memory Ninette de Valois's entrance in *Fighting the Waves*. In *The Death of Cuchulain*, the **Old Man** recalls a "tragi-comedian dancer" who is no longer available for his plays—possibly a reference to Ninette de Valois.

REFERENCES: De Valois, Ninette. *Come Dance with Me*. London: H. Hamilton, 1957; De Valois, Ninette. *Invitation to the Ballet*. New York: Oxford University Press, 1938; De Valois, Ninette. *Step by Step*. London: W. H. Allen, 1977; Walker, Kathrine Sorley. *Ninette de Valois: Idealist without Illusions*. London: Hamish Hamilton, 1987.

DE VERE, AUBREY [THOMAS] (1814–1902), poet, essayist, and dramatist. De Vere was the third son of the writer Sir Aubrey de Vere and grew up on the family estate, Curragh Chase, **Limerick**. After graduating from **Trinity College**, Dublin, he met the leading English writers of the day, **Wordsworth, Tennyson**, and **Carlyle**, who became major influences. He joined the Oxford Movement in 1838 and, through the influence of John Henry Newman (1801–90) and Cardinal Henry Edward Manning (1808–92), left the Church of Ireland in 1851 to become a Roman Catholic. The remainder of his life was devoted to theology and contemplation. Independently wealthy, de Vere published his first book, *English Misrule and Irish Misdeeds*, in 1848. This was followed by a travel book, *Sketches of Greece and Turkey* (1850), and his first collection of poems, *The Sisters and Inisfail* (1867). An enlightened member of the landowning class in Ireland, he worked throughout his life for religious equality and supported the Irish Land Act of 1881 with his publication *Constitutional and Unconstitutional Political Action* (1881). Apart from his political and religious writings, de Vere wrote ballads and lyrics, but his major contribution to Irish literature was his spirited retelling of Irish myths and legends, among them *The Foray of Queen Maeve, The Sons of Usnach*, and *The Children of Lir* and his version of the colloquy ''Oiseen and Saint Patrick.'' De Vere is little read today, although he played some part in the development of a specific Irish literary consciousness, and WBY and his contemporaries were in his debt. WBY was aware of de Vere's place among older poets like **James Clarence Mangan** and **Sir Samuel Ferguson** but regretted that much of his work was modeled on English forms and that he was best known as a poet among English Catholics (*UP1*. 216, 381). He thought his few genuine successes memorable but elusive (*WL*. 232). In a letter written to **Katharine Tynan** (*WL*. 33), he noted that **John Todhunter** modeled a book of poems on de Vere's *The Sisters and Inisfail*, while in 1908, he announced the publication by **Cuala Press** of a selection of poems by de Vere and Ferguson, but the book did not appear. He included *Selections from the Poems of Aubrey de Vere*, edited by G. E. Woodberry, among his list of ''Best Irish Books'' (*UP1*. 387).

REFERENCES: De Vere, Aubrey. *Recollections of Aubrey de Vere*. New York: E. Arnold, 1897; Marcus, Phillip L. *Yeats and the Beginning of the Irish Renaissance*. Syracuse: Syracuse University Press, 1987; Reilly, Sister Mary Paraclita. *Aubrey de Vere: Victorian Observer*. Dublin: Clonmore & Reynolds, 1956; Winckler, Paul A., and Stone, William V. ''Aubrey Thomas de Vere, 1814–1902: A Bibliography.'' *Victorian Newsletter*, no. 10, supp. (1956).

DHOYA. *See JOHN SHERMAN AND DHOYA*.

DIARMUID. *See* **GRANIA**.

DIARMUID. *See* **MacMURROUGH, DIARMUID**.

DIARMUID AND GRANIA [also *Diarmid and Grania*], three-act play written by WBY and **George Moore**. It was performed at the request of the **Irish Literary Theatre** by F. R. Benson and his Shakespearean Company at the Gaiety Theatre, Dublin, October 1901. The incidental music was composed by **Sir Edward Elgar**. *Diarmuid and Grania*, which shared the bill with **Douglas Hyde's** *Casadh an tSúgáin*, directed by **W. G. Fay**, tells the story of the lovers **Diarmuid** and **Grania** from the time when Grania refuses to marry the aging **Fionn** and elopes with her lover Diarmuid. The play ends with the death of the heroic

Diarmuid. The cast of English actors included Benson and his wife, who played the title roles, and the young Henry Ainley, who acted in *At the Hawk's Well* in 1916. Reaction to the Benson production from the Dublin press was negative, principally because the actors in this most popular of Irish legends were English. This offended the nationalist sensibilities of the audience and critics. The play suffered because it was accompanied by the one-act comedy by Douglas Hyde, in which the actors, directed by W. G. Fay, impressed with their authenticity and raw energy, making the professional actors, who were already on unfamiliar ground in an Irish mythological drama, appear stilted and mannered. The collaboration between Moore and WBY, too, had been an uneasy one, predictably so since the original plan was for Moore to write the play in French, which **Lady Gregory** would translate into her brand of local dialect known as Kiltartanese, before WBY gave it a final polish! It marked the beginning of Moore's disenchantment with the leaders and ideals of the Irish Literary Theatre. WBY did not include the play in collected editions of his work. It remained unpublished during his lifetime and was published for the first time in *The Dublin Magazine*, April–June 1951. The cast in the first production was as follows: Cormac, Alfred Brydone; Fionn Mac Cumhal, Frank Rodney; Diarmuid, F. R. Benson; **Goll**, Charles Bibby; **Oisin**, Henry Ainley; **Caoilte**, E. Harcourt Williams; Spearmen, G. Wallace Johnstone, Walter Hampden, Stuart Edgar; Niall, Matheson Lang; **Conan**, Arthur Whitby; Old Man, H. O. Nicholson; Shepherd, Mr. Owen; Boy, Ella Tarrant; Young Man, Joan Mackinlay; Grania, Mrs. F. R. Benson; **Laban**, Lucy Franklein.

REFERENCES: Hogan, Robert, and Kilroy, James. *The Irish Literary Theatre, 1899–1901.* Dublin: Dolmen, 1975; Miller, Liam. *The Noble Drama of W. B. Yeats.* Dublin: Dolmen, 1977; Saddlemyer, Ann. '' 'All Art Is a Collaboration'? George Moore and Edward Martyn.'' In *The World of W. B. Yeats*, ed. Robin Skelton and Ann Saddlemyer. Seattle: University of Washington Press, 1965.

DIONYSUS, god of wine and fertility in Greek mythology. He was the son of Zeus and was characteristically attended by a drunken, licentious group of satyrs and nymphs. Many festivals were held in his honor, the best known being the Spring Festival, or Greater Dionysia, held each year in Athens. From the music and orgiastic rituals of this festival emerged the Greek dramas written by Aeschylus, Aristophanes, and **Sophocles**. The worshippers of Dionysus are described by WBY in *The Resurrection* (*CPl.* 585).

DISCOVERIES, collection of essays by WBY. The volume, which was published by the **Dun Emer Press** in 1907, in a limited edition of 200 copies, contained a series of twenty-one short essays, some of which were little more than a paragraph in length. They had previously appeared, unsigned, under the title ''My Thoughts and My Second Thoughts'' in the *Gentleman's Magazine* (September, October, and November 1906). A circular design of a charging unicorn by **Robert Gregory** was printed on the title page. This was a favorite symbol of WBY. The essays were included in ***The Cutting of an Agate*** (1912).

REFERENCE: Oppel, Frances Nesbitt. *Mask and Tragedy: Yeats and Nietzsche, 1902–10.* Charlottesville: University Press of Virginia, 1987.

DOLMETSCH, ARNOLD (1858–1940), composer and Early Music enthusiast. He was born in Le Mans, France, of French and Swiss parentage. He studied at the Brussels Conservatory and, in 1882, enrolled as a pupil of Sir Hubert Parry at the Royal College of Music, London. In 1883, he accepted an appointment to teach violin at Dulwich College. In 1897, he composed the music for a production of *The Tempest*, directed by William Poel, the first of many collaborations. He began making and restoring musical instruments, one of which was purchased by **Herbert Horne**, who became a lifelong friend. Through Horne, he was introduced to a wide community of painters, poets, writers, and musicians, so that, by 1901, he was established at the center of London's intellectual elite, giving concerts and lectures on Renaissance and Baroque music. He accompanied Isadora Duncan in her Paris debut in 1903 and made a number of successful concert tours of the United States with his Early Music ensemble. In Boston, he was asked to open a workshop for the construction of early instruments. He accepted and remained in the United States for seven years. He returned to Europe in 1910 and, after living in France, returned to England in 1914 and settled in Haslemere, Surrey. In 1925, he began a series of Early Music festivals for which he made original instruments. Throughout his life, he pioneered the use of such instruments, including the recorder, and published collections of early songs and dances, among them *Select English Songs and Dialogues of the 16th and 17th Centuries* (1898) and *Interpretation of the Music of the 17th and 18th Centuries: Revealed by Contemporary Evidence* (1900). WBY and **Florence Farr** attended Dolmetsch's concerts in Charlotte Street, London. In 1901, they sought his help when they were experimenting with the speaking of verse to the accompaniment of a stringed instrument. Initially, WBY asked Dolmetsch to make a psaltery, an instrument that had originated in the Near East and had been used in Europe from the twelfth century to the Middle Ages. This would replace a less flexible instrument used by Florence Farr when she played the part of **Aleel** in ***The Countess Cathleen*** in May 1899. In his enthusiasm, Dolmetsch not only made the psaltery but also gave them valuable advice on the notation of spoken verse and its accompaniment—advice followed by Florence Farr with some success (*EI.* 16, 20, 21; *WL.* 354, 362). WBY's appreciation of Dolmetsch's skills and knowledge is contained in a letter he wrote inviting Dolmetsch to chair a lecture on ''Speaking to Musical Notes,'' which WBY gave at Clifford's Inn, London, 10 June 1902 (*KLIII.* 194–95). His poem ''The Players ask for a Blessing on the Psalteries and on Themselves'' (*CP.* 93) was performed at the lecture. Florence Farr's book *The Music of Speech* (1909) was dedicated to Dolmetsch and WBY.

REFERENCES: Campbell, Margaret. *Dolmetsch: The Man and His Work.* Seattle: University of Washington Press, 1975; Dolmetsch, Mabel. *Personal Recollections of Arnold*

Dolmetsch. New York: Da Capo, 1980; Ring, Layton, ed. *Renaissance Songs and Dances from the Library of Arnold Dolmetsch.* London: Universal Edition, 1959.

DONEGAL (Irish: *Dun-na-nGall*) [fort of the strangers], most northerly county in Ireland and part of the ancient province of **Ulster**. A remote, rugged region on the edge of the Atlantic Ocean, it was formerly known as *Tir Conaill*, the land of Conal, son of Niall of the Nine Hostages. From the tenth century, Donegal was the home of the O'Donnell family. In *The Countess Cathleen* (*CPl.* 37), the **First Merchant** claims to have seen the grain ships off the coast of Donegal during the Famine, while in ''Parnell'' (*LE.* 85), WBY recalls that the Irish nationalist Henry Harrison (1867–1954) had been arrested in Donegal for protesting against peasant evictions. It is also the setting for WBY's story ''The Man and His Boots'' (*MY.* 83–84), about a man who doubted the presence of ghosts in his house. **William Allingham** was born in Donegal and celebrated the local places in many of his poems.
    REFERENCE: McGarry, James P. *Place Names in the Writings of William Butler Yeats.* Gerrards Cross: Colin Smythe, 1976.

DONERAILE (Irish: *Dun-air-Aill*) [fort on the cliff], village near Mallow in **Cork** (county). It was the home of the ruling Desmond family until the late sixteenth century, when the fort and some 3,000 acres of land were granted to **Edmund Spenser**. In his essay ''Swedenborg, Mediums, and the Desolate Places'' (*LE.* 72), WBY recalls a shepherd in Doneraile who told him of the ghostly appearance of an aunt stark naked after death, while in ''Witches and Wizards and Irish Folk-Lore'' (*LE.* 74, 208), the old shepherd speaks of a magic wand with *Tetragrammaton* and *Agla* written on it—familiar words in Cabalism.
    REFERENCE: McGarry, James P. *Place Names in the Writings of William Butler Yeats.* Gerrards Cross: Colin Smythe, 1976.

DON JUAN, notorious Spanish libertine. There are many versions of his story. In the best known, he seduces the daughter of the Commendatore of Seville and then kills her father in a duel. When he invites a statue of his victim to a feast, it comes to life and drags Don Juan to hell. In a letter to **Lady Gregory** (*WL.* 525), WBY writes that in his poem ''On Those that hated 'The Playboy of the Western World,' 1907'' (*CP.* 124), he has compared **Arthur Griffith** and those who disapproved of **J. M. Synge's** play to the eunuchs who watch Don Juan riding through hell, in a picture by **Charles Ricketts**. He repeats the allusion in his Journal, adding that the ''cultivation of hatred . . . is the intellectual equivalent to the removal of the genitals'' (*M.* 176).

DONNE, JOHN (1572–1631), Jacobean poet and cleric. Donne was raised a Roman Catholic and educated at the universities of Oxford and Cambridge and at Lincoln's Inn, London. After returning from expeditions to Cádiz and the Azores with the earl of Essex in 1597, he became secretary to the powerful Sir Thomas Egerton, lord keeper of the seal. His poetry at that time consisted of love songs and lyrics, many of them sensual and sardonic. His marriage in 1601 to Anne More, a niece of Sir Thomas Egerton's wife, lost him his position at court, and his writing became more serious and philosophical. He was twice elected to Parliament, but at the request of James I of England, he took Holy Orders in the Anglican Church, after which he became royal chaplain and dean of St. Paul's Cathedral, London. He wrote powerful, innovative, religious, and metaphysical poetry, including the *Holy Sonnets*, which became a major inspiration to English poets during the middle years of the twentieth century, among them **T. S. Eliot**. WBY was an admirer of Donne and took some action to remove a "sentimental sensuality" from his own early work that he did not find in the poetry of Donne (*A.* 326). In 1912, he read with enthusiasm a definitive edition of Donne's poems by Herbert J. C. Grierson (*WL.* 570–71). Later, he wrote "To a Young Beauty" (*CP.* 157), in which he anticipated immortality in the company of Donne and **Walter Savage Landor**.

REFERENCE: Gardner, Helen L. *John Donne: A Collection of Critical Essays.* Englewood Cliffs, N.J.: Prentice-Hall, 1962.

DOONEY [ROCK], on the shores of **Lough Gill** in **Sligo** (county). The name may be derived from the Irish *Dun Aodh*, the fort of Aodh, or may just be the diminutive form of *Dun*, a little fort. In WBY's time, Dooney was a regular meeting place for dancing and fiddling on Sunday evenings. It is the setting for one of WBY's best-loved poems, "The Fiddler of Dooney" (*CP.* 82).

REFERENCE: McGarry, James P. *Place Names in the Writings of William Butler Yeats.* Gerrards Cross: Colin Smythe, 1976.

DOWDEN, EDWARD (1843–1913), scholar and literary critic. Dowden was born in **Cork**, the son of a linen draper. He entered **Trinity College**, Dublin, when he was sixteen years of age. There, he made the acquaintance of **John B. Yeats**, and they embarked upon a lifelong friendship during which Dowden generously lent the painter money and commissioned pictures from him. In 1867, four years after graduation, Dowden was appointed to the newly founded Chair of English Literature at Trinity College, a position that earned him power and prestige among Dublin intellectuals. He gained an international reputation with his books, among them *Shakespeare, His Mind and Art* (1875) and his *Life of Shelley* (1886), and promoted the poetry of **Walt Whitman**, then unrecognized in his own country. He married Mary Clerke in 1866 but later formed an attachment to one of his students, Elizabeth Dickinson West, whom he married in 1895, three years after the death of his first wife. Dowden invited WBY and his father to breakfast in his book-lined home in Rathgar, Dublin. There, he listened to the young poet reading his verses and made encouraging remarks (*A.* 85–87). Dowden hosted literary gatherings; indeed, it was at Dowden's home that the Dublin Lodge of the **Theosophical Society**, known as the **Dublin Hermetic Society**, was formed. Initially, WBY admired and respected Dowden, with something akin to hero worship, and his reputation benefited enormously from

Dowden's favorable comments on *The Wanderings of Oisin*. When Dowden refused to praise publicly the nineteenth-century Irish writers, like **Sir Samuel Ferguson**, WBY became critical and antagonistic (*UP1.* 89). Later, Dowden, who claimed he knew an Irish book "by its smell," made negative comments at a lecture, "The Poetry of Sir Samuel Ferguson," given in the Leinster Lecture Hall, Dublin, 14 January 1895 (*WL.* 245). The subsequent controversy, argued publicly by Dowden, WBY, **Standish [James] O'Grady**, and **T. W. Rolleston** in letters to the *Daily Express* (*UP1.* 347–49, 351–53, 383–87), was bitter and acrimonious. WBY writes of his disillusionment with Dowden, the man who had originally been a friend and an important influence, in "Ireland after Parnell" (*A.* 235–36). In his defense, Dowden always valued WBY as a poet, and his judgment of nineteenth-century Irish writers and WBY's contemporaries has proven correct. His critical work on **Shakespeare** is still a standard text.

REFERENCES: Boyd, Ernest A. *Appreciations and Depreciations: Irish Literary Studies.* New York: John Lane, 1918; Dowden, Elizabeth and Dowden, Hilda. *Letters of Edward Dowden and His Correspondents.* New York: Dutton, 1914; Ludwigson, Kathryn R. *Edward Dowden.* New York: Twayne, 1973; Patten, Eve. "A 'General Crowd of Small Singers': Yeats and Dowden Reassessed." *Yeats Annual* 12, 1996.

DOWN, county in the northeast of Ireland. It formed part of the ancient province of **Ulster**, the name derived from the Irish *Dun*, a fort. The county seat of Down is Downpatrick, where **St. Patrick** is reputedly buried. The county, which consists of rich, arable land, was settled by the Scots and English during the Plantation of Ulster in the seventeenth century and became a center of the prosperous linen industry in the eighteenth and nineteenth centuries. WBY's grandfather, **William Butler Yeats**, was Church of Ireland Rector of All Saints Parish, Tullylish, County Down. WBY alludes to him in the poem "Are You Content" (*CP.* 370). WBY's father was born in the rectory at Tullylish, while **Charles Johnston**, a close friend of WBY, lived in Ballykilbeg House, four miles from Downpatrick. The poet recalls visiting him there in 1891 (*M.* 45, 46), although he failed to find among the Scotch-Irish of north Down the legends that were so plentiful in the west of Ireland.

REFERENCE: McGarry, James P. *Place Names in the Writings of William Butler Yeats.* Gerrards Cross: Colin Smythe, 1976.

DOWSON, ERNEST (1867–1900), poet. Dowson was born in Kent, England. After his early education, which included periods in France and Italy, he went to Oxford University but left without completing his degree. At Oxford, he met **Lionel Johnson** and renewed that friendship when he became an active member of the **Rhymers' Club**, where he met WBY. Quiet and melancholic, he drank immoderately and frequented houses of ill-repute. In 1889, he met Adelaide (Missie) Foltinowitz, a Polish restaurant owner's daughter. Although she was only thirteen, he fell deeply in love with her, and she inspired much of his love poetry, including the well-known "Cynara." He dedicated his stories *Dilemmas*

(1895) to her. In 1894 and 1895, his parents died—his father from an overdose, his mother by hanging herself. He moved to France, but despite the success of his *Poems* (1896), he never recovered from the tragedy. The marriage of Adelaide Foltinowitz in 1897 to a waiter was a further blow (*A*. 310–12). Homeless and forgotten by his friends, he died of pneumonia and consumption at the age of thirty-three. WBY did not have a close relationship with Dowson, although he admired his verse, which he thought would prove of lasting quality. On a number of occasions, he claimed that he had recommended the publishing of *The Book of the Rhymers' Club* so that he might have copies of Dowson's poems (*A*. 301), while in addressing the poets of the Rhymers' Club in his poem "The Grey Rock" (*CP*. 115), he singled out Dowson and Lionel Johnson for special praise. Writing of Dowson in his autobiography, it is clear that he was concerned about him but knew too little of his destructive lifestyle until it was too late (*A*. 303, 327, 328, 399; *LE*. 90). Nine poems by Dowson were included in WBY's selection for *The Oxford Book of Modern Verse* (1936), and three books of Dowson's verse were in WBY's library (*OS*. nos. 542–44).

REFERENCES: Gardner, Joann. *Yeats and the Rhymers' Club: A Nineties' Perspective.* New York: Peter Lang, 1989; Halladay, Jean R. *Eight Late Victorian Poets Shaping the Artistic Sensibility of an Age.* Lewiston, N.Y.: E. Mellen, 1993; Longaher, Mark. *Ernest Dowson.* Philadelphia: University of Pennsylvania Press, 1967; Stanford, Derek, ed. *Three Poets of the Rhymers' Club: Ernest Dowson, Lionel Johnson, John Davidson.* Cheadle: Carcenet, 1974.

DRAMATIS PERSONAE, installment of WBY's autobiography. It was published in 1935 by **Cuala Press**, in an edition of 400 copies, and was principally an account of his association with **Lady Gregory** and the emergence of the **Irish National Theatre Society**, 1896–1902. *Dramatis Personae* was subsequently published by the Macmillan Company (New York, 1936) and included in *The Autobiography of William Butler Yeats* (1938). See also *Autobiographies*.

DREAMING OF THE BONES, THE, one-act verse play by WBY. It was published in *The Little Review* (January 1919) and subsequently in *Two Plays for Dancers* (1919) and *Four Plays for Dancers* (1921). In the play, a **Young Man**, a member of the Irish Republican Army, encounters the ghosts of **Diarmuid** and **Dervorgilla**, who were responsible for bringing the Normans to Ireland in the twelfth century. The lovers have been condemned to wander the countryside unable to touch until they find someone to pardon their crime. They ask the Young Man to forgive them, but he refuses to do so, and they must continue their restless wanderings. The structure and presentation closely parallel the **Noh** play *Nishikigi*, which WBY read in a translation by **Ernest Fenollosa**. The central action, however, is based on "Hanrahan's Vision," a story that WBY published in *Stories of Red Hanrahan* (1897) (*MY*. 246–52), in which Diarmuid and Dervorgilla appear to the poet **Hanrahan** on **Ben Bulben** and ask forgiveness, but it is denied them. **Lady Gregory's** *Dervorgilla* (1911) is another possible source. A successful reading of *The Dreaming of the Bones* was given at the home of **Oliver St. John Gogarty** in 1917, but WBY continued to work on the opening and closing lyrics and intensified the atmosphere (*WL*. 629). The first performance took place at the **Abbey Theatre**, 6 December 1931, with the following cast: Young Man, W. O'Gorman; Stranger, J. Stephenson; Girl, Nesta Brooking; Chorus, Joseph O'Neill, T. Browne (flute), Julie Grey (zither), Doreen Cuthbert (percussion). It was directed by Udolphus Wright, with music by Dr. J. F. Larchet. At the request of WBY, **Walter Rummel** had written music for the play, but it was thought too difficult and was not used.

REFERENCES: Bradley, Anthony. *William Butler Yeats*. New York: Frederick Ungar, 1979; Ellis, Sylvia C. *The Plays of W. B. Yeats: Yeats and the Dancer*. London: Macmillan, 1995; Jeffares, A. Norman, and Knowland, A. S. *A Commentary on the Collected Plays of W. B. Yeats*. London: Macmillan, 1975; Miller, Liam. *The Noble Drama of W. B. Yeats*. Dublin: Dolmen, 1977; Taylor, Richard. *A Reader's Guide to the Plays of W. B. Yeats*. New York: St. Martin's, 1984.

DROMAHAIR (Irish: *Drom-Dha-Eithiar*) [ridge of the two demons], village in County Leitrim, close to the **Sligo** border. Dromahair is on the banks of the River Bonnet, which flows into **Lough Gill**. In "A Teller of Tales" (*MY*. 5), WBY describes a storyteller from Dromahair, Paddy Flynn, who claimed it was haunted by fairies. Dromahair on a crowded Fair Day is the setting for the first verse of WBY's poem "The Man Who Dreamed of Faeryland" (*CP*. 49). See also "Kidnappers" (*MY*. 70).

REFERENCE: McGarry, James P. *Place Names in the Writings of William Butler Yeats*. Gerrards Cross: Colin Smythe, 1976.

DRUMCLIFF (Irish: *Druim-Chliach*) [ridge of the hazels], small town at the head of Drumcliff Bay. Drumcliff lies approximately five miles north of **Sligo** (town). To the southwest of Drumcliff is the towering mass of **Ben Bulben**, while four miles northeast is **Lissadell**, the home of the **Gore-Booth** family. WBY collected fairy lore around Drumcliff, and in his essay "Drumcliff and Rosses" (*MY*. 88–94), he describes the door to fairyland, high on the slopes of Ben Bulben, from which the fairy riders emerge each evening to roam over the plain of Drumcliff below. WBY's great-grandfather, **Rev. John Yeats**, was rector of St. Columba's Church in the Parish of Drumcliff. Adjacent to the church is an old Celtic cross, forty feet high, and nearby is the site of a monastic settlement founded by St. Columba in the sixth century. In "Are You Content" (*CP*. 370), WBY makes references to the cross and to his great-grandfather. WBY is buried in St. Columba's churchyard, the final lines from his poem "Under Ben Bulben" (*CP*. 397) cut on his tombstone.

REFERENCES: Allen, James Lovic. *Yeats's Epitaph: A Key to Symbolic Unity in His Life and Work*. Washington, D.C.: University Press of America, 1982; McGarry, James P. *Place Names in the Writings of William Butler Yeats*. Gerrards Cross: Colin Smythe, 1976.

DUBLIN CASTLE, seat of English power in Ireland from the thirteenth century until 1922. Built on high ground, 1204–28, to defend the city of Dublin from attack, the castle, which is off Dame Street, consists of four drum towers and a gatehouse. From the 1760s, visiting English monarchs were entertained there, and it was the setting for society events presided over by the viceroy. The castle season began in February with the Lord Lieutenant's Levee and ended with St. Patrick's Ball in March, when all the young society ladies were received by the viceroy in the Throne Room. Among the women who were presented were **Maud Gonne** and the **Countess Markiewicz**, before they embraced the Nationalist cause. During the Easter Rising of 1916, an attempt was made to occupy the castle, but it failed. The fine state apartments are still used for state functions, and the castle now houses the Heraldic Museum and the Genealogical Office. In his essay "Edmund Spenser" (*EI.* 362), WBY recalls that **Red Hugh O'Donnell** was imprisoned in the castle for four years, while in *The Unicorn from the Stars*, the hero Martin is making a golden coach for the Lord Lieutenant at Dublin Castle (*CPl.* 330, 341). In *The Pot of Broth* (*CPl.* 102) the **Tramp** claims that the Lord Lieutenant would have given Dublin Castle in exchange for his miraculous stone. In "Ireland after Parnell" (*A.* 233), WBY writes that he avoided those who had associations with the castle so as not to give the impression that he attacked some Nationalist opinion only to flatter the Unionists. Dublin Castle is open to visitors.

REFERENCES: McGarry, James P. *Place Names in the Writings of William Butler Yeats.* Gerrards Cross: Colin Smythe, 1976; O Broin, Leon. *Dublin Castle and the 1916 Rising.* New York: New York University Press, 1971.

DUBLIN HERMETIC SOCIETY, mystical association. It was formed in 1885 by WBY, with **AE, John Eglinton**, and **Charles Johnston**, to promote the study of oriental religions and theosophy. According to WBY in "The Poetry of AE" (*UP2.* 121), it met initially in a dilapidated house in York Street, Dublin, and then moved to Adelaide Road. WBY chaired the first meeting. The Dublin Hermetic Society subsequently became the Dublin Lodge of the **Theosophical Society** (*WL.* 592).

DUFFY, SIR CHARLES GAVAN (1816–1903), political activist and journalist. He was born in Monaghan (town), the son of a Catholic shopkeeper, and was largely self-educated. As a young man, he began to write for prominent Nationalist newspapers, and from 1839 to 1842, he successfully edited the *Belfast Vindicator*, a pro-**Daniel O'Connell** biweekly. In 1842, with **Thomas Davis** and John Blake Dillon, he founded *The Nation*, a radical weekly newspaper. Through his association with **John Mitchel**, whom he appointed editor of *The Nation*, he grew increasingly opposed to the more moderate policies of Daniel O'Connell and helped form a militant breakaway group, the Irish Confederation. Appalled by the horrors of the Irish Famine, he chose to work for reform by constitutional means. He entered the English Parliament as M.P. for New Ross in 1852 and organized a group of some fifty Irish members whose objective was to oppose any government that did not support the demands of the Irish Tenant League. In 1855, frustrated with the British parliamentary process, and factionalism within the Irish Nationalist movement, he emigrated to Australia to practice law. He again entered politics, and after his election to the State Parliament of Victoria in 1856, he was given a ministerial post in 1857 and appointed prime minister of Victoria, 1871–72, and Speaker of the Victoria House of Assembly, 1876–80. He was knighted in 1873. Because of ill health, he returned to Europe in 1880 and resided in the south of France, where he devoted himself to writing his memoirs and a history of Thomas Davis. In 1886, he published *The League of the North and South, 1850–54* (1886), reminiscences of his political activism in Ireland, and an autobiography, *My Life in Two Hemispheres* (1898). He was elected first president of the **Irish Literary Society** in 1892 and editor of the **New Irish Library**, a revival of a scheme successfully organized by the Young Irelanders in 1845 and edited by Gavan Duffy. WBY was antagonistic toward Gavan Duffy, believing him not only a poor writer but also one out of touch with contemporary thinking on Ireland (*A.* 224–28). When Duffy became editor of the New Irish Library, WBY was unhappy at the appointment and unsuccessfully challenged Duffy's leadership and choice of books. The limited success of the project gave WBY some satisfaction, and it was with irony that he proposed the vote of appreciation to Duffy on his resignation from the presidency of the Irish Literary Society in 1899. For his part, Duffy distrusted WBY, finding his poetry obscure and his politics questionable.

REFERENCES: Hogan, Robert, ed. *Dictionary of Irish Literature.* Rev. ed. Westport, Conn.: Greenwood, 1996; Marcus, Phillip L. *Yeats and the Beginning of the Irish Renaissance.* Syracuse: Syracuse University Press, 1987; Pearl, Cyril. *The Three Lives of Gavan Duffy.* Kensington: New South Wales University Press, 1979.

DULAC, EDMUND (1882–1953), illustrator, designer, and musician. He was born in Toulouse, France, and trained at the Académie Julienne in Paris. Between 1905 and 1918, he established himself as an outstanding illustrator in both line and color, particularly for his imaginative and decorative illustrations of well-known classics, like **Milton's** *Comus*, Robert Louis Stevenson's *Treasure Island*, Edward Fitzgerald's translation of *The Rubáiyát of Omar Khayyam*, and Laurence Housman's *The Arabian Nights.* He specialized in illustrating fairy stories, among them *The Sleeping Beauty* (1910) and *Edmund Dulac's Fairy Book* (1916). He held his first one-man show of portraits, illustrations, and caricatures in London in 1908 and took up permanent residence in London in 1912. As an illustrator, Dulac was influenced by the Pre-Raphaelites, Japanese prints, and his contemporary, Gustav Klimt. He preferred a decorative rather than a realistic effect in his illustrations, while his subjects were not overlit but flattened out, with the foreground and the horizon sharing the same plane. He worked in many fields of illustration, including portraits, postage stamps, commemorative medals, posters, and playing cards. Dulac met WBY shortly after arriving in

London, and they became lifelong friends—although they had a major quarrel in the 1930s. They attended séances together, and Dulac illustrated three of WBY's books and one of the *Broadsides* (1937). He devised the logo for three of WBY's books published by the **Cuala Press**. WBY's most productive collaboration with him, however, was the first production of *At the Hawk's Well* in 1916. Although WBY was involved in the presentation, much of its success was due to Dulac, who designed the costumes and lighting and the decorative cloth for the folding and unfolding of the curtain. He wrote the music, made masks for the **Old Man** and the **Young Man**, and played the part of the First Musician (*WL.* 609–12). This was the only stage production on which WBY and Dulac collaborated, although WBY continued to recommend elements of Dulac's designs for productions of his later plays *The Only Jealousy of Emer* (*CPl.* 281) and *The Dreaming of the Bones* (*CPl.* 433). In an early draft of his last play, *The Death of Cuchulain*, he suggests that the Old Man in the prologue should wear a mask like that worn by the Old Man in *At the Hawk's Well*. On seeing Dulac's masks and costumes used in a production of *At the Hawk's Well* in 1933, WBY relived the excitement of the first production and dedicated to Dulac *The Winding Stair and Other Poems* (1933). The Dulac masks are now in the possession of **Michael Yeats**. Dulac's music and costume designs for *At the Hawk's Well* are reproduced in *Four Plays for Dancers* (1921) (*WL.* 645). Dulac collaborated with WBY on four poetry broadcasts in 1937, "In the Poet's Pub," "In the Poet's Parlour," "My Own Poetry," and "My Own Poetry Again," writing some of the music and directing the singers. WBY wrote to Dulac about his setting for the poem "The Three Bushes," which was sung at an **Irish Academy of Letters** Dinner, May, 1937 (*WL.* 890). Dulac's painting also inspired the poem "On a Picture of a Black Centaur by Edmund Dulac" (*CP.* 242). In 1948, Dulac gave a talk to the **Irish Literary Society** in London, "Yeats as I Knew Him." He did two caricatures of WBY, one of him as Giraldus, used in the first edition of *A Vision* (1925), and the other as an aesthete, posed with an Irish harp.

REFERENCES: Dulac, Edmund. "Yeats as I Knew Him." *Irish Writing* 8 (July 1949); Larkin, David, ed. *Edmund Dulac: 1882–1953.* New York: Scribner, 1975; Loizeaux, Elizabeth Bergmann. *Yeats and the Visual Arts.* New Brunswick and London: Rutgers University Press, 1986; White, Colin. *Edmund Dulac.* London: Studio Vista, 1976.

DUNDALK. *See* **DUN DEALGAN**.

DUN DEALGAN (Irish: *Dún Dealgan*) [the fort of Dealga], now the city of Dundalk in County Louth. Dun Dealgan is believed to have been the site of **Cuchulain's** fort at the head of the Gap of the North. In WBY's play *On Baile's Strand*, the scene is a great hall at Dundealgan (*sic*). Near Cuchulain's fort was

Baile's Strand, now called Seatown. The legendary hero killed his son at Baile's Strand (*CPl.* 247, 699, 701).

REFERENCES: Mac Cana, Proinsias. *Celtic Mythology*. Feltham, Middlesex: Newnes, 1983; McGarry, James P. *Place Names in the Writings of William Butler Yeats*. Gerrards Cross: Colin Smythe, 1976.

DUN EMER PRESS, publishing house. It was founded by **Elizabeth (Lolly) Yeats** in 1902 as part of a larger project, Dun Emer Industries. This was the brainchild of Evelyn Gleeson, who, in 1902, returned from London to Ireland with the intention of starting a business dedicated to the training and employment of Irish women in arts and crafts. The business, which included weaving, embroidery, bookbinding, and printing, was housed in a large country house, renamed Dun Emer, in the village of Dundrum, outside Dublin. The Dun Emer Press, which used a handpress bought from a provincial newspaper, was dedicated to the publication of new books by Irish authors. WBY was invited to be editor, a position he readily accepted since it gave him the control and influence he lacked with the major English presses. The first book to be published by Dun Emer was WBY's *In the Seven Woods* (1903), followed by *The Nuts of Knowledge* (1903) by **AE**. Later titles included *The Love Songs of Connacht* (1904) by **Douglas Hyde**, WBY's *Stories of Red Hanrahan* (1905), *Twenty-one Poems* (1905) by **Lionel Johnson,** *Some Essays and Passages* (1905) by **John Eglinton,** *Sixteen Poems* (1905) by **William Allingham, Lady Gregory's** *A Book of Saints and Wonders* (1906), *Twenty-one Poems* (1907) by **Katharine Tynan**, and WBY's *Discoveries* (1907), the final book to appear under the Dun Emer imprint. From the early days of the project there had been tension between the Yeats family and Evelyn Gleeson. In May 1908, it was decided to move the press and the embroidery workshops, supervised by **Lily Yeats**, to a new location in Churchtown. Thus, the Cuala Industries, which included the **Cuala Press**, was formed. Evelyn Gleeson retained the name Dun Emer for her own enterprise.

REFERENCES: Miller, Liam. "The Dun Emer and the Cuala Press." In *The World of W. B. Yeats*, ed. Robin Skelton and Ann Saddlemyer. Seattle: University of Washington Press, 1965; Miller, Liam. *The Dun Emer, Later the Cuala Press*. Dublin: Dolmen, 1973; Murphy, William M. *Family Secrets: William Butler Yeats and His Relatives*. Syracuse, N.Y.: Syracuse University Press, 1995.

DUNSANY, LORD [EDWARD JOHN MORETON DRAX PLUNKETT] (1878– 1957), soldier, playwright, and short story writer. He was born in London and educated at Eton and the military academy at Sandhurst. He served in the Boer War with the Coldstream Guards, then returned to his family's Irish estate, Dunsany Castle, near **Tara**, to devote himself to farming and writing. After his marriage in 1904, he published *The Gods of Pegana* (1905), a book of short stories. This was followed by *Time and the Gods* (1906) and *The Sword of*

Welleran (1908). His first play, *The Glittering Gate* (1909), was produced at the **Abbey Theatre** (*M*. 210), while his first London production was *The Gods of the Mountain*, which was presented at the Haymarket Theatre in 1911. Three later plays were produced at the Abbey Theatre: *King Argimenes and the Unknown Warrior* (1911), *A Night at an Inn* (1919), and *The Tents of the Arabs* (1920). At the outbreak of World War I in 1914, he joined the Royal Inniskilling Fusiliers. In 1916, on a visit to Ireland, he came to the aid of British soldiers in the Easter Rising and was wounded. He later saw frontline combat in France. An international chess player, big game hunter, and entertaining lecturer, his books of fantasy and make-believe were popular, but he never achieved scholarly critical success. While friendly with WBY, who supported the productions of his plays at the Abbey Theatre, he did not embrace the nationalist aspirations of the majority of Irish writers. He remained intensely loyal to England, and his writings were essentially apolitical. His collection *Selections from the Writings of Lord Dunsany* was published by the **Cuala Press** in 1912.

REFERENCES: Amory, Mark. *A Biography of Lord Dunsany*. London: Collins, 1972; Bierstadt, Edward Hale. *Dunsany the Dramatist*. Boston: Little, Brown, 1917; Boyd, Ernest A. *Appreciations and Depreciations: Irish Literary Studies*. New York: John Lane, 1918; Saul, George Brandon. "Strange Gods in Far Places: The Short Stories of Lord Dunsany." *Arizona Quarterly* 19 (autumn 1963).

DURAS (Irish: *Dubh-ros*) [dark promontory], **County Clare**, between **Kinvara** and **Aughanish**. Duras was the summer home of Comte Florimond de Basterot of Bordeaux. There, WBY, **Lady Gregory**, and **Edward Martyn** strolled in the gardens and formulated their ideas for an Irish National Theatre (*A*. 380, 381). Duras House is now a Youth Hostel. In *The King's Threshold* (*CPl*. 117, 118), the poet **Seanchan**, who is on a hunger strike, is offered dulse (edible seaweed) and pigeons' eggs from Duras. In "Dust Hath Closed Helen's Eye" (*MY*. 28), WBY quotes an old man from Duras who believed that the legendary **Mary Hynes**, who lived in the area, had been taken away by the **Sídhe**.

REFERENCE: McGarry, James P. *Place Names in the Writings of William Butler Yeats*. Gerrards Cross: Colin Smythe, 1976.

E

EADE'S GRAMMAR SCHOOL. *See* **SLIGO GRAMMAR SCHOOL**.

EARDLEY CRESCENT, Yeats family residence. When **John B. Yeats** and his family returned to London in 1887, they rented a house at 58 Eardley Crescent in South Kensington. The house was situated behind the newly built Earl's Court Exhibition Hall, where Buffalo Bill and his American Indians were performing. The family was not happy living there, the house being old, dark, and noisy. Soon after their arrival, **Susan Yeats** suffered the first of her strokes and was taken to her sister's home in the north of England. She did not return until after the family moved to **Blenheim Road**, March 1888. The house in Eardley Crescent was owned by Mrs. Wheeler, and previous occupants had been the Dublin-born Keeling family. The house is described by Elsa D'Esterre-Keeling in her book *In Thoughtland and in Dreamland* (1890).

REFERENCES: Murphy, William M. *Family Secrets: William Butler Yeats and His Relatives.* Syracuse, N.Y.: Syracuse University Press, 1995; Murphy, William M. *Prodigal Father: The Life of John Butler Yeats (1839–1922).* Ithaca and London: Cornell University Press, 1978.

EARLY, BIDDY, local character and folk healer associated with **Ballylee, Galway** (county). She lived in a cottage about two miles from Feakle, thirteen miles southeast of **Coole Park**. Her cottage still stands by the roadside. In "Dust Hath Closed Helen's Eye" (*MY*. 22), WBY claims to have visited the tower at Ballylee to speak with the miller about Biddy Early and her miraculous cures. Most of his article "Ireland Bewitched" (*UP2*. 168–183) is devoted to the stories told about her and her association with the **Sídhe**, and he refers to her in his poem "I walked among the Seven Woods of Coole" (*CP*. 469). Although she took little money for her cures, Biddy Early accepted gifts of spirits, tobacco, and other goods, so that she was reputed to be a wealthy woman—hence, the remark in *The Pot of Broth* (*CPl.* 104) that Sibby will be as rich as Biddy Early now that she has the miraculous stone. **Lady Gregory** accompanied WBY on his visits to local people to enquire about Biddy Early's healing powers.

REFERENCE: Gregory, Lady, and Yeats, W. B. *Visions and Beliefs in the West of Ireland, Collected and Arranged by Lady Gregory; with Two Essays and Notes by W. B. Yeats.* 1920. Reprint, New York: Oxford University Press, 1970.

ECHTGE. *See* **SLIEVE ECHTGE**.

EDAIN. *See* **ÉTAIN**.

EDEN. According to the Judaic-Christian bible, Eden was the paradise garden created by God for the first humans, **Adam** and Eve. When they ate of the forbidden fruit of the tree of knowledge, they were expelled from the garden. No specific location for Eden has been found, although claims have been made for its location, particularly in Mesopotamia. WBY makes references to Eden in the poems ''Veronica's Napkin'' (*CP.* 270) and ''I walked among the Seven Woods of Coole'' (*CP.* 469).

EDGEWORTH, MARIA (1767–1849), novelist. Maria Edgeworth was born at Black Bourton, Oxfordshire, England, but moved to Ireland to the family home in Edgeworthstown when she was fifteen. Among the eldest of a large family, with many stepbrothers and -sisters (her father, Richard Lovell Edgeworth, married four times and had twenty-two children), she assisted her father in the running of his large Irish estate. Together, they developed a humane approach to their tenants and devised a model system of education for the younger children in the household. Encouraged by her father, Maria Edgeworth published *Letters to Literary Ladies* (1795) and *The Parent's Assistant* (1796). She collaborated with her father in the writing of *Practical Education* (1798). These books on model parenting and education were popular and influential in England and America. Her major novel, *Castle Rackrent*, in which she described several generations of Anglo-Irish gentry through the eyes of a faithful retainer, was published in 1800. It established Edgeworth as the first regional novelist, and she became a literary celebrity in London and in Europe. In addition to her duties on her father's estate, she maintained a prolific output of novels, short stories, and children's stories, including *Belinda* (1801), *Ennui* (1809), *The Absentee* (1812), and *Ormond* (1817). Her *Tales of Fashionable Life* (1809–12), published in six volumes, earned her a steady income. After her father's death in 1817, she devoted herself increasingly to her tenants, and during the Great Famine, she worked tirelessly to relieve their hardship and suffering. In her Anglo-Irish novels *Castle Rackrent, The Absentee*, and *Ormond*, Maria Edgeworth attacked with skill, subtlety, and humor the irresponsibility of the landlord class and revealed to English readers the reality of a life in Ireland of which they were largely unaware. In "J. M. Synge and the Ireland of His Time" (*EI.* 322), WBY compared Maria Edgeworth to **J. M. Synge**, and he included *Castle Rackrent* in his list of the "Best Irish Books" (*UP1.* 385). Nevertheless, in his 1896 review of *The Life of William Carleton* (*UP1.* 394–97), he was dismissive of her Irishness, claiming that because Maria Edgeworth came from a privileged class, she knew little about Ireland and the Gaelic tradition. He asserted that her writing lacked national character, since she wrote only of the upper classes, without the support of history or folklorists.

REFERENCES: Butler, Marilyn. *Maria Edgeworth: A Literary Biography*. Oxford: Clarendon, 1972; Flanagan, Thomas. *The Irish Novelists 1800–1850*. New York: Columbia University Press, 1959; Harden, O. Elizabeth McW. *Maria Edgeworth's Art of Prose Fiction*. The Hague: Mouton, 1971; Hawthorne, Mark D. *Doubt and Dogma in Maria Edgeworth*. Gainesville: University of Florida Press, 1967; Newcomer, James. *Maria Edgeworth the Novelist, 1768–1849*. Fort Worth: Texas Christian University Press, 1967.

EDITH VILLAS, Yeats family residence. When **John B. Yeats** and his family returned to London in October 1874, they lived at 14 Edith Villas, a small house in North End (now West Kensington). WBY's youngest sister, Jane Grace Yeats, was born there 29 August 1875, but she died of bronchial pneumonia nine months later. When the rest of the family returned to **Sligo** for extended periods of time, WBY stayed with the Earle family at **Farnham Royal** in Buckinghamshire while his father painted nearby at Burnham Beeches. John B. Yeats took the opportunity to give WBY his first lessons in geography and chemistry. When the family returned to Edith Villas in 1877, WBY attended the **Godolphin School**, Hammersmith. 14 Edith Villas, which the Yeats family left in early 1879, was destroyed by German bombing during World War II. WBY recalls his childhood experiences at Edith Villas and Godolphin School in *Reveries over Childhood and Youth* (*A.* 29–42).

EGLINTON, JOHN. *See* **MAGEE, W[ILLIAM] K[IRKPATRICK]**.

ÉIRE, name commonly used for modern Ireland. Éire is derived from Ériu, a queen of the **Tuatha dé Danaan**. When the Milesians invaded Ireland, she promised that the land would always belong to the sons of Míl if it were named after her. See "To the Rose upon the Rood of Time" (*CP.* 35), "The Dedication to a Book of Stories Selected from the Irish Novelists" (*CP.* 51), and "Into the Twilight" (*CP.* 65).

REFERENCES: Dames, Michael. *Mythic Ireland*. 1992. Reprint, New York: Thames & Hudson, 1996; Ellis, Peter Berresford. *Dictionary of Celtic Mythology*. New York: Oxford University Press, 1992; Green, Miranda J. *Dictionary of Celtic Myth and Legend*. London: Thames & Hudson, 1992; Mac Cana, Proinsias. *Celtic Mythology*. Feltham, Middlesex: Newnes, 1983.

EITHNE INGUBA, mythological figure. In WBY's plays *The Only Jealousy of Emer* and *The Death of Cuchulain*, Eithne Inguba is the mistress of **Cuchulain**. In the first of the plays, she is invited by **Emer** to kiss the inert body of Cuchulain and to bring it back to life. Later, after his wife Emer has renounced his love, Cuchulain recovers and turns to his mistress for love and support. In *The Death of Cuchulain*, she is the treacherous messenger who, under the spell of the **Sídhe**, is sent to persuade Cuchulain to fight before morning. In the first production of *The Only Jealousy of Emer* in Amsterdam, April 1922, the part of Eithne Inguba was played by Sara Heyblom. The role of Eithne Inguba in the first production of *Fighting the Waves*, a prose version of *The Only Jealousy of Emer*, August 1929, was taken by Shelah Richards. In the first production of *The Death of Cuchulain* by the Lyric Theatre Company, December 1949, the part was acted by Ronnie Masterson.

ELGAR, SIR EDWARD (1857–1934), composer. He lived most of his life in Worcester, England, near where he was born. His father was an organist and music seller, and although he had some violin lessons, Elgar was largely self-taught. Accomplished in playing a number of instruments, he composed works of wide variety, for wind instruments, strings, and voices. His early reputation was based mainly on his choral works, and he only came to the first rank of composers with his cantata *Caractacus* (1898), the *"Enigma" Variations* (1899), and the oratorio *The Dream of Gerontius* (1900). **George Moore** was impressed with *Caractacus* when he heard it in Leeds in 1898. In 1901, he invited Elgar to compose incidental music for the first production of *Diarmuid and Grania*, written by Moore and WBY. George Moore's first request was for music to accompany the death of **Diarmuid**. This became a funeral march, but Elgar also composed horn calls and fragments of incidental music for the play. In *Dramatis Personae* (*A.* 443), WBY writes that Elgar's funeral march was one of only two things he could remember from the production! Moore hoped that Elgar would collaborate with him on an opera and pursued the project from 1901 until 1914, but nothing materialized. A recording of Elgar's music for *Diarmuid and Grania* (which he published as *Grania and Diarmid*), performed by the City of Birmingham Symphony Orchestra, conducted by Sir Simon Rattle, is available on EMI Classics.

REFERENCE: Sadie, Stanley, ed. *The Grove Concise Dictionary of Music*. London: Macmillan, 1988.

ELIOT, T[HOMAS] S[TEARNS] (1888–1965), poet, playwright, and literary critic. He was born in St. Louis, Missouri, and educated at Harvard, the Sorbonne, and Oxford University. In 1914, he decided to make his home in England, becoming a British subject in 1927. After a brief career as a teacher and as a clerk with the Foreign and Colonial Department of Lloyd's Bank, he joined the publishing firm of Faber and Faber in 1935. He remained with the company until his death. He is regarded as one of the most influential poets of the twentieth century, making, in the dry style and despairing content of his poetry, a profound impact on the younger British writers, among them **W. H. Auden, Stephen Spender**, and **Louis MacNeice**. He was a considerable critic and playwright and successfully revived the writing of plays in verse for the contemporary theater, including *Murder in the Cathedral* (1935), *The Family Reunion* (1939), and *The Cocktail Party* (1950). Among his outstanding poems are "The Love Song of J. Alfred Prufrock" (1915), "The Waste Land" (1922), "Ash Wednesday" (1930), and the *Four Quartets* (1936–42). He was awarded the **Nobel Prize for Literature** and the Order of Merit in 1948. WBY and he had a mutual friend in **Ezra Pound**. He was fundamentally opposed to WBY in his philosophical stance, and in his lecture "After Strange Gods," published in 1934, he was critical of the older poet's supernatural interests. During the 1930s, however, he met with WBY on several occasions and came to respect him as a poet of the highest order, and in an address, "The Poetry of W. B. Yeats," given at the **Abbey Theatre**, June 1940, he spoke warmly of WBY's generosity to him. Although he recognized his genius, WBY was out of sympathy with the pessimism of much of Eliot's poetry (*LE*. 97–100). In his introduction to *The Oxford Book of Modern Verse* (*LE*. 189–92), in which he included seven poems by Eliot, he writes of his plainness and coldness, his apparent lack of imagination, and his rejection of rhythm and metaphor in his early poetry. Fifteen titles by Eliot, including *Prufrock and Other Observations* (1917), *The Waste Land* (1923), *After Strange Gods* (1934), *Murder in the Cathedral* (1935), *Collected Poems: 1909–1935* (1936), and *The Use of Poetry and the Use of Criticism* (1937), were in WBY's library (*OS*. nos. 610–25a).

REFERENCES: Frazer, G. S. "W. B. Yeats and T. S. Eliot." In *T. S. Eliot: A Symposium for His Seventieth Birthday*, ed. Neville Braybrooke. New York: Farrar, Straus & Cudahy, 1958; Lightfoot, Marjorie. "*Purgatory* and *The Family Reunion*: In Pursuit of Prosodic Description." *Modern Drama*, 1964; North, Michael. *The Political Aesthetic of Yeats, Eliot and Pound*. Cambridge: Cambridge University Press, 1991; Parkinson, Thomas. *W. B. Yeats: The Later Poetry*. Berkeley: University of California Press, 1964; Smith, Stan. *The Origin of Modernism: Eliot, Pound, Yeats and the Rhetoric of Renewal*. New York: Harvester Wheatsheaf, 1994; Stead, C. K. *The New Poetic: Yeats to Eliot*. Philadelphia: University of Pennsylvania Press, 1987; Stead, C. K. *Pound, Yeats, Eliot, and the Modernist Movement*. New Brunswick, N.J.: Rutgers University Press, 1986; Surette, Leon. *The Birth of Modernism: Ezra Pound, T. S. Eliot, W. B. Yeats, and the Occult*. Buffalo: McGill-Queen's University Press, 1993; Wright, George T. *The Poet in the Poem: The Personae of Eliot, Yeats and Pound*. Berkeley: University of California Press, 1960.

ELLIS, EDWIN J[OHN] (1848–1916), poet and painter. The son of Alexander Sharp Ellis (1814–90), a noted Scottish mathematician and natural scientist, Edwin J. Ellis became a close friend and associate of **John B. Yeats** after they met at Heatherley's Art School, London, in 1868. Together they formed a painting group called "The Brotherhood," which included **J. T. Nettleship**. Ellis visited the Yeats family in **Fitzroy Road**, but his brash manner irritated **Susan**

Yeats, and she discouraged his visits. He married in Italy in 1870, but his wife died a year later, and he returned to London in 1872. He married again in 1882, a German widow, Phillipa Keller Edwards, and when the Yeats family returned to London in the late 1880s, he renewed his friendship with them. He took a keen interest in WBY's early writings and became a regular member of the **Rhymers' Club**. With Ellis, WBY embarked on the ambitious three-volume *Works of William Blake, Poetic, Symbolic and Critical* (1893), an important formative experience for the young writer. Despite some interference from Ellis's hysterical wife, who thought WBY had some mesmeric power over her and refused to allow him to visit her husband, the work on **Blake** was the most important editorial work of WBY's life. Appreciative of the collaboration, WBY reviewed two collections of Ellis's verse, *Fate in Arcadia and Other Poems* (1892) (*UP1*. 234–37) and *Seen in Three Days* (1893) (*UP1*. 317–20). In May 1892, Ellis contributed the frontispiece to a second issue of *The Wanderings of Oisin*, and in 1895, WBY dedicated to him a revised version of the poem. He based his verse drama *The King's Threshold* on Ellis's *Sancan the Bard* (1895), although WBY claimed he had originally given the story to Ellis. In 1905, Ellis and his wife settled in Darmstadt, Germany. There, he completed his two-volume *Poetical Works of William Blake* (1906) and published a biography, *The Real Blake*, in 1907. In 1911, he suffered the first of a series of severe strokes. WBY visited him in Folkestone in August 1913 but found him paralyzed and unable to speak. He died in Germany, November 1916. When they worked on Blake together, WBY and Ellis spent much time in each other's company, researching and arguing over interpretations and conducting psychic experiments. It is clear from those occasions when WBY quotes Ellis that he was profoundly influenced by the older poet. He dismissed Ellis as a painter, finding his work academic and commonplace but thought highly of a number of his poems, quoting from them and encouraging others to read them (*A*. 159–64). He admired Ellis's psychic intuition and his mental ability to express deep philosophical issues in symbolic or abstract form (*M*. 28–31). Nevertheless, he wrote a guarded review of Ellis's poetry collection *Seen in Three Days*, being particularly bothered by the obscurity of the symbolism (*UP1*. 317–20). He included an excerpt from one of Ellis's long poems, ''Himself,'' in *The Oxford Book of Modern Verse* (1936).

REFERENCE: Murphy, William M. *Prodigal Father: The Life of John Butler Yeats (1839–1922)*. Ithaca, N.Y.: Cornell University Press, 1978.

ELSINORE [LODGE], villa at **Rosses Point** belonging to WBY's great-uncle **William Middleton**. Built by a smuggler, John Black, the house passed to a family called Cooper, and then to William Middleton. It was reputed to be haunted. The Middleton family spent summers at Elsinore and winters at Avena House. As a boy, WBY visited the house and played with his Middleton cousins (*A*. 15). He rowed in the mouth of the Garravogue River and fished for skate and herring. He listened to the mysterious stories told by the sailors on the wharf and on the boats that ran between **Sligo** (town) and Rosses Point. Through the Middletons, he was introduced to local folklore, while his cousin **Lucy Middleton**, who was gifted with second sight, told him stories about the supernatural. Later, Elsinore Lodge passed to his reclusive cousin **Henry Middleton**, whom WBY recalls in ''Three Songs to the One Burden'' (*CP*. 371).

REFERENCE: McGarry, James P. *Place Names in the Writings of William Butler Yeats*. Gerrards Cross: Colin Smythe, 1976.

EMAIN MACHA [The Twins of Macha], royal seat of the ancient province of **Ulster**. Emain Macha features prominently in the Ulster Cycle of mythological stories since it is the home of **Conchubar** and the **Red Branch**. The name derives from Macha, a name shared by three war goddesses in Irish mythology. One foresees the terrible events of the epic *Táin Bó Cuailnge* and dies of a broken heart on one of the twelve plains cleared by her husband and named after her. The second Macha rules over Ireland, forcefully gaining dominance over all challengers to her reign and punishing them by forcing them to build a fort at Emain Macha. The third Macha marries a mortal, and when her husband leaves to go to the large assembly of Ulstermen, she advises him not to boast of her there. Her husband ignores her request, and when he sees the king's horses at the assembly, he claims that his wife can race any of them and win. Macha is sent for and is compelled to race against the royal horses. She wins, but as she crosses the finish line, she gives birth to twins. Dying from pain and exhaustion, she lays a curse on the men of Ulster—that in times of trouble, they will suffer the same pains as she and that every adult male will be as weak as a woman in childbirth. Thus, when **Queen Maeve** attacks Ulster, all the men are prostrate. It is left to the youthful champion **Cuchulain** to defend the province against the might of **Connacht**. The site of Emain Macha is thought to be Navan Fort, a hill about two miles outside the modern city of Armagh (Irish: *Ard Macha*), where there are remains of circular ramparts. It may be, however, that the twin hills of Navan Fort and Armagh constitute the original site. Recent excavations suggest that Emain Macha flourished from 300 B.C. to A.D. 450 and that the Heroic Age in Ireland ended with its destruction. In *The Death of Cuchulain* (*CPl*. 695), **Eithne Inguba** reports that barns and houses at Emain Macha are being burned by the men of Connacht. Emain Macha is referred to in the poems ''The Madness of King Goll'' (*CP*. 17) and ''Baile and Aillinn'' (*CP*. 459). Navan Fort has been recently opened to the public, and there is a fine visitor's center adjacent to the site.

REFERENCES: Dames, Michael. *Mythic Ireland*. 1992. Reprint, New York: Thames & Hudson, 1996; Ellis, Peter Berresford. *Dictionary of Celtic Mythology*. New York: Oxford University Press, 1992; Green, Miranda J. *Dictionary of Celtic Myth and Legend*. London: Thames & Hudson, 1992; Mac Cana, Proinsias. *Celtic Mythology*. Feltham, Middlesex: Newnes, 1983; McGarry, James P. *Place Names in the Writings of William Butler Yeats*. Gerrards Cross: Colin Smythe, 1976.

EMER, wife to **Cuchulain**. She was the daughter of Forgall Manach and was reputedly chosen as his wife by Cuchulain because of the size of her bladder—a large bladder was thought to predict fertility. The relationship with her husband was strong but stormy, chiefly because he was attractive to women, especially the **Sídhe**. Before his death, Cuchulain had a vision of his wife Emer being thrown from the ramparts at **Emain Macha**. He hurried there to find her unharmed. When she attempted to dissuade him from returning to the battle, he disobeyed her and went to his death. Emer appears as a major character in four of WBY's plays on the life and death of Cuchulain. She is a loyal defender of her husband's bravery and courage in *The Green Helmet*. In *The Only Jealousy of Emer*, and its later version *Fighting the Waves*, she renounces her husband's love so that he may return safely from the land of the dead. In *The Death of Cuchulain*, she sends a letter with **Eithne Inguba**, her husband's mistress, warning him not to fight until **Conall Caernach** arrives with reinforcements. He fails to heed her warning, and after his death at the climax of the play, she performs a dance expressing a range of emotions, from rage to triumph. Among those who played the role of Emer at the **Abbey Theatre** were **Sara Allgood** and Eileen Crowe.

REFERENCES: Ellis, Peter Berresford. *Dictionary of Celtic Mythology*. New York: Oxford University Press, 1992; Green, Miranda J. *Dictionary of Celtic Myth and Legend*. London: Thames & Hudson, 1992.

EMERY, MRS. EDWARD. *See* **FARR, FLORENCE**.

EMMET, ROBERT (1778–1803), patriot. He was born in Dublin, the son of a Protestant physician who was in the service of the Lord Lieutenant. His older brother, Thomas Addis Emmet, who was a member of the United Irishmen, was arrested for his part in the 1798 Rebellion and exiled from Ireland. In 1793, at the age of fifteen, Emmet entered **Trinity College**, Dublin, and, following his brother's example, joined the United Irishmen. As a protest at the Lord Chancellor's attempt to assess the extent of student support for the nationalist organization, he left Trinity in 1802 and traveled in Europe. In France, he and other United Irishmen planned a further rebellion in Ireland. He met with Napoleon and Talleyrand to enlist help from the French, but when it was not forthcoming, he returned to Ireland to organize the rebellion himself. He lived in hiding in Dublin, secretly buying guns and recruiting volunteers. In July 1803, with a small, disorganized army, he led an abortive attack on **Dublin Castle**. The brutal killing of Lord Kilwarden, the Lord Chief Justice, turned the people of Dublin against Emmet, and he was forced into hiding in County Wicklow. In August 1803, he was arrested while trying to see his sweetheart, Sarah Curran, daughter of the eminent lawyer John Philpot Curran. After being tried and found guilty of treason, he was hanged in a public street in Dublin. Robert Emmet was a passionate visionary who acted without guile. His plans for rebellion were foolhardy and known to the English. After his execution, he became one of the heroes of Ireland's struggle for independence, with many ballads and songs written about his idealism and courage. In *Reveries over Childhood and Youth* (*A.* 21), WBY claims that his great-grandfather, **Rev. John Yeats**, had been a friend of Emmet and was suspected of being an accomplice in the rebellion. He is the country scholar that WBY refers to in "Pardon, old Fathers" (*CP.* 113). For WBY, Emmet became a symbol of that heroic Ireland that he wished modern Ireland to emulate. His longest and most sustained comments on him were made at the Emmet Centenary celebrations sponsored by **Clan-na-Gael** in New York, 28 February 1904 (*UP2.* 311–27). In his speech, WBY described in rich detail Emmet's rebellion, his heroism on the scaffold, and the development of a national consciousness inspired by his example. In "September 1913" (*CP.* 120), he measures the Dublin merchant class against Emmet's ideals and finds it wanting.

REFERENCE: Guiney, Louise Imogen. *Robert Emmet: A Survey of His Rebellion and His Romance*. London: David Nutt, 1904.

EMPEDOCLES (c. 495–435 B.C.), Greek philosopher. He believed all matter to be composed of four underived and indestructible substances—earth, air, fire, and water, joined together by love (Concord) and separated by strife (Discord). He claimed that motion is the only change possible and that apparent changes in an object are in fact changes of position in the basic particles. Thus, he first stated a principle central to modern physics. The impact of Empedocles's ideas on his society is referred to by WBY in "The Gyres" (*CP.* 337), and he cites Empedocles on the principles of Discord and Concord in "The Great Wheel" (*AV.* 67–68).

REFERENCES: Jaspers, Karl. *The Great Philosophers*. Trans. Edith Ehrlich and Leonard Ehrlich. New York: Harcourt Brace, 1994; Kingsley, Peter. *Ancient Philosophy, Mystery, and Magic: Empedocles and Pythagorean Tradition*. Oxford: Clarendon, 1995; Smertenko, Clara E. M. *On the Interpretation of Empedocles*. New York: Garland, 1980.

EOCHAID, KING, High King of Ireland. In a board game, his wife **Étain** is won by **Midhir**, king of the **Sídhe**, and together they fly away as birds to Midhir's castle at Bri Leith. Eochaid pursues them but is fooled into accepting Étain's identical daughter as his wife while Étain stays with Midhir. In another version of the story, Eochaid forces Midhir to give up his wife. In "The Two Kings" (*CP.* 503), Eochaid discovers his wife's intense loyalty to him.

REFERENCES: Dames, Michael. *Mythic Ireland*. 1992. Reprint, New York: Thames & Hudson, 1996; Ellis, Peter Berresford. *Dictionary of Celtic Mythology*. New York: Oxford University Press, 1992; Mac Cana, Proinsias. *Celtic Mythology*. Feltham, Middlesex: Newnes, 1983; McGarry, James P. *Place Names in the Writings of William Butler Yeats*. Gerrards Cross: Colin Smythe, 1976.

EPHESUS, ancient Greek city of Asia Minor. It was one of the wealthiest cities of Asia. It was taken by **Alexander the Great** in 334 B.C. After his death, when his empire was in decline, the city was captured by the Romans. Ephesus became a center of early Christianity and was visited by St. Paul, who addressed one of his letters to the congregation there. According to legend, seven sleepers were immured in a cave near Ephesus during the persecution of the Christians by the Roman emperor Decius (A.D. 201–51). They awoke 200 years later and were taken before Emperor Theodosius II (A.D. 401–50), their story confirming his faith. The decline of Alexander's empire and the legend of the sleepers are referred to by WBY in the poem "On a Picture of a Black Centaur by Edmund Dulac" (*CP*. 242).

ERASMUS SMITH HIGH SCHOOL. When the Yeats family returned to Ireland in 1881, WBY attended the Erasmus Smith High School, Harcourt Street, Dublin. The school was one of a number founded in Ireland by the philanthropist Erasmus Smith (1611–91), a London merchant. The school undertook to educate local children "in the fear of God, and good literature, and to speak the English tongue." In 1669, the Erasmus Smith High Schools were placed under Episcopalian supervision by Royal Charter. At sixteen and a half, the tall, gangling WBY was older than the other boys in his class, who regarded him as something of an oddity. Possibly because of poor eyesight, he appeared standoffish, and he had difficulty accepting opinions other than his own. Among his classmates were **John Eglinton** and **F. J. Gregg**. The atmosphere in the classroom was informal, but the students worked hard. WBY, a naturally bright student, found the workload at the school demanding, especially in Classics, and he was poor at literature because grammar was emphasized at the expense of expressive content. Games and hobbies were discouraged—a blow to WBY's interest in insect collecting. At school, WBY discovered chess, a hobby that brought him into contact with **Charles Johnston**, with whom he later formed the **Dublin Hermetic Society**. When he left the Erasmus Smith High School in December 1883, he convinced his father that his math and Classics were not up to standard for entrance to **Trinity College**, Dublin, and he elected to go to the **Metropolitan College of Art**.

REFERENCES: Christy, M. A. "Yeats's Teacher." *Times Literary Supplement*, 20 May 1965; Eglinton, John. "Yeats and His Story." In *Irish Literary Portraits*. London: Macmillan, 1935.

ERCOLE, DUKE OF FERRARA (1431–1505), member of the powerful Este family who ruled **Ferrara** in northern Italy, 1208–1598. Ercole, like other members of his family, was a generous patron of the arts. His court became the most brilliant in Europe. Literature and art were patronized, and industry and commerce flourished. Duke Ercole's daughter, Beatrice, was considered one of the most beautiful and astute women of the Italian Renaissance. As wife of the duke of Milan, she, too, was a patroness of the arts and attracted to her court many prominent writers and painters, among them **Baldassare Castiglione**. In "To a Wealthy Man who promised a Second Subscription to the Dublin Municipal

Gallery if it were proved the People wanted Pictures'' (*CP*. 119), WBY cites Duke Ercole as an example of a patron who intrinsically valued the arts.

REFERENCES: Gundersheimer, Werner L., ed. *Art and Life at the Court of Ercole I d'Este*. Geneve: Librairie Droz, 1972; Salvadori, Corinna. *Yeats and Castiglione: Poet and Courtier*. Dublin: Allen Figgis, 1965.

ERVINE, ST. JOHN [GREER] (1883–1971), dramatist, novelist, and critic. St. John Ervine was born in Belfast and started work at the age of fourteen in an insurance office. In 1900, he moved to London, where he met **George Bernard Shaw** and found success as a writer. After four of his early plays—*Mixed Marriage* (1911), *The Magnanimous Lover* (1912), *The Critics* (1913), and *The Orangeman* (1914)—had been produced at the **Abbey Theatre**, he was appointed manager in the fall of 1915. It was an inopportune appointment. As a Protestant from the North of Ireland, Ervine was opposed to Home Rule. He was openly critical of the Dublin critics, and when relationships between him and the Abbey actors became hostile, he was dismissed by WBY and **Lady Gregory** in May 1916. He went into military service and in 1918 was severely wounded. He settled in Devon, England, where he maintained a steady output of work, including plays, theater reviews, and biographies. His plays continued to be produced at the Abbey Theatre, among them *Boyd's Shop* (1936), *William John Mawhinney* (1940), and *Friends and Relations* (1941). He wrote adulatory biographies of the **Ulster** leaders Lord Edward Carson and Lord Craigavon, together with an unsympathetic account of the life of **Oscar Wilde** and a massive biography of his friend George Bernard Shaw. He was invited by WBY to be a founder member of the **Irish Academy of Letters** (*WL*. 717, 801).

REFERENCES: Boyd, John. ''St. John Ervine, a Biographical Note.'' *Threshold* 25 (summer 1974); Ervine, St. John. *Some Impression of My Elders*. New York: Macmillan, 1922; Ervine, St. John. ''After the Abbey.'' *New Ireland* 2, 4 March 1916; Hogan, Robert, ed. *Dictionary of Irish Literature*. Rev. ed. Westport, Conn.: Greenwood, 1996; Hunt, Hugh. *The Abbey: Ireland's National Theatre, 1904–1979*. Dublin: Gill & Macmillan, 1979; Ireland, Denis. ''Red Brick City and Its Dramatist: A Note on St. John Ervine.'' *Envoy* 1 (March 1950).

ESSAYS AND INTRODUCTIONS, collection of essays by WBY. The volume was published by the Macmillan Company in 1961, with the approval of **Mrs. W. B. Yeats**. It consisted principally of essays previously published in *Ideas of Good and Evil* (1903) and *The Cutting of an Agate* (1919). The introduction to the collection had been written by WBY in 1937, but publication was suspended because of World War II.

ESTRANGEMENT, collection of entries from WBY's diary. The volume was published by the **Cuala Press** in 1926 in a limited edition of 300 copies. It consisted of fifty entries from a diary that WBY kept in 1909. *Estrangement* was included in *Autobiographies* (1955).

ÉTAIN, fairy goddess. She is married to **Midhir,** king of the **Sídhe.** His first wife, jealous of Midhir's love for Étain, changes her into a fly, and she is blown to the palace of the High King of **Ulster,** where she is swallowed in a cup of wine by Edar, wife of one of the Ulster heroes. Étain is then reborn as a mortal child. When she becomes a woman, she is married to **Eochaid,** High King of Ireland. Midhir pursues her and eventually wins her back from Eochaid in a game of chess. In some versions of the story, after Midhir has taken her back to his **sídh,** Eochaid threatens to destroy the fairy mound. Terrified, Midhir returns her to the High King. In ***Deirdre*** (*CPl.* 177–78), the Musicians sing a song about Queen Étain and the extremes of passion, while in ***The Land of Heart's Desire*** (*CPl.* 55), the young wife, who is torn between the love of her husband and a desire to be with the fairies, claims to have been reading the story of Étain and her journey to the timeless land of Faery.

REFERENCES: Dames, Michael. *Mythic Ireland.* 1992. Reprint, New York: Thames & Hudson, 1996; Ellis, Peter Berresford. *Dictionary of Celtic Mythology.* New York: Oxford University Press, 1992; Green, Miranda J. *Dictionary of Celtic Myth and Legend.* London: Thames & Hudson, 1992; Mac Cana, Proinsias. *Celtic Mythology.* Feltham, Middlesex: Newnes, 1983.

EUROPA, princess of ancient Greece. Europa was the daughter of Agenor, king of Tyre, and sister of Cadmus. According to legend, Zeus appeared to her in the shape of a white bull and carried her off to Crete. There, she bore him three sons, **Minos,** Sarpedon, and **Rhadamanthus** Later, she married the king of Crete, who adopted the children. See also "Crazy Jane Reproved" (*CP.* 291).

EUROTAS, river in ancient Greece on which stood the city-state of **Sparta. Leda** was reputedly bathing in the Eurotas when she was visited by Zeus in the guise of a swan. In the poem "Lullaby" (*CP.* 300), WBY refers to the legend.

F
_____

FAERY CHILD, character in WBY's play *The Land of Heart's Desire*. In the play, the Faery Child sings of a paradise in which all are happy and no one gets old. She is welcomed by the **Bruin** family and with her mesmeric dancing entices Mary, the young bride, to leave her husband and follow her to fairyland, the Land of Heart's Desire. In the first production at the Avenue Theatre, London, March 1894, the Faery Child was played by Dorothy Paget, daughter of **H. M. Paget** and niece to **Florence Farr**.

FAIR HEAD (Irish: *Beann Mhor*) [large peak], rocky promontory in County Antrim, in the northeast of Ireland. In *The Countess Cathleen* (*CPl.* 30), the **First Merchant** convinces the **Countess** of her misfortune when he tells her that her ships are becalmed off the coast of Fair Head.
  REFERENCE: McGarry, James P. *Place Names in the Writings of William Butler Yeats.* Gerrards Cross: Colin Smythe, 1976.

FAIRY AND FOLK TALES OF THE IRISH PEASANTRY, collection of stories and legends. The anthology was selected and edited by WBY and published in 1888 by Walter Scott, London, Thomas Whittaker, New York, and W. J. Gage and Company, Toronto. It was dedicated to **AE** and included short stories and anecdotes by many of the major Irish writers, including **William Allingham, William Carleton,** and **Douglas Hyde**. The introduction and notes were by WBY (*Pl.* 3–22).
  REFERENCES: O'Shea, Edward. "Yeats's Revisions in Fairy and Folk Tales." *Southern Folklore Quarterly* 38 (Summer 1974). Thuente, Mary Helen. *W. B. Yeats and Irish Folklore.* Dublin: Gill & Macmillan, 1980.

FALIAS, mythical city. According to tradition, the **Tuatha dé Danaan** came to Ireland from the cities of Falias, Findrias, Gorias, and Murias, bringing with them their talismans of cunning and magic lore. From Falias, they brought the Stone of Destiny (Irish: *Lia Fail*), which was placed at **Tara**. It roared in acceptance of a new king of Ireland. From Gorias, they brought the Spear of **Lugh**. Anyone who carried it was invincible. From Findrias, they brought the Sword of Nuada. No one ever escaped from its deadly blade. From Murias was brought the Dagda's Cauldron, which satisfied all who partook of it. WBY refers to the four cities in "Baile and Aillinn" (*CP.* 459).

REFERENCES: Ellis, Peter Berresford. *Dictionary of Celtic Mythology.* New York: Oxford University Press, 1992; Mac Cana, Proinsias. *Celtic Mythology.* Feltham, Middlesex: Newnes, 1983.

FAND, woman of the **Sídhe**. Fand is the wife of **Manannán**, sea god and ruler of the country of the dead. In WBY's *At the Hawk's Well*, she appears as the Guardian of the Well, and as the Woman of the Sídhe in *The Only Jealousy of Emer*. In both plays, Fand attempts to distract **Cuchulain**. In *At the Hawk's Well*, she transforms from the guardian of the waters of immortality into a hawk-woman who successfully distracts the youthful hero from the waters. In *The Only Jealousy of Emer*, she promises the **Ghost of Cuchulain** an eternity of love in the Otherworld and relief from mortal cares. He is about to go with her, but his wife **Emer** renounces his love, and he rejects the Woman of the Sídhe. In a version of the story told by **Lady Gregory** in *Cuchulain of Muirthemne* (1902), Cuchulain goes with Fand to the Otherworld. When his wife arrives with fifty women to bring him back, Cuchulain insists he will always love his wife and cannot understand why Emer will not let him enjoy the company of Fand. Manannán, the deserted husband, causes Cuchulain to fall ill for a year, administers a drink of forgetfulness to him and to Emer, and passes his cloak between Fand and Cuchulain to ensure they will never meet again. Fand is a companion of the **Fool** in *On Baile's Strand* (*CPl.* 248), and there are references to her in "The Secret Rose" (*CP.* 77), "Under the Moon" (*CP.* 91), and "Mortal Help" (*MY.* 9).

REFERENCES: Ellis, Peter Berresford. *Dictionary of Celtic Mythology.* New York: Oxford University Press, 1992; Mac Cana, Proinsias. *Celtic Mythology.* Feltham, Middlesex: Newnes, 1983.

FARNHAM ROYAL, small village near Eton and Slough in the southeast corner of Buckinghamshire, England. WBY went there in the fall of 1876, when his father was painting landscapes at nearby Burnham Beeches. They lodged at Beech Villa, a guest house for visiting artists run by Joseph Earl and his wife Elizabeth. The house was later demolished to make way for Woodgate Garage, which stands on the main road through the village. In *Reveries over Childhood and Youth* (*A.* 28, 29), WBY recalls playing in the nearby woods, fishing in the pond, and shooting sparrows with one of the local boys.

FARR, FLORENCE (1860–1917), actress, writer, and feminist. She was born in Bromley, Kent, the daughter of William Farr, a noted statistician. She attended Cheltenham Ladies' College and Queen's College, London. She wished to be a schoolteacher but became an actress instead. In 1884, she married a young actor, Edward Emery, a member of a distinguished family of actors. He proved to be profligate and soon after the marriage, he emigrated to America and was never heard from again. She obtained a divorce in 1895. At this time, Florence Farr had a close relationship with **George Bernard Shaw**, who encouraged her career on the stage, although he became frustrated at her lack of discipline and unwillingness to work. WBY first saw her acting in 1890 in **John Todhunter's** *A Sicilian Idyll* in **Bedford Park**. He was impressed with her beauty, her sense of rhythm, and her beautiful voice but noted that she placed little value on these gifts, dressing without care as if contemptuous of her beauty's power (*A.* 120–22). In 1891, she played Rebecca West in the first London production of **Ibsen's** *Rosmersholm*, and in 1892, she appeared in the Independent Theatre's production of Shaw's *Widowers' Houses*. In 1894, she produced a series of plays at the Avenue Theatre, London, including *The Land of Heart's Desire*, the first performance of a play by WBY on the public stage (*A.* 280–81). In 1899, she was appointed general manager for the first season of the **Irish Literary Theatre** and played **Aleel** in *The Countess Cathleen*, the only performance in the first production that satisfied WBY (*A.* 413, 415, 417). In 1908, she acted with **Mrs. Patrick Campbell** in *The Thunderbolt* by Sir Arthur W. Pinero. Throughout this time, she was a member of various occult societies. In 1890, she joined **The Order of the Golden Dawn** and became Praemonstratrix in 1895. After the expulsion of **MacGregor Mathers**, she took charge of the London Temple, the Isis-Urania, although WBY and **Annie F. Horniman** had serious reservations about her leadership. She left to join the **Theosophical Society** in 1902 and, in July 1905, produced *The Shadowy Waters* at a Theosophical Convention in London, playing the role of **Dectora** (*WL.* 451). Florence Farr had a knowledge of music, and in the early years of the century, she and WBY embarked on a project to recover the ancient art of verse speaking to the accompaniment of a stringed instrument, the fulfillment of a long-held dream for WBY. With the help of **Arnold Dolmetsch**, they evolved a successful method. A detailed account of their developing ideas and progress is given by WBY in his ''Speaking to the Psaltery'' (*EI.* 13–27). Florence Farr toured the United States in 1907, sponsored by **John Quinn**, and on her return contributed articles on women's issues to the *New Age*. She was the author of a short novel, *The Dancing Faun*, as well as an esoteric pamphlet, *Egyptian Magic*. She collaborated with **Olivia Shakespear** on two verse plays, *The Beloved of Hathor* and *The Shrine of the Golden Hawk*, presented for two performances by the Egyptian Society in 1902 (*UP2.* 266–67). In 1912, disillusioned with her lack of recognition as an actress, she left England to take up an appointment as headmistress of Ramanathan College, a Vedanist seminary for girls in Ceylon. WBY noted her departure with regret. They continued to correspond until her death from cancer in 1917. He pays tribute to her in "All Souls' Night" (*CP*. 256), a poem written after her death.

REFERENCES: Bax, Clifford. *Florence Farr, Bernard Shaw, and W. B. Yeats*. Dublin: Cuala, 1941; Farr, Florence. *The Music of Speech*. London: Elkin Mathews, 1909; Johnson, Josephine. *Bernard Shaw's "New Woman."* Totowa, N.J.: Rowman & Littlefield, 1975.

FASCISM. In the early 1930s, WBY was reassessing his whole political attitude. The Ireland that he and his fellow writers promoted had failed to materialize, and in his old age, WBY was becoming increasingly impatient and angry. Having seen **Eamon de Valera**, as he believed, carried to power on the shoulders of the mob, the upper classes caring nothing for Ireland except as a venue for sport, and the rest of the population "drowned in religious and political fanaticism," WBY was entirely disillusioned. His remedy lay in a cultural rebirth, a realignment of traditional values of discipline and order, a unity of culture. Such a renewal, however, could not be achieved by democratic means—the fanaticism of the mob was impervious to persuasion and argument. Hence, in 1933, he supported the formation of an organization of Blueshirts, under the command of **General Eoin O'Duffy** (*WL*. 811–15). The movement was neofascist, and although WBY might have been unaware of the consequences of such an authoritarian regime, he embraced its ideas with enthusiasm. His intention was to set up a meritocracy of the educated classes. That they might be Protestant and members of the Ascendancy had special appeal, re-creating dreams of those earlier times when members of this elite class discovered for Ireland a newfound authority and independence. When **William T. Cosgrave** resigned the leadership of the Opposition in the Irish Parliament, a new coalition party, United Ireland, was formed from Cumann na nGaedheal, the National Centre Party, and the Young Ireland Association, under the leadership of General O'Duffy. For them, WBY wrote his "Three Songs to the Same Tune" (*CP*. 320), to be sung to the Irish tune "**O'Donnell Abu**." When his support of O'Duffy's Blueshirts waned, he rewrote the songs as "Three Marching Songs" (*CP*. 377), intending that no one should sing them. Yet the use of force to bring about a unity of culture remained a reasoned proposition for WBY, not only for Ireland but for the whole of Europe, a concept he explores in his note to "Three Songs to the Same Tune" (*VP*. 543–44) and "Commentary on the Three Songs" (*VP*. 835–36).

REFERENCES: Freyer, Grattan. *W. B. Yeats and the Anti-Democratic Tradition*. Dublin: Gill & Macmillan, 1981; Krimm, Bernard G. *W. B. Yeats and the Emergence of the Irish Free State, 1918–1939: Living in the Explosion*. Troy, N.Y.: Whitston, 1981; O'Brien, Conor Cruise. "Passion and Cunning: Politics of Yeats." In *In Excited Reverie*, ed. A. N. Jeffares and K. G. W. Cross. London: Macmillan, 1965; Stanfield, Paul S. *Yeats and Politics in the 1930s*. New York: St. Martin's, 1988.

FATHER HART, elderly priest in WBY's play *The Land of Heart's Desire*. As a representative of the Church, he attempts to persuade Mary **Bruin** from following the **Faery Child** to the Land of Heart's Desire, but he is unsuccessful. The role of Father Hart in the first production of the play at the Avenue Theatre, London, March 1894, was played by G. R. Foss.

FATHER JOHN, sympathetic priest in WBY's play *The Unicorn from the Stars*. At the opening of the play, he ministers to Martin **Hearne** as he recovers from a trance and speaks about the voices he has heard. He tries unsuccessfully to persuade Martin that his voices may be from the devil. Later, when he realizes that Martin may be in touch with the voice of God, he refuses to bring him back from a trance. The part of Father John in the first production of *The Unicorn from the Stars*, November 1907, was played by Ernest Vaughan.

FAY, [FRANCES JOHN] FRANK (1870–1931), actor, teacher, and cofounder of the **Abbey Theatre**. Born in Dublin, he was educated at Marlborough Street School and worked as a clerk with a firm of Dublin accountants, Craig & Gardner. He was active with his brother **W. G. Fay** in the formation of the Ormonde Dramatic Society, founded to produce the work of new Irish playwrights. An ardent student of the innovations of the Théâtre Libre in Paris, the National Theatre in Bergen, and the Independent Theatre in London, he was invited to produce for the Inghínidhe na hÉireann (Daughters of Ireland), a revolutionary society established by **Maud Gonne**. Through her, he met WBY. In April 1902, under the name W. G. Fay's National Dramatic Company, his brother premiered WBY's *Cathleen Ni Houlihan* in **St. Teresa's Hall**, Dublin. The success of this production led to the formation of the **Irish National Theatre Society**, later the Abbey Theatre. During the formative years of the Abbey, Frank Fay and his brother introduced WBY to stagecraft and acquainted him with current theater practice, in particular the naturalistic theater of André Antoine (1858–1943) and the stylized acting of Constant Coquelin (1841–1909). Frank Fay distinguished himself as an actor and teacher, with special skills in verse speaking— an interest he shared with WBY. He created the leading roles in a number of WBY's plays, including the **Fool** in *The Hour-Glass* (1903), **Seanchan** in *The King's Threshold* (1903), **Forgael** in *The Shadowy Waters* (1904), **Cuchulain** in *On Baile's Strand* (1904), **Naoise** in *Deirdre* (1906), and Martin **Hearne** in *The Unicorn from the Stars* (1907). With his brother's resignation from the Abbey, in 1908, he, too, left the company. He toured England for several years with a number of Shakespearian companies and acted with the prestigious Birmingham Repertory Theatre. He returned to Dublin in 1921 and spent his final years as a respected teacher of acting and elocution. He read poetry regularly on the radio and produced some of the first plays to be broadcast from **Radio Éireann**. Unlike his brother, he did not resign from the Irish National Theatre Society and returned to the Abbey Theatre in the twenty-fifth anniversary productions of *The Hour-Glass* and *The King's Threshold*. In *On the Boiler* (*LE.* 226), among his most memorable moments at the Abbey Theatre, WBY includes

Frank Fay's entrance as the friar in the last act of *The Well of the Saints* by **J. M. Synge**, performed at the Abbey Theatre, 1905.

REFERENCES: Fay, Gerard. *The Abbey Theatre, Cradle of Genius.* Dublin: Clonmore & Reynolds, 1958; Fay, W. G., and Carswell, Catherine. *The Fays of the Abbey Theatre.* London: Rich & Cowan 1935; Hogan, Robert, and Kilroy, James. *The Abbey Theatre: The Years of Synge 1905–1909.* Dublin: Dolmen, 1978; Hogan, Robert, and Kilroy, James. *Laying the Foundations.* Dublin: Dolmen, 1976; Hunt, Hugh. *The Abbey: Ireland's National Theatre, 1904–1978.* Dublin: Gill and Macmillan, 1979; Robinson, Lennox. *Ireland's Abbey Theatre: A History.* London: Sidgwick and Jackson, 1951.

FAY, W[ILLIAM] G[EORGE] (1872–1947), actor and play producer. He was born in Dublin and educated at Belvedere College. After leaving school at sixteen, he worked as a scene painter at the Gaiety Theatre, Dublin, before becoming an agent for Lloyd's Mexican Circus and traveling throughout Ireland posting playbills and arranging for the hire of performance sites. Later, he toured England and Ireland, playing minor roles with small companies, until economics forced him to return to Dublin to work as an electrician. Undeterred in his ambition to devote himself to the theater, and with the help of his elder brother **Frank**, he formed a community theater company, the Ormonde Dramatic Society, to present the work of new Irish playwrights. This society, which performed not only plays in English but also the first plays in Irish to be seen in Dublin, became the basis of W. G. Fay's Irish National Dramatic Company, which produced in 1902, **AE's** *Deirdre* and WBY's *Cathleen Ni Houlihan* (A. 449, 451, 452). This company, which became the **Irish National Dramatic Society**, was transformed into the **Irish National Theatre Society** (1903), later the **Abbey Theatre**. Much of the early success of the Abbey productions was due to W. G. Fay's disciplined management, his knowledge of stagecraft, and his skills as a comic actor. Indeed, he was the only original member of the Abbey Company to have experience of the professional stage. During his period with the company, he created leading roles in a succession of WBY's dramas, including Peter **Gillane** in *Cathleen Ni Houlihan* (1902), a **Tramp** in *The Pot of Broth* (1902), the **Mayor of Kinvara** in *The King's Threshold* (1903), the **Fool** in *On Baile's Strand* (1904), and **Johnny Bocach** in *The Unicorn from the Stars* (1907). He acted the role of Christy Mahon in the first production of **J. M. Synge's** *The Playboy of the Western World* (1907). In 1906, WBY dedicated *On Baile's Strand* "to William Fay, because of the beautiful fantasy of his playing of the character of the Fool." In 1907, concerned about the discipline of the actors, Fay demanded that he should be recognized as manager and producer of the Abbey. On 13 January 1908, after an acrimonious struggle with WBY and **Lady Gregory**, W. G. Fay resigned. He and his brother Frank formed a company to perform Irish plays in the United States, under the management of Charles Frohman. Although they had permission to present plays from the repertory of the Abbey Theatre, they incurred the wrath of WBY and Lady Gregory when the company was promoted as the Irish National Theatre Company of Dublin. The name was changed after **John Quinn** threatened legal action. The resignation of W. G. Fay and its aftermath were painful for WBY, contributing to his nervous breakdown in early 1909 (*M*. 140–41, 143–44). After 1909, W. G. Fay worked for brief periods in Birmingham, Nottingham, and Glasgow, before settling in London. There he remained until the end of his life, working regularly as an actor and producer and appearing in a number of films, including *Odd Man Out*. He never acted again at the Abbey. In 1935, he published, with C. Carswell, *The Fays of the Abbey Theatre*, telling his side of the power struggle that led to his resignation from the theater he had helped to found.

REFERENCES: Fay, Gerard. *The Abbey Theatre, Cradle of Genius*. Dublin: Clonmore & Reynolds, 1958; Hogan, Robert, and Kilroy, James. *The Abbey Theatre: The Years of Synge 1905–1909*. Dublin: Dolmen, 1978; Hogan, Robert, and Kilroy, James. *Laying the Foundations*. Dublin: Dolmen, 1976; Hunt, Hugh. *The Abbey: Ireland's National Theatre, 1904–1978*. Dublin: Gill and Macmillan, 1979; Robinson, Lennox. *Ireland's Abbey Theatre: A History*. London: Sidgwick and Jackson, 1951.

FEDELM, character in WBY's play *The King's Threshold*. She is the sweetheart of **Seanchan** and unsuccessfully tries to persuade him to give up his hunger strike and return home with her. The role of Fedelm was played by Máire Nic Shiubhlaigh in the first production of the play in the **Molesworth Hall**, Dublin, October 1903.

FELL, H[ERBERT] GRANVILLE (1872–1951), English graphic artist and illustrator. He exhibited at the Royal Academy in London in 1891. WBY first saw his work in the fall of 1894, at an exhibition at the Royal Institute of Painters in Water Colors. He was impressed (*KLI*. 462). When **Charles Shannon** was unable to design *Poems* (1895), WBY chose Fell to design the title page. In the event, he was disappointed with the design, which featured an angel and a serpent in gold on a brown background. Fell later became art editor of the *Ladies' Field* and the *Strand Magazine* and art critic for *Queen*. His designs for the *Book of Job* and the *Song of Solomon* were named as ''books of the year'' by *The Studio* (winter 1899–1900).

FENOLLOSA, ERNEST [FRANCISCO] (1853–1908), scholar and educator. He was born in Salem, Massachusetts, and graduated in philosophy and sociology from Harvard in 1874. He taught at Tokyo Imperial University, 1878–90, and recognized that with the thrust toward modernization in Japan many of the ancient Japanese traditions were being lost through national neglect. He dedicated himself to their preservation. In 1881, he financed a major exhibition of Japanese art in Tokyo. This became a catalyst for a renewed interest in classical Japanese painting and the founding of the Tokyo Fine Arts School. He translated some fifty texts from the Japanese **Noh** and vigorously resisted any attempts to update this traditional Japanese theater form. In 1890, he was appointed curator of the Oriental Department of Boston Museum. He resigned in 1897 and returned to Japan. But his pioneering work there had been so successful that the Japanese scholars, who now wished to take full control of their heritage, resented his return and treated him with coolness. He returned to the United States as a professor at Columbia University. After his early death in London, his second wife, Mary McNeil Fenollosa, dedicated herself to ensuring that her husband's work in Oriental studies was recognized. She published his *Epochs of Chinese and Japanese Art* (1912) and persuaded **Ezra Pound** to edit her husband's collection of Noh dramas. When Pound stayed with WBY in **Stone Cottage**, Sussex, in 1913, he was working on Fenollosa's translations. WBY realized that in the Japanese Noh he had found a model for his own lyric drama, and he contributed an introduction for Fenollosa's *Certain Noble Plays of Japan*, published by the **Cuala Press** in 1916.

REFERENCES: Brooks, Van Wyck. *Fenollosa and His Circle.* New York: Dutton, 1962; Fenollosa, Ernest. *Certain Noble Plays of Japan.* Churchtown, Dundrum: Cuala, 1916; Fenollosa, Ernest, and Pound, Ezra. *Noh or Accomplishment: A Study of the Classical Stage of Japan.* London: Macmillan, 1916.

FERGUS [Mac ROICH], legendary king of **Ulster**. He appears most prominently in the Ulster Cycle of mythological stories of the **Red Branch**. He was king of Ulster until he was tricked out of his throne by his mistress, **Nessa**, who promised him her favors only if he allowed her son **Conchubar** to reign for one year. Fergus agreed, but Conchubar proved so popular with the people that Fergus went into exile, choosing to live a peaceful life hunting in the woods. In the story "Deirdre and the Sons of Uisnech," Fergus travels to Scotland to persuade the lovers **Deirdre** and **Naoise** to return home, assuring them they will come to no harm. When Fergus is lured away by **Barach**, Naoise is killed by order of Conchubar, and Deirdre kills herself. Disgusted by Conchubar's treachery, Fergus exiles himself to **Connacht**. There, he becomes the lover of **Queen Maeve**. In the mythological saga *Táin Bó Cuailnge*, Fergus accompanies Maeve on the epic cattle raid. His strategy almost wins the day, but when he is reminded of a personal oath by **Cuchulain**, he retreats, taking most of the Connacht soldiers with him. WBY alludes to Fergus the poet-king and to Fergus, the author of the "Cattle Raid of Cooley," in his review "The Poetry of Sir Samuel Ferguson" (*UP1*. 91, 99). In *Deirdre*, he portrays Fergus sympathetically. In "Fergus and the Druid" (*CP*. 36) and "Who Goes with Fergus?" (*CP*. 48), Fergus is a mask for the poet who seeks wisdom from an ancient seer, a guise that WBY also adopts in "To the Rose upon the Rood of Time" (*CP*. 35).

REFERENCES: Ellis, Peter Berresford. *Dictionary of Celtic Mythology.* New York: Oxford University Press, 1992; Green, Miranda J. *Dictionary of Celtic Myth and Legend.* London: Thames & Hudson, 1992; Mac Cana, Proinsias. *Celtic Mythology.* Feltham, Middlesex: Newnes, 1983.

FERGUSON, SIR SAMUEL (1810–86), poet and antiquary. He was born at 23 High Street, Belfast. After his early education at Royal Belfast Academical Institution, he graduated from **Trinity College**, Dublin, and was called to the Irish Bar in 1838. He practiced law until his retirement in 1867. He was active politically but later withdrew to devote himself to scholarship and poetry. In 1867, he was appointed deputy-keeper of the public records of Ireland. His reorganization of a neglected department was recognized in 1878 by a knighthood. He contributed many articles to the Protestant *Dublin University Magazine*, encouraging collaboration and understanding between the two traditions in Ireland, the Anglo-Irish and the Gael, but it was as a poet that he had his most profound impact. Having taught himself Irish, he turned to the ancient Irish epics for inspiration. His *Lays of the Western Gael* (1865), *Congal: An Epic Poem in Five Books* (1872), and *Deirdre* (1880) stimulated a keen interest in his country's cultural heritage, while his home at 20 North Great George's Street, Dublin, and later at Strand Lodge, **Howth**, County Dublin, became an open house to anyone interested in Irish art, literature, or music. He became president of the **Royal Irish Academy** in 1882. His writing was not always serious: An early work, *Father Tom and the Pope* (1838), was a comic satire on Irish education. He wrote many articles on Irish antiquities, while his important work on the ancient Ogham inscriptions in Ireland, Wales, and Scotland was edited by his widow after his death. Ferguson was of central importance in the early poetic development of WBY. He introduced the young poet to the poetic possibilities in the old legends, and WBY was quick to champion the cause of the older writer. Conscious that Ferguson had been neglected as a poet, WBY was critical of his father's old friend **Edward Dowden** for not doing enough to promote Ferguson's reputation (*UP1*. 348), while WBY's inclusion of himself in the company of Ferguson, **Thomas Davis**, and **James Clarence Mangan** in his poem "To Ireland in the Coming Times" (*CP*. 56) aroused amusement and scorn from his contemporaries (*WL*. 213). His enthusiastic (and first published) article "The Poetry of Sir Samuel Ferguson—I" (*Irish Fireside*, 9 August 1886) (*UP1*. 81–87) and "The Poetry of Sir Samuel Ferguson—II" (*Dublin University Review*, November 1886) (*UP1*. 88–104), published on the death of Ferguson, were influential in gaining a fuller recognition of Ferguson's influence on succeeding Irish writers. WBY included *Father Tom and the Pope*, *Lays of the Western Gael*, and the poem *Conary* in his list of "Best Irish Books" (*UP1*. 383–87; *WL*. 247, 248). Later, he revised his opinion of Ferguson, finding praise for his achievements, but concluding that his poetry was "monotonous in cadence and clumsy in language" (*UP1*. 363). Ferguson is buried in the churchyard of Donegore, County Antrim, once the site of an ancient ecclesiastical settlement.

REFERENCES: Brown, Malcolm. *Sir Samuel Ferguson*. Lewisburg, Pa.: Bucknell University Press, 1973; Marcus, Phillip L. *Yeats and the Beginning of the Irish Renaissance*. Syracuse: Syracuse University Press, 1987; O'Driscoll, Robert. *An Ascendancy of the Heart: Ferguson and the Beginnings of Modern Irish Literature in English*. Dublin: Dolmen, 1976; Welch, Robert. "Sir Samuel Ferguson: The Two Races of Ireland." In *Irish Poetry from Moore to Yeats*. Totowa, N.J.: Barnes & Noble, 1980; Yeats, William

Butler, and Kinsella, Thomas. *Davis, Mangan, Ferguson?: Tradition and the Irish Writer.* Dublin: Dolmen, 1971.

FERRARA, city in northern Italy. Ferrara was a major center of commerce and art during the Renaissance, when it was ruled over by the Este family. WBY visited the city with **Lady Gregory** and her son **Robert** during a tour of Italy in 1907. In the poem "The People" (*CP.* 169), written in 1915, the poet regrets that he must devote so much of his time and energy to life in Dublin, where he is not fully appreciated, when he might be in Ferrara.

FIANNA, elite band of warriors led by **Fionn Mac Cumhal**. The Fianna are reputed to have been formed in 300 B.C. by Fiachadh, High King of Ireland. They consisted of twenty-five battalions, and membership could only be acquired by undergoing a series of ordeals as proof of exceptional skills and bravery. The Fianna were hunters as well as warriors. They had an affinity with nature and the capacity to move easily from the natural world of stags and wild boars to the supernatural world of the **Sídhe**. For this reason, the stories of the Fianna are more in the tradition of those mythological tales that became part of European literature from medieval times than the heroic, quasi-historical stories of **Cuchulain** and the **Red Branch**. The exploits of the Fianna are recorded in the Fenian Cycle (also known as the Ossianic Cycle), thought to date from the third century A.D. The eight major parts of the cycle were brought together in the *Colloquy of the Old Men* (Irish: *Agallamh na Seanórach*), a twelfth-century frame-story based on the premise that the warriors **Oisin** and **Caoilte** survived into the Christian era and encountered **St. Patrick**, to whom they recounted their adventures in a mood of nostalgia and regret for past conquests. WBY drew heavily on the legends of the Fianna in his early writings, most notably in *The Wanderings of Oisin* (1889), "Baile and Aillinn" (1903), *Crossways* (1889), and *The Rose* (1893).
REFERENCES: Dames, Michael. *Mythic Ireland.* 1992. Reprint, New York: Thames & Hudson, 1996; Ellis, Peter Berresford. *Dictionary of Celtic Mythology.* New York: Oxford University Press, 1992; Green, Miranda J. *Dictionary of Celtic Myth and Legend.* London: Thames & Hudson, 1992; Mac Cana, Proinsias. *Celtic Mythology.* Feltham, Middlesex: Newnes, 1983.

FIELD, MICHAEL (pseud.). *See* **BRADLEY, KATHARINE [HARRIS].**

FIGHTING THE WAVES, one-act play in prose by WBY. It was a reworking of the verse play *The Only Jealousy of Emer* and was written after WBY saw photographs of the masks made by **Hildo Krop** for a 1922 production of *The Only Jealousy of Emer* in Amsterdam. WBY was so impressed that he rewrote the play in prose and invited **Ninette de Valois** to choreograph the production using the Krop masks. *Fighting the Waves* was successfully performed in the **Peacock Theatre**, 13 August 1929. The cast, which included members of the

Abbey School of Ballet, was: **Cuchulain**, Michael J. Dolan; **Emer**, Meriel Moore; **Eithne Inguba**, Shelah Richards; Singer, J. Stevenson; **Ghost of Cuchulain**, Hedley Briggs; Chorus of Waves, Chris Sheehan, Mai Kiernan, Cepta Cullen, Doreen Cuthbert, Margaret Horgan, Thelma Murphy. Ninette de Valois danced the role of **Fand**. The music was composed by **George Antheil**, while the decorative curtain and costumes were designed by Dolly Travers Smith, wife of **Lennox Robinson**, who directed the production. The text of *Fighting the Waves* was published in ***Wheels and Butterflies*** (1934), when it was dedicated to Hildo Krop.

REFERENCES: Bjersby, Birgit. *The Interpretation of the Cuchulain Legend in the Works of W. B. Yeats.* Folcroft, Pa.: Folcroft, 1969; Miller, Liam. *The Noble Drama of W. B. Yeats.* Dublin: Dolmen, 1977.

FIGURE OF CUCHULAIN. *See* CUCHULAIN.

FINDRIAS. *See* **FALIAS**.

FINIVARAGH [also Finvarra, Finavarra, Finbar, Finnbarr] (Irish: *Fionnbharr*), master of the elements and king of the **Sídhe**. Finivaragh lived at **Cruachmaa** and was regarded as king of the **Connacht** fairies. As the old gods degenerated in folk memory, Finivaragh became king of all the fairies of Ireland. WBY's title for ''The Poet Pleads with the Elemental Powers'' (*CP*. 80), published in *The Second Book of the Rhymers' Club* (1894), was ''A Mystical Prayer for the Masters of the Elements, Finvarra, Feacra, and Caolte.'' In a letter to **John Quinn** (*KLIII*. 389), WBY movingly writes that if he could have one wish from Finivaragh, it would be to have his plays acted in Ireland and throughout the world. See also ''The Cradles of Gold'' (*UP1*. 417).

FINVARA (Irish: *Fidh an Mhara*) [the wood by the sea], rocky headland on the northern coast of **County Clare**. In ***The Dreaming of the Bones*** (*CPl*. 435), the **Young Man** claims he has been told to wait on the rocky shore under Finvara for a boat to take him to safety.

FIONN Mac CUMHAL [also Mac Cumhail, Mac Cumhaill], mythological Irish hero. He was the son of Cumhal of Clan Bascna and was born after the murder of his father. Reared by the Druids, he received from them the gift of prophecy and an affinity with the natural world. When he grew to manhood, he avenged his father's murder, and on his arrival at the royal court at **Tara**, he was made leader of the **Fianna**. Under his leadership, the Fianna grew in strength and reputation, performing many supernatural acts of hunting and fighting. He married Sava, a woman who had been transformed into a fawn, and they had a son, **Oisin**. The aging Fionn, having fallen in love with the youthful **Grania**, arranged the death of her lover **Diarmuid**. When she came to him as his bride, Fionn was ridiculed by the other warriors of the Fianna. He is said to have drowned in the **Boyne**. His exploits are told with relish in the many tales of the Fenian Cycle.

REFERENCES: Dames, Michael. *Mythic Ireland*. 1992. Reprint, New York: Thames & Hudson, 1996; Ellis, Peter Berresford. *Dictionary of Celtic Mythology*. New York: Oxford University Press, 1992; Green, Miranda J. *Dictionary of Celtic Myth and Legend*. London: Thames & Hudson, 1992; Mac Cana, Proinsias. *Celtic Mythology*. Feltham, Middlesex: Newnes, 1983.

FIRBOLG, mythological race of short, black-haired warriors. The Firbolg were known as "bag men," the name thought to have been given to them during a period of enslavement in Thrace, when they had to carry bags of earth from the fertile valleys to the rocky uplands. They were defeated by the **Tuatha dé Danaan** at the first battle of **Moytura**. Those who survived fled to the west of Ireland, and to the **Aran Islands**, where they built the massive stone fort of Dun Aengus on Inishmore. Those killed were buried at Carrowmore in **Sligo** (county), under the shadow of **Knocknarea**, the site of the largest Neolithic burial site in Ireland. Recent archaeological research suggests the tombs may have been built before 4000 B.C. The burial mounds of the Firbolg at Carrowmore are mentioned in *The Wanderings of Oisin* (*CP*. 409). According to WBY, the Firbolg unsuccessfully waged war with the **Fomorians** before the coming of the Tuatha dé Danaan (*VP*. 795).

REFERENCES: Dames, Michael. *Mythic Ireland*. 1992. Reprint, New York: Thames & Hudson, 1996; Ellis, Peter Berresford. *Dictionary of Celtic Mythology*. New York: Oxford University Press, 1992; Green, Miranda J. *Dictionary of Celtic Myth and Legend*. London: Thames & Hudson, 1992; Mac Cana, Proinsias. *Celtic Mythology*. Feltham, Middlesex: Newnes, 1983.

FITZGERALD, BARRY (1888–1961), actor. He was born William Joseph Shields in Dublin. After completing his education at Merchant Taylors' School, Dublin, he joined the Civil Service in 1911. His first acting experience was with a community drama group, the Kincora Players, and in 1917, he joined the **Abbey Theatre** as a part-time actor, taking the name Barry Fitzgerald. Only in 1929 did he resign from the Civil Service to become a full-time actor. In 1919, he played the First Old Man in WBY's *The Player Queen*. He was **Creon** in WBY's *Sophocles' King Oedipus* (1926) and *Sophocles' Oedipus at Colonus* (1927). At the Abbey, he gave many consummate comedic performances, especially in the plays of **Sean O'Casey**, and was named best character actor by the New York critics for the role of Fluther Good in the 1934 U.S. tour of *The Plough and the Stars*. In 1937, he moved to Hollywood, where he stayed for over twenty years. He returned to Ireland in the late 1950s and died in Dublin.

REFERENCES: Hunt, Hugh. *The Abbey: Ireland's National Theatre, 1904–1978*. Dublin: Gill & Macmillan, 1979; Robinson, Lennox. *Ireland's Abbey Theatre: A History*. London: Sidgwick and Jackson, 1951.

FITZGERALD, LORD EDWARD (1763–98), patriot. He was the son of James Fitzgerald, earl of Kildare, and lived much of his early life in France. A Prot-

estant, he joined the British army in 1779 and fought in the American Revolution, being severely wounded in the battle of Eutaw Springs. He was elected
M.P. for Athy and Kildare, but frustrated by the lack of reforms under English
rule in Ireland, and drawn by the successes of the French Revolution, he went
to Paris in 1792. His expulsion from the British army for his avowed republicanism only intensified his resolve to force the English to leave Ireland. He
joined the Society of United Irishmen in 1796. In 1798, he was in Ireland,
supervising the final arrangements for an Irish rebellion, when he was betrayed
to the English. He died of wounds received when he was arrested by Major Sirr,
who was godfather to several of WBY's ''great-great-grandfather's children''
(*A.* 21). For WBY, Lord Edward was one of the memorable figures of modern
Ireland, to be spoken of in company with **Jonathan Swift** and **Charles Stewart
Parnell** (*LE.* 209). His sacrifice was an example, like that of **Robert Emmet**
and **Wolfe Tone**, to all those involved in the setting up of a new and free Ireland.
WBY names Lord Edward among the heroic Irish martyrs in his poems ''Sep-
tember 1913'' (*CP.* 120) and ''Parnell's Funeral'' (*CP.* 319), while in ''Sixteen
Dead Men'' (*CP.* 205), he elevates those executed in the 1916 Easter Rising to
his exalted company.

REFERENCES: Byrne, Patrick. *Lord Edward Fitzgerald.* Dublin: Talbot, 1955; Lindsey,
John. *The Shining Life and Death of Lord Edward Fitzgerald.* London and New York:
Rich & Cowan, 1949.

FITZROY ROAD, London residence of the Yeats family. When **John B. Yeats**
moved from Dublin to London in 1867, he rented a three-story home at 23
Fitzroy Road, near Regent's Park. His wife and two young children joined him
in July 1867. It was the birthplace of WBY's younger brothers, Robert and
Jack, and of his sister **Lolly**. John B. Yeats remained in the house until the
lease expired in 1873, but his wife and children spent the four summers, 1868–
71, in **Sligo**. In July 1872, they left Fitzroy Road for Ireland and did not return.
In *Reveries over Childhood and Youth* (*A.* 5), WBY briefly recalls looking out
the window of 23 Fitzroy Road and seeing some boys playing in the street.

FLAUBERT, GUSTAVE (1821–80), novelist. He was born in Rouen, the son of
a French surgeon. He suffered from a nervous illness that limited his ability to
travel, and so he spent most of his life at his home at Croisset, near Rouen,
with his mother and a niece. He studied law but decided to become a writer.
His first work, *Novembre*, was written when he was twenty-one, but it was the
publication of his realist masterpiece *Madame Bovary* (1857) that brought him
national attention. For this novel, in which he depicted the frustrations of a
romantic young woman married to a rural doctor, he was prosecuted on moral
grounds, but he won the case. His other works include *Salammbô* (1862), *A
Sentimental Education* (1910), and the satirical *Bouvard and Pécuchet* (1881).
In 1903, WBY complained to the **National Library of Ireland** about the absence of books by Flaubert in the collection (*UP2.* 305). In ''The Autumn of

the Body'' (*EI.* 189–90), he observes that Flaubert wrote unforgettable scenes crowded with historical detail, while in his review of *Aglavaine and Selysette* by **Maeterlinck**, he claims Flaubert's *La Tentation de Saint Antoine* as the last important work of the old Romantic period (*UP2.* 52). WBY owned four books by Flaubert (*OS.* nos. 679–82).

REFERENCES: Lottman, Herbert R. *Flaubert: A Biography.* Boston: Little, Brown, 1989; Spenser, Philip H. *Flaubert: A Biography.* London: Faber & Faber, 1952; Troyat, Henri. *Flaubert.* Trans. Joan Pinkham. New York: Viking, 1992.

FOMORIANS. *See* **BALOR**.

FOOL, fictional character. The Fool appears in three plays by WBY, *The Hour-Glass, On Baile's Strand*, and *The Herne's Egg*. In *The Hour-Glass*, he is called **Teigue**, while in *The Herne's Egg*, he is Tom Fool. In the first version of *On Baile's Strand*, the Fool is named **Barach**. There is a reference to Seaghan the Fool in ''The Shadowy Waters'' (*CP.* 478). The introduction of the Fool into *The Hour-Glass* marks the first time that WBY includes in his drama a character outside the mainstream of society. In the three plays, the Fool is a low-life character, who, in addition to providing comic relief, possesses intuitive knowledge not yet available to the protagonist. He is an intermediary between the world of spirits and of men. In the first production of *The Hour-Glass* in 1903, the role of Teigue was taken by **Frank Fay**, while in *On Baile's Strand*, first performed in 1904, Barach the Fool was played by **W. G. Fay**. In the first production of *The Herne's Egg* by the Lyric Theatre Company, Dublin, 1950, Tom the Fool was acted by Patrick Nolan. **Tom O'Roughley** is the name of the wise fool in the poem ''Tom O'Roughley'' (*CP.* 158).

FORGAEL, fictional character. In *The Shadowy Waters*, he is in charge of a pirate ship and is leading his sailors on a mysterious quest. Believing him to be insane, they plot his murder, but they are prevented from doing so by the loyal **Aibric**. When they bring the captured **Dectora** to him, he seduces her with his music. At the conclusion of the play, Forgael and Dectora sail away together. In a note to the play, published in *The Arrow* (November 1906), WBY describes Forgael as a sea king of ancient Ireland. The role of Forgael was played in the first production of *The Shadowy Waters*, January 1904, by **Frank Fay**.

FOUNTAIN COURT, Middle Temple, London. In October 1895, WBY left the family home in **Bedford Park** to share rooms with **Arthur Symons** at 2 Fountain Court, a wide, tree-shaded court, west of Middle Temple Lane. WBY's quarters consisted of two small rooms at the top of the building, overlooking Essex Street. Symons occupied two adjoining rooms that overlooked Fountain Court. For WBY, the rooms at Fountain Court provided him with his first taste of freedom from his family (*A.* 322). They gave him the privacy to entertain

Olivia Shakespear, although when he first invited her and her friend **Valentine Fox** to tea, he went to buy a cake and locked himself out (*M*. 86–87). When his relationship with Olivia Shakespear intensified, WBY moved from Fountain Court in March 1896 to rooms in **Woburn Buildings**.

FOUR PLAYS FOR DANCERS, collection of plays by WBY. Published in 1921 by Macmillan and Company, the collection consists of *At the Hawk's Well, The Only Jealousy of Emer, The Dreaming of the Bones*, and *Calvary*. All four plays, modeled on the Japanese **Noh**, are in verse, with opening and closing lyrics, while the dramatic action concludes with a climactic dance. *Four Plays for Dancers* includes a note by WBY on the first performance of *At the Hawk's Well* and commentary on the other three plays. Music for *The Dreaming of the Bones* by **Walter Rummel**, together with **Edmund Dulac's** music, illustrations for the costumes, masks, and decorative cloth for *At the Hawk's Well*, accompany the texts.

FOX, [ELIZABETH] VALENTINE (1861–1931), close acquaintance and confidante of **Olivia Shakespear**. Valentine was the daughter of Captain David Stewart Ogilvy, a Scottish adventurer. In 1889, she married Thomas Hamilton Fox, a member of a wealthy family of brewers, and went to live in Keston, Kent. Unhappily married herself, she played a vital role in the relationship between WBY and Olivia Shakespear. She encouraged the relationship, acting as a sponsor, but she discouraged them from running away together, advising them to consummate the relationship but to do so covertly (*M*. 87–88). WBY and Olivia Shakespear followed her advice. In 1902, Valentine and her husband moved to London. There, she began a twenty-year affair with a wealthy barrister, Arthur Petersen. He was unmarried, and to avoid scandal, Valentine Fox, with her husband and daughter Ruth, moved in with him. The arrangement lasted until Petersen's death in 1922. The friendship with Olivia Shakespear was also maintained.
    REFERENCE: Harwood, John. *Olivia Shakespear and W. B. Yeats: After Long Silence*. New York: St. Martin's, 1989.

FRENCH, MRS., named in ''The Tower'' (*CP*. 218). Mrs. French lived in Peterswell, **Galway** (county). She was overheard to say she wished a local squire's ears were cut off. Later, at dinner, a servant presented her with the ears. The story is told in *Recollections of Jonah Barrington*, a copy of which was in WBY's library (*OS*. no. 120).
    REFERENCE: Barrington, Sir Jonah. *Recollections of Jonah Barrington*. Dublin and London: Talbot, T. Fisher Unwin, 1918.

FULL MOON IN MARCH, A, collection of poems and two plays. It was published by Macmillan and Company in 1935. The volume contains the plays *A Full*

Moon in March and *The King of the Great Clock Tower* (verse) and eighteen poems. Of the poems, "Two Songs Rewritten for the Tune's Sake" (*CP.* 325) had been published previously in *The Collected Plays of W. B. Yeats* (1934). All the other poems had been included in *The King of the Great Clock Tower* (1934), with the exception of four of the Supernatural Songs: "Ribh in Ecstasy" (*CP.* 329), "There" (*CP.* 329), "What Magic Drum?" (*CP.* 331), and "Whence Had They Come?" (*CP.* 332). The poems and plays in the collection were written after the death of **Lady Gregory**, and are generally considered to contain some of WBY's lesser writings. He himself struggled with the collection, as he described to **Dorothy Wellesley** (*WL.* 843). The play *A Full Moon in March* opens and closes with a chorus which presents the theme of the play, the union of spirit and matter, represented by a **Queen** and a **Swineherd**. Offended by the earthiness of the Swineherd and his insolent and suggestive speech, the Queen has him beheaded. In death, she achieves union with his severed head, in an erotic dance reminiscent of Salomé with the head of John the Baptist. The dance takes place at the full moon in March, the vernal equinox, and is an image of cyclical renewal. *A Full Moon in March* was not performed in WBY's lifetime.

REFERENCES: Bradley, Anthony. *William Butler Yeats.* New York: Frederick Ungar, 1979; Ellis, Sylvia C. *The Plays of W. B. Yeats: Yeats and the Dancer.* London: Macmillan, 1995; Miller, Liam. *The Noble Drama of W. B. Yeats.* Dublin: Dolmen, 1977; Taylor, Richard. *A Reader's Guide to the Plays of W. B. Yeats.* New York: St. Martin's, 1984.

FULLER, LOÏE (1862–1928), dancer and actress. She was born in Fullersburg, Ill., and from childhood acted in vaudeville and stock theater productions across the United States. While appearing in a production in New York in 1891, she developed her famous skirt dance, in which she manipulated yards of diaphanous fabric and explored the possibilities of colored lights playing on the swirling folds. In 1892, she performed at the Folies Bergère in Paris. Her arrival coincided with the beginnings of the Art Nouveau movement and the emergence of the Symbolists. She became the *doyenne* of the French intellectuals, inspiring tributes from the most distinguished writers and painters, among them **Mallarmé**. Such was her popularity that the management of the Folies Bergère effected costly alterations to the stage so that she might incorporate her novel effects. She launched the European careers of **Ruth St. Denis** and Maud Allen and promoted a company of Japanese dancers, among them Sado Yacco. WBY refers to this company as Chinese dancers in "Nineteen Hundred and Nineteen" (*CP.* 232). In "The Message to the Folk-Lorist" (*UP1* 285), WBY makes a reference "to the poetry of cigarettes and black coffee, of absinthe, and the skirt dance."

REFERENCES: Ellis, Sylvia C. *The Plays of W. B. Yeats: Yeats and the Dancer.* London: Macmillan, 1995; Kermode, Frank. ''Poet and Dancer before Diaghilev.'' In *Modern Essays*. London: William Collins Sons, 1958); Kermode, Frank. *Romantic Image*. London: Routledge & Kegan Paul, 1957; Sommer, Sally R. ''Loïe Fuller.'' *The Drama Review* 19 (March 1975).

FURTHER ROSSES. *See* **ROSSES, THE**.

G

GABHRA, site of the last battle of the Fenian Cycle. In A.D. 284, after the death of **Fionn Mac Cumhal**, the High King of Ireland determined to destroy the **Fianna** at the battle of Gabhra, near Garristown, Dublin (county). **Oscar**, the commander of the Fianna, killed the High King but was himself mortally wounded. While his body was being carried from the field, Fionn Mac Cumhal returned from **Tir-nan-Oge** to mourn his grandson. See also *The Wanderings of Oisin* (*CP*. 410).

REFERENCE: McGarry, James P. *Place Names in the Writings of William Butler Yeats.* Gerrards Cross: Colin Smythe, 1976.

GAEL, THE, a weekly paper published in Dublin by the Gaelic Athletic Association (GAA). *The Gael* first appeared in spring 1887, and although it was principally a sports paper, it included short stories, poems, and articles of literary merit. The literary editor was **John O'Leary**, and among the contributors were **Katharine Tynan, Douglas Hyde** and **John Todhunter**. An article by WBY on **Fionn Mac Cumhal** was published 23 April 1887. After a controversy with a rival nationalist paper, *The Gael* was suspended by the GAA and ceased publication, January 1888. While it was short-lived, *The Gael* was nevertheless an important outlet for the emerging talents of the Irish renaissance. *The Gael* was also the name of a separate New York publication.

GALILEE, farming region in northern Israel and the scene of the early ministry of **Christ**. WBY recalls the simplicity of life in biblical Galilee in his poem ''A Prayer on going into my House'' (*CP*. 183), while the impact of Christ, the Galilean, on the Greek and Roman civilizations is recalled in the final chorus of *The Resurrection* (*CPl*. 594).

GALWAY, city and county in the west of Ireland. WBY developed a strong association with Galway through **Lady Gregory** and other notable figures of the Irish renaissance, among them **Edward Martyn** and **George Moore**. In the 1890s, he visited homes in Galway, collecting folklore for his collection *The Celtic Twilight* (1893). It was while visiting homes in the area that WBY saw **Thoor Ballylee**, which he later bought and restored. Galway, for him, came to represent a place of peace and contentment, far from the rigors of life in London and Dublin, a place where the beggar and the nobleman still lived harmoniously, side by side. Galway is recalled in the elegy ''In Memory of Major Robert Gregory'' (*CP*. 148) and in many of the poems contained in the collections *The Wild Swans at Coole, The Tower*, and *The Winding Stair*.

REFERENCES: McGarry, James P. *Place Names in the Writings of William Butler Yeats*. Gerrards Cross: Colin Smythe, 1976; Smythe, Colin. *A Guide to Coole Park, Co. Galway: Home of Lady Gregory*. Gerrards Cross: Colin Smythe, 1973.

GARNETT, EDWARD (1868–1937), publisher's reader. He was the son of Richard Garnett (1835–1906), Keeper of Printed Books at the **British Museum**. He joined the publishing firm of **T. Fisher Unwin** in 1888 and quickly rose to reading manuscripts. He remained with them for ten years and then moved to other major publishing houses. During his career, Garnett fostered the talents of Joseph Conrad, Ford Madox Ford, John Galsworthy, D. H. Lawrence, and others. He was instrumental in having T. Fisher Unwin publish WBY's early works (*WL*. 157, 165). In 1892, WBY unsuccessfully badgered Garnett to use his influence to prevent **Sir Charles Gavan Duffy** from controlling the **New Irish Library** project (*WL*. 215, 216, 217, 222, 223, 225). After a quarrel, when Garnett published a negative review of **Lady Gregory's** *Cuchulain of Muirthemne* in 1903, the friendship between WBY and Garnett ended. In 1904, WBY wrote asking him to invite **Padraic Colum** to review for *The Speaker* (*KLIII*. 578–79). Garnett does not appear to have responded to the request. WBY may have contributed a positive, but unsigned, review of Garnett's *An Imaged World: Poems in Prose* (1894) to *The Speaker*, 8 September 1894 (*UP1*. 341–43).

REFERENCE: Jefferson, George. *Edward Garnett: A Life in Literature*. London: Cape, 1982.

GELLÉE, CLAUDE. *See* **CLAUDE**.

GENERAL POST OFFICE, O'Connell Street, Dublin. Built 1814–18, it was designed by Francis Johnston and, during the Easter Rising of 1916, was held by **James Connolly** and **Padraic Pearse**, who read the Proclamation of the Irish Republic from its steps. It was shelled during the Civil War in 1922, and only the facade of the original building was left standing. The **Young Man** in *The Dreaming of the Bones* (*CPl*. 435) claims to have fought in the Post Office during the Easter Rising, and it is the subject of the last verse in the final chorus of *The Death of Cuchulain* (*CPl*. 704–5). In *On the Boiler* (*LE*. 224), WBY reflects that just as Americans date their ancestry back to the *Mayflower*, future generations of wealthy Irish will date theirs back to the Post Office. The statue of **Cuchulain** by **Oliver Sheppard** now stands in the renovated lobby.

GEORGE'S VILLE, birthplace of WBY. The house at No. 1 George's Ville, now 5 Sandymount Avenue, Dublin, was the first home of **John B. Yeats** and his bride **Susan Pollexfen**. They moved to George's Ville in September 1863, and it was there that WBY was born, 13 June 1865. The house was a six-roomed, red-brick, Victorian duplex, with granite steps up to the front door and plate glass windows. It was half a mile from **Sandymount Castle**, the substantial dwelling of John B. Yeats's uncle **Robert Corbet**. The Yeats family lived at George's Ville until they moved to **Fitzroy Road**, London, in early 1867.

REFERENCE: Murphy, William M. *Prodigal Father: The Life of John Butler Yeats (1839–1922)*. Ithaca: Cornell University Press, 1978.

GHOST OF CUCHULAIN. *See* **CUCHULAIN**.

GILLANE [also Gillan], family name in WBY's play *Cathleen Ni Houlihan*. At the beginning of the action, Bridget and Peter Gillane are preoccupied with the marriage next day of their son Michael to **Delia Cahel**. When an Old Woman, **Cathleen Ni Houlihan**, appears, they offer her traditional hospitality. Despite the entreaties of Delia, Michael responds to the Old Woman and goes off to join the French, who have just landed off the coast at **Killala**. In the first production of *Cathleen Ni Houlihan*, April 1902, Peter Gillane was played by **W. G. Fay**, Bridget Gillane by Maire T. Quinn, Michael Gillane by Dudley Digges, and Patrick Gillane by C. Caulfield.

GILLIGAN, FATHER PETER, central character in ''The Ballad of Father Gilligan'' (*CP*. 52). According to WBY, his story was based upon an old folk legend from Castleisland, County Kerry (*VP*. 132, 800).

GIORGIONE (c. 1478–1510), landscape painter. Almost nothing is known of Giorgione's life except that he was born in Venice, had a reputation for charm, and died of the plague in his early thirties. His work, which is distinguished by its subject matter (bucolic landscapes bathed in warm, golden light), had a liberating influence on sixteenth-century Venetian painters. In *The Death of Synge* (*A*. 502), WBY wrote that his room at **Coole Park** was hung with many prints, among them the work of Giorgione. See also ''Upon a Dying Lady'' (*CP*. 177).

GIRNAR, holy mountain in India, in the Gir Hills, east of Junagadh. In *An Indian Monk: His Life and Adventures,* **Shri Purohit Swami** gives an account of climbing Girnar and walking in the sacred footprints of the god **Dattatreya**. WBY wrote the introduction to this work when it was first published in 1932 (*LE*. 132–38).

GLASNEVIN, suburb of north Dublin. It contains a large cemetery, known in history and literature as Glasnevin, though its name correctly is Prospect Cemetery. Since 1831, Glasnevin has been the traditional burial place for the heroes of Ireland. Among those buried there are **Daniel O'Connell, Sir Roger Casement, Sir Charles Gavan Duffy, Charles Stewart Parnell**, and **Countess Markiewicz**. WBY recalls Parnell's grave at Glasnevin in the moving tribute, to **Hugh Lane** in "To a Shade" (*CP*. 123). See also "Parnell's Funeral" (*CP*. 319).

REFERENCE: McGarry, James P. *Place Names in the Writings of William Butler Yeats.* Gerrards Cross: Colin Smythe, 1976.

GLEN AT ALT. *See* **ALT**.

GLENCAR (Irish: *Gleann an Chairthe*) [Glen of the Standing Stone], nine miles northeast of **Sligo** (town). The glen runs to the sea at **Drumcliff**, with **Ben Bulben** to the north and **Cope's Mountain** to the south. Several waterfalls flow into Glencar Lake. The best known, which is near Siberry's cottage where WBY and **Arthur Symons** stayed for a time in 1896, is the setting for "The Stolen Child" (*CP*. 20) and "Towards Break of Day" (*CP*. 208). The other notable waterfall in Glencar drops 300 feet from a ridge on Ben Bulben. When the wind is southerly, the water is blown upwards, giving the waterfall its name, the Stream against the Height (Irish: *Sruth-in-aghaidh-an-Aird*). In "The Mountain Tomb" (*CP*. 136), WBY describes this waterfall.

REFERENCE: McGarry, James P. *Place Names in the Writings of William Butler Yeats.* Gerrards Cross: Colin Smythe, 1976.

GLENDALOUGH (Irish: *Gleann Da Locha*) [glen of the two lakes], site of a monastic settlement founded by St. Kevin (d. 618), one mile west of Laragh in County Wicklow. Glendalough became a center of European learning during the eleventh and twelfth centuries. Today, it is distinguished by its round tower, stone crosses, and scenic beauty. **Iseult Gonne** lived at Laragh with her husband Francis Stuart. See also "Under the Round Tower" (*CP*. 154) and "Stream and Sun at Glendalough" (*CP*. 288).

REFERENCE: McGarry, James P. *Place Names in the Writings of William Butler Yeats.* Gerrards Cross: Colin Smythe, 1976.

GOBAN (Irish: *Goibhniu*), kitchen god and smith. Goban was host of the Otherworld and renowned for his ale, which gave immortality to all who drank it. He could make a sword or a spear with only three blows of a hammer. In "The Hour before Dawn" (*CP*. 131), there is a reference to Goban's mountain top. This is Slieve Anieran, a mountain in **Sligo** (county), where Goban made weapons for the **Tuatha dé Danaan**. See also "The Grey Rock" (*CP*. 115).

REFERENCE: McGarry, James P. *Place Names in the Writings of William Butler Yeats.* Gerrards Cross: Colin Smythe, 1976.

GODOLPHIN SCHOOL. When WBY was living with his family at **Edith Villas**, Chiswick, London, in 1877, he attended the Godolphin School in Iffley Road, Hammersmith. The school, founded in 1856, catered for the sons of struggling professional men. Having previously been tutored by his father, WBY was pleased to attend his first school, but he thought it rough, and he disliked being teased and isolated for his Irishness. He did not distinguish himself scholastically. In his first term, spring 1877, he was ranked twenty-first out of a class of thirty-one boys, while in the summer term of 1878, he was placed sixteenth out of twenty-one. His best subject was Classics, although he won a prize for chemistry, and in school sports in 1879, he won a silver cup for the half-mile race. He attended Godolphin School, early 1877–81, when his family returned to Ireland. The school was closed in 1900, and from 1906, the premises housed the Godolphin and Latymer School for Girls.

GOETHE, JOHANN WOLFGANG VON (1749–1832), poet, dramatist, and novelist. He was born in Frankfurt, Germany, the son of Johann Kaspar Goethe, an imperial councillor, and Katharine, daughter of the mayor of Frankfurt. After a happy childhood, which he describes in his autobiography *Poetry and Truth* (1811), he studied law at the University of Leipzig and at Strasbourg. Under the influence of the philosophers Rousseau and **Spinoza**, he developed the mystical feeling for nature that informs all his major work. With the success of his early drama *Götz von Berlichingen* (1773), the first work of the *Sturm und Drang* (storm and stress) movement, and the autobiographical novel *The Sorrows of Young Werther* (1774), Goethe was appointed chief minister of state at the court of Charles Augustus, duke of Saxe-Weimar, where he remained for the rest of his life. Inspired by a visit to Italy, 1786–88, he wrote *Egmont* (1788), *Roman Elegies* (1788), *Torquato Tasso* (1789), *Hermann and Dorothea* (1797), and the final version of the drama *Iphigenia in Tauris* (1787). The first part of his masterpiece, the dramatic poem *Faust*, was published in 1808. His close friendship with the dramatist Schiller, and his intense relationships with women, inspired some of his finest lyrics. His works were translated into English, notably by **Thomas Carlyle**. WBY admired Goethe, seeing in him the complete man, to be named in the company of **Homer, Dante**, and **Shakespeare**. Although he read no German, he was familiar with *Faust* (a copy of which he had in his library). This, he believed, was the only one of Goethe's works to have moved "the imagination of the world" (*UP2.* 141). In "Aphorisms of Yoga" (*LE.* 178–79), he expresses his admiration for Goethe's genius and claims *Wilhelm Meister's Apprenticeship* (1796) influenced him in his youth. He quotes from the work in *Per Amica Silentia Lunae* (*LE.* 11). He later refers to Goethe in a discussion on creativity and the subconscious (*LE.* 17).

REFERENCES: Boyle, Nicholas. *Goethe: The Poet and the Age*. Oxford: Clarendon, 1991; Friedenthal, Richard. *Goethe: His Life and Times*. London: Weidenfeld & Nicolson, 1993.

GOGARTY, OLIVER ST. JOHN (1878–1957), surgeon and man of letters. He was born in Dublin and attended Jesuit schools in Ireland and England before taking a medical degree at **Trinity College**, Dublin, in 1907. A classics scholar, who twice won the Vice-Chancellor's Prize at Trinity for verse, he went to Oxford University, hoping to emulate **Oscar Wilde** by winning the Newdigate Prize. In the event, he was placed second. He returned to Dublin, where he set up a successful practice as an ear-nose-and-throat specialist. He had been writing poetry from his undergraduate days, but the conservative traditions of the medical profession in Dublin precluded Gogarty from publishing under his own name. He used the pseudonym ''Gideon Ousley'' when his plays *A Serious Thing* (1919) and *The Enchanted Trousers* (1919) were performed at the **Abbey Theatre.** *Blight: The Tragedy of Dublin* (1917), which he wrote with Joseph O'Connor, was produced at the Abbey Theatre, December 1917, under the pseudonym A and O. Only in 1923 did he shed the mask of anonymity with *An Offering of Swans and Other Poems* (1924), published by the **Cuala Press** in 1924, with a preface by WBY (*PI.* 154–55), and *Wild Apples* (1930), for which WBY again wrote the preface (*PI.* 172–74). Although he was a committed writer, his literary reputation was overshadowed by his extravagant and, at times, malevolent behavior, so that he was considered more of a dilettante than a serious artist. In 1939, after losing a libel suit, he left Ireland and spent the rest of his life in the United States, writing prolifically. His *Collected Poems* was published in 1951. WBY was a friend of Gogarty and spent much time in his company in Dublin and at Renvyle House, Gogarty's country house in **Connemara**. In 1910, WBY lived in Fairfield, a house owned by Gogarty in Glasnevin, Dublin. Both were members of the **Irish Senate** from 1922, a venue that provided Gogarty with an opportunity to exercise his lively, Rabelaisian wit, much admired by WBY. In January 1923, during the Irish Civil War, Gogarty was taken prisoner by Republicans and escaped from his captors by swimming the River Liffey. In ''Modern Poetry: A Broadcast'' (*LE.* 100–101), WBY pays tribute to Gogarty's bravery. WBY based an early version of *Sophocles' King Oedipus* on a verse translation by Gogarty (it was later abandoned), and he included seventeen of Gogarty's poems in *The Oxford Book of Modern Verse* (1936), praising him as an outstanding lyric poet (*LE.* 187). A copy of Gogarty's *Selected Poems* (1933) was in WBY's library (*OS.* no. 756). Gogarty wrote extensively about his relationship with WBY, most notably in *As I Was Going Down Sackville Street* (1937), *Mourning Became Mrs Spendlove* (1946), *Rolling Down the Lea* (1950), and *It Isn't That Time of Year at All! An Unpremeditated Autobiography* (1954). He contributed to the special Yeats issue of *The Arrow* (1939) and wrote *William Butler Yeats: A Memoir* (1963).

REFERENCES: Carens, James F. *Surpassing Wit: Oliver St. John Gogarty, His Poetry and His Prose.* New York: Columbia University Press, 1979; Carens, James F. ''Gogarty and Yeats.'' In *Modern Irish Literature*, ed. Raymond J. Porter and James D. Brophy. New York: Twayne, 1972; Gogarty, Oliver St. John. *William Butler Yeats: A Memoir.* Dublin: Dolmen, 1963. Hogan, Robert, ed. *Dictionary of Irish Literature*. Rev. ed. Westport, Conn.: Greenwood, 1996; Lyons, J. B. *Oliver St. John Gogarty*. Lewisburg, Pa.: Bucknell University Press, 1976; O'Connor, Ulick. *Oliver St. John Gogarty: A Poet and His Times*. London: Cape, 1964.

GOLDEN HELMET, THE. *See* **GREEN HELMET, THE.**

GOLDEN PEAK, Hemakuta, sacred Indian mountain. It is north of the Himalayas and is sometimes identified with Mount **Kailas**, the paradise of Siva. See also "Anashuya and Vijaya" (*CP*. 13).

REFERENCES: O'Flaherty, Wendy Doniger, trans. *Hindu Myths: A Sourcebook Translated from the Sanskrit*. Harmondsworth, Middlesex: Penguin, 1975; Zimmer, Heinrich. *Myths and Symbols in Indian Art and Civilization*. Ed. Joseph Campbell. Washington, D.C.: Bollingen Foundation, 1946.

GOLDSMITH, OLIVER (1730–74), playwright, novelist, and essayist. He was born in Kilkenny West, County Westmeath, the son of the Reverend Charles Goldsmith, a Church of Ireland clergyman. Soon after his birth, the family moved to nearby Lissoy, where he spent his childhood. He attended schools in Edgeworthstown and Dublin and graduated from **Trinity College** in 1749. After refusing church ordination, he studied medicine at Edinburgh University, 1752–54, but left without completing his medical degree. He moved to London in 1756 and, in some desperation, turned to writing. His first book to arouse interest was *Citizen of the World, or, Letters from a Chinese Philosopher* (1762), a series of whimsical essays that looked at London society through the eyes of a Chinese visitor. He followed this success with the long, nostalgic poem "The Deserted Village" (1770), modeled on his native village of Lissoy. Goldsmith excelled as a novelist with *The Vicar of Wakefield* (1766), but it was with his two realistic comedies, *The Good Natur'd Man* (1768) and *She Stoops to Conquer* (1773), that he made his most profound impact on the theater of his day, replacing the sentimental comedy of manners with a robust drama, rich in humanity and insight. He made much money from his writing but his extravagance and overgenerous nature kept him poor. WBY appreciated Goldsmith's simple, sensitive nature, his intense imagination, and his delight in the common life that shocked so many of his contemporaries (*EI*. 402). Early in his career, WBY believed that Goldsmith, although born in Ireland, was essentially an English writer (*UP2*. 328). Later he revised his youthful opinions, making favorable comparisons between Goldsmith and **J. M. Synge** and naming him with **Jonathan Swift** and **George Berkeley** in "The Seven Sages" (*CP*. 271) and "Blood and the Moon" (*CP*. 267).

REFERENCES: Ginger, John. *The Notable Man: The Life and Times of Oliver Goldsmith*. London: Hamilton, 1977; Hogan, Robert, ed. *Dictionary of Irish Literature*. Rev. ed. Westport, Conn.: Greenwood, 1996; Wibberley, Leonard. *The Good-Natured Man: A Portrait of Oliver Goldsmith*. New York: Morrow, 1979.

GOLL (blind of one eye), Irish mythological king. There are several persons named Goll in Celtic mythology. The best known is Goll Mac Morna, who killed **Fionn Mac Cumhal's** father and became leader of the **Fianna**. In a note to his poem "The Madness of King Goll" (*CP*. 17), WBY writes that Goll "lived in Ireland about the third century" (*VP*. 857). The king lost his reason in a battle and fled to a glen, since called the Glen of the Lunatics (Irish: *Glen-na-Galt*). WBY states that the valley is in **Cork** (county), giving as his source Eugene O'Curry's *Manuscript Materials of Ancient Irish History* (1878). "The Madness of King Goll" was published in the *Leisure Hour*, September 1887, under the title "King Goll, an Irish Legend," with an illustration by **John B. Yeats**. In 1924, WBY recalled his father doing a painting of him as King Goll tearing strings out of a harp (*WL*. 705).

GONNE, ISEULT (1894–1954), daughter of **Maud Gonne**. WBY first met her in 1910, when he stayed with her mother at Colleville, Normandy. He introduced her to the poems of **Rabindranath Tagore**, and she read him the contemporary French poets **Francis Jammes** and **Charles Péguy**. WBY and she met again in 1912, and he was inspired by her dancing to write "To a Child Dancing in the Wind" (*CP*. 136). In the summer of 1916, she acted as his secretary. With her innocence and beauty, he found her attractive and reminiscent of her mother, feelings he explored in the poems "Two Years Later" (*CP*. 137) and "Men Improve with the Years" (*CP*. 152). At the same time, her youth made him conscious of his own middle age. In the spring of 1917, having been finally rejected by Maud Gonne, he proposed marriage to Iseult—a proposal that had the approval of **Lady Gregory** and **Olivia Shakespear**. Although she was fond of him, Iseult looked upon him more as an uncle than a lover (she called him Uncle Willie) and refused his offer. In May 1917, he addressed *Per Amica Silentia Lunae* (*LE*. 1, 32–33) to her. He again proposed marriage in September 1917 and was upset when she refused. (*WL*. 629–32). After his marriage to **Georgie Hyde-Lees**, 20 October 1917, he felt responsibility for Iseult, finding her a job in the School of Oriental Languages, London. Georgie Hyde-Lees and Iseult became friends, but his relationship with Iseult continued to trouble WBY. He wrote of the inappropriateness of his feelings in "Owen Aherne and his Dancers" (*CP*. 247) and reflected on his responsibilities in "Two Songs of a Fool" (*CP*. 190). He encouraged her to marry **Lennox Robinson**, but in 1920, she married the novelist Francis Stuart, then seventeen years of age. They had a child, but the marriage was unhappy, causing Maud Gonne so much distress that in letters to WBY she asked him to intervene. He refers to the destructive marriage in the poem "Why should not Old Men be Mad" (*CP*. 388). Iseult is the subject of Part IV of the poem "A Man Young and Old" (*CP*. 249), written in 1926–27.

REFERENCES: Elborn, Geoffrey. *Francis Stuart: A Life*. Dublin: Raven Arts, 1990; Stuart, Francis. *Black List, Section H*. Carbondale: Southern Illinois University Press,

1971; White, Anna MacBride, and Jeffares, A. Norman, eds. *The Gonne-Yeats Letters: 1893–1938.* New York: W. W. Norton, 1992.

GONNE, KATHLEEN (1868–1919), younger sister of **Maud Gonne**. She was born near the **Curragh** Military Camp, County Kildare, where her father, Captain Thomas Gonne, was in military service. After the death of her mother in 1871, she formed a close companionship with her sister. They lived for a time in **Howth** before moving to the south of France. Later, they traveled to Europe with their father. After his death in 1886, the two sisters were cared for in London by their uncle, William Gonne. Kathleen, who was quieter and more subdued than her sister, was a talented musician and studied art at the Slade. She was presented at court in 1888 and a year later married Captain (later Major-General) Thomas David Pilcher (1858–1928), who commanded a flying column in the Boer War. The family moved to Dublin in the mid-1890s, when Pilcher was appointed deputy assistant adjutant-general of Dublin. Later, they returned to London. She divorced her husband in the first decade of the century, and in March 1915, her favorite son, Tommy, was killed leading a platoon in France. Her health deteriorated, and she moved to Switzerland, where she died. WBY had a close friendship with her, sometimes dining with her in London. ''Adam's Curse'' (*CP.* 88), written in 1901, records such an occasion.

REFERENCE: White, Anna MacBride, and Jeffares, A. Norman, eds. *The Gonne-Yeats Letters: 1893–1938.* New York: W. W. Norton, 1992.

GONNE, [EDITH] MAUD (1866–1953), political activist. She was born in Surrey, the daughter of Thomas Gonne, captain in the British army, and spent her childhood in Ireland, where her father's regiment was stationed at the **Curragh**, County Kildare. After the death of her mother in 1871, she and her sister **Kathleen** were cared for by a nurse in **Howth**, County Dublin, before they moved for health reasons to the south of France. When her father returned to Ireland in 1882, Maud, a noted beauty, acted as his hostess until his death in 1886. She went to London to live with her father's elder brother, Uncle William, but she contracted pneumonia and journeyed to France to convalesce. In France, she fell in love with Lucien Millevoye, a Boulangist politician, and in 1888, she returned to Paris as his mistress. She had become interested in Irish nationalism, and through **C. H. Oldham**, she was introduced to **John O'Leary** and his sister **Ellen**. In January 1889, the latter gave her a letter of introduction to the Yeats family, then living at **Bedford Park**, London. From the moment he was introduced, WBY became infatuated with her, and he spent the next years trying to meet her expectations as a political activist. He proposed marriage on many occasions, but she always refused. Unknown to WBY, she had a son by Millevoye in January 1890. The child died some months later, while his mother was campaigning in England for the release of Fenian prisoners. She was initiated into **The Order of the Golden Dawn**, November 1891, and in 1892, she helped WBY with the foundation of the **National Literary Society**. She returned to France in 1893 and conceived a second child by Millevoye.

WBY visited her in Paris in February 1894, unaware that she was pregnant. Her daughter **Iseult Gonne** was born 6 August 1894. In 1897, WBY helped Maud Gonne found L'Association Irlandaise and joined her during the anti-Jubilee demonstrations that she organized in Dublin, July 1897. In 1898, he traveled with her on a lecture tour of England and Scotland to promote the **Wolfe Tone** Centenary celebrations. She and WBY grew spiritually closer, and in late 1898, they discussed the formation of an Order of Celtic Mysteries to be established in the Castle of Heroes on Lough Key. With the outbreak of the Boer War in 1899, she was politically active in the pro-Boer Transvaal Committee. She ended her relationship with Millevoye, who had taken another mistress, and formed a liaison with **John MacBride**. During Queen Victoria's visit to Dublin in 1900, she organized a counterdemonstration of 40,000 schoolchildren who swore an oath of undying hatred for England. She moved to Dublin in 1902 and made a triumphant appearance in WBY's play *Cathleen Ni Houlihan*. After joining the Catholic Church, she married MacBride on 21 February 1903. WBY was on a lecture tour at the time and was shocked by the news. Her son, Sean, was born in January 1904, but already the marriage was failing, and in 1905 she sued for divorce. Her accusations of physical abuse and sexual promiscuity against MacBride antagonized the people of Dublin, and having been granted custody of the child, she left for France, spending the next years in Paris and at Colleville in Normandy. WBY visited her in Paris in 1908, and they met in London in 1909. She visited Dublin in 1910, and he became a regular visitor to her home in Normandy. With the execution of MacBride for his part in the 1916 Easter Rising, WBY renewed his offer of marriage. When she refused, he turned his attention to her daughter Iseult. Maud Gonne wished to return to Ireland, but she was proscribed. In January 1918, she journeyed in disguise to Dublin but she was arrested and returned to England, where she was imprisoned for six months on suspicion of being involved in a pro-German plot. On her release, she again illegally entered Ireland, but WBY refused to allow her into her Dublin home at 76 St. Stephen's Green, which he had rented from her, because his wife was ill with pneumonia and expecting their first child. Although the friendship was strained for many years, Maud Gonne continued to call upon his help with family problems, especially when Iseult married the novelist Francis Stuart. She settled permanently in Dublin in 1918 and gave active support to **Eamon de Valera** during the Civil War of 1922. Her house was raided by the Free State authorities, and her son, who was a member of the Irish Republican Army (IRA), was interned. She was imprisoned in January 1923 but released after a hunger strike. Despite her activism, she was then of marginal importance in the political affairs of the Irish Free State. In 1936, she stood unsuccessfully for Cumann Poblachta na hEireann, a political party organized by her son. Her memoirs, *A Servant of the Queen*, in which she includes an account of her relationship with WBY, were published in 1938. WBY has written about her extensively, not only in his poetry but also in his autobiographical writings. From their first meeting, she became his muse, and he celebrated her beauty in poem after poem, from the early love lyrics like ''The Rose of the World'' (*CP*. 41), ''The Pity of Love''

(*CP*. 45), "The Sorrow of Love" (*CP*. 45), "When You are Old" (*CP*. 46), "The White Birds" (*CP*. 46), "The Countess Cathleen in Paradise" (*CP*. 48), "The Two Trees" (*CP*. 54), "He Hears the Cry of the Sedge" (*CP*. 75), "He thinks of those who have Spoken Evil of His Beloved" (*CP*. 75), "The Secret Rose" (*CP*. 77), "The Poet Pleads with the Elemental Powers" (*CP*. 80), "In the Seven Woods" (*CP*. 85), "The Arrow" (*CP*. 85), "The Folly of Being Comforted" (*CP*. 86), "Never Give all the Heart" (*CP*. 87), "Adam's Curse" (*CP*. 88), "Red Hanrahan's Song about Ireland" (*CP*. 90), and "O Do Not Love Too Long" (*CP*. 93) to the poems and plays in which he mythologized her as **Helen, Cathleen Ni Houlihan, Pallas Athene, Dectora**, and **Deirdre**, including "A Woman Homer Sung" (*CP*. 100), "Words" (*CP*. 100), "No Second Troy" (*CP*. 101), "Reconciliation" (*CP*. 102), "King and No King" (*CP*. 102), "Peace" (*CP*. 103), "Against Unworthy Praise" (*CP*. 103), "When Helen Lived" (*CP*. 124), "Fallen Majesty" (*CP*. 138), "Friends" (*CP*. 139), "The Cold Heaven" (*CP*. 140), "That the Night Come" (*CP*. 140), *The Shadowy Waters*, and *Deirdre*. After his marriage in 1917, the number of references to Maud Gonne in the poems decreased.

REFERENCES: Coxhead, Elizabeth. *Daughters of Erin: Five Women of the Irish Renascence*. London: Secker & Warburg, 1965; Cardozo, Nancy. *Maud Gonne: Lucky Eyes and a High Heart*. London: Gollancz, 1978; Freyer, Grattan. *W. B. Yeats and the Anti-Democratic Tradition*. Dublin: Gill & Macmillan, 1981; Gonne MacBride, Maud. *A Servant of the Queen*. Dublin: Golden Eagle Books, 1938; White, Anna MacBride, and Jeffares, A. Norman. *The Gonne-Yeats Letters: 1893–1938*. New York: W. W. Norton, 1992.

GONNE, MAY [Mrs. Bertie-Clay] (1863–1929), cousin of **Maud Gonne**. She trained as a nurse and became guardian of **Iseult Gonne** after Maud Gonne's marriage to **John MacBride**. In 1902, she married N. S. Bertie-Clay, a civil servant with the Foreign Service in India. She was a close friend and confidante of her cousin, especially during Maud's separation and divorce from MacBride. WBY visited her in London, and she encouraged his efforts to convince Maud Gonne to marry him (*M*. 50). She was a member of **The Order of the Golden Dawn** from 1900.

REFERENCE: White, Anna MacBride, and Jeffares, A. Norman, eds. *The Gonne-Yeats Letters: 1893–1938*. New York: W. W. Norton, 1992.

GORE-BOOTH, CONSTANCE [GEORGINA]. *See* **MARKIEWICZ, COUNTESS**.

GORE-BOOTH, EVA [SELENA] (1870–1926), poet, dramatist, and social worker. She was born at **Lissadell, Sligo** (county), daughter of Sir Henry Gore-Booth and sister to **Constance** and Mabel Gore-Booth (1880–1955). She had just returned home from extensive travels with her father in the West Indies and America when she met WBY in November 1894. He spent time in her company, finding her a sympathetic listener, and told her of his disappointed love for **Maud Gonne**. Indeed, he came close to asking her to marry him (*M*. 78–79). In 1897, she moved to Manchester, England. There, she attempted to promote women's rights and to organize women textile workers into trade unions. She attempted to cultivate her inner self through the study of Neoplatonism and Indian mysticism. A prolific writer, she published *Poems* in 1898 and, between 1904 and 1918, completed ten volumes of verse, including *The Death of Fionavar* (1916). Her verse drama about **Cuchulain,** *Unseen Kings* (1904), was considered for production by the **Irish National Theatre Society**. Worn out by overwork and ill health, she died in Hampstead, London, at the age of fifty-six. WBY encouraged her writing by reading her poems and sending her material of Irish interest (*WL*. 256–57). He immortalized her fragile beauty in his poem "In Memory of Eva Gore-Booth and Con Markiewicz" (*CP*. 263), an elegy written in 1927, after her death.

REFERENCES: Fletcher, Ian. "Yeats and Lissadell." In *W. B. Yeats and His Contemporaries*. Brighton, Sussex: Harvester, 1987; Hogan, Robert, ed. *Dictionary of Irish Literature*. Rev. ed. Westport, Conn.: Greenwood, 1996; Marreco, Anne. *The Rebel Countess: The Life and Times of Constance Markievicz* [*sic*]. London: Weidenfeld & Nicolson, 1967.

GORIAS. *See* **FALIAS**.

GORT, market town in **Galway** (county). Gort is one and a half miles from **Lady Gregory's** estate at **Coole Park** and close to WBY's home at **Thoor Ballylee**. It is associated with **Guaire**, king of **Connacht** in the sixth century. In WBY's play *The King's Threshold*, the poet **Seanchan** is on hunger strike outside Guaire's palace in Gort. In "Certain Noble Plays of Japan" (*EI*. 233), WBY regrets that he did not have the opportunity to describe the rocky landscape of modern Gort. See also "The Three Beggars" (*CP*. 124) and "To Be Carved on a Stone at Thoor Ballylee" (*CP*. 214).

REFERENCE: McGarry, James P. *Place Names in the Writings of William Butler Yeats*. Gerrards Cross: Colin Smythe, 1976.

GOSSE, SIR EDMUND [WILLIAM] (1849–1928), English poet, biographer, and literary critic. Son of the naturalist Philip Henry Gosse, he started work at seventeen as an assistant librarian in the **British Museum**. From 1884 to 1890, he lectured in English literature at Trinity College, Cambridge. Later, he was librarian in the House of Lords (1904–14). He achieved some prominence as a poet with his *On Viol and Flute* (1873) and *New Poems* (1879), but it was as a critic that he made his most significant contribution to literature. With his *Studies in the Literature of Northern Europe* (1879), he introduced the drama of **Henrik Ibsen** and other Scandinavian authors to the English public. He wrote scholarly biographies of Thomas Gray (1882), **John Donne** (1899), and **Algernon Swinburne** (1917), while *Father and Son* (1907), an account of his relationship with his father, became a classic. He was knighted in 1925. As a child, WBY was fascinated by Gosse's *King Erik* (1876), a five-act tragedy in blank verse, but by 1886, he was dismissive of his poetry (*UP1*. 92). In 1895, Gosse responded favorably to a gift of WBY's *Poems* (1895), and they became friends. Gosse used his considerable influence to secure WBY a Civil List pension in 1910 (*WL*. 550), and he chaired events to raise money for the **Abbey Theatre**. Their friendship was not always equable, however, particularly when WBY was awarded the **Nobel Prize for Literature** in 1923, an award that Gosse interpreted as an anti-British gesture from the Swedes. He wrote a nit-picking review in *The Sunday Times* of *The Bounty of Sweden*, to which WBY responded (*UP2*. 453–54).

REFERENCES: Thwaite, Ann. *Edmund Gosse: A Literary Landscape, 1849–1928*. Chicago: University of Chicago Press, 1984; Woolf, James D. *Sir Edmund Gosse*. New York: Twayne, 1972.

GRANIA [also Gráinne], fated lover from the Fenian Cycle of Irish mythology. Grania elopes with **Diarmuid** just as she is about to be married to the aging **Fionn Mac Cumhal**. For the next sixteen years, the lovers move from place to place throughout Ireland, until Diarmuid is fatally wounded on **Ben Bulben** by a magic boar. Only Fionn can save his life, but he refuses, and the love god **Aengus** takes the body to his palace at Brugh-na-Boinne. Fionn persuades Grania to return home with him as his bride, but when they enter the assembly of the Fenian knights, they are greeted with uncontrollable laughter. In WBY's poem "A Faery Song" (*CP*. 43), the fairies sing a lullaby to Diarmuid and Grania as they celebrate their wedding night under a cromlech, a massive structure consisting of a large flat stone resting on three or more upright stones. Many of the cromlechs in Ireland are still associated with the wanderings of Diarmuid and Grania. Their tragic story provided the plot for *Diarmuid and Grania* (1901), the play on which WBY collaborated with **George Moore**. There is a reference to the two lovers in "Upon a Dying Lady" (*CP*. 177) and to Grania in *The Wanderings of Oisin* (*CP*. 438).

REFERENCE: Dames, Michael. *Mythic Ireland*. 1992. Reprint, New York: Thames & Hudson, 1996.

GRATTAN, HENRY (1746–1820), patriot and statesman. He was born in Dublin and educated at **Trinity College** and the Middle Temple, London. He entered the Irish Parliament in Dublin in 1775 and quickly established himself as a brilliant orator and parliamentary leader. Through his efforts, he enabled the Irish Parliament in 1782 to gain a measure of independence from the English Parliament, forming what came to be known as Grattan's Parliament. Although he was Protestant, he worked for Catholic Emancipation and gained for Catholics the right to vote in Ireland. When a measure to enable Catholics to sit in

Parliament was vetoed by King George III, Grattan retired from the Irish Parliament in 1797, but his work for reform and independence was a catalyst to the 1798 Rebellion led by **Lord Edward Fitzgerald** and **Wolfe Tone**. He made a brief return to the Irish Parliament in 1800, when he unsuccessfully attempted to prevent the adoption of the Act of Union, and the Irish Parliament was dissolved. From 1805, despite deteriorating health, he sat in the English Parliament in London but took little part in debate, except in support of Catholic Emancipation. WBY was conscious of Grattan as one of the dominant Protestant leaders of Ireland in the eighteenth century and believed Grattan's Parliament represented a high point of Irish history, enabling the Irish gentry to rise to a greatness in eloquence, architecture, and literature unparalleled in 700 years of Irish history.

REFERENCES: Foster, R. F. *Modern Ireland 1600–1972.* 1988. Reprint, London: Penguin, 1989; Gwynn, Stephen L. *Henry Grattan and His Times.* Westport, Conn.: Greenwood, 1971.

GREAT MOTHER, earth goddess. In ancient Middle Eastern religion, and in Greece, Rome, and western Asia, she was the mother goddess, the symbol of fertility. As the creative force in nature, she was worshipped under many names, including Astarte, Cybele, Isis, and Demeter. Later, her cult involved the worship of a male deity, whose death and resurrection symbolized the regenerative power of the earth. See also ''Colonus Praise'' (*CP.* 245) and ''Parnell's Funeral'' (*CP.* 319).

GREAT SMARAGDINE TABLET, Hermetic work on alchemy. Written in medieval Latin, the Great Smaragdine Tablet was published in 1541 and attributed to the Egyptian god of writing, Thoth, or Hermes Trismegistus. See also ''Ribh Denounces Patrick'' (*CP.* 328).

GREEK, THE, character in WBY's play *The Resurrection.* At the opening of the action, The Greek, a disciple of **Christ**, is guarding the room where the other disciples are gathered after the crucifixion. He debates with **The Hebrew** the nature of the Messiah, insisting that Christ was pure spirit. When Christ appears, he touches the heart, convinced that it is a phantom. When he discovers the heart is beating, he is terrified but articulates the significance of the Christian era to the old Mediterranean civilization. In the first production of *The Resurrection*, July 1934, the role of The Greek was played by Denis Carey.

GREEN HELMET, THE, one-act heroic farce in verse by WBY. *The Green Helmet*, a later version of *The Golden Helmet*, a one-act play in prose that had been produced at the **Abbey Theatre**, March 1908, was published by the **Cuala Press** in 1910. The action of the play was based on two stories from **Lady Gregory's** *Cuchulain of Muirthemne*, ''The Feast of Bricriu'' and ''The Championship of Ulster.'' It was written in ballad meter inspired by **Wilfred Scawen**

Blunt in his play *Fand*. In WBY's play, the **Red Man** tests the warriors of Ireland by challenging them to repay an old debt—one of them must allow him to cut off his head. Only **Cuchulain** volunteers, and for his bravery, he is rewarded with the Green Helmet, the mark of a true hero. The play was first performed at the Abbey Theatre, February 1910, as a curtain raiser to a production of **J. M. Synge's** *The Playboy of the Western World*. The pairing was an apt one. *The Green Helmet* is a satire, and commentators have made connections between the meanness of heroic Ireland as it is presented in the play and the rowdy reception accorded the first production of *The Playboy*—indeed, in the course of the action, **Emer's** speech on behalf of her husband is drowned out by a vociferous mob. The cast of the first production was: Cuchulain, J. M. Kerrigan; **Conall**, Arthur Sinclair; **Laegaire**, Fred O'Donovan; Laeg, Sidney J. Morgan; Emer, **Sara Allgood**; Conal's Wife, **Máire O'Neill**; Laegaire's Wife, Eithne Magee; Red Man, Ambrose Power; Scullions, Horse Boys, and Blackmen, Eric Gorman, J. A. O'Rourke, John Carrick, F. R. Harford, T. Maloney, T. Durkin, and P. Byrne.

REFERENCES: Bjersby, Birgit. *The Interpretation of the Cuchulain Legend in the Works of W. B. Yeats*. Folcroft, Pa.: Folcroft, 1969; Henn, T. R. ''*The Green Helmet* and *Responsibilities*.'' In *An Honored Guest: New Essays on W. B. Yeats*, ed. Denis Donoghue and J. R. Mulryne. London: Edward Arnold, 1965; Miller, Liam. *The Noble Drama of W. B. Yeats*. Dublin: Dolmen, 1977; Taylor, Richard. *A Reader's Guide to the Plays of W. B. Yeats*. New York: St. Martin's, 1984.

GREEN HELMET AND OTHER POEMS, THE, collection of poems and a play by WBY. The collection was published by the **Cuala Press** in 1910, in a limited edition of 400 copies. The volume contained the text of WBY's heroic farce *The Green Helmet*, in addition to a series of short poems reflecting the poet's increasing rejection of the romantic nostalgia of his earlier verse in favor of a more direct, conversational and public style. The writing in this collection coincided with his increased responsibilities as a director of the **Abbey Theatre** and the more public role he chose to play in Ireland's political controversies. Even in those poems that addressed **Maud Gonne**, he was able to distance his personal feelings and transform her into a public persona as **Helen**. The 1912 Macmillan edition of *The Green Helmet and Other Poems* added six more poems.

GREENLANDS, unfenced area of sand hills at **Rosses Point, Sligo** (county). In the poem ''Three Songs to the One Burden'' (*CP*. 371), WBY recalls **Henry Middleton** walking over the Greenlands each Sunday afternoon.

REFERENCE: McGarry, James P. *Place Names in the Writings of William Butler Yeats*. Gerrards Cross: Colin Smythe, 1976.

GREGG, F[REDERICK] J[AMES], (1864–1927), journalist. He was a contemporary of WBY at the **Erasmus Smith High School** and visited the Yeats family when they lived in **Ashfield Terrace**, Dublin. In 1891, he immigrated to the United States, where he worked as a journalist on the *New York Evening Sun* and *Vanity Fair*. He formed an intimate friendship with **John Quinn**, who nicknamed him "El Greggo," and reintroduced him to **John B. Yeats** in 1909. Gregg was one of the small group who cared for the elderly painter in his final years in New York and, with Quinn and Jeanne Robert Foster, helped to plan his funeral, February 1922. He published an obituary of Quinn in the *Evening Sun*, 29 July 1924. Gregg's early poems were published in the *Irish Monthly* and in *Poems and Ballads of Young Ireland* (1888), edited by WBY.

    REFERENCE: Reid, B. L. *The Man from New York: John Quinn and His Friends*. New York: Oxford University Press, 1968.

GREGORY, ANNE [Mrs. de Winton] (b. 1911), older daughter of **Robert Gregory** and grandchild of **Lady Gregory**. She wrote *Me and Nu: Childhood at Coole* (1970), in which she describes living with her grandmother at Coole and at the Gregory summer home, Mount Vernon, in the **Burren**. She gives a child's perspective of WBY and other literary visitors to **Coole Park**. She is the subject of WBY's charming poem "For Anne Gregory" (*CP*. 277). She and her sister Catherine Gregory Kennedy returned from England in 1992 to open a Visitors Center in Coole Park.

    REFERENCE: Gregory, Anne. *Me and Nu: Childhood at Coole*. Gerrards Cross: Colin Smythe, 1970.

GREGORY, LADY [ISABELLA] AUGUSTA (1852–1932), playwright and patron. She was the seventh daughter of Dudley Persse, a member of the Anglo-Irish Ascendancy, and was born in the family home at **Roxborough, Galway** (county). In 1880, she married Sir William Gregory, a former governor of Ceylon and owner of **Coole Park**, a nearby estate. With her husband, she traveled widely in Europe and the Middle East and led an active social life in London. Her son, **Robert**, was born in London, 1881, and later that year she began an affair with **Wilfred Scawen Blunt**, under whose influence she wrote the political pamphlet *Arabi and His Household* (1882). Her sonnet sequence, *A Woman's Sonnets* (1892), was inspired by their relationship. After the death of her elderly husband in March 1892, she returned to Coole Park. She met WBY for the first time in 1894, but their friendship did not begin until the summer of 1896, when they met at **Tulira Castle**, the home of **Edward Martyn**. The following year, WBY spent the first of twenty summers at Coole Park, and it was there, and in her London apartment, that Lady Gregory and he formulated plans for an **Irish Literary Theatre**. She published an edition of her husband's autobiography in 1894 and, with WBY's encouragement, began collecting local folklore, which she published in *A Book of Saints and Wonders* (1906), *The Kiltartan History Book* (1909), *The Kiltartan Wonder Book* (1910), and *Visions and Beliefs in the West of Ireland* (1920). In the next years, she devoted herself totally to the cause of cultural nationalism, publishing her literary essays, *Ideals in Ireland*, in 1901.

Not only did she assist WBY with his early plays in dialect, but she also published her version of the **Ulster** mythological tales, *Cuchulain of Muirthemne* (1902), which WBY thought unequaled in English. She translated stories and plays from the Gaelic by **Douglas Hyde** and began to write a series of popular plays, including *The Jackdaw* (1901) and *Twenty-five* (1901). When the **Abbey Theatre** opened in 1904, her folk comedy *Spreading the News* shared the bill with WBY's *On Baile's Strand*. From then until her death, she was actively involved with the day-to-day administration of the Abbey. In January 1909, she took seriously ill from a cerebral hemorrhage. She recovered and, in 1911, accompanied the Abbey on their first tour of the United States, when riots broke out in Philadelphia over the production of **J. M. Synge's** *The Playboy of the Western World*. In the United States, she met **John Quinn**, with whom she had a brief affair. She led the Abbey Theatre's tours of the United States in 1912 and 1913. Her nephew **Hugh Lane** was drowned when the *Lusitania* was torpedoed in May 1915, and her son Robert, a major in the Royal Flying Corps, was shot down and killed over northern Italy in January 1918. In 1923, she had a first operation for breast cancer, and in April 1924, the family home at Roxborough was burned down by the Republicans. In 1927, Coole Park estate was sold to the Forestry Commission, but she was able to lease the house for the remaining five years of her life. From the early years of their relationship, WBY and Lady Gregory were mutually beneficial to each other. She provided him with patronage; he introduced her into literary circles in London and Dublin. She was a surrogate mother figure who cared for his health and welfare, while after 1918, he took the place of her devoted son. Together, they established and sustained the Abbey Theatre, a tribute to their mutual genius. WBY repaid many of his debts of gratitude to Lady Gregory through the tributes he wrote and those poems that chronicle the end of the Anglo-Irish tradition. He names her in ''Beautiful Lofty Things'' (*CP*. 348), and in ''The Municipal Gallery Revisited'' (*CP*. 368), she is included, with J. M. Synge, among his special friends. Five poems by Lady Gregory, translations from the Irish, were selected by WBY for *The Oxford Book of Modern Verse* (1936).

REFERENCES: Adams, Hazard. *Lady Gregory*. Lewisburg, Pa.: Bucknell University Press, 1973; Coxhead, Elizabeth. *Lady Gregory: A Literary Portrait*. Gerrards Cross: Colin Smythe, 1966; Saddlemyer, Ann. ''Augusta Gregory, Irish Nationalist.'' In *Myth and Reality in Irish Literature*, ed. Joseph Ronsley. Waterloo, Ontario: Wilfred Laurier University Press, 1977; Saddlemyer, Ann. *In Defense of Lady Gregory, Playwright*. Dublin: Dolmen, 1966; Torchiana, Donald T. *W. B. Yeats & Georgian Ireland*. Oxford: Oxford University Press, 1966.

GREGORY, [MAJOR] ROBERT (1881–1918), only child of Sir William and **Lady Gregory**. He was born in England and educated at Harrow, a prestigious English school. After attending Oxford University, he studied art at the Slade School in London and with the painter Jacques Emile Blanche in Paris. Before completing his studies, he assisted with designs for *The Hour-Glass* (1903) and designed *The Shadowy Waters* (1904), *Kincora* (1905), and *Deirdre* (1906), all produced by the **Irish National Theatre Society**. In 1907, he visited Italy with his mother and WBY, and after his marriage later that year, he lived much of his time at **Coole Park** with his wife Margaret and their three children, Richard, **Anne**, and Catherine. When **Mrs. Patrick Campbell** played in a revival of *Deirdre* in 1908, he designed the setting and costumes. In October 1914, an exhibition of his paintings opened at the Chenil Gallery, London. In 1915, he joined the army as a second lieutenant in the 4th Connaught Rangers. Later, he joined the Royal Flying Corps and rose to the rank of temporary major. In July 1917, he was awarded the Military Cross for gallantry and devotion to duty. On 23 January 1918, he was shot down in error—according to the records of the Royal Flying Corps—while returning to base in northern Italy. Robert Gregory was a promising painter and an able sportsman, excelling at cricket, boxing, rifle shooting, and horse riding. He had a generous nature, keen intelligence, and a deep love of Ireland. As a tribute to his talents, WBY wrote the elegy "An Irish Airman Foresees his Death" (*CP*. 152), and the longer poems "In Memory of Major Robert Gregory" (*CP*. 148) and "Shepherd and Goatherd" (*CP*. 159). In these, he celebrates Gregory as a twentieth-century Renaissance man—cultured, multitalented, and heroic. Later, he wrote "Reprisals" (*VP*. 791), a bitter poem about Gregory's death in Italy and the Black and Tans at Coole Park. This was published posthumously. WBY contributed a moving appreciation of Robert Gregory to *The Observer*, 17 February 1918 (*UP2*. 429–31). His portrait, painted by **Charles Shannon** in 1906, now hangs in the **Municipal Gallery of Modern Art**.

REFERENCES: Gordon, D. J., ed. "In Memory of Major Robert Gregory." In *W. B. Yeats: Images of a Poet*. Manchester: University of Manchester Press, 1961; Smythe, Colin, ed. *Robert Gregory, 1881–1918: A Centenary Tribute*. Gerrards Cross: Colin Smythe, 1981; Torchiana, Donald T. *W. B. Yeats & Georgian Ireland*. Oxford: Oxford University Press, 1966.

GREGORY'S WOOD. *See* **SEVEN WOODS**.

GREY ROCK [Craglee] (Irish: *Craig Liath*), stone monument in **County Clare**. Grey Rock is associated with Aoibheal (also Aoibheall, Aoibhell, Eevell, Aoife), one of the **Sídhe**. She was a fairy mistress (Irish: *leanán sídhe*). If a man rejected her, she became his slave; if he accepted her, he became her slave. Most Gaelic poets had their *leanán sídhe*, or fairy muse, who fed off them until they wasted away. In his essay "The Midnight Court" (*EX*. 281–86), WBY notes that Brian Merriman set his extravagant poem at the court of Eevell of Craglee, while in "The Crucifixion of the Outcast" (*MY*. 152), Aoibheal of the Grey Rock is named by the lay brother as one of the pagan demons praised by the poet Cumhal. See also "The Grey Rock" (*CP*. 115).

REFERENCE: McGarry, James P. *Place Names in the Writings of William Butler Yeats*. Gerrards Cross: Colin Smythe, 1976.

GRIFFITH, ARTHUR (1871–1922), political leader. He was born in Dublin and educated at the Christian Brothers School, Strand Street. A founder of the Celtic Literary Society, 1893, he was active in the Gaelic League and the Irish Republican Brotherhood, 1893–1910. He fought for the Boers, 1897–99, and edited a pro-Boer newspaper. Returning to Ireland in 1899, he and his friend **William Rooney** founded the radical nationalist weekly *The United Irishman*, modeled on **John Mitchel's** journal of the same name. As joint editor of the paper, Griffith advocated a policy of passive resistance to England (although he did not discount the possibility of an armed rebellion in the future) and the setting up of a national assembly in Dublin, a plan modeled on the "Hungarian Policy" outlined in his book *The Resurrection of Hungary: A Parallel for Ireland* (1904). He advocated, too, a policy of Irish self-dependence in culture, education, and economics. To promote these objectives, he founded Cumann na nGaedheal in 1900, a nationalist organization later reconstructed as Sinn Féin, meaning "we ourselves," to emphasize the notion of economic and political autonomy. He joined the Irish National Volunteers in 1913 and vehemently opposed the recruitment of Irishmen to fight for Britain in the 1914–18 war. He did not take part in the Easter Rising in 1916, but he was imprisoned by the British, nonetheless, and in the general election of 1918, representing Sinn Féin, he was elected M.P. for East Cavan. Sinn Féin scored an overwhelming majority in the election and proclaimed themselves the legitimate government of an Irish Republic, abstaining from the British Parliament at Westminster. For his part in a campaign of civil resistance, Griffith was arrested, November 1920. On his release, he headed the Irish delegation in the Treaty negotiations with England and successfully defended the Anglo-Irish Treaty in **Dáil Éireann** as the best opportunity for Ireland to gain her freedom. After the pro-Treaty candidates won the election of June 1922, Griffith was elected president of the Dáil. Civil war broke out, June 1922, and Griffith died from a brain hemorrhage, August 1922. In the early years of the Irish Dramatic Movement, Griffith and WBY were political allies (*WL.* 352–53). In his account of the demonstrations at the first performance of ***The Countess Cathleen*** (1899), WBY writes that Griffith brought men to applaud everything in the play that they thought the Catholic Church would not like (*A.* 416), and Griffith was enthusiastic about the sentiments expressed in ***Cathleen Ni Houlihan*** (1902). Later, their opposing views on art and nationality brought them into conflict, and the friendship deteriorated, especially after Griffith's paper attacked as anti-Irish **J. M. Synge's** *In the Shadow of the Glen* and *The Playboy of the Western World*. From 1905, *The United Irishman* and its successor *Sinn Féin* constantly provoked WBY with snide remarks about the **Abbey Theatre** and its associates. They questioned the motives of **Hugh Lane** because he was a professional picture dealer, but the inference was withdrawn after it was challenged by WBY (*KLIII.* 688). WBY and Griffith became personally antagonistic. For WBY, Griffith represented intellect outside the sanctity of culture, and he attributed to him motives of jealousy and envy (*WL.* 525). He expresses these feelings about Griffith in the poem

"On those that hated 'The Playboy of the Western World,' 1907" (*CP*. 124). Yet during his internment in 1918, Griffith persuaded the governor of Gloucester Jail to give the Irish prisoners a special dinner to celebrate WBY's birthday. In his poem "The Municipal Gallery Revisited" (*CP*. 368), WBY recalls Griffith's portrait painted by **Sir John Lavery**.

REFERENCES: Colum, Padraic. *Ourselves Alone! The Story of Arthur Griffith and the Origin of the Irish Free State*. New York: Crown, 1959; Davis, Richard P. *Arthur Griffith*. Dundalk: Dundalgan, 1976; Glandon, Virginia E. *Arthur Griffith and the Advanced-Nationalist Press: Ireland, 1900–1922*. New York: P. Lang, 1985; Younger, Calton. *Arthur Griffith*. Dublin: Gill & Macmillan, 1981; Younger, Calton. *A State of Disunion: Arthur Griffith, Michael Collins, James Craig, Eamon De Valera*. London: Muller, 1972.

GUAIRE (d. 663), king of **Connacht**. Guaire, who was renowned for his generosity, lived at Dun Guaire Castle, near **Kinvara**. He presented **St. Colman** with the monastery of Kilmacduagh and is reputed to have hosted Irish poets and their followers at his castle. In *The King's Threshold* (*CPl*. 107), Guaire appeals to the people to persuade the poet **Seanchan** to give up his hunger strike, caused by his having removed him from the Council of State. He is unsuccessful in his efforts, and Seanchan dies. King Guaire is a central figure in the poem "The Three Beggars" (*CP*. 124).

GUARDIAN OF THE WELL, THE. *See* **FAND**.

GUIDO. *See* **CAVALCANTI, GUIDO**.

GUIDOBALDO, DUKE OF URBINO (1472–1508), member of the Montefeltro family who ruled the Italian duchy of **Urbino** from the late twelfth century. Guidobaldo's father was Federico, who amassed a fortune by his military achievements and built the palace of Urbino. His heir, Guidobaldo, was physically infirm. He established a reputation for his generosity, refinement, and patronage of the arts. WBY visited the town of Urbino with **Lady Gregory** in 1907 and was impressed with its setting on the slopes of the Apennines. In his poem "To a Wealthy Man who promised a Second Subscription to the Dublin Municipal Gallery if it were proved the People wanted Pictures" (*CP*. 119), WBY cites Guidobaldo as a model patron. **Baldassare Castiglione's** account of life at the Montefeltro court, in *The Book of the Courtier* (1518), is regarded as one of the outstanding literary accomplishments of its time.

REFERENCES: Salvadori, Corinna. *Yeats and Castiglione: Poet and Courtier*. Dublin: Allen Figgis, 1965; Symonds, J. Addington. "The Revival of Learning." In *The Renaissance in Italy*. London: Murray, 1915.

GWYNN, STEPHEN [LUCIUS] (1864–1950), scholar, politician, and writer. He was born and educated at St. Columba's College, Rathfarnham, County Dublin, where his father was warden. Grandson of the Irish patriot William Smith

O'Brien, he graduated from Brasenose College, **Oxford**, and became a Classics teacher. In 1896, he left teaching to become a free-lance journalist in London. In 1906, he joined the Irish Parliamentary Party and served as M.P. for **Galway** (city), 1906–18. Although he was fifty when World War I broke out, he joined the Connaught Rangers and served in France. After the war, he retired from politics to concentrate on writing. He published biographies, including studies of **Jonathan Swift** and **Oliver Goldsmith**, in addition to *The Masters of English Literature* (1904), *Collected Poems* (1923), and an autobiography, *Experiences of a Literary Man* (1926). A friend of WBY, he met him at the **Contemporary Club**, where Gwynn was among the first to recognize WBY as the outstanding Irish poet. He wrote positive reviews of WBY and **Lady Gregory** in the *Fortnightly Review* (*WL.* 370, 390) and arranged for the **Irish National Theatre Society** to perform in London, May 1903 and March 1904 (*WL.* 399, 401, 410). Gwynn was an associate member of the **Irish Academy of Letters** and was honored with the Gregory Medal shortly before his death in Dublin at the age of eighty-six. His *Irish Literature and Drama in the English Language: A Short History* (1936) gives a firsthand account of the writers of the Irish Renaissance.

REFERENCES: Gwynn, Stephen L. *Irish Books and Irish People*. Freeport, N.Y.: Books for Libraries, 1969; Gwynn, Stephen L. "The Irish Literary Theatre." In *Irish Literature*, ed. Justin McCarthy. New York: Johnson Reprint, 1970; Gwynn, Stephen L., ed. *Scattering Branches: Tributes to the Memory of W. B. Yeats*. 1940. Reprint, Port Washington, N.Y.: Kennikat, 1965; Hogan, Robert, ed. *Dictionary of Irish Literature*. Rev. ed. Westport, Conn.: Greenwood, 1996.

GYLES, ALTHEA (1868–1949), graphic artist, illustrator, and minor poet. She was born into a wealthy Anglo-Irish family in Waterford. After quarreling with her family because she insisted on becoming a painter, she lived in poverty, first in Dublin, where she studied at the **Metropolitan School of Art** with WBY, and later in London, where she attended the Slade School with **Constance Gore-Booth**. She designed the covers for WBY's early publications *The Secret Rose* (1897), *Poems* (1899), and *The Wind among the Reeds* (1899), while elements of her designs were incorporated into the covers for *The Shadowy Waters* (1900) and *The Celtic Twilight* (1902). She made a drawing of a profile head of WBY. Her association with WBY lasted some ten years, but by November 1899, they had become estranged—after she insisted on bringing the publisher and pornographer **Leonard Smithers**, for whom she had designed *The Harlot's House* by **Oscar Wilde** and **Ernest Dowson's** *Decorations in Prose and Verse* (1899), to WBY's home at **Woburn Buildings** (*WL.* 330). She faded into obscurity, alone and in deteriorating health, but with the help of friends, among them **Arthur Symons**, Clifford Bax, and possibly WBY, her poems were published in reviews and magazines. She was included in *A Treasury of Irish Poetry in the English Tongue* (1900), with a brief biographical introduction by WBY (*PI.* 168). Despite requests from her family to return home, she insisted on living in miserable poverty in London, relying on the charity of friends. She died there, one of the last survivors of her social and artistic generation. WBY was impressed with her illustrations, which drew heavily on the symbol of the rose. He wrote enthusiastically of her work in ''A Symbolic Artist and the Coming of Symbolic Art,'' published with four of her drawings in *The Dome*, December 1898 (*M*. 283–86), claiming that her work was the opposite of decadent and rich with Blakean associations. He regretted, however, her lack of dedication and a talent that was never fulfilled. His most telling analysis of her is in ''Ireland after Parnell'' (*A*. 237–39), where she is not identified by name.

REFERENCES: Coldwell, Joan. '' 'Images That Yet Fresh Images Beget': A Note on Book-Covers.'' In *The World of W. B. Yeats*, ed. Robin Skelton and Ann Saddlemyer. Seattle: University of Washington Press, 1967; Fletcher, Ian. ''Poet and Designer: W. B. Yeats and Althea Gyles.'' In *W. B. Yeats and His Contemporaries*. Brighton, Sussex: Harvester, 1987; Gordon, D. J., ed. *W. B. Yeats: Images of a Poet*. Manchester: University of Manchester, 1961; Gould, Warwick; Marcus, Phillip L.; and Sidnell, Michael J., eds. *The Secret Rose: Stories by W. B. Yeats: A Variorum Edition*. London: Macmillan, 1981.

H

HALLAM, ARTHUR [HENRY] (1811–33), poet and essayist. He was the son of the English historian Henry Hallam and formed a close association with **Alfred, Lord Tennyson**, whom he met in 1828 at Trinity College, Cambridge. His early death inspired Tennyson to write the elegy "In Memoriam" (1850). Despite the brevity of his life, and limited output, Hallam exercised a considerable influence over WBY. In "Art and Ideas" (*EI.* 346–55), WBY claims that as a young poet he based his poetic principles on Hallam, whom he paraphrases in his Journal (*M.* 171, 179). He confirms his enthusiasm when he quotes him at some length in his essay "John Eglinton and Spiritual Art" (*UP2.* 130). In 1893, WBY wrote an enthusiastic review of *The Poems of Arthur Henry Hallam, Together with His Essay on the Lyrical Poems of Alfred Tennyson* (*UP1.* 276–78).

REFERENCES: Boas, Frederick S. *From Richardson to Pinero: Some Innovators and Idealists.* Freeport, N.Y.: Books for Libraries, 1969; Brookfield, Frances M. *The Cambridge Apostles.* New York: AMS Press, 1973.

HANRAHAN. *See* **RED HANRAHAN**.

HARDY, THOMAS (1840–1928), novelist and poet. He was born in Higher Bockhampton, a village near Dorchester, Dorset, and lived in the West Country most of his life, apart from a period in the 1860s when he was apprenticed to a church architect in London. His early novels were *Desperate Remedies* (1871) and *Under the Greenwood Tree* (1872), but his first success as a novelist came with *Far from the Madding Crowd* (1874). This was followed by *The Return of the Native* (1878), *The Mayor of Casterbridge* (1886), *Tess of the d'Urbervilles* (1891), and *Jude the Obscure* (1896). In 1896, in reaction to adverse criticism that his fatalistic works depicted indecency and immorality, he stopped writing novels. He turned to poetry and published *Wessex Poems* (1898), *Moments of Vision* (1917), and *The Dynasts* (1908), a historical drama in verse. WBY, impressed by his stark realism, included four poems by him in *The Oxford Book of Modern Verse* (1936): "Weathers" (1922), "The Night of Trafalgar" (1903), "At Casterbridge Fair" (1902), and "Snow in the Suburbs" (1925).

REFERENCES: Gibson, James. *Thomas Hardy: A Literary Life*. New York: St. Martin's, 1996; Pinion, F. B. *Thomas Hardy: His Life and Friends*. New York: St. Martin's, 1992; Williams, Charles. *Poetry at Present*. Freeport, N.Y.: Books for Libraries, 1969.

HAROLD'S CROSS, suburb of south Dublin. In WBY's play *The Words upon the Window-Pane* (*CPl.* 599), Cornelius Patterson keeps **Miss Mackenna** supplied with tips for the horse and greyhound racing at Harold's Cross. The Yeats home at **Ashfield Terrace** was in Harold's Cross.

REFERENCE: McGarry, James P. *Place Names in the Writings of William Butler Yeats*. Gerrards Cross: Colin Smythe, 1976.

HART LAKE [also Heart], small lake in **Sligo** (county), near the summit of the Ox Mountains. Hart Lake is the setting for WBY's poem "The Host of the Air" (*CP.* 63), based on a story told him by an old woman who lived nearby. WBY writes of the lake in "Kidnappers" (*MY.* 73), describing it as frequented by waterfowl and named, because of its shape, Heart Lake. Sources claim the original name for the lake was Loch Minnaun and that Hart Lake was derived from the Hart family who lived beside it.

REFERENCES: Kirby, Sheelah. *The Yeats Country*. Dublin: Dolmen, 1966; McGarry, James P. *Place Names in the Writings of William Butler Yeats*. Gerrards Cross: Colin Smythe, 1976.

HARUN AL-RASHID (766–809), caliph of Baghdad from 786. He was the younger son of the Caliph Mohammed al-Mahdi, third of the Abbasid dynasty to rule over Islam, and came to the throne after the sudden death of his older brother, Musa al-Hadi. During his reign, Baghdad became a prosperous center of world trade, and Harun Al-Rashid lavished his wealth on public works, new roads, and a system of canals between the Tigris and Euphrates. His palace occupied a third of the Round City of Baghdad, with magnificent gardens, banqueting halls, pavilions, libraries, laboratories, and harems containing hundreds of concubines and eunuchs. According to WBY, in a note to "The Gift of Harun Al-Rashid" (*VP.* 828), the generous caliph married a young wife who fell in love with him. In gratitude, he bestowed a bride on **Kusta Ben Luka**, his doctor and translator. "The Gift of Harun Al-Rashid" (*CP.* 513), written in 1923, is an account of WBY's developing relationship with his young wife, **Georgie Hyde-Lees**.

REFERENCE: Klonsky, Milton. "Harun al-Rashid." In *The Fabulous Ego: Absolute Power in History*. New York: Quadrangle/New York Times, 1974.

HAWK'S WELL [also Tullaghan Well, St. Patrick's Well], about one mile from the village of **Coolaney, Sligo** (county). It is probably the setting for *At the Hawk's Well*. It is said to have sprung up at the behest of **St. Patrick** and is remarkable because the water in the well ebbs and flows with the tide, despite its distance from the sea. Near the Hawk's Well is *Carraig-an-Seabhach*, or the Hawk's Rock. See also *The Only Jealousy of Emer* (*CPl.* 292) and *The Death of Cuchulain* (*CPl.* 699).

REFERENCES: Kirby, Sheelah. *The Yeats Country.* Dublin: Dolmen, 1966; McGarry, James P. *Place Names in the Writings of William Butler Yeats.* Gerrards Cross: Colin Smythe, 1976.

HEALD, EDITH SHACKLETON (1885–1976), journalist. She lived at The Chantry House, Steyning, Sussex, a sixteenth-century dwelling that she shared with her older sister, Nora Shackleton. Both were respected journalists. Edith began her career in the early 1900s with the *Manchester Sunday Chronicle*, before she moved to London's *Evening Standard*. A founder member of the PEN club and a suffragist, her writing was distinguished by its sharp wit and feminist bite. She was introduced to WBY by Helen Beauclerk, in 1937, and they corresponded frequently. In the final year of his life, when visiting England, WBY stayed for periods with **Dorothy Wellesley** and then moved to Edith Heald's at Steyning, where the "Yeats Room" was kept for his use. There, in April 1938, he worked on *Purgatory*, while in October, he began the prose draft of his last play, *The Death of Cuchulain*. At Christmas 1938, Heald and her friend Evelyn Marriott visited him in France, and she was present at his burial in **Roquebrune** a few weeks later. She arranged for a memorial tablet, designed by **Edmund Dulac**, to be placed at the cemetery in 1953. After WBY's death, Edith Heald had a lesbian affair with the painter Hannah Gluckstein, whom she met in 1943. It was a fraught relationship that persisted until her death. Heald's papers were sold at Christie's (London), 5 July 1978. They contained letters from WBY and manuscripts of some of the late poems. Most of the material was bought by Harvard University. The relationship between WBY and Heald found its way into fiction in Elizabeth Coxhead's *The Thankless Muse* (1967), in which WBY is the Cornish poet Thomas Laker.

REFERENCES: Coxhead, Elizabeth. *The Thankless Muse.* London: Secker & Warburg, 1967; Souhami, Diana. *Gluck 1895–1978: Her Biography.* London: Pandora, 1988.

HEARNE, family name in WBY's play *The Unicorn from the Stars*. Thomas Hearne is a coach builder who is working on a new gilded coach for the Lord Lieutenant in Dublin. His brother Andrew and his nephew Martin assist him in the workshop. At the beginning of the play, Thomas is embarrassed because his nephew is prone to visions. His brother Andrew believes the sickness to be the work of devils and is critical of the priest, **Father John**, because he has failed to cast them out. Martin wakens from a trance, insisting he has been given a message to destroy the Church and the Law. He sets fire to the gilded coach and leads a group of beggars on a rampage. He goes into another trance. He wakens to confess he was mistaken in his earlier actions. He is accidentally shot by the police when they arrive to arrest him. The role of Martin Hearne in the first production of *The Unicorn from the Stars*, November 1907, was played by **Frank Fay**. The role of Thomas Hearne was taken by Arthur Sinclair, and J. A. O'Rourke acted the part of Andrew Hearne.

HEBER [also Eber], son of Míl. After the Milesians conquered Ireland, he quarreled with his brothers about who should rule the country. Heber was eventually killed by his brother Heremon, who became the first Milesian king of Ireland. See also *The Wanderings of Oisin* (*CP*. 426).

HEBREW, THE, character in WBY's play *The Resurrection*. At the beginning of the action, he is guarding the eleven apostles who are in another room. He debates the nature of **Christ** with **The Greek**, relieved that, in his opinion, the crucified Christ was not a god but the best man who ever lived. When Christ appears, The Hebrew is confounded and speechless. The role of The Hebrew in the first production of *The Resurrection*, July 1934, was played by A. J. Leventhal.

HECTOR, leader of the Trojans. He was the son of **Priam** and the husband of Andromache. Courageous and devoted to his people, he was killed in the Trojan War by **Achilles**, in revenge for the slaying of Patrocles. See also ''The Phases of the Moon'' (*CP*. 183), ''His Memories'' (*CP*. 251), ''The Gyres'' (*CP*. 337), and *The Unicorn from the Stars* (*CPl*. 353).

HEGEL, [GEORG WILHELM] FRIEDRICH (1770–1831), philosopher. He was born in Stuttgart, Germany, the son of a government clerk. After studying theology at the University of Tübingen, he became a private tutor. He was appointed professor at the University of Jena in 1805 but resigned to edit a newspaper. He returned to academia when he accepted influential professorships at Heidelberg (1816–18) and Berlin (1818–31). His philosophical system, which he set down in a series of books, *Phenomenology of Mind* (1807), *Science of Logic* (1812–16), *Encyclopedia of the Philosophical Sciences* (1817), and *The Philosophy of History* (1858), included theories of ethics, aesthetics, history, politics, and religion. At its center was his ''dialectic,'' in which he claimed that a basic thesis generates its opposite—the antithesis. Their interaction leads to a synthesis that becomes the thesis in a new triad. This dialectic he applied to history; every nation breeds its opposite, conflicts with it, and through this conflict proceeds to a new nation. In discovering the dialectic, Hegel believed he had discovered a necessary law of nature. Thus, the course of history was determined by the dialectic; nothing could alter its course. His theory of history established him as the most important philosopher of the nineteenth century. In a letter to **Olivia Shakespear**, written in 1927, WBY claimed to be reading Hegel, and there are marginal strokes and underscorings in his copy of *The*

Logic of Hegel (*OS*. no. 869). Thereafter, there are numerous references to him in his essays and letters (*WL*. 725, 770, 781, 791, 813, 922). He quotes Hegel's theory of history in his "Introduction to *The Holy Mountain*" (*LE*. 151, 153–54), embracing Hegel's assertion that civilization, as we know it, started in Asia. In addition to *The Logic of Hegel*, he had a copy of *Hegel's Logic of World and Idea* (1929) in his library (*OS*. no. 868).

REFERENCES: Jaspers, Karl. *The Great Philosophers*. Trans. Edith Ehrlich & Leonard Ehrlich. New York: Harcourt Brace, 1994; Kaufman, Walter A. *Discovering the Mind*. New York: McGraw-Hill, 1980; Wiedmann, Franz. *Hegel: An Illustrated Biography*. Trans. Joachim Neugroschel. New York: Pegasus, 1968.

HELEN [OF TROY], most beautiful of all women in Greek mythology. Helen was the daughter of **Leda** and Zeus. She became the wife of Menelaus but was abducted by **Paris** and taken from **Sparta** to **Troy**. To recover Helen and avenge Menelaus, the Greeks waged war against the Trojans, the subject of **Homer's** epic *The Iliad*. When the war was over, Helen returned to Sparta with her husband Menelaus. Helen is the subject of WBY's poems "The Sorrow of Love" (*CP*. 45), "A Woman Homer Sung" (*CP*. 100), "No Second Troy" (*CP*. 101), and "When Helen Lived" (*CP*. 124). She is "Homer's paragon" in "The Double Vision of Michael Robartes" (*CP*. 194). In *The Player Queen* (*CPl*. 418), the Second Player boasts of acting in an old play, "The Fall of Troy," and reproaching Helen for the misery she caused, while in "An Enduring Heart" (*MY*. 36), WBY writes touchingly that his heart has been broken because he "loved Helen and all the lovely and fickle women of the world." In the broadcast "The Growth of a Poet" (*UP2*. 497), WBY speaks of Paris and Helen as the Irish **Diarmuid** and **Grania**. See also "The Tower" (*CP*. 218), "Lullaby" (*CP*. 300), "Three Marching Songs" (*CP*. 377), and "Why should not Old Men be Mad" (*CP*. 388).

HELICON, mountain in Boeotia, central Greece. Mount Helicon was sacred to the Muses and regarded as a source of poetic inspiration. Hippocrene, the fountain on Mount Helicon, was created by the foot of the flying horse Pegasus. WBY makes a somewhat ambiguous reference to Helicon in the poem "The Leaders of the Crowd" (*CP*. 207), where he appears to contrast the inspiration derived from Mount Helicon with the motivations of the gutter press in Dublin. See also *Sophocles' King Oedipus* (*CPl*. 507).

HENDERSON, MRS., character. In WBY's play *The Words upon the Window-Pane*, she is a Dublin-born medium who has come from London to conduct a séance for the Dublin Spiritualist's Association. Through her control Lulu, a child who died when she was five or six years old, the ebullient Mrs. Henderson calls up the spirits of **Jonathan Swift** and his companions, **Stella** and **Vanessa**. May Craig played the role of Mrs. Henderson in the first production of the play at the **Abbey Theatre**, November 1930.

HENLEY, W[ILLIAM] E[RNEST] (1849–1903), poet and critic. He was born in Gloucester, the son of a bookseller. In 1865, while attending the local grammar school, he contracted an illness that led to the amputation of his left leg. He worked for a short time in London as a freelance journalist, but with the recurrence of his illness and the onset of syphilis, he moved to Edinburgh under the care of Joseph Lister of the Royal Infirmary. For a time, he was a friend of Robert Louis Stevenson. In 1876, after his discharge from the hospital, he returned to London as the editor of the weekly *London*. When this ceased publication in 1879, he worked as a freelance journalist before his appointment as editor of the *Magazine of Art*. He returned to Edinburgh in 1888, as editor of the *Scots Observer* (later the *National Observer*) and remained there until his resignation in 1894, the year in which his six-year-old daughter died of cerebral meningitis. After her death, his own health deteriorated, causing him to give up journalism in 1897, when he retired on a Civil List pension. Among his published work was his collection of poems *The Song of the Sword* (1892). He was an editor of genius, with very pronounced tastes. He rejected the Pre-Raphaelites and the teachings of **Walter Pater**, and yet he was a powerful influence on the younger poets of the day, among them WBY, whom he met in 1888. WBY was critical of Henley as a poet (*A*. 295–96), but in "Four Years: 1887–1891" (*A*. 126–29), he acknowledged his debt to him as a passionate critic and man of vision. WBY, who visited him regularly at his home near **Bedford Park**, disagreed with Henley over almost everything, especially politics, but he admired him tremendously (*A*. 124–26). He was proud to be one of Henley's protégés (*M*. 37–40) and readily accepted his advice on the revision of his early poems. Four poems by Henley were included in WBY's selection for *The Oxford Book of Modern Verse* (1936).

REFERENCES: Cornford, L. Cope. *William Ernest Henley*. New York: Haskell House, 1972; Flora, Joseph M. *William Ernest Henley*. New York: Twayne, 1970.

HENRY STREET, in the center of Dublin. Henry Street is adjacent to the **General Post Office** (GPO), joining O'Connell Street and Mary Street. **Michael Joseph O'Rahilly** was killed in Henry Street, in the heavy fighting that followed the evacuation of the GPO during the 1916 Easter Rising. See also "The O'Rahilly" (*CP*. 354).

REFERENCE: McGarry, James P. *Place Names in the Writings of William Butler Yeats*. Gerrards Cross: Colin Smythe, 1976.

HERNE'S EGG, THE, play in six scenes. It was written by WBY in 1938 and published by Macmillan and Company in the same year. The source of the play was *Congal* (1872) by **Sir Samuel Ferguson**, but commentators have noticed similarities with *Seraphita* (1835) by **Honoré de Balzac**. The union of the priestess **Attracta** with the Great Herne is reminiscent of the reference to the sexual union between a mortal and a god in birdlike shape in the poem "Leda and the Swan" (*CP*. 241). Many stylistic elements in the writing and presentation are similar to those of Alfred Jarry's *Ubu Roi*, which WBY saw in Paris in 1896. The play also anticipates the Theatre of the Absurd. At the beginning of the action of *The Herne's Egg*, two kings, **Congal** and **Aedh**, are engaged in furious battle. They decide on a truce, and Aedh offers to host a celebratory banquet at **Tara**. Congal, despite the warnings of Attracta, gathers eggs belonging to the Great Herne, and Attracta, in revenge, invokes an ancient curse, telling him he will die at the hands of a **Fool**. At the feast, Congal, very drunk, feels insulted because he has been served a hen's egg in place of the Herne's eggs that he has collected. Aedh and he fight with table legs, having left their swords outside, and all the guests join in, armed with candlesticks and table legs. The fight continues offstage, but news is brought that Aedh is dead from a blow on the head. Congal, furious that his ritual feuding is at an end, blames the Great Herne and Attracta and insists he will revenge himself by raping Attracta. His men and he cast lots to decide the order in which they will rape her. The following morning, despite the protestations of Congal and his men, Attracta insists the Great Herne visited her in the night and made love to her. When Congal and his men contradict her, she invokes a curse that they will be reincarnated as beasts and vermin. To fulfill the prophecy, the Fool, armed with a cauldron lid for shield and a saucepan for helmet, wounds Congal with a kitchen spit. Congal, hoping to frustrate Attracta's prophecy, stands the spit upright and attempts to kill himself. Despite the last-minute intervention of Attracta, he dies at the moment a donkey conceives, so that Congal must be reborn as a donkey. The play was not performed in WBY's lifetime. Plans for a production at the **Abbey Theatre** in 1938 were aborted, much to WBY's relief, since he felt the play's Rabelaisian tone would offend the sensibilities of Dublin playgoers. The play premiered October 1950, when it was performed by Austin Clarke's Lyric Theatre Company, with the following cast: Congal, George Green; Aedh, Edward Golden; Corney, Alex Andrews; Mike, Jack MacGowran; Peter, Hugh Martin; Pat, Oliver Bradley; John, Gerald Mangan; James, Michael Reynaud; Malachi, Art O'Phelan; Mathias, Bart Bastable; Attracta, Eithne Dunne; Kate, Doreen Fitzpatrick; Agnes, Mary Fisher; Mary, Joan Stynes; Fool, Patrick Nolan; Soldiers, Frank Daly, Kevin Naughton, Jack Quinn, Kevin Redmond, Peadar Murphy. The play was directed by Josephine Albericci, with setting and costumes by **Anne Yeats**.

REFERENCES: Armstrong, Alison, ed. *The Herne's Egg: Manuscript Materials*. Ithaca and London: Cornell University Press, 1993; Bradley, Anthony. *William Butler Yeats*. New York: Frederick Ungar, 1979; Ellis, Sylvia C. *The Plays of W. B. Yeats: Yeats and the Dancer*. London: Macmillan, 1995; Miller, Liam. *The Noble Drama of W. B. Yeats*. Dublin: Dolmen, 1977; Taylor, Richard. *A Reader's Guide to the Plays of W. B. Yeats*. New York: St. Martin's, 1984.

HIGGINS, F[REDERICK] R[OBERT] (1896–1941), poet, editor, and playwright. He was born at Foxrock, **County Mayo**, and grew up in a Gaelic-speaking area of the west of Ireland, where he developed a passion for Irish folk songs and traditions. On leaving school, he was employed as an office boy and later became an official in the Irish labor movement. He contributed poems and articles to literary journals and, in 1924, published *The Salt Air*, a pamphlet containing six poems. When he published the anthologies *Island Blood* (1925), *The Dark Breed* (1927) and *Arable Holdings* (1933), he made the acquaintance of WBY, who thought him outstanding among the younger Irish poets. Together they edited *Broadsides* (1935), published by the **Cuala Press**. In 1935, Higgins was appointed to the board of the **Abbey Theatre**. He managed the Abbey company during their eight-month tour of the United States in 1937 and, in 1938, became managing director—an appointment that led to the resignation of fellow director **Frank O'Connor**. He was a director of the Cuala Press. Six of his poems were included in WBY's selection for ***The Oxford Book of Modern Verse*** (1936). A founding member and honorary secretary of the **Irish Academy of Letters**, he was awarded the Casement Medal for *Arable Holdings*. In 1940, he published *The Gap of Brightness*, which is believed to be his best work. His one-act play *A Deuce o' Jacks* was produced at the Abbey Theatre, September 1935, and published in the *Dublin Magazine*, 1936. At the Abbey Theatre Dramatic Festival, August 1938, he delivered a laudatory lecture entitled "W. B. Yeats."

REFERENCES: Higgins, F. R. "W. B. Yeats." In *Scattering Branches: Tributes to the Memory of W. B. Yeats*, ed. Stephen Gwynn. New York: Macmillan, 1940; Hunt, Hugh. *The Abbey: Ireland's National Theatre, 1904–1979*. Dublin: Gill & Macmillan, 1979; Kavanagh, Peter. *The Story of the Abbey Theatre*. New York: Devin-Adair 1950; MacManus, M. J. "A Bibliography of F. R. Higgins." *Dublin Magazine* 12 (1937); Rodgers, W. R., ed. "F. R. Higgins." In *Irish Literary Portraits*. New York: Taplinger, 1973.

HILL SEAT OF LAIGHEN, THE (Irish: *Dun Ailinne*), prehistoric hill fort near Kilcullen, County Kildare. It is claimed to be the oldest residence of the kings of **Leinster**. The Hill Seat of Laighen is associated with the god **Aengus**. After telling **Aillinn** of the death of her lover **Baile**, Aengus ran laughing to the hill, where he was joined by the two lovers, transformed into swans. See also "Baile and Aillinn" (*CP*. 463).

REFERENCE: McGarry, James P. *Place Names in the Writings of William Butler Yeats*. Gerrards Cross: Colin Smythe, 1976.

HINKSON, MRS. *See* **TYNAN, KATHARINE**.

HODGINS, ROSEANNA [Rose] (c. 1848–1930), Yeats family servant. She came from **Howth**, Dublin (county), and was taken into service when the family was living there in the mid-1880s. She traveled with them to London. Later, she was joined by another servant, Maria O'Brien. Both remained with the Yeats sisters **Lily** and **Lolly** when they returned to Ireland in 1902. Despite failing health,

Rose Hodgins continued to be hard-working and intensely loyal to all the family. She died in service.

REFERENCE: Murphy, William M. *Family Secrets: William Butler Yeats and His Relatives*. New York: Syracuse University Press, 1995.

HOMER, Greek poet. Little is known about his life except that he was poor and blind in his old age. He is believed to have composed his two epic poems, the *Iliad* and the *Odyssey*, before 700 B.C. In 1937, in "A General Introduction for My Work" (*LE.* 204), WBY wrote that he wished "to get back to Homer, to those that fed at his table," while in *The Death of Cuchulain* (*CPl.* 694), the **Old Man** of the prologue claims he will teach "the music of the beggar-man, Homer's music." Although he read him only in translation, WBY made a strong connection with Homer, principally through his interest in folktales and mythology but also in his philosophy. In his early reviews, Homer is consistently among those writers against whom he measures all others (*UP2.* 124, 131, 152), while Homer is identified with **Blind Raftery** and **Helen** becomes the mask for **Maud Gonne**. His interest, too, in having his poems spoken aloud or chanted to a musical accompaniment stemmed from his belief that Homer belonged to the oral tradition and sang his stirring epics aloud (*A.* 191). In 1893, when he was interviewed for the *Irish Theosophist*, he had a volume of Homer beside him (*UP1.* 298), while in his review of **Villiers de L'Isle Adam's** *Axël*, he measures the play against three standards of perfection, one of them being a few lines of Homer (*UP1.* 324). He was proud that he knew people who still read **Virgil** and Homer, among them **Robert Gregory** (*UP2.* 430) and **Oscar Wilde** (*A.* 138), and flattered when Wilde compared his art of storytelling to that of Homer (*A.* 135). He refers to Homer in the poems "A Woman Homer Sung" (*CP.* 100), "Peace" (*CP.* 103), "The Double Vision of Michael Robartes" (*CP.* 192), "The Tower" (*CP.* 218), "Meditations in Time of Civil War" (*CP.* 225), "Vacillation" (*CP.* 282), and "Mad as the Mist and Snow" (*CP.* 301).

REFERENCE: Bornstein, George, ed. *Ezra Pound among the Poets*. Chicago: University of Chicago Press, 1985.

HOPPER, NORA (1871–1906), poet, novelist, and journalist. She was born in Exeter, the daughter of Captain H. B. Hopper, and lived all her life in England. She worked as a freelance journalist and made an extensive study of Irish folklore. She came to the attention of WBY with *Ballads in Prose* (1894), which he claimed "haunted" him. He wrote enthusiastically about the collection and defended her against a charge of plagiarizing both his own verses and those of **Katharine Tynan** (*KLI.* 425–26). Indeed, Nora Hopper became his first protégée (*UP1.* 380). He included *Ballads in Prose* in his "Thirty Best Books" (*WL.* 247) and in "Best Irish Books" (*UP1.* 386), although he was less enthusiastic about her later work, which included *Under Quicken Boughs* (1896), *Songs of the Morning* (1900), and *Aquamarines* (1902). In 1903, she wrote the libretto for *The Sea Swan* (an Irish grand opera, with music by T. O'Brien Butler [1861–1915]), which was performed at the Theatre Royal, Dublin, December 1903. WBY writes of her favorably in "Irish National Literature, II: Contemporary Prose Writers" (*UP1*. 366–73). He contributed a short essay, "The Poems and Stories of Miss Nora Hopper," to the Dublin *Daily Express*, September 1898 (*UP2*. 124–28), a version of which was used to introduce Nora Hopper's poems in *A Treasury of Irish Poetry* (1900), edited by Stopford Brooke and **T. W. Rolleston**. In this essay, he writes persuasively of the delicacy of her verse and its essential mystery, but he is critical of her uncertainty over places in Ireland associated with her stories and legends.

REFERENCES: Hogan, Robert, ed. *Dictionary of Irish Literature*. Rev. ed. Westport, Conn.: Greenwood, 1996; Marcus, Phillip L. *Yeats and the Beginning of the Irish Renaissance*. Syracuse: Syracuse University Press, 1987.

HORACE [QUINTUS HORATIUS FLACCUS] (65–8 B.C.), Roman poet. He was the son of an educated freedman and studied at Rome and Athens. He fought at the battle of Philippi and, after returning to Rome, worked as a clerk. Through his friendship with **Virgil**, he was introduced to Maecenas, who became his benefactor and gave him the famous Sabine farm. There, Horace spent his later life, writing lyrics and satires that reflected his deep love of nature and the civilized spirit of his age. His major works, *Odes* and *Ars Poetica*, are distinguished by his mastery of poetic form and contain vivid descriptions of Roman life and the scenery of Italy. He has remained a major influence on English poetry to this day. In an early draft of his *Autobiography* (*M*. 74), WBY recalls **MacGregor Mathers**, with whom he stayed in Paris, coming down to breakfast carrying a copy of Horace. WBY names Horace in "Mad as the Mist and Snow" (*CP*. 301).

REFERENCE: Lyne, R. O. *Horace: Behind the Public Poetry*. New Haven: Yale University Press, 1995.

HORNE, HERBERT P[ERCY] (1864–1916), architect, art historian, poet, and member of the **Rhymers' Club**. He was born in Chelsea, London, and in 1885, two years after becoming apprenticed to the architect Arthur Macmurdo, he entered a partnership in the Century Guild, an association of artists dedicated to fine art and crafts. In 1892, he designed the Chapel of the Ascension in the Church of the Redeemer, Bayswater Road, London, said by WBY to be the smallest church in London (*LE*. 227). Horne shared a house at 20 Fitzroy Street, Bloomsbury, with Macmurdo, **Lionel Johnson**, and Selwyn Image. He introduced them to the poets who formed the Rhymers' Club, including WBY. From 1887 to 1891, Horne was editor of the *Hobby Horse*, which published the poems of WBY and many of the Rhymers. His volume of verse, *Diversi Colores*, was published in 1891. In 1900, he retired to Florence, Italy, where he wrote a biography of **Botticelli** (1908). After his death, his house in Florence was opened as a museum. WBY admired Horne for his taste and knowledge but suspected him of leaning unduly toward the eighteenth century. Later, he regretted a youthful prejudice that had prevented them from becoming friends. Horne's Chapel of the Ascension in the Church of the Redeemer was damaged during World War II and had to be razed.

REFERENCES: Fletcher, Ian. "Herbert Horne: The Earlier Phase." *English Miscellany: A Symposium of History, Literature and the Arts* (Rome), 1970; Horne, H. P. *Alessandro Filipepi, Commonly Called Sandro Botticelli, Painter of Florence.* London: Bell, 1908.

HORNIMAN, ANNIE [ELIZABETH] F[REDERICKA] (1860–1937), patron and benefactor. She was born in London into a wealthy English family of tea merchants. She studied art at the Slade School in London, 1882–86, and after visiting Germany, where she was impressed with the state-subsidized repertory system, she became interested in theater. Through an early friendship with Moina Bergson, she was introduced to **MacGregor Mathers**. He persuaded her to join **The Order of the Golden Dawn** in 1890, and it was there she met WBY, who shared with her his plans for an Irish national theater. After the marriage of Bergson and MacGregor Mathers, she became more intimately connected with Mathers, relying on his support through some personal crises. She arranged for him to be employed at her father's private museum in London and gave him an allowance. When the couple moved to Paris, her relations with them became strained, and she cut off the allowance. Mathers reacted by expelling her from The Order of the Golden Dawn in 1896. After a bitter struggle for control of the organization, she was reinstated in 1900 but resigned in 1903. She secretly funded **Florence Farr's** 1894 season of new plays at the Avenue Theatre, London (a season that included the first performance of WBY's *The Land of Heart's Desire*), and in 1903, having become an unpaid secretary to WBY, she designed the costumes for the first production of *The King's Threshold*. She leased the **Mechanics Institute** in Dublin in 1904 and paid for its restoration and conversion into the **Abbey Theatre**. She subsidized the Abbey productions, guaranteeing not only the actors' salaries but also the expenses of company tours to London—in addition to underwriting the publication of WBY's eight-volume *Collected Works* (1908). In all, she spent in excess of £10,000 on the Abbey. Despite her initial enthusiasm for the project, she became increasingly unhappy with the organization. Not only did she not always approve of the selection of plays, but she also found fault with the administration and believed the company to be antagonistic to her. She was jealous of the deepening artistic relationship between WBY and **Lady Gregory**. When the Abbey failed to close on the death of Edward VII in 1909, she saw the gesture as political and withdrew her subsidy. Her relationship with WBY was strained, especially when he refused to leave the Abbey to write for the Gaiety Theatre, Manchester, which she had opened in 1907. The Gaiety, which pioneered the British repertory theater system, became the major focus of her artistic interest until 1920, when the venture failed through lack of funds. She then traveled widely in Europe, especially Germany, where she indulged her interest in Wagnerian opera. She was honored for her services to the British theater in 1932. Despite her generosity to WBY and the Abbey Theatre, she has not been accorded recognition in Ireland, possibly because of her condescending attitude to the Irish and her opposition to Irish nationalism. WBY gives her scant attention in his writings.

REFERENCES: Flannery, James W. *Miss Annie Horniman and the Abbey Theatre*. Dublin: Dolmen, 1970; Frazier, Adrian. *Behind the Scenes: Yeats, Horniman, and the Struggle for the Abbey Theatre*. Berkeley: University of California Press, 1990; Gooddie, Sheila. *Annie Horniman: A Pioneer in the Theatre*. London: Methuen, 1990; Pogson, Rex. *Annie Horniman and the Gaiety Theatre, Manchester*. London: Rockliff, 1952.

HORTON, W[ILLIAM] T[HOMAS] (1864–1919), illustrator and visionary. He was born in Brussels of English parents. While he was still a boy, his family moved to Brighton, where he was enrolled at Brighton Grammar School, the school later attended by **Aubrey Beardsley**. He trained as an architect, but after his marriage, he embarked upon a career as an illustrator. Much influenced by **William Blake**, Horton had illustrations accepted by **Arthur Symons** for *The Savoy* (1896). He published a collection of his drawings under the title *A Book of Images* (1898), for which WBY contributed the introduction, although he purged it of all references to Horton when it was reprinted as "Symbolism in Painting" (*EI*. 146–52). Horton illustrated *The Grig's Book* (1900), a collection of nursery rhymes, and did drawings for three stories by Edgar Allan Poe, published by **Leonard Smithers**. In 1910, he illustrated his own poems in *The Way of the Soul: A Legend in Line and Verse*. When he was fifty, Horton, who had separated from his wife, had a relationship with Amy Audrey Locke, a writer with whom he lived until her death in 1916. He met WBY in the mid-1890s, and they were friends when WBY acted as his sponsor for his initiation into **The Order of the Golden Dawn**, March 1896—although Horton only remained in the Order for a few months. He was eccentric in mind and habits, unworldly, and highly judgmental. WBY tolerated him, and while they disagreed over many issues, especially WBY's pursuit of spiritualism, they maintained their friendship until Horton's death. Horton did a pen portrait of WBY, showing a haloed head surrounded with mystical symbols. A later profile drawing is possibly of WBY (*KLIII*. 106). Horton's platonic relationship with Amy Locke is recalled by WBY in "All Souls' Night" (*CP*. 256).

REFERENCES: Finneran, Richard. J., and Harper, George Mills. " 'He Loved Strange Thought': W. B. Yeats and William Thomas Horton." In *Yeats and the Occult*, ed. George Mills Harper. Toronto: Macmillan, 1975; Gordon, D. J., ed. *W. B. Yeats: Images of a Poet*. Manchester: University of Manchester, 1961; Harper, George Mills. *W. B. Yeats and W. T. Horton: The Record of an Occult Friendship*. Atlantic Highlands, N.J.: Humanities, 1980.

HOUR-GLASS, THE, one-act play by WBY. The earliest version of the play, in prose, was published in the *North American Review*, September 1903, and reprinted in 1904 and 1911. A new version in prose and verse, undertaken after WBY had embarked upon his artistic collaboration with **Gordon Craig**, was performed at the **Abbey Theatre**, November 1912, using the Craig screens. This version was published in *The Mask*, April 1913. The play was further revised in 1914 and included in *Responsibilities: Poems and a Play*. It is substantially this version that appears in *The Collected Plays of W. B. Yeats* (1934, 1952). In the play, which was based upon a folktale by **Lady Wilde** from her collection *Ancient Legends, Mystic Charms and Superstitions of Ireland* (1887), a **Wise Man** rejects the existence of the spiritual world, contradicting the **Fool**, who claims to have heard and seen proof of its existence. An **Angel** tells the Wise Man he has an hour to live and is destined for Hell unless he can find someone who believes in the spiritual world. In desperation, the Wise Man appeals to his wife and his pupils, but they contradict the existence of such a world, thinking that is what he wants them to say. Finally, the Wise Man recognizes that only in spiritual terror can the Truth emerge, and on his death, his soul, in the shape of a butterfly, is taken to Paradise. The play follows its source closely, including the final image of the butterfly, but the introduction of the Fool is a powerful innovation by WBY. The prose version of the play was performed by the **Irish National Theatre Society**, March 1903, with the following cast: Wise Man, J. Dudley Digges; **Bridget**, Maire T. Quinn; Children, Eithne and Padragan Nic Shiubhlaigh; Pupils, P. J. Kelly, **Seamus O'Sullivan, Padraic Colum**; Angel, Máire Nic Shiubhlaigh; Fool, **Frank Fay**.

REFERENCES: Bradley, Anthony. *William Butler Yeats*. New York: Frederick Ungar, 1979; Bushrui, S. B. "The Hour-Glass: Yeats's Revisions, 1903–1922." In *W. B. Yeats 1865–1939: Centenary Essays*, ed. D. E. S. Maxwell and S. B. Bushrui. Ibadan: Ibadan University Press, 1965; Miller, Liam. *The Noble Drama of W. B. Yeats*. Dublin: Dolmen, 1977; Phillips, Catherine, ed. *The Hour-Glass: Manuscript Materials*. Ithaca and London: Cornell University Press, 1994; Taylor, Richard. *A Reader's Guide to the Plays of W. B. Yeats*. New York: St. Martin's, 1984.

HOWTH, seaside resort near Dublin. WBY and his family lived in Howth, 1881–84, first in **Balscadden Cottage** and later in **Island View**, a house overlooking the harbor. It was one of the happiest periods for the Yeats family. **John B. Yeats** was teaching at the **Metropolitan College of Art**, WBY was attending a challenging school, **Erasmus Smith High School**, and his mother, **Susan Yeats**, was near the sea, in an environment that reminded her of her native **Sligo**. It was while there that WBY met **Laura Armstrong** (*A.* 76). **Maud Gonne** and her sister **Kathleen** lived in Howth after the death of their mother. In 1891, WBY and Maud Gonne spent a day on Howth Head and dined with Maud Gonne's old nurse in a cottage near Baily Lighthouse (*M.* 46). In 1895, Maud Gonne had a dream in which the ghost of WBY, dressed in priestlike garb, took her soul away and they wandered around the cliffs of Howth as they had done years before (*M*. 87). In "Beautiful Lofty Things" (*CP*. 348), WBY recalls Maud Gonne at Howth Station, waiting for a train.

REFERENCE: McGarry, James P. *Place Names in the Writings of William Butler Yeats*. Gerrards Cross: Colin Smythe, 1976.

HUGHES, JOHN (1864–1941), sculptor. He was born in Dublin and attended the **Metropolitan School of Art**, where he met WBY and the sculptor **Oliver Sheppard** and formed a friendship with **AE**. In 1890, he studied at the South Kensington Art School, London, returning to Dublin in 1894 to take up an appointment at his former art school. He exhibited at the Royal Academy, London, in 1897, 1898, and 1900. In 1902, after completing his first important commissions *Madonna and Child* and *Man of Sorrows* for St. Brendan's Cathedral, **Loughrea**, he moved to Paris, where he lived until about 1920 with his two sisters. They moved to Italy for six years, then returned to Paris. He continued to design public monuments for Dublin and other Irish towns, including a statue of Queen Victoria, now stored in Kilmainham Jail! In 1928, he gave up sculpture to earn a living playing flute in Paris cinemas. His *The Finding of Eurydice* is in the **Municipal Gallery of Modern Art**, Dublin, while a plaster bust of AE (1885–86) is in the Metropolitan School of Art. As a student, WBY and Hughes discussed philosophy together, but there appears to have been no contact after art school.

HUGO, VICTOR [MARIE] (1802–85), novelist, dramatist, and poet. The dominant figure in French literature during the nineteenth century, he was born in Besançon, the son of a general in Napoleon's army. He published his first book of verse, *Odes et poésies diverses*, in 1822, but it was his preface to the drama *Cromwell* (1827) that established him as the leader of the French Romantics. When his poetic drama *Hernani* was produced in 1830, it caused a literary battle between the Classicists and the supporters of Romanticism. His poetry, which included *Les Feuilles d'automne* (1831), *Les Chants du crépuscule* (1835), and *Les Rayons et les ombres* (1840), confirmed his reputation as the leading French poet of his day, but it was as a novelist that he achieved universal fame with his major epics *The Hunchback of Notre Dame* (1831) and *Les Misérables* (1862), both of which demonstrate his genius for portraying human suffering with passion and power. In 1851, because of his opposition to Napoleon III, he was exiled to the Channel Islands. There he remained for almost twenty years, until his triumphant return to Paris in 1870, when he was feted and elected to the National Assembly and the French Senate. He was buried in the Pantheon. As a youth, WBY claims to have read all of Victor Hugo's novels (*A*. 87) and to have been much influenced by his poetry (*EI*. 356). When he first met **Maud Gonne**, he told her his ambition was to be an Irish Victor Hugo (*M*. 41). He quotes frequently from Hugo, and at his meeting with **Paul Verlaine** in Paris, it was of Hugo that they spoke (*A*. 342).

REFERENCE: Juin, Hubert. *Victor Hugo*. Paris: Flammarion, 1980.

HYDE, DOUGLAS (1860–1949), author, scholar, and first president of Ireland. He was the son of a Protestant rector in Frenchpark, County Roscommon. Educated at home, he was a Classical scholar, fluent in Hebrew, German, and French, and he taught himself Irish through contact with the local people, recording stories from the oral tradition and collecting books written in the Irish language. He was an undergraduate at **Trinity College**, Dublin, in the early 1880s when he met WBY. They developed a friendship, and although Hyde found WBY an excessive talker, they spent much time in each other's company. He was an active member of the **Contemporary Club**, debating regularly with **John O'Leary, Dr. George Sigerson**, and **T. W. Rolleston**. He began writing nationalist poetry while at Trinity, under the pseudonym An Craoibhin Aoibhinn (pleasing little branch), and published his first poems in Irish in *The Irishman* and *The Shamrock*. He translated poems from the old Irish, rendering them into simple, evocative English that preserved the feeling and mood of the original. In his *Love Songs of Connacht* (1893), he printed most of the poems three times, giving the original Irish version, together with a free translation and a literal version. Yet in ''A Plea for the Irish Language,'' which he contributed to the *Dublin University Review*, August 1885, he argued that Irish nationalism would be better served by a revival of the Irish language than the development of an Irish literature in English. This was the theme of his inaugural lecture as president of the **National Literary Society**, November 1892 (*A*. 396; *M*. 58), a lecture that had far-reaching repercussions. In 1893, he was elected the first president of the Gaelic League, a nonpolitical organization founded to preserve Irish as the national language and to create a modern literature in Irish. Under his leadership, the Gaelic League flourished. By 1905, it had 550 branches throughout Ireland, including one formed by **Lady Gregory**. It became a vital force in the national revival, but when militant nationalists in the movement began to insist that language and politics could not be kept apart, Hyde resigned his presidency in 1915 to devote himself to literary and academic pursuits. From 1908 to 1932, he was professor of Modern Irish at University College, Dublin, and he served on the University Senate from 1909 to 1919. He retired to his home near Frenchpark, County Roscommon, and was reluctantly co-opted as a senator of the Irish Free State (1932–37). In 1938, he was appointed first president of Ireland, a post he retained until 1944. Hyde was a playwright and amateur actor. The first play in Irish produced at a professional theater in Ireland was Hyde's *Casadh an tSugáin* (*The Twisting of the Rope*), produced by the **Irish Literary Theatre** in 1901, with Hyde in the leading role. He wrote other plays in Irish, sometimes from scenarios contributed by WBY and Lady Gregory, and he worked with WBY on *Where There Is Nothing*. Indeed, scholars argue that Hyde contributed to WBY's *The Unicorn from the Stars*. WBY writes of his first encounters with Hyde, of his intriguing, peasantlike appearance, his habit of taking snuff, and his liking for poteen, in *The Trembling of the Veil* (*A*. 216–19). He was opposed to Hyde's proposal to de-Anglicize Ireland through the medium of all things Irish, arguing that a national literature might be created that was Irish in spirit and English in language (*UP1*. 255–56). He observes that Hyde's genius for folk poetry was ruined by political pressure from the Gaelic League (*A*. 218–19; *M*. 54). WBY was staying with Hyde in County Roscommon when he first saw **Castle Rock** and conceived of forming an Order of Celtic Mysteries (*A*. 253; *M*. 123). He chose three of Hyde's stories from the Irish for the collection *Fairy and Folk Tales of the Irish Peasantry* (1888) and included six of his poems in *Poems and Ballads of Young Ireland* (1888). In 1890, he found a publisher for Hyde's influential work *Beside the Fire: A Collection of Irish Gaelic Folk Stories* (1890), a first attempt to convey Irish folklore in a true Anglo-Irish idiom, and wrote a laudatory review in the *National Observer*, February 1891 (*UP1*. 186–90). He included four books by Hyde in his list of "Best Irish Books" (*UP1*. 386–87; *WL*. 247–50). WBY appeals to Craoibhin Aoibhinn in "At the Abbey Theatre" (*CP*. 107) and recalls him in "Coole Park 1929" (*CP*. 273).

REFERENCES: Conner, Lester. "The Importance of Douglas Hyde to the Irish Literary Renaissance." In *Modern Irish Literature: Essays in Honor of William York Tindall*, ed. Raymond J. Porter and James D. Brophy. New York: Twayne, 1972; Daly, Dominic. *The Young Douglas Hyde: The Dawn of the Irish Revolution and Renaissance 1874–1893*. Totowa, N.J.: Rowman & Littlefield, 1974; Marcus, Phillip L. *Yeats and the Beginning of the Irish Renaissance*. Syracuse: Syracuse University Press, 1987; McMahon, Sean. "Art and Life Blended: Douglas Hyde and the Literary Revival." *Éire* 14, no. 3 (1979); McMahon, Sean. "*Casadh an tSugáin*: The First Irish Play." *Éire* 12, no. 4 (1977); Meir, Colin. *The Ballads and Songs of W. B. Yeats: The Anglo-Irish Heritage in Subject and Style*. London: Macmillan, 1974.

HYDE-LEES, [BERTHA] GEORGE. *See* YEATS, [BERTHA] GEORGE (GEORGIE) [HYDE-LEES].

HYNES, MARY (d. 1840), noted beauty who lived at **Ballylee, Galway** (county), in the early nineteenth century. Mary Hynes fascinated the men of the surrounding area. They fought for a glimpse of her at fairs or hurling matches, and many asked to marry her, but she refused. One man reputedly tried to visit her after he had been drinking in a local pub and was drowned in the bog at **Cloone**. She interested WBY, not only because of her associations with Ballylee but also because her beauty had inspired the blind poet **Raftery**. For her, Raftery wrote the lyric "Mary Hynes, or the Posy Bright," translated by **Lady Gregory** and quoted by WBY in "Dust Hath Closed Helen's Eye" (*MY*. 22–30). Like **Helen** and **Maud Gonne**, Mary Hynes had caused suffering and pain to those captivated by her charms. In "The Literary Movement in Ireland" (*UP2*. 189–90), WBY tells of meeting an old woman who remembered how beautiful Mary Hynes had been and believed her death at an early age was probably the work of fairies, who took her away. She is the unnamed woman "commended by a song" in "The Tower" (*CP*. 218).

REFERENCE: Byrne, Donn. *Blind Raftery and his Wife Hilaria*. New York and London: the Century Co., 1924.

I

IBSEN, HENRIK (1828–1906), poet and dramatist. He was born and educated in Norway and as a student was drawn to radical politics. From 1851 to 1864, he was active in the Norwegian theater, first as a stage manager with the National Stage in Bergen and later as director of the Norwegian Theater in Oslo. After his early plays met with only moderate success, he went to Italy in 1864 and remained abroad until 1891. It was in Italy and in Germany that he wrote the bulk of the plays that established him as the most important figure in nineteenth-century European drama. These plays range from the early folk plays and poetic dramas, including the tragedy *Brand* (1866) and the existentialist *Peer Gynt* (1867), to the important social dramas *A Doll's House* (1879), *Ghosts* (1881), *An Enemy of the People* (1882), *The Wild Duck* (1884), *The Lady from the Sea* (1888), and *Hedda Gabler* (1890). On his return to Norway, he wrote the symbolic dramas *The Master Builder* (1892), *John Gabriel Borkman* (1896), and *When We Dead Awaken* (1899). WBY was quick to recognize Ibsen's contribution to the development of contemporary literature (*EI.* 186, 187), and in a lecture given to the **Irish Literary Society** in 1899 (*UP2.* 153–58), he used Ibsen and his Scandinavian theater as a model for the development of an Irish national theater. Later, he deplored the influence of Ibsen's realistic problem plays on the English stage (*UP1.* 322), but in his review of *Brand* and *Peer Gynt* (*UP1.* 344–46), he asserted that in these early poetic dramas the playwright had created works of art in which he never sank to the level of mere theorist or preacher. He disliked *A Doll's House*, the first of Ibsen's plays to be performed in England (*A.* 279), but he wrote of Ibsen as a "logician without rancor" and challenged those who found him morbid and gloomy (*LE.* 43).

REFERENCES: Beyer, Edvard. *Ibsen: The Man and His Work.* Trans. Marie Wells. New York: Taplinger, 1978; Meyer, Michael L. *Henrik Ibsen: A Biography.* 3 vols.

Garden City, N.Y.: Doubleday, 1967–70; Northam, John. *Ibsen: A Critical Study*. Cambridge: University Press, 1973.

IDEAS OF GOOD AND EVIL, collection of essays. It was published by **A. H. Bullen** in May 1903 and contained nineteen essays that WBY had written between 1896 and 1903. Many of them had been published previously in magazines and periodicals. All of the essays were later republished in *Essays and Introductions* (1961). The title, *Ideas of Good and Evil*, was taken from a collection of poems by **William Blake,** *Life and Works of William Blake* (1880), selected and edited by **Dante Gabriel Rossetti**.

INCHY WOOD. *See* **SEVEN WOODS**.

INISHEER. *See* **ARAN ISLANDS**.

INISHMAAN. *See* **ARAN ISLANDS**.

INISHMORE. *See* **ARAN ISLANDS**.

INISHMURRAY (Irish: *Inis Muirí*), island in the Atlantic, four miles off the coast of **Sligo** (county). The island was named for St. Muireadhach, bishop of **Killala**. On the island, which is no longer inhabited, is a well-preserved monastery, founded by St. Molaise in the sixth century. See also ''The Ballad of Father O'Hart'' (*CP*. 25).
    REFERENCE: McGarry, James P. *Place Names in the Writings of William Butler Yeats*. Gerrards Cross: Colin Smythe, 1976.

INNISFREE (Irish: *Inis Fraoigh*) [Heather Island], island in **Lough Gill, Sligo** (county). The island appealed to WBY because it had associations with fairy lore. It was believed that an enchanted mountain ash grew there and that its berries could either poison a mortal or endow him with magical powers (*VP*. 742). WBY wished some day to live on the island of Innisfree, seeking wisdom, and one evening, he slept outdoors at **Sleuth Wood** to watch the island in the early dawn (*A*. 71–72). It is the setting for one of WBY's best-loved poems, ''The Lake Isle of Innisfree'' (*CP*. 44). He wrote the poem in London, when he was homesick for Sligo (*A*. 153). See also *JS*. 57.
    REFERENCES: Alspach, Russell K. *Yeats and Innisfree*. Dublin: Dolmen, 1965; Gould, Warwick. ''Yeats as Aborigine.'' In *Four Decades of Poetry, 1890–1930*. Vol. 2. (1978); McGarry, James P. *Place Names in the Writings of William Butler Yeats*. Gerrards Cross: Colin Smythe, 1976.

IN THE SEVEN WOODS, collection of poems and a play. It was the first book published by the **Dun Emer Press** in 1903, in an edition of 325 copies. Subtitled *Being Poems Chiefly of the Irish Heroic Age*, the edition contained ten short poems, two longer poems, and the play *On Baile's Strand*. The short poems were "In the Seven Woods" (*CP*. 85), "The Arrow" (*CP*. 85), "The Folly of Being Comforted" (*CP*. 86), "The Withering of the Boughs" (*CP*. 87), "Adam's Curse" (*CP*. 88), "Red Hanrahan's Song about Ireland" (*CP*. 90), "The Old Men Admiring Themselves in the Water" (*CP*. 91), "Under the Moon" (*CP*. 91), "The Players Ask for a Blessing on the Psalteries and on Themselves" (*CP*. 93), and "The Happy Townland" (*CP*. 94). The longer poems were "The Old Age of Queen Maeve" (*CP*. 451) and "Baile and Aillinn" (*CP*. 459). Three poems, "Old Memory" (*CP*. 86), "Never Give all the Heart" (*CP*. 87), and "The Entrance of Deirdre" (later removed), were added to the 1906 edition, while two others, "The Ragged [later Hollow] Wood" (*CP*. 92) and "O Do Not Love Too Long" (*CP*. 93), were included in 1908. The volume takes its title from the **Seven Woods** in **Coole Park, Galway** (county).

INVER AMERGIN (Irish: *Inbhear Amhairgain*) [estuary of Amergin], mouth of the Avoca River in County Wicklow. Inver Amergin was associated with the poet and seer Amergin, son of Míl. He was renowned for his judgment on who should rule Ireland after the Milesians conquered it from the **Tuatha dé Danaan**. He is reputed to have written the first poem in Irish. See also "The Madness of King Goll" (*CP*. 17). Another Amergin was a Druid in the service of **Conchubar**.

REFERENCE: McGarry, James P. *Place Names in the Writings of William Butler Yeats.* Gerrards Cross: Colin Smythe, 1976.

IRISH ACADEMY OF LETTERS. In 1926, WBY, **AE**, and **Lennox Robinson** wrote to the president of the **Royal Irish Academy** suggesting that an autonomous committee of writers, modeled on the French Institute, should be appointed. The matter was delayed for some years, and only in 1932 was approval given. In a letter to prospective academicians, it was emphasized that the Academy would be a powerful force in combating literary censorship in Ireland. For WBY, the setting up of the Academy, opposed by the Catholic press in Ireland, fired his enthusiasm and gave him renewed vigor. He visited the United States in 1932 and was successful in raising money to endow the annual Gregory Medal, named in memory of **Lady Gregory**. The medal was designed by Maurice Lambert. The Academy gave three other annual awards: the Harmsworth Award, the Casement Award, and the O'Growney Award (for books in Gaelic). All three awards, which had cash prizes, have now lapsed. In a late essay, "Commentary on the Three Songs" (*VP*. 836), WBY, contrasting the honor accorded writers in Poland and Ireland, mentions that the Irish Academy met in rooms hired for five shillings a night.

REFERENCE: Raifeartaigh, T. O., ed. *Royal Irish Academy: A Bicentennial History.* Dublin: the Academy, 1985.

IRISH LITERARY SOCIETY. It was founded by WBY and **T. W. Rolleston** in London, May 1892, to bring together the Irish writers domiciled in London to promote a national culture. A preliminary meeting was held at WBY's home in **Blenheim Road**, 28 December 1891, when WBY introduced Rolleston to **John Todhunter, D. J. O'Donoghue**, and W. P. Ryan, all members of the Southwark Irish Literary Club, formed in 1883 to promote Irish culture but by then in decline. At the inaugural meeting of the Irish Literary Society, which took place in the Caledonian Hotel, London, May 1892, **Sir Charles Gavan Duffy** was appointed president, and Rolleston, secretary. WBY did not attend the meeting because he was in Ireland organizing the setting up of the **National Literary Society**. In his absence, he was appointed to the committee of fourteen. Most of the Irish writers in London became members, including **Oscar Wilde** and his mother **Lady Wilde**. The inaugural lecture, ''The Need and Use of Getting Irish Literature into the English Tongue,'' was given in March 1893 by Stopford Brooke. In the following years, the Society supported the **New Irish Library**, held classes in the Irish language, and launched the periodicals *The Irish Home Reading Magazine* (1894) and the *Irish Literary Society Gazette*. The Society promoted the Irish Text Society, which aimed to publish important works in Gaelic, and the Irish Folk Song Society, particularly noted for the Petrie Collection of Irish Music, edited by Sir Charles Stanford, and organized the visits of the **Irish National Theatre Society** to London in 1903 and 1904. WBY resigned from the Society in 1901 after **George Moore's** application for membership was opposed (*A*. 433). He was reinstated as an honorary member. WBY writes about the setting up of the Irish Literary Society in *Dramatis Personae* (*A*. 395–96).

IRISH LITERARY THEATRE, national theater movement. The idea for such a theater grew out of a discussion that WBY had with **Lady Gregory** and **Edward Martyn** in the summer of 1897. While WBY had entertained the idea for some time, it was only with the energy of Lady Gregory and the financial resources of Martyn that the idea was able to get off the ground. It was hoped to mount the first production of the Irish Literary Theatre in 1898, the anniversary of the 1798 Rebellion, but because of Patent Laws, it proved impossible to find a suitable venue in Dublin. In the event, the Patent Laws were amended, and the first productions of the Irish Literary Theatre took place a year later in the **Antient Concert Rooms**, 8–10 May 1899, when WBY's *The Countess Cathleen* and Edward Martyn's *The Heather Field* were performed. Both plays were cast and rehearsed in London by **George Moore** and **Florence Farr**. The second season took place on 19–20 February 1900, when Edward Martyn's *Maeve* was produced with **Alice Milligan's** *The Last Feast of the Fianna* and *The Bending of the Bough* by George Moore. For the third and final program, 21 October 1901, *Diarmuid and Grania*, written by WBY and George Moore, was presented with *Casadh an tSugain* by **Douglas Hyde**. The play by Moore and WBY, performed by F. R. Benson's professional acting company from England, was in sharp contrast to Hyde's play in Gaelic, performed by local community actors, directed by **W. G. Fay**. WBY was impressed with the naturalness and spontaneity of the players trained by Fay and his brother **Frank**. This prepared the way for the next development in the emergence of a national theater, the formation, in 1902, of W. G. Fay's National Dramatic Society, later to become the **Irish National Theatre Society**.

REFERENCES: Flannery, James W. *W. B. Yeats and the Idea of a Theatre: The Early Abbey Theatre in Theory and Practice*. New Haven: Yale University Press, 1976; Robinson, Lennox. *Ireland's Abbey Theatre: A History, 1899–1951*. London: Sidgwick & Jackson, 1951.

IRISH NATIONAL DRAMATIC SOCIETY, theater company. It grew out of several theater companies that **W. G. Fay** had founded in Dublin under various names, including the Ormonde Drama Company, W. G. Fay's Ormonde Dramatic Society, the Irish National Dramatic Company, and W. G. Fay's National Dramatic Society. With the success of WBY's *Cathleen Ni Houlihan*, April 1902, W. G. and his brother **Frank** decided to form a theater company to produce only Irish drama. Thus, the Irish National Dramatic Society was constituted, 9 August 1902. Since WBY had expressed interest, he was elected president, with **Maud Gonne, Douglas Hyde**, and **AE** as vice presidents. For their first production in the **Antient Concert Rooms**, 29–31 October 1902, the company produced *The Sleep of the King* and *The Racing Lug*, both by **James Cousins;** *The Laying of the Foundations* by Frederick Ryan; WBY's *The Pot of Broth*; and a play in Irish, *Eilís agus An Bhean Deírce*, by P. T. MacFhionnlaoich. The company was under the control of W. G. Fay; he chose the plays and directed the players. His selection of plays caused some controversy among the elected officers, the result of which was the drawing up, in February 1903, of a set of rules and a more specific statement of artistic policy based on the ideals of the **Irish Literary Theatre**. The Society, which was registered under the Friendly Societies Act as a cooperative, not a commercial, venture, was renamed the **Irish National Theatre Society**. A reading committee, consisting of WBY, AE, **Padraic Colum**, and the Fays, was set up. With the formation of the Irish National Theatre Society, W. G. Fay and his brother effectively lost control of the company they had brought into being.

REFERENCES: Hunt, Hugh. *The Abbey: Ireland's National Theatre, 1904–1979*. Dublin: Gill & Macmillan, 1979; Robinson, Lennox. *Ireland's Abbey Theatre: A History, 1899–1951*. London: Sidgwick & Jackson, 1951.

IRISH NATIONAL THEATRE SOCIETY. *See* **ABBEY THEATRE**.

IRISH SENATE. *See* **DÁIL ÉIREANN**.

IRVING, SIR HENRY (1838–1905), actor. He was born Jonathan Henry Brodribb in Somerset, England. His family intended that he should enter the Church, but he joined a professional theater company in 1856 to become an actor, changing his name to Henry Irving. He played hundreds of roles in the provinces before he settled in London, 1867. There, at the Lyceum Theatre in 1871, he had a major success as Matthias in *The Bells*. He became manager and leading actor of the Lyceum Theatre in 1878, and with Ellen Terry as his leading lady, he dominated the English stage until 1903, most notably in **Shakespeare**. His most famous role was Hamlet, which he first played in 1878. He was the first English actor to be knighted (1895). Irving was noted for his dynamic stage presence and fine speaking, although his style was mannered, even by contemporary standards. WBY was taken by his father to see Irving in *Hamlet* in 1874. In *Reveries over Childhood and Youth* (*A*. 47), he writes of the impact the actor made on him, an ''image of heroic self-possession,'' an image recalled in ''A Nativity'' (*CP*. 387). **Gordon Craig**, who acted with Irving, offered to show him the script of *The Hour-Glass* (*WL*. 375), but nothing came from the gesture.

REFERENCE: Craig, Edward Gordon. *Henry Irving*. New York: Longmans, Green, 1930.

ISLAND OF STATUES, THE, verse play. WBY reputedly began *The Island of Statues* for **Laura Armstrong**, a distant cousin, with whom he was in love. Described as an ''Arcadian Faery Tale—in Two Acts,'' the play appeared in serial form in the *Dublin University Review*, April–July 1885. The final installment, Act 2, Scene III, was included in *The Wanderings of Oisin and Other Poems* (1889). **AE** published a further fifty-three lines in ''A Celtic Christmas,'' the Christmas number of *The Irish Homestead*, December 1899. WBY did not reprint the play in any future volume of his work. He dropped from subsequent collections the short scene published in *The Wanderings of Oisin and Other Poems*, with the exception of the opening fifteen lines of Act 2, Scene III, which he published in *Poems* (1895) as ''The Cloak, the Boat, and the Shoes'' (*CP*. 10). The action of *The Island of Statues* takes place on an island, ruled over by an enchantress. Almintor, a hunter, visits the enchanted island to find a mysterious flower for Naschina, whom he loves. He chooses the wrong flower and is turned to stone. Naschina, resolved to find her love, dresses as a shepherd boy and journeys to the island. On the way, she meets two shepherds who are in love with her. They do not recognize her but tell her they are both in love with the same girl. To resolve the problem, they decide to fight a duel, and one of them is killed. On the island, the enchantress falls in love with Naschina, and a prophecy is uncovered. Only a shepherdess, for whom a lover has died, may find the mysterious flower. Naschina reveals her identity. She finds the flower and restores her lover Almintor to life. The enchantress dies. There is no record of any performances of the play.

REFERENCE: Bornstein, George, ed. *The Early Poetry, Vol. 1: Mosada and the Island of Statues*. Ithaca and London: Cornell University Press, 1987.

ISLAND VIEW. *See* **BALSCADDEN COTTAGE**.

ISOLDE [Iseult], one of the tragic lovers in *Tristram and Isolde*, an Anglo-Norman romance. **Tristram** journeys to Ireland to bring the beautiful Isolde back to Cornwall to be the bride of his uncle, King Mark. Tragedy emerges when Isolde and Tristram unknowingly swallow a potion that makes them fall in love. Their story is echoed in many Celtic elopement stories, most particularly in the tale of **Diarmuid** and **Grania**. WBY was impressed with **Laurence Binyon's** poem "Tristram's End" (*LE*. 94, 188), which he included in *The Oxford Book of Modern Verse* (1936).

ITH (Irish: *Magh Itha*) [Plain of Corn], **Donegal** (county), near the mouth of the Finn River where it enters Lough Foyle. Ith was a mythical invader of Ireland. He first saw Ireland from his father's tower in Spain and embarked with ninety men to visit it. Asked by the **Tuatha dé Danaan** to decide for them who should rule Ireland now that they had overcome the **Fomorians**, it became clear that Ith wanted the position for himself. The Tuatha dé Danaan killed him and returned his body to Spain. His compatriots, the Milesians, avenged him by conquering Ireland. See also "The Madness of King Goll" (*CP*. 17).
    REFERENCE: McGarry, James P. *Place Names in the Writings of William Butler Yeats.* Gerrards Cross: Colin Smythe, 1976.

ITO, MICHIO (1893–1961), dancer and choreographer. He was born in Tokyo, the eldest son of a well-to-do Japanese family. As the grandson of a samurai, he was given the opportunity to observe his native culture, including the **Noh**, and he had early training in Kabuki. In 1912, he traveled to Europe to study Western dance and attended the Dalcroze Institute in Hellerau, just outside Dresden. When the war broke out in 1914, he moved to London. There, he frequented the Café Royal, where he made the acquaintance of **Ezra Pound**. He was invited to dance at the home of **Lady Ottoline Morrell**. This was the first of a number of such invitations, leading to an engagement at the Coliseum Theatre. WBY was at this time working on his play *At the Hawk's Well*, modeled on the Japanese Noh. For him, Ito, who was now living in Pound's old rooms at 10 Church Walk, prepared a special performance of a Noh dance, in a costume made by **Charles Ricketts** and **Edmund Dulac**. It was a preparation for the work that WBY and Ito did together for the premiere of *At the Hawk's Well*, in which Ito danced the role of **The Guardian of the Well**. He later performed, at society gatherings, a series of traditional Japanese dances, to the accompaniment of poems by Masirni Utchiyama, translated by Pound. Because of the war in Europe, Ito moved to the United States, where, in November 1916, he directed and designed the Kabuki play *Bushido* for the Washington Square Players, while in July 1918, he directed and danced in the American premiere of *At the Hawk's Well* (*WL*. 651–52). Dulac's costumes and masks were used, but a new musical setting was composed by Kosaku Yamada. The following month, Ito toured the East Coast with a dance program that included *At the Hawk's Well*. In 1923, he staged for the Thursday Evening Club the first performance outside Japan of the Noh play *Hagoromo*. From 1919 to 1929, he performed and directed a series of revues, plays, musicals, and operas. These included *The*

Faithful by **John Masefield** and *Sister Beatrice* by **Maurice Maeterlinck**. In 1929, he went on tour to the West Coast. He remained in California for the next thirteen years, teaching and directing a wide range of productions, including opera and ballet. After Pearl Harbor, Ito was briefly interned in the United States. He moved back to Japan, where he introduced the plays of WBY at the Michio Ito Dancing Institute. Ito's contribution to the development of WBY's Noh drama has not been fully acknowledged. As Curtis Bradford points out in *Yeats at Work* (1965), because of Ito's talent, as rehearsals for *At the Hawk's Well* progressed, WBY cut songs and speeches and relied more and more on the dance.

REFERENCES: Caldwell, Helen. *Michio Ito: The Dancer and His Dances*. Berkeley: University of California Press, 1977; Carruthers, Ian. "A Translation of Fifteen Pages of Michio Ito's Autobiography." *Canadian Journal of Irish Studies* 2:1 (May 1975); Oshima, Shotaro. *W. B. Yeats and Japan*. Tokyo: Hokuseido, 1965; Reck, Michael. *Ezra Pound: A Close-up*. New York: McGraw-Hill, 1967; Sekine, Masaru. "Yeats and the Noh." In *Irish Writers and the Theatre*, ed. Okifumi Komesu and Masaru Sekine. Savage, Md.: Barnes & Noble, 1990.

J

JACK THE JOURNEYMAN, lamented lover of **Crazy Jane** in the poem "Crazy Jane and the Bishop" (*CP*. 290), and "Crazy Jane and Jack the Journeyman" (*CP*. 292). See also *The Pot of Broth* (*CPl*. 93).

JAFFER, vizier of Baghdad from 786 to 803. Jaffer was imprisoned by the caliph, **Harun Al-Rashid**. In "The Gift of Harun Al-Rashid" (*CP*. 513), the caliph has Jaffer put to death for a reason unknown to his subjects.

JAMMES, FRANCIS (1868–1938), poet and short story writer. He was born and lived all his life in the French Pyrenees. A Symbolist, his writing is distinguished by a deep religious faith and a joyous optimism arising out of the simple pleasures of rural life. His collections of verse include *De l'angélus de l' aube à l'angélus du soir* (1898) and *Les Géorgiques Chrétiennes* (1912). WBY was introduced to his poetry in 1917, when he visited **Iseult Gonne** in Normandy (*LE*. 33). She read him "Le Poète et l'oiseau: poème dialogué" from Jammes's collection *Le Deuil des primevères: 1898–1900* (1917), which WBY retained for his library (*OS*. no. 1012).
  REFERENCE: Lowell, Amy. *Six French Poets*. New York: Macmillan, 1915.

JOHN, AUGUSTUS [EDWIN] (1878–1961), painter. He was born in Wales, the son of a solicitor, and studied painting at the Slade School in London. With his exhibition at the Carfax Gallery in 1899, he achieved a reputation for his elegant drawings and vigorous portraits. In 1901, he became an instructor at an art school in **Liverpool**, and on his return to London, he was appointed coprincipal of the Chelsea Art School, 1903–7. He became an itinerant artist, moving from place to place with his first wife, Ida Nettleship, and his mistress, later his second wife, Dorothy (Dorelia) McNeill. In 1909, the wealthy American art collector **John Quinn** became his patron. After a period as an official war artist in Paris, he emerged as a painter of celebrities, among them **Thomas Hardy, George Bernard Shaw, James Joyce**, and **Sean O'Casey**. Many of his later society portraits showed flair but little substance, and his reputation declined. He was elected to the Royal Academy in 1928. John was a complex man, flamboyant and domineering, with a tendency to melancholia, but his dynamic personality and dashing good looks captivated those with whom he came in contact. Bohemian in dress and lifestyle, he became friendly with WBY in 1907, when both were guests of **Lady Gregory** at **Coole Park**. John did many drawings of WBY and later worked them into a fine etching and a portrait in oils—the portrait being among his best works. The etching was to have been included in WBY's *Collected Works* (1908), but it was not used until *The Collected Poems of W. B. Yeats* (1933). John completed a portrait of the mature WBY in 1930. WBY was fascinated by John's personality and eccentric lifestyle and shared this enthusiasm with **Florence Farr** and John Quinn (*WL*. 492–93, 496–97). In 1930, WBY writes about John's early portrait of him, concluding that the artist had uncovered WBY's "outlawed solitude" (*EX*. 308).

REFERENCES: Easton, Malcolm. *Augustus John*. London: H. M. S. O., 1975; Holroyd, Michael. *Augustus John: A Biography*. New York: Holt, Rinehart & Winston, 1975; Rothenstein, Sir John. *Augustus John*. London: Beaverbrook Newspapers, 1962.

JOHN BULL, stereotypical Englishman. The nickname was first used by Dr. John Arbuthnot (1667–1735), Scottish author, physician to Queen Anne and friend of **Jonathan Swift**. In 1712, Arbuthnot published five satirical pamphlets on the policies of the Whig Party in the British Parliament. In these he introduced the character John Bull. WBY uses the term derisively in "The Ghost of Roger Casement" (*CP*. 352). Dr. Arbuthnot is referred to in WBY's play *The Words upon the Window-Pane* (*CPl*. 609).

JOHN SHERMAN, title character. In WBY's novel *John Sherman* (1891), the hero must choose between life in London and life in Ireland, and between a sophisticated Englishwoman and his Irish sweetheart. John Sherman leaves his home in Ballah to live in London. There he becomes engaged to a wealthy Englishwoman, Margaret Leland. When he realizes that the engagement is a mistake, he arranges for her to meet the pompous clergyman, William Howard. The two fall in love, and Sherman, released from the engagement, returns to Ballah to marry his childhood sweetheart, Mary Carton. In the novel, Ballah is synonymous with **Sligo** (town), while the character of John Sherman is modeled on WBY himself and his cousin **Henry Middleton**.

REFERENCES: Finneran, Richard J., ed. *John Sherman and Dhoya: The Collected Works of W. B. Yeats*. Vol. XII. New York: Macmillan, 1991; Murphy, William M. "W. B. Yeats's John Sherman: An Irish Poet's Declaration of Independence." *Irish University Review* 9, no. 1 (1979).

JOHN SHERMAN. See ***JOHN SHERMAN AND DHOYA***.

JOHN SHERMAN AND DHOYA, publication. Written under the pseudonym Ganconagh (love-talker), an Irish spirit, *John Sherman and Dhoya* (1891) was published in London by **T. Fisher Unwin** in the Pseudonym Library Series and in the United States by Cassell Publishing Company as part of the Unknown Library. The volume consisted of *John Sherman*, a realistic short novel, and *Dhoya*, a short mythological story. In *John Sherman*, the eponymous hero must choose between London and Ballah, a town in the west of Ireland. In *Dhoya*, a mortal has a relationship with a fairy. *John Sherman and Dhoya* was republished with the subtitle *Two Early Stories* as volume seven of *Collected Works* (1908). It was then excluded from the canon.
     REFERENCE: Finneran, Richard J., ed. *John Sherman and Dhoya: The Collected Works of W. B. Yeats*. Vol. XII. New York: Macmillan, 1991.

JOHNSON, ESTHER [Stella] (1682–1728), intimate friend of **Jonathan Swift**. She met Swift in 1689, when he tutored her at Moor Park, Surrey, the home of Sir William Temple (she was the daughter of Temple's widowed housekeeper). Swift, after he was ordained in 1695, returned to Ireland to take up a church appointment. While there, Sir William Temple died, leaving Esther Johnson £1500, and in 1700, when Swift suggested she should come to live in Ireland, she moved to Dublin with her companion Rebecca Dingley. Despite the amorous attentions of **Hester van Homrigh** (Vanessa), Swift maintained a devoted friendship with Esther Johnson, whom he called Stella, until her death. The nature of the relationship has been the cause of much speculation. In the play ***The Words upon the Window-Pane*** (*CPl.* 613), WBY quotes from her poem "Stella to Dr. Swift on His Birth-day November 30, 1721" and concludes that her relationship with Swift was intellectual and platonic, not sexual. She predeceased Swift and is buried alongside him in St. Patrick's Cathedral, Dublin. WBY refers to her in the poem "The Seven Sages" (*CP.* 271).
     REFERENCES: Williams, Harold, ed. *Jonathan Swift: Journal to Stella*. Oxford: Clarendon, 1958.

JOHNSON, LIONEL [PIGOT] (1867–1902), poet. He was born at Broadstairs, Kent, and from an early age immersed himself in Greek and Latin studies, first at Winchester College and, from 1886, at New College, **Oxford**, where he came under the influence of **Walter Pater**. He moved to London, staying with **Herbert Horne** at 20 Fitzroy Street, and contributed articles and reviews to various periodicals. In 1889, after admiring WBY's ***The Wanderings of Oisin***, he met the author, and they formed a close friendship. Together, they were members of the **Rhymers' Club**, and Johnson took a keen interest in the **Irish Literary Society**, convincing himself that he had Irish ancestors. He converted to Catholicism in 1891. He published his first book, *The Art of Thomas Hardy*, in 1894, the year in which he introduced his cousin **Olivia Shakespear** to WBY.

His verse, which had appeared in *The Yellow Book*, was collected in *Poems* (1895) and *Ireland with Other Poems* (1897). He edited with Eleanor Hull the *Irish Home Reading Magazine*, 1894. Always something of an eccentric, a loner who slept by day and wrote by night, he became an alcoholic and died accidentally when he fell and fractured his skull in a public house in Fleet Street. During the 1890s, he was WBY's closest friend in London (until he was replaced by **Arthur Symons**) and, with his erudition, grace, and cultured manner, exercised a profound influence on the young Irishman. WBY acknowledged his debt to Johnson in the poems "The Grey Rock" (*CP*. 115–18) and "In Memory of Major Robert Gregory" (*CP*. 148). He dedicated **The Rose** to him and wrote about him at length in "The Tragic Generation" (*A*. 279–349). He included six poems by Johnson in his selections for **The Oxford Book of Modern Verse** (1936). Six titles by Johnson were in WBY's library (*OS*. nos. 1018–23).

REFERENCES: Alford, Norman. *The Rhymers' Club: Poets of the Tragic Generation.* New York: St. Martin's, 1994; Cevasco, George A. *Three Decadent Poets: Ernest Dowson, John Gray, and Lionel Johnson, an Annotated Bibliography.* New York: Garland, 1990; Fletcher, Ian. *W. B. Yeats and His Contemporaries.* Brighton, Sussex: Harvester, 1987; Gardner, Joann. *Yeats and the Rhymers' Club: A Nineties' Perspective.* New York: Peter Lang, 1989; Halladay, Jean R. *Eight Late Victorian Poets Shaping the Artistic Sensibility of an Age.* Lewiston, N.Y.: E. Mellen, 1993; Stanford, Derek, ed. *Three Poets of the Rhymers' Club: Ernest Dowson, Lionel Johnson, John Davidson.* Cheadle: Carcenet, 1974.

JOHNSTON, CHARLES (1867–1931), journalist. He was born near Downpatrick, **County Down**, the son of William Johnston, M.P. for South Belfast and a leader of the Orange Order. He met WBY when they were schoolboys at **Erasmus Smith High School**. Although Johnston was a brilliant student, he was regarded as conceited and arrogant by other pupils. WBY and he formed a friendship and spent much time in each other's company, playing chess and going on outings. Johnston was interested in theosophy, and together they read A. P. Sinnott's *Esoteric Buddhism*. In 1885, they formed the **Dublin Hermetic Society** and invited **Mohini Chatterjee** to address them (*A*. 90–92). After graduating from **Trinity College**, Dublin, Johnston moved to London in 1887. He became a member of the **Theosophical Society** and introduced WBY to **Madame Blavatsky**. With his outgoing personality, Johnston so impressed Blavatsky that she groomed him for leadership of the organization if he remained single. He did not honor the commitment, and in 1888, to Madame Blavatsky's disgust, he married her niece, Vera de Yakhontov (*WL*. 90). Soon after his marriage, Johnston joined the Indian Civil Service and served eighteen months as assistant magistrate in India, visiting Bombay, Madras, Calcutta, and Allahabad. In 1890, he returned to England and retired from the Indian Civil Service on medical grounds. In 1896, he and his wife emigrated to the United States, becoming citizens in 1903. In New York, Johnston worked as a journalist, contributing articles on Eastern subjects to newspapers and periodicals, among them the *New York Times Book Review, North American Review, Atlantic Monthly*, and *The Gael* (New York). He taught Sanskrit at Columbia University and translated books from Russian, German, and Sanskrit. He made the acquaintance of **John Quinn** and was invited to be president of the short-lived New York branch of the **Irish Literary Society** (*WL*. 403). He was on the platform when WBY addressed **Clan-na-Gael** in New York, on the occasion of the anniversary celebrations for **Robert Emmet**. Through Quinn, Johnston renewed his friendship with **John B. Yeats**, after the painter moved to New York in 1908. Johnston's friendship with WBY was most intense in the late 1880s and early 1900s, when WBY visited him at the family home, Ballykilbeg House, Downpatrick (*M*. 45–46). With time and distance, the friendship cooled, but Johnston's early influence on WBY's lifelong interest in the occult and Eastern philosophy cannot be overestimated.

REFERENCE: Boyd, Ernest. *Ireland's Literary Renaissance*. New York: Macmillan, 1937.

JONSON, BEN (1572–1637), dramatist, essayist, and poet. He was born in England, and after serving as a soldier in Flanders, he became an actor. He achieved his first success as a dramatist in London with *Every Man in His Humour* (1598), a play in which **William Shakespeare** acted. The following year, during a trial in which he was accused of killing another actor, he wrote a companion piece, *Every Man Out of His Humour*. After his acquittal, he became a court favorite, writing elegant masques for James I, who succeeded to the English throne in 1603. Jonson embarked on his memorable satirical dramas, *Volpone; or The Fox* (1606), *The Alchemist* (1610), and *Bartholomew Fair* (1614), all characterized by inventive plots and scorching wit. With these comic masterpieces, which insightfully ridiculed the follies of the age through the exaggeration of the ''humours,'' Jonson confirmed his stature as the outstanding English comic playwright after Shakespeare. Among his love poems are the engaging lyrics ''Drink to me only with thine eyes'' and ''Come, my Celia, let us prove.'' WBY studied Jonson in 1906, intending to write an essay on him and the English court, as he had done on **Edmund Spenser** (*WL*. 478–79), but the essay was never written. From his many references to Jonson, it is clear that he admired the Elizabethan poet not only for his lyrics but also for his prose and drama. He saw Jonson's *The Silent Woman* performed in 1905 (*WL*. 450) and was moved by a production of *Volpone*, which he saw in **Oxford** in 1921 (*WL*. 664–65). He claims to have been influenced, while writing his early verse dramas, by Jonson's unfinished play *The Sad Shepherd* (*UP2*. 508). In the short poem ''While I, from that reed-throated Whisperer'' (*CP*. 143), he quotes from the Epilogue to Jonson's early satire *The Poetaster* (1601), and in ''What is 'Popular Poetry'?'' (*EI*. 7), he cites Jonson's line ''Beauty like sorrow dwelleth everywhere.''

REFERENCES: Harris, Daniel A. ''Coole Transformed: The Country House Poem.'' In *Yeats: Coole Park & Ballylee*. Baltimore: Johns Hopkins University Press, 1974.

JOYCE, JAMES [AUGUSTINE] (1882–1941), novelist, playwright, and poet. He was born in Dublin and educated at Clongowes Wood College. Later, he attended University College, Dublin (UCD), where he studied languages and developed an intense interest in modern drama. He began publishing essays while still at university; his article on **Ibsen's** *When We Dead Awaken*, published in the *Fortnightly Review*, April 1900, drew praise from Ibsen himself. On graduation from UCD, he decided to become a medical doctor and, in 1902, went to Paris to pursue his studies. Unable to support himself, he returned to Ireland, but in 1904, having fallen in love with Nora Barnacle, he left with her for Zürich. The couple moved to Pola, and later Trieste, where Joyce supported himself as a writer by teaching English in the Berlitz school. In 1912, he returned to Ireland to arrange for the publication of *Dubliners*, his collection of short stories. After disagreements with the publisher and resistance from those who thought the stories were libelous and offensive, he left Ireland and never returned. *Dubliners* was first published in London (1914). Joyce spent the war years 1914–18 in Zürich, working on his novel *A Portrait of the Artist as a Young Man* (1916), a rewriting of an earlier fragment, *Stephen Hero*, begun in 1904. Positive response to the publication of *A Portrait of the Artist* and *Dubliners* encouraged him to continue with his epic novel *Ulysses*. Publication of the controversial *Ulysses* was delayed by obscenity charges until 1922, when it was published in Paris, although it continued to be banned in the United States and England until the 1930s. *Finnegan's Wake*, Joyce's final work, which he regarded as his best, was published in 1939. He wrote three volumes of poetry, *Chamber Music* (1907), *Pomes Pennyeach* (1927), and *Collected Poems* (1937), and a naturalistic play *Exiles* (1918), which WBY rejected for the **Abbey Theatre**. As writers, WBY and Joyce were fundamentally opposed. Unlike WBY, who encouraged an escapist, antinaturalistic writing about the rural Irish peasant, Joyce, influenced by Ibsen, and writing in the manner of the French and Russian naturalists, satirized the city dwellers of Dublin mercilessly and without sentimentality. In 1899, Joyce refused to join his fellow UCD students in their condemnation of *The Countess Cathleen*, but in an article, "The Day of the Rabblement," published in 1901, he was critical of WBY and the ideals of the **Irish Literary Theatre**. WBY recognized Joyce's talent, even though he did not fully understand it, and in 1902, he introduced Joyce to important literary contacts in London (*WL*. 386). Initially, Joyce rejected the senior poet's advice, believing him to be old-fashioned and out of date (he reportedly told WBY that he had met him too late), but he came to value his poetry, most of which he could recite from memory. He acknowledged his debt in a letter, written in 1932, declining membership of the **Irish Academy of Letters**. Three poems by Joyce were included in WBY's selection for *The Oxford Book of Modern Verse* (1936).

REFERENCES: Beja, Morris. *James Joyce: A Literary Life*. Columbus: Ohio State University Press, 1992; Ellman, Richard. *James Joyce*. New York: Oxford University Press, 1982; Kain, Richard M. *Dublin in the Age of William Butler Yeats and James Joyce*.

Norman: University of Oklahoma Press, 1967; Rodgers, W. R., ed. "James Joyce." In *Irish Literary Portraits*. New York: Taplinger, 1973; Watson, George J. *Irish Identity and the Literary Revival: Synge, Yeats, Joyce, and O'Casey*. Washington, D.C.: Catholic University of America Press, 1994; Wilson, Edmund. *Axel's Castle: A Study in the Imaginative Literature of 1870–1930*. 1931. Reprint New York and London: Scribner's, 1969.

JOYCE, P[ATRICK] W[ESTON] (1827–1914), historian, teacher, and collector of Irish music. He was born in Ballyorgan, **Limerick** (county), and educated at local hedge schools. After becoming a teacher, he continued with his own education at **Trinity College**, Dublin, graduating in 1861. He joined the Commissioners of National Education, a body responsible for the national school system, in 1845 and remained with them until his retirement in 1893. He published a number of books on Irish history and the Irish language, among them *The Origin and History of Irish Names of Places* (1869–70), *Old Celtic Romances* (1879), *A Child's History of Ireland* (1897), *A Social History of Ancient Ireland* (1903), and *English as We Speak It in Ireland* (1910). He collected Irish music, which he published as *Ancient Irish Music* (1873), and was elected president of the Royal Society of Antiquaries in 1906. WBY included Joyce's "Fergus O'Mara and the Air-Demons" in his anthology *Irish Fairy Tales* (1892). Two of the stories in *Old Celtic Romances* may have influenced the writing of *The Wanderings of Oisin*, since WBY's poem follows the plot of Joyce's "Oisin in Tirnanoge," and the bird imagery of the second island owes something to Joyce's "The Voyage of Maildun," in which an "isle of birds" is described in detail. In his list of "Best Irish Books" (*UP1*. 386;*WL*. 247), WBY included Joyce's *Old Celtic Romances* and *A Short History of Ireland*. He admired the latter's impartiality but regretted the colorless style. Joyce's *Social History of Ancient Ireland* was consulted by **Annie F. Horniman** when she was designing costumes for *The King's Threshold*.

REFERENCES: Hogan, Robert, ed. *Dictionary of Irish Literature*. Rev. ed. Westport, Conn.: Greenwood, 1996; Marcus, Phillip L. *Yeats and the Beginning of the Irish Renaissance*. Syracuse: Syracuse University Press, 1987; Unterecker, John. *A Reader's Guide to W. B. Yeats*. London: Thames & Hudson, 1967.

JUAN. *See* **DON JUAN**.

JUDAS, disciple who betrayed **Christ**. In WBY's play *Calvary*, he appears to Christ on the road to Calvary. He claims that having betrayed Christ to the Roman authorities he has exercised his right to choose. Thus, he is outside Christ's power and therefore more powerful than the god. The Roman soldiers order him to support the cross on which Christ is to be crucified.

K

KAILAS. *See* **MERU**.

KAMA, god of desire in Hindu mythology. A handsome young man, surrounded by nymphs, he is usually depicted shooting love darts made of flowers. He is the Hindu equivalent of **Aengus**. See also ''Anashuya and Vijaya'' (*CP*. 12).

REFERENCE: O'Flaherty, Wendy Doniger, trans. *Hindu Myths: A Sourcebook Translated from the Sanskrit*. Harmondsworth, Middlesex: Penguin, 1975.

KAVANAGH, ROSE (1859–91), poet and journalist. She was born at Killadroy, near Omagh, County Tyrone. She moved to Dublin in the late 1870s to study at the Royal Dublin Society (now the National College of Art) and was introduced to WBY through her friendship with **Katharine Tynan** and **Ellen O'Leary**. She contributed to various Irish and American periodicals and was editor of the *Shamrock* and *Irish Fireside*. Her regular feature article for children, ''Uncle Remus to His Nieces and Nephews,'' appeared in *Irish Fireside* and later in *The Weekly Freeman*. Three of her poems were included in WBY's *Poems and Ballads of Young Ireland* (1888). After her early death from consumption, WBY wrote a tribute to her in the *Boston Pilot*, April 1891 (*LNI*. 40–44), in which he admired the delicacy of her poetry, its gentle lyricism, and meditative mood.

KEATS, JOHN (1795–1821), poet. He was born in London, the son of a livery stable keeper. In 1811, he was apprenticed to a surgeon, but after meeting the poet Leigh Hunt, he became a full-time writer in 1817. His early work, which included ''I Stood Tip-toe upon a Little Hill'' and the longer poem ''Endymion,'' was attacked by *Blackwood's Magazine* and the *Quarterly Review* (1818).

In that year, his brother Tom died from tuberculosis, and he began his passionate, yet painful relationship with Fanny Brawne. After he contracted tuberculosis, he sailed for Italy and died soon after. His poems, especially the odes
written in 1820, ''Ode to a Nightingale,'' ''Ode on a Grecian Urn,'' and ''Ode
to Autumn,'' are among the finest in English. As a boy, WBY read and discussed
Keats with his father, **John B. Yeats**. He admired his fiery, brooding imagination (*M*. 203), and in his references to Keats in articles and essays, he names
him and **Shelley** among the outstanding lyricists. His early play *The Island of
Statues* was influenced by Keats and Shelley (*UP2*. 508). WBY movingly describes Keats in his poem ''Ego Dominus Tuus'' (*CP*. 180).

REFERENCES: Eddins, Dwight. *Yeats: The Nineteenth Century Matrix*. Tuscaloosa:
University of Alabama Press, 1971; Ende, Stuart A. ''Yeats's 'Dialogues with the Voice
of Enchantment.' '' In *Keats and the Sublime*. New Haven: Yale University Press, 1976;
Jones, James Land. *Adam's Dream: Mythic Consciousness in Keats and Yeats*. Athens:
University of Georgia Press, 1975; Leavy, Barbara Fass. ''Artist and Philistine.'' In *La
Belle Dame sans Merci and the Aesthetics of Romanticism*. Detroit: Wayne State Uni-
versity Press, 1974; Magaw, Malcolm. ''Yeats and Keats: The Poetics of Romanticism.''
Bucknell Review XIII (1965).

KEDRON [also Kidron], river valley east of Jerusalem. In ''The Travail of Passion'' (*CP*. 78), Kedron is associated with Gethsemane, the garden near the
foothills of the Mount of Olives where **Christ** prayed before being taken captive
by the Roman authorities.

KEGAN PAUL. *See* **PAUL, [CHARLES] KEGAN**.

KILCLUAN (Irish: *Cill-Cluain*) [church of the meadow], near Ballinasloe, **Galway** (county). In *The Hour-Glass* (*CPl*. 304), the **Fool** observes that because
of the religious skepticism of the **Wise Man**, the church bells in Kilcluan are
no longer ringing, and the people are snoring in their beds.

REFERENCE: McGarry, James P. *Place Names in the Writings of William Butler Yeats*.
Gerrards Cross: Colin Smythe, 1976.

KILGLASS (Irish: *Cill Ghlas*) [green church], townland in **Sligo** (county). In
WBY's play *Cathleen Ni Houlihan* (*CPl*. 81), Peter thinks the Old Woman,
Cathleen Ni Houlihan, might be the Widow Casey that was evicted at Kilglass.

REFERENCE: McGarry, James P. *Place Names in the Writings of William Butler Yeats*.
Gerrards Cross: Colin Smythe, 1976.

KILLALA (Irish: *Cill Ala*) [church of Ala], on the west coast of Ireland. In
County Mayo, Killala was the site of the French landing to support the Irish
during the unsuccessful 1798 Rebellion. It is the setting for the **Gillane** cottage
in WBY's play *Cathleen Ni Houlihan*, and at the end of the play, loud cheering

announces the arrival of the French soldiers. The area around Killala is rich in megalithic monuments and churches dating from the ninth century.

REFERENCE: McGarry, James P. *Place Names in the Writings of William Butler Yeats*. Gerrards Cross: Colin Smythe, 1976.

KILTARTAN [church of St. Tartan], barony near **Coole Park, Galway** (county). In "Dust Hath Closed Helen's Eye" (*MY*. 22), WBY writes that **Ballylee** is in the barony of Kiltartan, while in "An Irish Airman Foresees His Death" (*CP*. 152), he associates **Major Robert Gregory** with Kiltartan Cross, a crossroads in the area. The Kiltartan River, referred to in *The Cat and the Moon* (*CPl*. 462), flows into Coole Lake. The dialect that **Lady Gregory** used in her folk plays and in her adaptations of Molière came to be known as Kiltartanese.

REFERENCE: McGarry, James P. *Place Names in the Writings of William Butler Yeats*. Gerrards Cross: Colin Smythe, 1976.

KILVARNET (Irish: *Cill Bhearnais*) [church in the gap], townland near the village of Ballinacarrow, **Sligo** (county). In "The Fiddler of Dooney" (*CP*. 82), the fiddler claims that his brother is a priest in Kilvarnet. An important historical guide to the townland is *History, Antiquities, and Present State of the Parishes of Ballisadare and Kilvarnet in the County of Sligo* (Dublin, 1878), written by **Father Terence O'Rorke**.

REFERENCE: McGarry, James P. *Place Names in the Writings of William Butler Yeats*. Gerrards Cross: Colin Smythe, 1976.

KING. In WBY's play *The King of the Great Clock Tower*, the pompous King is a powerful ruler of his court. His **Queen**, however, remains inexplicably silent. When an arrogant **Stroller** insists the Queen will dance and sing for him, the jealous King has him beheaded. The Stroller's prophecy is fulfilled. The role of the King in the first performance of *The King of the Great Clock Tower*, July 1934, was played by **F. J. McCormick**.

KING, RICHARD ASHE (1839–1932), editor and journalist. He was born in **County Clare**. A practicing clergyman in the Church of Ireland, he retired about 1885 to live in a cottage at Blackrock, near Dublin, and devote himself to writing. He wrote biographies of **Jonathan Swift** and **Oliver Goldsmith** and a number of serials and popular novels under his own name and the pseudonym "Basil." A founding member of the **National Literary Society**, and its president, 1925–32, his *Swift in Ireland* (1896) was published by the **New Irish Library** and favorably reviewed by WBY (*UP1*. 407). As a young man, WBY visited his home and sought his help (*M*. 54). He admired his gentle, amiable nature and dedicated to him *Early Poems and Stories* (1925), recalling "The Silenced Sister," a controversial lecture that Richard Ashe King gave to the National Literary Society in 1894. The lecture, in which King claimed that Irish literature had been overwhelmed with partisan rhetoric, met with an intensity of criticism unexpected by King, but he was defended by WBY in letters to *United Ireland* (*UP1*. 306–10).

REFERENCES: Dalsimer, Adele M. "Yeats's Unchanging Swift." *Éire* (1974); King, Richard A. *Swift in Ireland*. 1895. Reprint, Folcroft, Pa.: Folcroft, 1969; Marcus, Phillip L. *Yeats and the Beginning of the Irish Renaissance*. Syracuse: Syracuse University Press, 1987.

KING OF THE GREAT CLOCK TOWER, THE, one-act play. The play, originally written by WBY in prose, was performed at the **Abbey Theatre**, July 1934. This version was published in *Life and Letters*, November 1934. Because of criticism from friends, principally **Ezra Pound**, he rewrote the play in verse— although he recommended the prose version for performance. The verse version, which he dedicated to the dancer **Ninette de Valois**, was published in *A Full Moon in March* (1935) and later in *The Herne's Egg and Other Plays* (1938) and *The Collected Plays of W. B. Yeats* (1952). In the play, which opens and closes with a chorus sung by two musicians, a masked **Stroller** comes to a court ruled over by a tyrannical **King** and his silent, masked **Queen**. The Stroller declares that after the Queen has danced for him, he will sing, and the Queen will kiss his mouth. In his anger, the King has the Stroller beheaded. In the climactic dance, the Queen fulfills the Stroller's prophecy. In the first performance at the Abbey Theatre, the cast was as follows: King, **F. J. McCormick**; Queen, Ninette de Valois; Stroller, Denis O'Dea; First Attendant, Robert Irwin; Second Attendant, Joseph O'Neill. The music was composed by Arthur Duff, and the costumes were designed by Dolly Travers Smith. The masks were by George Atkinson and the lighting by Udolphus Wright. The play was directed by **Lennox Robinson**.

REFERENCES: Bradley, Anthony. *William Butler Yeats*. New York: Frederick Ungar, 1979; Ellis, Sylvia C. *The Plays of W. B. Yeats: Yeats and the Dancer*. London: Macmillan, 1995; Jeffares, A. N., and Knowland, A. S. *A Commentary on the Collected Plays of W. B. Yeats*. London: Macmillan, 1975; Miller, Liam. *The Noble Drama of W. B. Yeats*. Dublin: Dolmen, 1977; Taylor, Richard. *A Reader's Guide to the Plays of W. B. Yeats*. New York: St. Martin's, 1984.

KING'S THRESHOLD, THE, one-act verse play by WBY. It was printed in the *United Irishman*, September 1903, and subsequently published in *The Hour-Glass and Other Plays* (1904) and *Plays in Prose and Verse* (1922). It was included in *The Collected Plays of W. B. Yeats* (1934, 1952). The setting of the play is outside King **Guaire's** castle at **Gort**. An idealistic poet, **Seanchan**, is on hunger strike in protest against his exclusion from the King's council— an ancient right enjoyed by the poets of Ireland. The King attempts to bribe him into giving up his hunger strike, sending to him, in turn, his Pupils, the **Mayor of Kinvara**, the beautiful **Fedelm**, and others. Seanchan resists their entreaties and dies, proclaiming his triumph. In the early versions, King Guaire relents at the end of the play, and Seanchan resumes his place on the King's council. In 1922, after the death from hunger strike of Terence MacSwiney, in protest against continued English injustices, WBY altered the ending, substituting the death of Seanchan. The plot of *The King's Threshold* was based on old Irish romances, namely, a Middle Irish tale, *Immtheacht na Tromdaimhe*, and **Lady Wilde's** *Ancient Legends of Ireland*, while WBY acknowledged his debt to *Sancan the Bard*, a play written in the early 1890s by **Edwin J. Ellis**. *The King's Threshold* was first performed by the **Irish National Theatre Society** at the **Molesworth Hall**, Dublin, October 1903, in a production financed by **Annie F. Horniman**, who also designed and made the costumes. The cast was: Seanchan, **Frank Fay**; King Guaire, P. J. Kelly; Lord Chamberlain, **Seamus O'Sullivan**; Soldier, William Conroy; Monk, S. Sheridan-Neill; Mayor, **W. G. Fay**; Cripples, **Padraic Colum**, E. Davis; Court Ladies, Honor Saville, Dora Melville; Princesses, **Sara Allgood**, Dora Gunning; Fedelm, Máire Nic Shiubhlaigh; Servants, P. MacShiubhlaigh, P. Josephs; Pupils, G. Roberts, C. NicChormac. A prologue was written for the first production and appeared in the version of the play printed in the *United Irishman*. It was not used because the company was too small to spare an actor to perform it. The published play was dedicated to Frank Fay.

REFERENCES: Bradley, Anthony. *William Butler Yeats*. New York: Frederick Ungar, 1979; Miller, Liam. *The Noble Drama of W. B. Yeats*. Dublin: Dolmen, 1977; Oppel, Frances Nesbitt. *Mask and Tragedy: Yeats and Nietzsche, 1902–10*. Charlottesville: University Press of Virginia, 1987; Taylor, Richard. *A Reader's Guide to the Plays of W. B. Yeats*. New York: St. Martin's, 1984.

KINSALE (Irish: *Cionn tSáile*) [head of the sea], seaport in **Cork** (county). Kinsale was the scene of a decisive battle in 1601, when the Irish and their Spanish allies were defeated by Elizabeth I of England. This defeat marked the end of a long and intense period of Irish resistance to English rule and effectively brought to an end the Gaelic civilization in Ireland. James II landed in Kinsale in 1689, on his way to the Battle of the **Boyne**, and after his defeat by **William III**, he sailed from Kinsale into exile. **Hugh Lane** was among the 1,195 passengers drowned, when the *Lusitania* was torpedoed by the Germans off the coast of Kinsale in 1915. Kinsale is the home of **Moll Magee** in WBY's "The Ballad of Moll Magee" (*CP*. 25).

REFERENCE: McGarry, James P. *Place Names in the Writings of William Butler Yeats*. Gerrards Cross: Colin Smythe, 1976.

KINSELLA, JOHN, fictional character. See "John Kinsella's Lament for Mrs. Mary Moore" (*CP*. 383). In a letter to **Edith Shackleton Heald**, WBY describes John Kinsella as an aging farmer, regretting the brevity of life and love (*WL*. 912).

KINVARA (Irish: *Ceann-Mhara*) [the head of the sea], market town on the coast of **Galway** (county). In *The King's Threshold*, the **Mayor of Kinvara** tries to persuade **Seanchan** to give up his hunger strike, claiming he is showing dis-respect to his home town. In *The Unicorn from the Stars* (*CPl.* 332), there are references to passers-by making a noise as they go to the Fair of Kinvara. A short distance from Kinvara is the sixteenth-century Dun Guaire Castle, built on the site of the former castle of **Guaire**, king of **Connacht**.

REFERENCE: McGarry, James P. *Place Names in the Writings of William Butler Yeats.* Gerrards Cross: Colin Smythe, 1976.

KIPLING, [JOSEPH] RUDYARD (1865–1936), poet, novelist, and children's au-thor. He was born in Bombay, India, the son of English parents, and educated in England at the United Services College, Westward Ho! After completing his education in 1882, he went back to India as a journalist with the *Lahore Civil and Military Gazette*. There, he wrote some of his most popular verse, including *Departmental Ditties* (1886) and *Barrack-Room Ballads* (1892), which appealed to the militant imperialism of the British Empire during the Victorian period. In 1889, he traveled to China and Japan and returned to London to find himself famous. In 1892, after his marriage to Caroline Balestier, he moved to Vermont. He remained there for four years, writing the children's stories for which he is best remembered, *The Jungle Book* (1894), *The Second Jungle Book* (1895), *Kim* (1901), *Just So Stories* (1902), and *Captains Courageous* (1897). Because of quarrels with his American in-laws, he returned to England in 1897 and settled in Sussex, the setting for *Puck of Pook's Hill*, published in 1906. The following year, he became England's first winner of the **Nobel Prize for Lit-erature**. WBY and he were contemporaries, but in the early years of the century, Kipling was better known and respected as a poet. They shared a mutual friend in **W. E. Henley** but did not spend any time in each other's company. In early writings, WBY is uncharacteristically cautious in his response to Kipling (*UP2.* 42). In private letters, however, he is censorious of Kipling's superficiality and use of rhetoric (*WL.* 413, 534, 710). In his introduction to *The Oxford Book of Modern Verse* (1936), he castigates Kipling for his opinions and politics and observes that his poems imitate the old ballads in manner only and not in form (*LE.* 185). He included two poems by Kipling in the anthology, "A St. Helena Lullaby" and "The Looking-glass: A Country Dance," both recommended by **Dorothy Wellesley** (*WL.* 877).

REFERENCES: Laski, Marghanita. *From Palm to Pine: Rudyard Kipling Abroad and At Home*. London: Sidgwick & Jackson, 1987; Seymour-Smith, Martin. *Rudyard Kipling*. New York: St. Martin's, 1989; Wilson, Angus. *The Strange Ride of Rudyard Kipling: His Life and Works*. New York: Viking, 1978.

KNOCKNAREA [also Knocknareagh] (Irish: *Cnoc-na-riaghadh*) [hill of the ex-ecutions], mountain to the south of **Sligo** (county). Knocknarea dominates the two bays of Sligo and **Ballisodare**. WBY had been familiar with it from child-hood, when he stayed with his grandparents at **Merville**. Later, he visited **George Pollexfen** at his summer home, Moyle Lodge, which looked across

Memory Harbour to Knocknarea. The burial cairn at its summit, known locally as Maeve's Cairn (*Miosgán Maebha*), is associated with **Maeve**, queen of **Connacht**, although she may not be buried there. The cairn is 80 feet high, with a circumference of 630 feet at the base, sloping to 300 feet at the top. Nearby is a smaller monument, said to be the tomb of Eoghan Bel, a warrior king whose dying wish was to be buried upright with his javelin in his hand and his face to the north so that he might better see the men of **Ulster** fleeing before the men of Connacht. It is to this tomb that WBY refers in "The Black Tower" (*CP*. 396). The warrior **Oisin** is reputed to have slipped from his horse at the foot of Knocknarea, finding himself a wizened old man, a legend that WBY uses in *The Wanderings of Oisin* (*CP*. 409). In WBY's poem "The Hosting of the Sídhe" (*CP*. 61), the mountain is associated with the **Sídhe**. In "And Fair, Fierce Women" (*MY*. 57–59), WBY tells of a woman in Sligo who had seen Queen Maeve coming over the mountain and was awed by her striking appearance, while in *The Countess Cathleen* (*CPL*. 17–18), the poet **Aleel** describes Maeve's tomb on Knocknarea. See also "Drumcliff and Rosses" (*MY*. 88–94), "The Ballad of Father O'Hart" (*CP*. 23), "The Valley of the Black Pig" (*CP*. 73), "Red Hanrahan's Song about Ireland" (*CP*. 90), and "The Alternative Song for the Severed Head" (*CP*. 324).

REFERENCES: Kirby, Sheelah. *The Yeats Country*. Dublin: Dolmen, 1966; McGarry, James P. *Place Names in the Writings of William Butler Yeats*. Gerrards Cross: Colin Smythe, 1976.

KNOCKNASHEE [also Cnoc-na-Sidha] (Irish: *Cnoc na Sídhe*) [hill of the fairies]. The name is fairly common in Ireland. In the vicinity of **Collooney, Sligo** (county), there are two hills, both called Knocknashee. One is in the parish of Achonry, County Sligo, while the other is nearby, in Boyle, County Roscommon. It is not certain which of them WBY has in mind in "The Ballad of Father O'Hart" (*CP*. 24). In "The Crucifixion of the Outcast" (*MY*. 152–53), the abbot denounces those who praise old gods and heroes, including Red Aodh of Cnoc-na-Sidha. This is most likely a reference to Cnoc-na-Sidha near Ballyshannon, **Donegal** (county), the home of Red Aodh, father of Macha, who may have given her name to **Emain Macha**.

REFERENCE: McGarry, James P. *Place Names in the Writings of William Butler Yeats*. Gerrards Cross: Colin Smythe, 1976.

KROP, HILDO (1884–1972), Dutch sculptor. He made the masks for the 1922 production of *The Only Jealousy of Emer* in Amsterdam. The play, translated into Dutch by Hélène Swarth, was directed by Albert van Dalsum (b. 1889), a leading actor-manager interested in innovative, stylized theater. The production, which was successfully presented in the Hollandsche Stadsschouwburg, Amsterdam, April 1922, was revived in 1923, 1924, and 1926. Krop made the masks in papier maché, cast over plaster originals. He later cast them in bronze. In 1927, WBY saw photographs of these bronzes, which are now displayed in the

Stadsschouwburg. He was encouraged to rewrite *The Only Jealousy of Emer* so that a production might be mounted placing emphasis on the masks, music, and dancing. The production of *Fighting the Waves*, with masks by Hildo Krop, music by **George Antheil**, and choreography by **Ninette de Valois**, was performed in the **Peacock Theatre** in 1929.

REFERENCE: Miller, Liam. *The Noble Drama of W. B. Yeats*. Dublin: Dolmen, 1977.

KUBLA KHAN [also Khubilai Khan] (1215–94), grandson of Genghis Khan. A Mongol general, he defeated the ruling Sung dynasty in China to become the first Mongol emperor but he was less successful in his attempts to conquer Japan, Southeast Asia, and Indonesia. To govern China required special skills. Kubla Khan was a tolerant ruler, a patron of arts and scholarship, and he opened up China to Western travelers, many of whom visited him in his magnificent palace at Shang-tu. This city in Southeastern Mongolia was the model for Coleridge's idyllic city of **Xanadu** in the poem ''Kubla Khan.'' In *The Player Queen* (*CPl*. 418), the First Player recalls that when he performed in Xanadu, Kubla Khan was envious of his voice and presence.

REFERENCE: Rossabi, Morris. *Khubilai Khan: His Life and Times*. Berkeley: University of California Press, 1988.

KUSTA BEN LUKA (c. 820–892), Arabian translator and doctor. Legend tells how Kusta Ben Luka was warned in a dream to accept the caliph's gift of a bride despite his plans to live out his final years as a monk. His bride soon began to talk in her sleep, and to Kusta's amazement, he learned those philosophies and profound thoughts for which he had been searching all his life. In ''The Gift of Harun Al-Rashid'' (*CP*. 513), WBY alludes to his own marriage and his fortunate discovery that his wife, **Georgie Hyde-Lees**, had the gift of automatic writing. See also WBY's note to ''An Image from a Past Life'' (*VP*. 821).

REFERENCE: Unterecker, John. *A Reader's Guide to W. B. Yeats*. Reprint. Syracuse: Syracuse University Press, 1996.

KYLE-DORTHA. *See* **SEVEN WOODS**.

KYLE-NA-NO. *See* **SEVEN WOODS**.

KYTELER, LADY ALICE, wealthy noblewoman. According to Holinshed's *Chronicle of Ireland*, Lady Kyteler lived in Kilkenny during the fourteenth century. In 1324, she was accused by Richard de Ledrede, bishop of Ossory, of having sexual intercourse with an evil spirit called **Robert Artisson**, to whom she sacrificed cocks and peacocks' eyes. She was tried and found guilty. Her maid Petronilla, an accomplice, was burned at the stake, but Lady Kyteler was taken secretly to England. A sacramental wafer with the print of the devil and ointment to grease a pole on which she reputedly flew around the neighborhood were found in her home in Kilkenny. An account of her trial, *A Contemporary Narrative of the Proceedings against Dame Alice Kyteler, Prosecuted for Sor-*

cery in 1324, by Richard Ledrede, Bishop of Ossory, was published in London by the Camden Society in 1843. WBY refers to Lady Kyteler in ''Nineteen Hundred and Nineteen'' (*CP*. 232).

REFERENCE: Seymour, St. John D. *Irish Witchcraft and Demonology*. 1913. Reprint, New York: Barnes & Noble, 1972.

L

LABAN (Irish: *Lí Ban*) [a woman's beauty], woman of the **Sídhe**. A sister of **Fand**, Laban is transformed into an otter when she neglects a magic well in her care. She appears as a Druidess in *Diarmuid and Grania*. In "Under the Moon" (*CP*. 91), WBY associates Laban with those women, like Fand and **Niamh**, who act out mankind's animal natures, merging past and present, psychic and physical, spiritual and temporal. Laban is the name of a small village near **Ardrahan**.

LAEGAIRE [also Laeghaire], mythological **Ulster** warrior. In WBY's play *The Green Helmet,* **Conall** and he are hiding from the **Red Man**, who is returning to claim his part of a bargain, agreed two years earlier, in which he is to cut the head off one of the Ulster champions. The Red Man appears with a gift, a Green Helmet, to be worn by the bravest of the warriors. Laegaire disputes the prize, and **Cuchulain** throws it into the sea. When **Emer**, Cuchulain's wife, sings a song in praise of her husband, the other wives insist on drowning out the song with a deafening noise of horns, clapping, and shouting. In the midst of the chaos, the Red Man challenges each of the Ulster heroes to complete the bargain. The cowardly Laegaire refuses, and Cuchulain kneels in his place. The role of Laegaire in the first production of the play, February 1910, was played by Fred O'Donovan. Laegaire is named among the kings in *On Baile's Strand* (*CPl*. 269, 277).

LAIGHEN. *See* **LEINSTER**.

LALLY, BIDDY, beggar. In WBY's play *The Unicorn from the Stars*, she is one of four opportunist beggars who help the misguided hero Martin **Hearne** when he responds to his voices and attacks the local community. The other beggars, who loot and pillage the countryside, are **Johnny Bocach, Paudeen**, and Nanny. Biddy Lally is credited with witchcraft and recommends bringing Martin out of a trance with herbs. In the first production of the play at the **Abbey Theatre**, Dublin, November 1907, the role of Biddy Lally was played by **Máire O'Neill**.

LAME BEGGAR, character in *The Cat and the Moon*. He and his companion, the **Blind Beggar**, are journeying toward the holy well of **St. Colman**, hoping for a cure. The Lame Beggar travels on the Blind Beggar's back. When the saint offers him the choice of physical wholeness or blessedness, the Lame Beggar chooses the latter. He is rewarded by seeing the saint. When the Blind Beggar leaves the stage, having beaten the Lame Beggar, the saint climbs on the Lame Beggar's back and tells him to dance. He throws away his stick and gradually gains the power of his legs. He exits dancing. The role of the Lame Beggar was played in the first production at the **Abbey Theatre**, September 1931, by W. O'Gorman.

LAND OF HEART'S DESIRE, THE, one-act play by WBY. *The Land of Heart's Desire* was the first play by WBY to be produced commercially. It had its premiere at the Avenue Theatre, Northumberland Avenue, London, during a season mounted by **Florence Farr**, with the financial backing of **Annie F. Horniman**. The play, which opened as a curtain raiser to **John Todhunter's** *The Comedy of Sighs*, was published by **T. Fisher Unwin**, and copies were on sale at the first performance, 29 March 1894. The poster was designed by **Aubrey Beardsley**. When Todhunter's play closed on 14 April 1894, *The Land of Heart's Desire* continued with *Arms and the Man* by **George Bernard Shaw**. WBY gives an account of the production in ''The Tragic Generation'' (*A.* 280–83). The play takes place in a cottage in **Sligo** and shows a young newly married woman, Mary **Bruin**, torn between her responsibilities as a wife and her wish to escape with the fairies to the Land of Heart's Desire. The action is not based on any particular story, but the theme is a familiar one in WBY's early work. He wrote the play at the request of Florence Farr, whose niece, Dorothy Paget, created the role of the **Faery Child**. The cast of the first production was: Maurteen Bruin, James Welch; Bridget Bruin, Charlotte Morland; Shawn Bruin, A. E. W. Mason; Mary Bruin, Winifred Fraser; Father Hart, G. R. Foss; Faery Child, Dorothy Paget. WBY later thought the play sentimental (*A.* 437) and made extensive revisions before a production at the **Abbey Theatre** in 1912 (*VP.* 211–12).

REFERENCES: Ellis, Sylvia C. *The Plays of W. B. Yeats: Yeats and the Dancer.* London: Macmillan, 1995; Miller, Liam. *The Noble Drama of W. B. Yeats.* Dublin: Dolmen, 1977; Smythe, Colin. ''A Note on Some of Yeats's Revisions for *The Land of Heart's Desire*.'' In *Yeats and the Theatre*, ed. Robert O'Driscoll and Lorna Reynolds. Niagara Falls, N.Y.: Maclean–Hunter, 1975.

LANDOR, WALTER SAVAGE (1775–1864), author and poet. He was born in Warwick and educated at Rugby and Trinity College, **Oxford**. After quarreling

with his father, he moved to Wales. There he wrote the poem *Gebir* (1798) and
met Lord Aylmer, the father of Rose Aylmer, whose death at the age of twenty
had moved Landor to write the elegy that bears her name. After his marriage
in 1811, Landor lived in Bath. In 1858, he inherited the family estates and
moved permanently to Italy. His best-known writings are *Imaginary Conversations* (1824–53), a series of nearly 150 prose dialogues between well-known
people. His verse ranges from epics to lyrics, some with a moving simplicity
and emotional power, although today he remains largely unstudied and unread.
WBY considered Landor one of the "great lesser writers" (*A.* 273). He mentions
him in "To a Young Beauty" (*CP.* 157), and there is an obscure reference to
Landor in "A Nativity" (*CP.* 387). Copies of Landor's books (*OS.* nos. 1080–
84) and John Foster's *Walter Savage Landor: A Biography* (*OS.* no. 690) were
in WBY's library.

REFERENCES: Dilworth, Ernest Nevin. *Walter Savage Landor.* New York: Twayne,
1971; Elvin, Malcolm. *Savage Landor.* New York: Macmillan, 1941; Evans, Edward
Waterman. *Walter Savage Landor: A Critical Study.* Folcroft, Pa.: Folcroft, 1969; Super,
R. H. *Walter Savage Landor: A Biography.* London: John Calder, 1957.

LANE, [SIR] HUGH [PERCY] (1875–1915), art collector and critic. He was born
in **Cork** (county), the son of a rector in the Church of Ireland. In 1893, he
joined the firm of Colnaghi, an established London art dealer, and at the age of
twenty-three, with little capital, he opened his own gallery in Pall Mall, London.
With his extraordinary appreciation of modern painting, especially the work of
the French Impressionists, he quickly gained a reputation as a critic and art
dealer. He was knighted in 1909. His interest in Irish art was awakened after
seeing a joint exhibition of paintings by **John B. Yeats** and Nathaniel Hone in
Dublin in 1901 and meeting WBY at **Coole Park**, the home of his mother's
younger sister, **Lady Gregory**. He mounted an exhibition of modern paintings
at the Royal Hibernian Academy in 1904 and offered thirty-nine pictures from
the collection to the Dublin Corporation, on condition that they build a permanent gallery to house them and raise funds to buy the rest of the collection.
The paintings included works by Corot, Courbet, Daumier, Degas, Monet, Ber-
the Morisot, together with Manet's *Le Concert aux Tuileries* and Renoir's *Les
Parapluies.* He favored a gallery designed by Sir Edward Lutyens over the River
Liffey. When the Dublin Corporation refused, and some members of the Royal
Hibernian Academy objected to the purchase of the additional pictures, Lane
withdrew his offer and willed the paintings to the National Gallery in London.
He continued to promote Irish art, however, commissioning portraits of prominent Irish men and women from artists like John B. Yeats and Sir William
Orpen. He was appointed director of the **National Gallery of Ireland** in 1914
and, in February 1915, added an unwitnessed codicil to his will, restoring the
collection to Dublin. He went down with the S.S. *Lusitania* when it was torpedoed in the Atlantic by the Germans, May 1915. The National Gallery in
London claimed the paintings, and controversy over the ownership was carried

on for many years, with Lady Gregory and WBY mounting an intensive campaign to have the pictures returned to Dublin. The matter was only resolved in 1959, when the National Gallery in London and the Irish government agreed to share the pictures on a loan basis every five years. Although WBY and Hugh Lane were not especially fond of each other, the poet was incensed by the attitude of the Dublin Corporation and some notable Dubliners to the Lane controversy. His feelings were expressed in a series of letters he wrote to the press (*UP2*. 330–31, 414–29, 431–32, 473–76) and in five poems. The first of the poems, "To a Wealthy Man who promised a Second Subscription to the Dublin Municipal Gallery if it were proved the People wanted Pictures" (*CP.* 119), was directed at Lord Ardilaun, who argued that money should only be given if the public demonstrated the desire for a gallery (*WL.* 573). The other poems are "September 1913" (*CP.* 120), "To a Friend whose Work has come to Nothing" (*CP.* 122), "Paudeen" (*CP.* 122), and "To a Shade" (*CP.* 123). WBY acknowledges Lane's contribution to Irish art when he recalls him in "The Municipal Gallery Revisited" (*CP.* 368).

REFERENCES: Bodkin, Thomas. *Hugh Lane and His Pictures*. Dublin: The Arts Council, 1956; Gregory, Lady. *Hugh Lane's Life and Achievements, with Some Account of the Dublin Galleries*. London: Murray, 1921.

LAST POEMS AND TWO PLAYS, collection of poetry and plays. It was published in 1939 by **Cuala Press** in the order dictated by WBY before his death. *Last Poems and Two Plays* contains some of the poet's most memorable work, including "Under Ben Bulben" (*CP.* 397), "Cuchulain Comforted" (*CP.* 395), "The Statues" (*CP.* 375), "Long-Legged Fly" (*CP.* 381), "Man and the Echo" (*CP.* 393), and "The Circus Animals' Desertion" (*CP.* 391). The plays in the volume are **Purgatory** and **The Death of Cuchulain**. When *Last Poems and Two Plays* was published by Macmillan and Company in 1940, three poems were added: "Why should not old men be mad" (*CP.* 388), "The Statesman's Holiday" (*CP.* 389), and "Crazy Jane on the Mountain" (*CP.* 390). The dominant mood of the collection is one of tragic gaiety, as the poet contemplates his death in the midst of a misguided and violent world, confident that the new age will bring a return to traditional values. In **Collected Poems** (1950), the poems from *Last Poems and Two Plays* and *New Poems* (1938) were grouped together under the subheading "Last Poems," in an order decided by the editors.

REFERENCES: Bradford, Curtis. *Yeats's "Last Poems" Again*. Dublin: Dolmen, 1965; Mulryne, J. R. "The *Last Poems*." In *An Honored Guest: New Essays on W. B. Yeats*, ed. Denis Donoghue and J. R. Mulryne. London: Edward Arnold, 1965; Stallworthy, Jon. *Yeats's Last Poems: A Casebook*. London: Macmillan, 1968.

LAVERY, HAZEL (1880–1935), second wife of the painter **Sir John Lavery**. She was born Hazel Martyn, in Chicago, and gained a reputation for her beauty. She was a talented painter and in 1925 completed a portrait of **George Bernard Shaw**. She met Sir John Lavery while on holiday in Brittany with her mother, and although he was almost twice her age, she was attracted to him. She married a young surgeon, but he died soon after the wedding, and five years later, in 1910, she married Lavery, a widower. She was an ideal companion for the painter, charming and sophisticated, and she encouraged him to take a sympathetic interest in Irish affairs. In 1923, he was commissioned by the Irish government to paint a portrait of Hazel Lavery. It has appeared on Irish banknotes since 1923. She died in 1935, after a long illness. In the poem, ''The Municipal Gallery Revisited'' (*CP*. 368), WBY refers to two paintings of her by her husband: *Hazel Lavery at Her Easel* and *The Unfinished Harmony*.

REFERENCE: Lavery, Sir John. *The Life of a Painter*. Boston: Little, Brown, 1940.

LAVERY, SIR JOHN (1856–1941), portrait and landscape painter. He was born in Belfast, but after the early death of his parents, he lived with relatives in Scotland. He trained at the Glasgow School of Art and at Heatherley's Academy in London (the same school that **John B. Yeats** attended). After further training in Paris, he returned to Scotland, where he became a freelance painter in 1879, at the age of twenty-three. He achieved early success, and an invitation to paint the state visit of Queen Victoria to the Glasgow Exhibition, in 1888, established his reputation as a court painter and helped him make connections with the social and political elite in London, among them Winston Churchill, Ramsey MacDonald, and Lady Cunard. He moved to London in 1890, the year he first visited Morocco, to which he retreated each winter. He was knighted in 1918 and made a freeman of both Dublin and Belfast. He was sympathetic to the nationalist cause in Ireland, although he managed to maintain a friendship with the **Ulster** leaders. He painted scenes from contemporary social and political life and received commissions for portraits of many Irish politicians, including Michael Collins, **Eamon de Valera, Gavan Duffy**, Lord Edward Carson, and writers **George Moore** and **Dora Sigerson Shorter**. The Irish government commissioned a portrait of his second wife **Hazel**, which appeared on Irish banknotes from 1923. In his poem ''The Municipal Gallery Revisited'' (*CP*. 368), WBY writes movingly of a number of Lavery's pictures, including *The Court of Criminal Appeal* (his painting of the trial of **Sir Roger Casement**), *St. Patrick's Purgatory, Blessing of the Colours*, and his portraits of **Arthur Griffith** and **Kevin O'Higgins**.

REFERENCES: Lavery, Sir John. *British Artists at the Front*. London: Country Life, 1918; Lavery, Sir John. *The Life of a Painter*. Boston: Little, Brown, 1940.

LAWLESS, [HONORABLE] EMILY (1845–1913), poet and novelist. She was born at Lyons Castle, County Kildare, daughter of the wealthy Sir Nicholas Lawless, later Lord Cloncurry. She spent much of her childhood with her mother's family, the Kirwans of **Castle Hackett**, and this fostered her love of Irish history and romance. In 1886, she published *Hurrish*, a novel about the Land League in Ireland. It was praised by Gladstone, who became her friend and correspondent. *With Essex in Ireland* (1890) was originally published as an authentic contemporary document; only later did she admit authorship. The romance *Grania: The Story of an Island* (1892) was set in the **Aran Islands**, while *Maelcho* (1894), a historical novel, dealt with the sixteenth-century Desmond Rebellion. Other works included her *Story of Ireland* (1887) and a biography of **Maria Edgeworth** (1904). Her most highly rated work was *With the Wild Geese* (1902), a volume of ballads and verse containing her moving poems "After Aughrim" and "Clare Coast." She died in Surrey, England, having moved there for health reasons and because she felt out of touch with nationalist trends in Ireland. WBY, although an admirer, was not uncritical of her portrayal of the Irish character. In "Irish National Literature, II: Contemporary Prose Writers—Mr. O'Grady, Miss Lawless, Miss Barlow, Miss Hopper, and the Folk-Lorists" (*UP1*. 369–70), he praises her intellect and ability to write feelingly when describing visions and visionaries but observes that, otherwise, her writing is based on stock caricatures of the English and the Irish. WBY included *Maelcho* and *Essex in Ireland* among his "Best Irish Books" (*UP1*. 386; *WL*. 247).

   REFERENCE: Hogan, Robert, ed. *Dictionary of Irish Literature*. Rev. ed. Westport, Conn.: Greenwood, 1996.

LAWRENCE AND BULLEN. *See* **BULLEN, A[RTHUR] H[ENRY]**.

LAZARUS, brother of **Martha** and **Mary**. In the New Testament of the Christian bible, Jesus raises Lazarus from the dead. In WBY's play *Calvary*, Lazarus recalls the peace and contentment of death. Conscious of his freedom in death, and aware that with the resurrection of **Christ** he can never be free again, he challenges Christ, who is making his way to his crucifixion.

LEAMY, EDMUND (1848–1904), politician, editor, and writer. He was born in Waterford. After qualifying as a lawyer, he abandoned law for politics and was elected Nationalist M.P. for Waterford in 1880, for N.E. **Cork** in 1885, for South **Sligo** in 1887, and for Kildare in 1900. He was a supporter of the Irish parliamentary leader **Charles Stewart Parnell**, and after a split in the Irish Party in 1890, he became editor of the Parnellite paper, *United Ireland*. Leamy's verse appeared in Irish journals, and he published two volumes of short stories, *Irish Fairy Tales* (1889) and *The Fairy Minstrel of Glenmalure* (1899). His play *Cupid in Kerry* was produced in Dublin, 1906. As editor of *United Ireland*, Leamy was sympathetic to WBY's ideals of a national literature, publishing a number of his articles and letters.

LECTURE TOURS. WBY made four lecture tours to the United States and Canada, 1903–4, 1914, 1920, and 1932–33. Each was a success, and he met the rigors of these nationwide tours with courtesy, humor, and total professionalism. He was impressed with the American people, admiring their enthusiasm, their lack of religious prejudice, and their interest in education, especially evident in the heavily endowed colleges and universities. However, reflecting on American education in "America and the Arts," which he wrote for *The Metropolitan Magazine* (*UP2*. 338–42), he was critical of the "intellectual indolence" of the Americans and felt their commitment to democracy resulted in uniformity. He began his first lecture tour at Yale University, 11 November 1903. He lectured at many colleges, including Smith, Amherst, Mount Holyoke, University of Pennsylvania, Bryn Mawr, Vassar, Berkeley, and McGill University, Montreal. He made presentations in major cities throughout the United States, including New York, Washington, Chicago, Indianapolis, San José, and Sacramento. His most important lecture was at Carnegie Hall, New York, 3 January 1904, when he spoke on "The Intellectual Revival in Ireland." **Clan-na-Gael** requested that he take part in the anniversary celebrations for **Robert Emmet**. He reluctantly agreed and gave an outstanding address on "Emmet the Apostle of Irish Liberty" (*UP2*. 313–27), 28 February 1904, at the Academy of Music, New York, before an audience that included the exiled Fenian O'Donovan Rossa (1831–1915). Anticipating trouble, he accompanied the **Abbey Theatre** when they presented *The Playboy of the Western World* in Boston, 16 October 1911. After an uneventful opening night, he left for New York, where he visited his father, before returning to London. WBY's second lecture tour began in early February 1914 and lasted through April 1914. A highlight of this visit was a banquet given by the Poetry Society of Chicago, which had awarded him a prize of £50 for his poem "The Grey Rock" (*CP*. 115). He made £500 from his trip in 1914. After his marriage to **Georgie Hyde-Lees** in 1917, he decided to do a further lecture tour to raise money to renovate and repair his Norman tower, **Thoor Ballylee**. His wife and he sailed for America on the *Carmania*, 6 January 1920, leaving the baby **Anne Yeats** in the care of his sister **Lily**. They stayed initially at the Algonquin Hotel, New York, and while WBY was away on the first part of his tour, extending through Toronto and Quebec, Mrs. Yeats took the opportunity to visit, almost daily, her father-in-law, **John B. Yeats**. On 29 January, the annual dinner of the Poetry Society of America was held at the Astor Hotel, New York, at which WBY was the guest of honor. The next part of the tour took WBY and his wife to the West, and they returned to New York in mid-April, before departing from Montreal, 29 May 1920. The tour was financially very rewarding. His final visit to the United States began in late 1932. Despite his uncertain health, he was determined to earn money, not only for the renovation of his new home, **Riversdale**, but also to raise funds for the **Irish Academy of Letters**. Mrs. Yeats did not accompany him. He lectured 26 October 1932 to 21 January 1933, and again the tour was lucrative, raising £700 for himself and a further £700 for the Irish Academy. In his biography *W. B. Yeats* (1943), Joseph Hone gives a detailed description of WBY the public speaker, "uneasy at first," who soon got into his stride and impressed with his "natural distinction of bearing, his gravity of utterance and his rhythm."

REFERENCE: Unterecker, John. *Yeats and Patrick McCartan: A Fenian Friendship.* Dublin: Dolmen, 1965.

LEDA, wife of Tyndareus, king of **Sparta**, in Greek mythology. According to legend, Leda was bathing in the **Eurotas**, when the god Zeus made love to her in the guise of a swan. The union produced **Helen** and the twins Castor and Pollux. In "Leda and the Swan" (*CP*. 241), a poem written 18 September 1923, WBY speculates on the feelings and thoughts of Leda at the height of her sexual encounter. There are references to Leda in "Lullaby" (*CP*. 300) and "Among School Children" (*CP*. 242). See also *The Player Queen* (*CPl*. 416) and *The Herne's Egg* (*CPl*. 649).

REFERENCE: Melchiori, Georgio. *The Whole Mystery of Art*. London: Routledge & Kegan Paul, 1960.

LE GALLIENNE, RICHARD [THOMAS] (1866–1947), poet, essayist, and novelist. He was educated at Liverpool College and moved to London in 1889, as personal secretary to the actor Wilson Barrett. Stunningly handsome, he socialized with members of London's artistic and literary establishment, including **Swinburne** and **William Morris**, and became a close friend of **Oscar Wilde** (whom he had met in Birkenhead in 1883). He was a founder member of the **Rhymers' Club**. After the publication of his collection of poems *Volumes in Folio* (1889), he was appointed reader for the publishing house Bodley Head, an appointment especially important to the poets of the Rhymers' Club, since it established a connection for them with a major publisher. The Bodley Head published the two anthologies produced by the Rhymers' Club (1892, 1894), in addition to books by individual Rhymers. The 1890s were productive years for Le Gallienne. He published *The Book-Bills of Narcissus* (1891), *English Poems* (1892), *The Religion of a Literary Man* (1893), and *Prose Fancies* (1894). He moved to the United States in 1905. WBY and Le Gallienne were introduced by **John Todhunter**. As reviewer for the *Speaker, Daily Chronicle*, and *Star*, Le Gallienne wrote favorably of WBY's work, including *The Countess Cathleen* (*KLI*. 320–21), although he was negative about *The Works of William Blake* (1893), which WBY had edited with **Edwin J. Ellis**. WBY praised Le Gallienne's contribution to the *Second Book of the Rhymers' Club* (*KLI*. 391) and gave encouragement and helpful advice in his letters (*KLI*. 346, 400–401).

REFERENCES: Alford, Norman. *The Rhymers' Club: Poets of the Tragic Generation*. New York: St. Martin's, 1994; Gardiner, Bruce. *The Rhymers' Club: A Social and Intellectual History*. New York: Garland, 1988; Gardner, Joann. *Yeats and the Rhymers' Club: A Nineties' Perspective*. New York: Peter Lang, 1989; Le Gallienne, Richard. *The Romantic '90s*. 1951. Reprint, London: Robin Clark, 1993.

LEINSTER (Irish: *Laighenster*) [place of broad spears], province of Ireland. One of the five original provinces, it is likely that it acquired its name from the Laighen, or broad spears, used by the Gauls when they inhabited the eastern part of Ireland during the third century B.C. The addition of *ster* (place) was made during the Norse settlement. The kings of Leinster had a residence on **The Hill Seat of Laighen**. The capital city of Ireland, Dublin, is in Leinster.

WBY recalls ghost stories he heard in a village in Leinster in "Village Ghosts" (*MY*. 15–21). See also "Baile and Aillinn" (*CP*. 459).

REFERENCES: Dames, Michael. *Mythic Ireland*. 1992. Reprint, London: Thames & Hudson, 1996; McGarry, James P. *Place Names in the Writings of William Butler Yeats*. Gerrards Cross: Colin Smythe, 1976.

LETTERS TO THE NEW ISLAND (1934), prose collection. *Letters to the New Island* comprises nineteen short essays on Irish folklore and literature, which WBY contributed to the Boston *Pilot* and the *Providence Sunday Journal* during the period 1888–92. The collection, which was published by Oxford University Press, was suggested by Horace Reynolds (1896–1965), a young American academic and student of Anglo-Irish literature, who met WBY in Ireland in 1927. WBY not only gave his approval for the collection, but he also took an active role in the publication. He wrote a preface to the edition, and recommended a cover design by **T. Sturge Moore**. He sent a photograph of his portrait by **H. M. Paget** for the frontispiece. In a recent edition (1989), edited by George Bornstein and Hugh Witemeyer, two essays, uncollected by Reynolds, are included.

LÉVI, ÉLIPHAS. *See* **CONSTANT, ABBÉ [ALPHONSE LOUIS]**.

LIMERICK (Irish: *Luimneach*) [bare area], county and city in southwest Ireland. The city, standing at the head of the Shannon estuary, is rich in history, having been captured by the Normans in the late twelfth century. Thomond Bridge, which crosses the River Shannon, is in the center of the city. In *The Pot of Broth* (*CPl*. 96), **John Coneely** accuses his wife **Sibby** of always thinking of the **Sídhe** ever since a neighbor found a pot of gold on the bridge at Limerick.

REFERENCE: McGarry, James P. *Place Names in the Writings of William Butler Yeats*. Gerrards Cross: Colin Smythe, 1976.

LINNELL, WILLIAM (1826–1906), artist. One of the family to whom WBY and **Edwin J. Ellis** dedicated their monumental study *The Works of William Blake* (1893). The family of three brothers, John (1821–1906), James Thomas (1823–1905), William, and their sisters, Elizabeth Anne (1820–1903) and Sarah (1830–?1908), owned original manuscripts by **William Blake**. These had been willed to them by their father John Linnell (1792–1882), a friend and patron of Blake. It was in the Linnell home in Redhill, Surrey, and in William Linnell's townhouse in Chelsea, that Ellis and WBY transcribed the Blake manuscripts in the late 1880s and early 1890s.

REFERENCE: Ellis, Edwin John, and Yeats, W. B., eds. *The Works of William Blake: Poetic, Symbolic and Critical*. 3 vols. London: Quaritch, 1893.

LISSADELL (Irish: *Lis-a-Doill*) [ring-fort of the blind man], home in **Sligo** (county) of **Eva Gore-Booth** and her sister **Constance**. The austere Georgian mansion, designed by Francis Goodwin in 1832 for the enlightened Sir Robert Gore-Booth, was built of limestone from **Ballisodare**. It stands at the foot of **Ben Bulben**, in the middle of a pine forest that runs down to **Drumcliff** Bay. The south front of the house, with its bay windows, looks over **Rosses Point** and across the water to **Knocknarea**. WBY first visited Lissadell, as a guest of the Gore-Booth family, in the winter of 1894; indeed, they were the first Irish aristocratic family to recognize him as a poet (*M*. 77–79). He was impressed with the fine interior, with its high ceilings, 100-foot-long gallery, and tasteful decoration. He admired the extensively wooded grounds, although he found the exterior of the house bare and uninteresting. He was conscious of the class differences between himself and the Gore-Booths but admired their sense of ordered tradition. He celebrates the house and its occupants in the moving elegy ''In Memory of Eva Gore-Booth and Con Markiewicz'' (*CP*. 263), written in 1927, some thirty-three years after his first visit. Since 1944, when the heir to the Gore-Booth estate was made a ward of the Irish state, the house and grounds have fallen into disrepair. Recently, there has been some attempt at renovation and restoration. In his early poem ''The Man Who Dreamed of Faeryland'' (*CP*. 49), WBY is referring not to Lissadell House but to the barony or townland of Lissadell in which the house is set.

REFERENCES: Fletcher, Ian. ''Yeats and Lissadell.'' In *W. B. Yeats and His Contemporaries*. Brighton, Sussex: Harvester, 1987; Gordon, D. J., ed. *W. B. Yeats: Images of a Poet*. Manchester, University of Manchester, 1961; Kirby, Sheelah. *The Yeats Country*. Dublin: Dolmen, 1966; McGarry, James P. *Place Names in the Writings of William Butler Yeats*. Gerrards Cross: Colin Smythe, 1976.

LIVERPOOL, port city in northwest England. As a boy, WBY boarded his **Pollexfen** grandfather's ship in Liverpool to take him on holiday to **Sligo**. In the poem ''In Memory of Alfred Pollexfen'' (*CP*. 175), he recalls Liverpool as the place where several of his uncles are buried. His sailor uncle, **John Pollexfen**, died and was buried in Liverpool, but WBY declares that his spirit has no true resting place on shore. See also ''Kidnappers'' (*M*. 74).

LOADSTONE MOUNTAIN, mythical mountain composed of the mineral magnetite. In one of the stories in Sir Richard Burton's translation of *Arabian Nights' Entertainment*, Sinbad the Sailor's ship is wrecked when it is pulled by magnetic force against the base of a loadstone (lodestone) mountain. An edition of *Sinbad the Sailor and Other Stories from the Arabian Nights* was illustrated by **Edmund Dulac**. See also ''A Prayer on going into my House'' (*CP*. 183).

LOCKE, JOHN (1632–1704), philosopher and political theorist. He was educated at Oxford University and returned there in 1660 as Professor of Greek, Rhetoric, and Philosophy. In 1675, he left England for France, where he made contacts with the leading thinkers in science and philosophy. He returned to England in 1679 but was considered by the government to be too radical in his views. He left for Holland, where he completed the famous *Essay Concerning Human Understanding* (1690). With the accession of **William III** to the English throne, he returned to London, where he became an occasional state adviser. He made important contributions to all fields of philosophy. He stressed the necessity of tolerating opposite opinion and maintained that each person can, with honesty and reason, see truth in differing aspects. He was distrustful of any metaphysical speculation and, as an empiricist, insisted that philosophy should be practical and grounded in human experience. He promulgated the view that the state, like the individual, should be governed by natural laws and that rights of property should be guarded, since each person has a right to the product of his or her labor. The theorists of the American Revolution drew heavily on his ideas, and the policy of checks and balances of the American Constitution was set down by Locke, as was the belief that revolution, under certain circumstances, is not only a right but an obligation. WBY disagreed with Locke, citing the instinctive behavior of birds in the nest and his young daughter **Anne's** acquisition of knowledge that anticipated experience (*A*. 270–72). He refers to Locke in the opening lines of "Fragments" (*CP*. 240).

REFERENCE: Locke, John. *An Essay Concerning Human Understanding*. 1690. Ed. Peter N. Nidditch. Oxford: Clarendon, 1975.

LOMAIR. *See* **BRAN**.

LONGHI, PIETRO (1702–85), painter. He is best known for his gentle satires of Venetian life. Most of his paintings are in Venetian collections. Among his works are *Domestic Group* and *Exhibition of a Rhinoceros*, now in the National Gallery, London, and four genre paintings owned by the Metropolitan Museum of Art, New York. In the poem "Upon a Dying Lady" (*CP*. 177), WBY refers to a panniered skirt worn by **Mabel Beardsley** that had been copied from a picture by Longhi.

REFERENCE: Pignatti, Terisio. *Pietro Longhi: Paintings and Drawings*. Trans. Pamela Waley. London: Phaidon, 1969.

LORRAIN, CLAUDE. *See* **CLAUDE**.

LOUGH DERG, small lake in **Donegal** (county). According to tradition, supported by the writings of Giraldus Cambrensis in his *Topography of Ireland* (1186) and the twelfth-century Roger of Wendover, **St. Patrick** fasted in a cave on an island in the lake and was rewarded with a vision of heaven and hell and purified of his sins. Thereafter, the island, Station Island, came to be known as St. Patrick's Purgatory. It rapidly became a place of pilgrimage, with many visions recorded, but in 1497, all pilgrimages were banned by the pope after an influential Dutch penitent had complained of seeing no visions there. Nevertheless, the practice continued, even after the Reformation, although the numbers of foreign pilgrims declined. In 1789, the cave was filled in by order of the

Catholic hierarchy. The pilgrimages continue today, taking place annually during the summer and lasting for three days. Pilgrims are required to fast, keep a twenty-four-hour vigil of continuous prayer, and complete three Stations of the Cross. Lough Derg is the setting for WBY's poem "The Pilgrim" (*CP*. 360), which appeared in *A Broadside*, no. 10 (October 1937). In his essay "If I were Four-and-Twenty" (*EX*. 266–67), he claims that if he were young again (the nature of the penance excludes the elderly), he would go on a pilgrimage to Lough Derg or **Cro-Patrick**, while in "The Celtic Element in Literature" (*EI*. 185), he paraphrases Ernest Renan, who believed that the visions seen at Lough Derg had a profound impact on the development of early European literature. There is also a Lough Derg in **County Clare** but it is not a place of pilgrimage.

REFERENCES: Dames, Michael. *Mythic Ireland*. 1992. Reprint, New York: Thames & Hudson, 1996; O'Connor, Rev. Canon Daniel. *St. Patrick's Purgatory, Lough Derg: Its History, Traditions, Legends, Antiquities, Topography, and Scenic Surroundings*. Dublin: Duffy, 1895.

LOUGH GILL (Irish: *Loch Gile*) [lake of brightness], picturesque lake, southeast of **Sligo** (town). It is approximately five miles long and one and a half miles wide. There are some eighteen islands in the lake, including **Church Island**, Cottage Island, and **Innisfree**—the setting for WBY's early poem "The Lake Isle of Innisfree" (*CP*. 44). Lough Gill and its environs had many associations for WBY. **Dooney** is on the southwest shore of the lake, near Cottage Island, while nearby is **Sleuth Wood** from which WBY could see Innisfree. **Dromahair** is to the southeast of Lough Gill. On the banks of Lough Gill, near Innisfree, is Cairns Hill. It is surmounted by a number of monolithic monuments, including a stone circle.

REFERENCE: McGarry, James P. *Place Names in the Writings of William Butler Yeats*. Gerrards Cross: Colin Smythe, 1976.

LOUGHREA (Irish: *Loch Riabhach*) [gray lake], large market town in **Galway** (county). To reach her home, **Lady Gregory** and her guests traveled by train from Dublin to Loughrea, before taking the coach to her estate at **Coole Park**. St. Brendan's Cathedral in the town is reputed for its stained glass windows by Evie Hone and **Sarah Purser** and fine sculptures by **John Hughes**.

REFERENCE: McGarry, James P. *Place Names in the Writings of William Butler Yeats*. Gerrards Cross: Colin Smythe, 1976.

LOUGH SWILLY (Irish: *Súileach*) [clear seeing], an inlet in **Donegal** (county). It was from Lough Swilly that the Flight of the Earls began in 1607. In 1798, **Wolfe Tone** sailed up the lough with 300 French soldiers, landing at Rathmullen. As WBY notes in "Edmund Spenser" (*EI*. 362–63), **Red Hugh O'Donnell** was lured on board a merchant ship moored in Lough Swilly and kidnapped.

REFERENCE: McGarry, James P. *Place Names in the Writings of William Butler Yeats*. Gerrards Cross: Colin Smythe, 1976.

LOVER, SAMUEL (1797–1868), songwriter and novelist. He was born in Dublin and studied to be a painter. After some success as a marine painter and miniaturist, he was elected to the Royal Hibernian Society in 1828. Increasingly, he turned to writing and published his first book, *Legends and Stories of Ireland* (1831), with his own illustrations. He was one of the founders of *The Dublin University Magazine* in 1833. After moving to London in 1835, he wrote the successful novels *Rory O'More* (1836) and *Handy Andy* (1842). In 1844, when his eyesight began to deteriorate, he toured England, the United States, and Canada with a program of his own ballads and sketches. This solo entertainment, *An Irish Evening*, was immensely popular and established his songs as the Irish standards of their day, among them "The Low-backed Car" and "Molly Bawn." WBY did not think highly of Lover, judging him not to be a poet of the people but a writer who promoted the stage-Irishman for the amusement of English audiences (*UP1*. 161–62). Nevertheless, he recognized that Lover drew for his stories on the only material available to him, and he includes his story "Barney O'Reirdan" in his list of "Best Irish Books" (*UP1*. 386; *WL*. 247).
  REFERENCE: Hogan, Robert, ed. *Dictionary of Irish Literature*. Rev. ed. Westport, Conn.: Greenwood, 1996.

LUGAIDH, KING, son of Cú Roí, king of **Munster**. He was the father of **Aillinn**, the tragic lover of **Baile**. In the epic *Táin Bó Cuailnge*, he planned to attack **Cuchulain**, but finding him weak after his battle with Ferdia at the Ford, he desisted. See also "Baile and Aillinn" (*CP*. 459).
  REFERENCE: Ellis, Peter Berresford. *Dictionary of Celtic Mythology*. New York: Oxford University Press, 1992.

LUGAIDH REDSTRIPE (Irish: *Lugaid Riab nDerg*), mythological figure from the **Red Branch** cycle. The son of Clothra, sister to **Queen Maeve**, he had three fathers. He was given the name Redstripe because his body was divided into three parts by red stripes, each part resembling an aspect of one of his fathers. In WBY's play *Deirdre* (*CPl*. 176), there is a reference to Lugaidh Redstripe and his wife, who suffered dreadful deaths.
  REFERENCE: Ellis, Peter Berresford. *Dictionary of Celtic Mythology*. New York: Oxford University Press, 1992.

LUGH [Lug], the sun god and father of **Cuchulain** by the mortal Dechtíre. Lugh was one of the most powerful of the **Tuatha dé Danaan**. He became ruler of the gods when he defeated his grandfather, **Balor** of the Evil-Eye, at the Battle of **Moytura**. He supported Cuchulain during his final battles in the *Táin Bó Cuailnge*. In his notes to **Lady Gregory's** *Visions and Beliefs in the West of Ireland* (*LE*. 260), WBY speaks of Cuchulain as the rebirth of Lugh. *Lughnasadh*, the feast of Lugh, one of the four major pagan festivals in Ireland, was celebrated in August to mark the harvesting of the crops.
  REFERENCES: Dames, Michael. *Mythic Ireland*. 1992. Reprint, New York: Thames & Hudson, 1996; Ellis, Peter Berresford. *Dictionary of Celtic Mythology*. New York: Ox-

ford University Press, 1992; Green, Miranda J. *Dictionary of Celtic Myth and Legend*. London: Thames & Hudson, 1992; Mac Cana, Proinsias. *Celtic Mythology*. Feltham, Middlesex: Newnes, 1983.

LUGNAGALL (Irish: *Lug na nGall*) [Hollow of the Strangers], townland on the south side of **Glencar** at the base of **Cope's Mountain**, in **Sligo** (county). From Lugnagall, it is possible to look down on **Drumcliff**. It is not far from **Knock-narea** and the fairy mountain of **Knocknashee**. In ''The Curse of the Fires and the Shadows'' (*MY*. 183), the English soldiers, who burn down the **Abbey of the White Friars**, are mysteriously led to their deaths on the steep slopes of Lugnagall, while in ''Hanrahan's Vision'' (*MY*. 248–52), the poet **Hanrahan** has a vision of the **Sídhe** while he sleeps on a ridge on Lugnagall. It is one of the settings in the poem ''The Man Who Dreamed of Faeryland'' (*CP*. 50).
      REFERENCE: McGarry, James P. *Place Names in the Writings of William Butler Yeats*. Gerrards Cross: Colin Smythe, 1976.

LUGNÉ-POË, AURÉLIAN-MARIE (1869–1940), actor, director, and theater manager. He was born in Villeneuve-lès-Avignon. After his studies at the Paris Conservatoire, he acted with Antoine at the Théâtre-Libre and, in 1886, founded the experimental theatre group Cercle des Escholiers. He became a supporter of Paul Fort, who introduced him to the work of the Symbolists, and he enthusiastically added the last name of Edgar Allan Poe to his own. At the Théâtre d'Art, he played a leading role in Fort's production of **Maurice Maeterlinck's** *The Intruder* (1891), and in his determination to stage another play by Maeterlinck, he established the celebrated Théâtre de l'Oeuvre in 1893 to perform *Pelléas and Mélisande*. At the Théâtre de l'Oeuvre, he promoted new writing and innovative staging, making a major contribution to the history of modern European theater. He staged the plays of **Ibsen, Strindberg**, and Gerhart Hauptmann, among others, and produced *Salomé* by **Oscar Wilde**. It was at the Théâtre de l'Oeuvre in 1896 that WBY attended the first performance of *Ubu Roi* by Alfred Jarry.
      REFERENCES: Jasper, Gertrude B. *Adventure in the Theatre: Lugné-Poë and the Theatre de L'Oeuvre to 1899*. New Brunswick, N.J.: Rutgers University Press, 1947; Robichez, Jacques. *Lugné-Poë*. Paris: L'Arche, 1955.

LUSITANIA, British passenger liner sunk off the Irish coast by a German submarine, 7 May 1915. Among the 1,195 lost was **Hugh Lane**, nephew of **Lady Gregory**. WBY had sailed on the *Lusitania* on one of his early visits to the United States. With the sinking of the *Lusitania*, American opinion swung in favor of entering World War I on the side of Britain and her Allies.

LYSTER, T[HOMAS] W[ILLIAM] (1855–1922), director and head librarian at the **National Library of Ireland**, 1895–1920. In a speech made at the unveiling of a memorial plaque to Lyster in the National Library, 27 March 1926 (*UP2*. 470–

72), WBY paid tribute to him as an outstanding scholar of literature, under whose guidance he had read Elizabethan literature. He revealed that Lyster had helped him revise the manuscript for *The Island of Statues* and taught him to correct proof sheets. WBY chaired the Lyster Memorial Committee that organized the occasion.

M

MacBRIDE, [MAJOR] JOHN (1868–1916), patriot. He was born in Westport, **County Mayo**, and educated at the Christian Brothers, Westport, and St. Malachy's College, Belfast. After working in a drapery business in Castlerea, County Roscommon, he moved to Dublin, where he was employed by Hugh Moore & Co., wholesale chemists and grocers. He joined the Irish Republican Brotherhood (IRB) and, in 1896, was sent on a mission to the United States. On his return, he emigrated to South Africa as an assayer in the Robinson gold mines near Johannesburg. When the Boer War broke out in 1899, he formed the Irish Transvaal Brigade to fight against the British and was commissioned as a major by President Kruger. When the brigade was disbanded, MacBride settled in Paris. He married **Maud Gonne** in 1903. After the birth of a son, Seán, he and his wife became estranged. They were legally separated in 1905. When MacBride returned to Ireland, he continued to be active in nationalist politics and was on the Supreme Council of the IRB in 1911. He worked for the Shannon Eel Fisheries in Athlone and as a minor official in the Dublin Waterworks. He was not a member of the Irish Volunteers but offered his services in the Easter Rising in 1916. As the only leader with military experience, he was appointed second in command of the garrison holding Jacob's biscuit factory. After the Rising, he was found guilty of high treason and shot. WBY had been bitterly disappointed when Maud Gonne married MacBride. Like others, he believed it to be a totally unsuitable match. During the period following her separation from MacBride, she took WBY fully into her confidence, telling him of MacBride's drunkenness and sexual improprieties with members of her household, among them **Iseult Gonne**. WBY wholly sided with her in her condemnation of MacBride's brutality and morality, but after 1916, he elevated MacBride to that circle of Irish patriots who had made the absolute sacrifice, listing him with **Thomas MacDonagh, Padraic Pearse**, and **James Connolly** in his elegy "Easter 1916" (*CP*. 202).

REFERENCES: Martin, Francis X. *Leaders and Men of the Easter Rising: Dublin 1916*. Ithaca, N.Y.: Cornell University Press, 1967; White, Anna MacBride, and Jeffares, A. Norman, eds. *The Gonne-Yeats Letters: 1893–1938*. New York: W. W. Norton, 1992.

MacBRIDE, MAUD GONNE. *See* **GONNE, MAUD**.

MacDONAGH, THOMAS (1878–1916), poet and patriot. He was born in Cloughjordan, County Tipperary, and educated at Rockwell College, **Cashel**. He spent some years in seminary but, after a personal religious crisis, left the priesthood to teach in Kilkenny. He joined the Gaelic League and, while on a visit to the **Aran Islands**, met **Padraic Pearse**. He published three volumes of verse, *Through the Ivory Gate* (1902), *April and May* (1903), and *The Golden Joy* (1906), and in 1908, he moved to Dublin to become the first teacher appointed by Pearse to St. Enda's School, near Rathfarnham. That same year, his play *When the Dawn Is Come* was produced by the **Abbey Theatre**. He was disappointed in the production and, for a time, became unsettled, withdrawing into isolation in the Dublin mountains. In 1912, his play *Metempsychosis*, in which WBY was satirized as Earl Winton-Winton de Winton, was produced by **Edward Martyn's** Theatre of Ireland. He began teaching at University College, Dublin, and appeared to find a new fulfillment in literature, reflected in his *Lyrical Poems* (1913). With **James Stephens** and **Padraic Colum**, he edited *The Irish Review* and embarked on the critical work *Literature in Ireland, Studies Irish and Anglo-Irish* (1916), published posthumously. In 1913, he joined the Irish Volunteers and was appointed Director of Training. In 1914, he was a founder, with Edward Martyn and Joseph Plunkett, of The Irish Theatre (1914–20). In 1915, he joined the Irish Republican Brotherhood and was a member of the military council that planned the Easter Rising in 1916. He signed the Proclamation of the Irish Republic and was in command of the garrison that held Jacob's biscuit factory. He was court-martialed and executed, May 1916. MacDonagh was introduced to WBY when his play was produced by the Abbey Theatre in 1908, and they met to discuss Ireland and the Gaelic language (*A*. 505–6). In *Estrangement* (*A*. 488), WBY recalls a conversation in which they discussed the destructiveness of contemporary journalism and the failure of the Gaelic League to foster a true Celtic spirit in the Irish language. In the elegy "Easter 1916" (*CP*. 202), WBY includes MacDonagh among those patriots who have been heroically transformed by the events of the Easter Rising, noting his sensitive nature and promise as a writer.

REFERENCES: MacDonagh, Donagh. "Plunkett and MacDonagh." In *Leaders and Men of the Easter Rising: Dublin 1916*, ed. F. X. Martin. London: Methuen, 1967; Parks, Edd Winfield, and Parks, Aileen Wells. *Thomas MacDonagh: The Man, the Patriot, the Writer*. Athens: University of Georgia Press, 1967.

MACKENNA, MISS, fictional character. In WBY's play *The Words upon the Window-Pane*, she is secretary to the Dublin Spiritualists' Association. According to **Dr. Trench**, she has corresponded with the spiritualist **Mrs. Henderson** and arranged for the hire of the rooms in which the séance is being held. She introduces the participants and tells them what is happening as the séance proceeds. The role of Miss Mackenna in the first production of the play at the **Abbey Theatre**, November 1930, was played by Shelah Richards.

MacKENNA, STEPHEN (1872–1934), classical scholar, translator, and journalist. He was born in **Liverpool** and, in the 1890s, moved to Paris. There he led a Bohemian life, mainly in the company of **J. M. Synge**, and formed friendships with **John O'Leary** and **Maud Gonne**. In 1897, he joined an international brigade to fight for Greece against Turkey. On his return, he worked in London and then moved to New York as a journalist with the *New York World*. In 1907, frustrated with American journalism, he returned to Dublin, where he became a leader writer for *The Freeman's Journal*. Among his friends in Dublin were **Padraic Colum, Thomas MacDonagh**, and **James Stephens**. Despite ill health and the protracted illness of his wife, he embarked upon a translation of **Plotinus** (1908, 1917), the work for which he is best known. He wanted to join MacDonagh in the Easter Rising in 1916 but was rejected because of his health. His wife died in 1923. Frustrated with the Anglo-Irish Treaty, he returned to England, where he made a modest living as a freelance journalist. In "Ireland after Parnell" (*A*. 230), WBY remembers, with gratitude, MacKenna's support during a dispute over the scheme to set up small libraries throughout Ireland. He had MacKenna's translation of Plotinus in his library (*OS*. nos. 1589–94).

REFERENCES: Dodds, E. R., ed. *Stephen MacKenna, Journal and Letters*. New York: William Morrow, 1936; Hogan, Robert, ed. *Dictionary of Irish Literature*. Rev. ed. Westport, Conn.: Greenwood, 1996.

MACLEOD, FIONA. *See* **SHARP, WILLIAM**.

MacMURROUGH, DIARMUID [also Dermot] (1090–1171), king of **Leinster**. Diarmuid is chiefly remembered for abducting **Dervorgilla**, wife of Tiernan O'Rourke of **Breiffny**. Diarmuid was then defeated by the Irish chieftains who outlawed him for his treachery and Dervorgilla restored to her husband. To recover his kingdom, Diarmuid invited the help of Henry II, the English king, promising in return to hold the land as Henry's vassal. Although Henry was too engaged with other business to take part himself, he gave Diarmuid letters patent authorizing any of his subjects to help him. In 1170, Richard de Clare, called Strongbow, landed in Ireland, captured Waterford, and married Diarmuid's daughter **Aoife**. MacMurrough took Dublin later that year but died soon after, apparently unrepentant for his actions. When Henry II arrived in person toward the end of 1171, he received the submission of natives and invaders alike, so beginning the subjection of Ireland to England. WBY dramatized the remorse of Diarmuid and Dervorgilla in his play *The Dreaming of the Bones*. The two lovers, identified as the **Stranger** and a **Young Girl**, appeal to a **Young Man** to forgive them for bringing the Normans to Ireland. The role of the Stranger in the first performance of the play, at the **Abbey Theatre**, December 1931, was played by J. Stephenson.

REFERENCE: Flanagan, Marie T. *Irish Society, Anglo–Norman Settlers, Angevin Kingship: Interactions in Ireland in the late Twelfth Century*. New York: Oxford University Press, 1989.

MacNEICE, LOUIS (1907–1963), poet. He was born in Belfast, Northern Ireland, and grew up in the neighboring town of **Carrickfergus**, where his father was rector of the local Church of Ireland. He was educated at Marlborough College and at Oxford University. After teaching in Birmingham and at Bedford College, University of London, he joined the **BBC** in 1940 as a writer and producer. He remained there until his death. Regarded as a leading English poet, he was associated with a group of socially and politically conscious writers, which included **Stephen Spender, C. Day Lewis**, and **W. H. Auden**. His first book of verse was *Blind Fireworks* (1929), but he is best known for his longer poems *Autumn Journal* (1939) and *Autumn Sequel* (1954). He wrote verse plays for radio, among them *Christopher Columbus* (1944) and *The Dark Tower* (1947). WBY was out of sympathy with MacNeice and the younger, satirical writers of the 1930s, believing their social passion was misplaced in poetry. He saw them very firmly as a group, but in his introduction to *The Oxford Book of Modern Verse* (*LE*. 201), in which he included four of MacNeice's poems, he noted that MacNeice looked at the modern world with greater horror than his contemporary, C. Day Lewis (*LE*. 201). A copy of MacNeice's *Poems* (1935) was in WBY's library (*OS*. no. 1199).

REFERENCES: Brown, Terence. *Louis MacNeice: Sceptical Vision*. Dublin: Gill & Macmillan, 1975; MacNeice, Louis. *The Poetry of W. B. Yeats*. New York: Oxford University Press, 1969; Maxwell, D. E. S. *Poets of the Thirties*. New York: Barnes & Noble, 1969; McDonald, Peter. *Louis MacNeice: The Poet in His Contexts*. Oxford: Clarendon Press, 1991; O'Neill, Michael, and Reeves, Gareth. *Auden, MacNeice, and Spender: The Thirties Poetry*. New York: St. Martin's, 1992; Stallworthy, Jon. *Louis MacNeice*. London: Faber & Faber, 1995.

MAETERLINCK, MAURICE (1862–1949), Belgian playwright. He was educated by Jesuits and practiced law before becoming a playwright. With his major Symbolist dramas, including *Pelléas and Mélisande* (1892), *Sister Beatrice* (1894), *The Interior* (1894), *Aglavaine and Selysette* (1896), and *Monna Vanna* (1902), and his fantasies *The Bluebird* (1908) and *The Betrothal* (1918), Maeterlinck was a dominant figure in European drama at the turn of the century. His work is largely of academic interest today. WBY was introduced to Maeterlinck's work in the mid-1890s (*A*. 193) and believed he was of the company of **Mallarmé, Puvis de Chavannes**, and **Villiers de l'Isle-Adam**, and those other visionaries like **Keats, Blake,** and **Edward Calvert**, who were liberating art from the bonds of realism to evolve a higher reality of the imagination. WBY was influenced in his early verse plays by Maeterlinck's abstract symbolism and by his ability to create a timeless world of myth and reverie (*EI.* 334). Through Maeterlinck, WBY was convinced of the power of verse in the theater and the use of minimum scenery to produce a maximum aesthetic effect, although he had some reservations about him as a dramatist, finding that he sometimes touched the nerves and not the heart (*WL.* 255). When he saw *The Bluebird* in 1909, he thought it a ''meretricious pantomime'' (*WL.* 541). WBY reviewed Maeterlinck's book of essays *The Treasure of the Humble* (*UP2.* 45–47) and *Aglavaine and Selysette* (*UP2.* 51–54). In 1902, he was anxious to see a London performance of *Monna Vanna*, produced by **Lugné-Poë**, less for the play than for the staging and production (*WL.* 375).

REFERENCE: Mahony, Patrick. *Maurice Maeterlinck: Mystic and Dramatist.* Washington, D.C.: Institute for the Study of Man, 1984.

MAEVE, QUEEN (Irish: *Mebh, Maebh*) [she who intoxicates], mythological goddess queen of **Connacht**. She ruled from her capital at **Cruachan** (County Roscommon) and was the dominant partner in the relationship with her husband **Ailill**. She had a lover, **Fergus Mac Roich**, who had a reputation for his sexual prowess. She appears in the Ulster Cycle of tales as a scheming, promiscuous woman who declares war on **Ulster** out of greed and jealousy. Her husband has a magnificent White Bull, but she is covetous of the Ulster Brown Bull. When the men of Ulster refuse to give it to her, she leads her army northwards and encounters **Cuchulain**, the only Ulster hero not under the spell of Macha. Maeve's struggles with the Ulster champion form the basis of the *Táin Bó Cuailnge*. Maeve attempts to bribe Cuchulain with her daughter Finnebair and then sends her strongest champions against him. When she fails, she brings about his death by magic. She meets her own death at the hands of her nephew, Furbaidhe, in revenge for the murder of his mother, Clothra. Maeve is reputed to be buried beneath a cairn on **Knocknarea** in **Sligo** (county), but other sources insist she is buried at Cruachan. While she does not appear as an onstage character, she plays a threatening and decisive part in the action of WBY's plays *On Baile's Strand* and *The Death of Cuchulain*. In the poems ''Red Hanrahan's Song about Ireland'' (*CP.* 90) and *The Wanderings of Oisin* (*CP.* 409), WBY associates Maeve with Knocknarea. In ''And Fair, Fierce Women'' (*MY.* 57), he vividly describes her as a strong, handsome figure of about thirty, dressed in white, carrying a sword and a dagger.

REFERENCES: Ellis, Peter Berresford. *Dictionary of Celtic Mythology.* New York: Oxford University Press, 1992; Green, Miranda J. *Dictionary of Celtic Myth and Legend.* London: Thames & Hudson, 1992; Mac Cana, Proinsias. *Celtic Mythology.* Feltham, Middlesex: Newnes, 1983.

MAGEE, MOLL, fictional character. In ''The Ballad of Moll Magee'' (*CP.* 25), she tells of being rejected by her husband after she has killed her child. According to WBY, the poem was based on a story preached in the chapel at **Howth**, County Dublin (*VP*. 843).

MAGEE, W[ILLIAM] K[IRKPATRICK] (1869–1961), essayist. He was born in Dublin, the son of a Presbyterian minister, and attended **Erasmus Smith High School**, where he was a contemporary of WBY. His job as assistant librarian at the **National Library of Ireland** brought him into contact with the leading figures of the Irish Renaissance, among them **James Joyce**, who included him in the "Scylla and Charybdis" section of *Ulysses*. He was a prolific writer and, under the pseudonym John Eglinton, published books of essays, including *Two Essays on the Remnant* (1895), *Pebbles from a Brook* (1902), *Bards and Saints* (1906), and *Anglo-Irish Essays* (1917). From 1904, he edited the magazine, *Dana*. As a young man, Magee established a firm friendship with **AE** through his membership of the Dublin Lodge of the **Theosophical Society**. Later, he wrote *A Memoir of AE* (1937), which caused some protests because he had cited the Galway County Library Committee for a decision to burn the books of eminent authors, among them **George Bernard Shaw** (*LE*. 222). Magee edited the letters of **George Moore** (1929, 1942) and **Edward Dowden** (1914). In his final years he was out of sympathy with nationalist politics in Ireland and retired to Wales, later to England. WBY and Magee were founder members of the **Dublin Hermetic Society** and firm friends (*M*. 210–11). In some early reviews of his work, WBY, admiring Magee's "profound prose," thought him a writer of genius (*UP2*. 116, 121). In 1898, WBY and Magee became involved in a newspaper controversy, designed to alert the public to the **Irish Literary Theatre** and its objectives. The major point at issue was the suitability of Irish myths as subjects for Irish drama, with Magee and WBY appearing to take opposing sides in a series of letters to the Dublin *Daily Express* (*UP2*. 129–32). The controversy not only produced some heated debate but also resulted in the publication of the pamphlet *Literary Ideals in Ireland* (1899). Magee included a pen portrait of WBY in his *Irish Literary Portraits* (1935).

REFERENCES: Boyd, Ernest A. *Appreciations and Depreciations: Irish Literary Studies*. New York: John Lane, 1918; Eglinton, John. *Literary Ideals in Ireland*. New York: Lemma, 1973; Hogan, Robert, ed. *Dictionary of Irish Literature*. Rev. ed. Westport, Conn.: Greenwood, 1996; Lenoski, Daniel S. "Yeats, Eglinton, and Aestheticism." *Éire* 14, no. 4 (1979); Marcus, Phillip L. *Yeats and the Beginning of the Irish Renaissance*. Syracuse: Syracuse University Press, 1987.

MAGH AI (Irish: *Machaire*) [plain], County Roscommon. It was the ancestral home of the O'Conors, kings of **Connacht**, the oldest family in Europe. **Cruachan**, the royal seat of **Queen Maeve**, is a dominant feature of the plain. In "The Old Age of Queen Maeve" (*CP*. 451), Maeve is hailed as queen of Cruachan and Magh Ai.

REFERENCE: McGarry, James P. *Place Names in the Writings of William Butler Yeats*. Gerrards Cross: Colin Smythe, 1976.

MAGI, priestly caste of ancient Persia who practiced Zoroastrianism. The Magi were revered as wise men, and their reputed power over evil spirits gave rise to the word *magic*. In the Christian tradition, the Magi were wise men or kings who, following a star, brought gifts of gold, frankincense, and myrrh to the infant Jesus in a stable in Bethlehem. WBY sees the Magi as kings in "The Secret Rose" (*CP*. 77) and "The Magi" (*CP*. 141). He refers to the Magi following the star in "The Autumn of the Body" (*EI*. 190).

MAHAFFY, SIR JOHN PENTLAND (1839–1919), author and classical scholar. He was born in Switzerland of Irish parents and educated at home in **Donegal** (county). He entered **Trinity College**, Dublin, at sixteen and, after graduation, took Holy Orders, then essential to obtaining a fellowship at Trinity. As professor of Ancient History at the college, 1869–99, and later provost, Mahaffy was a major influence on generations of Trinity students, among them **Oscar Wilde**. He was an accomplished musician, excellent conversationalist, and a brilliant scholar, publishing *Principles of the Art of Conversation* in 1887. He wrote studies of the philosophers René Descartes and Immanuel Kant, published a history of Trinity College, and having deciphered some papyri discovered in Egypt, published *The Empire of the Ptolemies* (1895). Tall and red-haired, he was an imposing figure around Dublin, where his strong, authoritative, and conservative opinions both delighted and antagonized his contemporaries. He was at the center of Dublin's social and intellectual life, but he was vehemently opposed to Irish nationalism and the learning of Gaelic, insisting that no worthwhile literature existed in the language and that textbooks in Irish were laughable and indecent. Such attitudes from a senior academic were bitterly resented by members of the Gaelic League and those associated with the Celtic Revival, so that Mahaffy was heavily satirized and lampooned. At the Irish Convention of 1917, held at Trinity, he proposed that Ireland should move to a system of federal government like that of Switzerland, with **Ulster** as an autonomous province. His plan was not accepted. He is best known today for the number of books he published on the Ancient Greeks, including *Social Life in Greece from Homer to Menander* (1875), *Old Greek Education* (1882), *History of Classical Greek Literature* (1885), *Greek Life and Thought from the Age of Alexander to the Roman Conquest* (1897), and *What Have the Greeks Done for Modern Civilization?* (1909). He was president of the **Royal Irish Academy**, 1911–16, and was knighted for his services to academia in 1918. WBY was antagonistic toward Trinity College and saw Mahaffy as the representative of a reactionary pro-British institution, but he consulted with Mahaffy when the chair of English Literature at Trinity became vacant in 1911 (*WL*. 557).

REFERENCES: Hogan, Robert, ed. *Dictionary of Irish Literature*. Rev. ed. Westport, Conn.: Greenwood, 1996; O'Connor, Ulick. *Celtic Dawn: A Portrait of the Irish Literary Renaissance*. 1984. Reprint, London: Black Swan, 1985.

MAID QUIET. The identity of this character is obscure. The poem "Maid Quiet" (*CP*. 78) was published without a title in the *National Observer*, 24 December

1892. It appeared as "O'Sullivan the Red upon his Wanderings" (*New Review*, August 1897) and "Hanrahan laments because of his Wanderings" (***The Wind Among the Reeds***, 1899). The title was changed to "The Lover mourns because of his Wanderings" (*The Poetical Works of W. B. Yeats*, 1906) and finally to "Maid Quiet" (*Collected Works*, 1908). In early versions of the poem, the name Mother of Peace is substituted for Maid Quiet.

MAINES, children of **Queen Maeve** and **Ailill**. Traditionally, there were seven sons, each with the prefix Maine in his name. They joined their mother in the epic struggle *Táin Bó Cuailnge*, and one of them is reputed to have killed **Conchubar. Lady Gregory** named each of the Maine sons in her saga *Cuchulain of Muirthemne* (1902). In "The Hour before Dawn" (*CP.* 130), WBY refers to nine Maines brawling at **Cruachan**.

REFERENCES: Ellis, Peter Berresford. *Dictionary of Celtic Mythology.* New York: Oxford University Press, 1992.

MAJORCA, largest of the Balearic Islands in the Mediterranean. The mild climate and pleasing scenery of Majorca make it a favorite health and seaside resort. WBY and **Shri Purohit Swami** (accompanied by the Swami's friend, Mrs. Foden) visited Palma, the chief city of Majorca, December 1935 to April 1936. They stayed at the Hotel Terremar, where they hoped to complete a translation of *The Ten Principal Upanishads* (1937). The work was interrupted when WBY took seriously ill with nephritis and irregular heartbeat. **Mrs. Yeats** and the children, **Michael** and **Anne**, joined him in February 1936 and found him much recovered and able to continue with the translation. While Mrs. Yeats was with him, **Margot Ruddock** visited WBY for assurances about her poetry. She came to see him at the Casa Pastor, San Augustin, on a hillside outside Palma, the house to which he had moved with Mrs. Yeats.

REFERENCES: Purohit Swami, Shri, and Yeats, W. B. *The Ten Principal Upanishads.* London: Faber & Faber, 1937; Ruddock, Margot. *Almost I Tasted Ecstasy.* London: J. M. Dent & Sons, 1937.

MALLARMÉ, STÉPHANE (1842–98), French writer, teacher, and influential leader of the Symbolist movement in Europe during the late nineteenth century. Mallarmé became known for his translation, in 1875, of "The Raven" by Edgar Allan Poe. He followed this with a number of collections of poetry and prose, among them *L'Après-midi d'un faune* (1876), *Poésies* (1877), *Divagations* (1897), and *Vers et Prose* (1893). His ideas on sound and music in poetry had a profound influence, not only on the French but also on English and American poets. WBY was introduced to Mallarmé by **Arthur Symons**, and he acknowledged that Symons's translations of Mallarmé had a profound influence on the poems in ***The Wind Among the Reeds*** and ***The Shadowy Waters*** (*A.* 320). Despite having little French, WBY called at his home in Paris, February 1894. He was received by Mallarmé's wife, who advised him that her husband was in England on a lecture tour. From Mallarmé, WBY took the title for a section of his autobiography *The Trembling of the Veil* (*A.* 109, 315), and he recalls his debt to Mallarmé in a letter written to **Dorothy Wellesley**, May 1937 (*WL.* 887).

REFERENCES: Millan, Gordon. *A Throw of the Dice: The Life of Stéphane Mallarmé.* New York: Farrar, Straus & Giroux, 1994; Rabate, Jean-Michel. *The Ghosts of Modernity.* Gainesville: University Press of Florida, 1996.

MALLET, MRS., fictional character. In WBY's play *The Words upon the Window-Pane*, she is a widow. An Englishwoman, she claims that her husband, who was drowned at sea, continues to speak to her through the medium **Mrs. Henderson**, and so she regularly attends her séances. On this occasion, she wishes to ask her husband's advice about opening a tea-shop in Folkestone. In the course of the action, her husband attempts to speak to her but is driven away by the spirit of **Jonathan Swift**. In the first production of *The Words upon the Window-Pane*, the part of Mrs. Mallet was played by Eileen Crowe.

MANANNÁN [Mac LIR], son of the Irish sea god, Lir, and husband of **Fand**. Reputed to be handsome and a fine warrior, Manannán was one of the **Shape-Changers**, able to ride his horses, the sea waves, as if over a huge plain. As the sea god, he was capable of protecting Ireland with the element that surrounds it. He was the possessor of magical powers, skills, tricks, illusion, and wisdom. There is a reference to Manannán in WBY's "Three Songs to the One Burden" (*CP.* 371), while his terrifying seahorses are alluded to in the poem "He bids his Beloved be at Peace" (*CP.* 69). In a note to the latter poem (*VP.* 808), WBY associates Manannán with the **Fomorians** and the country of the dead and comments on the powerful symbol of the sea in Irish mythology. See also *The Green Helmet* (*CPl.* 231) and *The Only Jealousy of Emer* (*CPl.* 285, 287).

REFERENCES: Ellis, Peter Berresford. *Dictionary of Celtic Mythology.* New York: Oxford University Press, 1992; Green, Miranda J. *Dictionary of Celtic Myth and Legend.* London: Thames & Hudson, 1992; Mac Cana, Proinsias. *Celtic Mythology.* Feltham, Middlesex: Newnes, 1983.

MANCINI, ANTONIO (1852–1931), Italian artist. He was discovered by **Hugh Lane**, who persuaded him to come from Rome to Dublin. He set up his studio at 17 Harcourt Street in a house that later became the Dublin Municipal Gallery. In 1907, he drew a pastel portrait of WBY, which was much disliked by **John B. Yeats**. WBY, who regarded Mancini as one of the outstanding living painters, thought the portrait made him look like an Italian bandit (*WL.* 502, 504). It was used as the frontispiece to a volume of WBY's *Collected Works* (1908). In his poem "The Municipal Gallery Revisited" (*CP.* 368), WBY writes enthusiastically about Mancini's oil portrait of **Lady Gregory**. To achieve arresting highlights in his pictures, Mancini incorporated into the pigment pieces of tinfoil, glass, and mother of pearl. WBY refers to this technique in "Swedenborg, Mediums, and the Deserted Places" (*LE*. 62).

REFERENCE: Bodkin, Thomas. *Hugh Lane and His Pictures*. Dublin: Browne & Nolan, 1934.

MANGAN, JAMES CLARENCE (1803–49), poet. He was born in Dublin, the son of an impoverished grocer. After attending school in Saul's Court, Dublin, where he learned Latin, Spanish, French, and German, he worked for seven years as a scrivener, followed by three years as an attorney's clerk. He was later employed as a cataloguer in the library of **Trinity College**, Dublin. A period spent with the Ordnance Topographical Society in the company of George Petrie, Eugene O'Curry, and John O'Donovan encouraged him to study early Irish poetry and folklore. From these studies emerged a number of poems and translations based on Old Irish originals, including "The Woman of Three Cows," "Kathleen-Ny-Houlahan," and "Kincora." These poems revealed not only a deep commitment to Ireland but also a fine technique that inspired many of the later Irish writers, including WBY and **James Joyce**. Although he contributed to the first edition of *The Nation* in 1842, most of Mangan's poems and prose pieces appeared in *The Dublin University Magazine, The Spirit of the Nation* (1843), and *Poets and Poetry of Munster* (1849). He led a bohemian life, frequenting the seedier parts of Dublin and disappearing without explanation for days on end. He was eccentric in appearance, wearing green-tinted spectacles and a tall, witchlike hat over his prematurely snow-white hair. He had few friends. Worn out by poverty, overwork, an unhappy love affair, alcohol, and drugs, he died during the cholera epidemic of 1849. WBY, as a young man, identified with Mangan, the passionate, self-absorbed loner, claiming he was the outstanding poet of the early nineteenth-century, writing better verse than **Thomas Davis** (*A*. 516; *EI*. 256). He published a biographical note on Mangan, with a reference to his unhappy love affair, in *Irish Fireside*, 12 March 1887 (*UP1*. 115–19), and an appreciation of his intense genius in "Popular Ballad Poetry of Ireland" (*UP1*. 152–57), published in the *Leisure Hour*, November 1889. A further article, "Clarence Mangan's Love Affair" (*UP1*. 194–98), appeared in *United Ireland*, 22 August 1891. He published eight of Mangan's poems in his *Book of Irish Verse* (1895), including "Dark Rosaleen," in which, in the Gaelic tradition of the *Aisling*, the poet has a vision of Ireland as a beautiful and sorrowing woman waiting for salvation from over the sea. In the poem "To Ireland in the Coming Times" (*CP*. 56), WBY names himself in the company of Davis, Mangan, and **Sir Samuel Ferguson**. It was an added fascination for WBY that Mangan had claimed to be a visionary who saw a sphere of light around men's souls. In this, WBY compares him with **Emanuel Swedenborg** (*UP1*. 197).

REFERENCES: Donaghy, Henry J. *James Clarence Mangan*. New York: Twayne, 1974; Kilroy, James. *James Clarence Mangan*. Lewisburg, Pa.: Bucknell University Press, 1970; Marcus, Phillip L. *Yeats and the Beginning of the Irish Renaissance*. Syracuse:

Syracuse University Press, 1987; Welch, Robert. ''James Clarence Mangan: 'Apples from the Dead Sea Shore.' '' In *Irish Poetry from Moore to Yeats*. Totowa, N.J.: Barnes & Noble, 1980; Yeats, William Butler, and Kinsella, Thomas. *Davis, Mangan, Ferguson?: Tradition and the Irish Writer*. Dublin: Dolmen, 1970.

MANNIN, ETHEL (1900–1984), novelist and travel writer. She was born in London but lived for a time in Ireland, principally in **Connemara**. She was a prolific novelist, best known for her *Connemara Journal* (1927) and her sentimental novel *Late Have I Loved Thee* (1948). In *Two Studies in Integrity* (1954), she compares the writings of Irish novelists Gerald Griffen and Father Prout (Francis Mahoney). During the 1930s, Ethel Mannin was one of a group of women with whom WBY corresponded on an intimate basis. With her, he discussed his political views and his writing (*WL.* 845) and the critical response to **The Oxford Book of Modern Verse** (*WL.* 867, 871–73). He responded to her novels in a brief, superficial way, appearing reluctant to get involved in any critical assessment of her writing.

REFERENCES: Hogan, Robert, ed. *Dictionary of Irish Literature*. Rev. ed. Westport, Conn.: Greenwood, 1996; Mannin, Ethel. *Two Studies in Integrity: Gerald Griffen and Rev. Francis Mahoney*. London: Jarrolds, 1954; Welch, Robert, ed. *The Oxford Companion to Irish Literature*. Oxford: Clarendon, 1996.

MANSION HOUSE, official residence of Dublin's Lord Mayor. In *On the Boiler* (*LE.* 409), WBY roundly criticizes the Victorian additions to the fine Queen Anne building in Dawson Street, Dublin. Built in 1705 by Joshua Dawson, it has been the official residence of the city's Lord Mayor since 1715. After the Easter Rising of 1916, the first Irish Parliament met there in 1919 to adopt Ireland's declaration of independence. The Round Room, in which the 1921 Treaty between England and Ireland was signed, was added in 1821.

REFERENCES: Craig, Maurice. *Dublin 1660–1860*. Dublin: Figgis, 1969. McGarry, James P. *Place Names in the Writings of William Butler Yeats*. Gerrards Cross: Colin Smythe, 1976.

MANTEGNA, ANDREA (1431–1506), painter of the Italian **Quattrocento** period. He was born in Padua, northern Italy, where he painted the frescoes in the Eremitani Church while he was in his late teens. He moved to Mantua, where he consolidated his reputation for strong, dramatic paintings, executed with a strict attention to perspective, historical accuracy, and draftsmanship. He had a passion for the antique, evidenced in clothing and architecture, and yet he infused his statuesque figures with life and vitality. Among his early works was the St. Luke altarpiece in Milan, while his painting on the ceiling of the bridal chamber of the Gonzaga palace at Mantua was widely imitated. His frescoes in the Eremitani Church, including the outstanding *St. James Led to His Execution*, were almost entirely destroyed during the bombing of Italy in 1944. WBY was introduced to Mantegna's genius at the National Gallery in London by **Olivia**

Shakespear (*M*. 86), while prints of Mantegna, **Botticelli**, and other Italian painters hung in WBY's bedroom at **Coole Park** (*A*. 502). See also "Her Vision in the Wood" (*CP*. 312).

REFERENCES: Boorsch, Suzanne, ed. *Andrea Mantegna*. New York: Metropolitan Museum of Art, 1992; Lightbrown, R. W. *Mantegna*. Berkeley: University of California Press, 1986.

MAREOTIC LAKE, salt lake in Egypt. The Mareotic Lake (Lake Mareotis) is separated from the Mediterranean by a strip of land on which **Alexandria** is situated. It was one of the barren sites where early Christian monasticism flourished in the fourth century A.D. WBY was familiar with James Hannay's book *The Wisdom of the Desert*, which describes the settlements of the early monks and their use of military imagery in their spiritual struggles (*LE*. 108–9, 256). See also "Demon and Beast" (*CP*. 209) and "Under Ben Bulben" (*CP*. 397). In support of his argument that water is **Shelley's** symbol of existence, he recalls in "The Philosophy of Shelley's Poetry" (*EI*. 85) the journey of **The Witch of Atlas** through the Mareotic Lake.

REFERENCES: Hannay, Rev. James O. *The Spirit and Origin of Christian Monasticism*. London: Methuen, 1903; Hannay, Rev. James O. *The Wisdom of the Desert*. London: Methuen, 1904.

MARKIEWICZ, COUNTESS [CONSTANCE GEORGINA] (1868–1927), political leader and activist. She was born in London, the eldest daughter of the Anglo-Irish Sir Henry Gore-Booth, and educated by a governess in the ancestral home at **Lissadell**, near **Sligo** (town). In 1887, she was presented at the court of Queen Victoria and took her place as a member of Ireland's landed gentry, respected and admired by the country people around Sligo as a beauty and a fine horsewoman (*M*. 78). In 1893, she moved to London to study painting at the Slade School of Fine Arts. In 1898, she went to Paris to continue her studies and there met Count Casimir Dunin-Markiewicz (1874–1932), a Polish artist whom she married at St. Marylebone Parish Church, London, 29 September 1900. They returned to Dublin, where Constance and her husband wrote plays for the Theatre of Ireland, and the Count established himself as a portrait painter, becoming an active member of the Dublin Arts Club, where his friends included WBY and **AE**. Marriage and Dublin social life failed to satisfy Constance. In 1906, while renting a cottage in the Dublin Mountains, she read nationalist literature left behind by a previous tenant, **Padraic Colum**. It aroused her interest in her country's political struggle, and she became actively involved in nationalist politics. She joined the Executive of Sinn Féin and, in 1909, founded Na Fianna, a movement modeled on the Boy Scouts but militant in its organization and objectives. She supported **James Connolly** in the Transport Workers strike in 1913, and after her husband left for the Ukraine, she joined Connolly's left-wing Citizen Army in 1914 and took part in the Easter Rising of 1916 as deputy leader of the garrison that held St. Stephen's Green. She was subsequently sentenced to death but reprieved. She opposed the Anglo-Irish Treaty of 1921, but with the setting up of the Irish Free State in 1922, she was elected to the first Irish Parliament, **Dáil Éireann**, and appointed to the Cabinet as Secretary for Labor. Her extremist political views became increasingly irrelevant, and she spent her final years working with the poor in the slums of Dublin. She was buried in **Glasnevin**, with over 100,000 people attending her funeral. WBY's elegy, "In Memory of Eva Gore-Booth and Con Markiewicz" (*CP.* 263), written after her death, nostalgically recalls a visit that he made to the Gore-Booth sisters at Lissadell, in 1894, although he had visited Constance when she first arrived in London the previous year. As she became more militant in her opposition to English rule in Ireland, WBY and she held opposing views. In his poem "Easter, 1916" (*CP.* 202), while celebrating her heroism, he regrets her association with ignorant men, seeing in her action a betrayal of her aristocratic tradition. See also "On a Political Prisoner" (*CP.* 206).

REFERENCES: Coxhead, Elizabeth. *Daughters of Erin: Five Women of the Irish Renascence.* London: Secker & Warburg, 1965; Fletcher, Ian. "Yeats and Lissadell." In *W. B. Yeats and His Contemporaries.* Brighton, Sussex: Harvester, 1987; Freyer, Grattan. *W. B. Yeats and the Anti-Democratic Tradition.* Dublin: Gill & Macmillan, 1981; Marreco, Anne. *The Rebel Countess: The Life and Times of Constance Markievicz [sic].* London: Weidenfeld & Nicolson, 1967; O'Faolain, Sean. *Constance Markiewicz.* Reprint. London: Cresset Library, 1987; Van Voris, Jacqueline. *Constance de Markiewicz in the Cause of Ireland.* Amherst: University of Massachusetts Press, 1967.

MARLOWE, JULIA (1866–1950), American actress. She was born Sarah Frances Frost in Cumberland, England, and emigrated to the United States as a child. She began acting with a professional touring company in 1880 but left the stage in 1884 to study with Ada Dow, a noted actress. She made her New York debut in 1887 and, for the next ten years, toured throughout the United States in the major English classics. In 1904, she formed a partnership with the romantic actor Edward Hugh Sothern, and together they became the leading players of Shakespearean drama in America. In 1907, they appeared in London, where they impressed **Arthur Symons** and other English critics in their productions of *Hamlet, Romeo and Juliet,* and *Twelfth Night.* On their return to New York City, they performed, at popular prices, to an audience that previously could not afford to see **Shakespeare.** From 1909, they acted with their own permanent touring company throughout the United States and Europe, often presenting Shakespeare for audiences of schoolchildren. They married in London in 1911. In 1926, after an illness, Julia Marlowe retired from the stage, and the company had to disband. As an actress, she was noted for her beauty, pleasing voice, and the subtlety and restraint of her characterizations. WBY, who shared Symons's enthusiasm for Julia Marlowe, may have seen her act Juliet when he toured the United States in 1903–4, and he considered asking her to play in ***Deirdre.*** He comments favorably on her acting in "His Phoenix" (*CP.* 170).

REFERENCES: Russell, Charles Edward. *Julia Marlowe, Her Life and Art.* New York: Appleton, 1926; Sothern, Edward Hugh. *Julia Marlowe's Story.* Ed. Fairfax Downey.

New York: Rinehart, 1954; Symons, Arthur. *Great Acting in English: An Appreciation of Julia Marlowe and Edward Sothern on the English Stage*. London: Ballantyne, 1907.

MARTHA, sister to **Lazarus** and **Mary**. She welcomed Jesus to her home in Bethany. In WBY's play *Calvary*, she is one of the women who accompanies Mary, the mother of Jesus, to watch his Crucifixion.

MARTIN, COLONEL, central figure in the ballad "Colonel Martin" (*CP*. 361). He is thought to have been based on Colonel Richard Martin (1754–1834), a well-known duelist, who was M.P. for **Galway** and a colonel in the Galway Volunteers. According to contemporary accounts, Martin discovered his wife in bed with a wealthy man. He successfully sued for damages and distributed the money he was awarded to the poor. The story occurs in **Lady Gregory's** *Kiltartan History Book* (1926).

MARTIN, VIOLET [FLORENCE]. *See* **SOMERVILLE AND ROSS**.

MARTYN, EDWARD (1859–1923), playwright. He was born in the family home, **Tulira Castle**, in **Ardrahan, Galway** (county), and educated at Jesuit schools in Ireland and England. He graduated from **Christ Church** College, **Oxford**. Independently wealthy, he was something of an anomaly in Ireland being Catholic and a landowner. He was passionately interested in theater and began writing plays in the style of **Ibsen's** problem dramas. WBY stayed with him in 1896 and wrote a detailed account of the visit in *Dramatis Personae* (*A*. 385–87). A conversation with WBY and **Lady Gregory** led to the formation of the **Irish Literary Theatre** in 1899. Martyn subsidized the seasons, 1899–1901, during which the Irish Literary Theatre produced his plays *The Heather Field* (1899) and *Maeve* (1900). After the success of *The Heather Field*, WBY believed him to be the company's first playwright and included *Maeve* in the second season, together with *The Tale of the Town*, which Martyn was completing. When WBY and **George Moore**, who became involved as producer, read the text of *The Tale of the Town*, they realized it was unactable, and Moore admitted he had helped in the writing of Martyn's earlier plays. They discussed changes, and finally *The Tale of the Town* was substantially rewritten and produced as *The Bending of the Bough* (*A*. 426–27), with Moore acknowledged as the sole author. The action undermined and alienated Martyn, who felt increasingly at odds with WBY's personality and choice of plays. He effectively withdrew from the Irish Literary Theatre and its successor, the **Irish National Theatre Society**, but he helped found the short-lived theater company, the Theatre of Ireland, in 1906. A devout Catholic, Martyn became increasingly sympathetic to the cause of Irish nationalism. He supported the Gaelic League financially and was president of Sinn Féin, 1904–8. In 1914, with **Thomas MacDonagh** and Joseph Plunkett, he founded The Irish Theatre (1914–20). They hoped to present an alternative program to the **Abbey Theatre**, opening with Martyn's satire *The Dream Phy-*

sician (1914), but the public response to The Irish Theatre, whose productions included plays by **Maeterlinck** and **Strindberg**, in addition to new Irish playwrights like Eimar O'Duffy and John MacDonagh, was disappointing. With the closure of The Irish Theatre in 1920, Martyn, in poor health, retired to his country estate, where he led the life of a devout but eccentric recluse. WBY and Martyn, despite their early collaboration, were fundamentally opposed in their ideas on the theater. Martyn was never able to move beyond his early enthusiasm for naturalism, and he lacked the courage to challenge those who disagreed with the policy and choice of plays.

REFERENCES: Courtney, Sr. Marie-Therese. *Edward Martyn and the Irish Theatre.* New York: Vantage, 1956; Gwynn, Denis R. *Edward Martyn and the Irish Revival.* London: Cape, 1930; McFate, Patricia. "*The Bending of the Bough* and *The Heather Field.*" *Éire-Ireland* (spring 1973); Setterquist, Jan. *Ibsen and the Beginnings of Anglo-Irish Drama II: Edward Martyn.* Uppsala: Lundquist, 1960.

MARY [Maire Rua], peasant wife, character in WBY's play *The Countess Cathleen.* She is a woman of about forty years of age, the wife of **Shemus Rua** and mother of **Teigue.** She has faith in God that her family will survive the famine. In contrast to other members of her family and her neighbors, she challenges the demon **Merchants** and refuses to eat any food bought with their money. The role of Mary in the first production of *The Countess Cathleen,* May 1899, was played by Madame San Carolo.

MARY, name of the three women who, in the company of **Martha,** gathered on the hillside to watch the Crucifixion of **Christ** in WBY's play *Calvary* (*CPl.* 453). Although WBY affords them no individuality in the play, they are most likely to have been Mary, the mother of Christ, Mary Magdalene, and Mary, the sister of Martha and **Lazarus.** In the Gospels of the New Testament (Christian Bible), there are four different versions of the events of Christ's trial, sentence, death, and Resurrection. Another Mary, the mother of James, is named in two of them, while Christ's mother is not named in any. In WBY's play *The Resurrection* (*CPl.* 588), **The Syrian** declares that he met Mary, the mother of Jesus, Mary, the mother of James, and the other women on their way from Christ's tomb in a state of intense excitement because the body was nowhere to be seen. See also "The Countess Cathleen in Paradise" (*CP.* 48), "The Unappeasable Host" (*CP.* 65) and "A Stick of Incense" (*CP.* 383).

MASEFIELD, JOHN (1878–1967), poet and novelist. He was born in Ledbury, Hertfordshire, and became an apprentice on a merchant ship when he was fourteen, sailing around Cape Horn. In 1895, he was a bartender in New York City, but he returned to London in 1897, where he found employment as a bank clerk. He became a subeditor with *The Speaker* and began writing a Miscellany column for the *Manchester Guardian.* His early collections of poetry, *Salt-Water Ballads* (1902) and *Ballads* (1903), drew on his experiences at sea and were marked by an earthy authenticity. He served with the Red Cross during World War I and, on his return to England, published his popular poems *Reynard the Fox* (1919) and *Right Royal* (1920), both of which evoked a romantic nostalgia for the English countryside. His *Collected Poems* was published in 1923, and he was appointed Poet Laureate in 1930. He wrote plays, essays, and adventure stories, but his later work failed to match the authenticity and freshness of his early poems. He met WBY in 1900, when he sought the Irish poet's advice on becoming a writer, and was invited to WBY's Monday Nights "At Home." This was the beginning of a mutual friendship that lasted until WBY's death. The two poets spent much time in each other's company, and Masefield, liked as a person by **Lady Gregory** (although she was not enthusiastic about his poetry), was invited to **Coole Park**. In 1903, he married Constance Crommelin, an **Ulster** woman who had been educated at Cambridge. WBY thought her opinionated and overbearing and came to believe her influence was detrimental to Masefield's development as an artist—and yet he recognized that she took care of her husband, who had a delicate constitution (*KLIII*. 352). When the Yeats family was living in **Oxford**, the Masefields lived nearby at Boar's Hill, and they were invited to a celebration at **Riversdale** of WBY's seventieth birthday. WBY included six poems by Masefield in his selection for *The Oxford Book of Modern Verse* (1936). Twenty-seven books of verse and other writings by Masefield are known to have been in WBY's library (*OS.* nos. 1240–64).

REFERENCES: Babington Smith, Constance. *John Masefield: A Life*. New York: Macmillan, 1978; Fisher, Margery Turner. *John Masefield*. New York: H. Z. Walck, 1963; Masefield, John. *Some Memories of W. B. Yeats*. Dublin: Cuala, 1940; Sternlicht, Sanford. *John Masefield*. Boston: Twayne, 1977.

MATHERS, [SAMUEL LIDDELL] MacGREGOR [Comte de Glenstrae] (1854–1918), writer, cabalist, and eccentric. He was born in London and, on the early death of his father, moved with his mother to Bournemouth. In 1877 he became a Freemason, and later joined the Rosicrucians. He moved to London in 1885 to pursue a study of esoteric and mystical texts in the **British Museum** and, in 1887, published his translation of Knorr von Rosenroth's *The Kabbalah Unveiled*. He followed this influential work with a book on the links between the Tarot and the occult. At the invitation of Dr. William Wynn Westcott and Dr. W. R. Woodman, he joined **The Order of the Golden Dawn** in 1887 and, drawing on his knowledge of Freemasonry and Egyptology, evolved a series of elaborate rituals. In June 1890, he married the clairvoyant Moina Bergson, sister of the distinguished philosopher Henri Bergson. In the same year, WBY met Mathers in the British Museum and was shortly afterwards initiated into The Golden Dawn (*A*. 183–84). During this time, Mathers was curator of the Horniman Museum in Forest Hill, London. He was fired in 1891, but his patron, **Annie F. Horniman**, continued to support him financially when he moved with his wife to Paris, in 1892. He set up a Temple of the Golden Dawn in Paris in 1894, but his behavior became increasingly irrational. He assumed a Scottish name and title, MacGregor Mathers, Comte de Glenstrae, dressed extravagantly in Highland costume, and flirted with Scottish nationalism, although WBY doubted he had ever been to Scotland (*A.* 335–36). When it was apparent that he was neglecting his occult studies, Annie Horniman withdrew his pension in 1896. Mathers retaliated by expelling her from The Golden Dawn and refused, despite entreaties, to reinstate her. He accused the members of the London Temple of plotting against him and dispatched a fellow-adept, Aleister Crowley, to take possession of the society's premises and papers. WBY and his supporters resisted the takeover and expelled Mathers from the London Temple. Some London members remained loyal to him, but gradually he faded into obscurity. From their initial meeting in 1890, it is evident that WBY was profoundly influenced by Mathers in his practice of the occult (*A.* 182–88). The influence extended to WBY's writing. Through the experiments that Mathers and he conducted together, WBY learned a system of meditation that enabled him to contact a range of symbols from a source other than the "conscious or subconscious memory." Even when their friendship was strained, WBY continued to use the rituals learned from Mathers to invoke reverie, images, and dreams (*A.* 255, 258, 270). He visited Mathers in Paris in 1894, and again in 1896, when they discussed plans for a Celtic Order of Mysteries. Yet he found it difficult to accept Mathers's dictatorial attitudes to the affairs of The Golden Dawn, and their friendship cooled. His account of Mathers, which he included in a note to ***The Trembling of the Veil*** (*A.* 576), shocked Moina Bergson when she read it after her husband's death. Mathers is recalled in the poem "All Souls Night" (*CP.* 256).

REFERENCES: Bachchan, Harbans Rai. *W. B. Yeats and Occultism.* New York: Weiser, 1974; Harper, George Mills, ed. *Yeats and the Occult.* London: Macmillan, 1976; Harper, George Mills. *Yeats's Golden Dawn.* London: Macmillan, 1974; Moore, Virginia. *The Unicorn: William Butler Yeats' Search for Reality.* New York: Farrar, Straus & Giroux, 1973; Regardie, Israel. *The Golden Dawn: An Account of the Teachings, Rites and Ceremonies of the Order of the Golden Dawn.* St. Paul, Minn.: Llewellyn, 1989.

MATHEWS, ELKIN (1851–1921), publisher. He was born in Gravesend, near London, the son of a timber and slate merchant. After serving an apprenticeship with various booksellers in London and Bath, he opened an antiquarian bookshop in Exeter. In 1887, with his business partner John Lane, he formed the Bodley Head, a publishing house in Vigo Street, London. Both men seized the opportunity to publish limited edition books of fine quality, including **Richard Le Gallienne's** *Volumes in Folio* (1889), **John Todhunter's** *A Sicilian Idyll* (1890), **Arthur Symons's** *Silhouettes* (1892) and **Oscar Wilde's** *Salomé* (1894). The partnership was dissolved in 1894. Lane took the Bodley Head imprint, and Mathews, with the support of various poets, including WBY, continued to publish limited editions, most notably in the Vigo Cabinet series, which published some 150 volumes of poetry and prose, from writers as distinctive as **J. M. Synge, John Masefield**, and **Lord Dunsany**. During the period 1887–1921,

Mathews published many books central to the literary movements of the time,
and through his support of young writers, among them **Ezra Pound**, Mathews
made a major contribution to English literature in the early years of the twentieth
century. Among his few omissions were **James Joyce's** *Dubliners* (although he
had earlier published Joyce's *Chamber Music*) and the early poetry of **T. S.
Eliot**. WBY was introduced to Mathews by Richard Le Gallienne. Although he
was not a poet, Mathews attended the meetings of the **Rhymers' Club** and
published their collections of verse, *The Book of the Rhymers' Club* (1892) and
The Second Book of the Rhymers' Club (1894). The publisher's relationship
with WBY was intensified when he moved to **Bedford Park**, to a house next
door to the Yeats family, and joined in the various social gatherings of the
garden suburb. When Mathews broke from his partner John Lane and set up on
his own, WBY arranged for him to publish *The Wind Among the Reeds* (1899),
"The Tables of the Law," and "The Adoration of the Magi" (1904).

REFERENCE: Nelson, James G. *Elkin Mathews: Publisher to Yeats, Joyce, Pound.*
Madison: University of Wisconsin Press, 1989.

MAYO (Irish: *Magh-eó*) [plain of the yews], county on the west coast of Ireland.
Although it is mainly bog land, Mayo is scenically remote and beautiful. **George
Moore's** large estate and family home, Moore Hall, was on the shores of Lough
Carra, County Mayo. He is buried nearby, on Castle Island, where he had played
as a child with **Oscar Wilde. F. R. Higgins** came from County Mayo, while
Arnold Bax stayed at Renvyle House, later the home of **St. John Gogarty**. In
The Cat and the Moon (*CPl.* 465), the **Blind Beggar** claims to have heard
about the woman-hating holy man of **Laban** who was keeping company with
an old lecher from Mayo, while in *The Herne's Egg* (*CPl.* 667), the servant
Corney challenges **Congal's** account of his union with **Attracta**, saying he has
the lying tongue of a Mayo man. WBY associated Mayo and the neighboring
counties with fairy lore and folktales. In *Mythologies* (1959), he cites an old
Mayo woman as the source of many of his stories. This is very likely **Mary
Battle**.

REFERENCE: McGarry, James P. *Place Names in the Writings of William Butler Yeats.*
Gerrards Cross: Colin Smythe, 1976.

MAYOR OF KINVARA. *See* **KINVARA**.

McCORMICK, F. J. (1889–1947), actor. He was born Peter Judge, in Skerries,
County Dublin. After a brief career as a civil servant in Dublin and London, he
joined the **Abbey Theatre** company in 1918 and became the outstanding Irish
actor of his generation. He showed enormous range and versatility and excelled
in the early plays of **Sean O'Casey**. He was a fine speaker of verse, creating
the leading roles in a number of later verse plays by WBY, including *Sophocles'
King Oedipus* (1926) and *The King of the Great Clock Tower* (1934). He toured
the United States with the Abbey company and played in three major films, the

last being *Odd Man Out*, but he was not widely known outside Ireland. His roles in WBY's plays included The Tapster in ***The Player Queen*** (1919), **Oedipus** in *Sophocles' King Oedipus* and ***Sophocles' Oedipus at Colonus*** (1927), and Abraham Johnson in ***The Words upon the Window-Pane*** (1930).

REFERENCES: Hunt, Hugh. *The Abbey: Ireland's National Theatre: 1904–1979*. Dublin: Gill & Macmillan, 1979; Kavanagh, Peter. *Story of the Abbey Theatre, From Its Origin in 1899 to the Present*. New York: Devin-Adair, 1950; Robinson, Lennox. *Ireland's Abbey Theatre: A History, 1899–1951*. London: Sidgwick & Jackson, 1951.

McGRATH, JOHN (1864–1956), journalist and editor. He was born in Portaferry, **County Down**. As a young man, he contributed articles to *Young Ireland* and later joined the staff of the *Freeman's Journal*. When the paper switched its loyalties to the anti-Parnellites, he moved to *United Ireland*, where he succeeded **Edmund Leamy** as editor. On October 1891, he published an article accusing the anti-Parnellites of the murder of **Charles Stewart Parnell**. WBY refers to this article in *M*. 57. McGrath and WBY were mutually respectful of each other. In 1892, McGrath helped WBY promote the **National Literary Society** by publishing in *United Ireland* the article "Is Dublin the Intellectual Capital of the Irish Race?" WBY replied to the question in May 1892 (*UP1*. 222–25). While he was appreciative of McGrath's favorable review of ***The Celtic Twilight*** (1893), WBY challenged his assertions that the stories were not "founded upon fact," pointing out that they were literally true (*UP1*. 310). Later, McGrath challenged WBY's argument that the publication of *The Patriot Parliament* by **Thomas Davis** was not a good choice for the **New Irish Library** (*UP1*. 339). In an article that he contributed to the *Westminster Review*, July 1911, McGrath described the enigmatic WBY as the most interesting of all the literary contributors to *United Ireland*.

McTAGGART, JOHN McTAGGART [ELLIS] (1866–1925), philosopher. In his major books, he argued for a belief in the rebirth of the soul, which WBY believed to be the foundation of McTaggart's philosophical system (*LE*. 117; *VPl*. 934). WBY had read his major works, *Studies in Hegelian Cosmology* (1901) and *Human Immortality and Pre-existence* (1915). These, and a copy of *The Nature of Existence* (1921), all with extensive marginalia, were in WBY's library (*OS*. nos. 1200–1204). See also "A Bronze Head" (*CP*. 382) and "Bishop Berkeley" (*EI*. 406).

REFERENCES: Broad, Charles D. *Examination of McTaggart's Philosophy*. New York: Octagon, 1976; Dickinson, G. Lowes. *John McTaggart McTaggart*. Cambridge: The University Press, 1931; Geach, Peter T. *Truth, Love, and Immortality: An Introduction to McTaggart's Philosophy*. London: Hutchinson, 1979; Rochelle, Gerald. *Life and Philosophy of John McTaggart McTaggart: 1866–1925*. Lewiston, N.Y.: E. Mellen, 1991.

MEATH (Irish: *Mide*) [middle], one of the five provinces of ancient Ireland and a county in the east of modern Ireland. The whole of Ireland was ruled from

Tara, the seat of the High King and capital of Meath until the sixth century. Meath did not exist at the time of the epic *Táin Bó Cuailnge*. The smallest of the provinces, it only came into existence when the High King (*árd-ri*), Tuathal Teachmhair (A.D. 130–60), created a fifth province so that the High Kings would not be embroiled in the politics of the four existing provinces. The sovereignty of the new province still survives today in the term *Royal Meath*. In *The Countess Cathleen* (*CPl.* 37), which takes place during a famine, the **Merchants** claim to have seen 900 oxen being driven through Meath. In *The Herne's Egg* (*CPl.* 673), the **Fool** is jealous of another fool, Johnny from Meath.

REFERENCES: Casey, Christine. *North Leinster*. London: Penguin, 1993; McGarry, James P. *Place Names in the Writings of William Butler Yeats*. Gerrards Cross: Colin Smythe, 1976.

MECHANICS INSTITUTE. *See* **ABBEY THEATRE**.

MEDICI, COSIMO DE' (1389–1464), merchant and head of the powerful Italian banking family. After his father's death, he allied himself with the bourgeois and the people of Florence against the merchants of the city, notably the Albizzi and the Pazzi. In 1433, these merchants banished the whole Medici family from Florence. One year later, he returned and, with the support of the community, quickly became the ruler of the city-state. His fame as a leader was established by his dedication to the arts and to artists and scholars. He founded several libraries, including the San Marco, and an Academy for Greek Studies. He was patron to such artists as Brunnelleschi, Donatello, Ghiberti, and Luca della Robbia. In his poem "To a Wealthy Man who promised a Second Subscription to the Dublin Municipal Gallery if it were proved the People wanted Pictures" (*CP.* 119), WBY recalls Cosimo who, regardless of politics, built the San Marco Library so that Italy might discover through books the art and wisdom of ancient Greece.

REFERENCES: Ames-Lewis, Francis, ed. *Cosimo 'Il Vecchio' de' Medici, 1389–1464*. Oxford: Clarendon, 1992; Vernon, Katherine D. E. *Cosimo de' Medici*. Port Washington, N.Y.: Kennikat, 1970.

MEMOIRS, prose collection. Published by Macmillan and Company in 1972, this volume brings together WBY's Journal, begun in December 1908, and the unpublished draft of his autobiography, which he started in 1915. Both are transcribed and edited by Denis Donoghue. While parts of the Journal were published by WBY in *Estrangement* (1926) and *The Death of Synge* (1928) and a selection made by Curtis Bradford in *Reflections* (Cuala Press, 1970), the full text of the Journal was published for the first time in *Memoirs*.

REFERENCES: Hamburger, Michael. *Art as Second Nature: Occasional Pieces, 1950–74*. Cheadle: Carcenet New Press, 1975; Sidnell, Michael. "Yeats in the Light of Day: The Text and Some Editions." In *Editing British and American Literature, 1880–1920*, ed. Eric W. Domville. New York: Garland Publisher, 1976; Stallworthy, Jon. "An Irish Window: Remaking W. B. Yeats." *Encounter* 43 (August 1974).

MENDEL, GREGOR [JOHANN] (1822–84), Austrian scientist and monk. He is credited with making important discoveries in heredity, although the significance of some of his findings was not realized until after his death. He entered the Augustinian monastery at Brno in 1843, and after teaching in a local high school, he was appointed prelate of the monastery in 1869. At the same time, he conducted scientific experiments using garden peas and was the first to accurately record hybridization data over several generations of the pea family. His classic account of his findings was published in 1866 and issued in pamphlet form in England as *Experiments in Plant Hybridization*, but the value of this work was not recognized until it was confirmed by three eminent biologists in 1900. He anticipated the discovery that fertilization of the female egg involved only one male sex cell, but he did not publish his findings. WBY alludes to Mendel's experiments with sweet peas in a note to "The Second Coming" (*VP*. 823).
    REFERENCES: Iltis, Hugo. *Life of Mendel*. Trans. Eden Paul and Cedar Paul. New York: W. W. Norton, 1932.

MERCHANT, FIRST, fictional character. In WBY's play *The Countess Cathleen*, the First Merchant, accompanied by the Second Merchant, arrives in the famine-stricken land of Ireland. Pretending to be Christians, the demon Merchants announce they will buy souls for gold and pay the boy **Teigue** to announce the news. They intensify the distress of the **Countess Cathleen**, telling her untruths until she agrees to sell her soul to relieve the suffering of the poor and to have the souls that the Merchants have bought set free. In the first production of *The Countess Cathleen*, May 1899, the parts of the First and Second Merchant were played by Marcus St. John and Trevor Lowe.

MERCHANT, SECOND. *See* **MERCHANT, FIRST**.

MERRION SQUARE, WBY residence in Dublin. After returning to Dublin from **Oxford** in 1922, WBY purchased a Georgian row house at 82 Merrion Square, an exclusive area close to the center of the city. He writes about his first impressions of the house, which he lived in for six years, in a series of letters to **Olivia Shakespear** (*WL*. 677–78, 689). He was especially pleased with the large drawing room in which to hold his regular Monday evenings "At Home." His return to Dublin coincided with an escalation of the violence of the Civil War. After selling the house to an architect in 1928, he moved to a rented apartment at 42 Fitzwilliam Square, Dublin. His ownership of the house in Merrion Square coincided with the period during which he was a member of the **Irish Senate**.

MERU [Mount Kailas], the golden mountain and central peak of the world. Mount Kailas, which is in the Himalayan range of Tibet, is known as Meru in the *Mahabharata* and in the Vedas. It is placed at the center of Paradise in Hindu mythology. WBY wrote the poem "Meru" (*CP*. 333) in 1934, just after he had studied Hindu writings and written an introduction for **Shri Purohit Swami's** translation of *The Holy Mountain* (1934) (*LE*. 139–55).

REFERENCES: O'Flaherty, Wendy Doniger, trans. *Hindu Myths: A Sourcebook Translated from the Sanskrit*. Harmondsworth, Middlesex: Penguin, 1975; Zimmer, Heinrich. *Myths and Symbols in Indian Art and Civilization*. Ed. Joseph Campbell. Washington, D.C.: Bollingen Foundation, 1946.

MERVILLE, a **Pollexfen** residence. Situated on Church Hill, a road leading southwest from **Sligo** (town) to Magheraboy, it was a substantial double-fronted house owned by WBY's grandfather **William Pollexfen**. WBY lived in the house for two years when he was a child and writes about the experience in some detail in his autobiography *Reveries over Childhood and Youth*. They were confusing years for young WBY. At Merville, all was quiet and serious, and his Pollexfen grandparents were cold and undemonstrative, in sharp contrast to the warmth and affection he received at his Grandmama Yeats's house in Upper Leeson Street, Dublin. Merville was sold in 1885. It is now known as Nazareth House.

REFERENCES: McGarry, James P. *Place Names in the Writings of William Butler Yeats*. Gerrards Cross: Colin Smythe, 1976; Murphy, William M. *Prodigal Father: The Life of John Butler Yeats (1839–1922)*. Ithaca, N.Y.: Cornell University Press, 1978.

METROPOLITAN SCHOOL OF ART, Kildare Street, Dublin. WBY attended art classes at the Metropolitan School of Art, May 1884–July 1885, but while he was there, he gave up painting and drawing entirely, to concentrate on writing (*EI*. 4). His father, **John B. Yeats**, taught at the school, and it was there that WBY met **AE** and the sculptors **John Hughes** and **Oliver Sheppard** (*A*. 79–82).

MEYER, KUNO (1858–1919), philologist and scholar. He was born in Hamburg, Germany. As professor of Celtic Literature at the University of Berlin and professor of Teutonic Languages at University College, **Liverpool**, he made a substantial contribution to the study of Celtic mythology, providing the Celtic Renaissance with authoritative scholarship and support. He delivered an important paper, "The Present State of Celtic Studies," at the first Pan-Celtic Conference held in Dublin in 1901. In 1903, he founded the School of Irish Learning, Dublin, later absorbed into the **Royal Irish Academy**. WBY did not meet Kuno Meyer for many years, although the scholar was acquainted with his friends, among them **Lady Gregory**. In 1893, WBY enthusiastically reviewed Meyer's scholarly translation of *The Vision of MacConglinne* (*UP1*. 261–63) as "one of the most singular and suggestive Irish books" he had encountered, and he borrowed the plot for his story "The Crucifixion of the Outcast" (*MY*. 147–56).

REFERENCES: Colum, Padraic. *Irish Elegies*. Dublin: Dolmen, 1976; Meyer, Kuno. *Miscellanea Hibernica*. New York: Johnson Reprint Corp., 1967; Meyer, Kuno, trans. *Selections from Ancient Irish Poetry*. London: Constable, 1911; Meyer, Kuno, and Nutt, Alfred T. *The Voyage of Bran*. New York: AMS, 1972.

MICHAEL ROBARTES AND THE DANCER, book of poems. First published by the **Cuala Press** in 1921, this collection of poetry shows WBY reaching a new level of frankness and maturity in his handling of personal and political themes. His marriage to **Georgie Hyde-Lees** in 1917, and the birth of a daughter in 1919, gave him more personal security, but he was deeply troubled by world violence and those anarchic forces that he believed anticipated the end of the Christian era. The poems in the collection may be divided into groups. There are the political poems, like "Easter 1916" (*CP*. 202) and "Meditations in Time of Civil War" (*CP*. 225), which examine his response to the Easter Rising and the continuing unrest in Ireland. There are the personal poems, like "Solomon and the Witch" (*CP*. 199) and "A Prayer for My Daughter" (*CP*. 211), which reflect his feelings as husband and father. Finally, there are those poems that explore his evolving philosophical system, as in "The Second Coming" (*CP*. 210). The **Michael Robartes** of the title is a tough man-of-action, a fictional character, who first appeared in the story "Rosa Alchemica" (*MY*. 267). His death is alluded to in "The Adoration of the Magi" (*MY*. 310).

REFERENCES: Davie, Donald. "Michael Robartes and the Dancer." In *An Honoured Guest: New Essays on W. B. Yeats*, ed. Denis Donoghue and J. R. Mulryne. London: Edward Arnold, 1965; Parkinson, Thomas, and Brannen, Anne, eds. *Michael Robartes and the Dancer: Manuscript Materials by W. B. Yeats*. Ithaca: Cornell University Press, 1994.

MICHELANGELO [BUONARROTI] (1475–1564), sculptor, painter, and poet. He was born in Caprese, near Florence, to a family of small-scale bankers. When he was thirteen, he was apprenticed to Ghirlandajo but left after one year, having apparently completed his apprenticeship. He found a generous patron, Lorenzo de' Medici, but with the overthrow of the **Medici** in 1494, he left for Bologna, where he completed the Tomb and Shrine of St. Dominic (1494–95). He traveled to Rome, where he accepted private commissions and completed his *Pietá*, now in the Basilica of St. Peter. His success as a sculptor led to commissions for vast projects, most of which remained uncompleted. He was commanded by Pope Julius II to build his tomb. When the project was halted because of lack of funds, the pope required him to work on a less expensive project, the painting of the ceiling of the **Sistine Chapel** (1508–12). The Sistine Chapel was the most important consecrated space in the Vatican. Michelangelo placed twelve figures, seven prophets and five sibyls, around the edge of the ceiling and filled the central domed area with nine religious scenes: three of the Creation of the

World, three from the story of **Adam** and Eve, and three devoted to **Noah** and the Flood. As he proceeded, working from over the entrance door toward the High Altar, he became freer and more spontaneous in his painting. The figures, while retaining a monumental quality, were imbued with complex human feeling, images of heroic and tragic humanity. When the ceiling was completed, he returned to sculpture, carving *Moses* (1513–15) for the tomb of Pope Julius. On the accession of Pope Leo X, a son of his former patron, Lorenzo de' Medici, Michelangelo went back to Florence, where he was involved in projects connected with the prestige of the Medici family, including the remodeling of the Medici palace and the Medici Chapel at San Lorenzo (1520–34). He left Florence for the last time in 1534. He spent his final years in Rome, completing *The Last Judgment* (1534) for the end wall of the Sistine Chapel and designing the Capitoline Square, the dome of St. Peter's, and various other buildings. Michelangelo's statues *Morning* and *Night*, which WBY saw in the Medici Chapel in 1907, are mentioned by name in the poem "Michael Robartes and the Dancer" (*CP*. 197). The painter is referred to in "An Acre of Grass" (*CP*. 346), while in "Under Ben Bulben" (*CP*. 397) and "Long-Legged Fly" (*CP*. 381), WBY alludes to Michelangelo's painting of the Sistine Chapel ceiling. WBY kept reproductions of Michelangelo in his home and, on one occasion, brought a reproduction of *Adam* to the Board of Censors to support his argument against censoring **George Bernard Shaw's** *The Black Girl in Search of God*.

REFERENCES: Bull, George, and Porter, Peter, eds. *Michelangelo: Life, Letters, Poetry*. Oxford and New York: Oxford University Press, 1987; Leites, Nathan C. *Art and Life: Aspects of Michelangelo*. New York: New York University Press, 1986; Loizeaux, Elizabeth Bergmann. *Yeats and the Visual Arts*. New Brunswick and London: Rutgers University Press, 1986; Seymour, Charles. *Michelangelo: The Sistine Chapel Ceiling*. New York: Norton, 1972.

MICHELOZZO [DE BARTOLOMEO] (1396–1472), architect and sculptor. He was a pupil of Brunelleschi and together with the sculptors Donatello and Ghiberti established the Renaissance style in Italy. As court architect and art adviser, Michelozzo accompanied **Cosimo de' Medici** into exile in Venice in 1433. A year later, he returned with him to Florence, where he designed the San Marco Library. He designed the Medici-Riccardi palace at Florence, the Medici Chapel at Santa Croce, and the Medici villa at Fiesole, noted for its terraced gardens. WBY recalls the planning of the San Marco Library in "To a Wealthy Man who promised a Second Subscription to the Dublin Municipal Gallery if it Were proved the People Wanted Pictures" (*CP*. 119). He is likely to have encountered Michelozzo's work when he visited Italy with **Lady Gregory** in 1907.

REFERENCE: Caplow, Harriet McN. *Michelozzo*. New York: Garland, 1977.

MIDDLETON, HENRY, cousin of WBY. He was only a little older than the poet and a close friend when WBY visited the Middleton homes at **Ballisodare** and **The Rosses** as a boy. He was handsome but somewhat eccentric in dress and manner and, in his later years, became a recluse. When WBY and his wife visited him in 1919, the poet climbed over the wall of Middleton's estate, **Elsinore**, to discover him lounging in the untidy sitting room, dressed in a white summer suit, claiming he was too busy to see anyone. WBY recalls this image of Henry Middleton in one of his last poems, "Three Songs to the One Burden" (*CP*. 371), published posthumously in *The Spectator*, 26 May 1939. The central character in WBY's novel **John Sherman** (1891) is partially based on Henry Middleton.

REFERENCE: Murphy, William M. *The Yeats Family and the Pollexfens of Sligo.* Dublin: Dolmen, 1971.

MIDDLETON, LUCY, cousin of WBY. She visited her uncle **George Pollexfen** when the poet was staying with him in **Sligo**, 1894–95. Lucy Middleton was reputed to have "second sight," and WBY recalls using her as a clairvoyant in his occult experiments (*M*. 75–76).

REFERENCE: Murphy, William M. *The Yeats Family and the Pollexfens of Sligo.* Dublin: Dolmen, 1971.

MIDDLETON, WILLIAM (1770–1832), WBY's maternal great-grandfather. He was a partner in the **Sligo** shipowning firm of Middleton and Mills and a widower of forty-three when he married fifteen-year-old Elizabeth Pollexfen Middleton (1798–1853) from the Channel Islands. Having nursed the sick during the Famine, he contracted cholera and died in 1832. WBY had a romantic view of his great-grandfather Middleton. In the poem "Are You Content?" (*CP*. 370), he refers to him as a smuggler, while in *Autobiography* (*M*. 102), he writes that the ship bringing William Middleton's possessions to Sligo, including a sword and a fine clock, had been wrecked at sea. It is this "grandfather" whose courage WBY envies in *Reveries over Childhood and Youth* (*A*. 36).

REFERENCE: Murphy, William M. *The Yeats Family and the Pollexfens of Sligo.* Dublin: Dolmen, 1971.

MIDDLETON, WILLIAM (1820–82), son of **William Middleton** and great-uncle to WBY. He lived at **Elsinore, Rosses Point**, and was a partner of **William Pollexfen**, WBY's maternal grandfather, in the family shipping and grain business, Middleton and Pollexfen. The partners also owned the Sligo Steam Navigation Company. William Middleton was a shrewd businessman, and under him the company prospered. After his death, the family business went into decline.

REFERENCE: Murphy, William M. *The Yeats Family and the Pollexfens of Sligo.* Dublin: Dolmen, 1971.

MIDHIR, son of the Dagda, ruler of the **Sídhe**. He lives at the *sídh* (fairy mound) of Bri Leith (now Slieve Callory), west of Ardagh, County Longford, and enlists the help of **Aengus** to make **Étain**, the loveliest of all the women in Ireland, fall in love with him. He marries her and brings her to his palace, but his first wife is jealous and transforms her into a fly. When Étain is reborn as a mortal, she marries **King Eochaid**, but Midhir pursues her and wins her back in a game of chess. He embraces her, and together they rise up into the air and are seen flying away in the shape of swans. King Eochaid pursues them and threatens to destroy the *sídh*, but Midhir promises to return Étain if Eochaid can choose her from among fifty women—all in the likeness of Étain. King Eochaid does so but later discovers he has chosen not Étain his wife but his daughter. See also "Baile and Aillinn" (*CP*. 459) and "The Harp of Aengus" (*CP*. 471).

REFERENCES: Ellis, Peter Berresford. *Dictionary of Celtic Mythology*. New York: Oxford University Press, 1992; Green, Miranda J. *Dictionary of Celtic Myth and Legend*. London: Thames & Hudson, 1992; Mac Cana, Proinsias. *Celtic Mythology*. Feltham, Middlesex: Newnes, 1983.

MILLIGAN, ALICE (1866–1953), playwright, poet, and political activist. She was born in Omagh, County Tyrone, the daughter of a Protestant businessman. After her education at Methodist College, Belfast, and King's College, London, she determined to learn Irish and moved to Dublin. There, she became active in nationalist politics. As organizer for the Gaelic League, she staged historical tableaux to raise funds to promote the study of Irish. With her friend Ethna Carbery (pen name of Anna Johnston [1866–1902], the daughter of an **Ulster** Fenian), she founded the short-lived monthly papers *The Northern Patriot* and *The Shan Van Vocht*. She wrote one-act plays, among them *The Last Feast of the Fianna* and *Red Hugh*, featuring Irish mythological and historical figures. *The Last Feast of the Fianna* was presented by the **Irish Literary Theatre** in 1900, while *Red Hugh* was produced by **W. G. Fay** for a drama festival organized by Cumann na nGaedheal in 1901. In his article "Plans and Methods" (*UP2*. 202), WBY wrote that *The Last Feast of the Fianna* was like the old Irish drama, but later he admitted it was undramatic (*A*. 429). He was so impressed with the acting in *Red Hugh* that he gave W. G. Fay permission to perform **Cathleen Ni Houlihan** (*A*. 449). A later play by Alice Milligan, *The Daughter of Donagh*, was presented by the **Abbey Theatre** in 1920. She published a novel, *A Royal Democrat* (1892), in addition to books of poetry and a biography of **Wolfe Tone** (1898). Saddened by the political division of Ireland, she retired from politics in 1922 and wrote little for the rest of her life. Under the pseudonym Iris Olkryn, she sent a long letter to *United Ireland*, 16 December 1893, disagreeing with comments made by WBY that political rhetoric had hampered the literary arts in Ireland. In a reply (*UP1*. 306–7), WBY, who was favorably disposed toward her, acknowledged her "very beautiful letter."

REFERENCES: Hogan, Robert, ed. *Dictionary of Irish Literature*. Rev. ed. Westport, Conn.: Greenwood, 1996; MacDonagh, Thomas. "The Best Living Irish Poet." *The Irish Review*, no. 4 (September–November 1915); MacManus, Anna. *We Sang for Ireland: Poems of Ethna Carbery, Seamus MacManus, and Alice Milligan*. Dublin: Gill, 1950; Mangan, Henry, ed. *Poems by Alice Milligan*. Dublin: Gill, 1954.

MILTON, JOHN (1608–74), poet and pamphleteer. He was born in London and educated at St. Paul's School and Christ's College, Cambridge. He started writing while at college, and before he was thirty, he had produced some of the greatest poetry in the English language, including "Ode on the Morning of Christ's Nativity," "L'Allegro," "Il Penseroso," and the elegy "Lycidas." His masque *Comus*, which WBY cites in the prologue to *The Death of Cuchulain*, was written in 1634 to celebrate a reunion of the Egerton family at Ludlow Castle. After spending a year in Italy, he supported the Presbyterians in their efforts to reform the established Church of England. His *Areopagitica* (1644), which argued against government censorship, antagonized the supporters of **Oliver Cromwell**. He regained their favor in 1649, when he published *The Tenure of Kings and Magistrates*, a document that supported the imprisonment of Charles I and argued for his execution. He was appointed to a Latin secretaryship in the Commonwealth government, but with the restoration of Charles II to the English throne, he went into hiding in Finsbury, a London suburb. There he devoted himself to his monumental epics, *Paradise Lost* (1667) and *Paradise Regained* (1671). He escaped from London to Chalfont St. Giles during the Great Plague, 1665–66, and later returned to Finsbury, where he died. WBY regarded Milton as one of the greatest writers and spoke of him in the company of **Shakespeare** and **Dante**, all of whom scorned rhetoric and wrote out of personal experience. In his essays, WBY quotes frequently from *Paradise Lost*, while in "The Phases of the Moon" (*CP*. 183), he refers to "Milton's Platonist," an allusion to *The Lonely Tower*, an illustration by **Samuel Palmer** reproduced in *The Shorter Poems of John Milton* (1889). In his introduction to *The Oxford Book of Modern Verse* (*LE*. 202), writing about Gerard Manley Hopkins and "sprung rhythm," he notes that Milton used a similar rhythm in his *Samson Agonistes* (1671), while in "Four Years: 1887–1891" (*A*. 145), he remarks that when **William Morris** criticized Milton for his rhetoric, the observation reflected more on Morris than on Milton. A copy of *Paradise Lost*, published in 1906, with illustrations by **William Blake**, and three other books of Milton's verse were in WBY's library (*OS*. nos. 1319–22).

REFERENCES: Brown, Cedric C. *John Milton: A Literary Life*. New York: St. Martin's, 1995; Schiffhorst, Gerald J. *John Milton*. New York: Continuum, 1990.

MINNALOUSHE, black Persian cat belonging to **Maud Gonne** and her daughter **Iseult**. It is the name of the cat referred to by the First Musician in the opening and closing choruses of WBY's play *The Cat and the Moon* (*CPl*. 461).

MINOS, king of Crete, in Greek mythology. He was the son of Zeus and **Europa** and husband to Pasiphaë. His children with Pasiphaë were Androgeus, Ariadne, and Phaedra. In "The Delphic Oracle upon Plotinus" (*CP*. 307), WBY names him as one of the three judges who welcome the philosopher **Plotinus** to the Greek heaven. In his essay "Blake's Illustrations to Dante" (*EI*. 143), WBY describes the figure of Minos in a drawing by the little-known nineteenth-century German artist Adolph Stürler.

MITCHEL, JOHN (1815–75), journalist, author, and patriot. He was born near Dungiven, County Derry, the son of a Presbyterian minister. Educated at Newry Grammar School and **Trinity College**, Dublin, he worked for a time as a bank clerk in Derry and in a lawyer's office in Newry, **County Down**. About 1842, he met **Charles Gavan Duffy** and **Thomas Davis** and became involved in nationalist politics, as a member of the Young Ireland Society. In 1843, he qualified as a lawyer, joined the Repeal Association, and in 1845, replaced Thomas Davis on the staff of *The Nation*. One of the finest journalists of the century, he left *The Nation* in 1847 to found *The United Irishman*, which became a vehicle for his more radical views. He advocated the use of force to achieve agrarian reform in Ireland and, in 1848, was sentenced to transportation to a penal colony on charges of treason. Most of his sentence was spent in Tasmania (**Van Diemen's Land**), where he lived with his wife and children. In 1854, he published *Jail Journal*, an account of his five years in prison. He escaped to America, where he worked as a journalist, gaining notoriety for his defense of slavery. After the American Civil War, he became editor of the New York *Daily News*. Maintaining his extremist views of Irish politics, he returned to Ireland in 1874 and was elected M.P. for Tipperary, but he was declared ineligible because he was a convicted felon. The constituency reelected him in 1875, but he died a few days later. Among his many publications were his critical introductions to the poems of Thomas Davis and **James Clarence Mangan**, on which WBY drew heavily. WBY did not agree with Mitchel's call for a violent solution to the Irish problem, but he believed him to be the only prose writer of style among the Young Irelanders (*A*. 204). He quotes from Mitchel's *Jail Journal* in "Under Ben Bulben" (*CP*. 397) and includes it in his list of "Best Irish Books" (*UP1*. 386).

REFERENCES: Hogan, Robert, ed. *Dictionary of Irish Literature*. Rev. ed. Westport, Conn.: Greenwood, 1996; Mitchel, John. *Jail Journal: With an Introductory Narrative of Transactions in Ireland*, with a critical introduction by Thomas Flanagan. Dublin: University Press of Ireland, 1982; O'Hegarty, P. S. *John Mitchel: An Appreciation, with Some Account of Young Ireland*. Dublin: Maunsel, 1917.

MITCHELL, SUSAN [LANGSTAFF] (1866–1926), poet and satirist. She was born at Carrick-on-Shannon, County Leitrim, daughter of the manager of the Provincial Bank. Her father died when she was six, and she was sent to Dublin to live with two aunts. She attended a private school in Morehampton Road. In 1897, she went to London for treatment of an illness that impaired her hearing. There she remained for two years, staying with **John B. Yeats** and his family in **Bedford Park**, both as a companion to **Lily Yeats** and as a paying guest. In 1901, she became assistant editor of *The Irish Homestead* and its successor *The Irish Statesman*, both edited by her friend **AE**. Her first collection of satiric verse, *Aids to the Immortality of Certain Persons, Charitably Administered*, appeared in 1908. A collection of religious verse, *The Living Chalice*, appeared in 1908 (she dedicated the second edition in 1913 to John B. Yeats), while a further collection *Frankincense and Myrrh* was published in 1912. She was a generous and kind Dublin hostess, who numbered among her friends the leading members of the Irish Literary Revival, including WBY, but she maintained a running battle with **George Moore**, whose pompous manner and arrogance irritated her. Her wit and charm appear in her parody on the *Playboy* riots, *The Abbey Row, Not Edited by W. B. Yeats* (1907), and in *Secret Springs of Dublin Song* (1918), but she could be a severe and wounding critic. She published a vigorous, stinging article on WBY and his management of the **Abbey Theatre** in *Sinn Féin*, 8 May 1909, while in 1916, she contributed a mocking study of George Moore to a series called *Irishmen Today*.

REFERENCES: Hogan, Robert, ed. *Dictionary of Irish Literature*. Rev. ed. Westport, Conn.: Greenwood, 1996; Kain, Richard M. *Susan L. Mitchell*. Lewisburg, Pa.: Bucknell University Press, 1972; Murphy, William. *Family Secrets: William Butler Yeats and His Relatives*. Syracuse, N.Y.: Syracuse University Press, 1995.

MOLAY, JACQUES DE (1243–1314), last grand master of the Knights Templar. He took part in the defense of Palestine against the Saracens, but when the Templars were driven from the Holy Land, he moved to Cyprus to reorganize. Jealous of their power and wealth, Philip IV of France ordered the Knights Templar to be suppressed. Their property was confiscated, and de Molay, with many of the Knights, was summoned to France, where he was charged, in 1307, with heresy. All were tortured. De Molay admitted certain charges but recanted and was burned at the stake. In "Meditations in Time of Civil War" (*CP*. 225), WBY uses the cry of vengeance for his murder from de Molay's supporters as a symbol of imminent world disorder.

REFERENCES: Addison, Charles G. *The Knights Templar History*. 1912. Reprint, New York: AMS, 1978; Howarth, Stephen. *The Knights Templar*. 1982. Reprint, New York: Dorset, 1991.

MOLESWORTH HALL, home of the **Irish National Theatre Society**, 1903–4. When the **Irish Literary Theatre** merged with the **Irish National Dramatic Society** to form the Irish National Theatre Society, they acquired the use of premises at Molesworth Hall, in the center of Dublin, between Kildare Street and Dawson Street. The Molesworth Hall seated 300 people, while the stage was sixteen feet by twelve feet, with a sixteen-foot-high opening. The first performance of the new Society was given 14 March 1903, when WBY's *The Hour-Glass* was staged in a double bill with **Lady Gregory's** *Twenty-Five*. WBY lectured during the intermission on "The Reform of the Theatre," a model of a stage by **Gordon Craig** on the table beside him. The next performance of the Irish National Theatre Society was given 8 October 1903. The evening featured two premieres, WBY's *The King's Threshold* and **J. M.**

Synge's *In the Shadow of the Glen.* **Maud Gonne** and others left the hall as a mark of protest against Synge's play, in which a young woman leaves her elderly husband for a loquacious, young tramp. **Padraic Colum's** *The Broken Soil* was performed 3 December 1903, followed by WBY's ***The Shadowy Waters***, 14 January 1904, and Synge's *Riders to the Sea*, 25 January 1904. It was after the performance of *The King's Threshold* that WBY appealed from the stage for money to carry on the work of the new Society, and the wealthy **Annie F. Horniman** is reported to have said, "I will give you a theatre." The **Abbey Theatre** opened 27 December 1904.

REFERENCES: Hunt, Hugh. *The Abbey: Ireland's National Theatre, 1904–1979.* Dublin: Gill & Macmillan, 1979; Robinson, Lennox. *Ireland's Abbey Theatre: A History, 1899–1951.* London: Sidgwick and Jackson, 1951.

MONTASHIGI. *See* **MOTOSHIGÉ, BISHU OSAFUNÉ.**

MONTENEGRO, mountainous region in the former Yugoslavia. The region belonged to Serbia. It was part of the Turkish Empire from 1499 to 1799, when it was granted independence. In 1918, Montenegro was again united with Serbia, and in 1946, it became a Yugoslav republic. In the poem "The Statesman's Holiday" (*CP.* 389), WBY refers to a one-stringed Montenegrin lute that was given to him by **Lady Gregory** on her return from holiday in Europe, April 1901. In ***On the Boiler*** (*LE.* 250), he recalls someone in Monte Carlo talking about a man playing a stringed instrument. He follows this by quoting the poem "The Statesman's Holiday."

MOONEEN (Irish: *Moínín*) [little bog], townland adjacent to Esserkelly, near **Ardrahan, Galway** (county). There, **Robert Gregory**, a fine horseman, made a jump so dangerous that many of the onlookers were unable to watch him. See also "In Memory of Major Robert Gregory" (*CP.* 148).

REFERENCE: McGarry, James P. *Place Names in the Writings of William Butler Yeats.* Gerrards Cross: Colin Smythe, 1976.

MOORE, GEORGE [AUGUSTUS] (1852–1933), novelist and short story writer. Born in **Mayo** (county), the son of a wealthy landowner, he was educated at Oscott College, Birmingham, England. After the death of his father in 1870, he rebelled against his family traditions and went to Paris in 1873 to study painting. There, he made the acquaintance of the leading Impressionist painters, among them Manet, Monet, Renoir, Dégas, and Sisley. Frustrated with his painting talent, he moved to London, where he began writing poetry and novels modeled on **Balzac**, Zola, Huysmans, Henry James, and others. An early novel, *A Modern Lover* (1883), showed promise, but it was not until the publication of *Esther Waters*, in 1894, that he was recognized as a major literary talent. His reputation as an art and drama critic grew rapidly during this period. He was one of the founders of the Independent Theatre in 1890 and wrote *The Strike at Arlingford*

(1893), a drama modeled on **Ibsen**. With the formation of the **Irish Literary Theatre** in 1899, he enthusiastically joined WBY, **Edward Martyn**, and **Lady Gregory**, and as the person with the most theater experience, he helped direct the plays, and he rewrote Martyn's play *The Tale of the Town* as *The Bending of the Bough*. He thought WBY's ***The Countess Cathleen*** the best verse play written since **Shakespeare**, and they collaborated on the writing of ***Diarmuid and Grania***, which was presented at the Gaiety Theatre, Dublin, 1901, but the process was not a happy one. The personal difficulties he encountered with WBY and his literary associates forced him to return to London in 1911, but despite quarreling with WBY and almost every Irish literary figure of note, the years he spent in Dublin were among the most creatively invigorating of his career. His collection of short stories *The Untilled Field* (1903) and his novel *The Lake* (1905) were inspired by his return to Ireland. His three-volume autobiography, *Hail and Farewell* (1911, 1912, 1914), gave a highly subjective view of his years in Dublin and aroused bitter resentment from WBY and Lady Gregory. Although WBY and Moore collaborated in the writing of *Diarmuid and Grania*, their views of the drama were directly opposed. Moore believed totally in naturalism, while WBY was moved by symbol and suggestion. They were incompatible and quarreled a great deal (*A.* 434–36). In ***Dramatis Personae*** (*A.* 401–7), WBY writes about Moore, focusing on his coarseness, his argumentative nature, his lechery, and his vicious tongue. He describes the rehearsals for *The Countess Cathleen* (*A.* 413–18) and the rewriting of *The Tale of the Town* (*A.* 425–30). WBY satirizes Moore and his friendship with his cousin Edward Martyn in his short play ***The Cat and the Moon***.

REFERENCES: Brown, Malcolm. *George Moore: A Reconsideration.* Seattle: University of Washington Press, 1955; Cunard, Nancy. *GM: Memories of George Moore.* London: Hart-Davis, 1956; Henn, Thomas Rice. *Last Essays: Mainly on Anglo-Irish Literature.* New York: Barnes & Noble, 1976; Hogan, Robert, and Kilroy, James. *The Irish Literary Theatre, 1899–1901.* Dublin: Dolmen, 1975; Hone, Joseph. *The Life of George Moore.* New York: Macmillan, 1936; Hughes, Douglas, ed. *The Man of Wax: Critical Essays on George Moore.* New York: New York University Press, 1971.

MOORE, T[HOMAS] STURGE (1870–1944), poet, playwright, critic, and graphic designer. He was born in Hastings, England, the eldest son of Daniel Moore, a physician, and his second wife, Henrietta. He attended Dulwich College but had to leave because of illness and continued his education at home. He became a designer with the Vale Press and, in 1903, married his half cousin, Marie Appia. They had two children. Among his published works were *The Vine-Dresser and Other Poems* (1899), *Absalom* (1903), *Marianne* (1911), *The Powers of the Air* (1920), *Judas* (1923), and *The Unknown Known* (1939). WBY was introduced to T. Sturge Moore in 1899, and they formed a close collaboration, Moore helping with the verse speaking in the first production of ***The Countess Cathleen*** and with set designs for the **Abbey Theatre**, most notably ***The Hour-Glass*** (1903) and ***The Shadowy Waters*** (1904) (*KLIII.* 336–39). Their correspondence,

1901–37, reveals many insights into WBY's aesthetic tastes and his developing knowledge of stagecraft. As a designer, WBY found T. Sturge Moore impractical, and he was not impressed with his skills as a teacher of verse speaking (*KLIII.* 402). Their most satisfactory collaboration appeared to be in book design. Between 1916 and 1940, T. Sturge Moore designed the covers for twelve of WBY's books, including *Four Plays for Dancers* (1921), *The Tower* (1928), and *The Winding Stair and Other Poems* (1933), and was recommended by WBY to the young American academic Horace Reynolds for the cover design of *Letters to the New Island* (1934). He designed bookplates for members of WBY's family. In 1931, T. Sturge Moore introduced WBY to **Shri Purohit Swami**. WBY included six poems by T. Sturge Moore in *The Oxford Book of Modern Verse* (1936), and collections of his poems and plays were in WBY's library (*OS*. nos. 1358–76).

REFERENCES: Bridges, Ursula, ed. *W. B. Yeats and T. Sturge Moore: Their Correspondence, 1901–1937*. London: Routledge & Kegan Paul, 1953; Easton, Malcolm. *T. Sturge Moore (1870–1944): Contributions to the Art of the Book & Collaborations with Yeats: Catalogue of an Exhibition*. Hull: University of Hull, 1970.

MORRELL, LADY OTTOLINE (1873–1938), daughter of the sixth duke of Portland. With her husband, Philip Morrell, a Liberal M.P. whom she married in 1902, Lady Ottoline lived at the Manor House, Garsington, Oxfordshire, 1915–28, providing hospitality to writers and artists, among them Virginia Woolf and members of the Bloomsbury group. In 1928, the Morrells sold Garsington and moved to Gower Street, London. WBY visited Lady Ottoline when he was staying in **Oxford** during the 1920s (*WL*. 679, 725). It was in her London home, in 1916, that he first saw the dancer **Michio Ito**. In "Ancestral Houses" (*CP*. 225), he recalls the Italianate gardens of the manor house, with peacocks, fine lawns, graveled paths, and classical garden ornaments. The poem "Spilt Milk" (*CP*. 271) grew out of a discussion he had with Lady Ottoline.

REFERENCES: Darroch, Sandra Jobson. *Ottoline: The Life of Lady Ottoline Morrell.* New York: Coward, McCann & Geoghegan, 1975; Heilbrun, Carolyn G., ed. *Lady Ottoline's Album.* New York: Knopf, 1976; Morrell, Lady Ottoline. *Memoirs of Lady Ottoline Morrell: A Study in Friendship.* Ed. Robert Gathorne-Hardy. New York: Knopf, 1964; Seymour, Miranda. *Ottoline Morrell: Life on the Grand Scale.* New York: Farrar, Straus & Giroux, 1993.

MORRIGU (Irish: *Morrigan*) [phantom queen], goddess of war and death. She is a triple-aspected goddess, with the power to change her shape; one of the three daughters of **Cailitin**, killed with his twenty-seven sons by **Cuchulain** at the Battle of the Ford, during the *Táin Bó Cuailnge*. After his death, his wife gives birth to deformed triplets: the Morrigu, Bodb, and Macha. They are trained in magic arts by **Queen Maeve** and taught to hate Cuchulain. When Cuchulain meets the Morrigu in the guise of a young girl, he rejects her offer of love, and in revenge, she attacks him. In the ensuing struggle, she is wounded and vows to have his life. In WBY's play *The Death of Cuchulain*, the Morrigu appears as a great black bird, triumphantly alighting on Cuchulain's shoulder as he dies from wounds received in battle.

REFERENCES: Ellis, Peter Berresford. *Dictionary of Celtic Mythology*. New York: Oxford University Press, 1992; Green, Miranda J. *Dictionary of Celtic Myth and Legend*. London: Thames & Hudson, 1992; Mac Cana, Proinsias. *Celtic Mythology*. Feltham, Middlesex: Newnes, 1983.

MORRIS, WILLIAM (1834–96), poet, painter, craftsman, and socialist. He was born in London and educated at Marlborough College and Oxford University. He lived at Kelmscott House, Upper Mall, Hammersmith, a house formerly known as The Retreat but renamed by Morris after his country home at Kelmscott, near **Oxford**. His London home was the center of late nineteenth-century English political and aesthetic life. Literary acquaintances and members of the Socialist League met regularly at the nearby Hammersmith Club each Sunday evening to hear socialist lectures and debate. WBY attended these meetings and was one of a small elite invited to remain for supper in Kelmscott House, after the main business of the evening was over. He was flattered and enthusiastically records these visits, describing his pleasure at being part of a group that sat conversing with Morris around a long unpolished and unpainted table (*A*. 139–40). At these gatherings, WBY met **George Bernard Shaw**, Sydney Cockerell, and Prince Kropotkin, the anarchist, among others. He took French lessons at Kelmscott House, but when his father insisted that he take his sisters to the class, he decided to leave (*A*. 143). He had been familiar with Morris's writing since childhood, and later, he was to describe Morris's prose romances as the only books he ever read slowly so that he would not arrive too quickly at the end (*A*. 141). He first met Morris at the **Contemporary Club**, Dublin, 1886, when Morris spoke about socialism and read aloud his poem "Sigurd the Volsung" (1876). His strong, dynamic personality had a profound influence on WBY. He became a role model so that, in 1919, he could still say that Morris was his "chief of men" (*LE*. 42). In "Four Years: 1887–1891" (*A*. 141), written in 1922, he claimed that although he now thought little of Morris's poetry, if an angel offered him a choice, he would choose to live Morris's life rather than his own. In the essay "The Happiest of the Poets" (*EI*. 53–64), he praised *The Well at the World's End*, paying tribute to its inspired poetic vision. Morris was impressed with *The Wanderings of Oisin* and promised to write a review for his socialist magazine *The Commonweal* (1885–93), but the review did not appear (*A*. 146).

REFERENCES: Cullingford, Elizabeth. *Yeats, Ireland and Fascism*. New York and London: New York University Press, 1981; Faulkner, Peter. *William Morris and W. B. Yeats*. Dublin: Dolmen, 1962; Loizeaux, Elizabeth Bergmann. *Yeats and the Visual Arts*. New Brunswick and London: Rutgers University Press, 1986; Lourie, Margaret A. "The Embodiment of Dreams: William Morris' 'Blue Closet Group.' " *Victorian Poetry* 15, no. 2 (1977).

MOSADA, poetic drama. It appeared in the *Dublin University Review* in June 1886, and an offprint edition, with paper cover and a frontispiece by **John B. Yeats**, was published by Sealy, Bryers & Walker, Dublin, in 1886. It was WBY's first published work in book form. The text was included in *The Wanderings of Oisin and Other Poems* (1889), but it was not reprinted during the author's lifetime. In *Mosada*, which is set in fifteenth-century Spain, the central character is the Moorish girl Mosada. After being taken prisoner by the Inquisition, which is attempting to stamp out heathen practices among the Moors, she takes poison in her prison cell in Granada. As she lies dying, she is approached by Ebremar, the Grand Inquisitor. He reveals that he is her former lover, Gomez, and that he plans to forsake the Inquisition and run away with her. She dies in his arms. He resumes his former identity and leaves to watch the other prisoners being burned at the stake. The play is in three short scenes, each with a different setting, and there are five characters: Mosada and Ebremar, two Inquisitors, and Cola, a lame Moorish boy. There is no record of any production of the play. The play was reviewed by **Katharine Tynan** in the *Irish Monthly*, March 1887.

REFERENCE: Bornstein, George, ed. *The Early Poetry, Vol. 1: Mosada and the Island of Statues*. Ithaca and London: Cornell University Press, 1987.

MOTOSHIGÉ, BISHU OSAFUNÉ, fourteenth-century Japanese swordsmith in the era of Ōei (1394–1428). He made the short samurai sword that **Junzo Sato** gave to WBY on his American tour in 1920. The sword had been in the Sato family for 550 years. WBY was so overwhelmed by the gesture that he made provision in his will for the sword to be returned to Sato's family. In "A Dialogue of Self and Soul" (*CP*. 265), WBY misspells the name as "Montashigi."

MOUNTAIN OF ABIEGNOS. *See* **ABIEGNOS**.

MOYTURA (Irish: *Magh Tuiredh*) [plain of towers], plain overlooking Lough Arrow in **Sligo** (county). It was the site of two important battles in Irish mythology. In the first, the **Tuatha dé Danaan**, led by Nuada, successfully defeated the **Firbolg**. In the second battle, the Tuatha dé Danaan fought the **Fomorians**. The slaughter was great on both sides. Nuada was killed by **Balor**, who was, in turn, slain by **Lugh**. The second battle of Moytura heralded the demise of the Tuatha dé Danaan. After the Milesian invasion, they were driven underground, and with the coming of Christianity to Ireland, they lost their godlike power and were relegated to the status of fairies. See also *The Countess Cathleen* (*CPl.* 49).

REFERENCE: Dames, Michael. *Mythic Ireland*. 1992. Reprint, New York: Thames & Hudson, 1996.

MUCKANISH (Irish: *Inis-na-Muc*) [promontory of the seals], headland on the coast of **County Clare.** *Muc* is the Irish word for pig, and along the west coast, the seals are called sea-pigs. In WBY's play *The Dreaming of the Bones* (*CPl.* 435), the **Young Man** watches for a boat to put in at Muckanish to take him to safety.

REFERENCES: Ellis, Peter Berresford. *Dictionary of Celtic Mythology.* New York: Oxford University Press, 1992; McGarry, James P. *Place Names in the Writings of William Butler Yeats.* Gerrards Cross: Colin Smythe, 1976.

MUIRTHEMNE, fertile plain in County Louth, stretching from the Cooley Mountains to the **Boyne**. It was the site of the major battle in the epic *Táin Bó Cuailnge*, and **Cuchulain** had a home there. In WBY's dramatic poem "Baile and Aillinn" (*CP.* 459), the lovers plan to marry at Muirthemne, while in *The Death of Cuchulain* (*CPl.* 695), **Eithne Inguba** tells Cuchulain that **Queen Maeve** and her army have burned his home at Muirthemne.

REFERENCE: McGarry, James P. *Place Names in the Writings of William Butler Yeats.* Gerrards Cross: Colin Smythe, 1976.

MULHOLLAND, ROSA (1841–1921), poet, short story writer, and novelist. She was born in Belfast, Northern Ireland, the daughter of a Belfast doctor, and was educated at home. Charles Dickens encouraged her early work, printing her stories in *Household Words*, and she wrote a number of novels, from the early *Dunmara* (1864), published under the pseudonym Ruth Murray, to *The Wild Birds of Killeevy* (1883) and *The Return of Mary O'Murrough* (1910). Her best-known work was *A Fair Emigrant* (1888). Her collections of verse included *Narcissa's Ring* (1916) and *O'Loughlin of Clare* (1916). Having spent a good deal of her early life in the west of Ireland, she wrote with some understanding of the Irish peasantry, but in a style romantic and religious. In 1891, at the age of fifty, she married the historian John T. Gilbert (1829–98), secretary of the Dublin Public Record Office. He was the author of the significant *History of the City of Dublin* (1854) and *History of the Viceroys of Ireland*. After his death, Rosa Mulholland published a biography, *Life of Sir John T. Gilbert* (1905). WBY was pleased with her review of *The Wanderings of Oisin and Other Poems*, which appeared in the *Irish Monthly*, May 1899. He considered two of her short stories for inclusion in *Representative Irish Tales* but chose the hitherto unpublished "The Hungry Death," a sad love story, because he felt the other two might as easily have been set elsewhere than in Ireland. She was one of the few contemporaries included in H. Halliday Sparling's *Irish Minstrelsy* (1887).

REFERENCE: Hogan, Robert, ed. *Dictionary of Irish Literature.* Rev. ed. Westport, Conn.: Greenwood, 1996.

MUNICIPAL GALLERY OF MODERN ART, Dublin. Located in Parnell Square, it is housed in a building that was formerly Charlemont House, a magnificent three-storied mansion built for the Earl of Charlemont (1728–99), a patron of the arts. The present gallery opened in 1930, the collection being transferred from the Dublin Municipal Gallery, 17 Harcourt Street, Dublin. The Municipal Gallery of Modern Art houses a fine collection of Irish and European paintings, including part of the **Hugh Lane** bequest, and portraits of the outstanding personalities in Ireland through the early years of the twentieth century. In the elegy "The Municipal Gallery Revisited" (*CP.* 368), completed in September 1937, WBY catalogs those portraits of Irish heroes and men of letters, all friends and acquaintances, that had moved him on a recent visit to the gallery. He spoke of this visit when he addressed the **Irish Academy of Letters**, 17 August 1937, a speech later published in *A Speech and Two Poems* (1937). The gallery is now known as the Hugh Lane Municipal Gallery of Modern Art.

REFERENCE: McGarry, James P. *Place Names in the Writings of William Butler Yeats.* Gerrards Cross: Colin Smythe, 1976.

MUNSTER (Irish: *Mughan-ster*), most southerly of the four provinces of modern Ireland. According to tradition, when the **Tuatha dé Danaan** were ousted by the Milesians, they retreated to Munster, where they lived in the fairy mounds, or **sídh**. Thus, the province has a reputation for fairy lore and magic. There are a number of references to Munster in the writings of WBY. It is included in the poem "The Dedication to a Book of Stories Selected from the Irish Novelists" (*CP.* 51), while in *The Unicorn from the Stars* (*CPl.* 341), Martin, the hero, refers to a poem by Egan O'Rahilly, a Munster poet of the early eighteenth century. Traditionally, there has been rivalry between Munster and neighboring **Connacht**. In "Hanrahan and Cathleen, the Daughter of Houlihan" (*MY.* 213), the men are listening to a song about a Munster man and a Connacht man quarreling about their two provinces, while in *The Herne's Egg* (*CPl.* 663), Pat, a soldier from Connacht, challenges the ability of a Munster devil to do any mischief to a man from Connacht.

REFERENCE: McGarry, James P. *Place Names in the Writings of William Butler Yeats.* Gerrards Cross: Colin Smythe, 1976.

MURIAS. *See* **FALIAS**.

MURROUGH (Irish: *Murchadh*), son of **Brian Boru**, High King of Ireland. Murrough was killed by the Danes in 1014 at the Battle of **Clontarf**. In WBY's poem "The Grey Rock" (*CP.* 115), Murrough was joined in the battle by his friend Dubhlaing O'Hartagan, who had been promised by Aoibheal, a fairy goddess, 200 years of life if he refused to take part. Dubhlaing rejected her offer and died with Murrough. See also **Grey Rock**.

REFERENCE: Otway–Ruthven, A. J. *A History of Medieval Ireland.* New York: St. Martin's Press, 1980.

MYERS, FREDERIC [WILLIAM HENRY] (1843–1901), pioneer in psychical research. He was the founder of the Society for Psychical Research and the author of a number of influential books on spiritualism, including *Science and the*

Future Life (1893) and *Human Personality and Its Survival of Bodily Death* (1903), a study of subliminal consciousness. In a note to "Swedenborg, Mediums, and the Desolate Places" (*LE*. 60, 323), WBY acknowledges Myers as a major source for the essay, while in **The Words upon the Window-Pane** (*CPl*. 598), **John Corbet**, a Cambridge doctoral student, refers skeptically to Myers's *Human Personality*. See also "Poetry and Tradition" (*EI*. 249).

REFERENCES: Gauld, Alan. *The Founders of Psychical Research*. New York: Schocken, 1968. James, William, ed. "Frederic Myers' Services to Psychology." In *Memories and Studies*. New York: Greenwood, 1968; Myers, Frederic. *Human Personality and Its Survival of Bodily Death*. 1907. Reprint, New Hyde Park, N.Y.: University Books, 1961.

MYTHOLOGIES. *See* **CELTIC TWILIGHT, THE**.

N
―――――――――

NAOISE, eldest of the three sons of **Usna**. The story of Naoise and his lover **Deirdre** is told in the **Ulster** Cycle of mythological tales. Deirdre is kept in seclusion by **Conchubar**. She catches sight of Naoise when he is with his brothers, Ainnle and **Ardan**, and falls in love with him. Initially, Naoise resists her advances but then agrees to elope with her to Scotland. There, they ask for protection from the Scottish king. When Conchubar finds their whereabouts, he sends **Fergus Mac Roich** to bring them back to Ulster. Despite a warning given to Deirdre in a dream, they return home, assured of Fergus's protection. As they approach Conchubar's palace at **Emain Macha**, Fergus is tricked into accepting an invitation to a feast given by the treacherous **Barach**. In his absence, Naoise and his brothers are murdered. When she discovers the fate of the sons of Usna, Deirdre kills herself. In his play *Deirdre*, WBY movingly dramatizes the return of the lovers to Ulster and their subsequent deaths. Naoise's brothers do not appear in WBY's version. The role of Naoise in the first production, November 1906, was played by **Frank Fay**. See also *The Countess Cathleen* (*CPl.* 45), "Under the Moon" (*CP.* 91), and "Baile and Aillinn" (*CP.* 459).

REFERENCES: Ellis, Peter Berresford. *Dictionary of Celtic Mythology*. New York: Oxford University Press, 1992; Green, Miranda J. *Dictionary of Celtic Myth and Legend*. London: Thames & Hudson, 1992; Mac Cana, Proinsias. *Celtic Mythology*. Feltham, Middlesex: Newnes, 1983.

NASH, JOSEPH (1838–1922), illustrator and watercolorist. He was an illustrator with the *Graphic* and a member of the Royal Institute of Water-Colorists. When the Yeats family moved to **Bedford Park** in 1888, **John B. Yeats** became friendly with the other artists in the neighborhood, among them Joseph Nash, who lived at 36 The Avenue. They were both members of the Calumet, a club that met on alternate Sundays in members' houses. WBY's sisters were contemporaries of Nash's daughters and spent vacations at the Nash holiday home at Haslemere. In 1894, Nash attended occult meetings with WBY.

REFERENCE: Murphy, William M. *Prodigal Father: The Life of John Butler Yeats.* Ithaca: Cornell University Press, 1978.

NATIONAL GALLERY OF IRELAND. Located in **Merrion Square** West, the gallery, which houses a fine collection of classical painting from the major European schools, was opened in 1864. **Hugh Lane** was director from 1914 until his death on the S.S. *Lusitania* in 1915. WBY makes a number of references to the National Gallery in his correspondence about the Lane Bequest (*UP2.* 415, 422, 474–75). In recent years, the gallery, having benefited from a major bequest from **George Bernard Shaw**, has been renovated and refurbished. It is now among the leading galleries in Europe.

REFERENCES: McGarry, James P. *Place Names in the Writings of William Butler Yeats.* Gerrards Cross: Colin Smythe, 1976; White, James, ed. *W. B. Yeats: A Centenary Exhibition in the National Gallery of Ireland.* Dublin: National Gallery of Ireland, 1965.

NATIONAL LIBRARY OF IRELAND. Located in Kildare Street, Dublin, it was founded in 1877 and moved to its present premises in 1890. When he was in Dublin, WBY spent much time reading in the National Library. He was critical of the library's refusal to carry the works of **Flaubert** and **Nietzsche** (*UP2.* 305), and he regretted the lack of books on Celtic culture and the Irish language. He was appreciative of the work done by the library staff, especially **T. W. Lyster**, who as director of the National Library from 1895 to 1920 encouraged both WBY and **James Joyce**. After Lyster's death, WBY was chair of the memorial committee and read a tribute at the unveiling of a plaque to him (*UP2.* 470–72). The library holdings extend to well over half a million volumes, while the Department of Manuscripts holds the papers of the major Irish writers, including a large collection of Yeats material donated by **Michael B. Yeats**.

REFERENCE: McGarry, James P. *Place Names in the Writings of William Butler Yeats.* Gerrards Cross: Colin Smythe, 1976.

NATIONAL LITERARY SOCIETY (Dublin). The society was founded in 1892 by WBY and **John O'Leary** to promote a contemporary Irish literature and culture. The first president of the society was John O'Leary. WBY was one of seven vice presidents, and there was a Council of twenty members, reflecting the whole spectrum of political thought in Ireland. The inaugural meeting took place 16 August 1892, when **Dr. George Sigerson** delivered the address "Irish Literature: Its Origins, Environment, and Influence." Initially, the society met in the **Mansion House**, Dublin, but in December 1892, rooms were taken at 4 College Green. There, they held weekly meetings, lectures, discussions, and musical entertainments. Papers were read by members, usually at two-weekly intervals, and a series of public lectures was arranged in the Leinster Lecture Hall, Molesworth Street, Dublin. There were plans for art exhibitions and a network of lending libraries to be set up throughout Ireland. O'Leary was succeeded as president of the society by **Douglas Hyde**, whose lecture "The Necessity of De-Anglicising Ireland" led to the founding of the Gaelic League. From the formation of the National Literary Society, there was rivalry with the London-based **Irish Literary Society**. Although it had been formed only a few months earlier, in May 1892, the London-based society assumed it was the central organization, a claim supported by the *Daily Telegraph*, 7 March 1892, suggesting that since London was the capital of Ireland, London was the appropriate venue for an Irish national literary society. In a letter to *United Ireland*, 30 July 1892, WBY insisted that the Dublin society was wholly separate from the London-based organization (*KLI*. 306–7). The founding of the National Literary Society was of central importance to the development of the Irish Renaissance. It became an important pressure group, bringing fresh debate to bear on the legacy of the Irish writers of the nineteenth century and examining the need for a national literature that pursued aesthetic rather than political aims. Not only was WBY a founder, but he also devoted himself enthusiastically to the organization. On 26 January 1893, he gave a reading for the society of his play *The Countess Cathleen* and lectured on "Nationality and Literature," 19 May 1893. In addition to his other duties, he acted as secretary of the libraries subcommittee and undertook to establish libraries of Irish books in the provinces. With the help of **Maud Gonne**, he generated gifts of money and books, but he lost interest when his secretarial methods were criticized and books intended for rural libraries were directed to Dublin. Disagreements among its members eventually undermined the success of the Irish Literary Society. A disillusioned WBY writes in detail about the early struggles of the society in "Ireland after Parnell" (*A*. 202–8).

REFERENCE: Marcus, Phillip L. *Yeats and the Beginning of the Irish Renaissance.* Syracuse: Syracuse University Press, 1987.

NESSA, ambitious and powerful wife of Fachtna, king of **Ulster**. She sleeps with Cathbad the Druid and bears **Conchubar Mac Nessa**. On the death of Fachtna, his half brother, **Fergus Mac Roich**, becomes king. Fergus is infatuated with Nessa, but she agrees to marry him only on condition that her son Conchubar will rule for one year. At the end of the year, Conchubar refuses to give up the throne, and Fergus goes into exile. Nessa is mentioned as the wife of Fergus in WBY's dramatic poem "The Old Age of Queen Maeve" (*CPl*. 451).

REFERENCE: Ellis, Peter Berresford. *Dictionary of Celtic Mythology.* New York: Oxford University Press, 1992.

NETTLESHIP, J[OHN] T[RIVETT] (1841–1902), lawyer, writer, and illustrator. He was a close friend of **John B. Yeats**, who thought him a genius and the acknowledged leader among the informal association of artists called "The Brotherhood." Nettleship was an alcoholic, and although he went into recovery, he never fulfilled the promise that he showed in early work. WBY devotes several pages of his autobiography, ''Four Years: 1887–1891,'' to Nettleship (*A*. 155–59). He admired the passion and melancholic feeling of Nettleship's symbolic paintings, among them the now-lost *God Creating Evil*, and he wrote a review of Nettleship's work. It was WBY's first art review, but it was rejected for publication. He spent much time in conversation with Nettleship and wrote with sympathy and affection for this failed artist. Years later, he could still be moved by the imagery in Nettleship's early designs. Nettleship designed the frontispiece for the first edition of *The Countess Kathleen and Various Legends and Lyrics* (1892). In a presentation copy, given to **John Quinn** in March 1904, however, WBY notes that the illustration, which depicts **Cuchulain** fighting the waves, was disappointing (*KLI*. 306).

REFERENCES: Loizeaux, Elizabeth Bergmann. *Yeats and the Visual Arts*. New Brunswick and London: Rutgers University Press, 1986; Murphy, William M. *Prodigal Father: The Life of John Butler Yeats, 1839–1922*. Ithaca: Cornell University Press, 1978; Nettleship, John T. *Robert Browning: Essays and Thoughts*. New York: Scribner, 1901.

NEW IRISH LIBRARY, publication project. In 1892, as part of the activities of the **Irish Literary Society**, WBY proposed the promotion of a series of books by Irish authors, to be published by **T. Fisher Unwin** and distributed in Ireland. The plan was based on a successful scheme previously organized by the Young Irelanders, with **Charles Gavan Duffy** as editor. WBY intended that the books should reflect the creative and imaginative literature currently being produced by the younger Irish authors. Simultaneously, Gavan Duffy, who had recently returned from Australia, was exploring a revival of the Young Irelanders' scheme with a little-known Irish publisher in London, Edmund Downey. When it was realized that the project would be more viable with an established publisher, **T. W. Rolleston**, who was familiar with WBY's plans, persuaded Fisher Unwin to support Gavan Duffy's scheme in place of WBY's. When he realized what was happening, WBY wrote to friends for support and conducted a heated correspondence in the *Freeman's Journal*, September 1892. Unable to salvage his plan, he reluctantly went along with Gavan Duffy, afraid lest Fisher Unwin withdraw from the project. The only concession he was granted was the appointment of **Douglas Hyde** and Rolleston as subeditors. His fears were confirmed when Gavan Duffy chose for publication *Patriot Parliament*, a dry historical tract by **Thomas Davis**. Later titles in the twelve-volume series included books by **Standish [James] O'Grady, John Todhunter**, and **Richard Ashe King**, but, as WBY predicted, after the initial publication, the scheme under Gavan Duffy's editorship failed to generate interest.

REFERENCE: Marcus, Phillip L. *Yeats and the Beginning of the Irish Renaissance*. Syracuse: Syracuse University Press, 1987.

NEWTON, SIR ISAAC (1642–1727), physicist and philosopher. Educated at Cambridge University, he made important contributions to physics and mathematics, but he is probably best known for his discovery of the laws of gravity and motion. He experimented with light, breaking up white light into the colors of the spectrum by the use of a prism. In his experiments and discoveries, Newton influenced the materialist thinking of the eighteenth century. In his essay on **George Berkeley** (*EI*. 396–411), WBY approvingly notes that Newton's ideas were challenged by both Berkeley and **Jonathan Swift**, while in a letter to **Olivia Shakespear** (*WL*. 807), he claims to have rejected the rational thinking of Newton in favor of the teachings of **Emanuel Swedenborg**.

REFERENCES: Brewster, Sir David. *Memoirs of the Life, Writings and Discoveries of Sir Isaac Newton*. Edinburgh: T. Constable, 1855; De Morgan, Augustus. *Essays on the Life and Work of Newton*. Chicago: Open Court, 1914.

NIAMH [brightness or beauty], daughter of **Manannán**. In the Fenian Cycle of tales, Niamh, in the guise of a hornless deer, appears to **Oisin**. He falls in love and agrees to accompany her to **Tir-nan-Oge**. There they live an idyllic life in a world outside time. After 300 years, during which they visit three islands, Oisin wishes to return to a mortal life. He leaves Niamh with the promise that he will return to Tir-nan-Oge without his feet touching the ground. When he falls from his horse, Niamh's spell is broken, and Oisin dies. The story of Niamh and her adventures with Oisin in Tir-nan-Oge is told in *The Wanderings of Oisin* (*CP*. 409). See also *The King of the Great Clock Tower* (*CPl*. 633–34, 641), "The Hosting of the Sidhe" (*CP*. 61), "The Lover asks Forgiveness because of his Many Moods" (*CP*. 73), "News for the Delphic Oracle" (*CP*. 376), and "The Circus Animal's Desertion" (*CP*. 391).

REFERENCE: Ellis, Peter Berresford. *Dictionary of Celtic Mythology*. New York: Oxford University Press, 1992.

NICHOLAS II (1868–1918), last czar of Russia. He became czar in 1894, but after a period of economic and social unrest, in which he failed to take progressive action, he was forced to abdicate, March 1917. David Lloyd George, who was head of the British War Cabinet, offered the czar asylum in England in 1917 but later withdrew the offer because of the opposition of King George V, cousin to the czar, who was concerned the action would antagonize anti-monarchists in England. The czar's execution by the Bolsheviks in July 1918 caused revulsion in Europe, since the czar was related by birth and marriage to the major European royal houses. In *On the Boiler* (*LE*. 242), WBY suggests that George V had proposed that Nicholas and his family be granted asylum but had been opposed by Lloyd George. See also "Crazy Jane on the Mountain" (*CP*. 390).

REFERENCE: Lloyd George, David. *The War Memoirs of David Lloyd George*. London: Nicholas & Watson, 1934.

NIETZSCHE, FRIEDRICH [WILHELM] (1844–1900), German philosopher. Born the son of a minister, who died when Nietzsche was young, he was raised by his mother in an atmosphere of extreme piety, which he later rejected. He was professor of philology at Basel, 1869–79, but resigned due to a nervous illness and eye trouble. He moved from place to place, seeking to improve his health, and though often in great pain, he worked steadily at his writings until 1889 when he became insane. In its poetic grandeur, his work reveals the intensity and sensitivity of his mind. It is driven by a passion and a zeal that anticipate his later breakdown. In essence, Nietzsche proclaimed the superiority of the aristocrat, the survival of the mightiest. He condemned the morality of the masses, particularly the Christian ethic in which the noble being is put down, the weak upheld. Man's will should create the superman, outside good and evil, who would wipe out decadent democracy. His greatest work was *Thus Spake Zarathustra* (1883–91), a copy of which was sent to WBY by **John Quinn** in September 1902. In thanking Quinn for the gift, WBY claimed to be previously unacquainted with Nietzsche, and in a letter to **Lady Gregory**, written a short time later, he apologizes for not writing to her because he has been steeped in Nietzsche (*WL*. 379). The work appears to be a major influence on the reshaping of the play *Where There Is Nothing* and an inspiration for the character of Paul Ruttledge. Thus, as Katharine Worth has pointed out in her introduction to the play (1987), Paul follows Zarathustra in calling for the destruction of the old laws and to free the self to create what Nietzsche called "a thing beyond itself." Present, too, is the emphasis on laughter and drunkenness as a prelude to destructiveness. A year later, WBY appears to have grown tired of the Dionysian frenzy (*WL*. 403), but inspired by Nietzsche, he found in his poetry a new energy and directness with which to challenge the world instead of retreating from it. In a letter to the *Irish Times*, 8 October 1903, he complained that the **National Library of Ireland** refused to carry any books written by Nietzsche (*UP2*. 305). A number of works by Nietzsche, including Thomas Common's translation of *The Case of Wagner, Nietzsche Contra Wagner* and *The Twilight of the Idols* (1896, 1899), were in WBY's library (*OS*. nos. 1437–45).

REFERENCES: Bohlmann, Otto. *Yeats and Nietzsche*. London: Basingstoke, 1982; Harper, George Mills. "The Creator as Destroyer: Nietzschean Morality in Yeats's *Where There Is Nothing*." *Colby Library Quarterly* 15, no. 2 (1979); Heller, Erich. "Yeats and Nietzsche: Reflections on a Poet's Marginal Notes." *Encounter* (December 1969); Morgan, Margery M. "Shaw, Yeats, Nietzsche, and the Religion of Art." *Kosmos* (Melbourne) (1967); Oates, Joyce Carol. "Yeats: Violence, Tragedy, Mutability." In *The Edge of Impossibility: Tragic Forms in Literature*. New York: Vanguard, 1972; O'Brien, Conor Cruise. *The Suspecting Glance*. London: Faber & Faber, 1972; Oppel, Frances Nesbitt. *Mask and Tragedy: Yeats and Nietzsche, 1902–10*. Charlottesville: University Press of Virginia, 1987; Whitaker, Thomas R. "History as Vision." In *Swan and Shadow: Yeats's Dialogue with History*. Chapel Hill: University of North Carolina Press, 1964; Worth, Katharine. *Where There Is Nothing: The Unicorn from the Stars*. Washington, D.C.: Catholic University of America Press, 1987.

NINEVEH, capital city of the Assyrian Empire. Situated on the banks of the Tigris, Nineveh was at its height in the eighth and seventh centuries B.C. It fell to an alliance of the Medes, the Scythians, and the Babylonians, 612 B.C. Recent excavations have revealed palaces and a library containing one of the earliest bibliographical indexes yet discovered. In his essay "The Symbolism of Poetry" (*EI*. 158), WBY quotes a line about Nineveh from "Music and Moonlight," a poem by Arthur O'Shaughnessy, to support his argument that great things proceed from small, that only those things that seem "useless or very feeble" have any power. See also "Fragments" (*CP*. 240), "Vacillation" (*CP*. 282), and "Pages from a Diary in 1930" (*EX*. 337).

NOAH, builder of the Ark. In the Old Testament of the Judaic-Christian Bible (Genesis, chaps. 6–10), God tells Noah that a great Flood will destroy the earth. He instructs him to build an Ark and take on board his family, including his sons and their wives, and two of all living creatures, to ensure their survival. In *The Player Queen* (*CPl*. 403), the Prime Minister is arranging for a play to be presented at Court. He has chosen "The Tragical History of Noah's Flood," to be performed by a troupe of traveling players. Their leader **Septimus** will play Noah, and his wife **Decima**, wearing a mask, will act the part of Noah's wife. Some of the other actors will play the animals. In the event, the play of Noah is not performed. See also "Wisdom" (*CP*. 246).

NOBEL PRIZE FOR LITERATURE, prestigious prize awarded annually by the Royal Swedish Academy. WBY received the Nobel Prize for Literature in 1923. He traveled to Sweden for the ceremony, which took place in the Hall of the Swedish Academy, 10 December 1923. A few days later, he delivered a lecture to the Academy on "The Irish Dramatic Movement." The whole experience touched WBY greatly, and he was flattered to know that the Swedish royal family thought he had behaved like a courtier (*WL*. 827). He gives his impressions of the visit in *The Bounty of Sweden* (*A*. 531–58), written as a gesture of gratitude to the Swedish Academy and sharing his admiration for the courtly ceremony and protocol that reminded him of the court at **Urbino**, described by **Castiglione**.

NOH THEATRE, highly stylized Japanese theater form. WBY encountered Noh for the first time during the period 1913–16 when **Ezra Pound** was editing the writings of the art critic and historian **Ernest Fenollosa**. WBY was sharing a cottage with Pound in Sussex and was introduced to the characteristics of Noh by reading translations of the best-known Noh plays. Of special interest to WBY was the fact that the plays were in verse. They were highly concentrated in form and were performed for a small, distinguished audience. The stylization of form and presentation and the simplicity of the setting were attractive to WBY, while the masks worn by the leading performers had metaphysical as well as aesthetic appeal. In theme, Noh touched common areas of interest in its preoccupation with the occult and with the hallowing of certain places with old associations. WBY explored the form for the first time in *At the Hawk's Well* (1916) and continued to use it as a model for the majority of his later plays—even in those like ***The Words upon the Window-Pane*** and ***Purgatory***, which appear to be more realistic but in fact draw heavily on the traditions of Noh. He writes persuasively of the impact of Noh on his drama in "Certain Noble Plays of Japan" (*EI.* 221–37).

REFERENCES: Masaru, Sekine. *Yeats and the Noh: A Comparative Study.* Savage, Md.: Barnes & Noble, 1990; Nakamura, Yasuo. *Noh: The Classical Theatre.* New York: Weatherhill, 1971; Oshima, Shotaro. *W. B. Yeats and Japan.* Tokyo: Hokuseido, 1965; Pound, Ezra, and Fenollosa, Ernest. *The Classic Noh Theatre of Japan.* New York: New Directions, 1959; Qamber, Akhtar. *Yeats and the Noh, with Two Plays for Dancers by Yeats and Two Noh Plays.* New York: Weatherhill, 1974; Tsukai, Nobuko. *Ezra Pound and the Japanese Noh Plays.* Washington, D.C.: University Press of America, 1983.

NONA, fictional character. In WBY's play ***The Player Queen***, she is a member of the theater troupe that is to present a play at the court of the **Queen**. After persuading **Decima**, the leading lady, to come out of hiding, Nona confesses that **Septimus** and she are lovers and that she intends playing Decima's role of **Noah's** wife in the performance. When the mob attacks the castle, she escapes with Septimus. Later, she returns to dance for the court, unaware that Decima is now the Queen. In the first performance of *The Player Queen*, May 1919, the role of Nona was played by Edith Evans.

NUTT, ALFRED T[RUBNER] (1856–1910), editor. He was publisher and editor of the scholarly *Folklore Journal*, the organ of the Folk-Lore Society. WBY did some copying work for his father's publishing company, David Nutt, in 1888, and was resentful that they did not publish any of his folktales. With his scholarly approach to folklore, Alfred T. Nutt was critical of contemporary writers who wrote versions of the ancient stories. Although he understood Nutt's preference for the oral tradition, WBY felt that he was too scientific in his approach to folklore and stifled the imaginative retelling of the tales. However, in an enthusiastic review in *The Bookman*, September 1898 (*UP2.* 119–21), of an extended essay by Nutt on the Celtic beliefs about the soul (included in the two-volume *The Voyage of Bran* [1895, 1897]—a translation by **Kuno Meyer** of an early Irish saga, edited by Meyer and Nutt), WBY added that the whole book was one of three without which it would be impossible for the scholar to understand Celtic legend.

REFERENCE: Thuente, Mary Helen. *W. B. Yeats and Irish Folklore.* Dublin: Gill & Macmillan, 1980.

O

O'BRIEN, DONOUGH, Irish chieftain. In 1317, he invited the Scots to invade the ancient kingdom of **Thomond** in the west of Ireland. In the ensuing battle, Donough was killed at **Athenry** and buried in nearby **Corcomroe Abbey**. His tomb may be seen in the ruins of the abbey today. His story is recounted in WBY's play *The Dreaming of the Bones* (*CPl.* 439).

REFERENCE: Otway–Ruthven, A. J. *A History of Medieval Ireland.* New York: St. Martin's Press, 1980.

O'BYRNE, ruling family of County Wicklow until late Elizabethan times. Their castle was in the valley of Glenmalure. Members of the O'Byrne family are buried in the graveyard in **Glendalough**, adjacent to the monastic settlement founded by St. Kevin in the seventh century. See also "Under the Round Tower" (*CP.* 154).

REFERENCE: Otway–Ruthven, A. J. *A History of Medieval Ireland.* New York: St. Martin's Press, 1980.

O'CASEY, SEAN (1880–1964), playwright. He was born John Casey, in Dublin. His father, a commercial clerk, was largely self-educated and placed much value on learning. With his premature death, his wife and young family were left to face a severe fall in living standards. Thus, O'Casey had a difficult childhood that he chronicles in his autobiographical novels *I Knock at the Door* (1939) and *Pictures in the Hallway* (1942). As a Protestant, O'Casey felt alienated from his almost exclusively Catholic neighbors. In addition, he was unable to attend school regularly because of a chronic eye complaint, but he read voraciously. His extreme poverty encouraged him to turn to communism and left-wing politics. For a time, he was secretary of the Irish Citizen Army (the political wing of the Irish Transport and General Workers' Union). He eventually resigned in protest against its association with the middle-class nationalists of the Irish Volunteers. He learned Irish and joined the Gaelic League. O'Casey developed an early passion for the theater, largely through his brother who organized amateur theatricals. Not only did he act in excerpts from plays by **Shakespeare** and Dion Boucicault, but he took part in a professional production of Boucicault's *The Shaughraun* at the **Mechanics Institute**. In 1921, he submitted some one-act plays to the **Abbey Theatre**. They were poorly constructed and uneven in language and characterization, but, encouraged by **Lady Gregory**, O'Casey persisted with his writing. At the age of forty-three, he achieved success with *The Shadow of a Gunman*, which opened at the Abbey Theatre, April 1923. With the Abbey productions of *Juno and the Paycock* (1924), and the controversial *The Plough and the Stars* (1926), which WBY defended in a speech from the stage, he became established as a playwright of international significance. He was invited to **Coole Park** and carved his name on the famous Autograph Tree. Nevertheless, he was bewildered and hurt by the negative reactions to *The Plough and the Stars* from the Irish press and sections of the public. He gave up his laboring job and left for London to become a full-time writer. In 1927, he married Eileen Carey, a young actress who had started her career with the D'Oyly Carte Opera Company and appeared in the London productions of his plays. In 1928, *The Silver Tassie*, which introduced elements of expressionism into his well-known naturalistic style, was rejected by WBY and the board of the Abbey Theatre (*WL.* 740–44), a decision later regretted, certainly by Lady Gregory. O'Casey was furious and sent copies of the rejection letters from WBY, Lady Gregory, and **Lennox Robinson** to the London *Observer*. They were published 3 June 1928. Now it was WBY's turn to be furious. He considered the letters to be private and vowed to sue for breach of copyright—a threat he did not carry out. The controversy gained international attention, causing much embarrassment to WBY. O'Casey vowed never to return to Ireland—a threat he did carry out! A production of *The Silver Tassie* was staged in London, October 1929, starring Charles Laughton, and with settings by **Augustus John**. It was produced at the Abbey Theatre in 1935. In his *Autobiographies*, O'Casey writes eloquently of the personalities involved in the Abbey Theatre, especially Lady Gregory and WBY. He was grateful to them but felt he had been betrayed. The rejection of *The Silver Tassie* brought him permanent exile from Ireland— and he never wrote as well again. WBY's defense of *The Plough and the Stars* at the **National Literary Society** was published in the *Dublin Magazine*, June 1926 (*UP2.* 466–72). He remained bitter over *The Silver Tassie* controversy and continued to defend his position in a diary kept in 1930 (*EX.* 333, 339). See also *Dramatis Personae* (*A.* 416).

REFERENCES: Hogan, Robert G., and Burnham, Richard. *The Years of O'Casey, 1921– 1926: A Documentary History*. Newark, N.J.: University of Delaware Press, 1992; Kilroy, Thomas, ed. *Sean O'Casey*. Englewood Cliffs, N.J.: Prentice-Hall, 1975; Krause, David. *Sean O'Casey and His World*. London: Thames & Hudson, 1976; Krause, David. *Sean*

O'Casey, the Man and His Work. London: MacGibbon & Kee; New York: Macmillan, 1960; O'Casey, Eileen. *Sean*. Ed. J. C. Trewin. London: Macmillan, 1971.

OCHOROWICZ, JULIEN (1850–1917), psychologist and psychical researcher. He was born in Poland and became codirector, in 1907, of the Institut Général Psychologique, Paris. He conducted psychical research, principally on spirit materializations by the medium Stanislawa Tomczyk. WBY cites experiments by Ochorowicz in "Swedenborg, Mediums, and the Desolate Places" (*LE*. 65, 67), acknowledging as his source *Annals of Psychical Research*.

O'CONNELL, DANIEL (1775–1847), political leader. He was born near Cahirciveen, County Kerry, and adopted by a wealthy Catholic uncle at Derrynane. As a boy, he was fluent in Irish and became familiar with the traditional native Irish culture, but as a Catholic, he was not permitted to attend **Trinity College**, Dublin. He went to school in France and saw at first hand the atrocities of the French Revolution, which led him to reject violence for political motives. He studied law at Lincoln's Fields in London and read widely, evolving a political philosophy by reading Voltaire, Rousseau, and other liberal thinkers of his day. On his return to Ireland, after being called to the Irish Bar in 1798, he built up a large practice on the **Munster** circuit, where his rhetoric and knowledge of the rural Irish enabled him to be a very successful lawyer. He was appalled by the bloodshed that he saw in the wake of the 1798 Rebellion and vowed to reach a solution to the Irish problem by peaceful means. After the Act of Union was passed by the English Parliament in 1800, he determined to campaign for Catholic Emancipation to enable Catholics to enter Parliament and to hold civil and military offices. In 1823, he founded the Catholic Association, and encouraged by the Catholic clergy, he built up a nationwide movement. In the **Clare** election in 1828, he overwhelmingly defeated the government candidate, although as a Catholic he was not permitted to take his seat. The result of the election alarmed the English Parliament, who were concerned that this might be the beginning of another Irish rising, and they passed the Catholic Emancipation Bill in 1829. In 1832, thirty-nine pro-O'Connellites were returned to the English Parliament. Buoyant with success, O'Connell resigned his law practice to concentrate wholly on politics, determined that his next action must be the repeal of the Act of Union. In 1834, he introduced debate on repeal in the English Parliament, but it met with stern opposition from those who saw it as a move toward separatism. In 1840, the Repeal Association was founded by O'Connell. In 1841, a group of journalists, **Thomas Davis**, John Blake Dillon, and **Charles Gavan Duffy**, started *The Nation* newspaper and formed a splinter group, the Young Irelanders, which promoted a brand of romantic nationalism linked to an idealized cultural identity. In 1841, O'Connell was elected the first Catholic Lord Mayor of Dublin and began to organize huge political demonstrations throughout the country. To the alarm of the English Parliament, three quarters of a million people gathered to hear him speak at **Tara**. An even larger demonstration, planned for **Clontarf**, near Dublin, 8 October 1843, was banned by the English prime minister. O'Connell had the numerical support to defy the ban, but he was unwilling to risk violence and called off the demonstration. He was arrested and sentenced to a year's imprisonment for conspiracy. He only served three months, but by the time of his release, he had forfeited his credibility, the Repeal movement had lost its momentum, and there was dissension among the leaders, especially from the Young Irelanders who proposed physical force. O'Connell was now almost seventy and confused about the future. With the ravages of the Great Famine in 1845–47, he left Ireland for the last time in January 1847. He made a final appeal to the English Parliament, reminding them of the great injustices they had perpetrated in Ireland, and sailed for Rome. He died on the journey and was buried in **Glasnevin**, Dublin, under a round tower, 165 feet in height. Known as 'the Liberator,' O'Connell was Ireland's most popular Catholic leader, although he alienated the Protestants by playing the Catholic card. Large and burly, he had a commanding voice and dominating personality. He had an insatiable appetite for work and loved public display of any kind, bands, uniforms, and the iconography of shamrocks, wolfhounds, and round towers. He had a reputation for coarse humor and abusive behavior toward his opponents. WBY was out of sympathy with O'Connell, whom he thought a ''comedian'' (*CP*. 319; *M*. 213), contrasting his popular, grandiose style with the dignified aloofness of **Charles Stewart Parnell** (*A*. 195). He was critical of O'Connell, the practical politician, whose political compromises, although they may have led to the emergence of a Catholic middle class and gained some concessions from the English Parliament, failed to satisfy the patriots (*UP2*. 320).

REFERENCES: Foster, Roy F. *Modern Ireland 1600–1972*. 1988. Reprint, London: Penguin, 1989; MacDonagh, Oliver. *The Emancipist*. New York: St. Martin's Press, 1989. O'Ferrall, Fergus. *Catholic Emancipation: Daniel O'Connell and the Birth of Irish Democracy*. Dublin: Gill & Macmillan, 1985.

O'CONNOR, FRANK (1903–66), short story writer and man of letters. He was born Michael Frank O'Donovan in **Cork** (city) and grew up in impoverished conditions. He was fortunate to attend the local St. Patrick's National School, where one of his teachers was the nationalist Daniel Corkery. Not only did Corkery encourage his writing, but he also introduced him to the richness of native Irish culture and the Irish language. Under Corkery's influence, O'Connor became involved in the Civil War in 1922, fighting on the Republican side. He was captured and interned. On his release, he taught Irish, started a theater in Cork, and became a librarian in Wicklow, Cork, and Dublin. He first used the pseudonym Frank O'Connor in the mid-1920s, when he published poems, stories, articles, and reviews in *The Irish Statesman*, edited by **AE**. These led to his acceptance in Dublin literary circles, and he became a frequent visitor at the homes of WBY and AE. He published his first book of short stories, *Guests of the Nation*, in 1931 and followed it, a year later, with his novel *The Saint and*

Mary Kate. His major biography of the Irish patriot Michael Collins, *The Big Fellow*, appeared in 1937. From 1935 to 1939, he was a director of the **Abbey Theatre**. There he found himself supporting WBY during another difficult period in the Abbey's history. With the death of WBY, however, and after bitter differences with the other Abbey Theatre directors, he resigned from the theater, and from his library post, to retire to County Wicklow. There, he became the poetry editor of the new and influential literary magazine *The Bell*. He was elected to the **Irish Academy of Letters** in 1941. He published *Irish Miles* (1947) in which his account of cycling trips that he and his Welsh wife made to neglected megalithic burial sites, monasteries, and castles called national attention to Ireland's rich historical past. He broadcast frequently for the **BBC**, reading his own poems and stories and reminiscing about his association with major Irish literary figures, including WBY—indeed, his comments are among the most informative and entertaining of the many accounts of WBY as the elder statesman of Irish poets. As his writing became more closely associated with cultural and sexual repression in Ireland, the government banned much of his later work. With his personal life in disarray, and his artistic life in question, he felt socially and professionally isolated. He divorced in 1950 and the next year moved to the United States, where he gained a wider audience with his regular contributions to the *New Yorker* and other periodicals. He married again in 1953 and lectured at a number of major American universities, including Chicago and Harvard. After suffering a stroke, he returned to Dublin in 1961 and taught at **Trinity College**. Besides fiction, he wrote his autobiography in two volumes, *An Only Child* and *My Father's Son*. He translated from the Irish and wrote many books of travel and literary criticism. Seven poems by O'Connor, all of them from the Irish, were included in WBY's selection for ***The Oxford Book of Modern Verse*** (1936).

REFERENCES: Matthews, James H. *Frank O'Connor*. Lewisburg, Pa.: Bucknell University Press, 1976; Matthews, James. *Voices: A Life of Frank O'Connor*. New York: Atheneum, 1983; Rogers, W. R., ed. *Irish Literary Portraits*. New York: Taplinger, 1973; Wohlgelernter, Maurice. *Frank O'Connor: An Introduction*. New York: Columbia University Press, 1977.

OCRIS HEAD [also Aughris] (Irish: *Eachros*) [promontory of the horse], headland in **Sligo** (county). The coastline at Aughris Head is very treacherous. In ***The Land of Heart's Desire*** (*CPl*. 55), the priest claims that it was the scene of a Spanish shipwreck. This is likely to have been a vessel from the Armada, wrecked off the west coast of Ireland in 1588.

REFERENCE: McGarry, James P. *Place Names in the Writings of William Butler Yeats*. Gerrards Cross: Colin Smythe, 1976.

OCTOBER BLAST, collection of poems. It was published by **Cuala Press** in 1927 in an edition of 350 copies. The collection contained a number of WBY's most important poems, including "Sailing to Byzantium" (*CP*. 217), "The Tower" (*CP*. 218), and "Among School Children" (*CP*. 242). All of these were later included in *The Tower* (1928).

"O'DONNELL ABU" (Irish: *O Domhnaill Abu*), patriotic marching song. The words were written by Michael Joseph McCann (1824–83), professor at St. Jarleth's College, **Tuam, Mayo** (county), and a member of the Young Irelanders. They were published in *The Nation* in 1843 under the title "The Clan Connell War Song" and sung to a tune by Joseph Haliday (1775–1846), a military bandmaster from Carrick-on-Suir, County Tipperary. The ballad celebrates the bravery and prowess of the Irish chieftain **Red Hugh O'Donnell**. In 1933, when WBY wished to write a popular song to be sung in the streets of Dublin, he chose the tune of "O'Donnell Abu" for the setting. See also "Three Songs to the Same Tune" (*CP*. 320).

REFERENCES: Zimmermann, Georges-Denis. *Irish Political Street Ballads and Rebel Songs, 1780–1900*. Hatboro, Pa.: Folklore Associates, 1967.

O'DONNELL, F[RANK] HUGH (1848–1916), writer and politician. He was born in **Donegal** (county) and educated at Queen's College, **Galway** (city). He became a journalist in London with the *Morning Post* and, after entering politics, was elected M.P. for Galway (city) in 1874. He was unseated by petition and elected M.P. for Dungarvan, 1877–85. He was antagonistic toward the leader **Charles Stewart Parnell**, who effectively ended his political career in 1885 by expelling him from the Irish Party. In 1888, O'Donnell took a libel action against *The Times*, which had earlier conducted a smear campaign against Parnell by linking him and the Irish M.P.s with political assassination. The libel action, although unsuccessful, revived the public outcry against Parnell and led directly to the setting up of the Parnell Commission. O'Donnell retired abroad but later tried to reenter Irish politics. In 1897, he joined WBY as one of two delegates from the English centenary committee attending a plenary meeting in Dublin to organize the commemorative celebrations for the 1798 Rebellion (*M*. 110). WBY was friendly toward him, finding him able and amusing, but when he discovered that O'Donnell was the author of anonymous pamphlets slandering **Michael Davitt** and others, he had him proscribed. In revenge, O'Donnell distributed *Souls for Gold* (1899), in which he maligned WBY and accused him of anti-Catholic bias in his play *The Countess Cathleen*, thus alienating many Catholics from the Irish National Theatre movement. In 1900, O'Donnell was thought responsible for the arrest of a French spy who was friendly toward the Irish nationalist movement. He then appropriated from the Boers money intended to assist revolutionary action in Ireland. A death threat was issued by the Republicans, but WBY successfully appealed for leniency. O'Donnell showed his gratitude by distributing another anti-WBY pamphlet, *The Stage-*

Irishman of the Pseudo-Celtic Revival (1904). In 1910, O'Donnell published a distorted *History of the Irish Parliamentary Party*.

REFERENCES: Hone, Joseph. *W. B. Yeats: 1865–1939.* 1943. Reprint, London: Macmillan, 1962; O'Donnell, F. Hugh. *A History of the Irish Parliamentary Party.* Vol. 1. London: Longmans, 1910.

O'DONNELL, RED HUGH (c. 1571–1602), chief of the O'Donnells and lord of Tír Conaill. He was born in Ballyshannon, **Donegal** (county), the son of Sir Hugh O'Donnell. In 1587, Red Hugh was taken hostage by the English, who feared the anti-English militancy of the O'Donnell family. He was imprisoned in **Dublin Castle** but escaped after three years and returned to Donegal. After the death of his father, he was inaugurated chief of the O'Donnells in 1592 and embarked upon an aggressive policy to drive out the English. He seized **Sligo** and **Connacht** and, with **Hugh O'Neill**, won the Battle of the Yellow Ford in 1598. His fortunes changed in 1601, when he joined the Spanish commander Don Juan del Aquila, who had arrived in **Kinsale** with 3,400 troops. O'Donnell heroically marched south over snow-covered mountains to meet up with Hugh O'Neill, but the combined armies failed to form a cohesive fighting unit and were decisively beaten by the English within nine days. Red Hugh sailed for Spain to seek reinforcements. He was received with full honors by Spanish King Philip III, but he fell mysteriously ill and died at Simancas. He is thought to have been poisoned by a fellow Irishman in the pay of the English. Red Hugh O'Donnell is associated with Kinsale, the final battle of the old Gaelic order in Ireland. His military skill and bravery have made him one of Ireland's most glamorous heroes. In the 1800s, the members of the Young Irelanders marched to the song written in his honor, **"O'Donnell Abu."** In "Edmund Spenser" (*EI.* 362–63), WBY gives an account of how Red Hugh was taken prisoner as a boy and escaped. He includes *The Flight of the Eagle*, an account of Red Hugh by **Standish [James] O'Grady**, in his list of "Best Irish Books" (*UP1.* 386). See also "Three Songs to the Same Tune" (*CP.* 322).

REFERENCE: Falls, Cyril B. *Elizabeth's Irish Wars.* 1950. Reprint, New York: Barnes & Noble, 1970.

O'DONOGHUE, D[AVID] J[AMES] (1866–1917), scholar and librarian. He was born in Chelsea, London, and contributed articles to the *Dublin Evening Telegraph* and other periodicals. He was intensely interested in Irish literature and did valuable research in the **British Museum** before writing his important work *Dictionary of Irish Poets in Ireland* (1892). At a dinner given to mark the publication of the dictionary, WBY proposed the toast. O'Donoghue published *The Life of William Carleton* (1896), based on an incomplete autobiography of **Carleton** that he had discovered. WBY praised the work in his review in *The Bookman* (*UP1.* 394–97). O'Donoghue moved to Dublin around 1896 and ran a family publishing house started by his late brother. He continued to research Irish subjects and published *Life of Mangan* (1897) and *Life of Robert Emmet*

(1902). In 1909, he was appointed librarian of University College, Dublin. In "Ireland after Parnell" (*A*. 208), WBY recalled an occasion when O'Donoghue was thrown out of a tombstone maker's house because he was critical of the popular Irish songwriter and poet Thomas Moore.

REFERENCE: Hogan, Robert, ed. *Dictionary of Irish Literature*. Rev. ed. Westport, Conn.: Greenwood, 1996.

O'DONOVAN, MICHAEL [FRANK]. *See* **O'CONNOR, FRANK**.

O'DRISCOLL, fictional character. In the ballad "The Host of the Air" (*CP*. 63), O'Driscoll loses his bride to the **Sídhe**. WBY claimed to have based the ballad on a story he had heard from an old woman in **Ballisodare** (*VP*. 143).

O'DUFFY, GENERAL EOIN (1892–1944), engineer, architect, and military leader. Born in County Monaghan, he joined the Irish Republican Army in 1917 and fought against the British until the signing of the Anglo-Irish Treaty in 1921. In 1922, he was appointed chief of staff of the Irish Republican Army and first commissioner of the new police force, an Garda Síochána. He was dismissed from the police force by **Eamon de Valera** in 1932 and became leader of the Army Comrades Association (the Blueshirts), a fascist (see **fascism**) inspired organization with a penchant for marches, demonstrations, and antidemocratic rhetoric. With his emphasis on physical drill, discipline, and national service, O'Duffy attracted the youth of Ireland frustrated with political and economic instability. He proposed a Blueshirts march in Dublin, August 1933, but de Valera imposed martial law, and the parade was called off. With the resignation of **William T. Cosgrave** as leader of the opposition in **Dáil Éireann**, O'Duffy was elected leader of the newly formed coalition party, the United Irish Party, Fine Gael, in which Cumann na nGaedheal merged with the National Centre Party. Tensions mounted between the Blueshirts and the Irish Republican Army, and in 1934, with the whole Blueshirts movement in disarray, O'Duffy resigned from Fine Gael. In 1935, he launched the National Corporate Party. He openly supported Italy's Mussolini and led a pro-Franco Irish Brigade to Spain in 1936. On his return to Ireland six months later, he retired from politics. He died in 1944 and was given a state funeral. WBY was introduced to the Blueshirts by Captain Dermot MacManus and embraced the movement with enthusiasm (*WL*. 813–15). He wrote three marching songs for them under the title "Three Songs to the Same Tune" (*CP*. 320). For a time, General O'Duffy was a regular visitor to his home in Dublin, but WBY's commitment to the movement waned, and he revised the marching songs to make them unsingable. See also "Parnell's Funeral" (*CP*. 319).

REFERENCES: Cullingford, Elizabeth. *Yeats, Ireland and Fascism*. New York and London: New York University Press, 1981; Freyer, Grattan. *W. B. Yeats and the Anti-Democratic Tradition*. Dublin: Gill & Macmillan, 1981; Krimm, Bernard G. *W. B. Yeats and the Emergence of the Irish Free State, 1918–1939: Living in the Explosion*. Troy,

N.Y.: Whitston, 1981; Manning, Maurice. *The Blueshirts*. Toronto: University of Toronto Press, 1971; Stanfield, Paul S. *Yeats and Politics in the 1930s*. New York: St. Martin's, 1988.

ODYSSEUS, mythological king of Ithaca, Greece, and the husband of Penelope. He was a suitor of **Helen** and went to **Troy** to rescue her after she was taken from **Sparta** by **Paris. Homer's** *The Odyssey* tells of his adventures, from the fall of Troy until his return to Ithaca ten years later. He is referred to in WBY's poem "The Sorrow of Love" (*CP*. 45).

OEDIPUS, son of Laius, king of **Thebes**, and Jocasta. When they are told by the oracle that their child will grow up to kill his father and marry his mother, Laius and Jocasta leave him to die on a mountainside. He is rescued by a shepherd and raised as the son of the king of Corinth. Oedipus learns of the prophecy and, unaware of his real parents, escapes to Thebes. On the way, he meets and kills Laius. He solves the riddle of the **Sphinx** and, after marrying Jocasta, becomes king of Thebes. Insistent on finding the cause of a great plague and famine that are ravaging the city, he learns the truth and blinds himself. Jocasta commits suicide. Oedipus goes into exile with his daughters, Antigone and Ismene, and Jocasta's brother, **Creon**, becomes king. Oedipus's sons, Eteocles and Polyneices, quarrel over the throne and kill each other in battle. WBY's adaptations of *Sophocles' King Oedipus* and *Sophocles' Oedipus at Colonus* were performed at the **Abbey Theatre** in 1926 and 1927, respectively. See also "From the *Antigone*" (*CP*. 315). According to **Mrs. Yeats**, the poem and the adaptations were based on a translation by Paul Masqueray.

O'GRADY, STANDISH HAYES (1832–1915), engineer and scholar. A cousin of **Standish [James] O'Grady**, he was born at Erinagh House, Castleconnell, **Limerick** (county). He grew up in the Gaelic-speaking area of Cloonagh, attended Rugby School and **Trinity College**, Dublin, and developed an early interest in Irish manuscripts. He became president of the Ossianic Society in 1856. He immigrated to the United States, where he was employed as an engineer for thirty years. On his retirement, he returned to England, where he worked on his important *Catalogue of Irish Manuscripts in the British Museum*, although the work remained incomplete at his death. He published *Silva Gadelica* (1892), a collection of tales from old Irish manuscripts, which was given a favorable review by WBY in *The Bookman* (*UP1*. 372), except for some reservations about the Latin style. WBY included it in his list of "Best Irish Books" (*UP1*. 386; *WL*. 247). Despite his interest in old Irish manuscripts, Standish Hayes O'Grady was a strict Unionist, opposed to the nationalist movement—hence, his decision to retire to England. In his "General Introduction for My Work" (*LE*. 206), WBY notes that O'Grady would not join the **Irish Literary Society** because he thought it a Fenian organization.

REFERENCE: Welch, Robert, ed. *The Oxford Companion to Irish Literature*. Oxford: Clarendon, 1996.

O'GRADY, STANDISH [JAMES] (1846–1928), historian and novelist. He was born in Castletown Berehaven, **Cork** (county), the son of a Church of Ireland rector. He attended Tipperary Grammar School and graduated from **Trinity College**, Dublin. He was called to the Irish Bar in 1872 and practiced law before pursuing an interest in Irish history and mythology, which culminated in his two-volume *History of Ireland: Heroic Period* (1878) and *History of Ireland: Cuculain [sic] and His Contemporaries* (1880). Included in this influential work, which became the cornerstone of the Irish Literary Revival, are versions of the early heroic tales and sagas, albeit in a revised and florid form to meet the expectations of late-Victorian taste. After publishing a further *History of Ireland: Critical and Philosophical* (1881), he reprinted relevant portions of the earlier work as *Cuculain [sic]: An Epic* (1882). He wrote an account of **Fionn Mac Cumhal** in *Finn and His Companions* (1892) and embarked on a trilogy of adventure stories with **Cuchulain** as the hero: *The Coming of Cuculain [sic]* (1894), *In the Gates of the North* (1901), and *The Triumph and Passing of Cuculain [sic]* (1920). He wrote other historical novels, including *The Bog of Stars* (1893), *The Flight of the Eagle* (1897), and *Red Hugh's Captivity* (1889), the latter two based on the story of **Red Hugh O'Donnell**. At the same time, he was active in Unionist politics, proposing in his book *Toryism and the Tory Democracy* (1886) a partnership between the landlord and the peasant classes to revive Ireland's culture and economy. He was publisher of the weekly *All-Ireland Review* (1900–1907) and the leader writer for the *Daily Express*, a Unionist newspaper in Dublin. Frustrated with political events, he left Ireland in 1918 and died in the Isle of Wight. Despite the limitations of his writing, WBY credited him with being the driving force behind the Irish Literary Revival (*EI*. 512), although O'Grady objected to the **Irish Literary Theatre's** dramatizations of the myths and legends because he felt they degraded Irish ideals. He was a major inspiration to WBY and his contemporaries in their use of Irish myth and legend to evolve a distinctively modern Irish literature. He brought Old Irish literature to life for them and for the average reader (*A*. 219–21), and WBY coupled him with **John O'Leary** as two powerful influences on him as a young poet. In "Beautiful Lofty Things" (*CP*. 348), WBY recalls his speech at a dinner in honor of the Irish Literary Theatre, 11 May 1899, at which O'Grady, very drunk, predicted the Easter Rebellion of 1916 and moved the gathering to applause with his rhetoric. He describes the event in more detail in ***Dramatis Personae*** (*A*. 423–24). WBY includes six books by Standish O'Grady in his list of "Best Irish Books" (*UP1*. 385–87). A number of Standish O'Grady's books, including *The Coming of Cuculain*, were in WBY's library (*OS*. nos. 1490–93).

REFERENCES: Boyd, Ernest A. *Appreciations and Depreciations: Irish Literary Studies*. New York: John Lane, 1918; Freyer, Grattan. *W. B. Yeats and the Anti-Democratic Tradition*. Dublin: Gill & Macmillan, 1981; Hogan, Robert, ed. *Dictionary of Irish Literature*. Rev. ed. Westport, Conn.: Greenwood, 1996; Marcus, Phillip L. *Standish O'Grady*. Lewisburg, Pa.: Bucknell University Press, 1970; O'Grady, Hugh Art. *Standish James O'Grady: The Man and the Writer*. Dublin: Talbot, 1929.

O'HARA BROTHERS. *See* **BANIM, JOHN**.

O'HART, FATHER JOHN (d. 1739), eponymous character in "The Ballad of Father O'Hart" (*CP*. 23). A well-loved priest from the parishes of **Ballisodare** and **Kilvarnet** in **Sligo** (county), he lost his lands during the period 1695–1727, when strict laws, imposed by the Irish Parliament, prevented Catholics from owning property in Ireland. Father O'Hart was a friend of the harpist Turlough O'Carolan (1670–1738).

O'HIGGINS, KEVIN [CHRISTOPHER] (1892–1927), politician. Born at Stradbally, County Laois, he was educated at Clongowes Wood College, Maynooth College, and University College, Dublin. He joined Sinn Féin while a student and was imprisoned for six months for an anticonscription speech in 1918. He was elected M.P. for Queen's County in 1920 and T.D. (member of the **Dáil**) for South Dublin in 1922. When the Irish Free State was formed in 1922, he became minister for Economic Affairs, then minister for Justice and External Affairs and vice president of the Executive Council. His policy was for a free and undivided Ireland within the British Commonwealth. During the Civil War, he worked unremittingly to restore law and order and took the decision to execute seventy-seven Republicans for possession of arms. On 10 July 1927, he was assassinated on his way to Mass, most believed in retaliation for the Republican executions. WBY was stunned by his death, especially since both he and **Mrs. Yeats** had had a premonition of it (*WL*. 726–27). WBY regarded O'Higgins not only as a friend but also as one of the finest intellects of his day. He responded to his death with a letter of sympathy to Mrs. O'Higgins, which was published in the *Irish Times*, 14 July 1927. Later, he wrote two poems in response to his murder: "Death" (*CP*. 264) and "Blood and the Moon" (*CP*. 267). There is a reference to O'Higgins in "Parnell's Funeral" (*CP*. 319), and his portrait by **Sir John Lavery** is mentioned in "The Municipal Gallery Revisited" (*CP*. 368).

REFERENCES: Freyer, Grattan. *W. B. Yeats and the Anti-Democratic Tradition*. Dublin: Gill & Macmillan, 1981; Krimm, Bernard G. *W. B. Yeats and the Emergence of the Irish Free State, 1918–1939: Living in the Explosion*. Troy, N.Y.: Whitston, 1981; Stanfield, Paul S. *Yeats and Politics in the 1930s*. New York: St. Martin's, 1988.

OISIN, mythological warrior and poet. He is the son of **Fionn Mac Cumhal** and the goddess Sadb. His mother, enchanted by a Black Druid, comes to Fionn's country in the form of a deer. When the Druid reclaims Sadb, Fionn finds the child abandoned and names him Oisin (little fawn). Oisin, who grows up to be one of the **Fianna's** greatest champions, marries a stranger from another country, Eibhir. Bewitched by **Niamh**, a golden-haired enchantress, he eventually agrees to live with her in **Tir-nan-Oge**. For 300 years, they travel through three magical islands, but when Oisin longs to return for a time to his own land, Niamh warns him that if he sets a foot on the soil of his native country, he will never be able to return to her. While wandering happily at home again, he accidentally falls from his horse, returns to his mortal age, and dies. The travels of Oisin and Niamh in Tir-nan-Oge form the narrative of WBY's *The Wanderings of Oisin* (*CP*. 409). See also ''The Circus Animal's Desertion'' (*CP*. 391) and *The King of the Great Clock Tower* (*CPl*. 633).

REFERENCES: Ellis, Peter Berresford. *Dictionary of Celtic Mythology*. New York: Oxford University Press, 1992; Green, Miranda J. *Dictionary of Celtic Myth and Legend*. London: Thames & Hudson, 1992; Mac Cana, Proinsias. *Celtic Mythology*. Feltham, Middlesex: Newnes, 1983.

OLDHAM, C[HARLES] H[UBERT] (1860–1926), lawyer, economist, and professor of political economy at **Trinity College**, Dublin. He was deeply committed to nationalist politics and, in 1886, formed the Protestant Home Rule Association. A year earlier, in 1885, he founded the **Contemporary Club**, which WBY and his father **John B. Yeats** attended regularly for almost two years. Although he was only five years older than WBY, Oldham was one of the first to recognize his extraordinary talent, and in 1885, he published WBY's early poems and plays in the *Dublin University Review*. Impressed with the young poet's earnestness and knowledge, he introduced him to **Katharine Tynan**. Oldham was a close friend of **Maud Gonne** and was instrumental in helping her meet prominent nationalists in Dublin, including the veteran **John O'Leary** and his sister **Ellen**, in 1888. Although he joined the **National Literary Society** and collected books for the library scheme, he was not an active member. WBY took the opportunity of speaking at the Contemporary Club to overcome his shyness and to sharpen his debating skills on some of the best minds in Dublin. He was grateful to Oldham and recalls him with some affection in *Autobiography* (*M*. 55–57), finding him sensitive though somewhat rude.

REFERENCE: Murphy, William M. *Prodigal Father: The Life of John Butler Yeats, 1839–1922*. Ithaca: Cornell University Press, 1978.

OLD MAN, character. An Old Man appears as a major character in three of WBY's plays: *At the Hawk's Well, Purgatory*, and *The Death of Cuchulain*. He is a minor character in *The Player Queen*. In *At the Hawk's Well*, the Old Man waits by the well, hoping to drink from the waters of immortality. When the youthful **Cuchulain** arrives, he sees him as a rival and tries to persuade him to leave. He explains that he has waited there for fifty years. Three times, **The Guardian of the Well** has lured him into sleep, and when he wakes, he finds the stones of the well are wet. His story anticipates the action of the play. When The Guardian of the Well gives the sign that the waters are about to flow, the Old Man falls asleep under her magic power. Again, he has missed his opportunity. In *Purgatory*, the Old Man, haunted by the memory of his mother, brings his bastard son to the burned-out shell of the house where he claims to have been born, the son of a noble lady and her dissolute groom. He reveals the story of his parentage, vividly recreating his mother's wedding night with her drunken husband and his intense hatred of his widowed father, an obsession that ends in the father's murder. At the climax of the action, the Old Man viciously kills his bastard son. In *The Death of Cuchulain*, the Old Man appears as a Prologue. As the producer of the play, he prepares the audience for the action and the style of presentation. He is irascible and demanding, requiring that the audience be small in number and familiar with WBY's earlier plays about Cuchulain. He promises music, a dance by **Emer**, and severed heads represented by parallelograms of painted wood. WBY uses the device of an Old Man as the Prologue in a version of *The King's Threshold*, published in *The United Irishman*, September 1903. It was omitted in performance—apparently because there was a shortage of actors! In the first performance of *At the Hawk's Well*, April 1916, the Old Man was played by Allan Wade, while Michael Dolan performed the Old Man in *Purgatory* when it was presented at the **Abbey Theatre**, August 1938. When *The Death of Cuchulain* was premiered by the Lyric Theatre Company, Dublin, December 1949, the Old Man was acted by Art O'Murnaghan.

O'LEARY, ELLEN (1831–89), poet. Born in County Tipperary, she later moved with her brother, **John O'Leary**, to Dublin, where they were active in revolutionary politics. She facilitated the escape of the Fenian **James Stephens**, raising money to charter a ship to take him to safety in France. When her brother was exiled from Ireland, she returned to Tipperary but continued to work for the nationalist cause. She contributed ballads to *The Nation* and other periodicals in Ireland and the United States, and her collection *Lays of Country, Home and Friends* was published posthumously in Dublin in 1891. She was a close friend and frequent correspondent of **Katharine Tynan**, who contributed an obituary of her to the *Boston Pilot*, 9 November 1889. Ellen O'Leary, sharing her brother's enthusiasm, idolized the young poet WBY. It was she who gave **Maud Gonne** a letter of introduction to the Yeats family when they were living in **Bedford Park** in 1889, little realizing the impact that meeting would have on the life and work of WBY. He included her poem "A Legend of Tyrone" in his anthology *Poems and Ballads of Young Ireland* (1888) and wrote an introduction to her work when it was published in *The Poets and the Poetry of the Century* (1891) (*UP1*. 256–58). In *Reveries over Childhood and Youth* (*A*. 94, 95, 98), he recalls her with affection and admiration.

REFERENCES: Murphy, William M. *Prodigal Father: The Life of John Butler Yeats, 1839–1922*. Ithaca: Cornell University Press, 1978.

O'LEARY, JOHN (1830–1907), Fenian. Born in Tipperary, where he inherited some property, he was educated at **Erasmus Smith High School** and **Trinity College**, Dublin. He studied law, but when he discovered that barristers were required to take the oath of allegiance to the British crown, he turned from law to study medicine. He attended Queen's College in **Cork** and in **Galway**, but he became increasingly involved with the Fenian organization, the Irish Revolutionary Brotherhood (later the Irish Republican Brotherhood), and did not graduate. In 1848, his strong nationalist sympathies led him into skirmishes with the police, and he was jailed for some weeks at Clonmel. In 1855, he went to Paris, where he shared rooms with **Whistler** and **Swinburne**. On his return to Ireland, he was appointed editor of the official Fenian journal, *The Irish People*, which advocated the overthrow of British rule. In 1863, the paper was seized by the government. In February 1864, O'Leary was arrested and sentenced to twenty years of penal servitude, a term later commuted to nine years, on condition that he leave Ireland until the period of his sentence elapsed. He settled in Paris but returned to Dublin in 1885. He was cofounder and first president of the **National Literary Society** in 1892 and president of the Supreme Council of the Irish Republican Brotherhood until his death. John O'Leary was a man of great generosity of spirit and high moral integrity. In his later years, however, he found himself financially insecure and isolated from the mainstream of Irish politics. In 1896, O'Leary published his reminiscences, *Recollections of Fenians and Fenianism*, which WBY found dry and unreadable. He reviewed it for *The Bookman*, February 1897, but devoted most of the article to O'Leary and his influence on the younger generation (*UP2*. 35–37). WBY first spoke with John O'Leary in 1885. They met frequently thereafter at the **Contemporary Club** and at O'Leary's home in Terenure, where he kept a literary salon that included **Douglas Hyde, T. W. Rolleston, AE**, and **John B. Yeats**. O'Leary, with his particular brand of nationalism, became his mentor and was responsible for the young poet turning to Ireland for the theme of his first important work, *The Wanderings of Oisin* (*LE*. 205; *UP2*. 509). O'Leary obtained a major number of subscribers to guarantee the publication of the collection *The Wanderings of Oisin and Other Poems* (1889). WBY's admiration for him appears over and over in the poems and essays. In the poem "Beautiful Lofty Things" (*CP*. 348), his is the first image that comes to the poet's mind, the personification of godlike nobility, while in "September 1913" (*CP*. 120), WBY gives him mythical status, seeing his death in 1907 as the end of an era in Ireland. A portrait, painted by John B. Yeats in 1904, shows his fine presence and the noble head of "Beautiful Lofty Things."

REFERENCES: Bourke, Marcus. *John O'Leary*. Dublin: Anvil Press, 1967; Freyer, Grattan. *W. B. Yeats and the Anti-Democratic Tradition*. Dublin: Gill & Macmillan, 1981; Gordon, D. J., ed. *W. B. Yeats: Images of a Poet*. Manchester: University of Manchester, 1961; Hogan, Robert, ed. *Dictionary of Irish Literature*. Rev. ed. Westport, Conn.: Greenwood, 1996; Marcus, Phillip L. *Yeats and the Beginning of the Irish Renaissance*. Syracuse: Syracuse University Press, 1987; Murphy, William M. *Prodigal Father: The Life of John Butler Yeats, 1839–1922*. Ithaca: Cornell University Press, 1978.

OLLAVE (Irish: *Ollamh*), most senior group among the poets (or *filidh*) in Ancient Ireland. Highest of seven grades of poets, it took nine to twelve years of study to become a member of the group. Several hundred primary stories had to be memorized, and at least a hundred secondary tales, before the applicant could claim the title of Ollave. The *filidh* enjoyed a privileged position within the society and were reputed for their wisdom and keen knowledge of custom and traditions. See also "The Madness of King Goll" (*CP*. 17).

REFERENCE: Ellis, Peter Berresford. *Dictionary of Celtic Mythology*. New York: Oxford University Press, 1992.

ON BAILE'S STRAND, one-act play. The first play by WBY to feature the mythological hero **Cuchulain**, it was written in 1903 and published in the collection *In the Seven Woods* (1903). In the central action, **Conchubar**, the High King, attempts to persuade Cuchulain to take the oath of fealty. Cuchulain, a wild, free spirit, at first refuses but under pressure agrees. As the ritual is taking place, a **Young Man** arrives from **Aoife's** country in Scotland and challenges Cuchulain to a fight. Cuchulain is reluctant to get involved, but under pressure, he becomes angry and seizes Conchubar. When the High King alleges that he has been taken over by witchcraft, Cuchulain accepts the Young Man's challenge. Only when he has killed the Young Man does Cuchulain realize he is his son. The main action opens and concludes with an encounter between a **Fool** and a **Blind Man**. WBY's source for the plot was "The Only Son of Aoife" in **Lady Gregory's** *Cuchulain of Muirthemne* (1902), but WBY departs from the original in some significant details, introducing autobiographical references and textual layerings that distance the action from its source to produce a play rich with ambiguity and dramatic tension. The play, widely regarded as among WBY's best, had its premiere on the opening night of the **Abbey Theatre**, 27 December 1904. The cast was Cuchulain, **Frank Fay**; Conchubar, George Roberts; Daire (an Old King), Arthur Sinclair; Blind Man, **Seamus O'Sullivan**; Fool, **W. G. Fay**; Young Man, P. MacShiubhlaigh. The chorus included **Sara Allgood**.

REFERENCES: Bjersby, Birgit. *The Interpretation of the Cuchulain Legend in the Works of W. B. Yeats*. Folcroft, Pa.: Folcroft, 1969; Ellis, Sylvia C. *The Plays of W. B. Yeats: Yeats and the Dancer*. London: Macmillan, 1995; Miller, Liam. *The Noble Drama of W. B. Yeats*. Dublin: Dolmen, 1977; Oppel, Frances Nesbitt. *Mask and Tragedy: Yeats and Nietzsche, 1902–10*. Charlottesville: University Press of Virginia, 1987.

O'NEILL, HUGH (c. 1540–1616), last of the great Irish chieftains. Although he was born Catholic, he was educated at the Protestant court of Queen Elizabeth I and adopted English ways. He served in the English army in Ireland from 1568 and was critical of his people's resistance to the English crown. When he inherited the title earl of Tyrone in 1585, his attitude toward the English presence in Ireland became somewhat ambivalent. He harbored survivors from the Spanish Armada, which had been wrecked off the coast of Ireland in 1588, and in 1591, he helped **Red Hugh O'Donnell** escape from **Dublin Castle**. He was proclaimed a traitor and, with the help of Red Hugh, decisively defeated the English at the Battle of the Yellow Ford in 1598. When Queen Elizabeth sent the earl of Essex, with an army of 20,000 men, to engage O'Neill in battle, he successfully manipulated Essex to agree to a truce, for which Essex lost his head. By 1600, O'Neill commanded much power and esteem throughout Ireland

and was intent on destroying English domination. In September 1601, a Spanish army led by Don Juan del Aguila arrived at the port of **Kinsale** in the southwest of Ireland. O'Neill harassed **Leinster** and the English Pale around Dublin, hoping to distract the English army, but they refused to fall into the trap and besieged the Spanish on their arrival. O'Neill and O'Donnell hurried to Kinsale, and although they had the resources and manpower to defeat the English, they failed to cohere as a fighting unit and were defeated. O'Neill surrendered, much of his land was confiscated, and he was forbidden to practice his religion. In 1607, he led the Flight of the Earls into exile in Rome, where his final years were spent in depressive melancholy.

REFERENCES: Bardon, Jonathan. *A History of Ulster.* Belfast: Blackstaff, 1992; Foster, R. F. *Modern Ireland 1600–1972.* 1988. Reprint. London: Penguin, 1989.

O'NEILL, MÁIRE. *See* **ALLGOOD, MOLLY.**

O'NEILL, OWEN ROE (c. 1590–1649), nephew of **Hugh O'Neill**. He served with distinction in the Spanish military, 1610–40, but in 1642, with the onset of the Civil War in England, he accepted an offer from **Ulster** rebels to lead them in a Rising against the English. O'Neill, proclaiming his loyalty to the English king and the Royalists against **Cromwell** and the Parliamentarians, took the oath of Catholic Confederacy in Kilkenny, November 1642, and signed a peace agreement with **Ormonde**, the king's deputy in Ireland. He successfully defeated the Scottish Parliamentarians, an army composed of Scottish Planter stock stationed in Ulster, at Benburb, County Tyrone, in June 1646. With this victory, he emerged as the only Irish leader who might defeat Cromwell, who landed in Dublin, 15 August 1649, but his death on 6 November 1649 put an end to hopes of an Irish victory. In 1909, when WBY was reading **John F. Taylor's** biography *Owen Roe O'Neill* (1896), he noted in his Journal that in his "directness and simplicity of mind" Owen Roe O'Neill was akin to the contemporary Protestant Ascendancy class, while his enemies had much in common with contemporary Catholics (*M.* 195).

REFERENCES: Bardon, Jonathan. *A History of Ulster.* Belfast: Blackstaff, 1992; Foster, R. F. *Modern Ireland 1600–1972.* 1988. Reprint. London: Penguin, 1989; Taylor, John F. *Owen Roe O'Neill.* London: Unwin, 1896.

ONLY JEALOUSY OF EMER, THE, one-act play in verse by WBY. It was first published by the **Cuala Press** in *Two Plays for Dancers* (1919). In the play, which is written in the style of the Japanese **Noh**, the inert body of **Cuchulain** lies on a bed, while his wife **Emer** and his mistress **Eithne Inguba** mourn his death. Unknown to them, the body of Cuchulain has been taken over by the mischievous **Bricriu**, while the **Ghost of Cuchulain** crouches at the front of the stage. Bricriu tells Emer that Cuchulain will be restored to life if she renounces his love. After she is shown a dance, in which the Ghost of Cuchulain is seduced by **Fand**, Emer is forced to give up Cuchulain's love. He is restored to life and the arms of his mistress. The action of *The Only Jealousy of Emer* owes much to WBY's emerging philosophical system, later set down in *A Vision*, but the sources for the plot are "The Sickbed of Cuchulain," in **Lady Gregory's** *Cuchulain of Muirthemne* (1902), and the Noh drama *Aoi no Ue*, in which a noble lady lies unconscious while she is viciously attacked by the jealous incarnation of her husband's love. *The Only Jealousy of Emer* was first produced by Albert van Dalsum in Amsterdam in 1922, with masks by the Dutch sculptor **Hildo Krop**. The first production in English was presented by the Dublin Drama League at the **Abbey Theatre**, May 1926, in a program introduced by WBY. The cast was: Ghost of Cuchulain, **F. J. McCormick**; Figure of Cuchulain, Arthur Shields; Emer, Eileen Crowe; Eithne Inguba, Shelah Richards; Woman of the Sídhe, Norah McGuinness; Musicians, John Stephenson, T. Moran, E. Leeming. The play was directed by **Lennox Robinson** and choreographed by **Ninette de Valois**. The masks and costumes were designed by Norah McGuinness. See also *Fighting the Waves*.

REFERENCES: Bjersby, Birgit. *The Interpretation of the Cuchulain Legend in the Works of W. B. Yeats*. Folcroft, Pa.: Folcroft, 1969; Ellis, Sylvia C. *The Plays of W. B. Yeats: Yeats and the Dancer*. London: Macmillan, 1995; Miller, Liam. *The Noble Drama of W. B. Yeats*. Dublin: Dolmen, 1977; Taylor, Richard. *A Reader's Guide to the Plays of W. B. Yeats*. New York: St. Martin's, 1984.

ON THE BOILER, pamphlet. It was written by WBY and published by the **Cuala Press** in 1938, with a cover design by **Jack B. Yeats**. The name was derived from an old rusty boiler on the quay at **Sligo** (town), from which locals, including one known as "the great McCoy," made speeches. In his preface, WBY indicates that the pamphlet is the first in a series; he identifies with the mad McCoy and will use this forum to "denounce the general wickedness" of the world. There was only one issue of *On the Boiler*, since WBY died the following January. In addition to six short essays, the first issue contained the play *Purgatory* and the first printing of the poems "Why should Not Old Men be Mad?" (*CP.* 388), "The Statesman's Holiday" (*CP.* 389), and "Crazy Jane on the Mountain" (*CP.* 390).

OONA, fictional character. In WBY's play *The Countess Cathleen*, she is a sympathetic and protective Nurse to the heroine, the **Countess Cathleen**. The role in the first production, May 1899, was played by Anna Mather.

O'RAHILLY, MICHAEL JOSEPH [The O'Rahilly] (1875–1916). Born in County Kerry, he was a well-to-do country gentleman and head of the clan O'Rahilly. After becoming involved in nationalist politics, he moved to Dublin, where he became a member of the Gaelic League and wrote for the Sinn Féin press. In 1913, as cofounder of the Irish Volunteers, he opposed recruitment of Irish soldiers to fight for England in World War I. In 1914, he was prominent in an abortive attempt to land German arms at **Howth**, outside Dublin. Opposed to the Easter Rising, he took the countermanding orders to **Limerick** on Easter Sunday, 1916, before returning to Dublin the next day to join the garrison commanded by **James Connolly**. He was shot in **Henry Street**, Dublin, during the evacuation of the **General Post Office** on the following Friday. WBY celebrates his mad heroism in the ballad "The O'Rahilly" (*CP.* 354), written in January 1937 and first published in *New Poems* (1938). He is not to be confused with Egan O'Rahilly, a Gaelic poet, whom WBY quotes in his introduction to *The Oxford Book of Modern Verse* (*LE.* 186) and in "Ireland after Parnell" (*A.* 217).

REFERENCE: Bax, Arnold. *Farewell My Youth, and Other Writings.* Aldershot: Scolar, 1992.

ORCHIL, a **Fomorian** sorceress. According to **Standish [James] O'Grady** in *The Coming of Cuculain* [*sic*]*: A Romance of the Heroic Age* (1894), she ruled the Underworld. In *The Countess Cathleen* (*CPl.* 46), WBY gives a powerful description of Orchil as a vaporous demon with long talons, seducing the soul of the **Countess Cathleen** and taking it to the Underworld. See also "The Madness of King Goll" (*CP.* 17).

ORDER OF THE GOLDEN DAWN, THE, occult society. The Order, which was dedicated to the study of Rosicrucianism and ritual magic, was founded in 1888 by William Wynn Westcott, Dr. D. R. Woodman, and **MacGregor Mathers**. WBY joined The Order in 1890, and fellow members included **Florence Farr, John Todhunter, Annie F. Horniman, George Pollexfen**, and **Maud Gonne**. As members of the Outer (or First) Order, they were required to take an oath of submission, to undergo a series of initiation rituals, and to study alchemical and astrological symbolism, the Hebrew alphabet, the ten Sephiroth and twenty-two Paths of the Cabalistic Tree of Life, and the Tarot. In 1891, WBY progressed to the Second Order, which focused on the study and practice of magic. After MacGregor Mathers was expelled from the society in 1900, WBY was appointed Imperator of the Outer Order and Instructor in Mystical Philosophy to the Second. He remained a member of The Order after his marriage in 1917, but he allowed his membership to lapse around 1921, amid continuing dissension among fellow Adepts. WBY's occult experiments embarrassed many of his friends, not least his mentor **John O'Leary**. Yet the poet rigorously defended his esoteric interests and proved through his writing that the study of magic and the rituals of The Order of the Golden Dawn offered him a symbolic language that he translated into powerful poetic imagery.

REFERENCES: Bachchan, Harbans Rai. *W. B. Yeats and Occultism.* New York: Weiser, 1974; Greer, Mary K. *Women of the Golden Dawn: Rebels and Priestesses.* Rochester, Vermont: Park Street Press, 1995; Harper, George Mills, ed. *Yeats and the Occult.* London: Macmillan, 1976; Harper, George Mills. *Yeats's Golden Dawn.* London: Macmillan, 1974; Hough, Graham. *The Mystery Religion of W. B. Yeats.* Sussex: Harvester, 1984; Moore, Virginia. *The Unicorn: William Butler Yeats' Search for Reality.* New York:

Octagon, 1973; Regardie, Israel. *The Golden Dawn: An Account of the Teachings, Rites and Ceremonies of the Order of the Golden Dawn.* St. Paul, Minn.: Llewellyn, 1995.

O'RIORDAN, CONAL [HOLMES O'CONNELL] (1874–1948), novelist and playwright. He was born in Dublin, the son of an eminent barrister, Daniel O'Connell O'Riordan. After attending the Jesuit school, Belvedere College, he intended entering the military. A fall from a horse caused a permanent spinal injury, and he turned to literature and the stage. He appeared as Engstrand in the English premiere of *Ghosts* by **Henrik Ibsen** and published short stories and novels under the pseudonym F. Norreys Connell. With the resignation of **W. G. Fay** from the **Abbey Theatre** in 1908, he was appointed manager, principally because he was a playwright, in contrast to Fay who was an actor and stage manager. After the death of **J. M. Synge** in 1909, O'Riordan was chosen to replace him on the board. In May 1910, **Annie F. Horniman**, upset because the Abbey had failed to close to mark the death of Edward VII, demanded the dismissal of O'Riordan. WBY opposed such action, but O'Riordan, frustrated with the tensions between Annie Horniman and the Abbey board, resigned and moved to England. There, he had some commercial success with lightweight comedies and romantic novels. Of his plays, the most successful was *The Piper*, a fantasy about a group of Irish patriots involved in the Rising of 1798, who argue amongst themselves over a prisoner. It was produced by the Abbey Theatre in 1908—although the first performance caused angry disturbances, which had to be quelled by WBY. He argued persuasively before the audience that the play was a satire about Irish heroes, frustrated in their endeavors by endless arguments and talk, citing as his examples **Robert Emmet** and **Parnell** (*UP2*. 362–63). Another fantasy by O'Riordan, *Time*, despite the negative reviews of the critics, impressed WBY when it was produced at the Abbey, April 1909 (*M*. 206–7, 209).

REFERENCES: Hunt, Hugh. *The Abbey: Ireland's National Theatre, 1904–1979.* Dublin: Gill & Macmillan, 1979; Robinson, Lennox. *Ireland's Abbey Theatre: A History, 1899–1951.* London: Sidgwick & Jackson, 1951.

ORMONDE. *See* **BUTLER**.

O'RORKE, FATHER TERENCE, parish priest and local historian. He was the author of the important historical work *History, Antiquities, and Present State of the Parishes of Ballysadare and Kilvarnet in the County of Sligo* (Dublin, 1878). The account of the dispossession of **Father John O'Hart**, which appears in the book, provided a source for WBY's "The Ballad of Father O'Hart" (*CP*. 23). WBY may have been inspired by Father O'Rorke's description of the Hawk Rock in **Sligo** (county) for his setting of *At the Hawk's Well*. A further local history by O'Rorke, *The History of Sligo Town and County* (1889), was published by private subscription. Among the subscribers was **George Pollexfen**.

WBY makes reference to Father O'Rorke's histories in his 1888 publication *Fairy and Folk Tales of the Irish Peasantry*.
    REFERENCE: Kirby, Sheelah. *The Yeats Country*. Dublin: Dolmen, 1966.

O'ROUGHLEY, TOM, fictional character. The name for this wise fool may be derived from **Roughley**, in the north of **Sligo** (county), an area familiar to WBY. See "Tom O'Roughley" (*CP*. 158).

OSCAR [also Osgar], son of **Oisin** and grandson of **Fionn Mac Cumhal**. He is the bravest warrior among the **Fianna** and is given command of an elite battalion called the "Terrible Broom." He leads the Fianna in the Battle of **Gabhra** in which Cairbre, the High King of Ireland, tries to destroy the power of the Fianna. After killing Cairbre in single combat, Oscar is mortally wounded, and the Fianna are defeated. Fionn comes from the Otherworld to mourn him. Oscar's death is recalled by Oisin in *The Wanderings of Oisin* (*CP*. 410), while in *The King's Threshold* (*CPl*. 110), the poet **Seanchan** dreams he is in **Almhuin** with Fionn and Oscar. In "The Statesman's Holiday" (*CP*. 389), the name Oscar refers to **Oscar Wilde**.
    REFERENCE: Ellis, Peter Berresford. *Dictionary of Celtic Mythology*. New York: Oxford University Press, 1992.

O'SULLIVAN, SEAMUS (1879–1958), poet and writer. He was born James Sullivan Starkey in Dublin, the son of a chemist. A founding member of the **Irish National Theatre Society**, he played leading roles in the first production of a number of plays by WBY, including the **Chamberlain** in *The King's Threshold* (October 1903), **Aibric** in *The Shadowy Waters* (January 1904), and the **Blind Man** in *On Baile's Strand* (December 1904). The following year, he published his first book of poetry, *The Twilight People* (1905), a collection of poems reminiscent in mood and feeling of the early Pre-Raphaelite poetry of WBY. Then followed *Verses: Sacred and Profane* (1908) and *The Earth-Lover and Other Verses* (1909). An ardent supporter of the nationalist Sinn Féin movement and a close friend of **Arthur Griffith**, the Sinn Féin leader, it was only with his collection *Requiem and Other Poems* (1917) that O'Sullivan expressed his political feelings in his poetry. He became a close friend of WBY and other major writers, **AE**, **James Joyce**, and **Oliver St. John Gogarty**. In 1923, he founded *The Dublin Magazine*, which he edited until his death. Almost every Irish writer of note was a contributor. He made a major contribution to the development of Irish writing by publishing and encouraging younger talents like Austin Clarke, **F. R. Higgins**, Liam O'Flaherty, Patrick Kavanagh, and Samuel Beckett, in addition to the established writers like WBY. While he edited *The Dublin Magazine*, O'Sullivan published few poems of his own, although he did publish his prose collections *Common Adventures* (1926) and *The Rose and Bottle* (1946). He appeared to recognize that his greatest contribution to Irish literature lay in encouraging others. In recognition of this work, the **Irish Academy of Letters** presented him with its Gregory medal in 1957.

REFERENCES: Hogan, Robert, ed. *Dictionary of Irish Literature.* Rev. ed. Westport, Conn.: Greenwood, 1996; Miller, Liam, ed. *Retrospect: The Work of Seamus O'Sullivan and Estella F. Solomons.* Dublin: Dolmen, 1973.

OXFORD, English university city. WBY was impressed with Oxford when he stayed there with his father's friend **York Powell** in 1888 and studied in the Bodleian Library. Not only was it a center of learning, but it was also close to the homes of friends like **John Masefield, Robert Bridges**, and **Lady Ottoline Morrell**. In early 1918, soon after his marriage, WBY and his wife rented a house in Oxford, at 45 Broad Street. In October 1919, they moved to 4 Broad Street, and from there he could hear the bell of **Christ Church**, the tolling of which he recalls in "All Soul's Night" (*CP.* 256). At 4 Broad Street, he continued his tradition of Monday nights "At Home" for literary friends. In 1921, he moved first to Minchen's Cottage, Shillingford, Berkshire, and then to Cuttlebrook House, Thame, where his son **Michael** was born. He moved back to 4 Broad Street in late 1921 and remained there until 20 March 1922, when he returned permanently to Ireland. His last visit to Oxford was in May 1931, when he was awarded an honorary degree from Oxford University.

REFERENCE: Bowra, C. M. *Memories, 1898–1939.* Cambridge: Harvard University Press, 1967; Strong, L. A. G. *Green Memory.* London: Methuen, 1961.

OXFORD BOOK OF MODERN VERSE, THE, anthology. WBY was invited to edit *The Oxford Book of Modern Verse* in late 1934, and he began working on the project almost immediately. He decided the anthology should begin with the death of **Tennyson** and include the work of contemporary poets, many of whom were unfamiliar to him. To remedy this, he read voraciously during the spring and summer of 1935, a period when he was ill and confined to his room. Many of the anthologies in his library had poems removed from them for further consideration, often in consultation with **Dorothy Wellesley**. His wife made the selection of his own poems for inclusion. He completed a draft of his introduction before mid-October, and the book was published in November 1936. It aroused controversy because of the selection of so many poems by minor writers, most of them personal friends of WBY. Only eight poems about World War I were included, while Wilfred Owen and Robert Graves were omitted altogether. WBY's views on modern poetry in his introduction were vigorously challenged, and he rose to the debate, being never happier than when he had a fight on his hands. Principally because of the public controversy, 15,000 copies of the anthology were sold in the first three months, and sales remained high— something that pleased him greatly!

P

PACKET FOR EZRA POUND, A, collection of essays and two poems. The essays, which were published by the **Cuala Press** in 1929, were written as a tribute to the poet **Ezra Pound**. The collection included the poems "At Algeciras—A Meditation upon Death" (*CP*. 278), composed while WBY was recuperating from an illness in 1928, and "Mohini Chatterjee" (*CP*. 279), a poem recalling the advice of the Indian philosopher **Mohini Chatterjee**, whom the youthful WBY met in Dublin in 1885. The essay "Introduction to the Great Wheel," later used as the introduction to *A Vision* (1937), was part of the collection.

PAGET, H[ENRY] M[ARRIOTT], artist and illustrator. He was an early resident in **Bedford Park**, where he became friendly with **John B. Yeats** and painted a portrait of WBY, 6 April 1889. This portrait, which was reproduced as the frontispiece to *Letters to the New Island* (1934), is now in the Ulster Museum, Belfast. Paget's sister-in-law was **Florence Farr**, with whom he acted in the first production of **John Todhunter's** *A Sicilian Idyll* at the Bedford Park Clubhouse, May 1890. His daughter, Dorothy Paget, played the **Faery Child** in the first production of *The Land of Heart's Desire*, Avenue Theatre, London, 1894.

REFERENCE: Murphy, William M. *Prodigal Father: The Life of John Butler Yeats (1839–1922)*. Ithaca: Cornell University Press, 1978.

PAIRC-NA-CARRAIG. *See* **SEVEN WOODS.**

PAIRC-NA-LEE. *See* **SEVEN WOODS.**

PAIRC-NA-TARAV. *See* **SEVEN WOODS.**

PAISTIN FINN, title character in a **Munster** folk song. WBY used the song in *The Pot of Broth* and included it in his collection *A Full Moon in March* (1935). Paistin Finn means "Little Child of Fionn," which suggests the poem may be a popular version of a song from Irish mythology.

PALLAS ATHENE. *See* **ATHENE.**

PALMER, SAMUEL (1805–81), illustrator, landscape painter, and visionary. He was the leading figure in a group of artists who called themselves "the Ancients." Brought together by their devotion to the paintings and writings of **William Blake**, the group included **Edward Calvert**. Eccentric in dress and behavior, the Ancients met frequently in the village of Shoreham, Kent, where Palmer lived with his father. Palmer is known not only for his sepia drawings of moonlit landscapes but also for his landscapes of Italy and his etchings for the *Eclogues of Virgil* (1883) and *The Shorter Poems of John Milton* (1889), among them *The Bellman, The Lonely Tower, The Sleeping Shepherd*, and *The Early Ploughman*. In his poem "The Phases of the Moon" (*CP.* 183), WBY alludes to *The Lonely Tower*, an engraving that illustrated **John Milton's** "Il Penseroso" (1889). While it is not known how WBY became acquainted with the work of Samuel Palmer, it is likely to have been through his interest in Blake. He is thought to have read a short memoir of Palmer written by his son, A. H. Palmer, a year after his death. In his essay "A Symbolic Artist" (*UP2.* 135), he quotes from Palmer's *Life and Letters*, published by A. H. Palmer in 1892. In a monograph *Beulah to Byzantium*, Raymond Lister examines the connections between Palmer's use of moon imagery and the many references to the moon in WBY's poetry. He argues that WBY was much influenced by Palmer in the simple, natural landscape of the early poems like "The Lake Isle of Innisfree." WBY names Palmer with Blake and Calvert in his elegy "Under Ben Bulben" (*CP.* 397). He purchased thirteen slides by Palmer and Edward Calvert to illustrate a lecture, "William Blake and His School," that he gave at the **Abbey Theatre**, 14 April 1918, and on his American **Lecture Tour,** 1920.

REFERENCES: Binyon, Laurence. *The Followers of William Blake: Edward Calvert, Samuel Palmer, George Richmond and Their Circle.* New York: B. Blom, 1968; Gordon, D. J., ed. *W. B. Yeats: Images of a Poet.* Manchester: University of Manchester, 1961; Lister, Raymond. *Beulah to Byzantium: A Study of Parallels in the Works of W. B. Yeats, William Blake, Samuel Palmer & Edward Calvert.* In Dolmen Press Centenary Papers. Vol. II. Dublin: Dolmen, 1965; Lister, Raymond. *Samuel Palmer and "the Ancients."* Cambridge: Cambridge University Press, 1984; Loizeaux, Elizabeth Bergmann. *Yeats and the Visual Arts.* New Brunswick and London: Rutgers University Press, 1986; Malins, Edward. *Samuel Palmer's Italian Honeymoon.* London and New York: Oxford University Press, 1968.

PAN, son of Hermes, in Greek mythology. The rustic god of **Arcady,** whose mother was a mortal, he is depicted with a human body but with the legs and feet of a goat, and goat's horns, ears, and tail. He is associated with caves and caverns, and the music of the pipes that bear his name. WBY presents a graphic picture of him in "News for the Delphic Oracle" (*CP*. 376). See also ***Sophocles' King Oedipus*** (*CPl*. 507).

PARIS, son of **Priam**, king of **Troy**, in Greek mythology. After being abandoned on Mount Ida because of a prophecy that he would destroy Troy, he was rescued by shepherds. Later, he was invited to settle a dispute among the goddesses **Athene**, Hera, and Aphrodite. He judged in favor of Aphrodite, who promised him the most beautiful woman in the world. He visited **Sparta**, where he persuaded **Helen**, wife of King Menelaus, to elope with him. In revenge, the Greeks invaded Troy, and in the ensuing war, Paris was mortally wounded. See also "A Man Young and Old" (*CP*. 249) and "Lullaby" (*CP*. 300).

PARMENIDES (c. 514 B.C.–?), Greek philosopher. He opposed Heraclitus's belief in the theory of change, in which everything in the universe is in a constant state of flux. According to Parmenides, the world of reality, which may only be conceived by logic, is unchangeable and immovable. See also "The Gift of Harun Al-Rashid" (*CP*. 513).
    REFERENCE: Heidegger, Martin. *Parmenides*. Trans. Andre Schuwer and Richard Rojcewicz. Bloomington: Indiana University Press, 1992.

PARNELL, CHARLES STEWART (1846–91), politician and leader of the Irish Parliamentary Party. He was born in Avondale House, Rathdrum, County Wicklow, the son of a wealthy Protestant landowner with nationalist leanings. His mother was the daughter of Admiral Stewart of the U.S. Navy. Educated in England, he enrolled at Magdalene College, Cambridge, but left without taking a degree. Committed to the Irish Home Rule movement, he entered the British Parliament in 1875 as Home Rule M.P. for **Meath**. There he was so successful in his use of obstructionist techniques that he focused national attention on Irish social problems. He became the first president of the National Land League in 1879 and leader of the Irish Parliamentary Party a year later. His agitation on the Irish Land Question led to violence against landlords, and he was imprisoned by the British in October 1881. He was released in May 1882, under the "Kilmainham Treaty," and in Parliament, he cleverly played off the Liberal majority against the Tories to secure Prime Minister Gladstone's support for Irish Home Rule. At the general election of 1885, the Irish Party had a triumphant victory, winning almost every seat in the country, but Gladstone's Home Rule Bill, which faced fierce rancor from the Conservatives, was defeated, and Gladstone lost office in the next British election. From then until 1890, Parnell was at the peak of his career. Public opinion in Britain had swung in his favor, and he was undoubtedly the "uncrowned king of Ireland," reputed for his brilliant political maneuvers but emotionally cold and arrogant. In the late 1870s, he had formed an attachment to the society beauty Katharine (Kitty) O'Shea and, in 1889, was named corespondent in a divorce case brought by her husband Captain William Henry O'Shea (1840–1905). Parnell refused to defend the action, and the resultant scandal cost him the support not only of the Irish Parliamentary Party but also of the Irish Catholic hierarchy and the Liberal Party. In June 1891, he married Kitty O'Shea and died in her arms five months later. In the general election of 1892, the Irish Parliamentary Party was defeated by a huge majority. In October 1891, by sheer chance, WBY met **Maud Gonne** at Kingstown (Dun Laoghaire) harbor as she disembarked from the boat bringing Parnell's body to Ireland. At the time, WBY, in contrast to his contemporaries, like **James Joyce**, wrote little about the fallen hero, with the exception of a short poem "Mourn— and Then Onward!" (*VP*. 737), published in the Parnellite newspaper *United Ireland* but excluded from all editions of his **Collected Poems**. In 1913, he wrote about Parnell in the poem "To a Shade" (*CP*. 123), and he returned to the subject in the mid-1930s with "Parnell's Funeral" (*CP*. 319), "Come Gather Round Me, Parnellites" (*CP*. 355), and "Parnell" (*CP*. 359), in which the dead hero becomes a late mask for the aging poet looking at the world with a cold, dispassionate eye. In a Commentary on "A Parnellite at Parnell's Funeral," an early title for "Parnell's Funeral" (*VP*. 832–35), he associates the death of Parnell with the ending of a significant era in Irish history. He also writes of him in "Parnell" (*EI*. 486–90), an essay written in 1936 in response to a visit by Henry Harrison, author of *Parnell Vindicated*.

REFERENCES: Cullingford, Elizabeth. *Yeats, Ireland and Fascism*. New York and London: New York University Press, 1981; Foster, Robert F. *Charles Stewart Parnell: The Man and His Family*. Hassocks, England: Harvester; Atlantic Highlands, N.J.: Humanities, 1976; Freyer, Grattan. *W. B. Yeats and the Anti-Democratic Tradition*. Dublin: Gill & Macmillan, 1981; Kee, Robert. *The Laurel and the Ivy: The Story of Charles Stewart Parnell and Irish Nationalism*. London: Hamish Hamilton, 1993; Lyons, F. S. L. *Charles Stewart Parnell*. London: Collins, 1977.

PATER, WALTER [HORATIO] (1839–94), essayist and critic. He was born in London and educated at King's School, Canterbury, and Queen's College, **Oxford**, where he studied Greek philosophy and developed a passionate interest in classical studies. Elected a Fellow of Brasenose College, Oxford, at the age of twenty-five, he exercised a major influence on many of his students, including **Oscar Wilde** and Gerard Manley Hopkins, with his belief in the moral importance of artistic perfection and that art acknowledged no utilitarian function but existed for itself alone. His own style, which was distinguished by its clarity and precision, reflected this belief. His critical study "Winckelmann" was published in the *Westminster Review* in 1867. When it was included in *The Renaissance: Studies in Art and Poetry* (1873), a work that Wilde thought "the very flower of decadence," it established his reputation. His other outstanding works included the substantial *Marius the Epicurean* (1885), the philosophical *Imaginary Portraits* (1887), and *Plato and Platonism* (1893), which gave a literary interpretation of **Plato's** philosophy. Pater made a profound impression on the Pre-Raphaelite movement and the decadence of the late nineteenth century. He was the most admired literary authority of the **Rhymers' Club**, his name frequently on the lips of his devotees **Lionel Johnson** and **Arthur Symons**, who visited him in Oxford. Indeed, in "The Tragic Generation" (*A.* 303), writing of Pater, WBY suggests his philosophy, which concentrated on learning and the artistic life to the neglect of the personal, may have contributed to the unfulfilled lives of his disciples. It is apparent from WBY's early verse, and from the prose style of *The Secret Rose*, that Pater's views were influential on the impressionable young poet, in his richly ornamented cadences and the imaginative subject matter removed from everyday life. WBY acknowledges this influence in "The Tragic Generation" (*A.* 321). He recalls reading Pater in a Dublin garden (possibly the garden of **George Moore**, another follower of Pater), trying to convince himself that Pater was a poor writer because he perplexed him and made him doubt himself (*UP2.* 261). He included an extract from Pater's description of the *Mona Lisa* as the opening selection in *The Oxford Book of Modern Verse* (1936), and he had copies of Pater's *Marius the Epicurean* (2 vols.), *Plato and Platonism*, and *The Renaissance: Studies in Art and Poetry* in his library (*OS.* nos. 1537–39). See also "The Phases of the Moon" (*CP.* 183).

REFERENCES: Donoghue, Denis. *Walter Pater: Lover of Strange Souls*. New York: Alfred A. Knopf, 1995; Loizeaux, Elizabeth Bergmann. *Yeats and the Visual Arts*. New Brunswick and London: Rutgers University Press, 1986.

PAUDEEN, diminutive form of the Irish name *Padraic*. It is the name of one of the beggars in WBY's play *The Unicorn from the Stars*. It is used derogatively by WBY in his poem "To a Wealthy Man who promised a Second Subscription to the Dublin Municipal Gallery if it were proved the People wanted Pictures" (*CP.* 119).

PAUL, [CHARLES] KEGAN (1828–1902), publisher. He was born at White Lackington, near Ilminster, Somerset, the son of an Anglican minister, and claimed Irish descent through a maternal grandmother, Mary Kegan. He was educated at Eton College and Oxford University, and after teaching at Eton, he was ordained into the Church of England and became vicar of Sturminster Marshall, Dorset, in 1862. He encountered conflict with the Church hierarchy because of his radical and High Church views, and in 1874, he retired from the clergy and moved to London. He had always enjoyed the friendship of notable Victorian writers and, in 1877, took over the publishing house of Henry Samuel King. He was joined in 1881 by Alfred Chenevix Trench, son of the archbishop of Dublin. They published under the name of Kegan Paul, Trench & Company and followed a policy of encouraging younger writers of merit, among them **Katharine Tynan, Wilfred Scawen Blunt**, and WBY, whose poem *The Wanderings of Oisin* was published by Kegan Paul in 1889.

REFERENCE: Paul, Kegan. *Memories*. Hamden, Conn.: Archon, 1971.

PAVLOVA, ANNA [MATVEYEVNA] (1885–1931), Russian dancer. Trained at the Imperial Ballet School, St. Petersburg, she made her debut at the Marinsky Theatre in 1899, when she was fourteen. She came to prominence when she toured the major capitals of Europe in 1906 and 1908 and established her preeminence as a prima ballerina when she danced with Diaghilev's Russian Ballet in 1910. She was noted for her superb technique and moving interpretation in a range of classical ballets, including *Giselle*. Her greatest performance, however, was in *The Dying Swan*, composed for her by Michael Fokine from the music of Saint-Saëns. In "His Phoenix" (*CP*. 170), WBY celebrates her popularity in Europe.

REFERENCES: Kerensky, Oleg. *Anna Pavlova*. New York: Dutton, 1973; Money, Keith. *Anna Pavlova: Her Life and Art*. New York: Knopf, 1982.

PEACOCK THEATRE, experimental wing of the **Abbey Theatre**. When **Annie F. Horniman** took a lease on the **Mechanics Institute** in 1904, she did not acquire all of the building, which was still being used by the Institute. In 1925, when the Institute no longer existed, the whole building was acquired by WBY and the directors of the Abbey Theatre. A basement became a storeroom, the first floor was made into a café (it later housed the Abbey School of Acting), and a large room on the second floor was transformed into a small theater, the Peacock. The auditorium, which was decorated in the peacock colors of dark blue and green with a hint of gold, was raked and held 102 persons. The stage itself was small, but there was a scene dock and two large dressing rooms on an upper story. The first performance in the Peacock was given by Dublin's New Players, November 1925, but the Peacock later became an alternative space for performances of the Abbey School of Acting and the presentation of plays in the Irish language. In the fall of 1928, Hilton Edwards and Micheál Mac-Liammóir rented the Peacock. After presenting a number of productions on the small stage, they moved to the Gate Theatre and there strengthened their reputation for innovation and artistry. The Peacock Theatre was destroyed in the Abbey fire in 1951 but was included as a second theater in the new Abbey, which opened in 1966.

REFERENCES: Hunt, Hugh. *The Abbey: Ireland's National Theatre, 1904–1979*. Dublin: Gill & Macmillan, 1979; Robinson, Lennox. *Ireland's Abbey Theatre: A History, 1899–1951*. London: Sidgwick & Jackson, 1951.

PEARSE, PADRAIC [HENRY] (1879–1916), writer, teacher, scholar, and patriot. He was born in Dublin, the son of an English father and Irish mother, and educated by the Christian Brothers, Westland Row, Dublin, and at University College, Dublin. He completed a law degree at King's Inns, London, in 1901, and returned to Dublin to edit *An Claidheamh Soluis* (*The Sword of Light*), the official journal of the Gaelic League. In 1908, he founded St. Enda's, in Rathfarnham, County Dublin, a bilingual school committed to the development of an Irish culture through the Irish language. For his students, he wrote pageants

and plays, all with religious or heroic themes. These became increasingly didactic in tone, reflecting his personal growth from teacher to preacher, and
promulgated a message of heroic self-sacrifice for Ireland. He joined the Irish
Republican Brotherhood (IRB) in 1913. During the two years preceding the
Easter Rising in 1916, as the commander of the Irish Volunteers, he drew inspiration from the memory of **Robert Emmet** and was a passionate and dynamic
spokesman for Ireland's separation from England by physical force. He was a
member of the Military Council of the IRB and director of Military Operations.
In 1916, on the eve of the Easter Rising, he was appointed commander in chief
of the rebel forces, and as president of the short-lived Provisional Government,
he read the Proclamation of the Irish Republic from the steps of the **General
Post Office** (GPO) in the center of Dublin. The rebellion lasted five days. Pearse,
who held the GPO with **James Connolly**, surrendered with the other rebels and
was executed on 3 May 1916. In addition to his political activities, he translated
poetry from the Gaelic and was a prolific writer of plays, poems, and stories,
in both Irish and English. His play *The Singer* was performed at the **Abbey
Theatre** in 1942. WBY met Padraic Pearse on a number of occasions and shared
the platform with him at the centenary celebrations for **Thomas Davis** in 1914.
WBY was in England at the time of the Easter Rising, but he wrote to **Lady
Gregory** expressing his concern over the executions and his despondency about
the future (*WL*. 612–14). He admired the rebels, especially Pearse, recognizing
that through their single-mindedness and dedication they had been transformed
into men and women of heroic stature and accomplishment. He expressed these
feelings most powerfully in his elegy "Easter 1916" (*CP*. 202), the first of a
number of poems about the Easter Rising that he wrote over the next twenty-
three years. The others include "Sixteen Dead Men" (*CP*. 205), "The Rose
Tree" (*CP*. 206), "The O'Rahilly" (*CP*. 354), "The Statues" (*CP*. 375), and
the concluding lyric of *The Death of Cuchulain* (*CPl*. 704).

REFERENCES: Edwards, Ruth Dudley. *Patrick Pearse: The Triumph of Failure*. London: Gollancz, 1977; Hogan, Robert, ed. *Dictionary of Irish Literature*. Rev. ed. Westport, Conn.: Greenwood, 1996; Porter, Raymond J. *P. H. Pearse*. New York: Twayne,
1973.

PÉGUY, CHARLES [PIERRE] (1873–1914), poet and essayist. Born into an impoverished French family, he dedicated himself to socialism and worked tirelessly throughout his life for just causes. In 1900, he began editing *Cahiers de
la Quinzaine*, a periodical in which he published his own work and that of other
aspiring writers. Although not Catholic, his writings were deeply spiritual, and
he became one of the foremost Catholic writers in France. WBY was introduced
to his poetry by **Iseult Gonne**, who read him Péguy's dramatic poem *Mystère
de la Charité de Jeanne d'Arc* (1910), when he visited her in Normandy in 1917
(*LE*. 33). WBY shares his enthusiasm for the poetry of Péguy in "If I Were
Four-and-Twenty" (*LE*. 35–36).

REFERENCE: Villiers, Marjorie H. *Charles Péguy: A Study in Integrity*. Westport,
Conn.: Greenwood, 1975.

PELEUS, son of **Aeacus,** in Greek mythology. He captured **Thetis,** one of the Nereids, and married her on Mount Pelion. In the poem "News for the Delphic Oracle" (*CP.* 376), WBY describes Peleus staring at Thetis, infatuated by her beauty, as in the painting by Nicholas Poussin, *The Marriage of Peleus and Thetis,* which hangs in the **National Gallery of Ireland.**

PER AMICA SILENTIA LUNAE, collection of essays. Published by Macmillan and Company in 1918, they were written after WBY returned from visiting **Maud Gonne** in Normandy in 1917. The collection contained the poem "Ego Dominus Tuus" (*CP.* 180), in addition to a prologue and an epilogue written for **Iseult Gonne,** whom WBY addressed by the code name "Maurice" (*LE.* 33). The title of the collection is from **Virgil's** *Aeneid,* translated by WBY as "through the friendly silences of the moon" (*LE.* 293).

PERSEUS, son of Zeus and Danaë, in Greek mythology. His mother was the daughter of Acrisius, king of Argos. Warned by the oracle that his grandson will bring about his death, Acrisius sends Perseus and his mother out to sea to perish. They float to Seriphus, where King Polydectes rescues them and falls in love with Danaë. Perseus obstructs the relationship and is sent by the king to bring back the head of Medusa. The gods aid Perseus in his task, and on his journey back to Seriphas, he rescues Andromeda from a sea monster and marries her. He kills Polydectes because he is still making advances to his mother, returns to Argos, and while competing in a discus contest, accidentally kills his grandfather Acrisius. In the poem "Her Triumph" (*CP.* 310), WBY presents Perseus as a heroic lover. See also *Discoveries* (*EI.* 281).

PETRONIUS ARBITER (d. 66), satirist. Born into a wealthy Roman family, he was a lover of luxury and fine living. He was given the title Arbiter Elegantiae when he served at the court of the emperor Nero. When threatened with downfall, Petronius planned his own death. He opened his veins and made his dying a leisurely procedure, attended by celebrations and festivities. He is the author of the satire *Petronii Arbitri Satyricon,* most of which has been lost. He is best known for the surviving fragment *Cena Trimalchionis* (*Trimalchio's Dinner*), a humorous account of the tastes and activities of the newly rich vulgarian Trimalchio, a figure modeled on Nero. See also "Upon a Dying Lady" (*CP.* 177), in which WBY makes connections between the dignified attitude of the dying **Mabel Beardsley** and that of Petronius Arbiter.

REFERENCES: Bagnani, Gilbert. *Arbiter of Elegance: A Study of the Life and Works of C. Petronius.* Toronto: University of Toronto Press, 1954; Kelly, Walter K., ed. *Erotica: The Elegies of Propertius.* London, Bell, 1880.

PHIDIAS (c. 490–c. 432 B.C.), sculptor. Regarded by his contemporaries as the greatest artist of ancient Greece, he was said to have seen the images of the gods and revealed them to the world. He had a profound influence on later sculptors only through descriptions of his work, since it is believed there are no original examples of his sculpture in existence. His greatest achievements were the *Athena Parthenos* at Athens and *Zeus* in the temple at Olympia. Both were chryselephantine statues, while Zeus, seated on a highly ornamental throne, wore a cloak covered with sculptural decorations. A torso of **Athene**, now in Paris, is considered the nearest to the original work of Phidias to have survived, while the Parthenon frieze, attributed to Phidias, but probably executed by students from his designs, is now in the **British Museum**. In the poem ''Nineteen Hundred and Nineteen'' (*CP*. 232), WBY names Phidias's sculptures among the ''many ingenious lovely things'' that no longer exist. See also ''The Statues'' (*CP*. 375) and ''Under Ben Bulben'' (*CP*. 397).

REFERENCES: Gardner, Ernest A. *Six Greek Sculptors*. Freeport, N.Y.: Books for Libraries, 1967; Loizeaux, Elizabeth Bergmann. *Yeats and the Visual Arts*. New Brunswick and London: Rutgers University Press, 1986; Schrader, Hans. *Phidias*. Frankfurt am Main: Frankfurter, 1924.

PLARR, VICTOR [GUSTAVE] (1863–1929), poet and librarian. In the early 1890s, he was librarian of King's College, London, and in 1897, he was appointed librarian to the Royal College of Surgeons, a position that he held for thirty years. He was a member of the **Rhymers' Club** and contributed to the two anthologies that they published in 1892 and 1894. WBY favorably compared the quality of his verse with that of **Ernest Dowson, Lionel Johnson** and **Richard Le Gallienne** (*KLI*. 391). His poems were included in *The Garland of New Poetry by Various Writers* (1899), and his collection *In the Dorian Mood* was published in 1896. His *Men and Women of the Time* (1895) included a brief biographical note on WBY. His most significant work was the memoir *Ernest Dowson, 1887–1897: Reminiscences, Unpublished Letters and Marginalia* (1914). His *Collected Poems*, edited by Ian Fletcher, was published in 1974.

REFERENCES: Alford, Norman. *The Rhymers' Club: Poets of the Tragic Generation*. New York: St. Martin's, 1994; Gardiner, Bruce. *The Rhymers' Club: A Social and Intellectual History*. New York: Garland, 1988; Gardner, Joann. *Yeats and the Rhymers' Club: A Nineties' Perspective*. New York: Peter Lang, 1989.

PLATO (c. 429–347 B.C.), philosopher. He was born to a noble family and, in 407 B.C., became a pupil and friend of Socrates. In 388 B.C., after living for a time at the court of Dionysus the Elder, in Syracuse, he returned to Athens, where he founded the Academy, a school in which he taught philosophy and mathematics, until his death. All his known writings have survived, including his twenty-five *Dialogues*, thirteen *Epistles*, and some *Definitions*. His *Dialogues* constitute one of the most influential bodies of writing in the history of Western civilization. They are also considered great works of literature, distinguished by vivid prose and witty and perceptive portrayals of contemporary Greek life. Among his celebrated *Dialogues* are *Symposium*, on the love of beauty, *Phaedo*, on immortality, and *Philebus*, on the mean as the ethical ideal, but the best known is his *Republic*, an ideal state in which each class performs the tasks for which it is best suited. Thus, the philosopher rules, the soldier fights, and the worker toils. Ideas were central to Plato's thinking. They gave life and significance to the world of the senses and made existence purposeful. His best-known exposition of this theory was the "parable of the cave" in the *Republic*. He taught the preexistence of the soul and that knowledge is partly a recollection of a previous life. He believed the human soul was immortal because it was indestructible, and he believed in a world soul and in the existence of a creator who was responsible for the physical universe. Virtue was the harmony or health of the soul, in which the rational part ruled the other parts. In the poem "Among School Children" (*CP.* 242), WBY refers to Plato and to an idea from the *Symposium* in which Plato argues, through the character of the comic dramatist Aristophanes, that a man and woman were originally one body until divided in two by Zeus. Love is the search for lost unity. In "The Tower" (*CP.* 218), WBY rejects the abstract thought of Plato and **Plotinus**, preferring to find inspiration in the imagination and observation. See also "His Bargain" (*CP.* 299), "Mad as the Mist and Snow" (*CP.* 301), "What Then?" (*CP.* 347).

REFERENCE: Buchanan, Scott, ed. *The Portable Plato.* New York: Penguin, 1979.

PLAUTUS, [TITUS MACCIUS] (c. 254–184 B.C.), playwright. He is believed to have been born in northeast Italy. He wrote his plays in idiomatic Latin and is best known for his ingenious plots, coarse humor, and the creation of a range of comic figures, most notably the braggart-buffoon and parasite-slave, two stock figures who have appeared in the plays of major European writers since that time. WBY refers to performances of the plays of Plautus at the court of **Ercole, Duke of Ferrara**, in his poem "To a Wealthy Man who promised a Second Subscription to the Dublin Municipal Gallery if it were proved the People wanted Pictures" (*CP.* 119).

REFERENCES: Anderson, William S. *Barbarian Play: Plautus' Roman Comedy.* Toronto: University of Toronto Press, 1993; Segal, Erich. *Roman Laughter: The Comedy of Plautus.* New York: Oxford University Press, 1987.

PLAYER QUEEN, THE, full-length play in prose. The play, which WBY began writing in 1908, was not printed until 1922, when it appeared in *The Dial*. It was subsequently published in *Plays in Prose and Verse* (1922) and included in the ***Collected Plays of W. B. Yeats*** (1934, 1952). The action of the play takes place in an unspecified country, sometime in the past. The local people are angry with their **Queen**, whom they never see. A group of traveling players arrive at the Queen's castle to present a play about **Noah** and the Flood. The leading man is **Septimus**, a drunken poet, who complains about the poor reception he has received in the town and the behavior of his wife **Decima**, the leading actress, who has disappeared. An angry mob attacks the castle, and all the players flee. Decima comes out of hiding to find herself betrayed by Septimus, who has left with **Nona**, another actress. She is about to kill herself when the terrified Queen enters. They exchange clothes, and the Queen departs from the castle, leaving Decima in her place. All the people, with the exception of Septimus, and the Prime Minister, whom she has chosen to marry, unknowingly accept Decima as Queen. After she has been entertained by the traveling players, the new Queen offers them money and forbids them from returning to her kingdom. *The Player Queen* had its first production at the King's Hall, Covent Garden, London, May 1919, when it was performed by the London Stage Society. The cast was as follows: Decima, **Máire O'Neill**; First Old Man, Brember Wills; Second Old Man, Orlando Barnett; Septimus, Nicholas Hannen; Tom of the Hundred Tales, Cyril Wilson; Peter of the Purple Pelican, Ernest Warburton; Tapster, Ernest Meads; Old Beggar, Brember Wills; Prime Minister, Hubert Carter; Nona, Edith Evans; Queen, Gwen Richardson; Stage Manager, J. Leslie Frith. It was produced and designed by Archibald Welland. The first performance at the **Abbey Theatre** was given in December 1919.

REFERENCES: Bradley, Anthony. *William Butler Yeats*. New York: Frederick Ungar, 1979; Ellis, Sylvia C. *The Plays of W. B. Yeats: Yeats and the Dancer*. London: Macmillan, 1995; Miller, Liam. *The Noble Drama of W. B. Yeats*. Dublin: Dolmen, 1977; Taylor, Richard. *A Reader's Guide to the Plays of W. B. Yeats*. New York: St. Martin's, 1984.

PLAYS AND CONTROVERSIES, collection of six plays, an essay, and a preface. Published by Macmillan and Company, London, 1923, New York, 1924, and reprinted in London, 1927, this volume contains a long essay, ''The Irish Dramatic Movement,'' largely taken from the magazine *Samhain*, together with the early verse dramas *The Countess Cathleen* and *The Land of Heart's Desire* and the later plays for dancers, *At the Hawk's Well, The Only Jealousy of Emer, The Dreaming of the Bones*, and *Calvary*. The volume also includes a Note on each of the six plays, and a preface to *The Land of Heart's Desire*, together with music for *At The Hawk's Well* and *The Dreaming of the Bones*. The frontispiece is taken from a charcoal drawing of WBY by **John Singer Sargent**, dated 1908. Seven renderings by **Edmund Dulac** for costumes, masks, and the black cloth from *At the Hawk's Well* are also included.

PLAYS FOR AN IRISH THEATRE, collections of plays. They were published by **A. H. Bullen** in 1903, 1904, 1905, 1907 as volumes 1–5 of *Plays for an Irish Theatre*. The volumes contained: *Where There Is Nothing* (1903), *The Hour-Glass, Cathleen Ni Houlihan*, and *The Pot of Broth* (1904), *The King's Threshold* and *On Baile's Strand* (1904), **J. M. Synge's** *The Well of the Saints* (1905), with an introduction by WBY, and *Deirdre* (1907). An edition of seven plays by WBY, with designs by **Gordon Craig**, was published by Bullen at the Shakespeare Head Press in 1911, under the same title. This edition contained *Deirdre, The Green Helmet, On Baile's Strand, The King's Threshold, The Hour-Glass, Cathleen Ni Houlihan*, and *The Shadowy Waters*.

PLOTINUS (c. 205–270), mystic, philosopher, and founder of Neoplatonism. He was born in Lycopolis, Egypt, and studied philosophy in **Alexandria**—hence, WBY calls him "a stark Egyptian" in "Under Ben Bulben" (*CP*. 397). After 244, he opened a school in Rome and evolved his major philosophical ideas based on the teachings of **Plato**. He drew on other Greek philosophers, on Eastern Zoroastrianism, and on Hinduism. He explained the deity by developing the idea of emanation in which a powerful, all-embracing unity flows from a central source, making "the universe a single complex living creature, one from all." His rational ideas, infused with mysticism, had a profound impact on early Christian thinkers, among them St. Augustine, although Plotinus himself opposed Christianity. Later Neoplatonists imbued the central beliefs of Plotinus's philosophy with such disparate elements as divination, demonology, and astrology. In WBY's poem "The Delphic Oracle upon Plotinus" (*CP*. 306), the soul of the great philosopher is described entering heaven. Volumes of **Stephen MacKenna's** translation of Plotinus were in WBY's library (*OS*. nos. 1589–94). See also "The Tower" (*CP*. 218).

REFERENCES: Barnwell, William C. "The Blandness of Yeats' Rhadamanthus." *English Language Notes* 14, no. 3 (1977); Evangeliou, Christos. *Aristotle's Categories and Porphyry*. Leiden and New York: 1988; MacKenna, Stephen, trans. *Plotinus: The Ethical Treatises, Being the Treatises of the First Ennead with Porphyry's Life of Plotinus*. London: Medici Society, 1917.

POEMS, collection of poetry and two plays. The first edition of WBY's collected work, it was published in 1895 by **T. Fisher Unwin**. Seven hundred and seventy-five copies were printed, of which 25 were on vellum and signed by the author. WBY wrote to Fisher Unwin in October 1894, inviting him to publish a collected edition and specifying certain conditions, all of which were met. The projected title of the collection was *Under the Moon*, but this was dropped in favor of the simpler title. *Poems* (1895) contained *The Wanderings of Oisin, The Countess Cathleen*, and *The Land of Heart's Desire*, besides those poems in *Crossways* and *The Rose*.

POLLEXFEN, ALFRED [EDWARD] (1854–1916), WBY's youngest uncle. He was born in **Sligo** and, as a young man, joined his oldest brother, **Charles Pollexfen**, in the **Liverpool** offices of his father's company, the Sligo Steam Navigation Company. Unmarried, he spent many years there as a clerk and in his spare time held the post of secretary to the Dickens Society in Liverpool. On the death of his brother **George** in 1910, he returned to the family business in Sligo and lived alone in lodgings in the town until ill health forced him to enter a nursing home in Bray, County Wicklow, where he died. A gentle, sensitive man, he played the concertina and loved literature. WBY pays tribute to him in the poem "In Memory of Alfred Pollexfen" (*CP*. 175), written immediately after his death.

REFERENCES: Murphy, William M. *Family Secrets: William Butler Yeats and His Relatives*. Syracuse, N.Y.: Syracuse University Press, 1995; Murphy, William M. *Prod-*

igal Father: The Life of John Butler Yeats (1839–1922). Ithaca: Cornell University Press, 1978; Murphy, William M. *The Yeats Family and the Pollexfens of Sligo*. Dublin: Dolmen, 1971.

POLLEXFEN, CHARLES (1838–1923), WBY's uncle. He was born in **Sligo**, the eldest son of **William Pollexfen**. He met WBY's father, **John B. Yeats**, when they attended Atholl Academy in the Isle of Man. After returning to Sligo, Charles joined the marines. On his discharge, he was sent by his father to manage the affairs of the Sligo Steam Navigation Company in **Liverpool** and had little contact with WBY and his family. At school, John B. Yeats found him surly and unpleasant. Later, he thought him responsible for the dissolute lifestyle of Frederick Pollexfen (1852–1929), a younger brother who lived with him in Liverpool.

REFERENCES: Murphy, William M. *Family Secrets: William Butler Yeats and His Relatives*. Syracuse, N.Y.: Syracuse University Press, 1995; Murphy, William M. *The Yeats Family and the Pollexfens of Sligo*. Dublin: Dolmen, 1971.

POLLEXFEN, ELIZABETH [née Middleton] (1819–92), mother of **Susan Mary Yeats** and grandmother of WBY. She was born in Wine Street, **Sligo** (town), the daughter of Elizabeth Pollexfen and **William Middleton**. Educated at a local school and accomplished in painting and music, she married her mother's cousin, **William Pollexfen**, in 1837. She and her husband lived with her widowed mother in Wine Street until 1845, when their growing family necessitated a move to a larger house in Union Place, Sligo, where her mother died in 1853. Of her thirteen children, eleven survived childhood, while a number of them lived well into old age. After his marriage, William Pollexfen joined his brother-in-law, **William Middleton**, in the new firm of Middleton and Pollexfen. The business prospered, so that in 1867 the family left Union Place and moved to **Merville**, a large house on sixty acres of land on the outskirts of Sligo. In that year, William Middleton had enough spare capital to purchase the entire area of **The Rosses** nearby. Elizabeth Pollexfen was a gentle, kind woman who impressed others by her calmness, dignity, and good sense. She led a well-to-do, comfortable life, attended always by servants to whom she showed kindness and sympathy. She died 8 October 1892. Her funeral, which WBY attended, was reported in the *Sligo Champion*. In *Reveries over Childhood and Youth* (*A*. 9–13), WBY recalls his Pollexfen grandmother with affection. He stayed with her often when he was young and spent time in her company. He went visiting with her, and she was responsible for disciplining him and instilling in him good, respectable, moral behavior. It is with pride that he writes of her delicate paintings of flowers from her own garden.

REFERENCES: Murphy, William M. *Family Secrets: William Butler Yeats and His Relatives*. Syracuse, N.Y.: Syracuse University Press, 1995; Murphy, William M. *Prodigal Father: The Life of John Butler Yeats (1839–1922)*. Ithaca: Cornell University Press,

1978; Murphy, William M. *The Yeats Family and the Pollexfens of Sligo*. Dublin: Dolmen, 1971.

POLLEXFEN, GEORGE [THOMAS] (1839–1910), uncle of WBY. Born in **Sligo** (county), the second son of WBY's maternal grandparents, **William** and **Elizabeth Pollexfen**, he lived in Sligo most of his life. As a boy, he attended Atholl Academy in the Isle of Man with his brother **Charles Pollexfen**. There he became friends with WBY's father, **John B. Yeats**. It was on a visit to George Pollexfen in Sligo in 1862 that John B. Yeats met his future wife, **Susan Pollexfen**. After his father's death in 1892, George took over the family business. He had little head for commerce, however, and the company lost money. It was rescued by his brother-in-law, Arthur Jackson, and George Pollexfen assumed the role of foreman, content to live quietly at his home, **Thornhill**, with his housekeeper, **Mary Battle**. He was staunchly Protestant, a leading Freemason, and Unionist in politics. He became high sheriff of Sligo, presiding at county elections, attending the Assizes, and ensuring that writs were served and sentences executed. As a young man, George Pollexfen had been a competent jockey, racing under the name Paul Hamilton. He owned a racehorse, Dunmorgan, which won a number of handicap races in England and Ireland. His other skill was astrology, and after WBY introduced him to cabalistic magic (*A.* 258–60; *M.* 75–76), George found he had a talent for casting horoscopes. In December 1893, recruited by WBY, he joined **The Order of the Golden Dawn** and became involved in plans for a Celtic Order of Mysteries (*M.* 125). Possibly through this shared interest, George Pollexfen and WBY were firm friends (*M.* 79). He often provided an audience for his nephew's poetry and, for a time, gave the struggling young poet an allowance of £1 a week. In his final years, he suffered from melancholia and hypochondria, and his behavior became increasingly eccentric. As WBY observes, from winter to summer he passed through a series of woollens that had to be weighed. He died of abdominal cancer, and his funeral to St. John's Churchyard was attended by 2,000 mourners, among them members of the Masonic Order who threw acacia sprays on his grave. He left an estate of £50,000, which he divided equally among his brothers and sisters and their heirs. In his will, he showed no special favor to the Yeats family, much to the disgust of his brother-in-law, the penniless John B. Yeats. Of his many uncles, WBY spent the most time in the company of his Uncle George. Through him, WBY was able to continue his close associations with Sligo, begun when he was a boy, and to absorb the fascinating stories of the fairy world told to him by Mary Battle. WBY pays tribute to George Pollexfen's athleticism and riding skills in the poem "In Memory of Alfred Pollexfen" (*CP.* 176) and writes about his melancholia and eccentricities in *A.* 69–70.

REFERENCES: Gordon, D. J., ed. *W. B. Yeats: Images of a Poet*. Manchester: University of Manchester, 1961; Murphy, William M. *Family Secrets: William Butler Yeats and His Relatives*. Syracuse, N.Y.: Syracuse University Press, 1995; Murphy, William

M. *Prodigal Father: The Life of John Butler Yeats (1839–1922)*. Ithaca: Cornell University Press, 1978; Murphy, William M. *The Yeats Family and the Pollexfens of Sligo*. Dublin: Dolmen, 1971.

POLLEXFEN, JOHN ANTHONY (1845–1900), uncle of WBY. Born in **Sligo** (county), he went to sea as a young man and remained a sailor all his life. He was the most genial and companionable of the Pollexfen brothers. He lived with his wife Mary Jane at Blundellsands, just outside **Liverpool**. He died unexpectedly at the age of fifty-five, just after returning from a voyage to South Africa, transporting troops to fight the Boers. See also "In Memory of Alfred Pollexfen" (*CP*. 175).

REFERENCES: Murphy, William M. *Family Secrets: William Butler Yeats and His Relatives*. Syracuse, N.Y.: Syracuse University Press, 1995; Murphy, William M. *Prodigal Father: The Life of John Butler Yeats (1839–1922)*. Ithaca: Cornell University Press, 1978; Murphy, William M. *The Yeats Family and the Pollexfens of Sligo*. Dublin: Dolmen, 1971.

POLLEXFEN, SUSAN [MARY]. *See* **YEATS, SUSAN [MARY]**.

POLLEXFEN, WILLIAM (1811–1892), maternal grandfather of WBY. He was born at Berry Head, near the port of Brixham, Devonshire, and ran away to sea at the age of twelve. In his early twenties, he met his widowed cousin's daughter, **Elizabeth Middleton**. They married, and he joined her brother, **William Middleton**, in the Sligo Steam Navigation Company, a shipping firm that carried goods to and from America, Portugal, and Spain. The success of the company encouraged William Pollexfen and his brother-in-law to buy the flour mills at **Ballysodare**. The venture, known as "Middleton and Pollexfen," generated a considerable fortune. William Pollexfen, who was a solid citizen, standing no nonsense from his employees or his neighbors, moved with his family from a small house in **Sligo** (town) to the grand residence of **Merville**, set on sixty acres of land. There, he played the role of the patriarch, terrifying and fascinating his grandchildren by turn. WBY writes engagingly about him in *Reveries over Childhood and Youth* (*A*. 6–9, 12–13). WBY, although much in awe, observed those details that he recollected with such clarity years later: the great scar on his grandfather's hand made by a whaling hook, the bits of coral he kept in a cabinet, and the jar of water from the River Jordan. From the slated and glass turret of the offices in the center of Sligo, he watched with a telescope, every day, the comings and goings of his ships. He kept an axe by his bedside to deter burglars and, at the age of eighty, refused the advice of his doctor that he should take a little alcohol as a stimulant, lest it become a habit! The young WBY found it difficult not to confuse him with God. He conjectures that his delight in passionate men in literature may have been inspired by his grandfather and observes that when reading *King Lear*, it is the image of his grandfather he has in mind. William Pollexfen is referred to in the poems "In Memory of Alfred Pollexfen" (*CP.* 175) and "Are You Content?" (*CP.* 370).

REFERENCES: Murphy, William M. *Family Secrets: William Butler Yeats and His Relatives.* Syracuse, N.Y.: Syracuse University Press, 1995; Murphy, William M. *Prodigal Father: The Life of John Butler Yeats (1839–1922).* Ithaca: Cornell University Press, 1978; Murphy, William M. *The Yeats Family and the Pollexfens of Sligo.* Dublin: Dolmen, 1971.

PORPHYRY (233–c. 304), philosopher. He was born into a noble family in Syria. He studied philosophy under **Plotinus** and became his disciple, emerging as a leading teacher of the Neoplatonist school. Apart from his own treatises on rhetoric and literary themes, he wrote lives of Plotinus and **Pythagoras**. In "The Philosophy of Shelley's Poetry" (*EI.* 82–86), WBY refers to Porphyry's essay on the "Cave of the Nymphs," and he quotes from his *Life of Plotinus* in "Bishop Berkeley" (*LE.* 110). See also "Swedenborg, Mediums, and the Desolate Places" (*LE.* 67–68). A copy of Porphyry's *Life of Plotinus* (1917), translated by **Stephen MacKenna**, was in WBY's library (*OS.* no. 1589).

REFERENCE: Barnwell, William C. "The Blandness of Yeats' Rhadamanthus." *English Language Notes* 14, no. 3 (1977).

POST OFFICE. *See* **GENERAL POST OFFICE**.

POT OF BROTH, THE, one-act farce in prose by WBY. The play, originally called *The Beggarman*, was written in dialect, with the help of **Lady Gregory**. It was printed in *The Gael*, New York, September 1903, and subsequently in *The Hour-Glass and Other Plays* (1904), but it was omitted from WBY's *Collected Works* (1908) because he thought it slight and insubstantial. He took note of its continuing popularity when he included it in the ***Collected Plays of W. B. Yeats*** (1934, 1952). In *The Pot of Broth*, which is based on a West of Ireland folktale, a **Tramp** cheats a foolish husband and his shrewish wife out of their dinner. Although there are few references to Celtic mythology in the play, the central action of the play turns on a belief in magic, in which a common stone has the power to make fine broth. While writing the play, WBY was much involved with magic symbolism, and as Richard Taylor suggests in his study *A Reader's Guide to the Plays of W. B. Yeats* (1984), the major props in the play— the pot, ham bone, stone, and chicken—may have symbolic meaning and be related to the four talismans brought to Ireland by the **Tuatha dé Danaan**. *The Pot of Broth* was first performed, October 1902, in the **Antient Concert Rooms**, Dublin, with **W. G. Fay** as the Tramp, Maire T. Quinn as Sibby, and P. J. Kelly as the husband John. The production was directed by **Frank Fay**.

REFERENCES: Bradley, Anthony. *William Butler Yeats.* New York: Frederick Ungar, 1979; Ellis, Sylvia C. *The Plays of W. B. Yeats: Yeats and the Dancer.* London: Macmillan, 1995; Miller, Liam. *The Noble Drama of W. B. Yeats.* Dublin: Dolmen, 1977; Taylor, Richard. *A Reader's Guide to the Plays of W. B. Yeats.* New York: St. Martin's, 1984.

POUND, EZRA [LOOMIS] (1885–1972), poet and critic. He was born in the small mining town of Hailey, Idaho, the only child of Homer Loomis Pound who worked in the Federal Land Office. When his father was appointed to the U.S. Mint in Philadelphia, the family settled nearby, in Wyncote. He graduated from Hamilton College, Clinton, New York, in 1905, and after completing his M.A. at the University of Pennsylvania, he left the United States for Europe in 1907, eventually settling in England, where he hoped to meet WBY. He was soon in the company of the most influential literary men in London, including the publisher **Elkin Mathews**. In 1909, he published a book of poems, *Personae*, followed almost immediately by *Exultations* (1909) and *The Spirit of Romance* (1910). In his verse, he strove for economy in language and concreteness of imagery, seeking his models in Anglo-Saxon poetry, Greek and Latin classics, and the novels of **Gustave Flaubert**. In 1912, he became London correspondent for the influential magazine *Poetry* (Chicago) and in this capacity dominated contemporary critical thinking in Anglo-American verse. Having been a member of T. E. Hulme's ''school of images'' from his arrival in London, he became the leader of the Imagist movement, drawing up the first Imagist manifesto and editing the anthology *Des Imagistes* (1914). As a leading figure in Modernism, his influence on major twentieth-century writers, among them **T. S. Eliot, James Joyce**, Robert Frost, and D. H. Lawrence, is well documented. In 1914, he married Dorothy Shakespear, daughter of **Olivia Shakespear**. The marriage was not a happy one, and in 1924, he had an affair with the expatriate American violinist Olga Rudge. Dorothy remained faithful to him and, in 1925, bore him a son, Omar Pound, who was raised by Olivia Shakespear. With the end of World War I, Pound reacted to the pessimistic mood that pervaded England by publishing two of his finest works, ''Homage to Sextus Propertius'' (1919), about the British Empire in 1917, and *Hugh Selwyn Mauberley* (1920), a brilliantly observed and concise examination of the artist in postwar English society. In 1920, he moved to Paris, where he befriended the young novelist Ernest Hemingway, and in 1924, he settled in **Rapallo**, Italy, and remained there for the next twenty years. In 1930, under the title *A Draft of XXX Cantos*, he published parts of his long, autobiographical poem, begun in 1915, in which he attempted to reconstruct the history of civilization out of his own experience. While continuing to publish segments of *The Cantos* through the 1930s, he turned increasingly to economic history and politics, becoming an active supporter of Mussolini and **fascism**. Indicted in 1946 for treasonous broadcasts made during World War II, he was found mentally unfit to stand trial and confined to a U.S. mental hospital in Washington, D.C. He continued writing and publishing and, in 1949, was awarded the Bollingen Prize for his *Pisan Cantos*. Persistent protests were made to the U.S. government by leading writers and artists, and in 1958, after charges against him were dropped, he was released. His final years were spent in Italy, where he continued his major work, *The Cantos* (1925–60), left unfinished at his death. When he first arrived in London, 1908, WBY was the poet Pound most wanted to meet. WBY was in

Ireland attending to the affairs of the **Abbey Theatre**, but soon after his return, Olivia Shakespear and her daughter Dorothy brought Pound to **Woburn Buildings** to meet him, May 1909. From their introduction, WBY and Pound maintained a close friendship that lasted until WBY's death. Pound attended WBY's Monday evenings at Woburn Buildings, and through the winters of 1913–15, they rented **Stone Cottage** in Sussex, where Pound shared with WBY the papers of the Orientalist **Ernest Fenollosa**. He helped direct the first production of *At the Hawk's Well* and was best man when WBY married in 1917. He persuaded WBY to contribute to *Poetry* (Chicago) in October 1913 and is credited with being the single most powerful influence on the development of WBY's later poetry, the older poet often seeking his advice (*EI*. 145). Indeed, WBY rewrote his play *The King of the Great Clock Tower* (1934) because of negative comments by Pound. When WBY's health was failing in 1929, Pound arranged accommodation for him in Rapallo. There, he introduced him to **George Antheil**, who composed the music for *Fighting the Waves*. WBY writes about Pound in his "Introduction to *The Oxford Book of Modern Verse*" (*LE*. 192–94), while at a dinner given in his honor by the Poetry Society of Chicago in 1914, he commented that, in his opinion, Pound's poem "The Return" was the most beautiful poem to have been written in free verse (*UP2*. 414). Three poems by Pound were included in WBY's selection for *The Oxford Book of Modern Verse* (1936). He had wanted to include more, but the publisher thought Pound's fees too expensive!

REFERENCES: Cullingford, Elizabeth. *Yeats, Ireland and Fascism*. New York and London: New York University Press, 1981; Diggory, Terence. *Yeats and American Poetry: The Traditions of the Self*. Princeton: Princeton University Press, 1983; Ellman, Richard. *Eminent Domain: Yeats among Wilde, Joyce, Pound, Eliot, Auden*. New York: Oxford University Press, 1967; Litz, A. Walton. "Pound and Yeats: The Road to Stone Cottage." In *Ezra Pound among the Poets*, ed. George Bornstein. Chicago: University of Chicago Press, 1985; Materer, Timothy, ed. *The Selected Letters of Ezra Pound to John Quinn, 1915–1924*. Durham and London: Duke University Press, 1991; Paige, D. D., ed. *The Letters of Ezra Pound: 1907–1941*. London: Faber & Faber, 1951; Reid, B. L. *The Man from New York: John Quinn and His Friends*. New York: Oxford University Press, 1968.

POWELL, [FREDERICK] YORK (1850–1904), historian and scholar. He was Regius Professor of Modern History at Oxford University from 1894. A close friend of WBY's father, **John B. Yeats**, WBY stayed with him when he was working in the Bodleian Library, **Oxford**. York Powell had a house at 6 Priory Gardens, **Bedford Park**, 1881–1902, and contrived to spend as much time there as his Oxford duties would allow. With John B. Yeats, he was a member of the Calumet, a conversation club that met regularly on alternate Sundays in members' homes. Other members included **John Todhunter** and **H. M. Paget**. Although he was amiable and broad-minded, York Powell was anti-Semitic and pro-British Empire. He approved of WBY's writing but regretted his Celtic leanings. Nevertheless, he enabled him to get a copying job with the folklore publishers David Nutt. Anxious to help both father and son, he offered to recommend WBY for the post of subeditor of the pro-Unionist newspaper *The Manchester Courier*, but the young poet declined, much to his father's delight (*M.* 31). Two poems by York Powell, both of them from the French of Paul Fort, were included in WBY's selection for ***The Oxford Book of Modern Verse*** (1936). WBY describes York Powell as an impressive man of fine appearance whose genius lacked ambition and regrets he himself was too immature to value his erudition and conversation (*A.* 117–19).

REFERENCE: Elton, Oliver. *Frederick York Powell: A Life and a Selection from His Letters and Occasional Writings*. Oxford: Clarendon, 1906.

PRIAM, mythological king of **Troy**. He was husband to Hecuba and father to **Hector**, Troilus, Cassandra, and **Paris**. He suffered many misfortunes during the Trojan War and was finally killed by Neoptolemus. His murder is referred to in WBY's poem "The Sorrow of Love" (*CP.* 45).

PROPERTIUS, SEXTUS (c. 50–16 B.C.), Roman love poet. Born in Umbria, he was a member of a group associated with the Roman statesman and literary patron Maecenas. Propertius's poems are chiefly addressed to his mistress, Cynthia, and are distinguished by their passion and sincerity expressed in a formal, measured style. WBY's short poem "A Thought from Propertius" (*CP.* 172) is loosely based on the second poem of Book II by the Roman poet (c. 26 B.C.).

REFERENCES: Hooley, Daniel M. *The Classics in Paraphrase: Ezra Pound and Modern Translators of Latin Poetry*. Selinsgrove, Pa.: Susquehanna University Press, 1988; Sullivan, J. P. *Ezra Pound and Sextus Propertius: A Study in Creative Translation*. Austin: University of Texas Press, 1964.

PROTEUS, sea god in Greek mythology. He was a prophetic old man of the sea, noted for his ability to transform himself into different shapes. If he was seized and held, however, he could foretell the future. Because the audience at the **Abbey Theatre** continually changed their minds about what they wanted to see, WBY, in his poem "At the Abbey Theatre" (*CP.* 107), compared them with the ever-changing Proteus. It is of interest that, in this early sonnet, WBY refers to Proteus and not to **Manannán**, the shape-changing Irish god of the sea.

PUCK FAIR, a fair that is held annually, 9–11 August, in the town of Killorglin, County Kerry. In the fair, a white male goat is crowned and led through the streets on a decorated cart. Clearly connected with a pagan fertility festival, the modern fair still provides an opportunity for unbridled merrymaking. The young boy in WBY's play *Purgatory* was born in early August, around the time of the Puck Fair.

REFERENCE: McGarry, James P. *Place Names in the Writings of William Butler Yeats.* Gerrards Cross: Colin Smythe, 1976.

PURGATORY, one-act play in verse. WBY began working on the play in March 1938. It was first published in *On the Boiler* (1938) and subsequently in *Last Poems and Two Plays* (1939) and *Collected Plays of W. B. Yeats* (1952). The concentrated action of the play, which many judge to be among WBY's best, takes place in front of the ruins of a large house, with a withered tree in the background. An **Old Man**, who claims to have been born in the house, tells the Boy, his bastard son, that souls in purgatory return to the scene of their transgressions and must live through them again and again. The house belonged to his mother, a wealthy landowner, who was disinherited when she married her groom. He has come to the house on the anniversary of his mother's wedding night, the night he was conceived. After his mother died in childbirth, he was brought up by his father, who squandered the family money in gambling and alcohol. The Old Man reveals that he killed his drunken, abusive father, left him in the burning house, and ran away. He became a beggar and had his son to a tinker woman he met on the roads. Hearing hoofbeats, the Old Man relives the events of his mother's wedding night. The Boy, aware that his father is distracted, attempts to steal his money. In the ensuing struggle, the Old Man sees the ghost of his drunken father. Thinking to stop the corruption of the family passing to yet another generation, he kills his bastard son. The play ends as the Old Man realizes it is not in his power to release his mother's soul from its torment. There is no single source for the play, but themes and motifs, among them the hoofbeats, the bare tree, and the ruined house, may be seen in WBY's earlier works, including the novel John Sherman, the story "Happy and Unhappy Theologians" (*MY*. 42–46), and the play *The King of the Great Clock Tower* (*CPl*. 640). *Purgatory*, which some found theologically controversial, was presented at the **Abbey Theatre**, August 1938, with Michael J. Dolan as the Old Man and Liam Redmond as the Boy. The setting was designed by WBY's daughter, **Anne Butler Yeats**, and the play was directed by Hugh Hunt.

REFERENCES: Bradley, Anthony. *William Butler Yeats.* New York: Frederick Ungar, 1979; Miller, Liam. *The Noble Drama of W. B. Yeats.* Dublin: Dolmen, 1977; Siegel, Sandra F., ed. *Purgatory; Manuscript Materials.* Ithaca and London: Cornell University Press, 1986; Taylor, Richard. *A Reader's Guide to the Plays of W. B. Yeats.* New York: St. Martin's, 1984.

PUROHIT SWAMI, SHRI (1882–1941), Indian mystic and author. He was born Shankar Gajanan Purohit, the grandson of a Marátha millionaire, but chose to renounce worldly possessions to become a Brahmin monk. He arrived in London, 28 February 1931, and was introduced to WBY in June 1931 by **T. Sturge Moore**. WBY, attracted to Indian mysticism, was persuaded to write the introduction to the Swami's autobiography, *An Indian Monk: His Life and Adventures* (1932). He followed this with an introduction to his translation of *The Holy Mountain* (1934), written by Bhagwan Shri Hamsa, the Swami's teacher. In December 1935, WBY and Shri Purohit traveled to Palma, **Majorca**, where they embarked upon a translation of *The Ten Principal Upanishads* (1937). WBY took ill, and **Mrs. W. B. Yeats** joined them in February 1936. The translation completed, Shri Purohit sailed for India in May 1936, while WBY and his wife returned to Ireland. Three short poems by Shri Purohit, one from the Hindi, the others from Urdu, were included in WBY's selection for *The Oxford Book of Modern Verse* (1936).

REFERENCES: Harwood, John. *Olivia Shakespear and W. B. Yeats: After Long Silence.* London: Macmillan, 1989; Harwood, John. "Yeats, Shri Purohit Swami, and Mrs Foden." In *Yeats Annual, No. 6,* ed. Warwick Gould. London: Macmillan, 1988.

PURSER, SARAH (1848–1943), portrait painter and patroness of the arts. She was born in Kingstown (later Dun Laoghaire) and educated in Switzerland. Her father was a wealthy mill owner, but when his business failed in 1873, Sarah studied at the Dublin School of Art and in Paris to become a painter. After her portrait of the **Gore-Booth** sisters was exhibited at the Royal Academy in London, she was much in demand as a portrait painter to the British aristocracy. Thus, she made a secure living as an artist, but a shrewd investment in Guinness Brewery when it became a public company in 1886 made her a wealthy woman. In 1903, she and **Edward Martyn** founded a workshop An Tur Gloine (The Tower of Glass) to assist promising artists in stained glass, including Evie Hone and Michael Healey. Among their early commissions were the windows in the cathedral at **Loughrea**. She designed the windows for the vestibule of the new **Abbey Theatre** in 1904. From 1916, she and her brother John, professor of medicine at **Trinity College**, Dublin, each month held afternoon receptions at their home for the literary and intellectual elite of Dublin. An energetic, feisty woman, committed to Irish art and artists, she formed the Friends of the National Collections of Ireland in 1924 and was responsible for securing Charlemont House, Dublin, as the **Municipal Gallery of Modern Art**. She died at the age of ninety-five after a seizure, it is said, brought on by rage at the sight of the poor design for a new postage stamp issued in honor of **Douglas Hyde**. For most of her life she was a close friend of the Yeats family. Although she was concerned about the aimlessness of WBY's teenage years, once she read his poetry, she was convinced he was a writer and gave him much encouragement. After **John B. Yeats** was rejected by the Royal Hibernian Academy in 1901, she organized in Dublin, at her own expense, an exhibition of his work. WBY describes her caustic wit in *M*. 43–44, 60–61.

REFERENCES: Coxhead, Elizabeth. *Daughters of Erin: Five Women of the Irish Renascence.* London: Secker & Warburg, 1965; Marreco, Anne. *The Rebel Countess: The Life and Times of Constance Markievicz [sic].* London: Weidenfeld & Nicolson, 1967.

PUVIS DE CHAVANNES, PIERRE (1824–1898), Symbolist painter and muralist. He was born in Lyons, the son of a prosperous mining engineer who provided him with lifelong financial support. Virtually self-taught as a painter, he moved to Paris in the 1840s and gained a reputation as a fine muralist, a medium in which realism and trompe l'oeil were discouraged. His early works *War* and *Peace* were purchased for the newly built Musée de Picardie in Amiens, and his murals were commissioned for many of the major buildings in France, including the Hôtel de Ville in Paris. Toward the end of his life, he accepted an invitation to paint nine murals for the Boston Public Library. He developed his mature style in the 1870s, when he brought his flat, decorative, mural technique to easel painting. He made considerable impact on the French salons, especially with paintings like *The Poor Fisherman*. He was an original painter, without parallel in French art, but he was unclassifiable and lost popularity after his death. Despite some major retrospectives in the 1970s, he remains largely neglected today, although persuasive arguments have emphasized his influence on Gauguin, Vuillard, Odilon Redon, and Picasso, among others. Puvis de Chavannes's dreamlike paintings featured idyllic landscapes and mythological figures, while his subdued colors and chaste figures were reminiscent of Giotto. In his murals and easel paintings, he rejected conventional perspective, keeping the subject to the foreground, as in a frieze or tapestry. His backgrounds were often dim and misty and consisted of a series of horizontal stripes ascending in layers to an unusually high horizon, which successfully eradicated any depth in the picture. From the late 1890s, the French painter exercised a major influence on WBY, both in subject matter and style. In his essay "A Theatre of Beauty" (*UP2*. 398–99), he asserts that a designer should look for what is distinctive in his medium, and he cites the muralist Puvis de Chavannes to prove his point. His painterly, friezelike approach to space and design appealed to WBY and influenced the staging of his early plays *The Countess Cathleen* and *The Shadowy Waters*.

REFERENCES: Boucher, Marie Christine. *Catalogue des dessins et peintures de Puvis de Chavannes*. Paris: Association Française d'Action Artistique, 1979; Crastre, François. *Puvis de Chavannes*. New York: F. A. Stokes, 1912; D'Argencourt, Louise. *Puvis de Chavannes*. Ottawa: National Gallery of Canada, 1977; Gordon, D. J. *Images of a Poet*. Manchester: University of Manchester, 1961; Wattenmaker, Richard J. *Puvis de Chavannes and the Modern Tradition*. Toronto: Art Gallery of Ontario, 1975.

PYTHAGORAS (c. 582–c. 507 B.C.), Greek philosopher. His profound influence on music and mathematics is largely due to the Pythagoreans, a mystical brotherhood that he founded. Through them we know that he was a skilled mathematician who influenced Euclid, and he was the first to claim that the earth was a sphere revolving about a fixed axis. From the discovery of mathematical intervals between musical notes, the Pythagoreans taught that number was the basis of all things and that all relationships could be expressed numerically. His discovery of the numerical relationship between musical notes is referred to by

WBY in the poem "Among School Children" (*CP*. 242). See also "The Delphic Oracle upon Plotinus" (*CP*. 307), "The Statues" (*CP*. 375), and "News for the Delphic Oracle" (*CP*. 376).

REFERENCES: Guthrie, Kenneth Sylvan, trans. *The Pythagorean Sourcebook and Library: An Anthology of Ancient Writings Which Relate to Pythagoras and Pythagorean Philosophy*. Ed. David R. Fideler. Grand Rapids, Mich.: Phanes, 1987; Kingsley, Peter. *Ancient Philosophy, Mystery, and Magic: Empedocles and Pythagorean Tradition*. Oxford: Clarendon, 1995.

Q

QUATTROCENTO, pertaining to the art and literature of fifteenth-century Italy. The term is used by WBY in "Among School Children" (*CP.* 242), "Her Vision in the Wood" (*CP.* 312), and "Under Ben Bulben" (*CP.* 397).

QUEEN. The role of the Queen appears in three plays by WBY. In *The Player Queen*, she is the Queen of an unspecified country, whose people have turned against her. After they attack her castle, the terrified Queen persuades the actress **Decima** to assume her role and rule in her place. In *The King of the Great Clock Tower*, the Queen is the silent, imagelike consort of a domineering, jealous **King**. She is moved by the words and actions of the **Stroller** to dance and kiss his Severed Head, ultimately gaining ascendance over the King. In *A Full Moon in March*, the chaste Queen challenges the **Swineherd** to sing for her and win her hand. In response to his insults, she has him beheaded. The union of the Queen and the Swineherd, representing spirit and matter, is presented symbolically in an orgasmic dance. In the first production of *The Player Queen*, May 1919, the role of the Queen was played by Gwen Richardson. In *The King of the Great Clock Tower*, July 1934, the Queen was danced by **Ninette de Valois**. There is no record of a performance of *A Full Moon in March* in WBY's lifetime.

QUEENSTOWN, port in **Cork** (county). It was the point of embarkation for major passenger liners en route to the United States. Named after Queen Victoria in 1847, it reverted to its original name, Cobh, after 1922. WBY recalls **John Shawe-Taylor** showing courage during a fierce storm at Queenstown, leaping from a trans-Atlantic liner on to the tender sent to pick up the passengers as it was swept away from the ship (*EI*. 343).

REFERENCE: McGarry, James P. *Place Names in the Writings of William Butler Yeats*. Gerrards Cross: Colin Smythe, 1976.

QUINN, JOHN (1870–1924), lawyer and patron. He was born in Tiffin, Ohio, the son of Irish immigrant parents, and after attending the University of Michigan in the fall of 1888, he left to become private secretary to Governor Charles Foster, secretary of the treasury in Washington, D.C. He graduated from Georgetown University in 1893 and took a second degree at Harvard before moving to New York to specialize in financial law. From a young age, he had been a book collector, and he spent much of his free time in the study of contemporary literature and philosophy, including the works of WBY. He began collecting pictures, especially portraits and studies of literary subjects. In 1900, he became a junior partner in the law firm of Alexander and Colby. Within five years, he established himself as one of the most brilliant financial lawyers in New York, and in 1906, he set up his own company. Following the death of his mother, he visited Dublin and London for the first time in 1902 and made the acquaintance of the major Irish writers and painters. He bought ten paintings by **Jack Yeats** and commissioned from **John B. Yeats** a series of contemporary Irish portraits. On his return to the United States, he arranged for the copyrighting of WBY's play *Where There Is Nothing* and formed the Irish Literary Society of New York, which produced three short plays by WBY at Carnegie Hall (then the Carnegie Lyceum) before the society went into decline—ostensibly because of opposition from clerics who objected to WBY's appointment as a vice president. Quinn returned to Ireland in 1903, when he became a patron of the **Dun Emer Press**, and went on a walking tour with Jack Yeats. Back in New York, he arranged WBY's first lecture tour of the United States, giving him the use of his New York apartment and arranging for important business and media contacts. Quinn visited **Coole Park** in 1903, and he returned again in 1904, forming a deep attachment for **Lady Gregory**, with whom he had an affair during the **Abbey Theatre's** tour of the United States in 1911. In 1904, he accompanied WBY to London, where he was introduced to **Arthur Symons, Charles Ricketts**, and **Charles Shannon**. He organized a tour of the United States for **Florence Farr** in 1906, and when John B. Yeats moved to New York in 1907, Quinn maintained him financially. Indeed, he became a surrogate son to the elderly, eccentric painter. Increasingly frustrated with Ireland, however, and the negative, backbiting responses to its major writers, like **J. M. Synge**, he announced that he would henceforth concentrate on collecting paintings and manuscripts but not books. He visited England and Ireland for the last time in 1909 but preferred to spend most of his time in London with **Augustus John**, who impressed him so much he decided to become his patron. As his fortune grew, Quinn became obsessive as a collector. In 1911, he estimated his library to be some 6,000 or 7,000 volumes, while the walls of his apartment at 58

Central Park West were lined with paintings, with many stacked in bedrooms and closets. His friendship with WBY cooled when he accused WBY of trying to seduce his mistress, Dorothy Coates, but during the Abbey Theatre tour of the United States in 1914, WBY and he were reconciled, and he agreed to buy his manuscripts on an annual basis to help defray John B. Yeats's living expenses. He nursed the painter through his final illness and arranged his funeral in February 1922. As a gesture of thanks, WBY dedicated to him *The Trembling of the Veil* (1922). Quinn's early death from cancer was a shock to his friends in Europe and the United States, including the Yeats family and **Ezra Pound**. They had lost a sensitive, knowledgeable, and generous patron who had helped shape the art and literature of his time.

REFERENCES: Materer, Timothy, ed. *The Selected Letters of Ezra Pound to John Quinn, 1915–1924*. Durham and London: Duke University Press, 1991; Reid, B. L. *The Man from New York: John Quinn and His Friends*. New York: Oxford University Press, 1968.

R

RACHLIN. *See* **RATHLIN**.

RADIO ÉIREANN. *See* **BROADCASTS**.

RAFTERY, [ANTHONY] (1784–1834), poet and musician. Commonly known as **Blind Raftery**, he was born at Cilleaden, in **County Mayo**. After being blinded by smallpox in his youth, he became an itinerant fiddler, spending most of his life around **Gort** and **Loughrea**. He had no formal education, but he composed poems and ballads on contemporary events, among them **Daniel O'Connell's** victory in the **Clare** parliamentary election of 1828, a drowning tragedy at Anach Cuain, and the hanging of Anthony O'Daly, a captain in the Whiteboys. He wrote love songs, especially to the beautiful **Mary Hynes**, the miller's daughter. His most ambitious work, however, was *Seanchas na Sceiche*, a metrical history of Ireland. Raftery was buried at Killeeneen, **Galway** (county). His poems were preserved in the oral tradition until they were collected and edited by **Douglas Hyde** in *Songs Ascribed to Raftery* (1903). WBY, in *The Tower* (*CP*. 218), recalls Raftery's song celebrating Mary Hynes and its effect on those men who fell in love with her. He connects Raftery with **Homer**, who was also blind, and with himself, creator of the poet **Hanrahan**. See also "Dust Hath Closed Helen's Eye" (*M*. 22).

REFERENCES: Byrne, Donn. *Blind Raftery and His Wife Hilaria*. New York and London: The Century Co., 1924; Gregory, Lady. *Poets and Dreamers*. Port Washington, N.Y.: Kennikat, 1967.

RAPALLO, seaside town on the Mediterranean. WBY and his wife visited the town in Italy, February–April 1928, when he was recovering from a breakdown in his health. They returned there, November 1928 to late April 1929, staying in a large sunny apartment in the Via Americhe, which they filled with their own furniture and books. At Rapallo, he not only enjoyed the warmer weather but also the company of **Ezra Pound** and other literati, among them **T. S. Eliot** and Gerhart Hauptmann and the composer **George Antheil** (*WL.* 758). In December 1929, when he was again wintering in Rapallo, he collapsed with Malta fever. After a grave illness, he recovered and remained in the apartment until July 1930, when he returned to Ireland. This was his last visit to Rapallo. *A Packet for Ezra Pound* (1929) contains a description of the idyllic setting of the seaport.

REFERENCES: Aldington, Richard. *A. E. Housman and W. B. Yeats: Two Lectures.* 1955. Reprint, Folcroft, Pa.: Folcroft, 1973; Patmore, Derek, ed. *My Friends When Young: Memoirs of Brigit Patmore.* London: Heinemann, 1968.

RATHLIN [also Rachlin], island six miles off the coast of County Antrim. Some of the **Firbolg** are reputed to have moved to Rathlin after the battle of **Moytura**. Robert the Bruce, hiding on the island, allegedly found inspiration in the endeavors of a laborious spider. He returned to Scotland, where he successfully defeated the English. Although conditions are harsh on the island, there are still about 100 people living on Rathlin today. See also *The Wanderings of Oisin* (*CP.* 442).

REFERENCE: McGarry, James P. *Place Names in the Writings of William Butler Yeats.* Gerrards Cross: Colin Smythe, 1976.

RAVENNA, city in north-central Italy. It is noted for its fine Roman and Byzantine buildings and for the magnificent fifth- and sixth-century Byzantine mosaics, as in the octagonal Church of San Vitale, built in 547. WBY's visit to Ravenna with **Lady Gregory** in 1907 is recalled in the powerful visual imagery of "Sailing to Byzantium" (*CP.* 217). **Dante** died in Ravenna in 1321.

REFERENCES: Bovini, Giuseppe. *Ravenna.* Trans. Robert Erich Wolf. New York: H. N. Abrams, 1973; Bovini, Giuseppe. *Ravenna Mosaics.* Oxford: Phaidon, 1978; Gordon, D. J., ed. *W. B. Yeats: Images of a Poet.* Manchester: University of Manchester, 1961.

RED BRANCH, ancient order of heroic knights. The Red Branch was founded by **Rury**, king of **Ulster**, and husband of Maga, the daughter of the love god **Aengus**. The order was similar to the **Fianna** and was commissioned to protect the High King, **Conchubar**. The most powerful of the Red Branch knights was **Cuchulain**. See also "Cuchulain's Fight with the Sea" (*CP.* 37).

REFERENCES: Ellis, Peter Berresford. *Dictionary of Celtic Mythology.* New York: Oxford University Press, 1992; Gregory, Lady. *Cuchulain of Muirthemne: The Story of the Men of the Red Branch of Ulster.* 1902. Reprint. Gerrards Cross: Colin Smythe, 1976.

RED HANRAHAN, fictional poet. WBY created the fictional Red Hanrahan as one of his early masks in "Stories of Red Hanrahan" (*MY.* 213–61). He refers to his invention of the lecherous Hanrahan in "The Tower" (*CP*. 218), though according to Giles W. L. Telfer in *Yeats's Idea of the Gael* (1965), Hanrahan bears a marked resemblance to the Gaelic poet Eoghan Ruadh O'Suileabhan [Owen Roe O'Sullivan] (1748–84). Indeed, WBY initially named him O'Sullivan the Red, a name he used in the titles of a number of poems in *The Wind Among the Reeds*. "Stories of Red Hanrahan" was first published in *The Secret Rose* (1897). See also "Red Hanrahan's Song about Ireland" (*CP*. 90).

REFERENCES: Conner, Lester I. "A Matter of Character: Red Hanrahan and Crazy Jane." In *Yeats, Sligo & Ireland*. Ed. A. Norman Jeffares. Gerrards Cross: Colin Smythe, 1980; Sidnell, Michael J. "Versions of the Stories of Red Hanrahan." *Yeats Studies 1* (1971); Telfer, Giles W. L. *Yeats's Idea of the Gael*. Dublin: Dolmen, 1965.

RED MAN, character. In WBY's play *The Green Helmet*, he is the solar god who comes from the sea to challenge the men of **Ulster**. In his annual visit, the Red Man, attended by his cat-headed supporters, is the vegetation god, the source of solar energy. When **Cuchulain** proves to be the bravest of the Ulster champions, the Red Man places the Green Helmet on his head, a gesture symbolic of the link between Cuchulain and external, cosmic forces. The character is an invention of WBY, combining figures from two stories in **Lady Gregory's** *Cuchulain of Muirthemne:* **Bricriu**, who creates discord, and Cú Roí, who tests the champions of Ulster. Ambrose Power played the role of the Red Man in the first production of *The Green Helmet* at the **Abbey Theatre**, March 1908.

REFERENCES: Bradley, Anthony. *William Butler Yeats*. New York: Frederick Ungar, 1979; Gregory, Lady. *Cuchulain of Muirthemne: The Story of the Men of the Red Branch of Ulster*. 1902. Reprint. Gerrards Cross: Colin Smythe, 1976.

RED MOLL, fictitious one-eyed character in the poem "The Shadowy Waters" (*CP*. 473). She is a prostitute whom the sailors visit when in port. The name *moll* is traditionally used for a woman of low repute.

REDMOND, JOHN [EDWARD] (1856–1918), politician. He was born at Ballytrent, County Wexford, the son of William Redmond, M.P. for Wexford. After graduating from Clongowes Wood College and **Trinity College**, Dublin, he was clerk of the House of Commons at Westminster. He was elected M.P. for New Ross in 1881 and joined the Irish Parliamentary Party, offering his full support to **Charles Stewart Parnell**. He was called to the Irish Bar in 1886. With the fall of Parnell in 1890, he led a minority of the party until 1900, when he was elected leader of the reunited Irish Parliamentary Party. He successfully maneuvered the passing of the third Home Rule Bill in 1912 but alienated himself from the militant Sinn Féin movement when he opposed violence and showed a willingness to accept the partition of Ireland. During World War I, he attempted to recruit the Irish Volunteers to join the British forces, arguing that such an act would be rewarded with Home Rule when the war was over. The Easter Rising took him by surprise and effectively brought an end to his political influence. In 1902, in an interview for *The Echo*, a London paper, WBY acknowledged that Redmond had the support of the older Nationalists and the farming community but not the young people from the major cities. He went on to pay tribute to Redmond as a parliamentary leader, admiring his ability to take a wider view of the important issues and not be caught up in the emotion of the moment (*UP2*. 290).

REFERENCES: Foster, R. F. *Modern Ireland 1600–1972*. 1988. Reprint. London: Penguin Books, 1989; Kerr, S. Parnell. *What the Irish Regiments Have Done: With a Diary of a Visit to the Front by John E. Redmond M.P.* London: T. Fisher Unwin, 1916.

RED SEA, separates northeast Africa from the Arabian Peninsula. In his poem "A Prayer on going into my House" (*CP*. 183), WBY threatens that anyone who destroys the views from **Thoor Ballylee** by erecting a cottage or cutting down a tree will meet with dire consequences, including having their soul chained to the bottom of the Red Sea. It is worth noting that since the poem was written in 1917, the view has been altered by the building of a farmhouse, but, as far as is known, nothing untoward has happened to the inhabitants.

RESPONSIBILITIES: POEMS AND A PLAY, collection of poems and a play. When WBY published this collection in 1914, he was forty-nine years old and conscious of his position as a respected, public poet in Ireland. The poems reveal the tensions he feels between his social and private responsibilities. He despairs of the value system of the prevailing bourgeoisie, and in "September 1913" (*CP*. 120), he compares the preoccupations of the new Catholic middle class with the attitudes of the nationalist **John O'Leary** and those earlier heroes, **Lord Edward Fitzgerald, Robert Emmet**, and **Wolfe Tone**, who fought for Ireland regardless of personal loss or gain. The language of the collection is spare, and there is an absence of superfluous imagery, showing the influence of his friendship with **Ezra Pound**. The poet is conscious of this development in his verse, recognizing in "A Coat" (*CP*. 142) that the former decorative style obscured the meaning. The collection was first published by **Cuala Press** in 1914, in a collection of 400 copies, under the title *Responsibilities: Poems and a Play*. It was published in London and New York in 1916 as *Responsibilities and Other Poems*. The play, a new version of ***The Hour-Glass***, was included in all three publications.

REFERENCE: Henn, T. R. *"The Green Helmet and Responsibilities."* In *An Honored Guest: New Essays on W. B. Yeats*, ed. Denis Donoghue and J. R. Mulryne. London: Edward Arnold, 1965.

RESURRECTION, THE, one-act play in prose and verse by WBY. An early version of the play was published in *The Adelphi*, June 1927, and the final version was included in *Stories of Michael Robartes and His Friends* (1931), ***Wheels and Butterflies*** (1934), and ***Collected Plays of W. B. Yeats*** (1934, 1952). It was dedicated to **Junzo Sato**. In the play, which takes place in Jerusalem on the third day following the crucifixion of **Christ, The Greek** and **The Hebrew** are guarding the inner room where the eleven disciples are in hiding. They discuss their separate views of the dead Christ, the Hebrew believing him to be human, while the Greek insists he is a spirit. In the street, the worshippers of **Dionysus** celebrate with orgiastic rituals the death and resurrection of their pagan god. **The Syrian** appears with the news that Christ has risen. The Greek and Hebrew are skeptical and try to prevent him from telling the disciples. Outside, the followers of Dionysus are motionless and stare at the upper room. When the figure of Christ appears, The Hebrew is terrified, but The Greek, convinced that Christ is a spirit, reaches forward to touch the body. His skepticism is confounded when he discovers that the heart of the phantom is beating. While The Syrian describes the scene in the inner room, The Greek realizes the significance for civilization of the coming of Christ. The play, following the **Noh** model, opens and closes with a song for the folding and unfolding of the cloth, performed by three Musicians, and Christ wears a stylized mask. The first performance of *The Resurrection* was given at the **Abbey Theatre**, 30 July 1934. WBY, in a note to the play, anticipated that the subject matter might make it unsuitable for presentation on the public stage in England or Ireland. The innovation of a masked Christ caused some controversy, many in the audience believing the device to be irreligious and immoral. The cast was: The Hebrew, A. J. Leventhal; The Greek, Denis Carey; The Syrian, J. Winter; Christ, Liam Gaffney; Musicians, Michael J. Dolan, Robert Irwin. The production was directed by **Lennox Robinson**, with masks by George Atkinson and music by Arthur Duff.

REFERENCES: Bradley, Anthony. *William Butler Yeats*. New York: Frederick Ungar, 1979; Ellis, Sylvia C. *The Plays of W. B. Yeats: Yeats and the Dancer*. London: Macmillan, 1995; Miller, Liam. *The Noble Drama of W. B. Yeats*. Dublin: Dolmen, 1977; Taylor, Richard. *A Reader's Guide to the Plays of W. B. Yeats*. New York: St. Martin's, 1984.

REVERIES OVER CHILDHOOD AND YOUTH. See AUTOBIOGRAPHIES.

RHADAMANTHUS, son of Zeus and **Europa** in Greek mythology. He was one of the three judges of souls in the Underworld, the others being **Aeacus** and **Minos**. In WBY's poem ''The Delphic Oracle upon Plotinus'' (*CP*. 306), Rhadamanthus is one of the trio, whom **Porphyry** in his *Life of Plotinus* calls the ''Golden Race,'' who guide **Plotinus** on his way to heaven.

REFERENCE: Barnwell, William C. ''The Blandness of Yeats' Rhadamanthus.'' *English Language Notes* (University of Colorado) 14, no. 3 (1977).

RHYMERS' CLUB, association of poets. It is generally believed to have been founded by WBY and **Ernest Rhys** in 1890, although this has been challenged by those who assert the club grew out of informal readings at the home of Arthur Mackmurdo at 20 Fitzroy Street, London. The Rhymers' Club flourished from 1890 to 1894. WBY claimed he founded the club to avoid feelings of jealousy among the younger poets. He was eager to formulate an agreed artistic manifesto, but the other members were skeptical. From early 1890, they met weekly, sometimes in private homes, but more regularly in an upper room at **Ye Olde Cheshire Cheese** (*KLI.* 217). Membership was by election, and guests were permitted. Regular members of the club, in addition to WBY and Ernest Rhys, were Walter Crane, **John Davidson, Ernest Dowson, Edwin J. Ellis**, A. C. Hillier, **Herbert P. Horne**, Selwyn Image, **Lionel Johnson, Richard Le Gallienne, Victor Plarr**, Ernest Radford, **T. W. Rolleston**, and **John Todhunter. Arthur Symons** was an early member but lost interest. **Oscar Wilde** sometimes attended when a meeting was held in a private home. At various times, WBY invited **Maud Gonne, John O'Leary**, and the illustrator **J. T. Nettleship**. The club published two anthologies—*The Book of the Rhymers' Club* (1892) and *The Second Book of the Rhymers' Club* (1894). Each contained six poems by WBY. A third anthology was planned but never published. The demise of the Rhymers' Club coincided with the developing careers of its successful members, like WBY, Symons, Dowson, and Lionel Johnson. It broke up gradually, partly due to a lack of ideological coherence and partly because of the range of talent of its members. While it was in existence, the Rhymers' Club had a practical value. It provided members with companionship and a sensitive audience for their verse, and since many of the poets were freelance journalists, they reviewed each other's work frequently and sympathetically. WBY refined his poetic technique by reading his work aloud. He gained a sense of himself as an Irish poet, realizing that in his upbringing and education he was far removed from his English contemporaries. Later, with the deaths of Dowson and Johnson, and the suicide of Davidson, WBY mythologized the leading members of the Rhymers' Club in "The Tragic Generation" (*A.* 299–318), asserting that to maintain their integrity in a philistine world some had turned to a dissolute lifestyle and insisted on suffering and dying. Ernest Rhys and others have disputed this classification, since many of the Rhymers lived into comfortable old age, outliving WBY. In 1936, in his broadcast on "Modern Poetry" (*EI.* 491), he describes the Rhymers' Club with candor. His poem "The Grey Rock" (*CP.* 115) is addressed to those Rhymers with whom he met regularly at Ye Olde Cheshire Cheese.

REFERENCES: Alford, Norman. *The Rhymers' Club: Poets of the Tragic Generation.* New York: St. Martin's, 1994; Gardiner, Bruce. *The Rhymers' Club: A Social and Intellectual History.* New York: Garland, 1988; Gardner, Joann. *Yeats and the Rhymers' Club: A Nineties' Perspective.* New York: Peter Lang, 1989; Stanford, Derek, ed. *Three Poets of the Rhymers' Club: Ernest Dowson, Lionel Johnson, John Davidson.* Cheadle: Carcenet, 1974.

RHYS, ERNEST [PERCIVAL] (1859–1946), editor and poet. He was born in London and lived for a few years in Wales, but his formative years were spent in Newcastle-on-Tyne, England. In 1886, he moved to London to pursue a literary career and was commissioned by the publisher Walter Scott to edit the Camelot Series, a sixty-four-volume series of classical and modern writings. He met WBY in May 1887 at the home of **William Morris**, and the two became friends. After a visit to **Walt Whitman** in 1888, Rhys was able to relay to WBY that the American poet was enthusiastic about the poetry of **Sir Samuel Ferguson**, largely because of an article written by WBY. Apart from introducing him to other writers, including **Michael Field**, Rhys invited WBY to contribute *Fairy and Folk Tales of the Irish Peasantry* (1888) and *Stories from Carleton* (1889) to the Camelot Series. In January 1890, Rhys and WBY founded the **Rhymers' Club** (*A*. 165). Later that year, at a party given by WBY, Rhys met Grace Little, whom he married in January 1891. With the birth of his third child and the continued ill health of his wife, Rhys was in financial difficulties. He prepared a list of 153 titles and persuaded J. M. Dent to publish them under the imprint "Everyman's Library." The series was a financial success, but while Rhys added monthly to the list, he made little from the project. In 1914, Dent dispensed with his services, and Rhys returned to freelance journalism and editorial work. He produced books of verse, including *The Leaf Burners* (1918), and two volumes of autobiography. In his last years, he lectured in the United States, visited Europe, and called upon WBY in Dublin in 1925. From their first meeting, Yeats was attracted to the rather dreamy personality of Rhys, and they maintained a close relationship through the ensuing years. Rhys was much influenced by WBY, and in his *Welsh Ballads* (1898), which WBY reviewed for *The Bookman* (*UP2*. 91–94), he returned to his own mythological roots. Two of these poems, "The Song of the Graves" and "The Lament for Urien," were included in WBY's selection for *The Oxford Book of Modern Verse* (1936).

REFERENCES: Rhys, Ernest P. *Everyman Remembers*. New York: Cosmopolitan Book Corporation, 1931; Rhys, Ernest P. *The Prelude to Poetry: The English Poets in Defence and Praise of Their Art*. London: E. M. Dent, 1927; Rhys, Ernest P. *Wales England Wed: An Autobiography*. London: J. M. Dent, 1940.

RHYS, PROFESSOR SIR JOHN (1840–1915), Celtic scholar. He was principal of Jesus College, **Oxford**, and author of *Lectures on the Origin and Growth of Religion as Illustrated by Celtic Heathendom* (1888), a copy of which was in WBY's personal library (*OS*. no. 1741). WBY contemplated writing a review of the book when it was first published, but his plan never materialized. Nevertheless, he made references to the work in his writings, regarding it as one of three books without which Celtic legends could not be understood, the others being **Henri d'Arbois de Jubainville's** *Le Cycle mythologique irlandais et la mythologie celtique* and **Alfred T. Nutt's** commentary on **Kuno Meyer's** *The Voyage of Bran* (*UP2*. 119).

REFERENCE: Rhys, Sir John. *Celtic Folklore, Welsh and Manx*. 1901. Reprint, New York: B. Blom, 1972.

RIBH, fictional philosopher. An early Christian hermit, ninety years old, he is the central figure in a series of twelve poems written by WBY in 1934, under

the generic title ''Supernatural Songs'' (*CP*. 327), and published in the collection *A Full Moon in March* (1935). WBY included a ''Commentary on Supernatural Songs'' in *The King of the Great Clock Tower* (*VP*. 837–38), in
which he explained that Ribh was an imaginary critic of **St. Patrick**, his Christianity coming from early Egypt.

RICKETTS, CHARLES [DE SOUSY] (1866–1931), painter, stage designer, illustrator, publisher, printer, and collector. He was born in Geneva, the son of an
English naval officer and a French mother. As a child, he lived in France, Italy,
and England and received little formal education—although he was an avid
reader. He was orphaned at the age of sixteen and taken care of by a rich,
benevolent grandfather who enabled him to pursue a career in art. In 1882, he
was apprenticed to a wood engraver at the London City and Guilds Technical
Art School. There, he formed a relationship with the painter **Charles Shannon**,
which was to last throughout his lifetime. In 1887, Shannon and he set up home
at The Vale, King's Road, London, and Ricketts earned a modest living from
book illustration and commissions. At The Vale, they hosted many social evenings, which attracted the major figures in art and literature in London, including
Oscar Wilde. Ricketts's knowledge of European art and literature was remarkable. In 1889, Shannon and he published the first of four issues of *The Dial*, an
avant-garde periodical that was heavily influenced by the work of the French
Symbolists, then almost unknown outside France and Belgium. In 1891, four
books by Oscar Wilde, including *The Picture of Dorian Gray*, were published
with covers by Ricketts. These were the first of a number of book designs,
culminating in what is widely held to be his finest work, the design of Wilde's
The Sphinx (1894). In the early 1900s, after he had turned to painting with some
success, he began to design for the stage. His facility in drawing, coupled with
his love of theater, made him ideally suited to the medium. He had a superb
technical sense and quickly found himself in demand by the major theatrical
directors of the day. Between 1906 and his death in 1931, he designed over fifty
productions, and not content with simply designing the sets and costumes, he
painted costumes, scenery, and properties, in addition to lighting the stage.
Among his best-known stage designs are *The Winter's Tale*, produced by Harley
Granville Barker in 1912, and **George Bernard Shaw's** *St. Joan*, in 1924. He
met WBY in November 1899 and, for some years, exerted an enormous influence on him. He almost certainly introduced WBY to the work of the French
painters Gustave Moreau and **Puvis de Chavannes**. He offered advice to
WBY's sister **Elizabeth Yeats** on the setting up of the **Dun Emer Press** and
designed the covers for the first two volumes of Macmillan's collected edition
of WBY's *Later Poems* (1922) and *Plays in Prose and Verse* (1922). In stage
design, he gave the poet help of a very practical kind. It was Ricketts who
suggested making a set of costumes that would suit any number of plays, and
he advocated having one designer for setting, costumes, and lighting. He encouraged WBY to invite **Gordon Craig** to design *The Countess Cathleen* in

1903, offering to raise £600 to meet the cost. He designed the costumes for the first production of **J. M. Synge's** *The Well of the Saints* in 1908 and *The King's Threshold*, presented by the **Abbey Theatre** at the Court Theatre, London, in 1914. WBY admired the boldness of line and the simplicity of these latter designs and thought them the best stage costumes he had ever seen. He acknowledged his debt to Ricketts in *The Bounty of Sweden* (*A.* 550), naming him among the notable myth makers and mask makers of the age.

REFERENCES: Binnie, Eric. *The Theatrical Designs of Charles Ricketts.* Ann Arbor, Mich.: UMI Research Press, 1985; Calloway, Stephen. *Charles Ricketts: Subtle and Fantastic Decorator.* London: Thames & Hudson, 1979; Delaney, J. G. P. *Charles Ricketts: A Biography.* Oxford: Clarendon, 1990; Delaney, J. G. Paul. " 'Heirs of the Great Generation,' Yeats's Friendship with Charles Ricketts and Charles Shannon." *Yeats Annual*, no. 4 (1986); Loizeaux, Elizabeth Bergmann. *Yeats and the Visual Arts.* New Brunswick and London: Rutgers University Press, 1986.

RIVERSDALE, Yeats residence. It was WBY's last home in Ireland. He leased the stone farmhouse, with its four acres of land in rural Rathfarnham, County Dublin, in the summer of 1932, holding the lease for thirteen years. The house overlooked the Wicklow Mountains, which WBY could see from his bedroom window. He was especially proud of the fine garden at Riversdale, with its croquet lawn and orchards. In a letter to **Olivia Shakespear** (*WL.* 799), sent soon after he moved there, he writes of the house, which reminds him of something out of a woodcut by **Edward Calvert**, and of his contentment in the surroundings. The house and its gardens are the setting for his poem "An Acre of Grass" (*CP.* 346), written in November 1936.

REFERENCE: Hone, Joseph. *W. B. Yeats: 1865–1939.* 1943. Reprint, London: Macmillan, 1962.

ROBARTES, MICHAEL. *See MICHAEL ROBARTES AND THE DANCER.*

ROBINSON, [ESME STUART] LENNOX (1886–1958), playwright and theater director. He was born in Douglas, **Cork** (county), and educated at Bandon Grammar School. As a youth, he was deeply interested in music, but he became fascinated with the theater after seeing a touring production by the **Abbey Theatre** in Cork, 1907. He wrote his first play, *The Clancy Name*, in 1908. WBY recognized in the author a fellow playwright and Anglo-Irishman and had the play produced by the Abbey Theatre, where it ran for three months. Robinson was appointed manager of the Abbey in 1910, when the theater was going through a difficult period after **Annie F. Horniman** withdrew her financial support. He led the company on their controversial tour of the United States with *The Playboy of the Western World* but later resigned to devote himself to full-time writing. His next play, *The Whiteheaded Boy*, was accepted for production by WBY with little enthusiasm, but when it opened at the Abbey in 1916, it proved successful. He was reappointed manager in 1919 and was responsible for discovering **Sean O'Casey**, whose plays revived the failing fortunes of the Abbey. He directed the majority of the plays at the Abbey until he was replaced in 1934, first by Bladon Peake and then Hugh Hunt. Among his outstanding productions were O'Casey's *The Shadow of a Gunman* and *The Plough and the Stars*, Eugene O'Neill's *The Emperor Jones,* **Lady Gregory's** version of Molière's *The Would-Be Gentleman* and WBY's *The Player Queen* (December 1919), *Sophocles' King Oedipus* (December 1926), *Sophocles' Oedipus at Colonus* (September 1927), *Fighting the Waves* (August 1929), *The Resurrection* (July 1934), and *The King of the Great Clock Tower* (July 1934). As a dramatist, Robinson placed emphasis in hs plays on dialogue and characterization, with little attention given to staging. These were the qualities he brought to his productions, with the result that, under his leadership, the Abbey productions gradually became unimaginative and outmoded. Nevertheless, the immensity of his achievement may only be fully appreciated when it is realized that he was directing a play a month for many years, and the majority of his productions were of new plays. Appointed a director of the company in 1923 (a position he maintained until 1956), he was a loyal supporter of WBY and ensured the continuation of WBY's policies for a national theater. His own plays confirm his skills as a sound theater craftsman and proved popular additions to the Abbey repertoire. In the article "The Need for Audacity of Thought" (*UP2.* 464), WBY speaks of his vision of life as akin to the most celebrated writers, including **Strindberg, James Joyce**, and **J. M. Synge**. Among Robinson's later plays, the best are *The Far-off Hills* (1928) and *Drama at Inish* (1933). He was for many years director of the Abbey School of Acting. He lectured frequently in the United States and wrote two volumes of autobiography, *In Three Homes* (1938) and *Curtain Up* (1941). He edited *Further Letters of John B. Yeats* (1920), published by the **Cuala Press**, and Lady Gregory's *Journals* (1946). His book *Ireland's Abbey Theatre: A History, 1899–1951* (1951) remains a standard work on the early years of that theater.

REFERENCES: Hogan, Robert; Burnham, Richard; and Poteet, Daniel P. *Rise of the Realists, 1910–1915*. Dublin: Dolmen, 1979; Lowery, Robert G., ed. *Whirlwind in Dublin: The Plough and the Stars Riots*. Westport, Conn.: Greenwood, 1984; Mikhail, E. H., ed. *Abbey Theatre: Interviews and Recollections*. Totowa, N.J.: Barnes & Noble, 1988; O'Neill, Michael J. *Lennox Robinson*. New York: Twayne, 1964; Peterson, Richard F. "The Crane and the Swan: Lennox Robinson and William Butler Yeats." *Journal of Irish Literature* 9, no. 1 (1980); Robinson, Lennox. *Ireland's Abbey Theatre*. London: Sidgwick & Jackson, 1951; Robinson, Lennox, ed. *Irish Theatre; Lectures Delivered during the Abbey Theatre Festival, August 1938*. New York: Haskell House, 1971.

ROCK OF CASHEL, hill dominating the plains of County Tipperary. Perhaps Ireland's greatest landmark, it has on its summit an impressive collection of medieval monuments, a castle, a cathedral, a round tower, a Celtic Cross, and a beautiful chapel built by **Cormac** and consecrated in 1134. It was the seat of the **Munster** kings from the fourth to the eleventh century, when it was handed over as an ecclesiastical site by Muircheartaigh O'Brien. WBY refers to the Rock of Cashel and to Cormac's chapel, now a ruin, in the poem "The Double Vision of Michael Robartes" (*CP*. 192).

REFERENCE: McGarry, James P. *Place Names in the Writings of William Butler Yeats*. Gerrards Cross: Colin Smythe, 1976.

ROLLESTON, T[HOMAS] W[ILLIAM HAZEN] (1857–1920), poet, writer, and member of the **Rhymers' Club**. He was born at Glasshouse, Shinrone, County Offaly, the son of a county court judge. In 1879, after completing his education at St. Columba's College, and **Trinity College**, Dublin, he traveled to Germany, where he studied German language and literature. On his return to Ireland, he became a disciple of **John O'Leary** and, in 1883, founded the influential *Dublin University Review*, which he edited, May 1885–December 1886. He moved to London, where he became more closely associated with WBY. Together they formed the **Irish Literary Society**, with Rolleston as the first secretary, but tension developed between them when **Charles Gavan Duffy** became the editor of the **New Irish Library**. WBY felt betrayed by Rolleston, who had supported Gavan Duffy in the negotiations with the publisher **T. Fisher Unwin** (*M*. 81–83). In 1894, Rolleston returned to Dublin as secretary of the Irish Industrial Association. He accepted an official government post as organizer for the Department of Agriculture and published a pamphlet, *Ireland, the Empire and the War* (1900), that recanted his previously held views on Irish nationalism (*M*. 118). He was leader writer for the Dublin *Daily Express* and correspondent for the London *Daily Chronicle*. In 1908, he returned to London, where he lectured and reviewed for the German section of *The Times Literary Supplement*. He remained in London until his death. Among his many publications are *The Teachings of Epictetus* (1886), *A Life of Lessing* (1889), and *Imagination and Art in Gaelic Literature* (1900). His collections of verse and prose include *Sea-Spray* (1909), *The High Deeds of Finn* (1910), and *Myths and Legends of the Celtic Race* (1911). He edited with Stopford A. Brooke the important collection *A Treasury of Irish Poetry* (1900), acknowledging WBY to be "the first of the English writing poets" of the period. His poem "Clonmacnoise," by which he is best remembered, was included in WBY's selection for ***The Oxford Book of Modern Verse*** (1936).

REFERENCES: Frenz, Horst, ed. *Whitman and Rolleston: A Correspondence*. Bloomington: Indiana University Press, 1951; Hogan, Robert, ed. *Dictionary of Irish Literature*. Rev. ed. Westport, Conn.: Greenwood, 1996; Marcus, Phillip L. *Yeats and the Beginning of the Irish Renaissance*. Syracuse: Syracuse University Press, 1987; Rolleston, Charles Henry. *Portrait of an Irishman: A Biographical Sketch of T. W. Rolleston*. London: Methuen, 1939.

RONSARD, PIÈRRE DE (1525–85), French poet and courtier. He was the leader of a group of poets called La Pléiade, which he formed at the Collège de Coqueret. His canon of work was enormous, representing many themes but prin-

cipally deeply felt love and patriotism. His best-known love poems appear in
Sonnets pour Hélène (1578), translated by Humbert Wolfe in 1934. He wrote
two long patriotic poems in 1562, *Discours des misères de ce temps* and *Re-
montrances au peuple de France*. WBY's poem "At the Abbey Theatre" (*CP*.
107) was written in imitation of a sonnet by Ronsard, "Tyard, on me blasmoit,
à mon commencement."

REFERENCES: Armstrong, Elizabeth. *Ronsard and the Age of Gold*. London: Cambridge University Press, 1968; Cave, Terence. *Ronsard the Poet*. London: Methuen, 1973;
Wilson, Dudley B. *Ronsard: Poet of Nature*. Manchester: Manchester University Press,
1961; Wolfe, Humbert, trans. *Pierre de Ronsard: Sonnets for Helen*. London: Allen &
Unwin, 1972.

ROONEY, WILLIAM (1873–1901), poet and nationalist. He was born in Dublin
and attended the Christian Brothers School, Strand Street, where **Arthur Griffith** was a friend and fellow pupil. On leaving school, he worked as a solicitor's
clerk and became involved in nationalist politics, joining the Dublin Celtic Society. He contributed poems and articles to *United Ireland* and *The Shamrock*,
among other nationalist papers, and many in Dublin regarded him as the next
Thomas Davis. In the 1890s, Arthur Griffith and he founded *The United Irishman*, with Griffith as editor, but he overexerted himself, traveling around Ireland
to rally support for the Irish language and the nationalist cause. His premature
death in Dublin was a shock to WBY and his writer friends. His *Poems and
Ballads* (1902), edited by Arthur Griffith, and *Prose Writings* (1909) were published posthumously. WBY dedicated the first edition of ***Cathleen Ni Houlihan***
(1902) to his memory.

REFERENCE: Boylan, Henry. *A Dictionary of Irish Biography*. Dublin: Gill & Macmillan, 1978.

ROQUEBRUNE, small town in the south of France. In November 1938, WBY
and his wife stayed at the Hôtel Idéal Séjour, Cap Martin, some two kilometers
from Menton on the French Riviera. There, WBY wrote his last poems, "Cuchulain Comforted" (*CP*. 395), dated 13 January 1939, and "The Black Tower"
(*CP*. 396), dated 21 January 1939. On 26 January 1939, he made final correc-
tions to his play ***The Death of Cuchulain***. He died, Saturday, 28 January 1939,
and was buried in the graveyard of the Chapel of St. Pancrace at Roquebrune,
a nearby town that overlooks Cap Martin. His body remained there until it was
reinterred at **Drumcliff** in 1948. A memorial tablet, designed by **Edmund Dulac**
and bearing the simple inscription "William Butler Yeats 1865–1939," was
placed in the cemetery at Roquebrune in 1953.

REFERENCE: Souhami, Diana. "Yeats's Bones." In *Gluck, 1895–1978: Her Biography*. London: Pandora, 1988.

ROSE, THE, poetry collection. As with ***Crossways*** (1889), *The Rose* was not a
separate volume of poetry by WBY but a selection of early verse from ***The***

Wanderings of Oisin and Other Poems (1889) and *The Countess Kathleen and Various Legends and Lyrics* (1892), included in *Poems* (1895). The rose of the title comes from WBY's occult studies. In the 1890s, his membership in **The Order of the Golden Dawn** and his knowledge of the Rosicrucian and cabalistic doctrines provided him with universal symbols, like the rose and the tree, that he wove into the poems in this collection to add richness and meaning. This is apparent in the opening poem "To the Rose upon the Rood of Time" (*CP*. 35), where the poet asks the Rose, symbol of eternal beauty, to inspire him while he tells tales of Ireland's mythological past. The collection shows a marked development in feeling and content from the self-conscious poetry of *Crossways*, principally because the poet is dealing with material that arises directly from his own experience. It includes the poems written out of his frustrated, intense love for **Maud Gonne**, "The Pity of Love" (*CP*. 46), "When You Are Old" (*CP*. 45), and "The White Birds" (*CP*. 46), as well as those poems inspired by the ancient Irish myths, "Cuchulain's Fight with the Sea" (*CP*. 37), and the poet's emotional connections to his homeland, "The Lake Isle of Innisfree" (*CP*. 44). He is conscious of his role as an Irish poet linked with earlier generations of poets, responsible for restoring the ancient dignity of his people, as in "To Ireland in the Coming Times" (*CP*. 56). The poems in *The Rose* show the influence of **Percy Bysshe Shelley** and of **William Blake**, whose work he was editing at this time. The collection was dedicated to his friend **Lionel Johnson**, while the epigraph, first printed in the 1925 *Early Poems and Stories*, is from Book X, chapter 27, of the *Confessions* of St. Augustine. A translation from the Latin reads: "Too late I loved Thee, O Thou Beauty of ancient days, yet ever new! too late I loved Thee!"

REFERENCE: Adams, Hazard. *The Book of Yeats's Poems*. Tallahassee: Florida State University Press, 1990.

ROSENKREUZ, FATHER CHRISTIAN [also Rosicross] (b. 1378). He was born to a noble German family and placed, at the age of five, in a cloister to learn Greek and Latin. In 1394, on a pilgrimage to Damascus, he was initiated into an Arabian order, The Blood of the Lamb, taking the magic name Christian of the Rose Cross. He studied at an Egyptian Temple of the Order for three years, and after more years of study and teaching in Africa, Spain, and his native Germany, he began to initiate others and send them on missionary exploits, thus founding the modern Order of the Rosy Cross, or Rosicrucianism. Many adherents claim the order existed from the days of ancient Egypt. The secret teachings deal with cabalistic writings and occult symbols, which include the rosy cross, swastika, pyramid, tower, dolphin, and gong. Adepts are called Illuminati, and the society is variously called Brothers of the Rosy Cross, Rosy-Cross Knights, and Rosy-Cross Philosophers. According to Johann Valentin Andreae (1586–1654) in his *Fama Fraternitatis* (1614), the followers of Father Rosenkreuz had him buried in a tomb, lit with magic lamps, in a cavern in **Abiegnos**, the mystic mountain in the center of the earth. When the tomb was discovered

120 years later, his body lay undecayed in a still-lighted tomb. This story is the subject of WBY's poem "The Mountain Tomb" (*CP*. 136). WBY was initiated into the Hermetic **Order of the Golden Dawn** in 1893. The order was founded by **MacGregor Mathers**, Dr. William R. Woodman, and Dr. William Wynn Westcott, all of whom were officers of the Rosicrucian Society in England.

REFERENCES: Hough, Graham. *The Mystery Religion of W. B. Yeats*. Sussex: Harvester, 1984; Moore, Virginia. *The Unicorn: William Butler Yeats' Search for Reality*. New York: Octagon Books, 1973; Regardie, Israel. *The Golden Dawn: An Account of the Teachings, Rites and Ceremonies of the Order of the Golden Dawn*. St. Paul, Minn.: Llewellyn, 1995.

ROSS, MARTIN. *See* **SOMERVILLE AND ROSS**.

ROSSES, THE, seaside area in the parish of **Drumcliff**, five miles to the northwest of **Sligo** (town). It includes the village of Rosses Point and the surrounding plain, a sandy stretch covered with short grass. All the land at The Rosses and the house called **Elsinore** were owned by WBY's great-uncle **William Middleton**, while WBY's uncle **George Pollexfen**, who had a house called Moyle Lodge in the village of Rosses Point, usually spent his summers there. WBY visited the area, both as a child and as an adult, attracted by its reputation as a place haunted by fairies. He visited the Rosses Point regatta (*EX*. 407) and spoke with the pilots about ghosts and apparitions (*EI*. 513). In his essay "Drumcliff and Rosses" (*MY*. 88–94), he describes a cave in the area that led to pre-Christian forts and raths buried underground. The Rosses is the setting for a number of WBY's poems, including "The Stolen Child" (*CP*. 20) and "The Meditation of the Old Fisherman" (*CP*. 23). It is referred to in "At Algeciras—A Meditation upon Death" (*CP*. 278) and in "Alternative Song for the Severed Head" (*CP*. 324). In a note to "The Stolen Child" (*CP*. 20), WBY writes there is a place in Further Rosses where anyone falling asleep might waken "silly" because the fairies have taken away their souls.

REFERENCE: McGarry, James P. *Place Names in the Writings of William Butler Yeats*. Gerrards Cross: Colin Smythe, 1976.

ROSSES POINT. *See* **ROSSES, THE**.

ROSSETTI, DANTE GABRIEL [CHARLES] (1828–82), poet and painter. He was born in London and began writing when he was a student in the junior department at King's College (1836–41). He transferred to a drawing school in Bloomsbury and was accepted into the Royal Academy school in 1845. He read voraciously the work of the European classic writers and was fascinated by Edgar Allan Poe. His poem *The Blessed Damozel* was published in 1850, bringing him instant acclaim. Later, he translated a collection of poems from the Italian, *Dante and His Circle* (1874), and published his sonnet sequence *The House of Life* (1881). The first edition of his *Collected Poems* appeared in 1870, and he edited a selection of the poems of **William Blake** (1880), whom he had discovered through the purchase of a volume of Blake's designs and writings in 1847. In 1848, having met the painters Holman Hunt and John Everett Millais, he founded the Brotherhood of the Pre-Raphaelites. In his early paintings, he focused principally on religious subjects, but he later turned to painting scenes from **Shakespeare, Robert Browning**, and **Dante**. After 1856, he found inspiration in the Arthurian legends of Sir Thomas Malory and **Lord Tennyson**. By this time, the Pre-Raphaelite Brotherhood had broken up, and Rossetti had gained the patronage of **John Ruskin**. He formed a close friendship with **Sir Edward Burne-Jones** and **William Morris**, and together they embarked on a second phase of the Pre-Raphaelite movement. In 1860, he married the model Elizabeth Siddal, the subject of his painting *Beata Beatrix* (1863). Her death from an overdose of laudanum, after two years of marriage, caused him distress and led to a chloral dependence that affected his later years. Toward the end of the 1860s, he turned again to poetry. The critical response to his *Poems* (1871), especially from **Robert Buchanan**, who attacked him in the article ''The Fleshly School of Poetry,'' and the amount of chloral and alcohol that he took for insomnia led to a nervous collapse from which he never entirely recovered. In his painting, he turned from literary subjects to portraits of the classic female with long, flowing red hair, sensuous mouth, and erotic stare, painted in luxuriant colors. These late paintings, among them *The Blessed Damozel* (1871–79), *Proserpine* (1874), and *La Pia de' Tolomei* (1881), are now in major galleries, including the Tate Gallery, London, and the Metropolitan Museum in New York. Of the seven members of the Pre-Raphaelite Brotherhood, Rossetti was the most popular, and he was identified as the leading figure of the movement. During the 1880s and 1890s, books and articles on him outnumbered those devoted to the other painters. As a young poet, WBY, sharing his father's enthusiasm for Rossetti, claimed he ''was in all things Pre-Raphaelite'' (*A*. 114). Through his use of color, pattern, and his delight in form, Rossetti was the exemplar of ''art for art's sake,'' and WBY wished to articulate in poetry what Rossetti achieved in painting. Writing of the **Rhymers' Club**, WBY notes that of the many influences on the group, Rossetti's was perhaps the most powerful (*A*. 302). In ''The Happiest of Poets'' (*EI*. 53–64), he writes of Rossetti at some length, observing that in his paintings he ''saw the supernatural beauty, the impossible beauty'' (*EI*. 64), both of which are subjects in WBY's drama and verse, as in *The Shadowy Waters*. In his essay ''The Bounty of Sweden,'' he names Rossetti— before 1870—as one of the ''great myth-makers and mask-makers'' (*A*. 550), while in ''The Theatre'' (*EI*. 170), he insists that the theater of art must discover decorative and grave gestures such as delighted Rossetti. He had *The Collected Works of Dante Gabriel Rossetti* (1897), *The House of Life* (1904), and *Letters of Dante Gabriel Rossetti to William Allingham* in his personal library (*OS*. nos. 1789–91).

REFERENCES: Faldet, David S. *Visual Art and the Poetics of Rossetti, Morris, and Yeats*. Ann Arbor, Mich.: UMI, 1987; Hough, Graham. *The Last Romantics*. London:

Methuen, 1961; Loizeaux, Elizabeth Bergmann. *Yeats and the Visual Arts*. New Brunswick and London: Rutgers University Press, 1986; Richardson, James. *Vanishing Lives: Style and Self in Tennyson, Rossetti, Swinburne, and Yeats*. Charlottesville: University Press of Virginia, 1988.

ROUGHLEY (Irish: *Reachla*) [Raghly], headland on the north shore of **Sligo** Bay, west of **Drumcliff**. This headland can be seen from **Rosses Point**. In "The Thick Skull of the Fortunate" (*MY*. 95), WBY describes the wild, violent, red-haired descendants of Danish pirates who, he claims, still inhabit a remote seaside area called Roughley—although at the end of the story, he says he might have been thinking of Moughorow. WBY draws on the name for his fictitious **Fool** in the poem "Tom O'Roughley" (*CP*. 158).
    REFERENCE: McGarry, James P. *Place Names in the Writings of William Butler Yeats*. Gerrards Cross: Colin Smythe, 1976.

ROXBOROUGH, home of **Lady Gregory** in **Galway** (county). She lived there until her marriage in 1880. Roxborough House is about seven miles from **Coole Park**, between **Loughrea** and **Gort**. The home was commandeered by the Irish Republican Army in 1922 and subsequently burned to the ground. WBY refers to Roxborough in the poem "In Memory of Major Robert Gregory" (*CP*. 150).
    REFERENCE: McGarry, James P. *Place Names in the Writings of William Butler Yeats*. Gerrards Cross: Colin Smythe, 1976.

ROYAL IRISH ACADEMY, Ireland's major learned society. It was founded by royal charter in 1785 to promote research and the collection of materials relating to the history of Ireland. The Academy is especially noted for its fine collection of early Irish manuscripts, including the *Annals of the Four Masters* (1632–36). In more recent times, the Academy, whose headquarters are at 19 Dawson Street, Dublin, prepared and published a *Dictionary of the Irish Language* (1976). WBY writes of the founding of the Academy and its importance to the study of ancient Irish literature in "A General Introduction for My Work" (*EI*. 511).
    REFERENCE: Raifeartaigh, T. O., ed. *Royal Irish Academy: A Bicentennial History*. Dublin: The Academy, 1985.

RUA, SHEMUS, a peasant. In WBY's play *The Countess Cathleen*, he foolishly invites the **Merchants** into his home and persuades the other peasants to sell their souls for gold. The part of Shemus Rua in the first production at the **Antient Concert Rooms**, May 1899, was played by Valentine Grace. See also **Mary** and **Teigue**.

RUDDOCK, MARGOT (1907–51), English actress and writer. Margot Ruddock was the stage name of Margot Collis, who, in 1932, married Raymond Lovell, a director and leading man in regional theater in the north of England. In 1934, she corresponded with WBY to ask his help with the establishment of a poet's theater in London. They began a close friendship, and WBY visited her regularly on his visits to London. He rehearsed her for a performance of his poems at the Mercury Theatre, London, but the event did not take place, and he wrote for her the major role of the **Queen** in his play *A Full Moon in March*, so that she might act it. WBY was disappointed that she was only given a small role in his play *The Player Queen*, produced by the Little Theatre, London, October 1935. She visited WBY unexpectedly while he was in **Majorca** in the spring of 1936. She was in a distressed state, and in response to some encouraging words about her poetry, she went down to the shore and danced. She was temporarily confined to a mental institution in Barcelona, where she was visited by WBY and his wife. After she recovered from her illness, he wrote an introduction to five of her poems when they were published in *London Mercury*, July 1936 (*UP2*. 502–5). She published a book of poetry, *The Lemon Tree* (1936), for which he again wrote the introduction (*Pl*. 186–90). He insisted that she should play **Decima** in a production of *The Player Queen* scheduled to be performed at the **Abbey Theatre**, August 1936. The theater directors avoided a confrontation by producing *Deirdre* in its place! However, he arranged for Margot Ruddock to be the chief speaker in a series of poetry broadcasts he made for the **BBC** in 1937. According to George Barnes, who produced the broadcasts, she had a quality that WBY admired, "the ability to pass naturally and unselfconsciously from speech to song." Barnes claimed that she was incapable of reproducing the same interpretation from one performance to another, and he insisted on replacing her in a later broadcast. Shortly afterward, she was committed to a mental institution, where she remained for the rest of her life. WBY names her with **Lady Gregory** and **Maud Gonne** in his poem "Beautiful Lofty Things" (*CP*. 348), while in "A Crazed Girl" (*CP*. 348), he recalls her dancing on the shore at Majorca. It would appear she was still on his mind when he referred to her in the late poem "The Man and the Echo" (*CP*. 393), in which he reflected that his flattering comments on her poetry may have overwhelmed her unstable mind. He included seven of her short poems in his selection for *The Oxford Book of Verse* (1936) (*LE*. 236).

REFERENCE: McHugh, Roger, ed. *Ah! Sweet Dancer: W. B. Yeats—Margot Ruddock, a Correspondence*. New York: Macmillan, 1970.

RUMMEL, WALTER [MORSE] (1882–1953), pianist and composer. He was born into a family of distinguished pianists, among them his father Franz Rummel (1853–1901) and his grandfather Joseph Rummel (1818–80). He studied in Paris with Claude Debussy and became one of the finest contemporary interpreters of the composer's work. Rummel had a close personal relationship with **Ezra Pound**. They met in Paris in 1908, and Pound stayed with the young pianist when he visited Paris in 1910. They shared an interest in Early Music and together published *Hesternae Rosae* (1913), an edition of French troubadour songs, translated by Pound and arranged for voice and piano by Rummel. He spent a considerable amount of his time in London, giving private and public recitals. In June 1914, he gave the English premiere of twelve preludes by Debussy in the Aeolian Hall, London. As a composer, he had the reputation of combining the charm of Debussy with the romantic dreaminess of Schumann and César Franck. WBY was introduced to Rummel by Ezra Pound and very likely attended a private recital that Rummel gave at the home of **Olivia Shakespear**, 1913. In 1917, Rummel composed the settings for WBY's drama *The Dreaming of the Bones*, published in *Four Plays for Dancers* (1921). In his preface to *Four Plays for Dancers*, WBY refers to Rummel's music as beautiful but difficult. It was not used in the first production of the play at the **Abbey Theatre**, December 1931, because of its difficulty.

REFERENCE: Davidson, Peter. ''Music in Translation: Yeats; Pound; Rummel; Dulac.'' In *Yeats and the Noh: A Comparative Study*, ed. Masaru Sekine and Christopher Murray. Gerrards Cross: Colin Smythe, 1990.

RURY (Irish: *Rudraidhe*), founder of **Ulster** and High King of Ireland. He was reputed to be the son of Partholon, a legendary Greek settler in Lough Erne, County Fermanagh. Rury's royal court at **Emain Macha** was known for its splendor and as a center of chivalry and home of poetry. The men of Ulster were known as Clan Rudraidhe. In WBY's poem ''Baile and Aillinn'' (*CP*. 469), **Baile**, son of the Ulster goddess **Buan** and heir to the throne of Ulster, is said to be of ''Rury's seed.''

RUSKIN, JOHN (1819–1900), writer and critic. He was born in London, the son of a wealthy wine merchant. After showing an early talent in writing and drawing, he took lessons with the noted watercolorist Copley Fielding. In 1836, he began his studies at **Christ Church, Oxford**, winning the Newdigate prize for poetry in 1839. Although he graduated in 1842, his studies had been interrupted by a nervous illness that necessitated his spending the winter of 1840 in Italy. There, he began a thorough study of Italian painting, culminating in his influential work *Modern Painters* (5 vol., 1843–60), although the first volume was a spirited defense of the English painter J. M. Turner. He married Effie Chalmers Gray in 1848 and, with her, toured northern France, making an intensive study of the moral principles underlying medieval architecture for his book *The Seven Lamps of Architecture* (1849). He wrote *The Stones of Venice* (1851–53), in which he applied these general principles to Venetian architecture. In 1853, he championed the Pre-Raphaelite Brotherhood, not only becoming patron to **Dante Gabriel Rossetti** but also establishing friendships with **Edward Burne-Jones** and John Millais. His wife began an affair with Millais, and in 1854, she successfully sued for divorce. Although he was frequently ill and near to breakdown, Ruskin increasingly turned in his writing to questions of social justice and the nature of wealth. He published his views, which challenged the theories of political economy promulgated by the economist John Stuart Mill, in a series of essays in *The Cornhill Magazine*, but his ideas were unpopular and the editor, William Makepeace Thackeray, discontinued them. Ruskin reacted by publishing them under the title *Unto This Last* (1860). In the collection, and in *Munera Pulveris* (1862–63), he questioned the ugliness and waste of modern industrial England. His later works, among them *Sesame and Lilies* (1865), proposed radical social changes, including old-age pensions, public education, and trade unions. In his middle years, he fell in love with a young, well-born Irish woman, Rose La Touche, who was then sixteen years of age. Her parents opposed the relationship, but the affair continued until Rose's death some years later. In 1870, Ruskin was appointed Slade Professor at Oxford, the first professor of art in England. He was a successful lecturer and teacher, but because of continuing bouts of mental instability and mania, he resigned his professorship in 1879 and retired to the Lake District, where he spent his final years. From the numerous references to Ruskin in his writings, it is apparent that WBY admired him both as a writer of fine prose and as a social theorist. In the article "Irish Language and Irish Literature" (*UP2*. 240), he includes him with **Walter Pater, Shelley, Keats**, and **Wordsworth** as a writer who faced misunderstandings and misinterpretation because he spoke to the evils of the time. In the opening pages of *Autobiography* (*M*. 19), he writes that his reading of Ruskin's *Unto the Last* caused violent rows with his father, who was opposed to Ruskin's ideas. These rows clearly made such an impression upon WBY that he recalls them again in "Tomorrow's Revolution" (*LE*. 226), written in 1938. In "If I were Four-and-Twenty" (*LE*. 42), he asserts that unlike the great writers like **Dante** and **Shakespeare**, who were preoccupied with evil, Ruskin focused only on the good in human behavior, and thus, in the absence of an antagonist, his writing lacked character and a dramatic sense.

REFERENCES: Abse, Joan. *John Ruskin: The Passionate Moralist*. New York: Knopf, 1980; Conner, Patrick. *Savage Ruskin*. Detroit: Wayne State University Press, 1979; Hewison, Robert. *John Ruskin: The Argument of the Eye*. London: Thames & Hudson, 1976; Hunt, John Dixon. *The Wider Sea*. New York: Viking, 1982.

RUSSELL, GEORGE [WILLIAM] (1867–1935), poet, painter, and theosophist. Born in Lurgan, County Armagh, Russell, who wrote under the pseudonym AE, moved with his family to Dublin in 1878. He was educated at the Art School, Kildare Street, and at Dr. C. W. Benson's School in Rathmines. After he left school in 1884, he attended evening classes at the **Metropolitan School of Art**. There he met WBY, who encouraged his painting and his spiritual interests and introduced him to **Katharine Tynan**. While at art school, Russell became interested in theosophy. In 1888, he was a founder member of the Dublin Lodge of the **Theosophical Society** and, from 1891 to 1897, lived with members of the Society at 3 Upper Ely Place. WBY sometimes stayed there on his visits to Dublin. Also living at 3 Upper Ely Place was Violet North, whom Russell married in 1898. Although he admired Violet North, WBY disapproved of the marriage (*WL*. 299–300). With the publication of *Homeward: Songs by the Way* (1894), Russell acquired a reputation as the Irish **William Blake** and was considered the equal of WBY in talent and promise. In 1897, WBY dedicated *The*

Secret Rose to Russell, regarding him as his closest friend (*LE.* 156–57). For a time, he took an active interest in the development of a national theater. His play *Deirdre*—about which WBY was critical (*WL.* 365, 367–68)—was produced by **W. G. Fay** in April 1902. He was elected vice president of the **Irish National Theatre Society** in 1902, and although he helped transform the society from an amateur company into a more professional organization, proposing the formation of a new society with control vested in a board of directors, he resigned in 1905, unhappy with the new professional structure. He was an engaging host and conversationalist, and his Dublin home at 17 Rathgar Avenue became a center for philosophical and artistic debate. He exercised a considerable influence over the younger Irish writers, among them **Padraic Colum, Frank O'Connor**, and **Seamus O'Sullivan**—although WBY was skeptical of his overly tolerant influence and wrote "To a Poet, Who would have me Praise certain Bad Poets, Imitators of His and Mine" (*CP.* 105) as a rebuff. Unlike WBY, Russell did not devote himself solely to literature. From 1890, he was a draper's clerk, and from 1897, he was an official of the Irish Agricultural Organization Society. This post required traveling throughout Ireland, organizing rural banks, and writing on economic affairs for agricultural journals. He was editor of the *Irish Homestead* (1905–23) and *The Irish Statesman* (1923–30), periodicals of the Irish Agricultural Organization Society that published Irish writers, including WBY and Katharine Tynan—but he refused to publish WBY's poem "Leda and the Swan" (*CP.* 241), claiming it was open to misinterpretation. From 1913, he was active in politics and argued vehemently for a free Ireland made up of two federal states, North and South. He approved the setting up of the Irish Free State in 1922, but disillusioned with politics, he refused to become a senator. He visited Paris for the first time in 1926 and gave lecture tours of the United States in 1928, 1930, and 1934. He was a founder member of the **Irish Academy of Letters** in 1932 and, with WBY and **George Bernard Shaw**, was awarded the prestigious Gregory Medal in 1935. After the death of his wife, he retired to London in 1933 and died of cancer in a small nursing home in Bournemouth, England, in 1935. WBY attended his funeral in Dublin (*WL.* 838). Despite his early promise, with the publication of successive books, including *Collected Poems* (1913), *Gods of War* (1915), *The Candle of Vision* (1919), *Midsummer Eve* (1928), *The Avatars* (1933), and *The House of Titans and Other Poems* (1934), it became apparent that Russell was not developing as a writer, principally because he was too remote and abstract in his thinking. Unlike WBY, Russell failed to evolve a poetic style that successfully blended the esoteric with the concrete and the personal. Hence, his poetic writing remained vague and remote. WBY admired the visionary Russell, comparing him on more than one occasion with the eighteenth-century mystic **Emanuel Swedenborg** (*EI.* 412–15). WBY and Russell had an intense relationship, but each was highly critical of the other (*WL.* 344–45, 477), and although their friendship lasted until Russell's death, there were periods when the relationship was strained (they were estranged 1905–13), especially as WBY's reputation blossomed while his friend's declined. WBY was influenced by Russell's deep spirituality and religious temperament but regretted that his visionary friend allowed himself to be distracted from his creative writing by his work with the Irish Agricultural Organization Society (*LE*. 156–57). He became frustrated with Russell because he felt he scorned technique and book learning, trusting his visions to do the work of the intellect (*M*. 147). Yet he admired the subtlety and delicacy of Russell's early poems (*WL*. 231–32), and in his essay "My Friend's Book'' (*EI*. 412–18), he wrote a sustained, generous review of Russell's *Song and Its Fountain* (1932). He encouraged the publication of *Some Passages from the Letters of AE to W. B. Yeats* (Dublin: Cuala, 1936) and included eight poems by Russell in his selection for *The Oxford Book of Modern Verse* (1936). He writes in depth about Russell and their relationship in *The Trembling of the Veil* (*A*. 236–49).

REFERENCES: Davis, Robert B. *George William Russell ("AE")*. Boston: Twayne, 1977; Howarth, Herbert. *The Irish Writers 1880–1940*. London: Rockliff, 1958; Kain, Richard M., and O'Brien, James H. *George Russell (A.E.)*. Lewisburg, Pa.: Bucknell University Press, 1976; Marcus, Phillip L. *Yeats and the Beginning of the Irish Renaissance*. Syracuse: Syracuse University Press, 1987; Summerfield, Henry. *That Myriad-Minded Man: A Biography of G. W. Russell—"A.E."* Totowa, N.J.: Rowman & Littlefield, 1975.

S

SALAMIS, island in the Saronic Gulf of the Aegean Sea. It was the site of a battle in 480 B.C., when the Greek fleet defeated the Persians, the first important naval battle in recorded history. In "The Statues" (*CP*. 375), WBY reflects that Europe was not born from this decisive battle but rather from the artistry and technical skill of Greek sculptors.

SALLEY GARDENS, setting for one of WBY's best-known lyrics, "Down by the Salley Gardens" (*CP*. 22). They are possibly the salley or willow gardens on the banks of the river at **Ballysodare**. Salley rods were used in basket making and in the thatching of cottages. In a note, WBY claims he based the poem on some lines sung to him by an old peasant woman at Ballysodare (*VP*. 90). His version follows closely the opening two verses of the text of a ballad in the P. J. McCall Ballad Collection in the **National Library of Ireland**.

REFERENCES: Kirby, Sheelah. *The Yeats Country*. Dublin: Dolmen, 1966; McGarry, James P. *Place Names in the Writings of William Butler Yeats*. Gerrards Cross: Colin Smythe, 1976.

SAMHAIN, Celtic festival. It was held at the beginning of November and marked the end of summer. It was a pastoral festival, when farm animals were brought in from the fields, some to be slaughtered, some to be kept for breeding, and it was a time of ritual mourning for the death of summer, marked by fairs, markets, assemblies, and political discussions. It was considered a time of danger, of supernatural energy, when life and death were intertwined, and normal laws of time were suspended. Barriers between this world and the Otherworld were down, and humans could penetrate the fairy world, and vice versa. *Samhain* was the name given by WBY to the magazine, published in 1901 through 1906 and in 1908, that became the official organ for the **Irish National Theatre Society** (*EX*. 73–243). In *Samhain*, he developed his ideas on acting, on the speaking of verse, and on the choice of plays for a national theater. See also **Beltaine**.

REFERENCES: Dames, Michael. *Mythic Ireland*. 1992. Reprint, New York: Thames & Hudson, 1996; Ellis, Peter Berresford. *Dictionary of Celtic Mythology*. New York: Oxford University Press, 1992; Green, Miranda J. *Dictionary of Celtic Myth and Legend*. London: Thames & Hudson, 1992; Mac Cana, Proinsias. *Celtic Mythology*. Feltham, Middlesex: Newnes, 1983.

SANDYMOUNT CASTLE, home of WBY's great-uncle **Robert Corbet**. This eighteenth-century country house with Gothic battlements, a clock tower, and a cloister stood in the seaside village of Sandymount, some three miles southeast of the center of Dublin. It had extensive secluded grounds, with flower and fruit gardens, a lake with swans, and vistas overlooking Dublin Bay. The grounds were abundant in deer, and two tame eagles were chained on an island in the lake. When he retired from the clergy, WBY's grandfather, **Rev. William Butler Yeats**, resided near the castle in a small house separated from it by a high wall and a wicket gate. WBY's father, **John B. Yeats**, spent his student days there. After Robert Corbet committed suicide in 1872, the house was converted into a boys' school, and the house and grounds were substantially remodeled. WBY was born in **George's Ville**, about half a mile from the castle. WBY refers to his Sandymount relations in "Are You Content" (*CP*. 370). In a diary entry for 1930, recalling a book with the castle printed on the cover, WBY writes nostalgically of Sandymount Castle, making associations between it and **Coole Park** (*EX*. 318–19).

REFERENCE: McGarry, James P. *Place Names in the Writings of William Butler Yeats*. Gerrards Cross: Colin Smythe, 1976.

SARGENT, JOHN SINGER (1856–1925), painter. He was born in Florence, Italy, of American parents. He studied with the French master Carolus-Duran and received immediate recognition when his work was shown in Paris in 1878. In 1884, he moved to London. There he remained for most of his life, enjoying a reputation for his studies of contemporary celebrities, including WBY, of whom he made a charcoal drawing in April 1908. This drawing was used in WBY's *Collected Works* (1908) and in *Collected Plays of W. B. Yeats* (1952). Sargent's remark, that his portraits show people as they really are, was quoted by WBY in "Other Matters" (*LE*. 246).

REFERENCE: Fairbrother, Trevor J. *John Singer Sargent*. New York: Abrams, 1994.

SATO, JUNZO (1897–1981), Japanese diplomat and member of the Yeats Society of Japan. He attended a lecture given by WBY in Portland, Oregon, in March 1920, and was so moved by the occasion that he presented the poet with a favorite family sword, made some 550 years earlier by the master craftsman

Bishu Osafuné Motoshigé. WBY was deeply touched by the gesture and gave Sato, in return, a copy of his poems. He wrote an enthusiastic letter to **Edmund Dulac** describing the circumstances of the gift. Later, he dedicated the play *The Resurrection* (1934) to Junzo Sato. The ancient sword became for WBY a symbol of life and rebirth, and he made reference to it in "My Table" (*CP*. 227), "A Dialogue of Self and Soul" (*CP*. 265), and "Symbols" (*CP*. 270). In a diary entry for 1930 (*EX*. 320), he recalls the sword wrapped in a piece of fabric from a Japanese lady's court dress, the silk reminding him of the covering of a chair at **Coole Park** made from a court dress worn by **Lady Gregory**.

SATURN, Roman god of agriculture. His festival was the Saturnalia, 17 December, when all work stopped, moral restrictions eased, and gifts were exchanged. It became the most popular of all the Roman festivals and was later extended by seven days. Saturday, the end of the working week, was named for Saturn. A "long Saturnian sleep" is referred to by WBY in the poem "On a Picture of a Black Centaur by Edmund Dulac" (*CP*. 242).

SCANAVIN (Irish: *Sceanmhan*) [fine shingle], townland in **Sligo** (county). There is a well at Scanavin (Irish: *Tober Sceanmhan*), about a mile from **Collooney**. In the third stanza of the poem "The Man Who Dreamed of Faeryland" (*CP*. 49), the speaker, in old age, stands beside the well at Scanavin and thinks angrily of those who mocked him throughout his life.
    REFERENCE: McGarry, James P. *Place Names in the Writings of William Butler Yeats*. Gerrards Cross: Colin Smythe, 1976.

SCATHACH, female warrior in Celtic mythology. She was the daughter of Ard-Greimne of Lethra, and in her home in Alba (Scotland), she trained youths in the arts of war. **Cuchulain** was among her students, and it was from her he received his famous spear, the *Gae Bolg*. He joined her in battle against her sister **Aoife**. In *On Baile's Strand* (*CPl*. 275), Cuchulain enquires desperately if the young man he has just killed is Scathach's son.
    REFERENCES: Ellis, Peter Berresford. *Dictionary of Celtic Mythology*. New York: Oxford University Press, 1992; Green, Miranda J. *Dictionary of Celtic Myth and Legend*. London: Thames & Hudson, 1992; Mac Cana, Proinsias. *Celtic Mythology*. Feltham, Middlesex: Newnes, 1983.

SCEOLAN. *See* **BRAN**.

SCHOPENHAUER, ARTHUR (1788–1860), philosopher. He was born in Danzig, Prussia, the son of a wealthy merchant. In 1805, on the sudden death of his father, the family moved to Weimar, where his mother, Johanna Schopenhauer, a novelist and essayist, introduced him to **Goethe**, with whom he formed a close friendship. He entered the University of Göttingen in 1809 as a student of the natural sciences, but influenced by his study of the philosophers **Plato** and Immanuel Kant, he transferred to the University of Berlin as a humanities scholar and earned his Ph.D. from the University of Jena in 1813. Returning to Weimar, he came under the influence of the Orientalist Friedrich Majer, who introduced him to Indian mysticism. After a quarrel with his mother because of her frivolous lifestyle, he left Weimar for Dresden. There, he devoted himself to writing and to a philosophical system based on Plato, Kant, and the Indian *Upanishads*. For Schopenhauer, who is called the "philosopher of pessimism," the world was a constant conflict of intuitive wills and insatiable needs, which produced only suffering and pain. Pleasure was the absence of pain and might only be achieved through the saintly renunciation of desire, through selflessness, and through identification with the suffering of others. He developed these beliefs in his major philosophical work *The World as Will and Representation* (1818). He was appointed to the University of Berlin in 1820. He intended rivaling the popular **Hegel**, who already taught at the university and whose philosophy of rational idealism he directly opposed. He remained at Berlin for four years, but the students largely ignored him, and he gave only one lecture. In his frustration, Schopenhauer left the university to concentrate on writing. He settled in Frankfurt, a recluse, absorbed by his own studies and ignored by fellow philosophers, although he continued to publish, most notably *On the Will in Nature* (1836). Three publishers rejected his work, but when an obscure Berlin publisher accepted the two-volume *Parerga und Paralipomena* (1851), in which he dealt with individual topics, such as parapsychology, writing and style, women, and education, it marked the beginning of his worldwide acceptance. His influence intensified after his death. With his philosophical notions on the power of intuition, creativity, and the irrational, he had a profound impact on later German philosophers, most notably **Nietzsche**, and on writers and composers like **Richard Wagner**. In "Art and Ideas" (*EI*. 347), WBY claims to have read Schopenhauer at an impressionable age. Later, with his interest in Indian mysticism, the German philosopher possessed added appeal for WBY, and he refers to his understanding of "will" as the only true reality in his "Introduction to *The Holy Mountain*" (*LE*. 148, 153) and "The Ten Principal Upanishads" (*LE*. 172).

REFERENCES: Fox, Michael, ed. *Schopenhauer: His Philosophical Achievement.* Brighton, Sussex: Harvester, 1980; Gardiner, Patrick. *Schopenhauer.* Harmondsworth, Middlesex: Penguin, 1971.

SCOTT, SIR WALTER (1771–1832), novelist and poet. He was born in Edinburgh, Scotland, the son of a lawyer, and attended schools in Edinburgh and Kelso. From an early age, he showed a remarkable talent for poetry, and he read voraciously in a range of languages: Italian, Spanish, French, German, and Latin. He took a deep interest in Scottish history and passionately explored his native countryside. He became a lawyer, but it was quickly apparent that his interest was not in law but in literature. A study of German Romanticism led to his translation of **Goethe's** *Götz von Berlichingen* in 1799, but it was his collections of old Scottish ballads, *Minstrelsy of the Scottish Border* (1802, 1803), that brought him his first literary success. He followed this with his own poetic romances set in Scotland, *The Lay of the Last Minstrel* (1805), *Marmion* (1808), and *The Lady of the Lake* (1810). In 1814, he published the first of his historical novels, *Waverley*, which vividly brought to life a vanished Scottish Highland society. The novel's popularity led to a series of historical masterpieces known as the "Waverley Novels," including *Guy Mannering* (1815), *Old Mortality* (1816), *Rob Roy* (1818), *The Heart of Midlothian* (1818), and *The Bride of Lammermoor* (1819). He was made a baronet in 1820 and embarked upon the building and furnishing of a baronial hall at Abbotsford in Roxburgh. He was involved in a series of business deals financed with the proceeds of books that he had still to write. Having exhausted the major Scottish themes, he turned for inspiration to English history and elsewhere, writing *Ivanhoe* (1820), set in twelfth-century England, *Kenilworth* (1821), set in Elizabethan England, and *Quentin Durward* (1823), set in fifteenth-century France. A financial crash in 1825 left him heavily in debt, but he determined to repay his creditors. He succeeded, but in the process, his health was destroyed. WBY was ambivalent in his assessment of Scott. He acknowledged the part that he, like **Robert Burns**, played in the development of a Scottish national identity, and he saw his influence in the songs of **Thomas Davis** and later Irish writers. He credited him with beginning a modern medieval movement that became a major influence on art, religion, and literature during the nineteenth century (*UP2*. 71). In an early article, "The Poetry of R. D. Joyce" (*UP1*. 105), published in the *Irish Fireside* in 1886, he associates Scott with the bardic tradition of **Homer** and **Victor Hugo**, but in a Journal entry (*M*. 248), written in 1910, he is critical of Scott because he presented only an external and picturesque view of Scottish life, creating through literature what WBY disparagingly calls "a province" and not a nation (*EI*. 341). In "What is 'Popular Poetry'?" (*EI*. 6), he judges him a poet of the middle class, of those who have lost contact with the folk tradition, a point he reiterates in "The Literary Movement in Ireland" (*UP2*. 185). Finally, in "A Defence of the Abbey Theatre" (*UP2*. 468), he compares him unfavorably with **Synge** and **Lady Gregory**, claiming that he made a single Lowland dialect serve for all of Scotland, while his two fellow Irish writers had selected dialects for their plays from a knowledge that few other dialect writers could equal.

REFERENCES: Davie, Donald. *The Heyday of Sir Walter Scott*. London: Routledge & Kegan Paul, 1961; Johnson, Edgar. *Sir Walter Scott: The Great Unknown*. New York: Macmillan, 1970; Muir, Edwin. *Scott and Scotland: The Predicament of the Scottish Writer*. Folcroft, Pa.: Folcroft, 1971.

SEANCHAN, fictional poet. He is the leading character in WBY's play *The King's Threshold*. Seanchan is on hunger strike to protest his exclusion from King **Guaire's** council. The King, fearing he might be thought weak, justifies his position, insisting that only those men who rule the country should sit on the council, a decision that has the support of the army, the church, and the law. He sends Seanchan's pupils to bribe him with property, a pension, jewels, and clothes, but the offers are rejected. Others, including his sweetheart **Fedelm**, unsuccessfully attempt to dissuade Seanchan from his action. The King threatens his pupils with death if they do not persuade their master to give up the hunger strike. The pupils exhort Seanchan to die rather than give up the established right of the poets of Ireland, and the play ends with the pupils carrying their dead but triumphant master from the stage. The part of Seanchan in the first production at the **Abbey Theatre**, 1903, was played by **Frank Fay**, to whom WBY dedicated the published version of the play.

SECRET ROSE, THE, collection of stories. Published by **Lawrence and Bullen**, London, April 1897, *The Secret Rose* brought together seventeen stories that WBY had published in magazines and periodicals over the previous five years. These included "The Binding of the Hair," "The Wisdom of the King," and a series of stories about **Red Hanrahan**, "The Book of the Great Dhoul and Hanrahan the Red," "The Twisting of the Rope and Hanrahan the Red," "Kathleen the Daughter of Houlihan and Hanrahan the Red," "The Curse of Hanrahan the Red," "The Vision of Hanrahan the Red," and "The Death of Hanrahan the Red." The book was designed by **Althea Gyles** and included illustrations by **John B. Yeats**. It was dedicated to **AE**.

REFERENCES: Gould, Warwick; Marcus, Phillip L.; and Sidnell, Michael J., eds. *The Secret Rose: Stories by W. B. Yeats: A Variorum Edition.* London: Macmillan, 1981; Putzel, Steven D. *Reconstructing Yeats: The Secret Rose and the Wind among the Reeds.* Dublin: Gill & Macmillan, 1986.

SEPTIMUS, fictional poet. In WBY's play *The Player Queen*, he is the self-pitying and aggressive leading character who is drunk throughout most of the action. He and his theater troupe have come to present a play at the Court, but his wife **Decima**, who is also his leading lady, cannot be found. She is jealous of Septimus's affair with **Nona**, another member of the company. When Septimus runs off with Nona, his wife feels betrayed and chooses to take the place of the terrified **Queen**, whose subjects have revolted. The feckless nature of the character and his drunken appeals on behalf of poetry contrast with the intensity and commitment of **Seanchan**, the poet in *The King's Threshold*. The role of Septimus in the first production of *The Player Queen*, May 1919, was played by Nicholas Hannen.

SEVEN WOODS, collective name for the woods on **Lady Gregory's** estate at **Coole Park**. WBY knew the woods well, since he spent much time walking there during the many summers he spent at Coole Park. Indeed, they made such a profound impression on him that he thought of them as the "Enchanted Woods," the title of an essay in which he recalls the people he met there and the stories they shared with him (*MY.* 60). In the Seven Woods, the poet found

peace from the preoccupations of his personal life, from the concerns of the
Abbey Theatre, and from the cutthroat world of Irish politics. He names the
woods in "I walked among the Seven Woods of Coole" (*CP*. 469), the opening
poem of the collection *The Shadowy Waters* (1900), dedicated to Lady Gregory,
and they are the subject of the poem "In the Seven Woods" (*CP*. 85). The
Seven Woods are Shan-walla (Irish: *Sean Bhalla*) [old wall], Kyle-dortha (Irish:
Coill dortha) [dark wood], Kyle-na-no (Irish: *Coill na gCno*) [the wood of the
nuts], Pairc-na-lee (Irish: *Pairc na Laoi*) [field of calves], Pairc-na-carraig (Irish:
Pairc na gCarraig) [field of stones], Pairc-na-tarav (Irish: *Pairc na dTarbh*)
[field of the bulls], and Inchy Wood (Irish: *Coill na nInsi*) [wood of the water
meadows]. A frightened squirrel is the subject of "To a Squirrel at Kyle-na-
no" (*CP*. 175), while in **The King's Threshold** (*CPl*. 115), the Second Cripple
claims that on the death of a local poet thorn trees from Inchy Wood to **Kiltartan** withered. The canopy of leaves and branches in Kyle-na-no are mentioned in "While I, from that reed-throated Whisperer" (*CP*. 143). In "A Prayer
for my Daughter" (*CP*. 211), WBY refers to Gregory's Wood, a general name
for one of the Seven Woods. The poem was completed while the poet was
staying with his wife and daughter at **Thoor Ballylee**, close to Coole Park.

REFERENCE: Smythe, Colin. *A Guide to Coole Park, Co. Galway: Home of Lady
Gregory*. Gerrards Cross: Colin Smythe, 1973.

SHADOWY WATERS, THE, verse play. The poet and his muse provide the theme
for this semiautobiographical verse play. It first appeared in *Poems 1899–1905*
(1906), but an "Acting Version" was included in *The Poetical Works of W. B.
Yeats*, Vol. II (1907). Having stolen her from her husband, **Forgael**, a poet
philosopher with a magic harp, woos **Dectora**, and they enter into a mystical
marriage. A source for the play was the story "The Birth of Cuchulain," from
Lady Gregory's *Cuchulain of Muirthemne* (1902), in which Dectora, the wife
of Sualtim, was carried off on her wedding day by the god **Lugh**. WBY initially
wrote the work as a dramatic poem, and after giving it to some actors to speak,
he was encouraged to rewrite it for the stage. While the play takes place in the
mythological past, it is rooted in WBY's private philosophy and experience. He
revised it many times, always trying to make it more stageworthy, and it is
central to his development as a playwright. The first production of *The Shadowy
Waters*, a version written in 1900 and described in the program as "a dramatic
poem," was given by the **Irish National Theatre Society**, 14 January 1904, in
the **Molesworth Hall**, Dublin. The part of Forgael was played by **Frank Fay**,
and Dectora by Máire Nic Shiubhlaigh. The scenery, with its striking dark blue
and dark green color scheme and a boat and sail painted green, gold, and copper,
was designed by **Robert Gregory**.

REFERENCES: Byrd, Thomas L. Jr. *The Early Poetry of W. B. Yeats: The Poetic Quest*.
Port Washington, N.Y.: Kennikat, 1978; Ellis, Sylvia C. *The Plays of W. B. Yeats: Yeats
and the Dancer*. London: Macmillan, 1995; Miller, Liam. *The Noble Drama of W. B.
Yeats*. Dublin: Dolmen, 1977; Oppel, Frances Nesbitt. *Mask and Tragedy: Yeats and
Nietzsche, 1902–10*. Charlottesville: University Press of Virginia, 1987.

SHAKESPEAR, OLIVIA (1863–1938), novelist and friend of WBY. She was the second child of Major-General Henry Tod Tucker and Harriet Maria Johnson. She married Hope Shakespear, a well-to-do solicitor fourteen years her senior, in 1885, and they had one child, Dorothy, born in 1886. Olivia Shakespear's marriage was unfulfilling, and in 1894, when she first saw WBY at a literary dinner, she asked her cousin **Lionel Johnson** to introduce her. This was the beginning of a friendship that provided WBY with some solace and comfort from the uncertainty of his relationship with **Maud Gonne**. They became lovers after WBY moved to his own rooms in **Woburn Buildings**, early in 1896, but were estranged a year later when Olivia Shakespear realized he loved Maud Gonne (*M*. 89). The relationship with Olivia Shakespear had a profound effect on his poetry. From the poem "He bids his Beloved be at Peace" (*CP*. 69), it is apparent that she, and not Maud Gonne, was instrumental in helping him find a deeper sensuality in his writing and that through their relationship he became more in touch with reality. In his autobiographical writings, WBY refers to her as Diana Vernon, one of **Sir Walter Scott's** heroines. The breakup of the relationship is the focus of the poems "The Lover mourns for the Loss of Love" (*CP*. 68) and "He reproves the Curlew" (*CP*. 69). After a period, the friendship, but not the relationship, was resumed. WBY recalls the liaison in "The Travail of Passion" (*CP*. 78), "Friends" (*CP*. 139), "The Empty Cup," Part V of the poem "A Man Young and Old" (*CP*. 249), and "After Long Silence" (*CP*. 301). Olivia Shakespear introduced **Ezra Pound** to WBY in 1909, and in 1911, her brother Harry Tucker married Edith Ellen Hyde-Lees, whose daughter by an earlier marriage became WBY's wife. Olivia Shakespear's daughter, Dorothy, married Ezra Pound, much against her parents' wishes. The marriage was unhappy. Hope Shakespear died in 1923, and from 1926 until her death, Olivia Shakespear took care of her grandson, Omar Pound. She was a highly intelligent woman, well-read in English, French, and Italian literature. She was a sensitive and talented novelist: her novella *Beauty's Hour* appeared in *The Savoy*, August, September 1896. Her other novels include *The Journey of High Honor* (1894), *The False Laurel* (1896), and *Rupert Armstrong* (1898). She collaborated with **Florence Farr** in the writing of two short plays, *The Beloved of Hathor* and *The Shrine of the Golden Hawk*. Both plays were produced by the Egyptian Society, London, January 1902, and were sensitively reviewed by WBY (*UP2*. 266–67). Even after his marriage in 1917, WBY and Olivia Shakespear corresponded frequently—indeed, the poet wrote fuller letters to her than to any of his other friends—and he called on her when he was in London. After her death, Ezra Pound returned to the Yeats family many of the letters WBY had written to her.

    REFERENCES: Freyer, Grattan. *W. B. Yeats and the Anti-Democratic Tradition*. Dublin: Gill & Macmillan, 1981; Harwood, John. "Olivia Shakespear: Letters to W. B. Yeats." In *Yeats Annual, No. 6*, ed. Warwick Gould. London: Macmillan, 1988; Harwood, John. *Olivia Shakespear and W. B. Yeats: After Long Silence*. London: Macmillan, 1989.

SHAKESPEARE, WILLIAM (1564–1616), dramatist and poet. He was born in Stratford-upon-Avon, the son of John Shakespeare and Mary Arden. His father, a burgess of the borough of Stratford, was appointed alderman in 1565 and later bailiff. In this capacity, he had the responsibility for engaging traveling theater groups to perform in the town. Stratford had a fine grammar school, which William Shakespeare very likely attended since he had such a knowledge of language and the classics. In 1582, he married Anne Hathaway, and after the birth of their three children, he traveled to London, leaving the family in Stratford. By the early 1590s, he had achieved some prominence in London as an actor and a playwright, and in 1592, he published his narrative poem *Venus and Adonis*. In 1594, he joined the Lord Chamberlain's Men (later, the King's Men) as a playwright and actor. In 1599, he became a part owner of the Globe Theatre, where his finest tragedies, *Hamlet, Othello, King Lear*, and *Macbeth*, were performed, in addition to *Twelfth Night* and *Measure for Measure*. His plays were performed at court, at the Inns of Court (the residences of London's legal societies), and at country houses when the King's Men went on tour. He wrote little after 1612 and retired to Stratford. He is buried in the chancel of Holy Trinity Church. WBY was introduced to Shakespeare by his father, who read passages from the plays to him as a child and took him to see **Henry Irving** as Hamlet, a performance recalled in the poems "Lapis Lazuli" (*CP.* 338) and "The Nativity" (*CP.* 387), both written in the 1930s. He sought every opportunity to see Shakespeare performed in London, and he visited the Stratford Memorial Theatre in 1901, 1902, 1904, 1905, 1908, and 1909. He read Shakespeare avidly, and when asked in 1932 to name the writers who had moved him, he put Shakespeare at the head of the list (*LE.* 129). He observed a Celtic influence on Shakespeare's characters and imagery (*EI.* 176, 177, 185; *UP2.* 206). For WBY, Shakespeare, with his exuberant passion, his love of people, and his disdain for the crowd, was a product of a pre-Renaissance England, to be named with the outstanding folk poets of earlier times (*LE.* 103). Shakespeare was a model writer and forged a national character through his work, like **Goethe, Dante**, and **Homer**. In trying to revive poetry in the theater, WBY took as his inspiration the poetic drama of Shakespeare, although in his later critical writings, he asserts that Shakespeare diluted his art by catering to the popular taste. He writes about his 1901 visit in "At Stratford-on-Avon" (*EI.* 96–110; *UP2.* 247–51).

REFERENCES: Desai, Rupin W. *Yeats's Shakespeare.* Evanston: Northwestern University Press, 1971; Nevo, Ruth. "Yeats, Shakespeare and Nationalism." In *Literature and Nationalism*, ed. Vincent Newey and Ann Thompson. Savage, Md.: Barnes & Noble, 1991; Kleinstück, J. "Yeats and Shakespeare." In *Centenary Essays on the Art of W. B. Yeats*, ed. D. E. S. Maxwell and S. B. Bushrui. Ibadan: Ibadan University Press, 1965; Perrine, Laurence. "Yeats and Shakespeare: 'The Old Stone Cross.' " *Modern British Literature* 3, no. 2 (1978).

SHANNON, CHARLES [HAZELWOOD] (1863–1937), painter and lithographer. He was born in Quarrington, Lincolnshire, the son of the Reverend Frederick

William Shannon, rector of the local Anglican church. After attending St. John's, Leatherhead, a school for the sons of clergymen, he transferred to the City and Guilds Technical Art School, Kennington, London, to study wood engraving. There, he met his lifelong companion **Charles Ricketts**, and they set up house at The Vale, King's Road, London. Their home became the center of an impressive circle of writers and painters, among them WBY. Initially, Shannon was regarded as the more promising artist and painted many portraits, including one of WBY, commissioned by **John Quinn** and reproduced as the frontispiece in *Collected Works* (1908), Vol. III. As Ricketts found increasing success as a designer, the situation was reversed, and Shannon became disillusioned and withdrawn. In 1929, while hanging a large painting at his home, he had a serious accident, which rendered him unconscious for nine days. Though he recovered consciousness, his mind was affected, and he lived as an invalid for the remainder of his life. Among his best works are *Bunch of Grapes* and *Lady with the Green Fan*, both owned by the **Municipal Gallery of Modern Art**. WBY met Shannon and Ricketts in the late 1890s, when he visited them at The Vale. They were collectors of painting and sculpture, and through them, WBY developed his taste for classical sculpture, so that in ''Four Years: 1887–1891'' (*A.* 169), he acknowledged them not only as friends but also ''in certain matters my chief instructors.'' In 1895, when working on *Poems*, WBY, who had admired a Shannon drawing, ''Shepherd in a Mist'' (*The Dial*, 1892), hoped he would design the cover (*KLI.* 439), but Shannon was unable to do so.

REFERENCE: Delaney, J. G. P. *Charles Ricketts: A Biography.* Oxford: Clarendon, 1990.

SHAN-WALLA. *See* **SEVEN WOODS**.

SHAPE-CHANGERS, supernatural beings with the power to metamorphose. In Celtic mythology, shape-changing is a common motif in which gods and divine creatures transform themselves into human or animal form, at will. The **Sídhe** are Shape-Changers. Thus, in WBY's play *At the Hawk's Well,* **The Guardian of the Well** transforms herself into a Hawk to distract **Cuchulain** from the magic water, while in the climactic dance, she appears as both woman and hawk. **Bricriu** masquerades as the **Figure of Cuchulain** in *The Only Jealousy of Emer*, while **Fand** is a seductress who attempts to lure the **Ghost of Cuchulain** to the Otherworld. In *The Death of Cuchulain*, the **Morrigu**, war goddess, reveals herself to the dying Cuchulain as a woman headed like a crow.

REFERENCE: Green, Miranda J. *Dictionary of Celtic Myth and Legend.* London: Thames & Hudson, 1992.

SHARP, WILLIAM (1855–1905), poet, novelist, biographer, and editor. He was born and grew up in the Western Highlands of Scotland but emigrated to Australia because of ill health. In 1879, he returned to London, where he became heavily influenced in his writing by the Pre-Raphaelites, principally **Dante Ga-**

briel Rossetti. In 1892, he published a biography of Rossetti, in addition to biographies of **Percy Bysshe Shelley** (1887), Heinrich Heine (1888), and **Robert Browning** (1890). From 1893, he wrote under the pseudonym **Fiona Macleod**, a fictitious writer with whom he carried on a lifelong correspondence. For her, he evolved a second literary style, quite distinct from his other writings, which he signed with his own name. Among the books published under the pseudonym were *The Divine Adventure: Iona* (1912), *The Dominion of Dreams* (1912), *Under the Dark Star* (1912), and *The Winged Destiny: Studies in the Spiritual History of the Gael* (1913). His play *The House of Usna*, a retelling of the **Deirdre** legend, was performed by the Stage Society, London, on 29 April 1900. WBY knew Sharp from 1888. He admired his psychic powers, and together they experimented with visions and trances. He was introduced to Fiona Macleod in the mid-1890s and corresponded with her, believing she really existed. He was pleased to have a Scots contributor to the Celtic Renaissance. He was impressed with her work, and when reviewing *From the Hills of Dream: Mountain Songs and Island Runes* in 1896, he commented on her authentic voice and use of Gaelic mythology (*UP1*. 421–24). When he became aware of the deception, he justified Sharp's behavior by insisting that he had been taken over by another persona while in a state of trance. In "The Tragic Generation" (*A.* 340–41), however, WBY speaks of Sharp as unreliable and given to fantasy.

REFERENCES: Fackler, Herbert V. *That Tragic Queen: The Deirdre Legend in Anglo-Irish Literature*. Salzburg, Austria: University of Salzburg, 1978; Halloran, William F. "W. B. Yeats and William Sharp: The Archer Vision." *English Language Notes* (University of Colorado) 6 (1969); Sharp, Elizabeth A. *William Sharp: A Memoir by His Wife*. London: Heinemann, 1910.

SHAW, GEORGE BERNARD (1856–1950), dramatist and critic. He was born in Dublin, the son of an unsuccessful grain merchant. He was educated at Wesley College but left school at fifteen because his family could not afford to send him to **Trinity College**, Dublin. He entered a land agency as a clerk. When his mother, a singer, left Dublin to seek work in London in 1876, Shaw joined her and tentatively began to pursue a career in the arts. For a time, he was a ghostwriter for George Vandeleur Lee, his mother's teacher and mentor, contributing articles on music to a weekly paper, *The Hornet*. Over the next few years, he wrote a number of novels, printed serially in socialist periodicals. He joined the newly formed Fabian Society in 1884 and was transformed from a shy young man into a speaker renowned for his audacity, wit, and remarkable ability to hold an audience. While working for the Fabian Society, writing much of their pamphlet material, he became a reviewer, contributing art reviews for *The World*, 1885–88, music criticism, under the pseudonym Corno di Bassetto, for *The Star*, 1889–90, and drama critiques for the *Saturday Review*, 1895–98, among others. By 1892, his first play, *Widowers' Houses*, had been produced. There followed *The Philanderer* (1893), *Mrs. Warren's Profession* (1893), *Arms and the Man* (1894), and *Candida* and *You Never Can Tell* (1900). In 1897,

The Devil's Disciple was acclaimed in New York, earning more than £2,000 in royalties. The following year, Shaw collapsed from overwork and was nursed back to health by Charlotte Payne-Townshend, whom he had met at the home of Sidney and Beatrice Webb. They married in 1898 and settled in Ayot St. Lawrence, Hertfordshire, 1906. Almost every year, there was a new play from Shaw, although it was not until Harley Granville-Barker took over the Royal Court Theatre and produced his work that Shaw was recognized as a genius. He was awarded the **Nobel Prize for Literature** in 1925. WBY met Shaw for the first time in February 1888, at the home of **William Morris**. Their dislike of each other was mutual, and WBY observed that Shaw was known only as a public speaker at street corners and socialist demonstrations. He was envious that Shaw, a "coldblooded Socialist," and **Oscar Wilde** had the whole of literary London waiting to hear what they would say next (*UP1.* 204–5). In 1894, his play *The Land of Heart's Desire* shared the bill with Shaw's *Arms and the Man* at the Avenue Theatre, London (*A.* 281–83), at a time when Shaw was having an affair with **Florence Farr**. Although he held ambivalent feelings towards Shaw, who had little time for the early Celtic Twilight posings of WBY, he respected him more and more for his great comic talent, his energy, his impartiality, and his bruising wit. Shaw's *John Bull's Other Island* was written at the request of WBY and offered to the **Irish National Theatre Society** in 1904, but the play needed stagecraft beyond the capability of the inexperienced Dublin company, especially in the leading role of Broadbent. In 1909, WBY and **Lady Gregory** defied the English censor and produced at the **Abbey Theatre** *The Shewing-Up of Blanco Posnet* (*UP2.* 377–80).

REFERENCES: Bax, Clifford, ed. *Florence Farr, Bernard Shaw and W. B. Yeats.* Dublin: Cuala, 1941; Coolidge, Olivia E. *George Bernard Shaw.* Boston: Houghton Mifflin, 1968; Laurence, Dan. H., and Grene, Nicholas. *Shaw, Lady Gregory and the Abbey.* Gerrards Cross: Colin Smythe, 1993; Peters, Margot. *Bernard Shaw and the Actresses.* Garden City, N.Y.: Doubleday, 1980; Ussher, Arland. *Three Great Irishmen: Shaw, Yeats, Joyce.* New York: Devin-Adair, 1953.

SHAWE-TAYLOR, [CAPTAIN] JOHN (1866–1911), landlord, soldier, and horseman. He was **Lady Gregory's** nephew, the son of her sister Elizabeth and Walter Shawe-Taylor, and lived at **Castle Taylor**, near Craughwell, **Galway** (county). A fine horseman, he joined the Cheshire Regiment in 1889 and became a captain ten years later. Having served in the Boer War, he was invalided with enteric fever and retired from the British army in 1901. He devoted himself to many causes in Ireland, helping landlords and Nationalist leaders resolve land problems and promoting a conference on the organization of the national university. Wyndham's Land Act (1903), which enabled the tenant class to acquire land at fair prices, came about largely through Shawe-Taylor's efforts—as WBY pointed out in a letter to the *Freeman's Journal*, 13 July 1903 (*UP2.* 304). He was active in the Gaelic League and established a model village near his home at *Ardrahan* to promote home industries and local products. His early death in

London was a profound shock to Nationalists and Unionists alike. For WBY, he was an example of the Renaissance man. In a tribute to Shawe-Taylor in *The Cutting of an Agate* (*EI*. 343–45), he writes of him enthusiastically as handsome and courageous, a natural leader, possessing, too, a deep commitment to religion, selflessness, and purity of motive, which distinguished him and his class. In "Coole Park, 1929" (*CP*. 273), WBY names Shawe-Taylor, and his cousin **Hugh Lane**, among those who gravitated to and were enriched by Lady Gregory and the noble tradition she maintained.

REFERENCE: Torchiana, Donald T. *W. B. Yeats & Georgian Ireland*. Oxford: Oxford University Press, 1966.

SHEBA, QUEEN OF, ruler of a region in Arabia. She ruled during the reign of **Solomon**, whom she visited in Jerusalem. Her relationship with the Hebrew king is the subject of "Solomon to Sheba" (*CP*. 155) and "Solomon and the Witch" (*CP*. 199). In both poems, Sheba and Solomon are masks for WBY and his wife. Writing of Solomon and Sheba in *Estrangement* (*A*. 464), WBY reflects on the discipline of love in which each holds up a mirror to the other, each creating a mask. See also "On Woman" (*CP*. 164).

REFERENCES: Levine, Faye. *Solomon & Sheba*. New York: R. Marek, 1980; Pearn, Norman Stone. *Quest for Sheba*. London: Nicholson & Watson, Ltd., 1937; Pritchard, James Bennett, ed. *Solomon and Sheba*. London: Phaidon, 1974.

SHELLEY, PERCY BYSSHE (1792–1822), poet and radical thinker. He was born at Field Place, near Horsham, Sussex, and educated at Eton and Oxford University. Early in 1811, he published anonymously the pamphlet *The Necessity of Atheism*, for which he was expelled from Oxford. Shocked by his son's unorthodox views, his father, Timothy Shelley, stopped his allowance and ceased all communication with him. In August 1811, Shelley eloped to Scotland with his sister's friend, Harriet Westbrook, then sixteen years old. They married and for three years lived precariously while he worked on his radical pamphlets and *Queen Mab* (1813), in which he denounced the priesthood, the monarchy, and commerce. In 1812, Shelley and his wife visited Dublin, where he addressed the Aggregate Meeting of the Catholics of Ireland—adherents to Catholic emancipation and repeal of the Act of Union—and distributed 500 copies of his seditious pamphlet *Address to the Irish People*. Despite a hostile reception, Shelley made another visit to Ireland in 1813. In 1814, after beginning an affair with Mary Wollstonecraft Godwin, he became estranged from his pregnant wife. His finances improved when he successfully entered into a legal dispute with his father and was awarded a lump sum of £7,400 and an annual annuity of £1,000. His *Alastor* was published in 1916, the year he visited Switzerland and formed a friendship with **Lord Byron**, spending much time in his company, reading, sailing, and making excursions around the Swiss lakes. On his return to England, the suicide of his wife and of his friend Fanny Imlay intensified his personal problems, but a month later, he married Mary Godwin. *The Revolt of Islam* was published in early 1818, and later that year, he left England and settled permanently in Italy. Domestic and financial problems continued, but it was in Italy that he produced the work on which his reputation rests, including the odes "To a Skylark," "Ode to the West Wind," "The Cloud," and "Ode to Liberty." They were published with the drama *Prometheus Unbound* in 1820. The struggle for Greek independence led to the writing of "Hellas," while the death of **John Keats**, in 1821, inspired the elegy "Adonais," in which Shelley asserts the eternity of beauty. His friendship with Byron, though often an uneasy one, continued, and they were together in Pisa, from November 1821 to July 1822, when Shelley drowned while sailing in the Bay of Lerici. As George Bornstein writes in the introduction to his study *Yeats and Shelley* (1970), WBY based his concept of both poet and poetry on Shelley, to whom he was introduced by **John B. Yeats**. His father not only read *Prometheus Unbound* to him when he was a child but also continued to discuss Shelley in his correspondence, 1906–17. WBY maintained his interest in Shelley throughout his life, imitating him in his early plays and poems and later rejecting him, while continuing to borrow his images and symbols. He even went so far as to inhabit a tower at **Ballylee**, like the title character of Shelley's poem "Prince Athanase" (1817), whom WBY refers to as a "visionary prince" in "The Phases of the Moon" (*CP.* 183). In 1938, he made a pilgrimage to Shelley's birthplace at Field Place. WBY's early understanding of Shelley is contained in the essay "The Philosophy of Shelley's Poetry" (*EI.* 65–95), written in the early 1900s, while his later reflections are contained in "Prometheus Unbound" (*LE.* 118–22), written in 1932.

REFERENCES: Bloom, Harold. *Yeats.* New York: Oxford, 1970; Bornstein, George. *Yeats and Shelley.* Chicago: University of Chicago Press, 1970; Bridle, John Lewis. *A Shelley Chronology.* Basingstoke: Macmillan, 1993; Hodgart, Patricia. *A Preface to Shelley.* London: Longman, 1985; O'Neill, Michael. *Percy Bysshe Shelley: A Literary Life.* New York: St. Martin's, 1990; Hone, Joseph, ed. *John Butler Yeats: Letters to His Son W. B. Yeats and Others 1869–1922.* 1944. Reprint, London: Secker & Warburg, 1983.

SHEPPARD, OLIVER (1865–1941), sculptor. He was born in Cookstown, County Tyrone, the son of Simpson Sheppard, a sculptor. Soon after he was born, the family moved to Dublin. He attended the **Metropolitan School of Art**, where he met WBY, and, in 1888, won a scholarship to the South Kensington Art School, London. He studied there until 1891, when he moved to Paris for a year, before returning to England as an art teacher. In 1902, he accepted a teaching position at the Metropolitan School of Art, Dublin. Later, he was appointed professor of sculpture at the Royal Hibernian Academy. Sheppard's work was Celtic in inspiration. He was highly regarded among British and Irish sculptors and exhibited at the prestigious Royal Academy in London, 1891–1928. He was a founder member of the Royal Society of British Sculptors. His sculpture *The Death of Cuchulain*, completed in Dublin, c. 1911–12, was later chosen to commemorate the Easter Rising of 1916. It stands in the **General**

Post Office in the center of Dublin. WBY refers to this work in the final lyric of *The Death of Cuchulain* (*CPl.* 705).

REFERENCE: Boylan, Henry. *A Dictionary of Irish Biography*. Dublin: Gill & Macmillan, 1978.

SHORTER, DORA [MARY] SIGERSON (1866–1918), novelist, short story writer, and poet. She was the daughter of eminent neurologist **Dr. George Sigerson** and a close friend of **Katharine Tynan**, under whose influence she published *Verses* (1893). In 1896, she married Clement K. Shorter (1857–1926), editor of the *Sketch* and the *Illustrated London News*, and moved to London. She and her husband often entertained WBY, and she was a frequent visitor to the discussion groups that met at the homes of various artistic and literary figures. She visited the Yeats family in **Bedford Park**, where in 1900 **John B. Yeats** did a pencil sketch of her in the flyleaf of a book, now in the James Augustine Healy Collection of Irish Literature, Colby College, Maine. She was a founder member of the Pan Celtic Society, whose membership included Katharine Tynan, **John O'Leary**, and **John Todhunter** but not WBY, who claimed he did not join the group because he might have incurred their displeasure by criticizing them (*M.* 55). In his introduction to *A Book of Irish Verse Selected from the Modern Writers* (1895) (*Pl.* 108), WBY writes that Dora Sigerson has put the Irish stories into "vigorous modern rhyme" and that her poem "Ceann Dubh Deelish" should have a permanent place in Irish lyric poetry. In 1904, Clement Shorter, thinking that WBY believed that the Irish Literary Revival was all due to the talents of himself and **Lady Gregory**, challenged his overgenerous review of Lady Gregory's *Cuchulain of Muirthemne* in *The Bookman*, May 1903, and offered as better models the work of **Jonathan Swift, Edmund Burke**, and **Oliver Goldsmith**. WBY responded in a letter to *The Daily News*, 11 May 1904 (*UP2.* 328), denigrating the earlier translations of the old sagas and insisting that Swift, Burke, and Goldsmith seemed to be English, rather than Irish, writers.

REFERENCE: Shorter, Dora Sigerson. *Collected Poems*. Introd. George Meredith. London: Hodder & Stoughton, 1907.

SICILY, large island in the Mediterranean Sea. WBY and his wife visited Sicily during the winter of 1924–25 and took the opportunity to study Byzantine mosaics in the cathedral at Monreale. It was during this vacation that the first version of *A Vision* (1925) was completed. In "Parnell's Funeral" (*CP.* 319), there is a reference to the image of a boy and tree on a Sicilian coin. According to WBY, in his notes to "The Stirring of the Bones" (*A.* 577–78), the Sicilian coin he had in mind was from the fifth century B.C. and showed the Mother Goddess, a beautiful woman, sitting in a tree. The sacrificial killing of her son with an arrow symbolized the death and resurrection of the Tree-Spirit.

REFERENCES: Demus, Otto. *The Mosaics of Norman Sicily*. London: Routledge & Kegan Paul, 1950; Kitzinger, Ernst. *Mosaics of Monreale*. Palermo: S. F. Flaccovio, 1960.

SÍDH, mound or hill, dwelling place of spirits in Celtic Ireland. When the Milesians invaded Ireland, the **Tuatha dé Danaan** were driven underground and relegated to the status of ''fairy,'' or *aes sídhe* [people of the hills]. The Dagda, ruler of the Tuatha dé Danaan, assigned each sídh to the care of an overlord. This Happy Otherworld was a place of perpetual feasting, hunting, and revelry, where all remained forever young. In time, the term *sídh* became synonymous with the fairies who dwelt there, the Sídhe. In the poem ''The Hosting of the Sídhe,'' WBY refers to **Niamh**, the beautiful fairy queen, who so enchanted the mortal **Oisin** that he followed her to **Tir-nan-Oge**. Also mentioned in the poem is **Knocknarea**, the mountain where Oisin slipped from his horse and regained his mortal life. In WBY's plays, the Sídhe appear in a number of guises. **The Guardian of the Well** in *At the Hawk's Well* transforms into a hawk to distract the youthful **Cuchulain** from the miraculous water, while a **Woman of the Sidhe** appears in *The Only Jealousy of Emer* and attempts to seduce the **Ghost of Cuchulain**.

REFERENCES: Dames, Michael. *Mythic Ireland*. 1992. Reprint, New York: Thames & Hudson, 1996; Ellis, Peter Berresford. *Dictionary of Celtic Mythology*. New York: Oxford University Press, 1992; Green, Miranda J. *Dictionary of Celtic Myth and Legend*. London: Thames & Hudson, 1992; Mac Cana, Proinsias. *Celtic Mythology*. Feltham, Middlesex: Newnes, 1983.

SÍDHE. *See* **SÍDH**.

SIDNEY, SIR PHILIP (1554–86), poet, statesman, and soldier. He was a member of Queen Elizabeth's court and a model of the Elizabethan ideal of heroic living. He combined all that the age admired in deportment, character and talent and numbered among his friends the most learned scholars of Europe. He was handsome and proficient in horsemanship, with a proud, fiery temperament, and he had the highest sense of his duties to his sovereign and the state. He died heroically at the Battle of Zutphen in the Netherlands. Sidney was a major poet and, in his day, rivaled **Edmund Spenser**, over whom he exercised much influence. He wrote *Apologie for Poetrie* (1595), arguing the importance of poetry to the well-being of the courtier and the state. As an apt and fitting tribute, WBY compares **Robert Gregory** to Sidney, the perfect courtier, in the elegy ''In Memory of Major Robert Gregory'' (*CP*. 148).

REFERENCES: Duncan-Jones, Katherine. *Sir Philip Sidney: Courtier Poet*. New Haven: Yale University Press, 1991; Hamilton, Albert C. *Sir Philip Sidney: A Study of His Life and Works*. Cambridge and New York: Cambridge University Press, 1977; McCoy, Richard C. *Sir Philip Sidney: Rebellion in Arcadia*. New Brunswick, N.J.: Rutgers University Press, 1979.

SIGERSON, DORA. *See* **SHORTER, DORA [MARY] SIGERSON**.

SIGERSON, DR. GEORGE (1839–1925), neurologist, historian, and translator. He was born at Holy Hill, near Strabane, Northern Ireland, and educated at Letterkenny Academy and in France. He studied medicine in **Cork** and Paris, before setting up a prestigious practice in Dublin. Later, he was professor of zoology at Newman's Catholic University and a senator of the Irish Free State, 1922–25. His house at 3 Clare Street, Dublin, was a gathering place for all those interested in Irish literature and music. He was one of the founders of the Irish *Feis Ceoil* and a member of the **National Literary Society** from 1893 until his death. A prolific writer, he published poems and political essays and edited a number of anthologies of his own translations from the Irish, including *The Poets and Poetry of Munster* (1860) and *Bards of the Gael and Gall* (1897). His *Modern Ireland* (1868) was a representative collection of his political articles. The oldest of his four children, **Dora Sigerson**, herself a novelist and poet, married Clement Shorter, editor of the *Illustrated London News*. In his essay *Irish National Literature, II*, published in *The Bookman* in 1895 (*UP1*. 372), WBY praises Sigerson for his interpretation of Gaelic history and his denunciation of rhetoric. In *Autobiography* (*M*. 53), he describes Dr. Sigerson in detail, admiring his generosity but criticizing his lack of scholarship and courage in action. Among the policy decisions with which **W. G. Fay** took issue before leaving the **Abbey Theatre** in 1908 was the rejection of many new plays deemed by the board unsuitable for production. Faced with this allegation, WBY invited Dr. Sigerson and representatives of the National Literary Society to read these plays, promising that any they found worthy would be performed (*UP2*. 359, 361). Although a friend and supporter of WBY, Dr. Sigerson took **Charles Gavan Duffy's** side against WBY in the debate over the choice of books for the **New Irish Library** (*M*. 65, 66, 67).

REFERENCE: Sigerson, George. *Two Centuries of Irish History, 1691–1870*. London: Kegan Paul, Trench, 1888.

SISTINE CHAPEL, private chapel in the Vatican in Rome. It was built in 1473 for Pope Sixtus IV and is distinguished for its many frescoes by leading painters, among them Perugino, **Botticelli**, Ghirlandaio, and **Michelangelo**. WBY and his wife visited the Sistine Chapel during the winter of 1924–25. He was impressed by the religious scenes painted by Michelangelo on the chapel roof and bought reproductions to bring home with him. He celebrates Michelangelo's genius in the elegy "Under Ben Bulben" (*CP*. 397). See also "Michael Robartes and the Dancer" (*CP*. 197).

REFERENCES: Bergman, Robert P. *Splendor of the Popes: Treasures from the Sistine Chapel and the Vatican Museums and Library*. Baltimore, Md.: Walters Art Gallery, 1989; Hartt, Frederick. *The Sistine Chapel*. New York: Knopf, 1991; Lewine, Carol F. *The Sistine Chapel Walls and the Roman Liturgy*. University Park, Pa.: Penn State University, 1993; Pietrangeli, Carlo. *The Sistine Chapel: A Glorious Restoration*. New York: H. N. Abrams, 1994.

SLEUTH WOOD. *See* **SLISH WOOD**.

SLIEVE ECHTGE (Irish: *Sliabh Echtge*), desolate mountain range. It runs from **Loughrea** in **Galway** (county) to Lough Derg on the River Shannon in **County Clare** and was reputedly named for Echtge, one of the **Tuatha dé Danaan** who received the land as her marriage dowry. The mountain range, which is referred to in the poem "The Withering of the Boughs" (*CP.* 87), is now called Slieve Aughty. WBY and **Lady Gregory** visited homes in the area in search of folk stories and local lore. In "Red Hanrahan" (*MY.* 220–22), the poet, tired after a long journey, falls asleep on Slieve Echtge, and when he wakes, finds himself in the Happy Otherworld with the fairies. He rejects their offers of pleasure, power, courage, and knowledge and leaves their beautiful queen, Echtge, in a never-waking sleep. In "The Galway Plains" (*EI.* 211), the poet recalls visiting the area with Lady Gregory and looking over the surrounding landscape from the sides of Slieve Echtge, while in "The Philosophy of Shelley's Poetry" (*EI.* 77), he remembers reading **Shelley's** *Prometheus Unbound* in the woods of Drim-na-Rod in the Echtge Hills.
  REFERENCE: McGarry, James P. *Place Names in the Writings of William Butler Yeats.* Gerrards Cross: Colin Smythe, 1976.

SLIEVE FUADH, highest point of the mountain range in County Armagh, known in ancient times as the Fews. Slieve Fuadh, near Newtownhamilton, overlooks a mountain pass leading from the north to the south of Ireland. **Conall Caernach** guarded **Ulster** from this mountain in the epic *Táin Bó Cuailnge*, while **Cuchulain** brought his war horse, the Grey of Macha, from a lake on Slieve Fuadh, and it returned there after his death. WBY describes the horse's return to the lake in *The Death of Cuchulain* (*CPl.* 699). The mountain is associated with **Deirdre** and her lover **Naoise**, while in *The Herne's Egg* (*CPl.* 669), **Attracta** claims to have had sexual union with the Great Herne on Slieve Fuadh. See also "Aglavaine and Selysette" (*UP2.* 50).
  REFERENCE: McGarry, James P. *Place Names in the Writings of William Butler Yeats.* Gerrards Cross: Colin Smythe, 1976.

SLIEVENAMON (Irish: *Sliabh na mBan*) [the mountain of the woman], mountain in southeastern County Tipperary. It is reputed to be the home of Bodb Dearg, a king of the **Tuatha dé Danann**, and is the setting for the feast in "The Grey Rock" (*CP.* 115). In *Autobiography* (*M.* 124), WBY names it among "the old sacred places." In his "Introduction to 'Mandukya Upanishad,' " he notes that **Standish [James] O'Grady** had announced in a weekly article that Slievenamon would one day become more celebrated than Mount Olympus (*LE.* 157, 206).
  REFERENCE: McGarry, James P. *Place Names in the Writings of William Butler Yeats.* Gerrards Cross: Colin Smythe, 1976.

SLIGO, county and town in the west of Ireland. The town of Sligo is situated in a fertile river valley, with its busy harbor on an inlet of the Atlantic Ocean.

To the north of the town is **Ben Bulben**, and to the south the mountain of **Knocknarea**, associated with the warrior queen **Maeve**. Although he was born in Dublin, and spent a great deal of his boyhood in London, WBY looked upon Sligo as his spiritual home. Most of his relatives lived in or near Sligo, and during his childhood, he frequently visited them on holiday, traveling from **Liverpool** in ships belonging to the Sligo Steam Navigation Company, owned by his grandfather **William Pollexfen** and his great-uncle **William Middleton**. From July 1872, when he was seven years old, he stayed in Sligo for over two years. As the grandson of a shipowner, he was treated with deference by the local people, and he took pride in seeing his grandfather's boats coming into Sligo Harbor. Although he found the atmosphere in **Merville**, his grandparents' house, restrictive, he enjoyed the large garden, the two dogs, and the pony. He spent time with the stable boy, Johnny Healey, who read him Protestant Orange ballads. A Middleton cousin, with whom he went sailing, lived at **Rosses Point**, and he visited the waterfalls of **Glencar** and slept overnight in **Sleuth Wood** so that he might see the island of **Innisfree** at sunrise. In nearby **Ballisodare**, he heard fairy stories told him by bright-eyed Paddy Flynn. As a young man domiciled in London, WBY returned regularly to Sligo, usually staying with **George Pollexfen**, with whom he shared an interest in magic and the occult. The stories in *The Secret Rose* were taken down almost verbatim from **Mary Battle**, George Pollexfen's old servant, who claimed to have second sight. In Sligo stood some of the great houses of the Anglo-Irish Ascendancy, among them **Lissadell**, home of the **Gore-Booth** family, whom he visited for the first time in 1894. Many of his early poems in *Crossways, The Rose*, and *The Wind Among the Reeds* are set in Sligo and the surrounding countryside, while the town of Ballah in *John Sherman* is Sligo. It is to Sligo he returns in his final poems, and although there was a suggestion that he should be buried in St. Patrick's Cathedral, Dublin, he was interred, at his request, at **Drumcliff** in the shadow of Ben Bulben.

REFERENCES: Gordon, D. J., ed. *W. B. Yeats: Images of a Poet*. Manchester: University of Manchester, 1961; Kirby, Sheelah. *The Yeats Country*. Dublin: Dolmen, 1962; McGarry, James P. *Place Names in the Writings of William Butler Yeats*. Gerrards Cross: Colin Smythe, 1976; Murphy, William M. *The Yeats Family and the Pollexfens of Sligo*. Dublin: Dolmen, 1971.

SLIGO GRAMMAR SCHOOL, Protestant grammar school for boys, **Sligo** (town). The school, which opened in 1907, was known locally as Eade's Grammar School when Mr. Eade was the headmaster. See also "In Memory of Alfred Pollexfen" (*CP*. 175).

REFERENCE: McGarry, James P. *Place Names in the Writings of William Butler Yeats*. Gerrards Cross: Colin Smythe, 1976.

SLISH WOOD (Irish: *slios*) [sloped]. This rocky wooded area on the south shore of **Lough Gill, Sligo** (county), stretches from **Dooney Rock** to **Innisfree**. In *Reveries over Childhood and Youth* (*A.* 73), WBY calls it Slish Wood, the name by which it is known locally. In "The Stolen Child" (*CP*. 20), he refers to it as Sleuth Wood, the word *Sleuth* being derived from the Irish *Sliu*, a slope. As a young man, WBY slept overnight in the wood, hoping to see the island of Innisfree in the early dawn.

REFERENCES: Kirby, Sheelah. *The Yeats Country*. Dublin, Dolmen, 1966; McGarry, James P. *Place Names in the Writings of William Butler Yeats*. Gerrards Cross: Colin Smythe, 1976.

SMITHERS, LEONARD [CHARLES] (1861–1907), publisher. He was born in Sheffield, England, and after graduating from Wesley College, he practiced as a lawyer. In 1891, he moved to London, where he began to publish with H. S. Nichols, a bookseller. Eventually, he opened a secondhand bookstore in The Strand and expanded his publishing business to include fine editions and books of eroticism. He published two collections of **Aubrey Beardsley's** drawings and **Max Beerbohm's** first book of caricatures. After the decline of the controversial magazine *The Yellow Book* in 1895, he persuaded **Arthur Symons** to edit his new quarterly magazine, *The Savoy*, with illustrations by Aubrey Beardsley. As a friend of Arthur Symons, WBY agreed to contribute to the new venture, despite his intense dislike for Smithers (*M*. 90–92). WBY was opposed to the relationship between Smithers and **Althea Gyles** and forbade her to bring him to his Monday night's "At Home" in **Woburn Buildings**, although she disobeyed him (*WL*. 330, 332). The tension over Smithers may have contributed to the chilling of the friendship between WBY and Miss Gyles.

REFERENCES: Smithers, Leonard C., ed. *Oriental Tales: The Work of Thomas-Simon Gueullette*. London: Atheneum, 1901; Smithers, Leonard C. *The Thousand and One Quarters of an Hour: Tartarian Tales*. London: Private, 1901.

SOLOMON (d. 922 B.C.), son of David and Bathsheba. He succeeded his father as king of the Hebrews. He built the first Hebrew temple in Jerusalem and made foreign alliances, notably with Egypt and the Phoenicians, thereby ensuring a peaceful reign. He was renowned for his large harem. Solomon's wisdom was legendary, although as he grew older, he became more despotic, alienating his subjects. He is a mask for WBY in the three poems "Solomon to Sheba" (*CP*. 155), "On Woman" (*CP*. 164), and "Solomon and the Witch" (*CP*. 199).

REFERENCES: Gaubert, Henri. *Solomon the Magnificent*. Trans. Launcelot Sheppard and A. Manson. New York: Hastings House, 1970; Levine, Faye. *Solomon & Sheba*. New York: R. Marek, 1980; Maly, Eugene H. *The World of David and Solomon*. Englewood Cliffs, N.J.: Prentice-Hall, 1966.

SOMERVILLE, EDITH [ANNA OENONE]. *See* **SOMERVILLE AND ROSS**.

SOMERVILLE AND ROSS, collaborative authors **Edith [Anna Oenone] Somerville** (1858–1949) and **Violet Martin** (1862–1915). Edith Somerville was educated privately at her parents' home, Drishane, in **Cork** (county). She studied art in London and in Europe and throughout her life continued to paint and illustrate. In 1886, she met her second cousin, Violet Martin, who was born at Ross House, **Galway** (county), and educated at Alexandra College, Dublin. Their friendship led to the literary partnership Somerville and Ross, which continued very successfully until Martin's death—and even after, if we accept Somerville's assertion that she continued her collaboration through spiritualist communication. In 1889, they produced their first book, *An Irish Cousin*, a fine attempt at a Gothic novel. Its success led to commissions to write travel articles, to which Martin contributed the text and Somerville the illustrations. In 1889, they produced *Some Experiences of an Irish R.M.*, the first in a series of lively and amusing collections of short stories, among them *Further Experiences of an Irish R.M.* (1908) and *In Mr. Knox's Country* (1915), which gained them wide popularity. In 1894, however, they published *The Real Charlotte*, arguably the outstanding Anglo-Irish novel of the nineteenth century and the work that earned them a reputation as serious and important novelists, comparable with **Balzac** and George Eliot. In 1898, Violet Martin had a serious hunting accident from which she never fully recovered. After her death in 1915, Edith Somerville continued to acknowledge Violet Martin as coauthor. The best of these later works are *Mount Music* (1919) and *The Big House of Inver* (1952). In 1932, **Trinity College**, Dublin, conferred an honorary doctorate on the literary partnership. In addition to the books written with Edith Somerville, Violet Martin published two volumes of autobiographical essays, *Some Irish Yesterdays* (1906) and *Strayaways* (published posthumously in 1920). In 1932, Edith Somerville was elected a founder member of the **Irish Academy of Letters**. WBY met both Somerville and Ross socially. In "Irish National Literature, II" (*UP1*. 371), he has some praise for their portrayal of middle-class life in *The Real Charlotte*, but otherwise he appears to have ignored their literary efforts. He does not include them in his 1895 list of "Best Irish Books" (*UP1*. 385–87), a curious omission.

REFERENCES: Collis, Maurice. *Somerville and Ross*. London: Faber, 1968; Cronin, John. *Somerville and Ross*. Lewisburg, Pa.: Bucknell University Press, 1972; Cronin, Anthony. *Heritage Now: Irish Literature in the English Language*. New York: St. Martin's Press, 1982; Lewis, Gifford. *Somerville & Ross: The World of the Irish R.M.* New York: Viking, 1985; Robinson, Hilary. *Somerville & Ross: A Critical Appreciation*. New York: St. Martin's, 1980.

SOPHOCLES (496–406 B.C.), dramatist. He was born at **Colonus**, near Athens, the setting of his last play, *Oedipus at Colonus* (c. 407). He was celebrated as a dramatist in his lifetime, winning eighteen of the dramatic competitions associated with the annual festival of **Dionysus**, but only seven of his major plays survive, including *Oedipus the King* (c. 429), *Antigone* (c. 441), and *Electra* (date unknown). He was a fine theater craftsman and is credited with introducing a third actor into the drama and with heightening the dramatic involvement of the chorus. Since it was on the plays of Sophocles that **Aristotle** based his definition of tragedy in the *Poetics*, the influence of Sophocles on Western drama has been supreme. For WBY, Sophocles, like **Shakespeare**, was a writer whose genius defined the age. Two of WBY's outstanding dramatic achievements are his versions for the modern stage, *Sophocles' King Oedipus* and *Sophocles' Oedipus at Colonus*.

REFERENCES: Bates, William N. *Sophocles: Poet and Dramatist*. New York: Russell & Russell, 1969; Kitto, H. D. F. *Sophocles: Dramatist & Philosopher*. Westport, Conn.: Greenwood, 1981; Waldock, Arthur J. A. *Sophocles the Dramatist*. Cambridge: Cambridge University Press, 1966.

SOPHOCLES' KING OEDIPUS, one–act play. WBY saw a production of *Oedipus Rex* by **Sophocles** at the University of Notre Dame, when he was on an American tour, 1903–4. Since the play was banned by the English censor on the grounds of immorality, WBY determined to mount a production in Dublin. In 1905, he invited **Oliver St. John Gogarty**, a Greek scholar, to work on a translation. The result was not successful, and in 1912, WBY began work on his own version. He lost interest in it until 1926, when he completed it, using a translation by Paul Masqueray, a copy of which was in his library (*OS*. no. 1964). WBY's *Sophocles' King Oedipus* was successfully produced at the **Abbey Theatre**, 7 December 1926, with the following cast: **Oedipus, F. J. McCormick**; Jocasta, Eileen Crowe; **Creon, Barry Fitzgerald**; Priest, Eric Gorman; **Tiresias**, Michael J. Dolan; Boy, D. Breen; First Messenger, Arthur Shields; Herdsman, Gabriel J. Fallon; Second Messenger, P. J. Carolan; Nurse, May Craig; Children, Raymond and Edna Fardy; Servants, Tony Quinn, Michael Scott, C. Haughton; Leader of the Chorus, J. Stevenson; Chorus, Peter Nolan, Walter Dillon, T. Moran, M. Finn, D. Williams. The production was directed by **Lennox Robinson**. *Sophocles' King Oedipus* was published by Macmillan and Company in 1928 and included in *The Collected Plays of W. B. Yeats* (1934, 1952). It is in prose, with the choruses in verse. It was this version that Laurence Olivier used when he played the title role at the Old Vic, London, in 1945, and it was used by Tyrone Guthrie in his famed production in Stratford, Ontario, in 1954.

REFERENCES: Clark, David R., and McGuire, James B. "Yeats's Versions of Sophocles: Two Typescripts." In *Yeats and the Theatre*, ed. Robert O'Driscoll and Lorna Reynolds. Niagara Falls, N.Y.: Maclean-Hunter, 1975; Hogan, James C. *A Commentary on the Plays of Sophocles*. Carbondale: Southern Illinois University Press, 1991; Miller, Liam. *The Noble Drama of W. B. Yeats*. Dublin: Dolmen, 1977.

SOPHOCLES' OEDIPUS AT COLONUS, one-act play. WBY followed his version of *Sophocles' King Oedipus* with its sequel, *Sophocles' Oedipus at Colonus*, which he began writing in December 1926. The play chronicles the years of exile until **Oedipus's** death in a wood near **Colonus** and was published in *Collected Plays of W. B. Yeats* (1934, 1952). It was performed by the **Irish National Theatre Company** at the **Abbey Theatre**, September 1927, with the following cast: Oedipus, **F. J. McCormick**; Antigone, Shelah Richards; Ismene, K. Curling; Polyneices, Gabriel J. Fallon; **Theseus**, Michael J. Dolan; **Creon, Barry Fitzgerald**; A Stranger, Arthur Shields; A Messenger, P. J. Carolan; Leader of the Chorus, J. Stephenson; Chorus, Peter Nolan, Walter Dillon, T. Moran, M. Finn, M. Scott; Servants and Soldiers, U. Wright, C. Culhane, G. Green, J. Breen, P. Raymond, W. J. Scott. The production was directed by **Lennox Robinson**.

REFERENCES: Clark, David R., and McGuire, James B. "Yeats's Versions of Sophocles: Two Typescripts." *Yeats and the Theatre*, ed. Robert O'Driscoll and Lorna Reynolds. Niagara Falls, N.Y.: Maclean-Hunter, 1975; Hogan, James C. *A Commentary on the Plays of Sophocles*. Carbondale: Southern Illinois University Press, 1991; Miller, Liam. *The Noble Drama of W. B. Yeats*. Dublin: Dolmen, 1977.

SPARTA, city-state of ancient Greece. The inhabitants of Sparta prided themselves on their toughness and bravery and gave themselves totally to the pursuit of warfare. By the sixth century B.C., Sparta was the strongest city-state in Greece. In the Persian Wars, Sparta and Athens fought together. Afterward, the rivalry between these two city-states led to the Peloponnesian War, which wrecked the Athenian Empire. Sparta emerged victorious but was then decisively defeated by **Thebes**. The city was subsequently conquered by Macedon and fell into decline. In "The Curse of Cromwell" (*CP*. 350), there is a reference to the Spartan boy who stole a fox. He hid it in his clothes, and when caught, rather than admit his guilt, he let the fox gnaw him to death. The story comes from Plutarch's *Lives of Ten Orators*. In "Poetry and Tradition" (*EI*. 248), WBY refers to Lycurgus, the reformer of the Spartan constitution in the seventh century B.C.

REFERENCES: Fitzhardinge, L. F. *The Spartans*. London: Thames & Hudson, 1980; Henderson, Bernard W. *The Great War between Athens and Sparta*. New York: Arno, 1973; Lazenby, J. F. *The Spartan Army*. Warminster, England: Aris & Phillips, 1985.

SPECKLED BIRD, THE, unfinished novel. When WBY was planning the novel, he made visits to **Galway** (county) and the **Aran Islands** in 1896, and to Paris in 1897, for research. He wrote four different versions of the story, which deals with the artist and his search for spiritual reality. He abandoned the project in 1902 or 1903.

REFERENCE: Yeats, William Butler. *The Speckled Bird*. Ed. William H. O'Donnell. Toronto: McClelland & Stewart, 1976.

SPENDER, [SIR] STEPHEN (1909–95), poet, critic, and fiction writer. He was born near London, the son of Harold Spender, a journalist. As a child he was interested in painting but began writing poetry before he attended Oxford University in the late 1920s. He joined the Communist Party but later resigned as a member. His early poetry, published in *Twenty Poems* (1930) and *Poems* (1933), had a revolutionary fervor that many critics compared favorably with the work of **Percy Bysshe Shelley**, though others were antagonized by his communistic ideals. In his later work, *The Still Centre* (1939) and *Ruins and Beliefs* (1942), he fused contemporary imagery with personal experience to convey a deeply felt and highly charged emotional message about the social and political world of the 1930s. His collections of verse included *Selected Poems* (1965) and *The Generous Days* (1971), and he wrote books of criticism, among them *The Creative Element* (1953) and *The Struggle of the Modern* (1963), in which he called upon contemporary poets, including WBY, whom he accused of "aristocratic individualism," to discover a system of values that were not purely subjective but social and objective. In common with many critics, WBY saw Spender, with **W. H. Auden** and **C. Day-Lewis**, as a member of a radical group of socially committed poets who had forsworn personality in the cause of beliefs. It is in this context that WBY named Spender in "Modern Poetry" (*LE*. 95). Two of his poems were included in WBY's selection for *The Oxford Book of Modern Verse* (1936).

REFERENCES: Maxwell, D. E. S. *Poets of the Thirties*. New York: Barnes & Noble, 1969; Sternlicht, Sanford. *Stephen Spender*. New York: Macmillan, 1992; Weatherhead, A. K. *Stephen Spender and the Thirties*. Lewisburg, Pa.: Bucknell University Press, 1975.

SPENSER, EDMUND (1552–99), poet and courtier. His father was John Spenser, a free journeyman of the Merchant Taylors' Company, although in the *Prothalamion* Spenser claims to be descended from the titled Spensers of Althorpe, Northampton. He attended the Merchant Taylor's school and Cambridge University, where he studied mathematics, dialectics, perspective, astronomy, and Greek. In his education, he was profoundly influenced by **Plato** and contemporary philosophical writing, especially the Italian Neoplatonists. The influence of Platonic dialectics is apparent in every passage of argument in Spenser's poetry. He formed a friendship with **Sir Philip Sidney**, a courtier and poet who exemplified an ideal of courtly life, and Spenser determined on a court career. After Cambridge, Spenser went to Ireland in 1580, as secretary to Lord Grey, the Lord Deputy of Ireland. He lived mostly in or near Dublin, and since it was the Lord Deputy's official residence, he spent much time in **Dublin Castle**. After holding minor offices, he was granted the confiscated lands and castle of Kilcolman in **Cork** (county) and retired there in 1587 to devote himself to writing. He had achieved literary prominence with *The Shepheardes Calender* (1579) and, in 1589, went to London for the publication of *The Faerie Queen* (Books I–III, 1590), expecting to receive court preferment. When little was forthcoming because of his association with Sidney and courtiers like his patron, the earl of Leicester, and Sir Walter Raleigh, he returned to Ireland and described his London visit in *Colin Clout, Come Home Again* (1595). The same year saw the publication of *Astrophel*, an elegy for Sir Philip Sidney, and the sonnet sequences celebrating his courtship of Elizabeth Boyle, *Amoretti* and *Epithalamion*. In 1596, he completed *The Faerie Queen* (Books IV–VI), an allegorical statement of his moral, political, and religious beliefs in the court of

Gloriana, Elizabeth I. In 1596, he wrote a prose defense of Lord Grey's repressive, anti-Catholic policies in Ireland under the title *A View of the Present State of Ireland*, but it was not sanctioned for publication until 1633. In the Rebellion of 1598, led by **Hugh O'Neill**, Kilcolman Castle was burned. Spenser returned to London, where he died soon afterward. He is widely regarded as the finest lyricist in English after **Shakespeare**. As a young man, WBY wrote poetry and plays in the style of Spenser, in which shepherds and shepherdesses pursued a world of spiritual beauty in the fields of **Arcady** (*A*. 66, 92), and he edited an edition of the *Poems of Spenser*, published by the Caxton Publishing Company in 1906. In the poem "The Municipal Gallery Revisited" (*CP*. 368), he draws a parallel between Spenser's patron, the earl of Leicester, and his own patron, **Lady Gregory**. In his essay "Edmund Spenser" (*EI*. 356–83), he gives a long, detailed biographical study of Spenser and his poetry.

REFERENCES: Carpenter, Frederick I. *A Reference Guide to Edmund Spenser*. Chicago: University of Chicago Press, 1923; Sacks, Peter M. *The English Elegy: Studies in the Genre from Spenser to Yeats*. Baltimore: Johns Hopkins University Press, 1985; Waller, Gary F. *Edmund Spenser: A Literary Life*. New York: St. Martin's, 1994.

SPHINX, winged lion with a woman's head, in Greek mythology; recumbent animal form with man's head in Egyptian mythology. In the **Oedipus** legend, the Sphinx was sent to **Thebes** by Hera to ask the riddle about the three ages of man. After each failed attempt at a solution, a Theban was killed until Oedipus solved the riddle. The Sphinx died, and Oedipus became king of Thebes (*CPl*. 476). In his essay "Certain Noble Plays of Japan" (*EI*. 226), WBY muses that only the dead may fully possess being, thus explaining why we gaze with so much feeling on the face of the Sphinx. A Sphinx with a female torso is referred to in "The Double Vision of Michael Robartes" (*CP*. 192), while a man-headed Sphinx is featured in the poem "The Second Coming" (*CP*. 210). See also "Introduction to the Holy Mountain" (*LE*. 151).

REFERENCE: Hassan, Selim. *The Sphinx: Its History in the Light of Recent Excavations*. Cairo: Government Press, 1949.

SPINOZA, BARUCH [Benedict] (1632–77), philosopher. He was born near Amsterdam, a member of a Jewish community who had fled the Inquisition in Spain and Portugal. He was a lens grinder by profession, but he devoted much time to the reading of philosophy, especially the works of Descartes. When his views became too radical, he was barred from practicing his faith by his Jewish compatriots. Despite a withdrawn and modest nature, he was sought out by leading European philosophers. He refused a professorship at Heidelberg University, preferring the quiet life of a lens grinder to academia. His important works include *Ethics* (1677) and *Opera Posthuma* (1677). Spinoza's radical philosophy promotes belief in a God, infinite and all-embracing. All that exists is a manifestation of this God, sometimes called Nature, and nothing exists outside of it. Nothing finite has any substance, only the infinite. Free will and chance do not exist. Thus, the pursuit of egotism and passion limit the individual; only by accepting a place in the overall design can the individual achieve true freedom and fulfill his destiny. In his essay on ''Bishop Berkeley'' (*EI*. 396–411), WBY, who regretted the rationalist materialism of the philosophers **Isaac Newton** and **John Locke**, predicts that in two or three generations the ''movement of philosophy'' from Spinoza to **Friedrich Hegel** will be accepted as ''the greatest of all works of intellect.''

REFERENCES: Browne, Lewis. *Blessed Spinoza: A Biography of the Philosopher*. New York: Macmillan, 1932; Scruton, Roger. *Spinoza*. Oxford: Oxford University Press, 1986.

SPRING-RICE, SIR CECIL [ARTHUR] (1859–1918), British diplomat. He joined the foreign service in 1882 and held posts in Europe and Asia. He was minister to Persia, 1906–8, and to Sweden, 1908–12. In 1912, he was appointed British ambassador to the United States, a post he retained until his death. In the ballad ''Roger Casement'' (*CP*. 351), WBY accuses Spring-Rice of spreading the rumor about **Sir Roger Casement's** alleged homosexuality, possibly because he was forced to do so by the British government.

REFERENCES: Burton, David Henry. *Cecil Spring-Rice: A Diplomat's Life*. London: Associated University Presses, 1990; Gwynn, Stephen, ed. *Letters and Friendships of Sir Cecil Spring-Rice*. Freeport, N.Y.: Books for Libraries, 1972.

ST. ANTHONY (A.D. 251?–345), hermit and founder of Early Christian monasticism in Egypt. He went into total seclusion at the age of thirty-five and, for twenty years, is reputed to have repelled every temptation known to mankind. When he emerged from his isolation, he formed a monastic community that followed a strict regimen of solitude, except for worship and meals, and became a model for later monastic settlements. After some years, Anthony again went into seclusion, in the desert near **Thebaid**. There he lived out his long life. He is referred to in WBY's poem ''Demon and Beast'' (*CP*. 209). There was also a St. Anthony of Padua (1195–1231). He was renowned for his eloquence and is usually represented in paintings with the infant **Christ** in his arms. He is invoked by Roman Catholics to recover lost belongings.

REFERENCES: Hannay, Rev. J. O. *The Spirit and Origin of Christian Monasticism*. London: Methuen, 1903; Hannay, Rev. J. O. *The Wisdom of the Desert*. London: Methuen, 1904.

STARKEY, JAMES SULLIVAN. *See* **O'SULLIVAN, SEAMUS**.

ST. COLMAN'S WELL, near **Kiltartan, Galway** (county). The well, which is the setting for WBY's play *The Cat and the Moon*, is within a couple of miles of **Thoor Ballylee**. It was associated with St. Colman, the patron saint of the Cathedral Church of Kilmacduagh, near **Coole Park**. According to tradition, St. Colman was born near Kiltartan while his mother was in hiding. She wanted to baptize the child, but there was no water nearby. Miraculously, a fountain of water sprang forth from under an oak tree under which she had placed the child.

REFERENCE: McGarry, James P. *Place Names in the Writings of William Butler Yeats.* Gerrards Cross: Colin Smythe, 1976.

ST. DENIS, RUTH (1880–1968), dancer and choreographer. She was born Ruth Denis in Newark, New Jersey, and had little dance training. She toured as an actress and skirt dancer and, from 1904, took an interest in Egyptian dance. Her Hindu-inspired dance production *Radha* debuted in 1906 and was instantly popular. She toured the vaudeville circuit in Europe, 1906–8, and in the United States in 1910, gradually extending her repertoire with the composition of other dances, all on exotic themes, including *O-mika*, based on the Japanese **Noh**. In 1914, she married Ted Shawn, with whom she founded the Denishawn School of Dance in Los Angeles and New York. The relationship was not emotionally satisfying, but they remained together until 1932, organizing major tours and helping to bring about a recognition of modern dance as an independent art form. St. Denis's choreography, which consisted mainly of decorative and often two-dimensional poses, was highlighted by the theatrical use of color, light, and exotic costuming. WBY saw her dance in London in 1908, and in the poem "His Phoenix" (*CP.* 170), he includes her in a list of beautiful women with whom he compares **Maud Gonne**.

REFERENCES: Shelton, Suzanne. *Divine Dancer: A Biography of Ruth St. Denis.* Garden City, N.Y.: Doubleday, 1981; Sherman, Jane. *The Drama of Denishawn Dance.* Middletown, Conn.: Wesleyan University Press, 1979; Terry, Walter. *Miss Ruth: The "More Living Life" of Ruth St. Denis.* New York: Dodd, Mead, 1969.

STELLA. *See* **JOHNSON, ESTHER**.

STEPHENS, JAMES (1825–1901), founder of the Irish Republican Brotherhood. He was born in County Kilkenny and worked as a civil engineer. He was involved with **Daniel O'Connell** and his Repeal Association, but after joining the Young Ireland movement, he became more militant and took part in the abortive rising of 1848. He escaped to France, where he became convinced that a successful uprising against the English was possible. In 1858, he formed the Irish Republican Brotherhood, a branch of the Fenians, and visited the United States to solicit funds. He wrote his influential work *On the Future of Ireland* (1862) and, in 1863, founded a newspaper to further his cause, *The Irish People*, with **John O'Leary** as one of the editors. He visited the United States in 1864 and received the financial support of the Fenian movement in America for a proposed uprising in September 1865. The plan was discovered, and with the help of **Ellen O'Leary**, who mortgaged property to hire a boat, he escaped to France. He returned to the United States with the promise of another rising in 1867. When he postponed action, he was denounced as a traitor and deposed by younger activists. He fled again to France and earned a paltry living as a journalist and teacher. He returned to Ireland in the late 1880s with funds raised by friends but took no further part in revolutionary politics. In *Autobiography* (*M.* 132), WBY recalls visiting the "old Fenian leader" with **Maud Gonne**.

REFERENCE: Ryan, Desmond. *The Fenian Chief: A Biography of James Stephens.* Coral Gables, Fla.: University of Miami Press, 1967.

STEPHENS, JAMES (1882–1950), poet, novelist, and broadcaster. Always witty and whimsical, he spent his life telling tall stories about his birth, parentage, and personal life. He was very likely born in Dublin and, from 1903 to 1913, was employed as a scrivener in the Dublin law offices of Thomas Tighe, McCready & Son. In 1913, he moved to Paris but returned to Dublin in 1915. In 1918, he was appointed registrar of the **National Gallery of Ireland**, a post he held until 1925, when he left Ireland to live in London and Paris. His major writings were published in the early part of his life, among them *The Crock of Gold* (1912), *The Demi-Gods* (1914), *Deirdre* (1923), *In the Land of Youth* (1924), and *Collected Poems* (1926). In 1925, he embarked on a series of lecture tours of the United States, arranged principally by his friend **Padraic Colum**. From 1937, he became a regular contributor to the **BBC** in London and broadcast pithy reminiscences and impressions of the major figures in the Irish Literary Revival, including WBY. For many, these broadcasts constitute his most lasting work. Stephens, with other young Irish writers, was a friend of **AE**. WBY, who felt alienated from that circle, had Stephens and Colum in mind when he wrote "To a Poet, who would have me Praise certain Bad Poets, Imitators of His and Mine" (*CP*. 105). Later, he revised his opinion of both writers, admiring especially their translations from the Irish, and he praised Stephens as a folk poet in his broadcast on "Modern Poetry" (*LE*. 100). He included eight poems by Stephens in his selection for *The Oxford Book of Modern Verse* (1936), and eleven books by Stephens were in WBY's library, including *Collected Poems* (1931), *The Hill of Vision* (1912), and *Reincarnations* (1918) (*OS*. nos. 1997–2006).

REFERENCES: Bramsbäck, Birgit. *James Stephens: A Literary and Bibliographical Study.* Dublin: Hodges Figgis, 1959; Finneran, Richard J., ed. *Letters of James Stephens.* New York: Macmillan, 1974; Martin, Augustine. *James Stephens: A Critical Study.* Totowa, N.J.: Rowan & Littlefield, 1977; Pyle, Hilary. *James Stephens: His Work and an Account of His Life.* London: Routledge & Kegan Paul, 1965.

STILTJACK, MALACHI, character in WBY's poem "High Talk." The Book of Malachi, the last book in the Old Testament of the Judaic-Christian Bible, is a call by the prophet for the people to reject their lax and corrupt ways and return to their former faithfulness to God. In the poem "High Talk" (*CP*. 385), WBY sees the brilliance and wit of his friend **Oliver St. John Gogarty** as the defiant gesture of the artist, conscious of a heroic past, refusing to submit to the banalities of the present. He is dubbed Malachi as a reference to **James Joyce's**

Malachi (Buck) Mulligan in *Ulysses*, while Stilt-Jack is a verbal play on St. John, his middle name. Malachy was also a twelfth-century Irish saint.

REFERENCES: Carens, James F. *Surpassing Wit: Oliver St. John Gogarty*. New York: Columbia University Press, 1979; Carens, James F. "Gogarty and Yeats." *In Modern Irish Literature*, ed. Raymond J. Porter and James D. Brophy. New York: Twayne, 1972.

ST. MICHAEL, archangel in the Judaic, Christian, and Islamic traditions. As the highest-ranking angel, he is usually pictured as a prince or warrior with a sword, often fighting with the dragon (Satan) and dispatching him to Hell. In "The Happy Townland" (*CP*. 94) and "The Hour before Dawn" (*CP*. 130), WBY pictures Michael with a trumpet calling the dead at the Resurrection, a role assigned to Gabriel. He also makes this association in "J. M. Synge and the Ireland of his Time" (*EI*. 316) and in "Bishop Berkeley" (*LE*. 108). In "Journal" (*M*. 249), he recalls **Maud Gonne** lighting a candle to St. Michael at Mont-Saint-Michel, where the saint is reputed to have appeared. See also "The Rose of Peace" (*CP*. 41).

STONE COTTAGE, Yeats residence. WBY found the cottage in the fall of 1913, while he was visiting **Olivia Shakespear's** brother, Harry Tucker, who lived in the vicinity. Situated on a private road in Coleman's Hatch, Hartfield, East Sussex, about one hour's journey from London, the house had an unspoiled view of the Sussex heath to the front and a wood to the rear. With **Ezra Pound** as his secretary, WBY rented the cottage and stayed there for some months during the winters of 1913, 1914, and 1915, cared for by two sisters, the Misses Wellfare. While there, he read the translations by **Ernest Fenollosa** of **Noh** plays, which Pound was in the process of editing. He read the poetry of **Wordsworth**, and Icelandic sagas, and wrote not only poetry but his lectures for his 1914 American tour. He instructed Pound in spiritualism and astrology. Apart from trying to teach WBY fencing, Pound provided a critical audience for WBY's writings, encouraging him to explore a sparer, more concrete and sinewy verse, free from abstractions. Sometimes **Lady Gregory** came to Stone Cottage for weekends, bringing with her eligible young women, among them **Georgie Hyde-Lees**, whom WBY married in 1917. **Wilfred Scawen Blunt** lived in the area.

REFERENCE: Longenbach, James. *Stone Cottage*. New York: Oxford University Press, 1988.

ST. PATRICK (c. 385–461), patron saint of Ireland. There has always been dispute over his birthplace; many hold that it was near Dumbarton, Scotland, while others claim it was in the Celtic province of Brittany, France. In his *Confession*, there is evidence to support both claims. He was captured as a boy of sixteen by Celtic marauders, brought to Ireland, and sold as a slave to an Antrim chieftain. After seven years, he escaped to Gaul, where he entered the monastery at Lerins. He studied there for several years, returned home to live with relatives, and had a vision calling him back to Ireland to convert it to Christianity. He returned to the monastery to complete his studies. After twelve years, he was consecrated bishop and went to Ireland as a missionary in 432. He gained his first converts at **Tara**, the seat of the High King, and successfully defied the pagan priests when he lit the Paschal (Easter) fire on the hill of Slane. He used the existing social system of the country to convert the people, tribe by tribe. He modified the ancient laws of Ireland to harmonize with Christian practice. In 444 or 445 he established the archepiscopal see at Armagh and continued his missionary work until he had converted almost the whole island. He retired to Saul in 457, remaining there until his death. He was buried in Downpatrick, which became a great European shrine, until its sacking by the English in 1539. WBY's poem *The Wanderings of Oisin* (*CP*. 409) is based on a traditional Irish dialogue, ''The Colloquy of St. Patrick,'' in which **Oisin** recounts to the saint his adventures in **Tir-nan-Oge**, and St. Patrick, having listened with some interest, tells him the **Fianna** are in Hell. See also ''Ribh Denounces Patrick'' (*CP*. 328).

REFERENCES: Bieler, Ludwig. *Studies on the Life and Legend of St. Patrick*. Ed. Richard Sharpe. London: Variorum Reprints, 1986; Bury, J. B. *The Life of St. Patrick and His Place in History*. Freeport, N.Y.: Books for Libraries, 1971; Gallico, Paul. *The Steadfast Man: A Biography of St. Patrick*. Garden City, N.Y.: Doubleday, 1958; Hopkin, Alannah. *The Living Legend of St. Patrick*. New York: St. Martin's, 1989.

ST. PATRICK'S PURGATORY. *See* **LOUGH DERG**.

STRAFFORD, EARL OF (1593–1641), statesman and adviser to Charles I of England. Sir Thomas Wentworth, first earl of Strafford, was lord deputy of Ireland from 1633 to 1641. There, he imposed his autocratic will with such force and cruelty that he was hated by the native Irish. He extended the Plantation of **Ulster** by giving large tracts of land to English settlers and enforced strict observance of the Thirty-nine Articles of the Anglican Church. From 1639, he was joint-chief adviser to Charles I of England. In 1640, he raised an army in Ireland to fight recalcitrant Scots. When the Long Parliament assembled, he was accused of raising the army to use against English subjects. Although he was tried and found innocent of treason, the king was forced to sign a bill of attainder, and Strafford was beheaded. His portrait, attributed to the school of Van Dyck, is in the **National Gallery**, Dublin, and is referred to in WBY's poem ''Demon and Beast'' (*CP*. 209).

REFERENCES: Kearney, Hugh F. *Strafford in Ireland, 1633–41: A Study in Absolutism*. Cambridge: Cambridge University Press, 1989; Timmis, John H. *Thine Is the Kingdom: The Trial for Treason of Thomas Wentworth, Earl of Strafford*. Alabama: University of Alabama Press, 1974; Wedgwood, Cicely V. *Strafford: 1593–1641*. Westport, Conn.: Greenwood, 1970.

STRANGER. *See* **MacMURROUGH, DIARMUID**.

STRINDBERG, [JOHAN] AUGUST (1849–1912), playwright, novelist, and short story writer. He was born in Stockholm, the son of a former waitress and a bankrupt aristocrat who worked as a steamship agent. In his autobiography, *Son of a Servant* (1886), he tells of an emotionally troubled childhood of poverty and neglect. He attended the University of Uppsala, where he prepared to enter the church. Later, he changed to medicine but left Uppsala without completing a degree. He worked as a freelance journalist in Stockholm and, in 1874, became a librarian at the Royal Library. In 1877, he embarked upon the first of three disastrous marriages, and with the publication of his novel *The Red Room* (1879), a satirical view of Stockholm society, he became famous throughout Sweden. Mentally unstable, he traveled with his wife and young family around Europe. With the publication of his collection of short stories, *Married* (1884), he was prosecuted for blasphemy. Though acquitted, the trauma further affected his mind and led to a persecution mania that fueled his naturalistic dramas, *The Father* (1887), in which he expressed his negative view of women, and *Miss Julie* (1888), a psychological battle of the sexes. His marriage to Siri von Essen ended in divorce in 1891, and to his intense grief, he lost the custody of their four children. He traveled to Berlin, where, in 1892, he married the Austrian journalist Frida Uhl. They separated two years later, in Paris. The ensuing emotional stress led to a period of religious introspection and conversion that he described in *Inferno* (1897). In 1899, he returned to Stockholm, where he married the Norwegian actress Harriet Bosse (the marriage ended in divorce three years later), and he embarked upon the last triumphant phase of his work. His new-found religious faith was depicted in his later expressionistic plays, among them *A Dream Play* (1902) and *The Ghost Sonata* (1907), both of which reflected the influence of the mystic **Emanuel Swedenborg** and anticipated important theatrical developments in European drama in the twentieth century. Despite his national popularity, Strindberg was ignored by the Swedish Academy, a point raised by WBY when he went to Stockholm to receive the **Nobel Prize for Literature** in 1923. WBY was in the company of Strindberg in Paris, most likely in February 1894, when Strindberg was experimenting with the making of alchemical gold and the finding of the Philosopher's Stone (*A*. 347), although WBY admits to not knowing who he was until years later (*LE*. 32). He believed that it was from Strindberg that he first heard about nonnaturalistic staging (*A*. 538–39).

REFERENCES: Meyer, Michael. *Strindberg*. New York: Random, 1985; Morgan, Margery. *Strindberg*. London: Macmillan, 1985.

STROLLER, fictional character in WBY's play *The King of the Great Clock Tower*. The Stroller is a boastful stranger who, having heard of the **Queen**, arrives at court and insists on seeing her. Invoking the name of **Aengus**, he prophesies that the Queen will dance for him and kiss his mouth. For his insolence, the jealous **King** has him beheaded. When the prophecy is fulfilled, the

Queen triumphantly lifts his severed head on her shoulder, while the diminished King kneels at her feet.

ST. TERESA [St. Theresa of Avila] [1515–82], reformer and mystic. She was born into a wealthy Spanish family and entered the Carmelite Order about 1536. After a period of illness and religious doubt, she experienced a second conversion, which directed her toward mysticism and church reform through the founding of a house of Discalced (or Barefoot) Carmelites, living in strict observance of the laws of the Catholic Church. She met with opposition from dissolute and unreformed members of the Church but, in 1562, opened the Convent of St. Joseph, in Avila, the first of many convents to which she devoted her life. She was a tireless worker, possessing a persuasive charm, astuteness, humor, and good sense. With her associate St. John of the Cross, she stimulated a reawakening of religious fervor throughout Europe. She wrote a number of mystical works that are valued for their simplicity, directness, rich imagery, and spiritual insights. They include *Life* (1565), a spiritual autobiography, *Way of Perfection* (1565), *Interior Castle* (1577), and *Foundations* (1582), all considered among the greatest works of mystical literature. In the late 1920s, WBY read the *Interior Castle, Foundations*, and other books about St. Teresa, including *The Life of St. Teresa* (1911), in which Lady Lovat describes the body of St. Teresa after death, still intact even after many years, exuding a perfumed oil that embalmed the air of the tomb. It is to this miracle that WBY refers in "Oil and Blood" (*CP*. 270) and "Vacillation" (*CP*. 282).

REFERENCES: Auclair, Marcelle. *St. Teresa of Avila*. Trans. Kathleen Pond. New York: Pantheon, 1953; Clissold, Stephen. *St. Teresa of Avila*. New York: Seabury, 1979; Slade, Carole. *St. Teresa of Avila: Author of a Heroic Life*. Berkeley: University of California Press, 1995.

ST. TERESA'S HALL, public hall at 36 Clarendon Street, Dublin. The stage of St. Teresa's Hall was thirty feet by twenty feet, and the hall seated 300. The first production of WBY's play ***Cathleen Ni Houlihan*** was given there for three performances, April 1902. It was produced by **W. G. Fay's** Irish National Dramatic Company, with **Maud Gonne** in the title role. The success of this production, which was performed with **AE's** *Deirdre*, led to the foundation of the **Irish National Theatre Society** in 1903. WBY notes that the production was so popular that people had to be turned away (*EX*. 88–89).

REFERENCE: McGarry, James P. *Place Names in the Writings of William Butler Yeats*. Gerrards Cross: Colin Smythe, 1976.

SURRACHA. In WBY's play ***Deirdre*** (*CPl*. 178), the heroine tells the Chorus that her rubies were taken by her husband from the king of Surracha. It may be that Deirdre is referring to Sorcha, the Gaelic Underworld. *Sorcha* may be used to indicate any exotic country and does not denote a specific geographical location.

SWEDENBORG, EMANUEL (1688–1772), scientist, religious teacher, and mystic. He was born in Sweden, the son of a professor of theology, who was also chaplain to the royal court. In 1719, his father was elevated to a bishopric, and the family name was changed from Swedberg to Swedenborg. After graduating from the University of Uppsala, Emanuel Swedenborg spent some years traveling in Europe, a student of mathematics and the natural sciences. On his return to Sweden in 1716, he was appointed assessor of the Royal College of Mines. For the next thirty years, he devoted himself to engineering and to the publishing of many works on philosophy, humanism, the animal kingdom, the brain, the nature of the soul, and psychology. In 1744, he published *Journal of Dreams*, a record of an intensely painful religious crisis during which he had a vision of **Christ**. In April 1745, he claimed to have had a waking vision of Christ and to have been told to devote himself to interpreting the Scriptures and to communicating what had been revealed to him of Heaven and Hell, the world of spirits and the angels. Thereafter, he committed himself fully to the contemplation of spiritual matters, believing that God had revealed the inner doctrines of the divine word to him alone. From 1749 to 1771, he wrote thirty volumes, all of them in Latin, devoted to the revelations, including *Heavenly Arcana* (1749–56), *Apocalypse Explained* (1785–89), *On Heaven and Its Wonders and on Hell* (1758), and *True Christian Religion* (1771). The teachings of his New Church were set forth in 1757, and after his death, his disciples formed the Church of the New Jerusalem, a religious sect that survives until the present day. His visions and religious interpretations inspired many nineteenth-century writers, among them **Honoré de Balzac** and **Strindberg**. Influenced by **Edwin J. Ellis**, WBY began studying Swedenborg in the late 1880s, alongside the writings of other mystics like **Boehme** and **Blake** (*A*. 161), and he incorporated Swedenborg's ideas in his projected Order of Celtic Mysteries, which he worked on through the 1890s (*A*. 254). The writings of the Swedish mystic helped WBY understand the relationship between soul and matter, and he wrote about him at length in his essay "Swedenborg, Mediums, and the Desolate Places" (*LE*. 47–73), written in 1914 and published in **Lady Gregory's** *Visions and Beliefs in the West of Ireland* (1920). He had ten volumes of Swedenborg, many of them with extensive marginalia, in his library (*OS*. nos. 2036–40).

REFERENCES: Brock, Erland J., and Glenn, E. Bruce, eds. *Swedenborg and His Influence*. Bryn Athyn, Pa.: Academy of the New Church, 1988; Synnestvedt, Sig, ed. *The Essential Swedenborg*. New York: Swedenborg Foundation, 1977; Toksvig, Signe. *Emanuel Swedenborg: Scientist and Mystic*. New York: Swedenborg Foundation, 1983.

SWIFT, JONATHAN (1667–1745), prose satirist and cleric. He was born in Dublin, the son of an Englishman who settled there after the restoration of the English monarchy in 1660. He was sent to St. John's College in Kilkenny, then considered the best school in Ireland, and entered **Trinity College**, Dublin, in 1682. After his graduation, he was appointed secretary to Sir William Temple, a distant relative, at Moor Park, Surrey. He retained this position until Temple's death in 1699 but returned to Ireland in 1695 to be ordained into the Anglican Church as vicar of Kilroot, near Belfast. He started writing poetry in the early 1690s, but his true gift for prose satire did not emerge until he composed *A Tale of a Tub* (1704), a satirical attack on ''the numerous and gross corruptions in religion and learning'' in English society. With Temple's death in 1699, Swift returned to Ireland as chaplain and secretary to the Lord Justice, earl of Berkeley. He maintained contact with London, writing important religious and political pamphlets like ''Discourse of the Contests and Dissensions between the Nobles and the Commons in Athens and Rome,'' in which he showed that the balance of power between the English monarchy and Parliament was fatal to tyranny. In 1710, he returned to London. He viewed with apprehension the emerging power of the Nonconformist church at the expense of the Anglican community, a growth encouraged by the Whig administration in the Westminster Parliament. Although he had been a vigorous Whig supporter, he joined a new Tory administration, convinced they were more supportive of the Established Church. His reactions to the changing mood in England under the Tories were recorded in his *Journal to Stella* (1710–13). He became the Tories' chief pamphleteer and editor of the Tory journal, *The Examiner*, and was rewarded for his services by an appointment as dean of St. Patrick's Cathedral in Dublin in 1713, a reward that came as a disappointment since he had apparently expected more. Although born in Dublin, within sight of St. Patrick's, Swift did not regard himself as Irish. Yet on his permanent return, he vehemently identified with the dispossessed. With exuberant wit and political satire, he targeted the intransigence of the English government in their treatment of Ireland's social and economic problems. In ''Drapier's Letters'' (1724–25), he attacked an English government scheme to provide Ireland with debased coinage and painted such an exaggerated picture of the consequences that the coinage was withdrawn from circulation. In 1729, incensed by the sufferings of Dublin's poor, he published ''A Modest Proposal: for preventing the Children of poor People from being a Burthen *[sic]* to their Parents, or the Country, and for making them beneficial to the Publick,'' a letter written anonymously in the style of the public reformers of the day. In it he recommended the selling of Irish babies as culinary delicacies for the rich to alleviate Ireland's overpopulation and provide the parents with additional income. For these and other ironical pamphlets, he became a folk legend among the poor of Dublin. He published his greatest satire, *Gulliver's Travels*, in 1726. In the work, his hero, Lemuel Gulliver, sets out on a voyage and, by a series of mishaps, finds himself in strange lands. Swift disdainfully uses the range of races and societies that Gulliver encounters to reveal the follies and excesses of eighteenth-century society. He passionately indicts the whole of humankind, which he concludes is incapable of aspiring to any level above the bestial or the inhuman. He had suffered throughout his life from dizziness and nausea (now identified as Ménière's disease), a condition that made him, at times, irascible. As he grew older, he became violent and uncontrolled to a point bearing on insanity. He suffered a paralytic stroke and, in 1742, was declared incapable of caring for himself, and guardians were appointed. On his death, he left his savings to found St. Patrick's Hospital for the mentally ill. In his introduction to *The Words upon the Window-Pane*, the play in which Swift is a central player, WBY wrote: "Swift haunts me; he is always just round the next corner" (*EX*. 345). He had always admired Swift for his plain speaking (*UP1*. 308) and for his unique, passionate nature (*UP1*. 407), an admiration shared by **Lady Gregory**, but early in his career, WBY had rejected him, with **Burke, Berkeley**, and **Goldsmith**, as an English writer. Quoting from **Joyce**, he noted that there was more intensity in a single stanza of **James Clarence Mangan** than in all of Swift. In a row over the distribution of books for the **National Literary Society** in the early 1890s, he admitted to knowing little about Swift (*M*. 68), and in his dispute with **Edward Dowden** in 1895, he claimed that the works of Swift, among others, were not Irish literature because they were not about Irish subjects (*UP1*. 352). Nothing by Swift appeared in his list of "Best Irish Books." Yet in the late 1920s, Swift took hold of WBY, becoming for him a late mask that mirrored his own savage indignation at the passing of the old world order and the demise of a much-maligned Protestant ruling class in a new Ireland dominated by **Eamon de Valera** and the Catholic hierarchy (*LE*. 242). Thus, in a letter to *The Spectator*, September 1928, he attacks the Catholic Church's position on birth control and offers Swift's "A Modest Proposal" (*UP2*. 483) as a solution to the impending crisis of overpopulation. In the poem "Blood and the Moon" (*CP*. 267), written in 1927, he expresses his pride in an intellectual ancestry that includes Swift, while in "Parnell's Funeral" (*CP*. 319), he associates Swift with **Parnell**, both men of character isolated by their deeds from the howling mob. In "Swift's Epitaph" (*CP*. 277), a short poem that echoes in its language and imagery Swift's own epitaph, he celebrates Swift the libertarian. WBY's most fully developed statement on Swift and the two women in his life, **Stella** and **Vanessa**, is contained in his play *The Words upon the Window-Pane*, written in 1930. In it he dramatizes not only a question that has intrigued Swiftian scholars for generations, the nature of Swift's relationship with these two women (in a diary, kept in 1930, he notes that Swift "almost certainly hated sex"), but also the relationship between the life of the intellect (Stella) and the life of the body (Vanessa). In the play, **John Corbet** comments that he is writing an essay on Swift and Stella for his doctorate at Cambridge and intends to prove that in the eighteenth century "men of intellect reached the height of their power" and that all that is worthy in the Irish character and in architecture comes from that time. WBY had the seventeen-volume Thomas Sheridan edition of Swift's *Works* (1784) in his library (*OS*. no. 2043). See also "The Seven Sages" (*CP*. 271).

REFERENCES: Archibald, Douglas N. "The Words upon the Window-Pane and Yeats's Encounter with Jonathan Swift." In *Yeats and the Theatre*, ed. Robert O'Driscoll and Lorna Reynolds. Niagara Falls, N.Y.: Maclean-Hunter, 1975; Faulkner, Peter. *Yeats & the Eighteenth Century*. Dublin: Dolmen, 1965; Maxwell, D. E. S. "Swift's Dark Grove: Yeats and the Anglo-Irish Tradition." In *W. B. Yeats: Centenary Essays*, ed.

D.E.S. Maxwell and S. B. Bushrui. Ibadan: Ibadan University Press, 1965; Torchiana, Donald T. *W. B. Yeats & Georgian Ireland*. Oxford: Oxford University Press, 1966.

SWINBURNE, ALGERNON [CHARLES] (1837–1909), poet and critic. He was born in London, the son of an admiral in the British navy. He attended Balliol College, **Oxford**, where he met **William Morris, Edward Burne-Jones**, and **Dante Gabriel Rossetti**. He left Oxford in 1860 without a degree, but a generous allowance from his father enabled him to pursue a literary career. He achieved his first success as a writer with the poetic drama *Atalanta in Calydon* (1865), in which he re-created in English the form and style of the classic Greek tragedy. His *Poems and Ballads* (1866) were attacked by conservative critics for their overt sensuality and paganism, but they were praised by younger readers for their evocative imagery and technical inventiveness. A meeting in 1867 with Italian patriot Giuseppe Mazzini led to an enthusiasm for political freedom, a theme explored by Swinburne in his verse collections *A Song of Italy* (1867) and *Songs before Sunrise* (1871). His other poetic works included a dramatic trilogy, *Chastelard* (1865), *Bothwell* (1874), and *Mary Stuart* (1881); the second series of *Poems and Ballads* (1878); a long poem, *Tristram of Lyonesse* (1882); and the dramatic tragedy *Locrine* (1887). His literary criticism was prolific, ranging from his monographs *Shakespeare* (1880) and *Ben Jonson* (1889) to *Essays and Studies* (1875) and *Ave Atque Vale* (1867–68), an elegy on Baudelaire. His health was undermined by alcoholism and indulgent living. After a total breakdown in 1879, he was cared for by his friend Theodore Watts-Dunton, with whom he spent the last thirty years of his life. He continued to write fine works, but his most important poetry belonged to the earlier part of his life. Swinburne's musicality in language and rhythm was an early influence on the young WBY, but later he came to believe that Swinburne's rhetoric and choice of political themes for poetry had prevented him from writing a purer, simpler verse (*LE*. 31, 91, 183).

REFERENCES: Henderson, Philip. *Swinburne: Portrait of a Poet*. New York: Macmillan, 1974; Richardson, James. *Vanishing Lives: Style and Self in Tennyson, Rossetti, Swinburne, and Yeats*. Charlottesville: University Press of Virginia, 1988.

SWINEHERD, fictional character. In WBY's play *A Full Moon in March*, the Swineherd comes to the court of the cruel, chaste **Queen**, intending to marry her. In place of the expected song of courtship, he insults her, and she has him beheaded. When his head is brought to her, she indulges in a wild, sexual dance, climaxing in a kiss, representing the union of spirit and matter.

SYMONS, ARTHUR [WILLIAM] (1865–1945), poet and critic. He was born in Milford Haven, Pembrokeshire, and although his schooling was irregular, he determined to be a writer. During the 1890s, he was on the staff of the *Athenaeum* and *Saturday Review*. He contributed to *The Yellow Book* and became editor of *The Savoy* in 1896. He was a member of the **Rhymers' Club** and replaced **Lionel Johnson** as WBY's closest friend in London from the mid-1890s (*M*. 36). The two writers shared rooms at **Fountain Court** during the winter of 1895 and went on a tour of the West of Ireland together in 1896, visiting **Sligo, Coole Park, Tulira Castle** (the home of **Edward Martyn**), and the **Aran Islands**. Symons's account of the trip was published in *The Savoy*, October–December 1896. Sophisticated and urbane, Symons introduced WBY to the work of the French Symbolists **Mallarmé** and **Paul Verlaine** (*A*. 319–21). He acquainted him with the music hall, and the genesis of WBY's preoccupation with the dancer in his poems and dance plays is contained in early poems by Symons, among them "La Mélinite: Moulin Rouge" (1892) and "Nora on the Pavement" (1893). His seminal work *The Symbolist Movement in Literature* (1899), which he dedicated to WBY, had a profound influence on twentieth-century writers in English, including **T. S. Eliot**. In 1901, Symons married Rhoda Bowser, a musician, whose extravagant tastes and lifestyle caused him financial hardship and contributed to his mental breakdown in 1908. He recovered in 1910 but produced no further work of value, apart from *Confessions* (1930), a moving account of his illness. He published his first book of verse, *Days and Nights*, in 1889, followed by *An Introduction to the Study of Browning* (1889) and *Silhouettes* (1892). His important *Studies in the Seven Arts* was published in 1906. Other collections of verse by Symons included the daring *London Nights* (1895) and the decadent *Amoris Victima* (1897), both reviewed by WBY (*UP1*. 373–75; *UP2*. 38–42), and *A Book of Twenty Songs* (1905). WBY had nineteen titles by Symons in his personal library, including *The Symbolist Movement in Literature* (*OS*. nos. 2052–70). Three poems by Symons, including two poems from the French of Paul Verlaine, were included in WBY's selection for *The Oxford Book of Modern Verse* (1936).

REFERENCES: Ellis, Sylvia C. "The Dancer in Performance." In *The Plays of W. B. Yeats: Yeats and the Dancer*. London: Macmillan, 1995; Fletcher, Ian. "Symons, Yeats and the Demonic Dance." In *W. B. Yeats and His Contemporaries*. Brighton, Sussex: Harvester, 1987; Halladay, Jean R. *Eight Late Victorian Poets Shaping the Artistic Sensibility of an Age*. Lewiston, N.Y.: E. Mellen, 1993; Kermode, Frank. "Poet and Dancer before Diaghilev." In *Modern Essays*. London: Fontana, 1971.

SYNGE, [EDMUND] J[OHN] M[ILLINGTON] (1871–1909), playwright and poet. He was born in Rathfarnham, County Dublin, the son of a prosperous lawyer and a strong-willed mother, whose evangelical teachings he rejected after reading Darwin at the age of fourteen. He was educated privately, and at **Trinity College**, Dublin, where he graduated in 1892, winning prizes in Hebrew and Irish. After studying violin at the Royal Irish Academy of Music, he went to Germany in 1893, intending to become a professional musician, but after two years, he decided instead to devote himself to writing. He settled in Paris and enrolled at the Sorbonne, where he took classes with **Henri d'Arbois de Jubainville**, the noted Celtic scholar. He met WBY and **Maud Gonne** in Paris in 1896, and through them, he was introduced to many Irish nationalists (*A*. 343–

45, 567–70). He joined Maud Gonne's l'Irlande Libre but resigned when he realized it was a revolutionary and semimilitary movement. Since Synge had a knowledge of Irish, WBY, who had just returned from the **Aran Islands**, encouraged him to go there to find a theme and "to express a life that has never found expression." Synge made the first of his visits to the islands in 1898, staying in a cottage on **Inishmore**, while he shared the primitive lifestyle of the islanders and listened to their talk. His first account of his visit to the islands was published in the *New Ireland Review*, later that year. He returned to Aran each summer until 1902, when he gave up his small apartment in Paris to live permanently in Dublin. His first two one-act plays, *In the Shadow of the Glen* (1903) and *Riders to the Sea* (1904), were performed by the **Irish National Theatre Society**. Hostility from those who thought it inconceivable that any Irish woman should leave her farmer husband to run off with a tramp greeted *In the Shadow of the Glen*, but its reception by English critics confirmed what WBY had already known—that Synge was a genuine new voice in Irish theater. *The Well of the Saints* was produced at the **Abbey Theatre** in 1905, the year that Synge joined WBY and **Lady Gregory** on the Abbey Board of Directors. The production of *The Playboy of the Western World* at the Abbey in 1907 further antagonized those who thought Synge was demeaning the women and men of Ireland. Later that year, the Abbey produced *The Tinker's Wedding*. Synge's last play, *Deirdre of the Sorrows*, said to have been written for his sweetheart, the actress ***Máire O'Neill***, was produced posthumously in 1911. *The Aran Islands*, an account of his visits to the islands, written in 1901, was published in 1907. A morose, melancholy man, Synge had suffered poor health from childhood and, in 1897, had undergone an operation to remove an enlarged neck gland, the onset of Hodgkinson's disease, which eventually killed him. He had suffered bouts of emotional depression, particularly in the mid-1890s, when he proposed marriage to Cherrie Matheson and was refused. The public debate and outcry over *The Playboy* caused a further deterioration in his emotional health and may have contributed to his early death. For WBY, Synge, with his vivid language and earthy characterizations, was the major talent of the Irish theater, and he never ceased championing him in public debate and in print (*UP2*. 331–38; *EX*. 225–58). In the early 1900s, under the influence of Synge, WBY's poetry and drama lost some of their vagueness and self-consciousness, to become more direct and resilient in tone. The two writers spent time together, but they were not emotionally close. Synge had a persuasive manner, which WBY lacked, but his relaxed attitude frustrated his fellow directors at the Abbey. His death, however, was a profound shock to WBY and ultimately affected the development of the Abbey Theatre. WBY pays tribute to him in the poems "In Memory of Major Robert Gregory" (*CP*. 148), "Coole Park, 1929" (*CP*. 273), and "The Municipal Gallery Revisited" (*CP*. 368). His fullest account of Synge and his achievement is contained in "J. M. Synge and the Ireland of His Time" (*EI*. 311–42) and in his prefaces to *The Well of the Saints* and *Poems and Translations* (*EI*. 298–310). He records his death in some detail in *The Death* *of Synge* (extracts from a diary which WBY kept in 1909) (*A.* 506–19). Twelve poems and prose poems by Synge were included in WBY's selection for *The Oxford Book of Modern Verse* (1936).

REFERENCES: Gerstenberger, D. "Yeats and Synge: A Young Man's Ghost." In *Centenary Essays on the Art of W. B. Yeats*, ed. D. E. S. Maxwell and S. B. Bushrui. Ibadan: Ibadan University Press, 1965; Rodgers, W. R., ed. "J. M. Synge." In *Irish Literary Portraits*. New York: Taplinger, 1973; Synge, J. M. *Letters to Molly: John Millington Synge to Máire O'Neill.* Ed. Ann Saddlemyer. Cambridge, Mass.: Belknap, 1971; Synge, J. M. *Some Letters of John M. Synge to Lady Gregory and W. B. Yeats.* Ed. Ann Saddlemyer. Dublin: Cuala, 1971; *The Synge Manuscripts in the Library of Trinity College, Dublin.* Dublin: Dolmen, 1971.

SYRIAN, THE, disciple. In WBY's play *The Resurrection*, The Syrian brings the news that the women have been to the tomb and found that **Christ** has risen from the dead. **The Hebrew** and **The Greek**, who are both skeptical, try to prevent him telling the other disciples. The Syrian in the first production of *The Resurrection* at the **Abbey Theatre**, July 1934, was played by J. Winter.

T

TAGORE, RABINDRANATH (1861–1941), playwright, poet, musician, and teacher. He was born into a wealthy, talented, cosmopolitan Bengal family in Calcutta, India, the son of Devendranath Tagore (1817–1905), who had given up his wealth and become known as "Maharishi" (great sage). His older brother, Dwijendranath Tagore (1840–1926), was an outstanding poet, musician, and mathematician. Rabindranath Tagore attended the Bengal Academy but was not happy at school, and so his father took him to a summer home in the Himalayas and enabled the young boy to educate himself in literature and the sciences. He studied law in England for one year but returned to India, where he managed his family's large estates and was active in the Indian nationalist movement. He turned to writing prose, poetry, and drama, all of it deeply lyrical and drawing heavily on the rich store of classical Indian literature, especially ancient Sanskrit scripture and the writings of Kalidasa, India's major poet. His early work celebrated his joy in the natural world, but after a series of family tragedies, his writing became more religious and philosophical. His prolific output won him a reputation in India as a teacher and philosopher, while translations of his work into English brought him international attention, principally through the energies of WBY, who met him in June 1912 at the home of William Rothenstein and wrote the introduction to *Gitanjali* (*EI.* 387–95), a collection of prose poems published in Europe, 1912. Tagore was awarded the **Nobel Prize for Literature** in 1913 and donated the cash prize to the school he had founded in India in 1901. Thereafter, he traveled throughout the world, becoming a major celebrity. His later works included *Balaka* (1914) and his novels *The Home and the World* (1919) and *Gora* (1924). He dedicated his collection *The Gardener* (1913) to WBY, who then wrote a short introduction to Tagore's play *The Post Office* (1913) (*PI.* 144), which was produced by the **Abbey Theatre** in 1913.

After his early admiration, WBY cooled in his enthusiasm for Tagore. He felt the Indian poet had become more interested in writing good English than good poetry and so had produced "sentimental rubbish" in a language not his own (*WL*. 834), but he included seven of his prose poems in the collection *The Oxford Book of Modern Verse* (1936). Twenty-six copies of books by Tagore, many of them uncut, were in WBY's library (*OS*. nos. 2077–2100).

REFERENCES: Bose, Abinash Chandra. *Three Mystic Poets: A Study of W. B. Yeats, AE, and Rabindranath Tagore*. Folcroft, Pa.: Folcroft, 1970; Dutta, Krishna, and Robinson, Andrew. *Rabindranath Tagore: The Myriad-Minded Man*. New York: St. Martin's, 1996; Henn, Katherine. *Rabindranath Tagore: A Bibliography*. Metuchen, N.J.: Scarecrow, 1985; Lago, Mary M., ed. *Imperfect Encounter: Letters of William Rothenstein and Rabindranath Tagore: 1911–1941*. Cambridge: Harvard University Press, 1972.

TÁIN BÓ CUAILNGE [also Cuailgne, Cualnge], mythological saga. Regarded as the greatest of the Irish sagas, and the oldest vernacular epic in Western literature, the *Táin Bó Cuailnge* tells of the battle for the Brown Bull of Cooley between **Maeve**, queen of **Connacht**, and the warriors of **Ulster**, chiefly **Cuchulain**. From internal evidence, the central myth, with a collection of pretales that lead up to the *Táin*, is traditionally believed to be contemporaneous with the life of **Christ**, but it was not written down until the medieval period. The saga is contained in a series of manuscripts, the oldest of which, *Lebor na hUidre*, the *Book of the Dun Cow*, was compiled by the monks in the monastery of Clonmacnoise during the twelfth century. This manuscript contains what is thought to be the earliest known form of the epic, but another version is found in the *Yellow Book of Lecan*, a late-fourteenth-century manuscript. With these sources, however, the *Táin* is incomplete. Missing is the motivation for the Cattle Raid, the cause of the illness that affects the Ulster warriors for much of the action, and the reason for **Fergus Mac Roich's** defection to Maeve's camp. These details are contained in other manuscripts, most notably in the *Book of Leinster*, which dates from the twelfth century. This is the most complete version of the saga and the one used by **Standish [James] O'Grady** for his abridged versions of the tales and by **Lady Gregory** for her *Cuchulain of Muirthemne*. The most interesting contemporary version of the epic is by Thomas Kinsella. It is a translation based mainly on the manuscripts of the *Book of the Dun Cow* and the *Yellow Book of Lecan*, with additional material from the *Book of Leinster*.

REFERENCES: Dames, Michael. *Mythic Ireland*. 1992. Reprint, New York: Thames & Hudson, 1996; Ellis, Peter Berresford. *Dictionary of Celtic Mythology*. New York: Oxford University Press, 1992; Kinsella, Thomas. *The Tain*. London: Oxford University Press, 1977; Mac Cana, Proinsias. *Celtic Mythology*. Feltham, Middlesex: Newnes, 1983; O'Rahilly, Cecile. *Táin Bó Cualnge*. Dublin: Dublin Institute for Advanced Studies, 1967.

TALMA, FRANÇOIS JOSEPH (1763–1826), French classical actor. He made his debut at the Comédie-Française in 1787 and, under the influence of the painter

Jacques Louis David (1748–1825), shocked the theater-going public by wearing a Roman toga in a production of Voltaire's *Brutus* in place of the accepted French dress. He rose to prominence in 1789 and was reputed for his passionate but exaggerated style of acting, in which gestures and facial expression preceded the words—"the way the lightning comes before thunder," according to a contemporary critic. He was radical in his politics and late in his career enjoyed the patronage of Napoleon. In *The Death of Cuchulain* (*CPl*. 693), an **Old Man**, speaking directly to the audience, claims to be "the son of Talma." See also "A Nativity" (*CP*. 387), written in 1936, and *On the Boiler* (*LE*. 227).

REFERENCE: Collins, Herbert F. *Talma: A Biography of an Actor*. New York: Hill & Wang, 1964.

TAMERLANE [also Tamburlaine, Timor, Timur the Lame] (c. 1336–1405), Mogul conqueror. He was the son of a tribal leader and declared himself to be descended from Ghengis Khan. In 1369, he became ruler of Samarkand and devoted his life to subduing other nations and slaughtering thousands as he captured cities and territories in Persia and India. He died while conducting an invasion of China and was buried at Samarkand. Although a Moslem, he was merciless to coreligionists as well as infidels. He was, by contrast, a strong supporter of the arts and sciences and was responsible for building large, impressive public works. His courage in the face of death is referred to in WBY's poem "Upon a Dying Lady" (*CP*. 177).

REFERENCES: Klonsky, Milton. "Tamerlane." In *The Fabulous Ego: Absolute Power in History*. New York: Quadrangle/New York Times, 1974; Lamb, Harold. *Tamerlane: The Earth Shaker*. Garden City, N.Y.: Garden City Publishing Co., 1928; Manz, Beatrice F. *The Rise and Rule of Tamerlane*. Cambridge: Cambridge University Press, 1989.

TARA (Irish: *Teamhair*) [conspicuous place], seat of the ancient High Kings of Ireland. It is located six miles south of Navan, on the main Dublin-Navan Road. Rising some 300 feet, Tara was situated in the central province **Meath**, surrounded by the four other provinces of the ancient pentarchy during the Iron Age. When it was at the height of its power, it was the site of the Feast of Tara (*Feis Temhra*), held to inaugurate a new king and to solemnize the union between his kingship and the local earth goddess. Tara declined in importance with the coming of Christianity. The site of Tara today is described by WBY in "Gods and Fighting Men" (*EX*. 14–15). It is a large, grass-covered hill, but closer inspection reveals evidence of megalithic earthworks, ramparts, and ditches. Early literature, such as the fourteenth-century *Yellow Book of Lecan*, suggests there were a number of buildings and monuments on or near the hill, the chief of them being the *Tech Midhchuarta* (The Hall of Mead-Circling), known also as the Hall of Warriors or House of Tara, and reputed for its size and magnificence. The Stone of Destiny, reputedly brought from **Falias**, was on the Mound of the Hostages. WBY may have had the Hall of Mead-Circling in mind in the poem "In Tara's Halls" (*CP*. 374). Some of the action of *The*

Herne's Egg takes place in the Banqueting Hall (another name for the Hall of Mead-Circling), while **Aedh**, king of Tara, is a character in the play. WBY visited the Hill of Tara in 1902 and was dismayed to find unauthorized diggings taking place there (*UP2*. 295). It is to this that he refers in the poem "In the Seven Woods" (*CP*. 85). See also "The Two Kings" (*CP*. 503).

REFERENCES: Dames, Michael. *Mythic Ireland*. 1992. Reprint, New York: Thames & Hudson, 1996; Enright, Michael J. *Iona, Tara, and Soissons: The Origin of the Royal Anointing Ritual*. Berlin and New York: De Gruyter, 1985; Macalister, R. A. S. *Tara: A Pagan Sanctuary of Ancient Ireland*. New York: Scribner's Sons, 1931.

TAYLOR, JOHN F[RANCIS] (1850–1902), Irish barrister and journalist. He was called to the English and Irish Bars and earned a reputation as a fine advocate and orator. As a disciple of **John O'Leary**, he was a determined nationalist and pugnacious debater. He did not agree, however, with agrarian agitation and vehemently attacked those who supported it, incurring thereby the wrath of William O'Brien, the editor of the *United Irishman*. He was a member of the **Irish Literary Society** and the Young Ireland Society, to whom he delivered the Inaugural Address on "Parliaments of Ireland." He met WBY at the **Contemporary Club** but was always antagonistic to him, possibly because he was jealous of O'Leary's enthusiasm for the younger poet. In a letter to the *Freeman's Journal*, 7 September 1892, Taylor questioned the logrolling of the poets of the **Rhymers' Club**, and he supported **Sir Charles Gavan Duffy** in his struggle for control of the **New Irish Library** with swingeing attacks on WBY and his circle, attacks that WBY responded to with enthusiasm (*UP1*. 240–44). WBY resented Taylor's influence over **Maud Gonne**, who regarded him as a close friend. Nevertheless, he praised Taylor as an outstanding orator, the greatest he had ever heard, but noted that his violent temper prevented him from achieving the recognition he deserved (*A*. 422–24). Taylor's defense of the study of Irish, which he gave to the Law Students' Debating Society on 24 October 1901, is quoted by WBY in *Reveries over Childhood and Youth* (*A*. 96–97).

TEIGUE, peasant son. In WBY's play *The Countess Cathleen*, he is a boy of fourteen who shares his father's skepticism about prayer and the help the family may expect from God during the famine. He is enthusiastic about the **Merchants** who come to his home and helps his father persuade the other peasants to barter their souls for gold. See also **Mary** and **Shemus Rua**.

TENNYSON, ALFRED, LORD (1809–92), poet. He was born the son of a Lincolnshire rector, and after attending Louth Grammar School for five years, he returned home to be educated by his father. He began writing poetry in his teens. In 1827, when his father's health deteriorated, he went to Trinity College, Cambridge. There he met **Arthur Hallam** and became a member of the exclusive Cambridge undergraduate group, the Apostles. His first book, *Poems,*

Chiefly Lyrical, was published in 1830. With the death of his father in 1831, he left Cambridge. In 1832, he published *Poems*, which included "The Lotus-Eaters" and "The Lady of Shalott," poems distinguished by their metrical variety, imagery, and verbal melody. The sudden death, a year later, of Arthur Hallam, who had not only been a close friend but had also written a eulogistic review of Tennyson's early work in *The Englishman's Magazine* of *Poems, Chiefly Lyrical*, was a profound blow. Out of his emotional pain, intensified by the mental instability of members of his family, he wrote some of his most memorable work, including "Locksley Hall," "Ulysses," and "Morte d'Arthur," long poems that expressed philosophic doubts in an increasingly materialistic age. He followed his anthology *Poems* (1842) with "In Memoriam" (1850), a long elegy sequence dedicated to Hallam, in which he attempted to reconcile traditional Victorian beliefs with the emerging theories of science. He married in 1850, the year he was appointed Poet Laureate, and embarked on a stable and secure period of his life. Between 1859 and 1888, he completed *Idylls of the King*, a retelling of the Arthurian epic in which he explored the intrusion of evil into Camelot because of the adulterous affair between Lancelot and Guinevere. The success of the epic confirmed his position as the chief spokesman for poetry in the Victorian age, but it demonstrated an increasingly moralistic tone that alienated some readers. In 1883, he was made a peer. In selecting poems for *The Oxford Book of Modern Verse* (1936), WBY chose the death of Tennyson as the end of Victorianism and the beginning of the modern era in poetry. When he went to art school in Dublin in the 1880s, he introduced his fellow students to the poetry of Tennyson (*A.* 81). Later, he was persistently critical of Tennyson because, in his mature verse, he focused on social, philosophical, and psychological complex issues rather than on the writing of pure poetry (*EI.* 113, 163, 190, 347; *LE.* 91). In 1892, the year of Tennyson's death, WBY wrote a respectful and balanced review of "The Death of Oenone" in *The Bookman* (*UP1.* 251–54).

REFERENCES: Francis, Elizabeth A., ed. *Tennyson: A Collection of Critical Essays.* Englewood Cliffs, N.J.: Prentice–Hall, 1980; Killham, John, ed. *Critical Essays on the Poetry of Tennyson.* New York: Barnes & Noble, 1960; Martin, Robert Bernard. *Tennyson: The Unquiet Heart.* Oxford: Oxford University Press, 1980; Richardson, James. *Vanishing Lives: Style and Self in Tennyson, Rossetti, Swinburne, and Yeats.* Charlottesville: University Press of Virginia, 1988.

THEBAID, district surrounding **Thebes**, royal capital of ancient Egypt. It was a center of Early Christian monasticism from the third century. Following the example of Jesus, religious ascetics, perceiving themselves to be at war with the forces of worldly evil, chose to live a hermit-like existence in the desert devoting themselves to prayer and religious service. This became a model for the development of Christian monasteries in the West. Thebaid is referred to in WBY's poem "Demon and Beast" (*CP*. 210) and in the essay "Bishop Berkeley" (*EI*. 405).

REFERENCES: Hannay, Rev. J. O. *The Spirit and Origin of Christian Monasticism*. London: Methuen, 1903; Hannay, Rev. J. O. *The Wisdom of the Desert*. London: Methuen, 1904.

THEBES, chief city of Boeotia in ancient Greece. According to legend, the city, which is northwest of Athens, was founded by Cadmus, the son of Agenor, king of Tyre. While searching for his sister **Europa**, who had been carried off by Zeus in the shape of a bull, Cadmus visited the oracle at **Delphi** and was told to settle where a cow lay down. The cow led him to the site of Thebes, where he built a citadel, the Cadmea. There, he killed a dragon and, on the advice of **Athene**, planted its teeth. They grew into an army of warriors, and when he set them fighting each other, only five survived. They became the ancestors of the Theban nobility. Cadmus himself was great-grandfather of Laius, father of **Oedipus**. WBY's version of *Sophocles' King Oedipus* takes place outside the royal palace in Thebes, where Oedipus is king. It is the setting for many of the Greek tragedies, including Aeschylus's *Seven Against Thebes*. The ruins of Cadmus's palace may still be seen in the modern city now called Thívai.

REFERENCE: Schefold, Karl. *Gods and Heroes in Late Archaic Greek Art*. Trans. Alan Griffiths. Cambridge: Cambridge University Press, 1992.

THEOSOPHICAL SOCIETY. *See* **BLAVATSKY, MADAME [HELENA PETROVNA]**.

THESEUS, mythological Greek warrior and king of Athens. He is the son of Aegeus and Aethra of Troezen. Following a promise that he should follow his father to Athens only when he is strong enough to lift a huge rock under which Aegeus has hidden a sword and sandals, Theseus succeeds at the age of sixteen and journeys to Athens. There, he is reunited with his father. He is sent against the Bull of Marathon and travels to Crete, where, with the help of Ariadne, he slays the Minotaur. When Aegeus kills himself, because he mistakenly thinks the Minotaur has killed his son, Theseus becomes king of Athens. He unites the warring communities of Attica and defeats the Amazons. In WBY's version of *Sophocles' Oedipus at Colonus,* **Oedipus**, near death, arrives at a wood on the outskirts of Athens and puts himself and his daughters under the generous protection of Theseus.

REFERENCE: Plutarch. *The Rise and Fall of Athens*. Trans. Ian Scott-Kilvert. Harmondsworth, Middlesex: Penguin, 1960.

THETIS, wife of **Peleus** and mother of **Achilles** in Greek mythology. She was loved by Zeus and Poseidon but was given in marriage to a mortal because it had been prophesied that her son would be greater than his father. In the poem "News for the Delphic Oracle" (*CP*. 376), WBY recalls the painting by Nicolas

Poussin, *The Marriage of Peleus and Thetis* (now titled *Acis and Galatea*), in which Peleus gazes admiringly at the naked figure of Thetis in front of him. The painting is in the **National Gallery of Ireland**.

THOMOND, ancient territory in the west of Ireland. It consisted mainly of the present **County Clare** and east **Galway** (county). Thomond was in the kingdom of **Connacht** but became part of **Munster** during the reign of James I of England in the seventeenth century. The rebellion of **Donough O'Brien** against the king of Thomond, in the early fourteenth century, is discussed by the **Young Man** and the **Stranger** in WBY's play *The Dreaming of the Bones* (*CPl.* 439).

REFERENCE: McGarry, James P. *Place Names in the Writings of William Butler Yeats.* Gerrards Cross: Colin Smythe, 1976.

THOOR BALLYLEE, tower at **Ballylee** (Irish: *Baile O'Liagh*), near **Gort, Galway** (county). Known locally as Ballylee Castle, it was one of thirty-two defensive towers built by the deBurgo family in the Galway area during the Norman period. It was later owned by Sir William Gregory, before it was taken over by the Congested Districts Board. WBY bought it in early 1917 for £35 and chose to call it Thoor Ballylee, combining a version of the Irish for tower (*tur* or *tor*) with the Anglicized name for the townland. He had seen the tower, which stands on the Cloone River, when he toured the area in 1900, and he included a description of it in "Dust Hath Closed Helen's Eye" (*MY.* 22). The tower, which was then inhabited by a farmer and his wife, fell into disrepair, and when WBY made a bid for the property in 1917, there was no roof, and the doors were rotten. After renovating the tower and the adjoining cottages, WBY and his wife and family moved there during the summer of 1919. With WBY's increasing duties as a senator and public figure, they were only able to stay there sporadically over the next years. They discovered that the first floor flooded at least once a year, and the damp was not helpful to WBY's health. The family did not return after 1929. Thoor Ballylee is the setting for the poems in the volume *The Tower* (1928) and is featured in the cover design by **T. Sturge Moore**. See also "A Prayer for my Daughter" (*CP.* 211) and "To be Carved on a Stone at Thoor Ballylee" (*CP.* 214). A lively description of the day-to-day life of the Yeats family at Thoor Ballylee is given by **Anne Yeats** in *Shenandoah*, summer 1965.

REFERENCES: Gordon, D. J., ed. *Images of a Poet.* Manchester: University of Manchester, 1961; Hanley, Mary. *Thoor Ballylee—Home of William Butler Yeats*, ed. Liam Miller. Dublin: Dolmen, 1965; Jeffares, A. Norman. "Poet's Tower." In *The Circus Animals: Essays on W. B. Yeats.* Stanford, Calif.: Stanford University Press, 1970.

THORNHILL, home of WBY's uncle **George Pollexfen**. It was one of a pair of Victorian semidetached houses on the Strandhill Road, a short distance out of **Sligo** (town). George Pollexfen had moved there from a notorious area of Sligo called the **Burrough**. WBY stayed with him at Thornhill, which he describes as "a little house about a quarter of a mile into the country" (*A*. 257). There they discussed the occult and conducted psychic experiments.

REFERENCES: Kirby, Sheelah. *The Yeats Country*. Dublin: Dolmen, 1966; McGarry, James P. *Place Names in the Writings of William Butler Yeats*. Gerrards Cross: Colin Smythe, 1976.

THREE ROCK MOUNTAIN [also Two Rock Mountain], mountain that overlooks Dublin from the southwest. In "My Friend's Book" (*EI*. 413), WBY writes that **AE** would sit on Two Rock Mountain inducing a state of trance so that he might see visions. In "Ireland after Parnell" (*A*. 240), he recalls vividly AE returning home from walking on the mountain. The mountain is referred to in WBY's poem "The Peacock" (*CP*. 135).

REFERENCE: McGarry, James P. *Place Names in the Writings of William Butler Yeats*. Gerrards Cross: Colin Smythe, 1976.

TIME AND THE WITCH VIVIEN, dramatic poem by WBY. Originally called *Vivien and Time*, it tells the story of Vivien, the proud, narcissistic enchantress who dies after losing at dice and chess to Father Time. The poem was written in 1884 for WBY's early love **Laura Armstrong**, who played the part of Vivien in an amateur performance at the home of Judge Wright in **Howth**, County Dublin. There is no record of who played Father Time in the reading. The poem was published in *The Wanderings of Oisin and Other Poems* (1889) but was not included in any later publications. There is no record of a professional production.

TIMON (c. 320–230 B.C.), skeptic and man of letters. Born into a poor family in Phlius, Greece, he worked as a dancer and studied philosophy. His tutor was Pyrrhon, accepted today as the father of Skepticism. Timon became popular as a lecturer and acquired a large fortune. In 275 B.C., he retired to Athens to devote himself to writing. Little remains of his vast output of tragedies, comedies, satyr plays, prose, and verse, but he is remembered for his bitter, sarcastic attacks on contemporary philosophers. Timon is the central character in **Shakespeare's** *Timon of Athens*. He loses his wealth and, in anger at the behavior of his friends who have deserted him, retires from society, accompanied only by the faithful Alcibiades. In his poem "An Acre of Grass" (*CP*. 346), WBY, in old age, asks for a Timon-like frenzy so that he may find truth.

TIMOR. *See* **TAMERLANE**.

TIRARAGH (Irish: *Tir-Fhiachrach*) [district of Fiachra], barony in **Sligo** (county) to the west of the Ox Mountains. See also "The Ballad of Father O'Hart" (*CP*. 23).

TIR CONAILL. *See* **DONEGAL**.

TIRESIAS, prophet. According to Greek mythology, he was blinded by **Athena** after seeing her bathe naked in a pool. In remorse, she gave him the power of prophecy. Tiresias appears in the role of visionary or seer throughout Greek literature. In *Sophocles' King Oedipus* (*CPl.* 482), he reveals that **Oedipus** himself is the murderer of Laius, but the proud king will not listen to him.

TIR-NAN-OGE [also Tír na nÓg], the Country of the Young, or the Happy Otherworld of Irish mythology. It is the land established by the vanquished **Tuatha dé Danaan**, where pain, age, and physical deterioration are never experienced. In a note included in **Lady Gregory's** *Visions and Beliefs in the West of Ireland* (1920), WBY observes that Tir-nan-Oge is variously described as under the earth or all about us. It is also commonly believed to be an island somewhere off the west coast of Ireland (*LE.* 278). In *Fairy and Folks Tales of the Irish Peasantry* (*Pl.* 20–21), WBY describes **Oisin's** visit to the Country of the Young, noting that it is often associated with the fairies and is thought to have three locations: the island of the living, the island of victories, and the land under the water. The timeless world of Tir-nan-Oge is the setting for the opening lyric in WBY's play *The King of the Great Clock Tower*, while in *The Wanderings of Oisin*, Oisin lives there for 300 years with **Niamh**.

REFERENCES: Dames, Michael. *Mythic Ireland.* 1992. Reprint, New York: Thames & Hudson, 1996; Green, Miranda J. *Dictionary of Celtic Myth and Legend.* London: Thames & Hudson, 1993.

TODHUNTER, JOHN (1839–1916), physician, poet, and playwright. He was born to a Quaker family in Dublin and educated at Quaker schools in Ireland and England. At sixteen, he was apprenticed to a firm of tea and sugar merchants, but he left in 1862 to study medicine at **Trinity College**, Dublin. There he won the vice chancellor's prize for English verse three times and formed a close friendship with **John B. Yeats**, whom he later supported by commissioning portraits and sketches. After completing his medical studies in 1870, he married Katharine Ball and settled in Dublin as resident physician at Cork Street Fever Hospital. He then accepted an appointment as professor of English at Alexandra College, Dublin. His wife died in childbirth in 1871, and the child died three years later. Todhunter decided to abandon medicine for literature, and after traveling abroad, he settled in **Bedford Park**, London, where he remained for the rest of his life. In 1879, he married Dora Louisa Digby, of Dublin, but her personality caused tensions between him and his friends, especially John B. Yeats. He published a number of collections of verse, among them *Laurella and Other Poems* (1876), *Forest Songs* (1881), and *How Dreams Come True* (1890), wrote *A Study of Shelley* (1880), and translated Heinrich Heine's *Book of Songs* (1907). His first play, *Alcestis*, was produced at Hengler's Circus in 1879. In the first production of *Helena in Troas* (1886), also presented at Hengler's Circus, **Herbert Beerbohm Tree** and his wife played the leading roles, while J. T. Grein's Independent Theatre staged *The Black Cat* in 1893. Yet it was an amateur production of his pastoral play *A Sicilian Idyll* that made an impression on WBY and gave the playwright the one major success of his life (*A.* 119–20; *LNI.* 36–39). He had persuaded Todhunter to write the play, hoping it would inaugurate a yearly arts festival in Bedford Park modeled on the festival of **Dionysus**, and it was produced at the Bedford Park Clubhouse during the week of 5 May 1890, with **Florence Farr** and her brother-in-law **H. M. Paget** in the leading roles. Although WBY later acknowledged he had overrated the play, he was impressed with the innovative staging and the simple lyricism of the verse (*UP1.* 191–94). The play was repeated for two performances at St. George's Hall, Regent Street, London, 1–2 July 1890. It was revived at the Vaudeville Theatre, London, 15–19 June 1891, in a double bill with Todhunter's *The Poison Flower*, for which WBY helped distribute complimentary tickets. When Florence Farr produced a season at the Avenue Theatre, London, March 1894, she opened with Todhunter's *A Comedy of Sighs* in a double bill with WBY's ***The Land of Heart's Desire***. The production was not successful. What had appealed to an esoteric audience in Bedford Park was not suitable for a commercial venue (*A.* 280–81). Todhunter helped WBY establish the **Irish Literary Society** and was a member of the **Rhymers' Club**. Under the influence of WBY, he turned his attention to Celtic subjects. *A Life of Patrick Sarsfield* (1895) and *Three Irish Bardic Tales* (1896) were issued by the **New Irish Library**. Other books on Irish themes included *From the Land of Dreams* (1918) and *Isolt of Ireland* (1927). Todhunter never developed into a major writer, but he had considerable influence over the young WBY, alerting him to the possibilities of poetic drama. WBY's ideas on staging, verse speaking, and characterization owed much to his early experience of seeing Todhunter's plays, and it is likely that Todhunter's work encouraged him to continue to write for the stage. WBY includes a short pen-portrait of Todhunter in "Four Years: 1887–1891" (*A.* 117).

REFERENCES: Hogan, Robert, ed. *Dictionary of Irish Literature.* Rev. ed. Westport, Conn.: Greenwood, 1996; Marcus, Phillip L. *Yeats and the Beginning of the Irish Renaissance.* Syracuse: Syracuse University Press, 1987.

TOM, servant. In the poem "Colonel Martin" (*CP.* 361), he assists his master **Colonel Martin** with the distribution of gold that the master has been awarded in a court action against his wife's lover. When the gold has been distributed, the master asks Tom if he has kept any for himself. He has not and so must spend his last days scraping a living by gathering seaweed on the seashore.

TOM THE LUNATIC, eponymous character in a series of three short poems that WBY wrote in the early 1930s. His name may have derived from the historical association of the name Tom with a foolish person, as in **Shakespeare's** "Poor Tom" in *King Lear.* The first of these poems is "Tom the Lunatic" (*CP.* 305), followed by "Tom at Cruachan" (*CP.* 306) and "Old Tom Again" (*CP.* 306).

TONE, [THEOBALD] WOLFE (1763–98), Protestant revolutionary leader and author. The son of a coach maker, he studied at **Trinity College**, Dublin. He was called to the Irish Bar in 1789, but his dislike for the practices of English law, and his admiration for the objectives of the French Revolution, turned him toward politics. In 1791, he formed the Society of United Irishmen, aimed at setting up an Irish Parliament entirely free from England and uniting Protestants and Catholics in opposition to English rule. After being implicated in a plot to organize a French invasion, he left Ireland for America in 1794. In 1796, he traveled to Paris and joined the French army as adjutant general of the Armée d'Angleterre. In the 1798 Rebellion, when the French troops arrived too late at **Killala, County Mayo** to help the Irish, Wolfe Tone was captured in a French frigate off the coast of **Donegal**, court-martialed, and sentenced to death for treason. His request to be shot as a soldier was disallowed, and he was sentenced to be hanged and disembowelled as a criminal. He committed suicide the morning the sentence was to be carried out. A biography, written by his son, was edited by Bulmer Hobson in 1919, and his *Letters*, edited by Bulmer Hobson, was published in 1920. In the poem ''September 1913'' (*CP*. 120), WBY names Wolfe Tone with **Lord Edward Fitzgerald** and **Robert Emmet** as representatives of those Irish heroes who sacrificed themselves for the ideals in which they so passionately believed. He includes Tone's autobiography in his list of ''Best Irish Books'' (*UP1*. 387). See also ''Parnell's Funeral'' (*CP*. 319).

REFERENCES: Boylan, Henry. *Theobald Wolfe Tone*. Dublin: Gill & Macmillan, 1981; Elliott, Marianne. *Wolfe Tone: Prophet of Irish Independence*. New Haven: Yale University Press, 1989.

TOWER, THE, collection of verse. It was published by Macmillan and Company in 1928, with cover design by **T. Sturge Moore**. The poems in this collection are among the finest that WBY wrote. They eloquently reflect his life as husband, father, senator of the Irish Free State, **Nobel Prize** winner, and celebrated poet. The mood of the collection is bitter, as the poet comes to terms with his own aging and with the political troubles in Ireland. Gone is his preoccupation with youth and physical beauty. He turns to the enrichment of the soul and to his own immortality, as in the opening poem ''Sailing to Byzantium'' (*CP*. 217). He withdraws, too, from the political violence around him by retreating into the tower, **Thoor Ballylee**, to write and to contemplate his philosophical ideas. As in the title poem, the tower becomes a powerful symbol for the poet himself, and throughout the collection, rich in symbol and imagery, the poet extends the meaning and significance of the poetry beyond the personal to the universal. The poems in *The Tower* were previously included in *Seven Poems and a Fragment* (1922), *The Cat and the Moon and Certain Poems* (1924), and *October Blast* (1927).

REFERENCE: Holloway, John. ''Style and World in *The Tower*.'' In *An Honored Guest: New Essays on W. B. Yeats*, ed. Denis Donoghue and J. R. Mulryne. London: Edward Arnold, 1965.

TRAMP [also Beggarman], fictional character. In WBY's play *The Pot of Broth*, he is a man of great charm and shrewdness who manipulates **Sibby Coneely**

and her husband into giving him a chicken, a ham bone, and a bottle of whisky in exchange for a worthless stone. The role of the Tramp in the first production, at the **Antient Concert Rooms**, October 1902, provided **W. G. Fay** with one of his most successful, comedic roles.

TREE, [HERBERT] BEERBOHM (1853–1917), actor and theater manager. He was born in London, the half brother of the critic and caricaturist **Max Beerbohm**. His father was a grain merchant who wished him to enter the family business. He found little joy in it, and in 1878, he became a professional actor, making his London debut the same year at the Olympic Theatre. He was soon playing major character roles in London and the English provinces. In 1887, he leased the Haymarket Theatre, London, and directed himself in leading roles, most notably, Falstaff and Richard II, although many critics considered his melodramatic roles in the popular *Trilby* and *Oliver Twist* to be his finest. He directed the contemporary plays of **Henrik Ibsen, Oscar Wilde** and **Maurice Maeterlinck**. In 1897, he built Her Majesty's Theatre, London, where he presented overelaborate and excessively staged productions of **Shakespeare**, including a presentation of *A Midsummer Night's Dream* in 1900, in which the stage was populated with real animals and real trees—leaving nothing to the imagination. Her Majesty's became his permanent theater home. WBY was not impressed with Beerbohm Tree's productions, considering them vulgar and meretricious (*WL*. 443). A presentation of **J. M. Synge's** *The Tinker's Wedding*, in 1909, so appalled him that he left after the first act. He later refused **Mrs. Patrick Campbell** permission to perform *The Player Queen* for Beerbohm Tree (*WL*. 538).

REFERENCES: Beerbohm, Max. *Sir Herbert Beerbohm Tree: Some Memories of Him and of His Art*. New York: B. Blom, 1969; Bingham, Madeleine. *The Great Lover: The Life and Art of Herbert Beerbohm Tree*. New York: Atheneum, 1968; Pearson, Hesketh. *Beerbohm Tree: His Life and Laughter*. New York: Harper, 1956.

TREMBLING OF THE VEIL, THE, volume of autobiography. WBY completed this section of his autobiography while he was staying at **Thoor Ballylee** in 1922. It was published in the same year by T. Werner Laurie, in an edition of 1,000 copies, each signed by the author. The volume consisted of five parts: Book I. Four Years: 1887–1891; Book II. Ireland after Parnell; Book III. Hodos Chameliontos; Book IV. The Tragic Generation; Book V. The Stirring of the Bones. Book I covers the years from his family's return to London and **Bedford Park** in 1887 through his connections with **William Morris, Madame Blavatsky**, and **MacGregor Mathers**. Book II deals with the setting up of the **Irish Literary Society**, his friendship with **John O'Leary** and Irish writers like **AE**, and his quarrel with **Gavan Duffy** over the **New Irish Library**. Book III explores his increasing interest in the occult, especially his collaborations with his uncle **George Pollexfen**. Book IV tells of the **Rhymers' Club** and the tragic lives lived by so many of the poets whose work he shared, while Book V examines his involvement in Dublin politics and finishes with the setting up of the **Irish Literary Theatre**. The title is from **Stéphane Mallarmé**, and the volume is dedicated to the American **John Quinn**. See *Autobiographies*.

TRENCH, DR., fictional character. In WBY's play *The Words upon the Window-Pane*, he is president of the Dublin Spiritualists' Association. He invites **John Corbet** to the séance and shares with him his knowledge of mediumship and the lodging house where the séance takes place. In the first production of the play, at the **Abbey Theatre**, November 1930, the role of Dr. Trench was played by P. J. Carolan.

TRINITY COLLEGE, Dublin. Situated in the center of Dublin, it was founded in 1592 during the reign of Queen Elizabeth I and is the oldest university in Ireland. It has been traditionally associated with the Protestant Anglo-Irish Ascendancy, with a distinguished roster of alumni, including **Robert Emmet, Wolfe Tone, Oscar Wilde**, and **J. M. Synge**. WBY's great-grandfather, grandfather, and father all graduated from Trinity, and it was expected that he would go there as well. He chose, instead, to attend art school. With the Celtic revival of the 1890s, he became increasingly antagonistic to Trinity, identifying it with traditional Protestant values and claiming that Trinity did not produce "artistic minds" (*EI.* 298). He was critical of the faculty, including **Edward Dowden**, and he responded negatively to those members of the **Rhymers' Club** who were Trinity graduates. Later, his attitude to the college changed, and he celebrated the great writers and thinkers of the eighteenth century, **Jonathan Swift, Oliver Goldsmith, George Berkeley**, and **Edmund Burke**, all of whom had gone there. On the death of Dowden in 1910, WBY was considered for a professorship but was not appointed. He received an honorary degree from Trinity in 1922. Trinity College, Dublin, is an independent academic institution and has no affiliations with Trinity College, Oxford, or Trinity College, Cambridge.
    REFERENCES: McDowell, R. B. *Trinity College, Dublin, 1592–1952: An Academic History*. Cambridge: Cambridge University Press, 1982; Edwards, P. W. ''Yeats and the Trinity Chair.'' *Hermathena*, CI (1955).

TRISTRAM [also Tristan, Trystan], one of the tragic lovers in *Tristram and Isolde*, an Anglo-Norman medieval romance that was written down in the late twelfth century. While there are many versions of the story, the basic plot involves Tristram journeying to Ireland, where he meets the beautiful **Isolde** and brings her back to Cornwall to be the bride of his uncle, King Mark. Tragedy develops when the couple unknowingly swallow a potion that makes them fall in love, and they are betrayed to King Mark. Tristram is banished but is killed by the King as he sings of his love for Isolde. The story of Tristram and Isolde was originally independent but later became incorporated into Arthurian legend when Tristram became one of **Arthur's** knights. The love of Tristram and Isolde provided for WBY one of the great myths of passionate self-sacrifice, and he refers to Tristram's absorption with Isolde in "Lullaby" (*CP*. 300). He was especially moved by the version of the Tristram and Isolde story told by **Laurence Binyon** in "Tristram's End" and included it in *The Oxford Book of Modern Verse* (1936). He makes a reference to Tristram and King Pellinore, from Malory's *Le Morte d'Arthur*, in his introduction to *Gitanjali* (*LE*. 170).

TROY, city in northwestern Anatolia. Because of its commanding position on the southern entrance to the Dardanelles, the straits linking the Black Sea and the Aegean Sea, the city of Troy was wealthy and strategically important to the ancient world. It was destroyed by the Greeks during the Trojan War, fought because of the abduction of **Helen** by **Paris**, and took on mythic status, principally in the writings of **Homer** in *The Iliad* and *The Odyssey* and through **Virgil's** *Aeneid*, which contains the best-known account of the sacking of the city. The site of the ancient city was excavated in the late nineteenth century, the Trojan legend having previously been regarded as myth, not history. The destruction of Troy is referred to by WBY in his poem "The Rose of the World" (*CP*. 41).

TUAM (Irish: *Tuaim-da-ghualann*) [the tumulus of the burial mounds], cathedral town in **Galway** (county). The town gained prominence during the twelfth century when it was the seat of Turlough O'Conor, king of **Connacht**. In "Mortal Help" (*MY*. 9), WBY recalls an old man telling him he had seen, when he was young and working in the fields near Tuam, a troop of fairies dressed in checkered clothes with red waistcoats. There is a reference to the bishop of Tuam in *Dramatis Personae* (*A*. 412).

REFERENCE: McGarry, James P. *Place Names in the Writings of William Butler Yeats.* Gerrards Cross, Colin Smythe, 1976.

TUATHA DÉ DANAAN, people of the goddess Danu, mother of all the gods. They inhabited pre-Christian Ireland before the coming of the Milesians. They had all the human virtues and vices and were associated with warmth and light, in contrast to the **Fomorians**, the powers of cold and darkness. The Tuatha dé Danaan fought two great battles, the first against the **Firbolg**, the second against the Fomorians. They possessed four talismans, the Stone of Fáil (which recognized a true king), the Spear of **Lugh** (which brought them victory), the Sword of Nuada (which made them invincible), and the Cauldron of the Dagda (which assured them of plenty). They were skilled in magic and Druidic lore. After the Battle of **Moytura**, in which they were defeated by the Milesians, they were ousted from the upper world and took to living in the **sídh** or fairy mounds of **Tir-nan-Oge**, no longer gods but fairies. A vivid picture of the Tuatha dé Danaan is given by WBY in "The Unappeasable Host" (*CP*. 65) and "The Withering of the Boughs" (*CP*. 87). He names among the sacred places of Ireland

Slievenamon, the home of Bodb Dearg, a king of the Tuatha dé Danaan (*M.* 125).

REFERENCES: Ellis, Peter Berresford. *Dictionary of Celtic Mythology*. New York: Oxford University Press, 1992; Green, Miranda J. *Dictionary of Celtic Myth and Legend*. London: Thames & Hudson, 1992; Mac Cana, Proinsias. *Celtic Mythology*. Feltham, Middlesex: Newnes, 1983.

TUBBER (Irish: *Tober*) [a well], village in **County Clare**. It is referred to in WBY's play *The Pot of Broth* (*CPl.* 92, 103). The **Tramp** in the play takes the boiled chicken in case he fails to reach the village of Tubber before nightfall.

REFERENCE: McGarry, James P. *Place Names in the Writings of William Butler Yeats*. Gerrards Cross: Colin Smythe, 1976.

TULIRA CASTLE, home of **Edward Martyn**, near **Ardrahan, Galway** (county). Formerly known as Burke Castle, it was substantially rebuilt in the Gothic style by Martyn's mother in 1882 after fire destroyed the house. The only original part left standing was the tower in which Martyn had his study. In *Dramatis Personae* (*A.* 385–87), WBY describes Tulira, which he visited for the first time in August 1896, in the company of **Arthur Symons**. He found the furniture in the drawing room excessive and vulgar, but he admired the fine paintings by Degas, Corot, Monet, and Utamaro on the walls. **Lady Gregory** paid a visit while WBY was staying at Tulira, reminded him that they had met in London, and invited him to visit her at **Coole Park**. The castle still remains habitable today.

REFERENCE: McGarry, James P. *Place Names in the Writings of William Butler Yeats*. Gerrards Cross: Colin Smythe, 1976.

TULLY. *See* **CICERO, [MARCUS TULLIUS]**.

TURNER, W[ALTER] J[AMES] (1889–1946), poet, music and art critic. He was born in Australia and immigrated to England in 1907. He spent several years working in commerce in London but gave up this profession to concentrate on music criticism. He was critic for the *Musical Standard* and the *New Statesman*. His first volume of poetry, which appeared in 1916, established him as a poet of merit, especially for the music of his verse and its philosophical content. In 1918, Turner married Delphine Dubuis, but the relationship was uneasy. His published works included the novels *Blow for Balloons* (1934), *Henry Airbubble in Search of a Circumference to His Breath* (1936), and *The Duchess of Popocatapetl* (1939). He wrote books of music criticism, *Beethoven; the Search for Reality, Orpheus, or The Music of the Future* (1926), *English Music, Variations on the Theme of Music*, and *Wagner*. He wrote experimental plays, among them *The Man Who Ate the Popomack* and *Smaragda's Lover*, both of which were published and performed. *Jupiter Translated* was performed in 1933. Among his many influential friends were Siegfried Sassoon, **James Stephens,**

Dorothy Wellesley, and **Lady Ottoline Morrell**. WBY was impressed with Turner's poetry; for a time they were close friends, and he included twelve of Turner's poems in *The Oxford Book of Modern Verse* (1936). In 1937, during rehearsals for the four poetry programs that WBY arranged for the **BBC**, Turner supported WBY in his efforts to restore poetry as a popular art form through unaccompanied ballads and songs. WBY had fourteen of Turner's books in his library (*OS.* nos. 2160–72).

REFERENCE: McKenna, Wayne. *W. J. Turner, Poet and Music Critic*. Gerrards Cross: Colin Smythe, 1990.

TWO PLAYS FOR DANCERS, collection of plays by WBY. It was published by the **Cuala Press** in 1919 in an edition of 400 copies. It contained two of WBY's plays written in the style of the Japanese **Noh,** *The Only Jealousy of Emer* and *The Dreaming of the Bones*, and a short preface in which WBY confirms his preference for this form of drama.

TWO ROCK MOUNTAIN. *See* **THREE ROCK MOUNTAIN**.

TYNAN, KATHARINE (1859–1931), poet and novelist. She was born in County Dublin, the daughter of Andrew Tynan, a wealthy farmer. In 1868, she moved with her family to a farm in Clondalkin, a village four and a half miles southwest of Dublin, on the Grand Canal. In her autobiography, *Twenty-five Years* (1913), she describes the family home, Whitehall, a charming thatched cottage and two-story annex set ten acres back from the main Tallaght to Clondalkin road. From 1869 to 1875, she attended the local convent school of St. Catherine of Drogheda. She published her first poem, "Dreamland," in *Young Ireland* in 1875, and with her collection *Louise de la Vallière*, which appeared in 1885, she became known as a successful poet. Although she was six years older than WBY, from 1885 to 1891, they were frequently in each other's company, often attending meetings of the Protestant Home Rule Association or the **Contemporary Club. John B. Yeats** painted her portrait, while WBY sat beside her in the studio reciting his poetry. They met, too, at the homes of **John O'Leary** and **Rose Kavanagh**. WBY valued her not only as a poet but also as a close companion through whom he could make contacts with those influential writers and editors who were her friends. She had no doubts about his poetic gifts, and in a review in *Irish Monthly*, March 1887, she hailed *Mosada* as a powerful and joyful work. After WBY and his family moved to London in 1887, she was a frequent correspondent. He stayed at Whitehall for two months, from 22 November 1887 to 26 January 1888, and again in August 1891. Indeed, on this last visit, it was believed by her family that WBY had proposed marriage to her, but she had refused him. From then on, the relationship cooled, and she is given scant attention in his autobiography. In 1893, she married Henry Albert Hinkson, a barrister and classics scholar, and they moved to England. There, she embarked upon a lucrative career in journalism, contributing articles on educational and feminist issues to English and American periodicals, including *The Pall Mall Gazette, The National Observer, The Providence Journal, The Catholic Worker*, and *The Boston Pilot*. She returned to Ireland when her husband was appointed resident magistrate for **County Mayo**. Despite her family's strong Republican sympathies, both she and her husband identified themselves as pro-British. With the death of her husband, she was forced to support her family of three children by her writing. She returned to England, where she lived for the rest of her life, maintaining an extraordinary output of novels, plays, poetry, and memoirs, including her four volumes of autobiography, *Twenty-five Years* (1913), *The Middle Years* (1916), *The Years of the Shadow* (1919), and *The Wandering Years* (1922). The first of these is especially interesting for the pen sketches it offers of the leading figures of the Irish Renaissance, principally WBY. Considered during the early years of the Celtic revival to be the most promising of the Irish poets, Tynan failed to develop as a writer. This was possibly due to the hack work she was called upon to do to support her family, but it also demonstrated an inability or unwillingness to reach below the external realities or go beyond her narrow Catholic and middle-class values. Among her published works are *Shamrocks* (1887), *Ballads and Lyrics* (1891), *The Way of a Maid* (1895), *Wind in the Trees: A Book of Country Verse* (1898), *Poems* (1901), *The Sweet Enemy* (1901), *Irish Poems* (1913), *Flower of Youth: Poems in War Time* (1915), and *The Holy War* (1916). WBY included her *Legends and Lyrics* [*sic*] in his list of "Best Irish Books" (*UP1*. 387).

REFERENCES: Fallon, Ann Connerton. *Katharine Tynan*. Boston: Twayne, 1979; Freyer, Grattan. *W. B. Yeats and the Anti-Democratic Tradition*. Dublin: Gill & Macmillan, 1981; Halladay, Jean R. *Eight Late Victorian Poets Shaping the Artistic Sensibility of an Age*. Lewiston, N.Y.: E. Mellen, 1993; Marcus, Phillip L. *Yeats and the Beginning of the Irish Renaissance*. Syracuse: Syracuse University Press, 1987; McHugh, Roger, ed. *Letters to Katharine Tynan*. New York: McMullen Books, 1953; Rose, Marilyn Gaddis. *Katharine Tynan*. Lewisburg, Pa.: Bucknell University Press, 1973.

U

UATHACH, daughter of **Scathach**. She became **Cuchulain's** mistress during the period of one year and a day when he was training on Scathach's Island (reputed to be the Isle of Skye, Scotland). In *On Baile's Strand* (*CPl.* 275), desperate to hear that it is not, as he fears, his own child by the warrior-queen **Aoife** he has slain, Cuchulain questions the **Blind Man**, who knows the truth. He asks if the **Young Man** was the son of Uathach or any of the other Scottish queens.

REFERENCE: Ellis, Peter Berresford. *Dictionary of Celtic Mythology*. New York: Oxford University Press, 1992.

ULADH. *See* **ULSTER**.

ULSTER (Irish: *Uladh*), most northerly of the ancient provinces of Ireland. It is likely that it encompassed all of the land north of a line from the River Drowes in the west to the River **Boyne** in the east. It took its name from the Ulaidh, the dominant people of Ulster. Theirs was an aristocratic warrior society, and a vivid picture of the lifestyle may be drawn from the epic *Táin Bó Cuailnge*. During this heroic age, believed to be contemporaneous with **Christ**, Ulster was ruled by **Conchubar** from his capital seat at **Emain Macha**. He was the focus of a group of knights of the **Red Branch**, among them **Cuchulain, Conall Caernach**, **Lagaire**, and **Fergus**. Conchubar fell in love with the fated **Deirdre**, who eloped with her lover **Naoise**, and it was at Emain Macha that Deirdre took her own life. When the epic *Táin Bó Cuailnge* was written down in the twelfth century, the Ulaidh ruled little more than the counties of Antrim and **Down**, the rest having been taken from them in the fifth century by Niall of the Nine Hostages, king of **Tara**. The Plantation of Ulster took place in the seventeenth century, when James I of England colonized the northern province with Scottish and English settlers. Since the partition of Ireland in 1922, the modern province of Ulster consists of counties Antrim, Down, Armagh, Tyrone, Fermanagh, and Londonderry. A number of WBY's closest associates, including **AE** and **Charles Johnston**, were from Ulster. His father, **John B. Yeats**, was born in Tullylish in County Down, the son of a local rector in the Church of Ireland. WBY made several trips to Ulster and to Belfast, its capital (*M.* 45, 59), although he was out of sympathy with the hardheaded Protestant Orangemen of the North. The ancient province of Ulster is mentioned by WBY in the poems "Under the Moon" (*CP.* 91) and "Baile and Aillinn" (*CP.* 459).

REFERENCES: Bardon, Jonathan. *A History of Ulster.* Belfast: Blackstaff, 1992; Dames, Michael. *Mythic Ireland.* 1992. Reprint, New York: Thames & Hudson, 1996; Ellis, Peter Berresford. *Dictionary of Celtic Mythology.* New York: Oxford University Press, 1992; Mac Cana, Proinsias. *Celtic Mythology.* Feltham, Middlesex: Newnes, 1983.

UNICORN FROM THE STARS, THE, three-act play in prose. It was published in New York, 1908, and subsequently in *The Unicorn from the Stars and Other Plays* (1908) and *Collected Works* (1908). It was included in ***The Collected Plays of W. B. Yeats*** (1934, 1952). *The Unicorn from the Stars* was based on an earlier five-act play, "Where There Is Nothing," which was apparently written by WBY in two weeks (with the help of **Lady Gregory** and **Douglas Hyde**) to keep **George Moore** from stealing the plot (*WL.* 503). Although "Where There Is Nothing" was published in *The United Irishman,* 1 November 1902, and performed at the Royal Court Theatre, London, 26 June 1904, WBY disliked the play and withdrew it from publication. Later, he decided to rewrite it with Lady Gregory. The action of *The Unicorn from the Stars,* which he claims is almost wholly Lady Gregory's in craft but his in thought (*VPl.* 712), concerns a young visionary, Martin **Hearne**. At the opening of the play, Martin awakens from a trance, claiming to have ridden a white unicorn and to have been given a command that he can no longer remember. When a thieving beggar exclaims, "Destruction on us all!," Martin recalls the instruction he has been given. Under the banner of a white unicorn, he exhorts the beggars to destroy the Law and the Church. They begin by setting fire to the golden coach being prepared for the Lord Lieutenant and then plunder and destroy a big house in the neighborhood. Martin, who has taken part in the attack, falls into another trance. When he wakes, he claims to have misunderstood the previous command. The battle was not against Law and the Church but was to be fought in the mind. Only when the self has rejected the world can one know the true joy of heaven— where there is nothing, there is God. As Martin shares this visionary dream, he is accidentally killed by the police, who have come to arrest the beggars. The action of the play is original, but it is based on the story "Where there is Nothing, there is God" included by WBY in ***The Secret Rose*** (1897) (*MY.* 184). The title *The Unicorn from the Stars* was taken from the third grade of **The Order of the Golden Dawn,** *Monocris de Astris* (the Unicorn from the Stars), and many references and symbols in the play are closely related to

WBY's occult studies, an aspect dealt with by Katharine Worth in her introduction to *Where There Is Nothing* and *The Unicorn from the Stars* (1987). The first performance was given at the **Abbey Theatre**, November 1907, with the following cast: **Father John**, Ernest Vaughan; Thomas Hearne, Arthur Sinclair; Andrew Hearne, J. A. O'Rourke; Martin Hearne, **Frank Fay; Johnny Bocach, W. G. Fay; Paudeen**, J. M. Kerrigan; **Biddy Lally, Máire O'Neill**; Nanny, Brigit O'Dempsey.

REFERENCES: Ellis, Sylvia C. *The Plays of W. B. Yeats: Yeats and the Dancer*. London: Macmillan, 1995; Miller, Liam. *The Noble Drama of W. B. Yeats*. Dublin: Dolmen, 1977; Oppel, Frances Nesbitt. *Mask and Tragedy: Yeats and Nietzsche, 1902–10*. Charlottesville: University Press of Virginia, 1987; Worth, Katharine, ed. *Where There Is Nothing: The Unicorn from the Stars*. Washington, D.C.: Catholic University of America Press, 1987.

UNWIN, T. FISHER (1848–1935), publisher. In 1882, T. Fisher Unwin bought the firm of Marshall Japp & Company and began publishing under his own imprint. Among his readers was **Edward Garnett**, who introduced him to WBY. Together, WBY and Unwin embarked on a plan to publish in England books of Irish interest. Despite the opposition of WBY, the series, which came to be known as the **New Irish Library**, was edited by **Sir Charles Gavan Duffy**. To WBY's satisfaction, the series proved unsuccessful. Unwin, however, was generous to WBY, publishing *John Sherman and Dhoya* (1891), *The Countess Kathleen and Various Legends and Lyrics* (1892), *The Land of Heart's Desire* (1894), and *Poems* (1895), in addition to the periodicals *Beltaine* (1899–1900) and *Samhain* (1902–4) and *Irish Fairy Tales* (1892), edited by WBY.

REFERENCE: Gerber, Helmut E., ed. *George Moore in Transition: Letters to T. Fisher Unwin and Lena Milman*. Detroit: Wayne State University Press, 1968.

URBINO, town in Italy. WBY visited Urbino while on a visit to Italy with **Lady Gregory** and her son **Robert** in April 1907. He was impressed with the great ducal palace, which had been converted from a fortress by Federico da Montefeltro, duke of Urbino, in the fifteenth century. In the beautifully proportioned palace, set picturesquely on a steep hill, the duke founded his schools of Art and Poetry, Mathematics and Humanism, and built a library, which was then the largest in Europe. For WBY, the court of Federico and his son **Guidobaldo** was a model of enlightenment, possessing all the virtues of the Italian Renaissance, celebrated in *The Book of the Courtier* (1528) by *Baldassare Castiglione*.

REFERENCE: Rotondi, Pasquale. *The Ducal Palace of Urbino: Its Architecture and Decoration*. New York: Transatlantic Arts, 1969.

USNA [also Usnach] [Irish: *Uisnach*], husband of Ebhla and father of **Naoise**, Ainnle, and **Ardan**. All three brothers were knights of the **Red Branch**, and their moving story is told in "The Fate of the Sons of Uisnech," a tale preserved in the *Yellow Book of Lecan* and later added to the **Ulster** Cycle as part of ***Táin Bó Cuailnge***. Ainnle and Ardan accompany the lovers Naoise and **Deirdre** to Scotland. **Conchubar**, the High King, lures them back to Ulster with fake promises and has all three brothers treacherously put to death. The story is dramatically told by WBY in his play ***Deirdre***. He refers to the sons of Usna in ***The Death of Cuchulain*** (*CPl.* 704) and to their death in ''The Rose of the World'' (*CP*. 41).

REFERENCES: Dames, Michael. *Mythic Ireland*. 1992. Reprint, New York: Thames & Hudson, 1996; Ellis, Peter Berresford. *Dictionary of Celtic Mythology*. New York: Oxford University Press, 1992; Mac Cana, Proinsias. *Celtic Mythology*. Feltham, Middlesex: Newnes, 1983.

USNACH. *See* **USNA**.

V

VALLEY OF THE BLACK PIG. According to WBY, the Valley of the Black Pig was believed to be the site of a battle in which Ireland's enemies would be finally vanquished (*CP*. 526–27). A number of possible locations throughout Ireland have been suggested, but in "The Chase of the Enchanted Pigs of Aenghus an Bhroga," published in *Transactions of the Ossianic Society* (1861), there is a reference to the Valley of the Black Pig in **Ulster**. There are remnants of Black Pig's Dyke in counties Cavan, Longford, and Leitrim, on the border between Ulster and the rest of Ireland, parts of a defensive wall intended to guard the passes into ancient Ulster. See also "The Valley of the Black Pig" (*CP*. 73).

REFERENCE: McGarry, James P. *Place Names in the Writings of William Butler Yeats*. Gerrards Cross: Colin Smythe, 1976.

VAN DIEMEN'S LAND, former name for Tasmania, an island state in southeast Australia. The island, which lies 150 miles from the mainland, was discovered in 1642 by Abel Tasman, a Dutch navigator, who named it Van Diemen's Land. In 1803, England took possession of the island and established a penal colony at Hobart, the capital. With the last shipment of convicts in 1853, the name was changed to Tasmania. It was federated as a state of the Commonwealth of Australia in 1901. **John Mitchel**, like others fighting for Irish independence, was tried for sedition in 1848 and sentenced to fourteen years' transportation to Van Diemen's Land. Thus, in the poems and ballads of the Young Ireland movement, the penal colony became a symbol of England's tyranny, as in "O Come All Ye Airy Bachelors," sung by **Johnny Bocach** in *The Unicorn from the Stars* (*CPl*. 354).

VANESSA. *See* **VAN HOMRIGH, HESTER**.

VAN HOMRIGH, HESTER (1691–1723), intimate friend of **Jonathan Swift**. She was the daughter of a rich Dutch merchant who became Lord Mayor of Dublin. While on a visit to London with her mother, in 1708, she met Swift at Dunstable. He took a fatherly interest in her, but she fell in love with him and moved to England. After she inherited a house from her father at Kildrogest (now **Celbridge**), near Dublin, she followed Swift to Ireland in 1714. For the following years, they met and exchanged passionate letters, Swift addressing her as Vanessa. In 1723, when rumors reached her of a marriage with **Esther Johnson** (**Stella**), she wrote to Stella to ascertain the truth. Furious, Swift rode to her home, confronted her with the letter, and left. They never met again, and Hester van Homrigh was dead one month later. Swift's poem ''Cadenus and Vanessa'' comments on the tragic shortcomings of a love relationship. In WBY's play *The Words upon the Window-Pane*, Vanessa speaks passionately of her love for Swift through the medium **Mrs. Henderson** (*CPl.* 609–11).

REFERENCE: Hardy, Evelyn. *The Conjured Spirit, Swift: A Study in the Relationship of Swift, Stella, and Vanessa*. 1949. Reprint, Westport, Conn.: Greenwood, 1973.

VERLAINE, PAUL (1844–96), poet. He was born in Metz, the only child of a French army officer. He went to a prestigious school in Paris and, after graduation, was employed by an insurance company and in the city government. He made the acquaintance of **Mallarmé** and **Villiers de L'Isle-Adam**, who introduced him to members of the Parnassian group and other contemporary writers. His first publication, *Poèms saturniens*, a collection of melancholy love poems, was published in 1863. In 1869, he married sixteen-year-old Mathilde Mauté, to whom he wrote *La bonne chanson*. His relationship with his wife was undermined by his infatuation with Arthur Rimbaud, who came to live with them in 1871. Verlaine then left his wife and infant son to travel with Rimbaud in France and Belgium. They moved to England, where Verlaine completed his *Romances sans paroles*, a collection of unsurpassed lyrical verse, published in 1874 while he was in prison in Mons for wounding Rimbaud in a quarrel. While in prison, Verlaine regretted the excesses of his profligate life. On his release, he rejected Rimbaud and moved to England, where he taught French and drawing in high schools and made the acquaintance of **Tennyson** and **Swinburne**. He returned to France in 1877 to find his ''Art poétique'' enthusiastically adopted by the young Symbolists. After a series of personal losses, and his failure to reestablish a relationship with his wife, he lapsed into alcoholism and debauchery in the bohemian demimonde of Paris. Verlaine was one of the first Symbolists, and his poetry, which draws on his intense personal life, is remarkable for an emotional depth that never fails to reveal an underlying honesty and naïveté, especially in the major collections *Romances sans paroles* (1874) and *Sagesse* (1881). His work loses much in translation, but **Arthur Symons** and **Ernest Dowson** made extremely good translations of his lyrics. WBY admired Verlaine; as a young man, he secretly envied the dissolute lifestyle out of which he could write such moving and sensual verse. He called with him at his home in the Rue St. Jacques, when he visited Paris for the first time, February 1894, and recorded his impressions of the visit in the *Savoy*, April 1896 (*UP1*. 398–99), and in "The Tragic Generation" (*A*. 341–42). In the course of the visit, the French poet discussed **Shakespeare, Maeterlinck, Victor Hugo**, and Tennyson. Of special interest were his observations on Villiers de L'Isle Adam's *Axël*, which WBY had just seen (*UP1*. 324–25). In "The Tree of Life" (*EI*. 270–72), WBY reflects that while the French poet drew on his own life in his poetry, he himself cared for nothing but visions and states of mind.

REFERENCES: Hillery, David. *Verlaine: Fixing an Image*. Durham: University of Durham, 1988; Rabate, Jean-Michel. *The Ghosts of Modernity*. Gainesville: University Press of Florida, 1996; Stephen, Philip. *Paul Verlaine and the Decadence*. Manchester: University of Manchester, 1974.

VERNON, DIANA. *See* **SHAKESPEAR, OLIVIA**.

VERONESE, PAOLO (1528–88), Italian painter of the Venetian school. Born Paolo Caliari, in Verona, he was responsible for the ceiling paintings in the ducal palace in Venice. He executed many works for the Church of San Sebastiano, in which he interpreted religious scenes in a secular and decorative manner, without reference to the supernatural. As a result, he was called before the Inquisition in 1573 and ordered to change details of *Christ in the House of Levi*, a painting that they claimed was filled with "buffoons and similar vulgarities." Veronese defended his right to introduce directly observed detail into a religious work, an attitude not generally accepted in Europe until the nineteenth century. Among his paintings are *The Rape of Europa, Triumph of Venice*, and *Venice Ruling with Justice and Peace*, all of which are in the ducal palace in Venice. His treatment of the human body is referred to by WBY in "Michael Robartes and the Dancer" (*CP*. 198).

REFERENCES: Rearick, William R. *The Art of Paolo Veronese, 1528–1588*. Cambridge: Cambridge University Press, 1988; Watson, Peter. *Wisdom and Strength: The Biography of a Renaissance Masterpiece*. New York: Doubleday, 1989.

VERONICA, a woman who is reputed to have given her veil (or napkin) to **Christ** on his way to Calvary. The veil, which retained the print of Christ's face, is preserved as a holy relic in the Vatican in Rome. Although known familiarly as Saint Veronica, she does not appear in the official calendar of saints. See "Veronica's Napkin" (*CP*. 270). In the poem, WBY refers to "Berenice's Hair." Veronica is the Latin form of the Greek **Berenice**.

VIJAYA, figure from Hindu mythology. He is a hunter in WBY's dramatic love poem "Anashuya and Vijaya" (*CP*. 10). His name means "victorious."

VILLIERS DE L'ISLE-ADAM, [PHILIPPE] AUGUSTE, [COMTE DE] (1838–89), French Symbolist writer and visionary. He was the son of an impoverished nobleman from Brittany in northern France who could trace his ancestry back to the eleventh century. After his arrival in Paris, Villiers de L'Isle-Adam became friends with Baudelaire and **Mallarmé**. He published his first novel, *Isis*, in 1862 but lived unrecognized and in poverty until the 1880s, when his major works *Les Contes cruels* (1883), *L'Eve future* (1886), and *Axël* (1886) achieved some popularity, especially among the youth of Paris. *Axël* is regarded as the first Symbolist drama and a milestone in theater history. It is a dramatic poem in prose in which two lovers sacrifice earthly wealth, power, and love to seek eternal life through death. This allegorical drama, which was not performed until after the author's death, premiered at a private performance at the Théâtre de la Gaîté Lyrique, Paris, 26 February 1894. WBY attended this premiere, accompanied by **Maud Gonne**, and was so moved by the play that he studiously tried to read it in the original, despite his scant knowledge of the French language. He discussed the production when he met **Paul Verlaine** (*UP1*. 399). In the preface to H. P. R. Finberg's translation of *Axël* (1925), WBY pays tribute to the influence of Villiers de L'Isle-Adam on his own verse, noting that his symbols dominated his imagination for many years (*UP1*. 322–25). Echoes of the language and imagery of *Axël* are to be found in *The Wind Among the Reeds* (1899) and in the final lines of *The Shadowy Waters* (*CPl*. 166–67). The production confirmed WBY's ideas about the staging of symbolic drama. A first edition of *Axël* and a copy of Finberg's translation were in WBY's library (*OS*. nos. 2200–2201).

REFERENCES: Raitt, A. W. *The Life of Villiers de L'Isle–Adam*. Oxford: Clarendon, 1981; Villiers de L'Isle-Adam, Philippe Auguste. *Axël*. Trans. June Guicharnaud. Englewood Cliffs, N.J.: Prentice-Hall, 1970.

VIRGIL (70–19 B.C.), Roman poet. He was born near Mantua and grew up on his father's farm. In 41 B.C., he journeyed to Rome, where he published *The Eclogues* (37 B.C.), an idealized picture of rural life in Italy. With *The Georgics* (30 B.C.), his poetry became more realistic, conveying a more truthful response to living and working in the country. The remainder of his life was devoted to his epic, *The Aeneid*. Virgil's writing had a profound influence on later writers, most notably **Dante**. WBY had copies of *The Eclogues of Virgil*, translated and illustrated by **Samuel Palmer**, and C. Davidson's *The Works of Virgil, Literally Translated into English Prose* (1875) in his library (*OS*. nos. 2202–3), and he admired **William Blake's** illustrations for an edition of Virgil's *Eclogue I* (1821), buying slides of seven of them to illustrate the lecture ''William Blake and His School,'' which he gave at the **Abbey Theatre**, 14 April 1918, and on his American **Lecture Tour** in 1920. In the essay ''Poetry and Tradition'' (*EI*. 246), WBY recalls the eighteenth-century Ireland of **Henry Grattan**, an ideal world where people still read Virgil and **Homer**. In *The Death of Cuchulain* (*CPl*. 693), the **Old Man** in the prologue also speaks of such a time.

REFERENCE: Wagenvoort, H. *Studies in Roman Literature, Culture, and Religion*. New York: Garland, 1978.

VISION, A, publication. Soon after his marriage in 1917, WBY discovered his wife had the gift of automatic writing, and for the next several years, he laboriously transcribed and organized this esoteric material from unknown communicators. It was published in 1926 by T. Werner Laurie in an edition of 600 copies, each signed by the author. After consolidating his ideas with readings from philosophy, principally **Plato** and the Neoplatonists, he produced a revised version in 1929, and a final version was published by the Macmillan Company in 1937. *A Vision* is in five parts: The Great Wheel; The Completed Symbol; The Soul of Judgment; The Great Year of the Ancients; and Dove or Swan. According to WBY's theory of the Great Wheel, history may be divided into 2,000-year cycles, with each cycle corresponding to one of twenty-eight phases of the moon. Men and women are classified on a scale of subjectivity to objectivity, each corresponding to twenty-six phases of the lunar month, since complete objectivity and complete subjectivity (phase one and phase fifteen, respectively) cannot exist. In his introduction to *A Vision*, WBY claims to have been told by the unknown communicators that they had come to give him "metaphors for poetry" (*AV*. 8). He believed the material had made a major contribution to his verse, chiefly to his collections *The Tower* and *The Winding Stair and Other Poems*. No work by WBY has caused more controversy than *A Vision*, although recent scholars suggest that his later poetry and drama cannot be fully understood without it.

REFERENCES: Frye, Northrop. "The Rising of the Moon: A Study of *A Vision*." In *An Honored Guest: New Essays on W. B. Yeats*, ed. Denis Donoghue and J. R. Mulryne. London: Edward Arnold, 1965; Hough, Graham. *The Mystery Religion of W. B. Yeats*. Sussex: Harvester, 1984; Malins, Edward, and Purkis, John. *A Preface to Yeats*. London: 1974. Reprint, Longman, 1994; Moore, Virginia. *The Unicorn: William Butler Yeats' Search for Reality*. New York: Octagon Books, 1973.

VON HÜGEL, BARON FRIEDRICH [FREIHERR] (1852–1925), theologian. He was born in Florence, the son of an Austrian diplomat. After his marriage in 1873, he settled in England, where he wrote the two works that profoundly influenced modern Catholicism: *The Mystical Element of Religion as Studied in Saint Catherine of Genoa and Her Friends* (1908) and *Eternal Life* (1912). Von Hügel was an independent thinker who advocated moral responsibility and the exercise of free will in addition to a belief in the supernatural life. WBY read von Hügel and admired his objectivity, but in Section VIII of "Vacillation" (*CP*. 282), he finally dismissed von Hügel's comforting religious doctrine.

REFERENCES: Barmann, Lawrence F. *Baron Friedrich von Hügel and the Modernist Crisis in England*. Cambridge: Cambridge University Press, 1972; Lester-Garland, L. *The Religious Philosophy of Baron F. von Hügel*. London: Dent, 1933.

W

WADDING, LUKE (1588–1657), Franciscan monk. He was born in Waterford, Ireland, to a wealthy Anglo-Catholic family and educated in the Irish College at Lisbon, Portugal. After becoming president of the Irish College at Salamanca, he moved to Rome, where he founded the College of St. Isadore. He was rector there for fourteen years. On his death, he bequeathed to the college 5,000 books and 800 manuscripts. Throughout his life, he maintained close connections with his native Ireland. His portrait by José Ribera (1588–1652), which is referred to by WBY in ''Demon and Beast'' (*CP*. 209), is in the **National Gallery of Ireland**.

REFERENCE: Share, Bernard. *Irish Lives: Biographies of Fifty Famous Irish Men and Women*. Dublin: Allen Figgis, 1971.

WAGNER, RICHARD (1813–83), composer and librettist. He was born in Leipzig, Germany, and attended Kreuzschule, Dresden, and Nicholaischule, Leipzig. He was an undistinguished scholar, but he was avidly interested in music and taught himself piano and composition. At Leipzig University, he disdained academic studies except for a detailed personal reading of the scores of the major composers, especially the quartets and symphonies of Beethoven. After many disappointments, his opera *Rienzi* (1838–40) was successfully performed in Dresden in 1842. *Der fliegende Holländer* (1841) was presented the following year, but its innovative integration of music and drama puzzled the audience. He was appointed conductor of the court opera and embarked upon writing a series of operas, beginning with *Tannhäuser* (1845) and *Lohengrin*, which brought the German Romantic movement to its culmination. He became involved in the German revolution of 1848–49 and was active in the Dresden uprising of 1849. When a warrant was issued for his arrest, he escaped to Zürich, unable to attend the premiere of *Lohengrin*, conducted at Weimar by Liszt. In exile, he explored a revolutionary style of music theater and published his aesthetic theories in a series of prose works, including *Art and Revolution, The Art Work of the Future*, and *Opera and Drama*. After studying the Siegfried legend and Norse myths, he embarked on his master work *Der Ring des Nibelungen* (1853–74), consisting of the tetralogy *Das Rheingold* (1853–54), *Die Walküre* (1854–56), *Siegfried* (1856–69), and *Götterdämmerung* (1874). In these operas, for which he wrote the libretti, he fused music and text, developing thematic phrases, later called leitmotiv, to characterize an episode or person. In 1861 he was allowed to return to Germany, but having lived an extravagant lifestyle abroad, he was penniless. He found a wealthy patron in Louis II, who invited him to take up residence in Munich and financed productions of his major works, including *Tristan und Isolde* (1857–59) and *Die Meistersinger von Nürnberg* (1862–67), his only comic opera. In 1872, Wagner moved to Bayreuth, Bavaria. There he built a theater, Das Festspielhaus, a performing space specially designed to meet the presentational demands of his music-dramas, and wrote his last work, *Parsifal* (1877–82), a sacred festival drama. The complete Ring Cycle was presented at Bayreuth in 1876, and since then, except for breaks during World Wars I and II, Bayreuth has presented annual festivals of Wagner's work. WBY was inspired by Wagner in the setting up of a national theater in Ireland, believing that with his range of operas on mythological themes, Wagner had given to Germany a soul in the same way that Greek tragedy had given an identity to ancient Greece. Thus, he believed him to be the most passionate influence in modern Europe (*UP2*. 125), while in *The Celtic Element of Literature* (*EI*. 186), he cites him, with **Ibsen** and **William Morris**, for having created a "new romance" out of the Scandinavian myths (*EI*. 186). In his essay *At Stratford-on-Avon* (*EI*. 99), he deplores the "half-round theatre" at Stratford, comparing it unfavorably with Wagner's theater at Bayreuth.

REFERENCE: Sabor, Rudolph. *The Real Wagner*. London: Deutsch, 1987.

WALSH, EDWARD (1805–50), translator and political activist. He was born in Londonderry, the son of a soldier from **Cork** (county). After being educated at a hedge-school, he became a hedge-schoolmaster. He was imprisoned for taking part in a tithe war and, on his release, became a teacher at a national school in Mallow, County Cork, and later in County Waterford. He was a teacher at the convict establishment at Spike Island, County Cork, but was dismissed because of his association with **John Mitchel**. He spent his final years in ill health and penury, teaching in the Cork workhouse. He contributed poems and articles to *The Nation* and the *Dublin Penny Journal*. Later, he was subeditor of *The Monitor*, a Dublin weekly. He is best known for his translations *Reliques of Irish Jacobite Poetry, with Metrical Translations* (1844) and *Irish Popular Songs, Translated with Notes* (1847). In his essay "Popular Ballad Poetry of Ireland" (*UP1*. 151–52), WBY writes movingly of Edward Walsh and his translations from the Gaelic, while in "Poetry and Tradition" (*EI*. 248), he acknowledges

Walsh as one of the early influences on his own use of rural Ireland as a source of inspiration. In an article on Irish fairies, he quotes Walsh's poem "The Fairy Nurse" (*UP1*. 178), a poem similar to WBY's "The Unappeasable Host" (*CP*. 65). Later, he was to prefer the translations from the Irish of **Douglas Hyde** to those of Walsh (*UP1*. 295).

REFERENCE: Kickham, Charles J. "Edward Walsh: A Memoir." In *The Valley Near Slievenamon*, ed. James Maher. Kilkenny: Kilkenny People, 1942.

WANDERINGS OF OISIN, THE. See WANDERINGS OF OISIN AND OTHER POEMS, THE.

WANDERINGS OF OISIN AND OTHER POEMS, THE, poetry collection. The volume contained the long, dramatic poem *The Wanderings of Oisin* in addition to thirteen other poems (later included in *Crossways*), among them "The Song of the Happy Shepherd" (*CP*. 7), "The Madness of King Goll" (*CP*. 17), "The Stolen Child" (*CP*. 20), "Down by the Salley Gardens" (*CP*. 22), and "The Ballad of Moll Magee" (*CP*. 25). The collection was first published by **Kegan Paul** in 1889. The title poem is in the form of a verse dialogue between the old warrior **Oisin** and **St. Patrick** and recounts Oisin's adventures in **Tir-nan-Oge** with the immortal **Niamh**. The poem is in three parts. In Part I, Oisin falls in love with Niamh and agrees to go with her to the Land of the Ever Young, where there is continuous music and dancing. In Part II, they visit the Island of Many Fears, while in Part III, they journey to the Island of Forgetfulness. The poem ends with Oisin returning to the mortal world. WBY is thought to have based his narrative on Bryan O'Looney's translation of the poem from the Gaelic, *The Lay of Oisin and the Land of Youth*, although it has been suggested that WBY worked from the Gaelic Union school edition of the poem, which contained a translation. WBY revised the poem many times and included it with other narrative poems at the end of his *Collected Poems* (1933). Before his death, however, he decided to place it at the front of the definitive edition of his poems, thus emphasizing its importance to his whole poetic output. *The Wanderings of Oisin* is dedicated to **Edwin J. Ellis**, with whom WBY collaborated on *The Works of William Blake* (1893).

REFERENCES: Dalsimer, A. M. "W. B. Yeats, *The Wanderings of Oisin*: Blueprint for a Renaissance." Éire II, no. 2 (1976); Telfer, Giles W. L. *Yeats's Idea of the Gael*. Dublin: Dolmen, 1965.

WATT, A[LEXANDER] P[OLLOCK] (1837–1914), literary agent. He was born in Edinburgh, Scotland. After working with his brother-in-law, who was a publisher, he set himself up as a literary agent, in time becoming the foremost in Britain. From June 1900, A. P. Watt represented WBY, placing his books and articles with publishers for a flat rate of ten percent. For this he contacted publishers, negotiated contracts, and ensured that financial obligations were met.

Since WBY's publishing affairs had been highly disorganized, it was a very satisfactory arrangement. Watt became WBY's exclusive agent in May 1901.

WATTS, GEORGE FREDERIC (1817–1904), painter and sculptor. After studying at the Royal Academy, London, he visited Italy and developed an enthusiasm for Venetian painting and Greek sculpture. On his return to London, where he became known as "England's **Michelangelo**," he completed a number of commissions for large, decorative murals, including the fresco *Justice* in Lincoln's Inn. He established himself as a leading society painter and influenced his contemporaries with his allegorical paintings, such as *Love and Life* (1885), *Love and Death*, and *Hope* (1886). **John B. Yeats** admired Watts, whose painting was distinguished by vibrant color and soft contours, and he shared his enthusiasm with WBY, who in "The Bounty of Sweden" (*A*. 550) named Watts among the "great myth-makers and mask-makers." WBY was impressed with Watts's portraits, including one of **William Morris** (1870) acquired by the National Gallery, London. A reproduction of this painting hung over his mantelpiece and inspired his description of Morris in "Four Years: 1887–91" (*A*. 141). In January 1906, on the occasion of a Watts's retrospective mounted by **Hugh Lane** in Dublin, WBY gave a lecture on Watts. In the lecture, "The Ideal in Art," he praised those paintings in which Watts was consciously trying not to be a prophet or preacher and acknowledged that he owed to Watts the recognition of the viability of Irish myth as sources for inspiration and expression (*UP2*. 342–45).

REFERENCES: Gaja, Katerine. *G. F. Watts in Italy: A Portrait of the Artist as a Young Man*. Florence: L. S. Olschki, 1995; Watts, Mary S. *George Frederic Watts*. London: Macmillan, 1912.

WELLESLEY, DOROTHY [VIOLET, DUCHESS OF WELLINGTON] (1889–1956), poet. She was born Dorothy Ashton, in Berkshire. In 1899, her mother, after the early death of her first husband, married the earl of Scarborough and introduced her daughter to the world of aristocratic privilege. After her own marriage in 1914 to Gerald, seventh duke of Wellington, Dorothy Wellesley lived at Penns in the Rocks, an eighteenth-century home in East Sussex. WBY stayed there in June 1935. He found, in the ordered gardens and sophisticated company, an atmosphere reminiscent of **Coole Park**. He returned to Penns in the Rocks for extended periods during 1937 and 1938. Dorothy Wellesley was a published poet before she met WBY (her first anthology had been published in 1920), but she lacked critical assessment. He read her poetry while making his selection for *The Oxford Book of Modern Verse* (1936), and he was impressed by its imagery and precision of style. It is apparent from his letters, and the many references to her in his essays, that Lady Dorothy became an important friend and literary confidante during the final four years of his life. He wrote an enthusiastic introduction for her anthology *Selections from the Poems of Dorothy Wellesley* (1936) and, with her, edited *Broadsides: A Collection of New Irish* *and English Songs* (1937). He included eight of her poems in *The Oxford Book of Modern Verse*, and he had copies of her *Poems of Ten Years: 1924–1934* (1934) and *Selections from the Poems of Dorothy Wellesley* in his library (*OS.* nos. 2235–36). His poem "To Dorothy Wellesley" (*CP.* 349) includes a reference to Lady Dorothy's Great Dane, named Brutus.

REFERENCES: O'Shea, Edward. "Yeats as Editor: Dorothy Wellesley's *Selections*." *English Language Notes* (December 1973); Wellesley, Dorothy. *Letters on Poetry from W. B. Yeats to Dorothy Wellesley*, ed. Kathleen Raine. 1940. Reprint, London: Oxford University Press, 1964.

WHEELS AND BUTTERFLIES, collection of plays and introductions by WBY. The volume, which was published by Macmillan and Company in London (1934) and New York (1935), consisted of four short plays: ***The Words upon the Window-Pane, Fighting the Waves*** (*VPl.* 528), ***The Resurrection***, and ***The Cat and the Moon***. It included introductions to all four plays. As he explained in a letter to **Olivia Shakespear** (*WL.* 779), the "Wheels" of the title were the introductions, intended for the many small societies meeting in Dublin, while the "Butterflies" were for his friends. The collection contained the music for *Fighting the Waves* composed by **George Antheil**.

WHERE THERE IS NOTHING. *See UNICORN FROM THE STARS, THE*.

WHISTLER, JAMES [ABBOTT] McNEILL (1834–1903), painter. He was born in Lowell, Massachusetts, the son of a civil engineer who was descended from an old British family with Irish connections. He attended the Military Academy at West Point but left to pursue a career as a painter. In 1855, he went to Paris, where he adopted a bohemian lifestyle, and became influenced by the realist painters Courbet and Fantin-Latour. He achieved some success when his work was exhibited in Paris in 1863, but, attracted by the Pre-Raphaelite movement, he moved to London. There he met **Dante Gabriel Rossetti** and acquired an appreciation for Japanese art, which influenced the color and style of much of his work, including *Rose and Silver: La Princesse du Pays de la Porcelaine* (1864), *Symphony in Grey and Green: The Ocean* (1866–67), *Arrangement in Grey and Black, No. 1: The Artist's Mother* (1873), and *Old Battersea Bridge: Nocturne—Blue and Gold* (1872–75). He adopted the credo "Art for art's sake," and influenced by the abstract nature of music, he gave musical titles to his paintings, among them *Symphony* and *Harmony*. He painted a series of nocturnes using a special technique modeled on the style of Oriental calligraphy. He excelled in book design, etching, and lithography, as well as pastel, and wrote critical essays that made a major contribution to art theory. In 1877 he brought a libel suit against **John Ruskin**, and although successful, the court costs were substantial and resulted in his bankruptcy. He left London for Venice in 1879. There he became a celebrity and produced fine works in pastels and watercolor. He returned to London, where he became a dominant figure in the social art world and engaged in controversy with **Oscar Wilde**. After his marriage in 1888, he spent his time increasingly in Paris. As an art student, WBY was pleased when an exhibition of Whistler's paintings was shown in Dublin at the Royal Hibernian Academy (*A*. 82), and in 1898, he wrote enthusiastically about Whistler's use of pattern and rhythm in pictures in which the human figure had almost disappeared (*M*. 283–84).

REFERENCES: Anderson, Ronald. *James McNeill Whistler: Beyond the Myth*. New York: Carroll & Graf, 1995; Fleming, Gordon H. *James Abbott McNeill Whistler: A Life*. New York: St. Martin's, 1991; Weintraub, Stanley. *Whistler: A Biography*. New York: Weybright and Talley, 1974.

WHITMAN, WALT[ER] (1819–92), poet. He was born in West Hills, New York, the son of a carpenter. After attending public school in Brooklyn, he became apprenticed to a local printer. Later he worked in a printing shop in New York City, before moving to Long Island in 1835 to teach in the county schools. In 1838, he edited a local newspaper, the *Long-Islander*, before returning to New York City to work as a printer and journalist. Becoming involved in Democratic politics, he was editor of the prestigious *Brooklyn Eagle* but lost his job when he supported the Free Soil Party. He moved for a time to New Orleans but returned to New York to devote himself to writing. In 1855, he published the poetry collection that established his reputation, *Leaves of Grass*. The volume, which contained twelve poems, including ''Song of Myself,'' was written in a verse form reminiscent of the King James version of the Bible. The poems proclaimed human freedom and were so unashamedly outspoken in their celebration of human sexuality that he had to publish and set some of the type himself. With his recognition by the American poet Ralph Waldo Emerson, he issued a second edition, in 1856, and a third in 1860. During the American Civil War (1861–65), he worked as a nurse in the Union Army hospitals in Washington, D.C. He published his war poetry in *Drum-Taps* (1865), a collection that reflected his deepening awareness of the significance of the Civil War, and *Sequel to Drum-Taps* (1865–66), which contained ''When Lilacs Last in the Dooryard Bloom'd,'' an elegy for Abraham Lincoln. His prose collection *Democratic Vistas* appeared in 1871. A stroke in 1873 left him partially paralyzed, and he returned to Camden, New Jersey, where he remained for the rest of his life. He continued revising and working on *Leaves of Grass*, work very important to the development of modern poetry in Europe and the United States. WBY admired Whitman and, as a young man, carried a copy of Whitman's poems around in his pocket. As he wrote to an unnamed correspondent, possibly in 1887, he believed Whitman to be ''the greatest teacher of these decades'' (*WL*. 32). He was influenced, as in so many of his likes and dislikes, by the enthusiasm of his father and by **Edward Dowden**, who was a personal friend of the American poet and responsible for Whitman's popularity in Europe at a time when he was ignored by the majority of American readers and critics. Modeling himself on his father, who imitated the gregarious Whitman, WBY sought out

the company of other poets and socialized—behavior that brought a sharp re-
proof from **John O'Leary**, who advised him to be solitary and aloof (*A.* 229).
It was an occasion for some pride when WBY learned that Whitman had read
with interest his article on **Sir Samuel Ferguson**, news brought to him by
Ernest Rhys after a visit to Whitman in 1888 (*KLI.* 49). WBY held up Whitman,
with Thoreau, Bret Harte, and George Washington Cable, as examples of those
writers who had made a successful break from the English model and created
a national literature in the United States (*UP1.* 256). Whitman's style influenced
WBY in his early writing, encouraging him to write out of himself, but he had
reservations later about the process. In his long account of **AE** and his failure
to develop as a poet, WBY wonders what would have happened if AE had not
read, as a young man, Whitman and Emerson, whose writings, he thought, had
become superficial because they lacked the "Vision of Evil" (*A.* 246).

    REFERENCES: Allen, Gay Wilson. *The Solitary Singer: A Critical Biography of Walt
Whitman*. New York: Macmillan, 1955; Callow, Philip. *From Noon to Starry Night: A
Life of Walt Whitman*. Chicago: Dee, 1992; Kaplan, Justin. *Walt Whitman: A Life*. New
York: Simon & Schuster, 1980; Knapp, Bettina L. *Walt Whitman*. New York: Continuum,
1993.

WILDE, LADY [JANE FRANCESCA] (c. 1824–96), writer and mother of **Oscar
Wilde**. She was born in Wexford, the daughter of a Dublin solicitor. As a young
woman, she was much influenced in her politics by **Thomas Davis**, and from
1844, she contributed fervent and declamatory poems and articles, under the
pen name "Speranza," to the nationalist paper *The Nation*. In 1851, she married
Sir William Wilde (1815–76), a distinguished surgeon and president of the
Royal Irish Academy. In 1857, she published her first collection of verse, *Ugo
Bassi: A Tale of the Italian Revolution*, followed by *Poems* (1864). After her
husband's death in 1876, she moved to London, where she conducted a successful salon. Her eccentric appearance, in black wig and exotic costumes of
the 1860s, amused many, but her wit was remarkable, and like her famous son,
she was much quoted by the literary set in London. She maintained her interest
in Ireland and published two books of folklore, now considered her best writing.
These are *Ancient Legends, Mystic Charms, and Superstitions of Ireland* (1887),
which WBY included in his list of "Best Irish Books" (*UP1.* 386), and *Ancient
Cures, Charms and Usages of Ireland* (1890), favorably reviewed by WBY in
"Tales from the Twilight" (*UP1.* 170–73) and described as "the most beautiful
gathering of Irish folklore in existence." Lady Wilde was awarded a Civil List
pension of £300 a year, but with Oscar Wilde's imprisonment (she had urged
him to stand trial rather than flee the country), she was socially ostracized and
sank into poverty. WBY was introduced to her by **Katharine Tynan** in the
summer of 1888. After that, he attended her salon, which was held each Saturday
afternoon at her home at Knightsbridge, London. Later, Lady Wilde and her
older son Willie moved to 146 Oakley Street, Chelsea, where she died.

    REFERENCES: Hogan, Robert, ed. *Dictionary of Irish Literature*. Rev. ed. Westport,
Conn.: Greenwood, 1996; White, Terence de Vere. *The Parents of Oscar Wilde*.

London: Hodder & Stoughton, 1967; Wyndham, Horace. *Speranza*. London: T. V. Boardman, 1951.

WILDE, OSCAR [FINGALL O'FLAHERTIE WILLS] (1854–1900), dramatist, essayist, poet, and wit. He was born in Dublin, the younger son of Sir William Wilde, a successful ear and eye surgeon and author of books on archaeology and folklore, and **Lady Wilde**. He was educated at Portora Royal School, Enniskillen, and **Trinity College**, Dublin, and received a scholarship to Oxford University, where he distinguished himself as a classical scholar and poet by winning the Newdigate Prize in 1878. While at Oxford he came under the influence of **Walter Pater** and **John Ruskin** and chose to live to the full their philosophy of the centrality of art in life. For Wilde, this meant not only writing about art but living it, so that he affected an aesthetic pose and promoted his stance with witty epigrams and flamboyant wit. In London, he became the center of an admiring social circle, and the butt of hostility from periodicals like *Punch*, while Gilbert and Sullivan satirized him as the fleshly poet Bunthorne in their comic opera *Patience*. He published *Poems* (1881), a volume of work derivative of the Pre-Raphaelites **Swinburne** and **Dante Gabriel Rossetti**, and in 1882, he made a yearlong lecture tour of the United States, extolling the virtues of a lifestyle devoted to beauty and art. In 1884 he married Constance Lloyd, the daughter of an Irish lawyer, and they had two children, Cyril and Vyvyan. He was a reviewer for the *Pall Mall Gazette* and editor of *Woman's World* (1887–89). He published his charming fairy tales *The Happy Prince and Other Tales* (1888) and his only novel *The Picture of Dorian Gray* (1891), in which sensual pleasure and moral turpitude corrupt a young aesthete. Yet it was in the theater that Wilde produced work of lasting value. His social comedies, *Lady Windermere's Fan, A Woman of No Importance, An Ideal Husband*, and *The Importance of Being Earnest*, showed him to be an innovative playwright, who used the conventional French well-made play, overlaid with searing wit and satire, to expose the frailties of the late-Victorian society. Increasingly, his social notoriety and literary successes led him to the pursuit of reckless pleasure, especially in the company of young men. His intense relationship with Lord Alfred Douglas, son of the Marquess of Queensberry, was the catalyst to his downfall. Having lost a civil libel action against the marquess, who accused him of being a sodomite, he was found guilty of criminal charges relating to homosexuality and imprisoned for two years (1895–97). In jail, he wrote the long, accusatory letter to Lord Alfred Douglas, **De Profundis** (1905), and on his release, the moving account of a hanging, *The Ballad of Reading Gaol* (1898). His final years were spent in France. His adoring mother, wife Constance, and his older brother Willie predeceased him. Wilde was the center of artistic and literary circles when WBY returned to London in the late 1880s, and they met soon after. Wilde was a member of the **Rhymers' Club** but seldom came to the gathering in **Ye Olde Cheshire Cheese** (WBY remembers him being there only once). WBY admired Wilde's larger-than-life personality, which reminded him of some figure from fifteenth-century Italy. He was impressed by his wit and conversation, believing it to be the best in London, and he noted that he drawled slowly, in "perfect sentences" (*A*. 130, 139), an observation recalled in the poem "The Statesman's Holiday" (*CP*. 389). He was invited to Christmas dinner with Wilde and his family in Tite Street, a measure of Wilde's generosity to the younger Irishman. Impressed with the unexpectedly austere, predominantly white decor of the dining room, he describes it in detail in "Four Years: 1887–1891" (*A*. 134–35). After the meal, Wilde read to him from the proofs of his essay "The Decay of Lying" (1889). He praised WBY as a poet and storyteller, flattering him by comparing him with **Homer** (*A*. 135–36). WBY was critical of Wilde, thinking his writing vague and overelaborate in cadence, except in the major plays, which were extensions of Wilde's own brilliant conversation, and in the fairy stories. His two reviews of Wilde's work, in *United Ireland*, September 1891, and *The Bookman*, March 1895, were not favorable (*UP1*. 202–5, 354–55). He was in **Sligo**, staying with his uncle **George Pollexfen**, when the news arrived of Wilde's libel action against the Marquess of Queensberry. During the trial, WBY was a sympathetic supporter. He admired the moral courage that Wilde and his family showed in the face of public rejection and disgrace. He collected letters of support from all the notable writers and intellectuals (except **Edward Dowden**, who refused) and delivered them to the Wilde home (*A*. 287). He includes a section from *The Ballad of Reading Gaol* in *The Oxford Book of Modern Verse*, quoting two of the best-known verses in his introduction (*EI*. 182–83). A story by Wilde, "The Doer of Good," in which **Christ** returns to find himself rejected by those he has healed, is the accepted source for WBY's dance play *Calvary*.

REFERENCES: Coakley, Davis. *Oscar Wilde: The Importance of Being Irish*. Dublin: Town House, 1994; Ellman, Richard. *The Uses of Decadence: Wilde, Yeats, Joyce*. Bennington, Vt.: Bennington College, 1983; Pine, Richard. *The Thief of Reason: Oscar Wilde and Modern Ireland*. New York: St. Martin's, 1995.

WILD SWANS AT COOLE, THE, title of a collection of poems by WBY. It was published by the **Cuala Press** in 1917, in an edition of 400 copies, the volume including the play *At the Hawk's Well*. When it was published by Macmillan and Company in 1919, the play was omitted and seventeen additional poems included, among them "An Irish Airman Foresees His Death" (*CP*. 152). Most of the poems in the volume were written between 1915 and 1918. "The Wild Swans at Coole" is the title of the opening poem in the collection, a poem set in **Coole Park**, the home of **Lady Gregory**, and written after WBY's final rejection by **Maud Gonne** in 1917. The poem reflects the poet's sense of mortality and loss, while the others in the collection show the changes that had occurred in the poet's life over the previous four years. After his rejection by Maud Gonne, he had been refused by her daughter **Iseult Gonne**. He then married **Georgie Hyde-Lees**, and together they embarked on the renovation of **Thoor Ballylee**, giving him a sense of direction and purpose. While many of the early poems in the collection explore a common theme of death, including "In Memory of Major Robert Gregory" (*CP*. 148) and "In Memory of Alfred Pollexfen" (*CP*. 175), his wife's automatic writing provided a catalyst for those later poems in which he evolved his philosophical system, most notably "The Double Vision of Michael Robartes" (*CP*. 192).

REFERENCES: Martin, Graham. "The Wild Swans at Coole." In *An Honored Guest: New Essays on W. B. Yeats*, ed. Denis Donoghue and J. R. Mulryne. London: Edward Arnold, 1965; Parrish, Stephen, ed. *The Wild Swans at Coole: Manuscript Materials.* Ithaca: Cornell University Press, 1994.

WILLIAM III (1650–1702), king of England, Scotland, and Ireland. He was the son of William II, prince of Orange. In 1677, he married Mary, the Protestant daughter of the future James II of England, and in 1688, he was invited to England by parliamentary leaders concerned at King James's overt Catholicism. William landed with an army and brought about the Glorious Revolution, in which James's army deserted and fled to France, and James was permitted to escape. In 1689, William accepted Parliament's proposal that he should reign jointly with his wife and signed the Bill of Rights, which recognized the supremacy of parliamentary power over royal power. In 1690, he defeated the exiled James at the Battle of the **Boyne**. In the poem "Lapis Lazuli" (*CP*. 338), WBY refers to William III as "King Billy," the name by which he is familiarly known to the Protestants of **Ulster**.

REFERENCES: Bardon, Jonathan. *A History of Ulster*. Belfast: Blackstaff, 1992; Foster, R. F. *Modern Ireland 1600–1972*. 1988. Reprint, London: Penguin, 1989.

WILSON, RICHARD (1714–82), English landscape painter. He was a disciple of **Claude** and, like him, went to Italy to sketch and paint visionary landscapes, among them *Lake Albano*. WBY recalls Wilson in "Under Ben Bulben" (*CP*. 397), in which he is listed with **Edward Calvert, William Blake**, and Claude, all visionary painters of the classical tradition.

REFERENCES: Constable, W. G. *Richard Wilson*. Cambridge, Mass.: Harvard University Press, 1953; Solkin, David H. *Richard Wilson: The Landscape of Reaction*. London: Tate Gallery, 1982; Wilson, Richard. *Catalogue of an Exhibition of Pictures by Richard Wilson and His Circle*. London: Tate Gallery, 1949; Wilson, Richard. *An Italian Sketchbook: Drawings Made by the Artist in Rome and Its Environs in the Year 1754*. Ed. Denys Sutton and Ann Clements. London: Routledge & Kegan Paul, 1968.

WIND AMONG THE REEDS, THE, collection of poetry by WBY. It was published in April 1899 by the Shakespeare Head Press, with a cover design by **Althea Gyles**. The collection represents a transition between the poems of *The Rose* (1893) and those of *In the Seven Woods* (1903) and shows the influence in language and symbol not only of his association with the poets of the **Rhymers' Club** but also of his interest in the French Symbolists. The writing in the poems, which include "The Song of Wandering Aengus" (*CP*. 66), "He bids his Beloved be at Peace" (*CP*. 69), "The Secret Rose" (*CP*. 77), and "He

Wishes for the Cloths of Heaven'' (*CP*. 81), shows a subtle shift from the posing and self-conscious commitment to Ireland of his earlier verse to a poetry infused with his personal feelings for **Maud Gonne** and the complications of his affair with **Olivia Shakespear**. Writing of these personal dilemmas through the medium of Irish mythology and the occult, he gives to the imagery a new-found energy and universality. While working on the collection, WBY was involved with the setting up of the **Irish Literary Theatre**. Of note, in the early versions of the poems in the collection is his use of masks, among them **Aedh, Michael Robartes**, and **Hanrahan**, through which he addresses his personal thoughts and feelings.

REFERENCE: Putzel, Steven D. *Reconstructing Yeats: The Secret Rose and The Wind among the Reeds*. Dublin: Gill & Macmillan, 1986.

WINDING STAIR AND OTHER POEMS, THE, collection of verse by WBY. It was published in 1929 by Fountain Press, New York. The volume takes its title from the spiral stone staircase of the Norman tower, **Thoor Ballylee**, and represents a ''return to life'' after the bitter and depressing mood of *The Tower*. While there is still some gloominess in those poems in which WBY remembers important friends, as in the elegy ''In Memory of Eva Gore-Booth and Con Markiewicz'' (*CP*. 263), or in the poems celebrating **Lady Gregory** and her home at **Coole Park**, the poet ultimately recognizes that life is not a choice between the flesh and the soul but that each is dependent on the other. The collection is dedicated to **Edmund Dulac**, while the design of the book cover is by **T. Sturge Moore**. The 1933 publication of *The Winding Stair and Other Poems* by Macmillan and Company also contained the poems from the collection *Words for Music Perhaps and Other Poems* (1932) and the poem ''Crazy Jane talks with the Bishop'' (*CP*. 294).

REFERENCE: ''On *The Winding Stair*.'' In *An Honored Guest: New Essays on W. B. Yeats*, ed. Denis Donoghue and J. R. Mulryne. London: Edward Arnold, 1965.

WINDY GAP (Irish: *Bearna-na-Gaeithe*), familiar place name throughout Ireland. In the poem ''Running to Paradise'' (*CP*. 129), WBY is very likely referring to Windy Gap, near Carraroe, **Sligo** (county).

REFERENCE: McGarry, James P. *Place Names in the Writings of William Butler Yeats*. Gerrards Cross: Colin Smythe, 1976.

WISE MAN, fictional character. In WBY's play *The Hour-Glass*, he ridicules the existence of a spiritual world that challenges his materialist philosophy. He is told by the **Angel** that he will die and go to Hell unless he can find someone who believes in an after world. He desperately questions his pupils and his wife and finally comes to an understanding of the reality of the spiritual world. As he dies, a white butterfly, which emerges from his mouth, is placed in a box to be opened in Paradise. The role of the Wise Man in the first production of

The Hour-Glass at the **Abbey Theatre**, March 1903, was played by Dudley Digges.

WITCH OF ATLAS. According to **Shelley**, in his poem "The Witch of Atlas" (1824), she was a Naiad who lay in a dark cave until she was carried down river in a boat. Once out of the cave, she was transformed by the rays of the sun into a cloud. For Shelley, the Witch of Atlas symbolized the beauty of wisdom. WBY describes her passage down the Nile into the **Mareotic Lake** (*EI.* 84–85). He continues the connection in his poem "Under Ben Bulben" (*CP.* 397).
   REFERENCE: Bornstein, George. *Yeats and Shelley.* Chicago: University of Chicago Press, 1970.

WOBURN BUILDINGS, WBY's London residence. He rented rooms at 18 Woburn Buildings (now 5 Woburn Walk) in 1896. The area, while convenient to the **British Museum** and Euston Station, was seedy, and WBY was regarded as something of an oddity by the other residents of the street. He occupied two floors of this row house and was cared for by the landlady Mrs. Old and her husband, a carpenter. One of the floors contained a sitting room and a kitchen, and there was a bedroom and a bathroom on the floor above. It was in Woburn Buildings that he held his weekly "Monday Evenings" for literary friends and acquaintances. In his book *Some Memories of W. B. Yeats,* **John Masefield**, a frequent visitor, describes the rooms with their Pre-Raphaelite colors and furnishings. The sitting room had dark brown walls, dark curtains hung on the windows, and chairs and tables of dark wood. Paintings by his father and younger brother decorated the walls, together with engravings by **William Blake**. The effect was tasteful but somber. From 1904, a dark blue lectern, with enormous candles on either side, displayed his prized Kelmscott Chaucer. After his marriage in 1917, his wife **Georgie** redecorated the rooms to reflect the current Voysey taste in decoration—unpainted furniture and earthy colors (*WL.* 634). In 1919, WBY decided to give up his London home and return permanently to Ireland.
   REFERENCES: Drinkwater, John. *Discovery: Being the Second Book of an Autobiography.* Boston: Houghton Mifflin, 1933; Masefield, John. *Some Memories of W. B. Yeats.* New York: Macmillan, 1940.

WOMAN OF THE SIDHE. *See* **FAND**.

WOOD, ANNIE BESANT (1847–1933), theosophist. She was an outspoken atheist and officer of the National Secular Society before she converted to theosophy in 1889. Her lectures, "Why I Became a Theosophist," presented in August 1889, received much press coverage. WBY worked with her in the Esoteric Section of the **Theosophical Society** in the fall and winter of 1889–90, recording some brief remarks about their experiments together in his Journal, October 1889

(*M*. 281–82). When the Society split into groups, following the death of **Madame Blavatsky** in 1891, Annie Besant became one of the rival leaders. In an appendix to *Visions and Beliefs in the West of Ireland*, WBY refers to her book *The Ancient Wisdom: An Outline of Theosophical Teachings* (1897) (*LE*. 266–68).

REFERENCES: Dinnage, Rosemary. *Annie Besant*. Harmondsworth, Middlesex: Penguin Books, 1986; Taylor, Anne. *Annie Besant: A Biography*. Oxford: Oxford University Press, 1992; West, Geoffrey. *Annie Besant*. New York: Viking, 1928; Williams, Gertrude L. M. *Passionate Pilgrim: A Life of Annie Besant*. London: John Hamilton, 1932.

WOODSTOCK ROAD, Yeats residence. In the spring of 1879, the Yeats family moved from **Edith Villas** to 8 Woodstock Road in the London suburb of **Bedford Park**. It was the largest and most elegant house the Yeatses had lived in as a family, with a room set aside as a school room, presided over by Miss Jowitt. While the younger children had lessons at home, WBY attended the nearby **Godolphin School**. In his *Reveries over Childhood and Youth* (*A*. 42–44), WBY describes the new garden suburb as an idyllic place. There he played hide-and-seek in unoccupied houses, planted sunflowers and love-lies-bleeding in the yard, and took dancing lessons in a brick tiled house decorated in peacock blue, with De Morgan tiles and **William Morris** wallpapers. The streets were not straight, as in the neighborhood of Edith Villas, and railings were wooden and not iron. It was a romantic, picture-book world, where even the people dressed like those in the storybooks. The Yeats family remained at Woodstock Road until the fall of 1881, when they returned to Ireland to live at **Balscadden Cottage, Howth**.

REFERENCES: Murphy, William M. *Family Secrets: William Butler Yeats and His Relatives*. Syracuse, N.Y.: Syracuse University Press, 1995; Murphy, William M. *Prodigal Father: The Life of John Butler Yeats (1839–1922)*. Ithaca: Cornell University Press, 1978.

WORDS FOR MUSIC PERHAPS AND OTHER POEMS, poetry collection. It was published in 1932 by the **Cuala Press**, in an edition of 450 copies. It included "Coole Park, 1929" (*CP*. 273), "Coole Park and Ballylee, 1931" (*CP*. 275), "For Anne Gregory" (*CP*. 277), and "Byzantium" (*CP*. 280), as well as the **Crazy Jane** poems, "Crazy Jane and the Bishop" (*CP*. 290), "Crazy Jane Reproved" (*CP*. 291), "Crazy Jane on the Day of Judgment" (*CP*. 291), "Crazy Jane and Jack the Journeyman" (*CP*. 292), "Crazy Jane on God" (*CP*. 293), and "Crazy Jane Grown Old looks at the Dancers" (*CP*. 295). All the poems in the collection were later included in *The Winding Stair and Other Poems* (1933).

WORDS UPON THE WINDOW-PANE, THE, one-act play in prose. The play was published in 1934 by the **Cuala Press** and subsequently included in *Wheels and Butterflies* (London, 1934; New York, 1935) and *The Collected Plays of*

W. B. Yeats (1934, 1952). A commentary on the play appeared in the *Dublin Magazine*, October–December 1931 and January–March 1932. WBY began the play in 1930 at **Coole Park** and dedicated it to his friend and patron **Lady Gregory**. At the time, he was reading **Jonathan Swift's** *Journal to Stella* and his correspondence with Alexander Pope and Henry St. John. *The Words upon the Window-Pane* focuses on the enigmatic relationship between Swift and the women who loved him, **Esther Johnson** (**Stella**) and **Hester van Homrigh** (**Vanessa**). The action takes place at a séance organized by the Dublin Spiritualists Association; the time is the present, and the setting is a house that had formerly belonged to friends of Swift. The séance is conducted by **Mrs. Henderson**, an experienced medium from England, for a group of believers and a young Cambridge skeptic, **John Corbet**, who recognizes the lines scratched on the windowpane as having been written for Swift by Stella. As the séance proceeds, it becomes apparent that the medium has been possessed by Swift and the two women. In a first exchange, Vanessa pleads with her lover for physical love. Swift rejects this, insisting that any offspring might inherit the madness that he believes he possesses. In the second exchange, he praises Stella for the platonic love she offers and quotes the lines written on the windowpane. Those attending the séance think it a failure, with the exception of Corbet and the president of the Dublin Spiritualists Association, **Dr. Trench**. As everyone leaves, Mrs. Henderson is again possessed by the spirit of Swift. WBY was encouraged to write the play by his wife (*EX.* 322). *The Words upon the Window-Pane* was first performed at the **Abbey Theatre**, November 1930, with the following cast: **Miss Mackenna**, Shelah Richards; Dr. Trench, P. J. Carolan; John Corbet, Arthur Shields; Cornelius Patterson, Michael J. Dolan; Abraham Johnson, **F. J. McCormick; Mrs. Mallet**, Eileen Crowe; Mrs. Henderson, May Craig. The play was directed by **Lennox Robinson**.

REFERENCES: Bradley, Anthony. *William Butler Yeats*. New York: Frederick Ungar, 1979; Miller, Liam. *The Noble Drama of W. B. Yeats*. Dublin: Dolmen, 1977; Taylor, Richard. *A Reader's Guide to the Plays of W. B. Yeats*. New York: St. Martin's, 1984.

WORDSWORTH, WILLIAM (1770–1850), poet. He was born in Cockermouth, in the north of England, and educated at Hawkshead Grammar School. He was an undistinguished student at St. John's College, Cambridge (1787–91). A walking tour in revolutionary France, summer of 1790, made a profound impact on him, and he became a vigorous republican sympathizer. After leaving university, he led an aimless life in London in the company of noted radicals, but in 1797, a legacy enabled him to move, with his sister Dorothy, to Alfoxden House, near Bristol. There he formed an intense friendship with the poet **Samuel Taylor Coleridge**, and they embarked upon the collection of poems published as *Lyrical Ballads* (1798). His manifesto, included in the second edition of 1800, set forth his approach to a new style of poetry, different in content, language, and tone from the measured, formal verse of the Neoclassicists. In 1799, he returned to his home country, the Lake District, where he remained for the rest of his life.

He married in 1802. He was appointed Poet Laureate in 1843, and it is generally agreed that his later work, in which he became moralistic and increasingly orthodox in his views, is inferior to the poetry of *Lyrical Ballads* and *Poems, in Two Volumes* (1807). For his inspiration, Wordsworth turned to nature, and his lyrical descriptions of flowers, birds, animals, and the simple folk of the English countryside made a profound impact. Yet it is in his longer, autobiographical poems, among them "Lines Composed a Few Miles above Tintern Abbey," "Ode: Intimations of Immortality," and *The Prelude*, that he makes his most profound statements about the relationship of humankind to the natural world. WBY, influenced by his father and members of his circle, was negative in his response to Wordsworth, going so far as to call him "a little disreputable" when compared with **Keats** and **Shelley** (*EI.* 347–48). In a review of **William Allingham**, he stated his preference for those poets who, unlike Wordsworth, belonged to the bardic tradition (*UP1.* 105). While he admired the vivid imagination that Wordsworth possessed (*EI.* 329), he was out of sympathy with the psychological intricacies of much of his poetry and the moralistic and utilitarian content of the late verse (*A.* 235, 313, 490). Nevertheless, in his poem "The Stolen Child" (*CP.* 20), and those ballads written in the 1930s, like "The O'Rahilly" (*CP.* 354), WBY shows Wordsworth's influence.

REFERENCES: Gill, Stephen. *William Wordsworth: A Life*. Oxford: Clarendon Press, 1989; Heaney, Seamus. "The Makings of a Music: Reflections on Wordsworth and Yeats." In *Preoccupations: Selected Prose, 1968–1978*. London: Faber & Faber, 1980.

X, Y, Z

XANADU, idyllic city. It is the site of the palace of **Kubla Khan** in the poem of the same name by **Samuel Taylor Coleridge** and is very likely based on Kubla Khan's capital of Cambulac. In *The Player Queen* (*CPl.* 418), the First Player boasts that he once acted at Xanadu, in a play called *The Fall of Troy*, and was much praised by Kubla Khan.

YEATS, ANNE [BUTLER] (b. 1919), daughter of WBY. Born in Dublin, she trained as a painter and designed the settings for a number of productions at the **Abbey Theatre**, including the first production of *Purgatory*, 1938. Unmarried, she lives in Dublin, where she enjoys a reputation as a successful painter and graphic artist. In "Father and Child" (*CP.* 308), WBY refers to an incident when Anne praised Fergus Fitzgerald, a visitor to the Yeats home. See also "A Prayer for My Daughter" (*CP.* 211), written soon after her birth.

REFERENCES: Murphy, William M. *Prodigal Father: The Life of John Butler Yeats (1839–1922)*. London and Ithaca: Cornell University Press, 1978; Unterecker, John. "An Interview with Anne Yeats." *Shenandoah*, Vol. XVI, (summer 1965).

YEATS, BENJAMIN (1750–95), WBY's great-great-grandfather. He was a wholesale dealer in linens in Dublin. He must have been a fairly successful man since he married **Mary Butler Yeats**, one of the descendants of the third duke of **Ormonde**.

YEATS, [BERTHA] GEORGE (GEORGIE) [HYDE-LEES] (1892–1968), wife of WBY. Known familiarly as Georgie, she was born at Hartley Wintney, near Odiham, in Hampshire, the daughter of William Gilbert Hyde-Lees (c. 1865–1909), a captain in the Militia, and Edith Ethel Woodmass (c. 1868–1942). Her parents separated soon after she was born, and Georgie Hyde-Lees lived with her mother, mainly in London but also traveling in Europe, where she learned Italian. She attended St. James's School, London, and a private school run by Miss Douglas in Kensington. Cultured and well-read, she became friendly with WBY in 1911, after the marriage of her mother to **Olivia Shakespear's** brother, Harry Tucker. They attended séances together, and WBY was her sponsor when she was initiated into **The Order of the Golden Dawn** in 1914. She married WBY on 20 October 1917, a few weeks after he proposed to her. Soon after the marriage, the discovery that she had the gift of automatic writing helped to intensify the relationship between WBY and his young bride. She proved an able wife for the aging poet. Not only did she provide for his personal needs, she also organized and corrected his manuscripts and facilitated his writing. She nursed him through some difficult illnesses in the late 1920s and 1930s and turned a blind eye to his flirtations with **Margot Ruddock, Dorothy Wellesley, Ethel Mannin**, and **Edith Shackleton Heald**, among others. She was a director of the **Cuala Press**. She is referred to by name in the poem "To be Carved on a Stone at Thoor Ballylee" (*CP*. 214), and there are allusions to her in a number of poems by WBY, including "Solomon to Sheba" (*CP*. 155), "Solomon and the Witch" (*CP*. 199), and "Two Songs of a Fool" (*CP*. 190) in which she appears as the speckled cat. See also "The Gift of Harun Al-Rashid" (*CP*. 513).

REFERENCE: Murphy, William M. *Prodigal Father: The Life of John Butler Yeats (1839–1922)*. London and Ithaca: Cornell University Press, 1978.

YEATS, ELIZABETH CORBET [LOLLY] (1868–1940), sister of WBY and founder of the **Cuala Press**. She was born in London and grew up in the family home in **Bedford Park**. She trained to be a kindergarten art teacher and taught privately, in addition to publishing three books on painting: *Brush Work* (1896), *Brush Work Studies of Flowers, Fruit and Animals* (1898), and *Elementary Brush Work Studies* (1899). Influenced by Emery Walker, the chief inspiration behind the private press movement in England, she developed an interest in the art of printing. On his recommendation, she took a month's course at the Women's Printing Society in London, and in July 1902, she joined Evelyn Gleeson in Dublin and founded the **Dun Emer Press**, part of Dun Emer Industries. Later, in 1908, she dissolved her association with Miss Gleeson because of personality differences and started the Cuala Press, which she ran until her death in 1940. A gifted artist, she designed embroidery, prints, and Christmas cards. She was neurotic and excitable by nature and much given to talking and complaining. She resented and resisted WBY's editorial control over the Cuala Press, and they had many quarrels. Observers, including **John B. Yeats**, noted that many of the quarrels arose because the two were temperamentally so alike. WBY himself noted the similarities between them (*M*. 156), fearing it was a form of inherited madness.

REFERENCES: Miller, Liam. *The Dun Emer Press, Later the Cuala Press*. Dublin: Dolmen, 1973; Murphy, William M. *Family Secrets: William Butler Yeats and His Relatives*. Syracuse, N.Y.: Syracuse University Press, 1995.

YEATS, ISAAC BUTT (1848–1930), uncle of WBY. He was in temperament and imagination directly the opposite of his older brother **John B. Yeats**—although they remained close friends, even when the latter moved to the United States. After taking a degree from **Trinity College**, Dublin, Isaac Yeats became secretary to the Artisan Drilling Company and lived a quiet, reclusive life on Morehampton Road, Dublin, close to where his maiden sisters Jenny and Gracie had a home. Later, he moved to 50 Wellington Road, Dublin, to live with his widowed sister Mary Letitia (1841?–95) and her daughter Edith Mary Wise. Shy, retiring, and conservative in tastes and habits, he was generous to John B. Yeats and his family, but as a Unionist, he remained politically opposed to his brother and WBY. There is a fine pencil sketch of Isaac Butt Yeats, drawn by John B. Yeats about 1904, now in the possession of **Michael B. Yeats**.

REFERENCE: Murphy, William M. *Prodigal Father: The Life of John Butler Yeats (1839–1922)*. London and Ithaca: Cornell University Press, 1978.

YEATS, JACK B[UTLER] (1871–1957), brother of WBY. The youngest son of **John B. Yeats**, he was born in London. Because of the illness of his mother, **Susan Yeats**, Jack grew up in **Sligo** with his maternal grandparents, with whom he lived until he was sixteen. Even when he returned to London in 1887 to attend the National Art Training School (later the Royal College of Art), in South Kensington, he continued to visit Sligo every year until his uncle **George Pollexfen** died in 1910. In contrast to his enigmatic and ambitious older brother, Jack Yeats was warm and uncomplicated, with a love of life and comedy and theatrical spectacles like the Wild West Show being presented at Earl's Court, London. He began illustrating for various journals while still at art school and, in 1894, married a fellow student, Mary Cottenham White (known as Cottie). They settled in Devon, in a rural cottage that they named Cashlauna Shelmiddy (Snails' Castle), Strete, near Dartmouth. The relationship was a secure and happy one that lasted until Cottie's death in 1947. Although Jack Yeats had been painting watercolors in the 1890s, it was his work as a black-and-white illustrator with an observant eye for character and detail that brought him early attention. In 1896, he sold his first drawing to *Punch*. This marked the beginning of a long association with the fashionable English periodical, to which he contributed until 1941, under the pseudonym W. Bird. With his developing interest in Irish nationalism, he turned increasingly for subjects and themes to the west of Ireland, especially to the locations in Sligo that he had known intimately as a child. He had a lifelong interest in nineteenth-century ballad sheets and produced his own version, initially printed by the **Dun Emer Press** and later under the imprint of the **Cuala Press**. A friendship with **J. M. Synge** led him to illustrate the latter's *The Aran Islands* and *In Wicklow, West Kerry and Connemara*. He began to paint in oils early in the 1900s and held yearly exhibitions in London and Dublin. It is these paintings, in which he chose Ireland and its people for his subject matter, that established his reputation as Ireland's outstanding painter of the early twentieth century. He and his wife left Devon for

Ireland in 1910 and settled at Greystones, outside Dublin. They later moved to 61 Marlborough Road, Dublin, where he recorded the life of the busy city with as much affection and insight as he had recorded the people and places of rural Ireland. In his early paintings, he introduced real and imaginary figures into the pictures of bars, beaches, and race courses. Later, he painted the figures of Irish legend and mythology. He was an accomplished writer of prose and short plays, among them *In Sand*, which was produced by the **Abbey Theatre** in 1949. WBY and his brother were not always on cordial terms. They differed politically, Jack Yeats rejecting his brother's stance on the Irish Free State of 1922. They differed in personality. Where WBY was a public figure ever willing to discuss and defend his art, Jack Yeats was a private man who preferred to let his art speak for him. While WBY was elitist, his brother was the chronicler of the common man. Jack Yeats was resentful of his brother's reputation, which threatened to submerge his own. When the name Yeats was mentioned, it was invariably the poet who was being referred to and not the painter. Indeed, it was only after WBY's death in 1939 that Jack Yeats received the critical acclaim that he so richly deserved. There are few references to Jack Yeats in his brother's writings. In *Reveries over Childhood and Youth* (*A*. 52, 68, 551), WBY recalls Jack's drawing and paintings, which remind him of the people and places they both knew in Sligo as children. WBY's collection *On the Boiler* was illustrated by Jack Yeats.

REFERENCES: Booth, John. *A Vision of Ireland: Jack B. Yeats*. Nairn, Scotland: Thomas & Lochar, 1992; McGreevy, Thomas. *Jack B. Yeats: An Appreciation and an Interpretation*. Dublin: Waddington, 1945; Murphy, William M. *Family Secrets: William Butler Yeats and His Relatives*. Syracuse, N.Y.: Syracuse University Press, 1995; Pyle, Hilary. *Jack B. Yeats: A Biography*. London: Andre Deutsch, 1970; Rosenthal, T. G. *Jack Yeats, 1871–1957*. London: Knowledge Publications, 1966.

YEATS, JANE GRACE CORBET (1811–76), WBY's paternal grandmother. She married **Rev. William Butler Yeats** at St. Mary's Church, Donnybrook, County Dublin, in November 1835. Her mother, Grace Armstrong, was the daughter of Captain Robert Armstrong of County Cavan and the grandniece of one of the duke of Marlborough's generals. It was through this connection that WBY was related to **Laura Armstrong**. Jane Grace Corbet Yeats was a spirited woman and a caring, disciplined mother to her nine children. Her firstborn was WBY's father **John B. Yeats**. After her husband's retirement in 1861, they lived near **Sandymount Castle**, the home of her brother **Robert Corbet**. She later moved to Upper Leeson Street, Dublin.

REFERENCES: Murphy, William M. *Prodigal Father: The Life of John Butler Yeats (1839–1922)*. London and Ithaca: Cornell University Press, 1978; Yeats, John Butler. *Early Memories*. Dublin: Cuala, 1923.

YEATS, JANE TAYLOR (1777–1842), wife of **Rev. John Yeats** and great-grandmother of WBY. She was the daughter of the politically influential William

Taylor, an official in **Dublin Castle**. Her son, **Rev. William Butler Yeats**, WBY's grandfather, was born in Dublin Castle.

REFERENCE: Murphy, William M. *Prodigal Father: The Life of John Butler Yeats (1839–1922)*. London and Ithaca: Cornell University Press, 1978.

YEATS, JERVIS (1670–1712), ancestor of WBY. While Dublin references to the names *Yeats, Yeates*, and *Yeatts* go back as far as 1671, Jervis Yeats is the earliest known ancestor in WBY's family records. He is listed as a Dublin wholesale linen merchant in 1712. His son and grandson, both named **Benjamin**, followed him into the business. It is believed the Yeats family came to Ireland from Yorkshire, England.

REFERENCES: Murphy, William M. *Family Secrets: William Butler Yeats and His Relatives*. Syracuse, N.Y.: Syracuse University Press, 1995; Murphy, William M. *Prodigal Father: The Life of John Butler Yeats (1839–1922)*. London and Ithaca: Cornell University Press, 1978.

YEATS, JOHN B[UTLER] (1839–1922), father of WBY. He was born in Tullylish, in the north of Ireland, the son of **Rev. William Butler Yeats**. He was educated at **Trinity College**, Dublin, intending to become a lawyer. He was called to the Irish Bar in 1866, after his marriage to **Susan Pollexfen** and the birth of their first child, WBY. A daughter, **Susan Mary (Lily)**, was born later that year. In 1867, he moved to London with his young family to study painting at Heatherley's Art School. A second daughter, **Elizabeth Corbet (Lolly)**, was born in 1868, when the family lived at **Fitzroy Road**. To pay for his tuition, John B. Yeats took out mortgages on some property that he had inherited at Thomastown, County Kildare. The family lived in extreme poverty in London, and in 1872, the Yeats family, which now consisted of two more sons, **Jack B.** and Robert Corbet, returned to **Sligo** with their mother. Over the next years, John B. Yeats and his family moved back and forth between Ireland and London, until 1888, when they settled in **Bedford Park**. In the meantime, Robert had died in Ireland, and a third daughter, Jane Grace, born in August 1875, died less than a year later. WBY's mother suffered a stroke in 1887, and her mental health gradually deteriorated until her death in 1900. John B. Yeats was not successful as a painter, lacking the confidence even to complete the few commissions he received. He was careless in his business arrangements and, in 1886, sold the remaining properties on his Irish estate to pay his debts. In 1901, assisted by his friend **Sarah Purser**, he had a successful showing of his paintings in Dublin, and he decided to return to Ireland. There he was moderately successful. He was at the center of a lively art scene and was commissioned by the American art patron **John Quinn** to paint the leading contemporary figures in Dublin, including **Douglas Hyde, George Moore, Standish [James] O'Grady**, and **J. M. Synge**. He took an active role in supporting **Hugh Lane** in the controversy over the building of a modern gallery in Dublin and challenged the audience from the stage during the first performance of Synge's

Playboy of the Western World (*A.* 483), an action recalled by WBY in his poem ''Beautiful Lofty Things'' (*CP.* 348). In 1907, he accompanied his daughter Lily to an Irish Exhibition in New York, where he remained for the rest of his life, despite deteriorating health and the entreaties of his family to return to Ireland. *Passages from the Letters of John Butler Yeats*, edited by **Ezra Pound**, was published in 1917, while his autobiographical account, *Early Memories*, was published by **Cuala Press** a year after his death. Other published collections are *Essays Irish and American* (1918) and *Further Letters of John Butler Yeats* (1920). John B. Yeats, with his sharp, enquiring mind and explosive passion, must have been the single most powerful influence on WBY as a writer. He took an active part in his education, challenging him aesthetically, intellectually, and philosophically. Much of what WBY said and wrote was in direct opposition to his father's views. Their differing opinions and interests led to intense verbal and emotional encounters (*LE.* 226; *M.* 19, 20). John B. Yeats provided a model for WBY of the brilliant but hopelessly impractical artist whose talents were consumed by socializing rather than by art. WBY was frustrated by his father's distrust of success. As a result, he modeled himself on ruthless, dominating men like **William Morris** and dedicated himself totally to the disciplined service of art. He writes in detail about his early relationship with his father in his autobiography *Reveries over Childhood and Youth*.

REFERENCES: Archibald, Douglas N. *John Butler Yeats*. Lewisburg: Bucknell University Press, 1974; Hogan, Robert, ed. *Dictionary of Irish Literature*. Westport, Conn.: Greenwood, 1979; Hone, Joseph, ed. *John Butler Yeats: Letters to His Son W. B. Yeats and Others, 1869–1922*. 1944. Reprint, Secker & Warburg, 1993. Loizeaux, Elizabeth Bergmann. *Yeats and the Visual Arts*. New Brunswick and London: Rutgers University Press, 1986; Murphy, William M. *Family Secrets: William Butler Yeats and His Relatives*. Syracuse, N.Y.: Syracuse University Press, 1995; Murphy, William M. *Prodigal Father: The Life of John Butler Yeats (1839–1922)*. London and Ithaca: Cornell University Press, 1978; White, James. *John Butler Yeats and the Irish Renaissance*. Dublin: Dolmen, 1972.

YEATS, MARY BUTLER (1751–1834), WBY's paternal great-great-grandmother. She was the daughter of Edmond **Butler**, a member of the distinguished **Ormonde** family that had settled in Ireland in the twelfth century, and married **Benjamin Yeats**. Through her, WBY's great-grandfather, **Rev. John Yeats**, traced his ancestry to the third duke of Ormonde and inherited 560 acres in Thomastown, County Kildare, as well as a house in Dorset Street, Dublin, and a silver cup dated 1534, inscribed with the Ormonde coat of arms. Through her grandfather, Abraham Voisin, Mary Butler Yeats was descended from Claude Voisin, a Huguenot who had arrived in Dublin in 1634.

REFERENCES: Murphy, William M. *Family Secrets: William Butler Yeats and His Relatives*. Syracuse, N.Y.: Syracuse University Press, 1995; Murphy, William M. *Prodigal Father: The Life of John Butler Yeats (1839–1922)*. London and Ithaca: Cornell University Press, 1978.

YEATS, MRS. W. B. *See* **YEATS, [BERTHA] GEORGE (GEORGIE) [HYDE-LEES]**.

YEATS, REV. JOHN (1774–1846), WBY's great-grandfather. He was the son of **Benjamin Yeats** and **Mary Butler Yeats**. After graduating from **Trinity College**, Dublin, he entered the Church of Ireland and was appointed rector of St. Columba's Parish Church in **Drumcliff, Sligo** (county), in 1811. It was a good living, worth about £4,000 pounds a year, and since "Parson John" had additional income from the property in County Kildare that he had inherited from his mother, he lived comfortably. He remained at St. Columba's until his death. A friend of the patriot **Robert Emmet**, he was a scholarly man, gentle, courteous, and tolerant, and was well liked by his Catholic neighbors, who on one occasion lit a bonfire to celebrate his return to Drumcliff from Dublin. He enjoyed a drink and is reputed to have concealed his liquor in a secret drawer in the rectory so that his wife, **Jane Taylor Yeats**, would not find it. On his death, he left a liquor bill of £400. Rev. John Yeats is referred to by WBY in "Are You Content?" (*CP.* 370) and "Under Ben Bulben" (*CP.* 397).

REFERENCES: Murphy, William M. *Family Secrets: William Butler Yeats and His Relatives.* Syracuse, N.Y.: Syracuse University Press, 1995; Murphy, William M. *Prodigal Father: The Life of John Butler Yeats (1839–1922).* London and Ithaca: Cornell University Press, 1978.

YEATS, REV. WILLIAM BUTLER (1806–62), WBY's paternal grandfather. He was born in **Dublin Castle**, the son of **Rev. John Yeats** and **Jane Taylor Yeats**. His childhood was spent in **Sligo**, where his father was rector of St. Columba's Parish Church, **Drumcliff**. A tall, good-looking man with red hair and brown eyes, he was admitted to **Trinity College**, Dublin, in 1828. While at Trinity, he lived for a year with his elderly grandmother, **Mary Butler Yeats**, in Great Cumberland Street, Dublin, and became friends with **Isaac Butt**. He was a fine horseman and always had his own horse. After graduation, he entered the Church of Ireland and was appointed curate of Moira Parish Church, **County Down**. The rector of the church, with whom he lived, objected to the appointment of the tall, horse-riding young man, believing him more suited to be a jockey than a clergyman. In November 1835, Rev. William Butler Yeats married **Jane Grace Corbet Yeats** at St. Mary's Church, Donnybrook, County Dublin. He accepted the rectorship of All Saints Parish Church, Tullylish, County Down, where his eldest son **John B. Yeats** was born in 1839—although no record of the birth appears in the parish records. Like his father, Rev. William Butler Yeats was a philosopher and a courteous gentleman, one of the "old school" of Church of Ireland clergy. As a rector in the puritanical north of Ireland, his liberal attitudes did not always meet with the approval of his congregation. He had a good relationship with the local Catholic priest, and during the cholera epidemic of 1845, he risked his own life by ministering to the poor and raising money for their relief. In 1846, he inherited from his father a house in Dorset

Street, Dublin, and 560 acres at Thomastown, County Kildare. The property was divided into seventeen farm tenancies, but since these were heavily mortgaged, the property made demands on Rev. William Butler Yeats's financial resources. He retired from All Saints Parish in ill health in 1861 and lived in a small house near the home of his brother-in-law **Robert Corbet** in Dublin. WBY refers to his grandfather in the poem "Are You Content?" (*CP*. 370).

REFERENCES: Murphy, William M. *Prodigal Father: The Life of John Butler Yeats (1839–1922).* London and Ithaca: Cornell University Press, 1978; Yeats, John Butler. *Early Memories.* Dublin: Cuala, 1923.

YEATS, SUSAN [MARY] (1841–1900), WBY's mother. She was the eldest daughter of **William** and **Elizabeth Pollexfen** and younger sister of **Charles** and **George Pollexfen**, whom **John B. Yeats** had met at Atholl Academy, on the Isle of Man. She met her future husband in September 1862, when John B. Yeats spent a holiday with her family in **Sligo**, and they became engaged before he returned to Dublin two weeks later. Although shy and withdrawn, she was regarded as being extremely pretty. She was lacking in humor and given to petulance. They married in St. John's Church, Sligo, 10 September 1863, and after honeymooning in **Galway**, they moved into **George's Ville**, 5 Sandymount Avenue, Dublin, where their first child WBY was born. Within the next ten years, Susan Yeats had given birth to six children (two of whom died in infancy) and seen her life change from the security of her family in County Sligo to the instability of marriage to a penniless painter. The period 1869–77 was especially traumatic for her. She moved back and forth between London and Sligo, sometimes without the children, who remained in Sligo, sometimes remaining in Sligo while her husband returned to London. In 1877, she suffered two strokes, possibly due to the financial and emotional burden imposed on her by her husband's irresponsible behavior. From early 1889, she gradually retreated from life, invalided to her room, unvisited by guests who called on WBY or her husband— including **Lady Gregory**, who, while she was being entertained in the home, was unaware of Susan's presence upstairs. In her illness, she was cared for by the family doctor and friend of her husband, Dr. Gordon-Hogg. She died suddenly on 3 January 1900 and was buried in Acton Rural Cemetery. WBY makes few references to her in his autobiography and other writings, but he writes about her love of Sligo and storytelling in *Reveries over Childhood and Youth* (*A*. 31). A plaque, paid for by her children, was erected in St. John's Church, Sligo.

REFERENCES: Murphy, William M. *Family Secrets: William Butler Yeats and His Relatives.* Syracuse, N.Y.: Syracuse University Press, 1995; Murphy, William M. *Prodigal Father: The Life of John Butler Yeats (1839–1922).* London and Ithaca: Cornell University Press, 1978.

YEATS, SUSAN MARY [LILY] (1866–1949), sister of WBY. She was born at Enniscrone, near **Sligo** (town), and moved with the family to London in 1867.

Like WBY and her younger sister, **Lolly**, Lily's childhood was spent moving frequently between England and Ireland, until the family settled in **Bedford Park** in 1888. Being closest to WBY in age, she and he were childhood companions, a close relationship that continued throughout their lives. Through WBY's association with **William Morris**, she studied embroidery with May Morris, his daughter, from 1889. She became her assistant but left in 1894 when tensions between her and May Morris, a demanding employer, became unbearable. With the setting up of the Dun Emer Guild, intended to train young Irish women in traditional arts and crafts, she returned to Ireland in 1902 to run the embroidery workshop. She continued with the workshop when she and her sister Lolly left Dun Emer in 1908 to set up Cuala Industries, home of the **Cuala Press**. Emotionally stable and clearheaded, Lily Yeats spent most of her life dealing with the unpredictable behavior of her younger, complaining sister, as well as managing the day-to-day affairs of Cuala Industries. The toll on her health was considerable. From childhood she had suffered from an overactive thyroid gland that caused fatigue and respiratory difficulties. In 1923, after a breakdown, she entered a nursing home for extended care. **Georgie Yeats** looked after the business until her return to health in 1925. A relapse in 1931 forced the closure of the workshop, although Lily continued to do fine embroidery pieces on a part-time basis until a stroke in 1943 left her partially paralyzed and housebound for her remaining years. She was a talented artist, a fine needlewoman, and a witty and entertaining writer, as evidenced by her letters to her family and friends. WBY commissioned at least two embroideries from her, *The Land of Youth* (1937) and *Innisfree* (1938), both designed by Diana Murphy (*LE.* 249).

REFERENCES: Murphy, William M. *Family Secrets: William Butler Yeats and His Relatives.* Syracuse, N.Y.: Syracuse University Press, 1995; Murphy, William M. *Prodigal Father: The Life of John Butler Yeats (1839–1922).* London and Ithaca: Cornell University Press, 1978.

YEATS, [WILLIAM] MICHAEL B[UTLER] (b. 1921), son of WBY. He was born at Cuttlebrook House, Thame, Oxfordshire, and moved with his family to Ireland in 1922. A lawyer by profession, he has devoted much of his life to public service as a member of the **Irish Senate** and as Irish representative to the European parliament in Brussels. He is married to harpist Grainne Ni Hegarty and has three daughters, Catriona (b. 1951), Siobhan (b. 1953), Sile (b. 1955), and a son Padraig (b. 1959). Much of his time has been spent caring for his father's literary interests, although in his own right he is an authority on Irish folksong about which he has written and lectured extensively. He has been generous to academics and donated major collections of WBY's manuscripts and private papers to the **National Library of Ireland**. He lives in Dalkey, outside Dublin. He is the subject of WBY's poem "A Prayer for my Son" (*CP.* 238), written in December 1921, some four months after his birth.

REFERENCES: Murphy, William M. *Family Secrets: William Butler Yeats and His Relatives.* Syracuse, N.Y.: Syracuse University Press, 1995; Murphy, William M. *Prod-*

igal Father: The Life of John Butler Yeats (1839–1922). London and Ithaca: Cornell University Press, 1978.

YOUNG GIRL. *See* **DERVORGILLA**.

YOUNG MAN. In WBY's play *The Dreaming of the Bones*, the Young Man, who claims he has fought in the **General Post Office** in Dublin during the Easter Rising, is waiting off the coast of **Clare** for a boat to take him to safety. He encounters the ghosts of **Diarmuid MacMurrough** and **Dervorgilla** but is unable to respond to their desire for forgiveness. The role of the Young Man in the first production of the play, at the **Abbey Theatre**, December 1931, was played by W. O'Gorman. In *On Baile's Strand*, a Young Man, who has been trained from his youth to fight **Cuchulain**, is sent from Scotland to Ireland to challenge the warrior in armed combat. Cuchulain kills the Young Man, only to discover it is his own son **Connla**. In the first production of *On Baile's Strand*, at the Abbey Theatre, December 1904, the Young Man was played by Prionnsias MacShiublaigh. The Young Man in *At the Hawk's Well*, played in the first production by Henry Ainley, identifies himself as Cuchulain.

ZEPPELIN, first rigid-framed airship. Designed by Graf von Zeppelin (1838–1917), a German army officer, it was used to bomb London during the 1914–18 war. Soon after his marriage to **Georgie Hyde-Lees** in October 1917, WBY and his wife left London for Ashdown Forest to escape the Zeppelin raids. WBY makes reference to the raids in ''Lapis Lazuli'' (*CP*. 338), written in July 1936.

Selected Bibliography

REFERENCE

Bibliographical Works

Wade, Allan. *A Bibliography of the Writings of W. B. Yeats*. Rev. Russell K. Alspach. London: Hart-Davis, 1968.

Reference Works

Domville, Eric, ed. *A Concordance to the Plays of W. B. Yeats*. 2 vols. Ithaca and London: Cornell University Press, 1972.

Finneran, Richard J., ed. *Anglo-Irish Literature: A Review of Research*. New York: Modern Language Association of America, 1976.

————. *Recent Research on Anglo-Irish Writers, a Supplement to Anglo-Irish Literature: A Review of Research*. New York: Modern Language Association of America, 1983.

Jeffares, A. Norman. *A New Commentary on the Poems of W. B. Yeats*. Stanford, Calif.: Stanford University Press, 1984.

Jeffares, A. Norman, and Knowland, A. S. *A Commentary on the Collected Plays of W. B. Yeats*. London: Macmillan, 1975.

Jochum, K. P. S. *W. B. Yeats: A Classified Bibliography of Criticism*. Champaign-Urbana: University of Illinois Press, 1978.

O'Shea, Edward. *A Descriptive Catalog of W. B. Yeats's Library*. New York and London: Garland, 1985.

Parrish, S. M., ed. *A Concordance to the Poems of W. B. Yeats*. Ithaca and London: Cornell University Press.

Saul, George Brandon. *Prolegomena to the Study of Yeats's Plays*. Philadelphia: University of Pennsylvania, 1958.

————. *Prolegomena to the Study of Yeats's Poems.* Philadelphia: University of Pennsylvania, 1957.

COLLECTED WORKS

Yeats, W. B. *Autobiographies.* 1955. Reprint, London: Macmillan, 1956.
————. *The Collected Plays of W. B. Yeats.* 1952. Reprint, London: Macmillan, 1977.
————. *The Collected Poems of W. B. Yeats.* 1950. Reprint, London: Macmillan, 1982.
————. *Essays and Introductions.* New York: Macmillan, 1961.
————. *Explorations.* Selected by Mrs. W. B. Yeats. New York: Macmillan, 1962.
————. *Mythologies.* New York: Macmillan, 1959.
————. *A Vision.* London: Macmillan, 1937.

Editions

Allt, Peter, and Alspach, Russell K., eds. *The Variorum Edition of the Poems of W. B. Yeats.* New York: Macmillan, 1968.
Alspach, Russell K., ed. *The Variorum Edition of the Plays of W. B. Yeats.* London: Macmillan, 1966.
Bornstein, George, ed. *Under the Moon: The Unpublished Early Poetry by William Butler Yeats.* New York: Scribner, 1995.
Bornstein, George, and Witemeyer, Hugh, eds. *Letters to the New Island: The Collected Works of W. B. Yeats.* Vol. VII. New York: Macmillan, 1989.
Donoghue, Denis, ed. *W. B. Yeats Memoirs: Autobiography—First Draft, Journal.* London: Macmillan, 1972.
Finneran, Richard J., ed. *John Sherman and Dhoya: The Collected Works of W. B. Yeats.* Vol. XII. New York: Macmillan, 1991.
————. *The Poems: The Collected Works of W. B. Yeats.* Vol. I. New York: Macmillan, 1989.
Frayne, John P., ed. *Uncollected Prose by W. B. Yeats 1: First Reviews and Articles, 1886–1896.* New York: Columbia University Press, 1970.
————. *Uncollected Prose by W. B. Yeats 2: Reviews, Articles and Other Miscellaneous Prose, 1897–1939.* New York: Columbia University Press, 1975.
Gould, Warwick, Marcus, Phillip L., and Sidnell, Michael J., eds. *The Secret Rose: Stories by W. B. Yeats: A Variorum Edition.* London: Macmillan, 1981.
O'Donnell, William H., ed. *Later Essays: The Collected Works of W. B. Yeats.* Vol. V. New York: Charles Scribner's Sons, 1994.
————. *Prefaces and Introductions: The Collected Works of W. B. Yeats.* Vol. VI. New York: Macmillan, 1989.
Pearce, Donald R. *The Senate Speeches of W. B. Yeats.* Bloomington: Indiana University Press, 1960.

LETTERS

Bax, Clifford, ed. *Florence Farr, Bernard Shaw and W. B. Yeats.* Dublin: Cuala, 1941.
Finneran, Richard J. *The Correspondence of Robert Bridges and W. B. Yeats.* London: Macmillan, 1977.

Hone, Joseph, ed. *John Butler Yeats: Letters to His Son W. B. Yeats and Others, 1869–1922*. 1944. Reprint, London: Secker & Warburg, 1983.

Kelly, John, and Domville, Eric, eds. *The Collected Letters of W. B. Yeats*. Vol. I, 1865–1895. Oxford: Clarendon Press, 1986.

Kelly, John, and Schuchard, Ronald, eds. *The Collected Letters of W. B. Yeats*. Vol. III, 1901–1904. Oxford: Clarendon Press, 1994.

McHugh, Roger, ed. *Ah! Sweet Dancer: W. B. Yeats—Margot Ruddock, a Correspondence*. New York: Macmillan, 1970.

———. *W. B. Yeats: Letters to Katharine Tynan*. New York: McMullen Books, 1953.

Wade, Allan, ed. *The Letters of W. B. Yeats*. New York: Octagon Books, 1980.

Wellesley, Dorothy. *Letters on Poetry from W. B. Yeats to Dorothy Wellesley*. Ed. Kathleen Raine. 1940. Reprint, London: Oxford University Press, 1964.

White, Anna MacBride, and Jeffares, A. Norman, eds. *The Gonne-Yeats Letters: 1893–1938*. New York: W. W. Norton, 1992.

BIOGRAPHY

Ellmann, Richard. *Yeats: The Man and the Masks*. London: Macmillan, 1948.

Foster, R. F. *W. B. Yeats: A Life. Part 1: The Apprentice Mage 1865–1914*. Oxford and New York: Oxford University Press, 1997.

Hone, Joseph. *W. B. Yeats: 1865–1939*. 1943. Reprint, London: Macmillan, 1962.

Jeffares, A. Norman. *W. B. Yeats: A New Biography*. New York: Farrar, Straus & Giroux, 1989.

———. *W. B. Yeats: Man and Poet*. London: Routledge & Kegan Paul, 1962.

MacLiammóir, Micheál, and Boland, Eavan. *W. B. Yeats and His World*. London: Thames & Hudson, 1971.

Murphy, William M. *The Yeats Family and the Pollexfens of Sligo*. Dublin: Dolmen, 1971.

Tuohy, Frank. *Yeats*. London: Macmillan, 1976.

CRITICISM

Adams, Hazard. *The Book of Yeats's Poems*. Tallahassee: Florida State University Press, 1991.

Bradford, Curtis. *Yeats at Work*. Carbondale: Southern Illinois University Press, 1965.

Donoghue, Denis. *Yeats*. London: Fontana, 1971.

Dorn, Karen. *Players and Painted Stage: The Theatre of W. B. Yeats*. Sussex: The Harvester Press, 1984.

Ellis, Sylvia C. *The Plays of W. B. Yeats: Yeats and the Dancer*. London: Macmillan, 1995.

Ellmann, Richard. *The Identity of Yeats*. London: Faber & Faber, 1954.

Engelberg, Edward. *The Vast Design: Patterns in W. B. Yeats's Aesthetic*. Toronto: University of Toronto, 1964.

Finneran, Richard J., Harper, George Mills, and Murphy, William M., eds. *Letters to W. B. Yeats*. 2 vols. New York: Columbia University Press, 1977.

Flannery, James W. *W. B. Yeats and the Idea of a Theatre: The Early Abbey Theatre in Theory and Practice*. New Haven: Yale University Press, 1976.

Gordon, D. J., ed. *W. B. Yeats: Images of a Poet*. Manchester: University of Manchester, 1961.

Gorski, William T. *Yeats and Alchemy*. Albany: State University of New York, 1996.

Harper, George M., ed. *Yeats and the Occult*. Toronto: Macmillan, 1975.

Henn, T. R. *The Lonely Tower: Studies in the Poetry of W. B. Yeats*. London: Methuen, 1950.

Jeffares, A. Norman. *W. B. Yeats: The Critical Heritage*. London: Routledge & Kegan Paul, 1977.

Larrissy, Edward. *Yeats the Poet: The Measures of Difference*. Hemel Hempstead, Herts.: Harvester Wheatsheaf, 1994.

Loizeaux, Elizabeth Bergmann. *Yeats and the Visual Arts*. New Brunswick and London: Rutgers University Press, 1986.

Malins, Edward, and Purkis, John. *A Preface to Yeats*. 1974. Reprint, London: Longman, 1994.

Meir, Colin. *The Ballads and Songs of W. B. Yeats: The Anglo-Irish Heritage in Subject and Style*. New York: Barnes & Noble, 1974.

Melchiori, Giorgio. *The Whole Mystery of Art: Pattern into Poetry in the Work of W. B. Yeats*. London: Routledge and Kegan Paul, 1960.

Moore, Virginia. *The Unicorn: William Butler Yeats' Search for Reality*. New York: Octagon Books, 1973.

Murphy, William M. *Family Secrets: William Butler Yeats and His Relatives*. Syracuse, N.Y.: Syracuse University Press, 1995.

O'Donnell, William H. *A Guide to the Prose Fiction of W. B. Yeats*. Ann Arbor, Mich.: UMI Research Press, 1983.

O'Driscoll, Robert, and Reynolds, Lorna, eds. *Yeats and the Theatre*. Niagara Falls, N.Y.: Maclean–Hunter, 1975.

Skelton, Robin, and Saddlemyer, Ann, eds. *The World of W. B. Yeats*. Seattle: University of Washington Press, (1965) 1967.

Stallworthy, Jon. *Between the Lines: Yeats's Poetry in the Making*. Oxford: Clarendon, 1965.

———. *Vision and Revision in Yeats's Last Poems*. Oxford: Clarendon, 1969.

Stauffer, Donald A. *The Golden Nightingale: Essays on Some Principles of Poetry in the Lyrics of William Butler Yeats*. 1949. Reprint, Folcroft, Pa.: Folcroft, 1969.

Thuente, Mary Helen. *W. B. Yeats and Irish Folklore*. Dublin: Gill & Macmillan, 1980.

Torchiana, Donald T. *W. B. Yeats & Georgian Ireland*. Oxford: Oxford University Press, 1966.

Unterecker, John. *A Reader's Guide to W. B. Yeats*. Reprint, Syracuse: Syracuse University Press, 1996.

———. *Yeats: A Collection of Critical Essays*. London: Prentice-Hall, 1963.

Whitaker, Thomas R. *Swan and Shadow: Yeats's Dialogue with History*. Chapel Hill: University of North Carolina, 1964.

Wilson, F. A. C. *W. B. Yeats and Tradition*. London: Gollancz, 1960.

GENERAL INTEREST

Bardon, Jonathan. *A History of Ulster*. Belfast: Blackstaff, 1992.

Brown, Malcolm. *The Politics of Irish Literature: From Thomas Davis to W. B. Yeats*. London: Allen & Unwin, 1972.

Dames, Michael. *Mythic Ireland*. 1992. Reprint, New York: Thames & Hudson, 1996.

Flanagan, Deirdre, and Flanagan, Laurence. *Irish Place Names*. Dublin: Gill & Macmillan, 1994.

Foster, R. F. *Modern Ireland 1600–1972*. 1988. Reprint, London: Penguin, 1989.

Gregory, Lady. *Cuchulain of Muirthemne: The Story of the Men of the Red Branch of Ulster*. 1902. Reprint, Gerrards Cross: Colin Smythe, 1976.

Hederman, M. P., and Kearney, R., eds. *The Crane Bag Book of Irish Studies*. Dublin: Blackwater, 1982.

Kinsella, Thomas, trans. *The Tain*. Dublin: Dolmen, 1969.

Maxwell, D. E. S. *A Critical History of Modern Irish Drama, 1891–1980*. Cambridge: Cambridge University Press, 1984.

Index

Main entries in the Encyclopedia are indicated by small capitals, and page numbers for each main entry are in bold type. Throughout, the abbreviation WBY is used for W. B. Yeats.

Along with general information and a listing of residences, the entry for WBY is divided into: Articles; Collections; Broadcasts; Lectures; Newspapers and Periodicals; Poems; Prefaces and Introductions; Works edited; Works reviewed. Additional information, such as his relationship with individuals, places and organizations, has been included at the end of the entry for the person or subject concerned.

In the interest of space, plays and collections of prose and verse which are the subject of main entries are included in the main index. They have not been listed under WBY's entry.

KILGLASS, County Sligo, **210**

KILLALA, County Mayo, 26, 73, 158, 195, **210–11**, 395

KILTARTAN, County Galway, 74, **211**, 352, 371

KILVARNET, County Sligo, **211**, 288

KING (*The King of the Great Clock Tower*), **211**, 212, 250, 376–77

KING, RICHARD ASHE (1839–1932), editor and journalist, **211–12**, 273; "The Silenced Sister", 211; *Swift in Ireland*, 211

King Billy. *See* WILLIAM III

King Lear, Shakespearean character, 40, 313, 354, 394

King of the Great Clock Tower, The [1934] (collection), 154, 332

KING OF THE GREAT CLOCK TOWER, THE [1935] (play), 7, 47, 70, 83, 97, 113, 154, 211, **212**, 250, 274, 289, 316, 318, 322, 334, 341, 376, 393

KING'S THRESHOLD, THE (1904), **212–13**, 261, 290, 333, 350, 352

—actors in, 12, 84, 143, 144, 297, 351

—cast of first production, 213

—characters in: BRIAN, 48; CHAMBERLAIN, 75, 297; FEDELM, 145, 351; GUAIRE, 75, 167, 175, 350; MAYOR OF KINVARA, 144, 213; SEANCHAN, 126, 143, 145, 167, 175, 350

—costume designs, 188, 208

—ANNIE F. HORNIMAN and, 188, 208, 213

—places named in, 13, 126, 167

—publication history, 53, 83, 212, 290, 309

—sources, 132, 213

KINSALE, County Cork, **213**, 284, 293

KINSELLA, JOHN, fictional, **213**

KINVARA, County Galway, 23, 126, 175, **213–14**

KIPLING, RUDYARD (1865–1936), poet and novelist, 34, **214**

KNOCKNAREA, County Sligo, 13, 30, 150, **214–15**, 227, 231, 237, 361, 364

KNOCKNASHEE, County Sligo, **215**, 231

KROP, HILDO (1884–1972), sculptor, 113, 148, **215–16**, 294

KUBLA KHAN (1215–1294), Mongol general, **216**, 426

KUSTA BEN LUKA (c. 820–892), Arabian doctor, 179, **216**

KYLE-DORTHA. *See* SEVEN WOODS

KYLE-NA-NO. *See* SEVEN WOODS

KYTELER, LADY ALICE, noblewoman, 19–20, **216–17**

LABAN, woman of the Sídhe, 115, **218**, 250

LAEGAIRE (*The Green Helmet*), 169, **218**

LAIGHEN. *See* LEINSTER

LALLY, BIDDY (*The Unicorn from the Stars*), 10, **218–19**, 403

LAME BEGGAR (*The Cat and the Moon*), 42, 61, 72, **219**

LAND OF HEART'S DESIRE, THE (1894), 7, 138, **219**, 404

—actors in, 11, 143, 219, 299

—characters in: BRUIN family, 52, 142; FAERY CHILD, 81, 90, 139, 142, 299; FATHER HART, 142–43

—first production, 32, 141, 188, 219, 357, 394

—places named in, 26, 81, 90, 282

—publishing history, 83, 219, 309, 310, 404

—sources, 219

LANDOR, WALTER SAVAGE (1775–1864), poet and critic, 47, 118, **219–20**

LANE, HUGH (1875–1915), art collector, 4, 38, 57, 93, 112, 159, 172, 174, 213, **220–21**, 231, 241, 268, 271, 358, 414, 430

LAST POEMS AND TWO PLAYS (1939), 83, 109, **221**, 318

LAVERY, HAZEL (1880–1935), wife of Sir John Lavery, **221–22**

LAVERY, SIR JOHN (1856–1941), painter, 68, 175, 221, **222**, 288

—paintings: *Blessing of the Colours*, 222; *The Court of Criminal Appeal*, 68, 222; *Hazel Lavery at her Easel*, 222; *St. Patrick's Purgatory*, 222; *The Unfinished Harmony*, 222

LAWLESS, EMILY (1845–1913), poet and novelist, **222–23**; *Essex in Ireland*, 222–23; *Maelcho*, 223

—works: *Rupert Armstrong*, 353; *Beauty's Hour*, 44; *The Beloved of Hathor*, 141; *The False Laurel*, 353; *The Journey of High Honor*, 353; *The Shrine of the Golden Hawk*, 141
—WBY: 44, 163; introduced by, 204, 353; relationship with, 152–53, 243–44, 353, 421; reminiscences, 24; writes to, 45, 52, 97, 112, 181, 253, 274, 333, 353, 415
SHAKESPEARE, WILLIAM (1564–1616), playwright and poet, 28, 55, 119, 160, 199, 206, 245, 259, 263, 279, 339, 343, **354**, 366, 370, 392, 394, 396, 408
Shakespeare Head Press, 53, 309, 420
SHANNON, CHARLES (1863–1937), painter and lithographer, 145, 173, 323, 332, **354–55**; portrait of Major Robert Gregory, 173; portrait of WBY, 355
SHAN-WALLA. *See* SEVEN WOODS
SHAPE-CHANGERS, supernatural beings, 241, **355**
SHARP, WILLIAM (1855–1905), writer, **355–56**; Fiona MacLeod (pseud.), 356
SHAW, GEORGE BERNARD (1856–1950), dramatist and critic, 11, 34, 65, 76, 90, 137, 141, 203, 219, 221, 238, 256, 265, 271, 332–33, 344, **356–57**
—works: *Arms and the Man*, 219, 356, 357; *The Black Girl in Search of God*, 256; *John Bull's Other Island*, 357; *The Shewing-Up of Blanco Posnet*, 11, 357
SHAWE-TAYLOR, JOHN (1866–1911), nephew of Lady Gregory, 322–23, **357–58**
SHEBA, QUEEN OF, **358**
SHELLEY, PERCY BYSSHE (1792–1822), poet, 58, 96, 210, 244, 337, 343, 356, **358–59**, 369, 422, 425; "Prince Athanase", 359
SHEPPARD, OLIVER (1865–1941), sculptor, 158, 191, 254, **359–60**; "The Death of Cuchulain" (sculpture), 359–60
Shields, Arthur (1896–1970), actor, 91, 294, 367, 368, 424
SHORTER, DORA SIGERSON (1866–1918), writer, 222, **360**

SICILY, Mediterranean island, 59, **360**
SÍDH, fairy mound, 257, **361**
SÍDHE, fairy people, 134, 148, 355
—FAND, **140**, 149
—FINIVARAGH, 149
—LABAN, 218
—MIDHIR, 135, 138, 257–58
—places associated with: BEN BULBEN, 35; BUAL'S HILL, 52; CRUACHMAA, 100; GREY ROCK, 173; KNOCKNAREA, 215; KNOCKNASHEE, 215; LUGNAGALL, 231
—WBY: references in works, 23, 126, 127, 173, 215, 218, 226, 231, 285; *AT THE HAWK'S WELL*, 21, 140, 355; *THE DEATH OF CUCHULAIN*, 130, 355; *THE ONLY JEALOUSY OF EMER*, 140, 355. *See also* Sídh
SIDNEY, SIR PHILIP (1554–86), poet and statesman, **361**, 369
SIGERSON, DORA, 362. *See also* SHORTER, DORA SIGERSON
SIGERSON, DR. GEORGE (1839–1925), neurologist and historian, 90, 192, 271, 360, **362**; "Irish Literature: Its Origins, Environment, and Influence" (lecture), 271
Sinclair, Arthur (1883–1951), actor, 10, 86, 110, 170, 181, 292, 404
Sinn Féin, political organization, 93, 112, 174, 244, 246, 288, 297
Sinn Féin, newspaper, 174, 261, 294
SISTINE CHAPEL, Rome, 6, 255–56, **362**
Slade School of Fine Arts, London, 164, 172, 176, 188, 202, 244
SLEUTH WOOD, 195, 229. *See also* Slish Wood
SLIEVE ECHTGE, County Galway, 34, 56, 100, **363**
SLIEVE FUADH, County Armagh, **363**
SLIEVENAMON, County Tipperary, **363**, 398–99
SLIGO, town and county, 151, 227, 294, 296, **363–64**, 430, 433
—places in: ABBEY OF WHITE FRIARS (Sligo Abbey), 3, 53, 231; ALT, 13, 82; BALLINAFAD, 26; BALLISODARE, 26, 84, 288, 346, 363; BALLYGAWLEY HILL, 26; BEN BULBEN, 35, 69, 91, 121, 159,

—exhibition of paintings in Dublin, 220, 319, 430
—moves to New York, 171, 206, 323, 431
—teaches at METROPOLITAN COLLEGE OF ART, 190, 254
—relatives, 427, 428, 429, 432, 433
—WBY: accompanies him to FARNHAM ROYAL, 129; attends CONTEMPORARY CLUB with, 289; breakfasts at home of EDWARD DOWDEN with, 118; frontispiece to MOSADA by, 266; influenced by, 57, 431; introduced to works of BALZAC by, 28; introduced to PERCY BYSSHE SHELLEY by, 359; portrait as GOLL by, 163; portrait by MANCINI disliked by, 241; reads JOHN KEATS with, 210; visits him in New York, 224
YEATS, MARY BUTLER (1751–1834), great-great-grandmother of WBY, 57, 426, **431**, 432
YEATS, MICHAEL B. (b. 1921), son of WBY, 73, 100, 124, 240, 271, 298, 428, **434**
YEATS, MRS. W. B., 137, 319. *See also* Yeats, Georgie
YEATS, REV. JOHN (1774–1846), great-grandfather of WBY, 87, 121, 135, 429, 431, **432**
YEATS, REV. WILLIAM BUTLER (1806–62), grandfather of WBY, 57, 119, 347, 429, 430, **432–33**
Yeats, Robert Corbet (1870–73), brother of WBY, 151, 430
YEATS, SUSAN (1841–1900), mother of WBY, 41, 127, 131–32, 158, 190, 311, 312, 428, 430, **433**
YEATS, SUSAN MARY [LILY] (1866–1949), sister of WBY, 41, 125, 185, 224, 260, 430, **433–34**
Yeats, William Butler (1865–1939): Ganconagh (pseud.), 204
—Monday Nights 'At Home', 33, 248, 253, 298, 316, 365, 422
—residences: ASHFIELD TERRACE, Dublin, 20, 28, 171, 179; BALSCADDEN COTTAGE, Howth, 27–28, 190, 423; BLENHEIM ROAD, London, 41–42, 127, 197;

Broad Street, OXFORD, 77, 298; Cuttlebrook House, Thame, Oxon., 298, 434; EARDLEY CRESCENT, London, 127; EDITH VILLAS, London, 129, 160, 423; FITZROY ROAD, London, 131, 151, 158, 430; Fitzwilliam Square, Dublin, 253; FOUNTAIN COURT, London, 42, 152–53, 382; GEORGE'S VILLE, Sandymount, Dublin, 158, 347, 433; ISLAND VIEW, HOWTH, 28, 190; MERRION SQUARE, Dublin, 100, 253; Minchen's Cottage, Shillingford, Berkshire, 298; RIVERSDALE, Rathfarnham, Dublin, 45, 55, 63, 224, 248, 333; STONE COTTAGE, Coleman's Hatch, Sussex, 146, 276, 316, 374; THOOR BALLYLEE, County Galway, 7, 23, 26–27, 87, 91, 157, 167, 224, 328, 352, 371, 391, 395, 396, 419, 421; WOBURN BUILDINGS, London, 32, 39, 50, 153, 176, 316, 353, 365, 422; WOODSTOCK ROAD, London, 33, 423
Yeats, William Butler, additional works by
—ARTICLES: ''America and the Arts'', 224; ''And Fair, Fierce Women'', 56, 215, 237; ''Aphorisms of Yoga'', 160; ''Aristotle of the Books'', 17; ''Art and Ideas'', 74, 178, 349; ''At Stratford-on-Avon'', 354, 412; ''Autumn of the Body, The'', 151–52, 329; ''Bishop Berkeley'', 7, 82, 251, 274, 314, 371, 374, 390; ''Blake's Illustrations to Dante'', 45, 259; ''Celtic Beliefs about the Soul'', 105, 277; ''Celtic Element in Literature, The'', 18, 19, 229, 412; ''Clarence Mangan's Love Affair'', 242; ''Commentary on 'A Parnellite at Parnell's Funeral' '', 302; ''Commentary on Supernatural Songs'', 332; ''Commentary on the Three Songs'', 142, 196; ''Defence of the Abbey Theatre, A'', 350; ''Drumcliff and Rosses'', 74, 121, 215, 338; ''Dust Hath Closed Helen's Eye'', 17, 27, 79, 81, 126, 127, 193, 211, 325, 391; ''Edmund Spenser'', 22, 92, 98, 122, 229, 284, 370; ''Ellen O'Leary'',